THE FOUR GOSPELS

The Four Gospels

Catholic Personal Study Edition

Editors:

Catherine Upchurch

Ronald D. Witherup, s.s.

Contributors:

Mary Elsbernd, o.s.f.

Leslie Hoppe, o.f.m.

Irene Nowell, o.s.b.

Catherine Upchurch

Macrina Wiederkehr, o.s.b.

Ronald D. Witherup, s.s.

LITTLE ROCK SCRIPTURE STUDY

*A ministry of the Diocese of Little Rock
in partnership with Liturgical Press*

The Four Gospels is an extract from the forthcoming *Little Rock Catholic Study Bible.*

Nihil Obstat: Erik T. Pohlmeier, *Censor Librorum.*
Imprimatur: ✝Anthony B. Taylor, Bishop of Little Rock, Arkansas, March 27, 2009.

NEW TESTAMENT
Nihil Obstat: Stephen J. Hartdegen, O.F.M., L.S.S., *Censor Deputatus.*
Imprimatur: ✝James A. Hickey, S.T.D., J.C.D., Archbishop of Washington, August 27, 1986.

Design by Ann Blattner.
Symbol design by Barbara Knutson.
Four evangelists design by Helen Siegl.
Line maps created by Clifford M. Yeary.
Photo research by Ann Blattner and Robin Pierzina, O.S.B.
Typography by Julie Surma.
Little Rock Scripture Study logo originally designed by Maria Estaún; modified by Lisa Walz.

1	2	3	4	5	6	7	8

Library of Congress Cataloging-in-Publication Data

Bible. N.T. Gospels. English. New American Standard. 2009.
   The Four Gospels : Catholic personal study edition / editors, Catherine Upchurch, Ronald D. Witherup ;
contributors, Mary Elsbernd . . . [et al.].
      p.   cm. — (Little Rock Scripture study)
   Includes indexes.
   ISBN 978-0-8146-3631-2 (pbk.)
   I. Upchurch, Catherine.   II. Witherup, Ronald D., 1950–   III. Elsbernd, Mary, 1946–   IV. Title.

BS2553.N45   2009
226'.052043—dc22

2009016401

Contents

Key to Symbols

 Brief summary of each gospel

 Author of the gospel

 Date of composition

 Description of content

 Description of main characters

 Definitions and explanations of terms and ideas

 Not-so-minor characters who move the story along

 Archaeological insights

 Social justice teachings

 Prayer starters

 Liturgical use of Scripture

May the Lord be in my mind, on my lips, and in my heart.

Preface

Around the world, before the gospel is proclaimed at Mass, all who are present cross themselves on the forehead, lips, and chest. In this gesture, we are reminded not only that the proclamation of the gospel is significant but also that the Good News of Jesus Christ should find a worthy dwelling in our thoughts, words, and deeds. *May the Lord be in my mind, on my lips, and in my heart* becomes our prayer as gospel people.

The four gospel accounts have always enjoyed pride of place in our lives as Catholics. They appear at the head of the New Testament as the prime testimony to Jesus of Nazareth, they are proclaimed at every Eucharist, and they provide the basis for reflection for those in the catechumenate process. In our eucharistic gatherings, the Book of the Gospels is carried in procession as Mass begins, and the proclamation of the gospel provides the crescendo for the Liturgy of the Word. Even our bodies and voices signal the importance of the Good News of Jesus Christ: we stand as an assembly, sing the "Alleluia" (or in Lent an alternate proclamation), and on occasion incense the gospel before it is proclaimed. There is no doubt that the fourfold gospel is the center of our spiritual formation.

Each of the four evangelists provides a "voice" for telling the story of Jesus and the coming of the kingdom of God. These voices act something like a choir. Each voice has its own strong tone and can be enjoyed independently. The four strong voices together create a song with depth, harmony, and even on occasion disharmony. Modern readers of the Bible benefit both from hearing the tone and range of each voice as well as the beauty of the voices together.

This book presents the four gospels of Matthew, Mark, Luke, and John, along with tools to help readers bridge the gap between the cultures and languages of the ancient Mediterranean world and our own. At the start of this volume, readers are presented with helpful background information that sets the stage for reading the biblical texts. At the close of this volume, readers will find information that describes the church's most common use of these texts in liturgy, along with a listing of the cycle of readings through the church year. The heart of this volume is in the middle where we find the text of the gospels themselves. The translation provided is the New American Bible, including the introduction to each gospel as well as footnotes and cross-references that are part of this Catholic translation. In addition, readers will find other useful information, photographs, and line maps inserted throughout the text to provide helpful insights for understanding and application.

Abbreviations

CCC *Catechism of the Catholic Church* (Latin version issued by Libreria Editrice Vaticana, 1994), United States Catholic Conference, 1994. English translation of the *Catechism of the Catholic Church: Modifications from the Editio Typica*, 1997, United States Catholic Conference

DV *Dei Verbum* (Dogmatic Constitution on Divine Revelation), promulgated by Vatican Council II, 1965

EJ *Economic Justice for All*, Pastoral Letter of United States Catholic Conference, 1986

GIRM *General Instruction of the Roman Missal*, United States Catholic Conference, 2003

GS *Gaudium et Spes* (Pastoral Constitution on the Church in the Modern World), promulgated by Vatican Council II, 1965

IBC *The Interpretation of the Bible in the Church*, promulgated by the Pontifical Biblical Commission, 1994

LXX *The Septuagint*—the name commonly assigned to the first Greek translation of the Hebrew Scriptures made in pre-Christian times

NAB New American Bible

NT New Testament

RM *Redemtoris Missio* (On the permanent validity of the church's missionary mandate), Encyclical of Pope John Paul II, 1990

Background to the Gospels

Ronald D. Witherup, S.S.

The experience of reading the gospels is enhanced by understanding in advance some background information pertinent to the gospels and other parts of the New Testament.

The gospels originated in the preaching of the early church. The process was rather long and complicated, beginning with the first disciples of Jesus who spoke of their faith experiences after the resurrection. This oral tradition began to take a discernible shape in literary form, eventually being written down for posterity. Decades after the events, the four evangelists we designate as Matthew, Mark, Luke, and John collected, edited, and shaped these oral and written traditions into the four canonical gospels. The process, which was somewhat overlapping, can be diagrammed as follows:

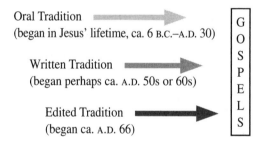

Oral Tradition
(began in Jesus' lifetime, ca. 6 B.C.–A.D. 30)

Written Tradition
(began perhaps ca. A.D. 50s or 60s)

Edited Tradition
(began ca. A.D. 66)

G
O
S
P
E
L
S

This process implies that the gospels contain various levels of tradition that reflect both the historical and theological interests of the early church. Scholars point to three layers evident in all four gospels, again somewhat overlapping, which date across the entire first Christian century:

- Stories, sayings, teachings, etc., from the lifetime of Jesus (ca. A.D. 1–30)

- Materials from the oral preaching of the apostles and early disciples (ca. A.D. 30–65)

- Materials shaped by the evangelists and their respective communities (ca. A.D. 65–100)

The *Catechism of the Catholic Church* (112) notes that these layers are part of church teaching concerning the origin of the gospels. Reaching bedrock history in such a multilayered reality can be tricky, but the gospels all reflect both historical and theological realities in the life of Jesus and the early church. Reading the gospels requires being mindful of this complex process.

The Synoptic Gospels

That the gospels have similar backgrounds is particularly evident in Matthew, Mark, and Luke. So close are they in outline, traditions about Jesus, and in other details, that they are clearly related literarily. In fact, they are known as the Synoptic Gospels because they can be viewed "with one eye" in parallel fashion.

Gospel Origins

The best scholarly hypothesis about the origin of the Synoptic Gospels is called the "Modified Two-Source Hypothesis." According to this theory, Mark is the oldest of the three Synoptics and was a primary source for Matthew and Luke. Scholars also hypothesize a second source, called "Q" (from the German word *Quelle*, "source"), which is actually the material in Matthew and Luke that is *not* found in Mark (mostly sayings). Matthew and Luke are thought to have used two other hypothetical sources unique to them, "M" and "L," respectively. This hypothesis is commonly diagrammed as follows:

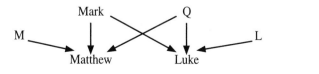

Christology in the New Testament

One of the most important aspects of the New Testament is obviously its teaching about Jesus Christ. The study of the significance of Jesus of Nazareth from a faith perspective is called Christology. The gospels in particular give evidence of many titles that were applied to Jesus in faith, titles that often had distinct historical and cultural backgrounds and profoundly different theological insights. Although paying attention to titles for Jesus is not the only way to arrive at christological insights, it is a helpful tool. The chart below describes briefly the most important *New Testament titles* or *designations* for Jesus.

Title/ Designation	Description and Background	References
Son of God	Title used in OT for divine beings in the heavenly court (Wis 5:5) or for the Davidic kings (2 Sm 7:14; Ps 2:7); in Greco-Roman world a title used of Caesar; became the most important theological title for Jesus, emphasizing his intimacy with God the Father and contributing eventually in post-NT times to the doctrine of the Trinity	Mt 1:1; 4:3, 6; 14:33; Mk 1:1; 15:39; Lk 1:35; Jn 1:49; Acts 9:20; Rom 1:4; 2 Cor 1:19; Gal 2:20
Son of Man	From Aramaic/Hebrew for "a human being" or member of the human race (Ez 2:1; 3:1, 10); became a title in Jewish apocalyptic literature for a victorious figure who would defeat Israel's enemies (Dn 7:13-14); Jesus likely used it as a roundabout reference for himself; became a title associated with Jesus' miracles, authority, suffering, death, and resurrection, and second coming in glory for judgment	Mt 8:20; 9:6; Mk 8:31-33; 9:30-32; 10:32-34; 13:26; Lk 18:8, 31; Jn 1:51; 9:35; Acts 7:56
Son of Abraham	Unique to Matthew, although implied elsewhere to emphasize Jesus' fulfillment of the promise to Abraham to become the father of many nations (Gn 15:4-5)	Mt 1:1; cf. Mt 8:11-12; Lk 1:55; Jn 8:52-58; Heb 2:13-20
Son of David	Title legitimizing Jesus' heritage in King David's lineage; most associated with Jesus' healing ministry; perhaps has background in the legend that Solomon, in addition to being wise, had healing properties	Mt 1:1; 9:27; 15:22; Mk 10:47-48; Lk 20:41
Messiah	From Greek *christos* and Hebrew *mashiach*, meaning "anointed one"; used of OT kings and prophets who were anointed for service; became identified in later Judaism with a victor who would overthrow the Romans and reestablish Israel to its glory; in Christianity became another name for Jesus as well as a title	Mt 1:1; Acts 2:36; 3:20

Lord	From Greek *kyrios*, which can simply mean "sir"; used in the LXX as a circumlocution for YHWH because of Hebrew Bible substitution of *'adonai* for God's name; most common title and form of address for Jesus applied to him after the resurrection, indicating his vindication in glory	Mt 14:30; 15:22; Mk 7:28; Lk 11:1, 39; 12:41; Jn 6:23; 9:38; Acts 2:36; Rom 10:9; 1 Cor 13:3; Phil 2:11
Suffering Servant	Not so much a title as a descriptive background to some NT passages; in fulfillment of the "songs" in Is 42:1-4; 49:1-6; 50:4-9; 52:13–53:12; merges with the Son of Man title above to form a "suffering Son of Man" image	Passion narratives of the gospels; cf. Mt 8:17
The Prophet	Title referring to the eschatological prophet who was expected to come in the end times for judgment	Jn 1:21; cf. Mk 8:28; Mt 16:14
Emmanuel	Hebrew meaning "God with us"; unique to Matthew; sees Jesus as fulfillment of Is 7:10-16, that God will provide help in time of need	Mt 1:23
Mari	Aramaic expression "my Lord" used respectfully of teachers; preserved in the early Christian liturgical acclamation "Maranatha" (Our Lord, come!)	1 Cor 16:22; Rev 22:20
Rabbi/Rabbouni Teacher	Hebrew/Aramaic for "my master"; used respectfully of teachers and has simply a polite connotation; similar to the Greek title "teacher"	Mk 10:35, 51; Jn 1:49; 20:16
The Word	Unique to Johannine literature; has Hellenistic-Jewish philosophical background in the preexistent *logos* who assisted God with creation (Prv 1–9)	Jn 1:1-5, 14; 1 Jn 1:1
Wisdom	Implicit in some NT documents rather than explicit; based upon OT notion of the preexistent "Wisdom Woman" who was with God at creation (Prv 1–9; Wis 7–9; Sir 24)	Mt 11:28-30; Jn 1:1-14; Col 1:15-20
New Adam	Unique to Paul; compares Jesus with Adam, the first human being, who failed to live up to God's purposes; Jesus thus introduces a "new creation"	1 Cor 15:22, 45-49; Rom 5:12-14
High Priest	Unique to Hebrews; uses the Jewish notion of the main priest in charge of the temple as fulfilled in Jesus; Jesus is both the sacrificial victim and the High Priest who offers sacrifice once and for all	Heb 4:14–8:6

A Suffering Messiah?

The origin of messianic expectation in the Bible is complex. The word "messiah" (Hebrew, *mashiach*; Greek, *christos*) simply means "anointed one." It was used most often for the Davidic king in Israel (1 Sm 10:1; Ps 2:2). Occasionally the term was applied to a foreigner who paradoxically accomplished YHWH's will (e.g., the Persian king Cyrus in Is 45:1). At the time of Jesus, Judaism exhibited distinctive expectations regarding a future messiah at the "end times." Some Jews expected a royal Davidic messiah, a political and military leader, who would cast off the Romans and restore Israel to its glory. The Essenes at Qumran expected at least two messiahs. One was a political messiah to challenge the Roman authorities; the second and more important one was a messiah in the priestly line of Aaron, who would restore true religious fervor in Israel.

Nowhere in Judaism, however, was there expectation of a *suffering* messiah. This is a strictly Christian concept formed on the basis of the experience of Jesus of Nazareth as crucified and risen Lord, a much different type of messiah than expected, one who suffered in order to bring God's salvation to human beings. Of the NT authors, only Luke develops the concept of a suffering messiah explicitly (see Lk 24:26, 46; Acts 17:3). Nevertheless, some OT texts about a "suffering righteous man" or other suffering figures influenced the development of the Christian concept of a suffering messiah whose pain and sacrifice vicariously saved people (Wis 2–5; Pss 22, 69; the Suffering Servant Songs of Deutero-Isaiah [esp. 52:13–53:12]).

Opponents of Jesus Portrayed in the New Testament

The gospels and Acts name numerous groups as *opponents of Jesus* and the early church. Modern readers can sometimes confuse them, in part because the gospels tend to see them uniformly as united against Jesus and his followers. Historically speaking, they were often very distinct groups with complex and independent histories. The following chart helps to set the record straight.

Opponents of Jesus	Description	References
Pharisees	Group of pious laity within Judaism that sought to preserve authentic Judaism but also allowed broad, oral interpretations of the Torah; influential between the 2nd cent. B.C. and the 1st cent. A.D.; only Jewish group to survive the destruction of Jerusalem (A.D. 70) and provide the foundation for rabbinic Judaism; believed in angels, spirits, and general resurrection of the dead	Mt 3:7; 12:14; 27:62; Mk 7:5; 12:13; Lk 6:7; 15:2; Jn 7:32; 18:3
Sadducees	Aristocratic group of leaders tied to the temple in Jerusalem and willing to cooperate with Roman authorities; opposed the Pharisaic belief in angels, spirits, and general resurrection of the dead; Matthew inaccurately portrays them as generally working together with Pharisees	Mt 3:7; 16:1; Mk 12:18; Lk 20:27; Acts 4:1; 5:17; 23:6-8

Scribes	Professionals who could read and write; were charged with preservation and interpretation of the Torah	Mt 2:4; 5:20; 23:13; Mk 2:16; 14:1; Lk 11:53; Jn 8:3; Acts 4:5; 6:12
Chief priests	A general term for the aristocratic priestly leaders of the temple in Jerusalem	Mt 2:4; Mk 11:18, 27
Elders of the people	Distinguished leaders representing the Jewish people on legal and judicial matters and tied to the temple	Mt 26:3, 47; Mk 11:27; 15:1; Lk 22:6; Acts 4:5-8
High Priest	Principal leader of the cultic rituals of the temple during the Second Temple period; often allied to political leaders; the only priest who had access to the Holy of Holies in the temple on the Day of Atonement	Mt 26:3, 57-65; Mk 14:53; Lk 22:54; Jn 11:49-51; 18:13-24; Acts 5:17-27
Herodians	Political supporters of Herod Antipas about whom little is known	Mt 22:16; Mk 3:6; 12:13
Sanhedrin	Literally, "council" or "assembly"; highest ruling body of elders in Judaism with legislative and judicial duties at the time of Jesus; presided over by the High Priest; the extent of their actual power at the time of Jesus is not clear	Mt 5:22; 26:59; Mk 14:55; 15:1; Lk 22:66; Jn 11:47; Acts 5:21; 6:12

We should emphasize that these people are not always portrayed negatively in the New Testament. Paul, for instance, trumpets his background as a Pharisee (Phil 3:5), although he counts his discipleship of Christ as far more significant. Also, the author of Matthew seems to identify himself as a scribe (13:52). The scribe in Mark 12:32 also receives Jesus' approval for his response about the essentials of the law. Some scribes of the Pharisaic party appear to defend Paul, nearly causing a riot (Acts 23:9).

In addition, it must be noted that another group prominent in the first century appears actually to have received the message of Jesus well. The Samaritans, whom the Jews despised as illegitimate "cousins" because of intermarriage with foreign peoples, come across as friendly toward Jesus and his followers (Lk 10:29-37; 17:16), but not in every instance (Lk 9:52). Jesus uses one as an illustration for good works (Lk 15:33-37). There is even evidence of strong success of Christian evangelization among the Samaritans (Jn 4:39-40; Acts 8:25), who likely constituted some segment of certain early Christian communities.

The Roman Empire as Background
for the New Testament

The *Roman system of government* during NT times, although somewhat fluid in nature, was hierarchically structured like a pyramid. At the top was the emperor ("caesar," a title derived from the family name of Julius Caesar) whose very word became law. Roman emperors varied in quality, but all were autocratic.

The image of the emperor was also intimately bound to Roman religion. Emperors were usually divinized, that is, declared to be divine. This could happen either after death or while the emperor still lived. Titles associated with Jesus in the NT were also secularly applied to emperors, such as savior (Lk 2:11), lord (Mt 14:28), and benefactor (Lk 22:25). This practice of promoting the worship of the emperor as a god challenged early Christians dearly. Not to bow down in worship to the emperor was tantamount to treason and usually brought a condemnation to death. The designation "friend of Caesar" (Jn 19:12) was likely an honorific title bestowed on those particularly loyal to the emperor.

The NT exhibits a mixed reaction to Roman governing authority. On one hand, the NT acknowledges the necessity of paying taxes (e.g., Jesus' saying in Mt 22:21 and par.; cf. Lk 23:2), participating in a government census (Lk 2:1-4), using citizenship to appeal for proper treatment under law (cf. Paul in Acts 25:8-12), and paying respect to lawful authority (Ti 3:1). The NT also implies the natural role of legal authority, especially when it narrates events that happened during the reign of certain emperors, governors, and the like (Lk 3:1; Acts 24:27).

On the other hand, the NT teaches that all secular legal authority comes ultimately from God (Jn 19:11). Not even the emperor can usurp this authority or take God's place, and there can be no assent to the emperor cult of divinization. The latter position obviously placed Christians in opposition to secular authority and led to charges of sedition against Jesus and later Christians (Lk 23:2-3; Acts 25:7-8) and to various persecutions, especially under the emperors Nero and Domitian.

The chart lists some of the key Roman governmental structures but leaves out the many complex levels of Roman government that developed over time.

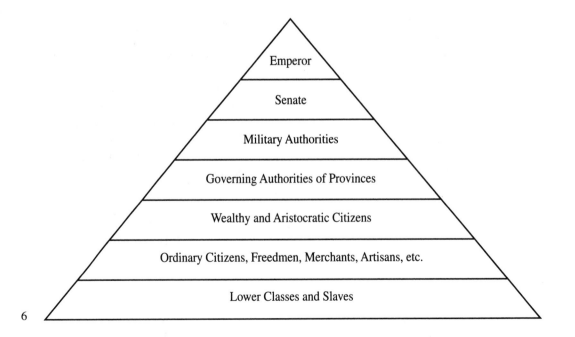

Emperor

Senate

Military Authorities

Governing Authorities of Provinces

Wealthy and Aristocratic Citizens

Ordinary Citizens, Freedmen, Merchants, Artisans, etc.

Lower Classes and Slaves

The position of the Gospel according to Matthew as the first of the four gospels in the New Testament reflects both the view that it was the first to be written, a view that goes back to the late second century A.D., and the esteem in which it was held by the church; no other was so frequently quoted in the noncanonical literature of earliest Christianity. Although the majority of scholars now reject the opinion about the time of its composition, the high estimation of this work remains. The reason for that becomes clear upon study of the way in which Matthew presents his story of Jesus, the demands of Christian discipleship, and the breaking-in of the new and final age through the ministry but particularly through the death and resurrection of Jesus.

The gospel begins with a narrative prologue (1:1–2:23), the first part of which is a genealogy of Jesus starting with Abraham, the father of Israel (1:1-17). Yet at the beginning of that genealogy Jesus is designated as "the son of David, the son of Abraham" (1:1). The kingly ancestor who lived about a thousand years after Abraham is named first, for this is the genealogy of Jesus Christ, the Messiah, the royal anointed one (1:16). In the first of the episodes of the infancy narrative that follow the genealogy, the mystery of Jesus' person is declared. He is conceived of a virgin by the power

SUMMARY

Matthew presents Jesus of Nazareth as a great teacher and Son of God, emphasizing that he is Emmanuel ("God with us"). It follows the story from the virginal conception of Jesus, through his public ministry, to his passion, death, and resurrection, and commissioning the disciples to evangelize the whole world.

Author: Unknown, but ancient tradition calls him "Matthew" and identifies him with the tax collector disciple of Jesus (Mt 9:9).

Date: After A.D. 70 and perhaps between A.D. 80–90.

Content: Virginal conception of Jesus; massacre of holy innocents; baptism of Jesus; five great sermons (Sermon on the Mount [5–7], Instruction to Disciples [10], Collection of Parables [13], Instruction on Church Discipline [18], Sermon about the Last Days [24–25]); miracles; Peter's confession of faith; transfiguration; passion, death, and resurrection of Jesus; resurrection appearance in Galilee; and the Great Commission.

Main Characters: Jesus of Nazareth, John the Baptist, Peter, James and John (the sons of Zebedee), faithful women of Galilee, some Jewish leaders who opposed Jesus, Judas Iscariot, Pontius Pilate.

of the Spirit of God (1:18-25). The first of the gospel's fulfillment citations, whose purpose it is to show that he was the one to whom the prophecies of Israel were pointing, occurs here (1:23): he shall be named Emmanuel, for in him God is with us.

The announcement of the birth of this newborn king of the Jews greatly troubles not only King Herod but all Jerusalem (2:1-3), yet the Gentile magi are overjoyed to find him and offer him their homage and their gifts (2:10-11). Thus his ultimate rejection by the mass of his own people and his acceptance by the Gentile nations is foreshadowed. He must be taken to Egypt to escape the murderous plan of Herod. By his sojourn there and his subsequent return after the king's death he relives the Exodus experience of Israel. The words of the Lord spoken through the prophet Hosea, "Out of Egypt I called my son," are fulfilled in him (2:15); if Israel was God's son, Jesus is so in a way far surpassing the dignity of that nation, as his marvelous birth and the unfolding of his story show (see 3:17; 4:1-11; 11:27; 14:33; 16:16; 27:54). Back in the land of Israel, he must be taken to Nazareth in Galilee because of the danger to his life in Judea, where Herod's son Archelaus is now ruling (2:22-23). The sufferings of Jesus in the infancy narrative anticipate those of his passion, and if his life is spared in spite of the dangers, it is because his destiny is finally to give it on the cross as "a ransom for many" (20:28). Thus the word of the angel will be fulfilled, ". . . he will save his people from their sins" (1:21; cf. 26:28).

In Matthew 4:12 Matthew begins his account of the ministry of Jesus, introducing it by the preparatory preaching of John the Baptist (3:1-12), the baptism of Jesus that culminates in God's proclaiming him his "beloved Son" (3:13-17), and the temptation in which he proves his true sonship by his victory over the devil's attempt to deflect him from the way of obedience to the Father (4:1-11). The central message of Jesus' preaching is the coming of the kingdom of heaven and the need for repentance, a complete change of heart and conduct, on the part of those who are to receive this great gift of God (4:17). Galilee is the setting for most of his ministry; he leaves there for Judea only in Matthew

19:1, and his ministry in Jerusalem, the goal of his journey, is limited to a few days (21:1–25:46).

In this extensive material there are five great discourses of Jesus, each concluding with the formula "When Jesus finished these words" or one closely similar (7:28; 11:1; 13:53; 19:1; 26:1). These are an important structure of the gospel. In every case the discourse is preceded by a narrative section, each narrative and discourse together constituting a "book" of the gospel. The discourses are, respectively, the "Sermon on the Mount" (5:3–7:27), the missionary discourse (10:5-42), the parable discourse (13:3-52), the "church order" discourse (18:3-35), and the eschatological discourse (24:4–25:46). In large measure the material of these discourses came to Matthew from his tradition, but his work in modifying and adding to what he had received is abundantly evident. No other evangelist gives the teaching of Jesus with such elegance and order as he.

In the "Sermon on the Mount" the theme of righteousness is prominent, and even at this early stage of the ministry the note of opposition is struck between Jesus and the Pharisees, who are designated as "the hypocrites" (6:2, 5, 16). The righteousness of his disciples must surpass that of the scribes and Pharisees; otherwise, in spite of their alleged following of Jesus, they will not enter into the kingdom of heaven (5:20). Righteousness means doing the will of the heavenly Father (7:21), and his will is proclaimed in a manner that is startling to all who have identified it with the law of Moses. The antitheses of the Sermon (5:21-48) both accept (5:21-30, 43-48) and reject (5:31-42) elements of that law, and in the former case the understanding of the law's demands is deepened and extended. The antitheses are the best commentary on the meaning of Jesus' claim that he has come not to abolish but to fulfill the law (5:17). What is meant by fulfillment of the law is not the demand to keep it exactly as it stood before the coming of Jesus, but rather his bringing the law to be a lasting expression of the will of God, and in that fulfillment there is much that will pass away. Should this appear contradictory to his saying that "until heaven and earth pass away" not even the

smallest part of the law will pass (5:18), that time of fulfillment is not the dissolution of the universe but the coming of the new age, which will occur with Jesus' death and resurrection. While righteousness in the new age will continue to mean conduct that is in accordance with the law, it will be conduct in accordance with the law as expounded and interpreted by Jesus (cf. 28:20, ". . . all that I have commanded you").

Though Jesus speaks harshly about the Pharisees in the Sermon, his judgment is not solely a condemnation of them. The Pharisees are portrayed as a negative example for his disciples, and his condemnation of those who claim to belong to him while disobeying his word is no less severe (7:21-23, 26-27).

In Matthew 4:23 a summary statement of Jesus' activity speaks not only of his teaching and proclaiming the gospel but of his "curing every disease and illness among the people"; this is repeated almost verbatim in Matthew 9:35. The narrative section that follows the Sermon on the Mount (8:1–9:38) is composed principally of accounts of those merciful deeds of Jesus, but it is far from being simply a collection of stories about miraculous cures. The nature of the community that Jesus will establish is shown; it will always be under the protection of him whose power can deal with all dangers (8:23-27), but it is only for those who are prepared to follow him at whatever cost (8:16-22), not only believing Israelites but Gentiles who have come to faith in him (8:10-12). The disciples begin to have some insight, however imperfect, into the mystery of Jesus' person. They wonder about him whom "the winds and the sea obey" (8:27), and they witness his bold declaration of the forgiveness of the paralytic's sins (9:2). That episode of the narrative moves on two levels. When the crowd sees the cure that testifies to the authority of Jesus, the Son of Man, to forgive sins (9:6), they glorify God "who had given such authority to human beings" (9:8). The forgiveness of sins is now not the prerogative of Jesus alone but of "human beings," that is, of the disciples who constitute the community of Jesus, the church. The ecclesial character of this narrative section could hardly be more plainly indicated.

The end of the section prepares for the discourse on the church's mission (10:5-42). Jesus is moved to pity at the sight of the crowds who are like sheep without a shepherd (9:36), and he sends out the twelve disciples to make the proclamation with which his own ministry began, "The kingdom of heaven is at hand" (10:7; cf. 4:17), and to drive out demons and cure the sick as he has done (10:1). Their mission is limited to Israel (10:5-6) as Jesus' own was (15:24), yet in 15:16 that perspective broadens and the discourse begins to speak of the mission that the disciples will have after the resurrection and of the severe persecution that will attend it (10:18). Again, the discourse moves on two levels: that of the time of Jesus and that of the time of the church.

The narrative section of the third book (11:2–12:50) deals with the growing opposition to Jesus. Hostility toward him has already been manifested (8:10; 9:3, 10-13, 34), but here it becomes more intense. The rejection of Jesus comes, as before, from Pharisees, who take "counsel against him to put him to death" (12:14) and repeat their earlier accusation that he drives out demons because he is in league with demonic power (12:22-24). But they are not alone in their rejection. Jesus complains of the lack of faith of "this generation" of Israelites (11:16-19) and reproaches the towns "where most of his mighty deeds had been done" for not heeding his call to repentance (11:20-24). This dark picture is relieved by Jesus' praise of the Father who has enabled "the childlike" to accept him (11:25-27), but on the whole the story is one of opposition to his word and blindness to the meaning of his deeds. The whole section ends with his declaring that not even the most intimate blood relationship with him counts for anything; his only true relatives are those who do the will of his heavenly Father (12:48-50).

The narrative of rejection leads up to the parable discourse (13:3-52). The reason given for Jesus' speaking to the crowds in parables is that they have hardened themselves against his clear teaching, unlike the disciples to whom knowledge of "the mysteries of the kingdom has been granted" (13:10-16). In Matthew 13:36 he dismisses the crowds and continues the discourse to his disciples alone, who

claim, at the end, to have understood all that he has said (13:51). But, lest the impression be given that the church of Jesus is made up only of true disciples, the explanation of the parable of the weeds among the wheat (13:37-43), as well as the parable of the net thrown into the sea "which collects fish of every kind" (13:47-49), shows that it is composed of both the righteous and the wicked, and that separation between the two will be made only at the time of the final judgment.

In the narrative that constitutes the first part of the fourth book of the gospel (13:54–17:27), Jesus is shown preparing for the establishment of his church with its teaching authority that will supplant the blind guidance of the Pharisees (15:13-14), whose teaching, curiously said to be that of the Sadducees also, is repudiated by Jesus as the norm for his disciples (16:6, 11-12). The church of Jesus will be built on Peter (16:18), who will be given authority to bind and loose on earth, an authority whose exercise will be confirmed in heaven (16:19). The metaphor of binding and loosing has a variety of meanings, among them that of giving authoritative teaching. This promise is made to Peter directly after he has confessed Jesus to be the Messiah, the Son of the living God (16:16), a confession that he has made as the result of revelation given to him by the heavenly Father (16:17); Matthew's ecclesiology is based on his high christology.

Directly after that confession Jesus begins to instruct his disciples about how he must go the way of suffering and death (16:21). Peter, who has been praised for his confession, protests against this and receives from Jesus the sharpest of rebukes for attempting to deflect Jesus from his God-appointed destiny. The future rock upon whom the church will be built is still a man of "little faith" (see 14:31). Both he and the other disciples must know not only that Jesus will have to suffer and die but that they too will have to follow him on the way of the cross if they are truly to be his disciples (16:24-25).

The discourse following this narrative (18:1-35) is often called the "church order" discourse, although that title is perhaps misleading since the emphasis is not on the structure of the church but on the care that the disciples must have for one another in respect to guarding each other's faith in Jesus (18:6-7), to seeking out those who have wandered from the fold (18:10-14), and to repeated forgiving of their fellow disciples who have offended them (18:21-35). But there is also the obligation to correct the sinful fellow Christian and, should one refuse to be corrected, separation from the community is demanded (18:15-18).

The narrative of the fifth book (19:1–23:39) begins with the departure of Jesus and his disciples from Galilee for Jerusalem. In the course of their journey Jesus for the third time predicts the passion that awaits him at Jerusalem and also his resurrection (20:17-19). At his entrance into the city he is hailed as the Son of David by the crowds accompanying him (21:9). He cleanses the temple (21:12-17), and in the few days of his Jerusalem ministry he engages in a series of controversies with the Jewish religious leaders (21:23-27; 22:15-22, 23-33, 34-40, 41-46), meanwhile speaking parables against them (21:28-32, 33-46), against all those Israelites who have rejected God's invitation to the messianic banquet (22:1-10), and against all, Jew and Gentile, who have accepted but have shown themselves unworthy of it (22:11-14). Once again, the perspective of the evangelist includes not only the time of Jesus' ministry but that of the preaching of the gospel after his resurrection. The narrative culminates in Jesus' denunciation of the scribes and Pharisees, reflecting not only his own opposition to them but that of Matthew's church (23:1-36), and in Jesus' lament over Jerusalem (23:37-39).

In the discourse of the fifth book (24:1–25:46), the last of the great structural discourses of the gospel, Jesus predicts the destruction of the temple and his own final coming. The time of the latter is unknown (24:36, 44), and the disciples are exhorted in various parables to live in readiness for it, a readiness that entails faithful attention to the duties of the interim period (24:45–25:30). The coming of Jesus will bring with it the great judgment by which the everlasting destiny of all will be determined (25:31-46).

The story of Jesus' passion and resurrection (26:1–28:20), the climax of the gospel, throws light on all that has preceded. In Matthew "righteousness" means both the faithful response to the will of God demanded of all to whom that will is announced and also the saving activity of God for his people (see 3:15; 5:6; 6:33). The passion supremely exemplifies both meanings of that central Matthean word. In Jesus' absolute faithfulness to the Father's will that he drink the cup of suffering (26:39), the incomparable model for Christian obedience is given; in his death "for the forgiveness of sins" (26:28), the saving power of God is manifested as never before.

Matthew's portrayal of Jesus in his passion combines both the majestic serenity of the obedient Son who goes his destined way in fulfillment of the scriptures (26:52-54), confident of his ultimate vindication by God, and the depths of fear and abandonment that he feels in face of death (26:38-39; 27:46). These two aspects are expressed by an Old Testament theme that occurs often in the narrative, i.e., the portrait of the suffering Righteous One who complains to God in his misery, but is certain of eventual deliverance from his terrible ordeal.

The passion-resurrection of God's Son means nothing less than the turn of the ages, a new stage of history, the coming of the Son of Man in his kingdom (28:18; cf. 16:28). That is the sense of the apocalyptic signs that accompany Jesus' death (27:51-53) and resurrection (28:2). Although the old age continues, as it will until the manifestation of Jesus' triumph at his parousia, the final age has now begun. This is known only to those who have seen the Risen One and to those, both Jews and Gentiles, who have believed in their announcement of Jesus' triumph and have themselves become his disciples (cf. 28:19). To them he is constantly, though invisibly, present (28:20), verifying the name Emmanuel, "God is with us" (cf. 1:23).

The questions of authorship, sources, and the time of composition of this gospel have received many answers, none of which can claim more than a greater or lesser degree of probability. The one now favored by the majority of scholars is the following.

The ancient tradition that the author was the disciple and apostle of Jesus named Matthew (see 10:3) is untenable because the gospel is based, in large part, on the Gospel according to Mark (almost all the verses of that gospel have been utilized in this), and it is hardly likely that a companion of Jesus would have followed so extensively an account that came from one who admittedly never had such an association rather than rely on his own memories. The attribution of the gospel to the disciple Matthew may have been due to his having been responsible for some of the traditions found in it, but that is far from certain.

The unknown author, whom we shall continue to call Matthew for the sake of convenience, drew not only upon the Gospel according to Mark but upon a large body of material (principally, sayings of Jesus) not found in Mark that corresponds, sometimes exactly, to material found also in the Gospel according to Luke. This material, called "Q" (probably from the first letter of the German word *Quelle*, meaning "source"), represents traditions, written and oral, used by both Matthew and Luke. Mark and Q are sources common to the two other synoptic gospels; hence the name the "Two-Source Theory" given to this explanation of the relation among the synoptics.

In addition to what Matthew drew from Mark and Q, his gospel contains material that is found only there. This is often designated "M," written or oral tradition that was available to the author. Since Mark was written shortly before or shortly after A.D. 70 (see Introduction to Mark), Matthew was composed certainly after that date, which marks the fall of Jerusalem to the Romans at the time of the First Jewish Revolt (A.D. 66–70), and probably at least a decade later since Matthew's use of Mark presupposes a wide diffusion of that gospel. The post-A.D. 70 date is confirmed within the text by Matthew 22:7, which refers to the destruction of Jerusalem.

As for the place where the gospel was composed, a plausible suggestion is that it was Antioch, the capital of the Roman province of Syria. That large and important city had a mixed population of Greek-speaking Gentiles and Jews. The tensions

between Jewish and Gentile Christians there in the time of Paul (see Gal 2:1-14) in respect to Christian obligation to observe Mosaic law are partially similar to tensions that can be seen between the two groups in Matthew's gospel. The church of Matthew, originally strongly Jewish Christian, had become one in which Gentile Christians were predominant. His gospel answers the question how obedience to the will of God is to be expressed by those who live after the "turn of the ages," the death and resurrection of Jesus.

The principal divisions of the Gospel according to Matthew are the following:

I. The Infancy Narrative (1:1–2:23)
II. The Proclamation of the Kingdom (3:1–7:29)
III. Ministry and Mission in Galilee (8:1–11:1)
IV. Opposition from Israel (11:2–13:53)
V. Jesus, the Kingdom, and the Church (13:54–18:35)
VI. Ministry in Judea and Jerusalem (19:1–25:46)
VII. The Passion and Resurrection (26:1–28:20)

I: The Infancy Narrative

The Genealogy of Jesus

1 [1]*[a]The book of the genealogy of Jesus Christ, the son of David, the son of Abraham.* [2][b]Abraham became the father of Isaac, Isaac the father of Jacob, Jacob the father of Judah and his brothers.[c] [3][d]Judah became the father of Perez and Zerah, whose mother was Tamar. Perez became the father of Hezron, Hezron the father of Ram, [4][e]Ram the father of Amminadab. Amminadab became the father of Nahshon, Nahshon the father of Salmon, [5][f]Salmon the father of Boaz, whose mother was Rahab. Boaz became the father of Obed, whose mother was Ruth. Obed became the father of Jesse, [6][g]Jesse the father of David the king.

David became the father of Solomon, whose mother had been the wife of Uriah. [7]*[h]Solomon became the father of Rehoboam, Rehoboam the father of Abijah, Abijah the father of Asaph. [8]Asaph became the father of Jehoshaphat, Jehoshaphat the father of Joram, Joram the father of Uzziah. [9]Uzziah became the father of Jotham, Jotham the father of Ahaz, Ahaz the father of Hezekiah. [10]Hezekiah became the father of Manasseh, Manasseh the father of Amos,* Amos the father of Josiah. [11]Josiah became the father of Jechoniah and his brothers at the time of the Babylonian exile.

[12][i]After the Babylonian exile, Jechoniah became the father of Shealtiel, Shealtiel the father of Zerubbabel, [13]Zerubbabel the father of Abiud. Abiud became the father of Eliakim, Eliakim the father of Azor, [14]Azor the father of Zadok. Zadok became the father of Achim, Achim the father of Eliud, [15]Eliud the father of Eleazar. Eleazar became the father of Matthan, Matthan the father of Jacob, [16]Jacob the father of Joseph, the husband of Mary. Of her was born Jesus who is called the Messiah.

[17]Thus the total number of generations from Abraham to David is fourteen generations; from David to the Babylonian exile, fourteen generations; from the Babylonian exile to the Messiah, fourteen generations.*

a
Gn 5:1 /
1 Chr 17:11 /
Gn 22:18

b
Lk 3:23-38

c
Gn 21:3;
25:26; 29:35;
1 Chr 2:1

d
Gn 38:29-30;
Ru 4:18;
1 Chr 2:4-9

e
Ru 4:19-20;
1 Chr 2:10-11

f
Ru 4:21-22;
1 Chr 2:11-12

g
2 Sm 12:24;
1 Chr 2:15; 3:5

h
2 Kgs 25:1-21;
1 Chr 3:10-15

i
1 Chr 3:16-19

1:1–2:23 The infancy narrative forms the prologue of the gospel. Consisting of a genealogy and five stories, it presents the coming of Jesus as the climax of Israel's history, and the events of his conception, birth, and early childhood as the fulfillment of Old Testament prophecy. The genealogy is probably traditional material that Matthew edited. In its first two sections (1:2-11) it was drawn from Ruth 4:18-22; 1 Chronicles 1–3. Except for Jechoniah, Shealtiel, and Zerubbabel, none of the names in the third section (1:12-16) is found in any Old Testament genealogy. While the genealogy shows the continuity of God's providential plan from Abraham on, discontinuity is also present. The women Tamar (1:3), Rahab and Ruth (1:5), and the wife of Uriah, Bathsheba (1:6), bore their sons through unions that were in varying degrees strange and unexpected. These "irregularities" culminate in the supreme "irregularity" of the Messiah's birth of a virgin mother; the age of fulfillment is inaugurated by a creative act of God. Drawing upon both biblical tradition and Jewish stories, Matthew portrays Jesus as reliving the Exodus experience of Israel and the persecutions of Moses. His rejection by his own people and his passion are foreshadowed by the troubled reaction of "all Jerusalem" to the question of the magi who are seeking the "newborn king of the Jews" (2:2-3), and by Herod's attempt to have him killed. The magi who do him homage prefigure the Gentiles who will accept the preaching of the gospel. The infancy narrative pro-

claims who Jesus is, the savior of his people from their sins (1:21), Emmanuel in whom "God is with us" (1:23), and the Son of God (2:15).

1:1 The Son of David, the son of Abraham: two links of the genealogical chain are singled out. Although the later, David is placed first in order to emphasize that Jesus is the royal Messiah. The mention of Abraham may be due not only to his being the father of the nation Israel but to Matthew's interest in the universal scope of Jesus' mission; cf. Genesis 22:18 ". . . in your descendants all the nations of the earth shall find blessing."

1:7 The successor of Abijah was not Asaph but Asa (see 1 Chr 3:10). Some textual witnesses read the latter name; however, **Asaph** is better attested. Matthew may have deliberately introduced the psalmist Asaph into the genealogy (and in 1:10 the prophet Amos) in order to show that Jesus is the fulfillment not only of the promises made to David (see 2 Sm 7) but of all the Old Testament.

1:10 Amos: some textual witnesses read **Amon**, who was the actual successor of Manasseh (see 1 Chr 3:14).

1:17 Matthew is concerned with fourteen generations, probably because fourteen is the numerical value of the Hebrew letters forming the name of David. In the second section of the genealogy (1:6b-11), three kings of Judah, Ahaziah, Joash, and Amaziah, have been omitted (see 1 Chr 3:11-12), so that there are fourteen

j
2:13, 19;
Lk 1:35

The Birth of Jesus

¹⁸*Now this is how the birth of Jesus Christ came about. When his mother Mary was betrothed to Joseph,* but before they lived together, she was found with child through the holy Spirit. ¹⁹Joseph her husband, since he was a righteous man,* yet unwilling to expose her to shame, decided to divorce her quietly. ^{20j}Such was his intention when, behold, the angel of the Lord* appeared to him in a dream and said, "Joseph, son of David, do not be afraid to take Mary your wife into your home. For it is through the holy Spirit that this child has been conceived in her. ²¹She will bear a son and you are to name him Jesus,* because he will save his people from their sins." ²²All this took place to fulfill what the Lord had said through the prophet:

In contrast to Matthew, Luke 1:26–2:14 has an extensive portrait of Mary the mother of Jesus, including the annunciation by Gabriel, the Canticle of Mary, and the visitation to Elizabeth.

Joseph, Dreamer Turned Activist

Dreamers are often said to be living in their own world, perhaps even an alternate universe. They're not often known as planners or doers. Every organization needs dreamers but most make sure they have plenty of worker bees on hand to turn a good dream into reality.

Joseph, husband of Mary and descendant of David, was a dreamer. Like the great Joseph of Genesis (ch. 37), it is in dreams that this Joseph finds his identity and calling. He dares to believe that God can and has revealed to him a new and awesome wonder. Rather than dwell in dreamland and leave the action to someone else, Joseph himself acts. He takes Mary as his wife. Another dream (Mt 2:13-14) leads him to take his young family to Egypt for protection. And in yet another dream, he finds the courage to return to Israel where he and Mary will raise Jesus in the tradition of their ancestors.

The story of Joseph illustrates that dreams can change the course of history, but only if we invest ourselves in their worth. The kingdom of God is just such a vision that is worthy of our life's effort.

Joseph the carpenter

---

generations in that section. Yet the third (1:12-16) apparently has only thirteen. Since Matthew here emphasizes that each section has fourteen, it is unlikely that the thirteen of the last was due to his oversight. Some scholars suggest that **Jesus who is called the Messiah** (1:16b) doubles the final member of the chain: **Jesus,** born within the family of David, opens up the new age as **Messiah,** so that in fact there are fourteen generations in the third section. This is perhaps too subtle, and the hypothesis of a slip not on the part of Matthew but of a later scribe seems likely. On **Messiah,** see the note on Luke 2:11.

1:18-25 This first story of the infancy narrative spells out what is summarily indicated in Matthew 1:16. The virginal conception of Jesus is the work of the Spirit of God. Joseph's decision to divorce Mary is overcome by the heavenly command that he take her into his home and accept the child as his own. The natural genealogical line is broken but the promises to David are fulfilled; through Joseph's adoption the child belongs to the family of David. Matthew sees the virginal conception as the fulfillment of Isaiah 7:14.

1:18 Betrothed to Joseph: betrothal was the first part of the marriage, constituting a man and woman as husband and wife.

Subsequent infidelity was considered adultery. The betrothal was followed some months later by the husband's taking his wife into his home, at which time normal married life began.

1:19 A righteous man: as a devout observer of the Mosaic law, Joseph wished to break his union with someone whom he suspected of gross violation of the law. It is commonly said that the law required him to do so, but the texts usually given in support of that view, e.g., Deuteronomy 22:20-21 do not clearly pertain to Joseph's situation. **Unwilling to expose her to shame**: the penalty for proved adultery was death by stoning; cf. Deuteronomy 22:21-23.

1:20 The angel of the Lord: in the Old Testament a common designation of God in communication with a human being. **In a dream**: see Matthew 2:13, 19, 22. These dreams may be meant to recall the dreams of Joseph, son of Jacob the patriarch (Gn 37:5–11:19). A closer parallel is the dream of Amram, father of Moses, related by Josephus (*Antiquities* 2, 9, 3; [par.] 212, 215–16).

1:21 Jesus: in first-century Judaism the Hebrew name Joshua (Greek *Iēsous*) meaning "Yahweh helps" was interpreted as "Yahweh saves."

²³*ᵏ"Behold, the virgin shall be with child and bear a son,
    and they shall name him Emmanuel,"

which means "God is with us." ²⁴When Joseph awoke, he did as the angel of the Lord had commanded him and took his wife into his home. ²⁵ˡHe had no relations with her until she bore a son,* and he named him Jesus.

k	Is 7:14 LXX
l	Lk 2:7
a	Nm 24:17

The Visit of the Magi

2¹*When Jesus was born in Bethlehem of Judea, in the days of King Herod,* behold, magi from the east arrived in Jerusalem, ²ᵃsaying, "Where is the newborn king of the Jews? We saw his star* at its rising and have come to do him homage." ³When King Herod heard this, he was greatly troubled, and all Jerusalem with him. ⁴Assembling all the chief priests and the scribes of the people, he inquired of

Emmanuel (Hebrew, "God with us") is a symbolic name in Isaiah, most likely referring to King Ahaz's son Hezekiah (Is 7:14). He is meant to give assurance to the king that God will not desert him and his people, and that he should not seek political alliances for self-defense. Matthew sees this prophetic word fulfilled in Jesus. Jesus is now the assurance that God has not abandoned the people.

Getting It Right . . . Which Herod?

The NT features several kings from the same royal family whose names are Herod. Antipater I, grandfather of Herod the Great, was the founder of the Herodian dynasty (second century B.C.). They were Idumeans who converted to Judaism. Readers must be attentive to which Herod is in view at any given time. Here Matthew refers to King Herod the Great, the great builder of magnificent structures in Jerusalem. The following chart will help keep the Herod family straight. After Herod's death, the Roman emperor divided Herod's kingdom among his three sons. All during the NT period the Herodian rulers relied extensively on the Roman emperors to reinforce their authority, a tactic that Herod the Great's father, Antipater II, had begun in the early first century B.C. The NT reference to certain "Herodians" likely refers to political supporters of Herod Antipas (Mt 22:16; Mk 3:6; 12:13).

Name	Description	Key NT References
Herod the Great	Ruled 37–4 B.C.; built the temple in Jerusalem, called the second temple	Mt 2:1-12
Archelaus (son)	Ruled 4 B.C.–A.D. 6; inherited Judea and Samaria as "king" from his father but was an ineffectual ruler removed rather quickly by Rome	Mt 2:22
Herod Antipas (son)	Ruled 4 B.C.–A.D. 39 as tetrarch of Galilee; beheaded John the Baptist, who opposed the marriage to his brother's wife Herodias	Mt 14:1; Mk 6:17; Lk 3:1, 19; 9:7; Acts 13:1
Philip the Tetrarch (son)	Ruled 4 B.C.–A.D. 34; Roman educated and capable ruler; expanded Panias and renamed it Caesarea Philippi	Mt 14:3; Mk 6:17; Lk 3:1
Herod Agrippa I	Ruled A.D. 41–44; beheaded James, son of John ca. A.D. 44	Acts 12:1-23
Herod Agrippa II	Ruled A.D. 53–93; supported Rome during the Jewish revolt A.D. 66–70	Acts 25:13–26:32
Herod Philip	Married to Herodias, who later married Antipas	Mk 6:17

1:23 God is with us: God's promise of deliverance to Judah in Isaiah's time is seen by Matthew as fulfilled in the birth of Jesus, in whom God is with his people. The name Emmanuel is alluded to at the end of the gospel where the risen Jesus assures his disciples of his continued presence, ". . . I am with you always, until the end of the age" (28:20).

1:25 Until she bore a son: the evangelist is concerned to emphasize that Joseph was not responsible for the conception of Jesus. The Greek word translated "until" does not imply normal marital conduct after Jesus' birth, nor does it exclude it.

2:1-12 The future rejection of Jesus by Israel and his acceptance by the Gentiles are retrojected into this scene of the narrative.

2:1 In the days of King Herod: Herod reigned from 37 to 4 B.C. **Magi**: originally a designation of the Persian priestly caste, the word became used of those who were regarded as having more than human knowledge. Matthew's magi are astrologers.

2:2 We saw his star: it was a common ancient belief that a new star appeared at the time of a ruler's birth. Matthew also draws upon the Old Testament story of Balaam who prophesied that "A star shall advance from Jacob" (Nm 24:17), though there the star means not an astral phenomenon but the king himself.

2:4 Herod's consultation with the chief priests and scribes has some similarity to a Jewish legend about the child Moses in which

b
Mi 5:1 /
2 Sm 5:2

c
Ps 72:10-11,
15; Is 60:6

d
Hos 11:1

them where the Messiah was to be born.* ⁵ᵇThey said to him, "In Bethlehem of Judea, for thus it has been written through the prophet:

> ⁶'And you, Bethlehem, land of Judah,
>   are by no means least among the
>   rulers of Judah;
> since from you shall come a ruler,
>   who is to shepherd my people
>   Israel.'"

Woodcut image of the magi's visit

⁷Then Herod called the magi secretly and ascertained from them the time of the star's appearance. ⁸He sent them to Bethlehem and said, "Go and search diligently for the child. When you have found him, bring me word, that I too may go and do him homage." ⁹After their audience with the king they set out. And behold, the star that they had seen at its rising preceded them, until it came and stopped over the place where the child was. ¹⁰They were overjoyed at seeing the star, ¹¹*ᶜand on entering the house they saw the child with Mary his mother. They prostrated themselves and did him homage. Then they opened their treasures and offered him gifts of gold, frankincense, and myrrh. ¹²And having been warned in a dream not to return to Herod, they departed for their country by another way.

Dreams feature in both OT and NT stories as vehicles for revealing God's will to human beings. In Genesis Jacob's dream expresses contact with God (Gn 28:12). Also, another Joseph is honored for his "dreams," though they make his brothers jealous; his ability to interpret Pharaoh's dreams properly saves him (Gn 37–41). In Matthew, God uses dreams to direct Joseph to accept Mary as his wife and Jesus as his son. The magi also receive dreams to avoid contact with the evil King Herod. Even Pilate's wife receives a dream that testifies to Jesus' innocence (Mt 27:19). Dreams, then, are a means of divine communication that can have serious consequences in human affairs.

The Flight to Egypt

¹³*When they had departed, behold, the angel of the Lord appeared to Joseph in a dream and said, "Rise, take the child and his mother, flee to Egypt,* and stay there until I tell you. Herod is going to search for the child to destroy him." ¹⁴Joseph rose and took the child and his mother by night and departed for Egypt. ¹⁵*ᵈHe stayed there until the death of Herod, that what the Lord had said through the prophet might be fulfilled, "Out of Egypt I called my son."

The Massacre of the Infants

¹⁶When Herod realized that he had been deceived by the magi, he became furious. He ordered

---

the "sacred scribes" warn Pharaoh about the imminent birth of one who will deliver Israel from Egypt and the king makes plans to destroy him.

2:11 Cf. Psalm 72:10; Psalm 72:15; Isaiah 60:6. These Old Testament texts led to the interpretation of the magi as Kings.

2:13-23 Biblical and nonbiblical traditions about Moses are here applied to the child Jesus, though the dominant Old Testament type is not Moses but Israel (2:15).

2:13 Flee to Egypt: Egypt was a traditional place of refuge for those fleeing from danger in Palestine (see 1 Kgs 11:40; Jer 26:21),

but the main reason why the child is to be taken to Egypt is that he may relive the Exodus experience of Israel.

2:15 The fulfillment citation is taken from Hosea 11:1. Israel, God's son, was called out of Egypt at the time of the Exodus; Jesus, the Son of God, will similarly be called out of that land in a new exodus. The father-son relationship between God and the nation is set in a higher key. Here the son is not a group adopted as "son of God," but the child who, as conceived by the holy Spirit, stands in unique relation to God. He is son of David and of Abraham, of Mary and of Joseph, but, above all, of God.

the massacre of all the boys in Bethlehem and its vicinity two years old and under, in accordance with the time he had ascertained from the magi. ¹⁷Then was fulfilled what had been said through Jeremiah the prophet:

> ¹⁸*ᵉ*"A voice was heard in Ramah,
>   sobbing and loud lamentation;
> Rachel weeping for her children,
>   and she would not be consoled,
>   since they were no more."

Traditional cave "house" in Nazareth

The Return from Egypt

¹⁹When Herod had died, behold, the angel of the Lord appeared in a dream to Joseph in Egypt ²⁰*ᶠ*and said, "Rise, take the child and his mother and go to the land of Israel, for those who sought the child's life are dead."* ²¹He rose, took the child and his mother, and went to the land of Israel. ²²But when he heard that Archelaus was ruling over Judea in place of his father Herod,* he was afraid to go back there. And because he had been warned in a dream, he departed for the region of Galilee. ²³*ᵍHe went and dwelt in a town called Nazareth, so that what had been spoken through the prophets might be fulfilled, "He shall be called a Nazorean."

II: The Proclamation of the Kingdom

The Preaching of John the Baptist

3 ¹*ᵃIn those days John the Baptist appeared, preaching in the desert of Judea* ²ᵇ[and] saying, "Repent,* for the kingdom of heaven is at hand!" ³*ᶜIt was of him that the prophet Isaiah had spoken when he said:

e
Jer 31:15

f
Ex 4:19

g
13:54; Mk 1:9;
Lk 2:39; 4:34;
Jn 19:19

a
Mk 1:2-8;
Lk 3:2-17

b
4:17; 10:7

c
Is 40:3

2:18 Jeremiah 31:15 portrays Rachel, wife of the patriarch Jacob, weeping for her children taken into exile at the time of the Assyrian invasion of the northern kingdom (722–21 B.C.). Bethlehem was traditionally identified with Ephrath, the place near which Rachel was buried (see Gn 35:19; 48:7), and the mourning of Rachel is here applied to her lost children of a later age. **Ramah**: about six miles north of Jerusalem. The lamentation of Rachel is so great as to be heard at a far distance.

2:20 For those who sought the child's life are dead: Moses, who had fled from Egypt because the Pharaoh sought to kill him (see Ex 2:15), was told to return there, "for all the men who sought your life are dead" (Ex 4:19).

2:22 With the agreement of the emperor Augustus, Archelaus received half of his father's kingdom, including Judea, after Herod's death. He had the title "ethnarch" (i.e., "ruler of a nation") and reigned from 4 B.C. to A.D. 6.

2:23 Nazareth . . . he shall be called a Nazorean: the tradition of Jesus' residence in Nazareth was firmly established, and Matthew sees it as being in accordance with the foreannounced plan of God. The town of Nazareth is not mentioned in the Old Testament, and no such prophecy can be found there. The vague expression "through the prophets" may be due to Matthew's seeing a connection between Nazareth and certain texts with are words with a remote similarity to the name of that town. Some such Old Testament texts are Isaiah 11:1 where the Davidic king of the future is called "a bud"

(*nēser*) that shall blossom from the roots of Jesse, and Judges 13:5, 7 where Samson, the future deliverer of Israel from the Philistines, is called one who shall be consecrated (a *nāzîr*) to God.

3:1-12 Here Matthew takes up the order of Jesus' ministry found in the gospel of Mark, beginning with the preparatory preaching of John the Baptist.

3:1 Unlike Luke, Matthew says nothing of the Baptist's origins and does not make him a relative of Jesus. **The desert of Judea**: the barren region west of the Dead Sea extending up the Jordan valley.

3:2 Repent: the Baptist calls for a change of heart and conduct, a turning of one's life from rebellion to obedience towards God. **The kingdom of heaven is at hand**: "heaven" (literally, "the heavens") is a substitute for the name "God" that was avoided by devout Jews of the time out of reverence. The expression "the kingdom of heaven" occurs only in the gospel of Matthew. It means the effective rule of God over his people. In its fullness it includes not only human obedience to God's word, but the triumph of God over physical evils, supremely over death. In the expectation found in Jewish apocalyptic, the kingdom was to be ushered in by a judgment in which sinners would be condemned and perish, an expectation shared by the Baptist. This was modified in Christian understanding where the kingdom was seen as being established in stages, culminating with the parousia of Jesus.

3:3 See the note on John 1:23.

21

MATTHEW

d
11:7-8;
2 Kgs 1:8;
Zec 13:4

e
12:34; 23:33;
Is 59:5

f
Jn 8:33, 39;
Rom 9:7-8;
Gal 4:21-31

g
Jn 1:26-27, 33;
Acts 1:5

h
13:30;
Is 41:16;
Jer 15:7

i
Mk 1:9-11;
Lk 3:21-22;
Jn 1:31-34

"A voice of one crying out in the desert,
'Prepare the way of the Lord,
make straight his paths.'"

[4]*[d]John wore clothing made of camel's hair and had a leather belt around his waist. His food was locusts and wild honey. [5]At that time Jerusalem, all Judea, and the whole region around the Jordan were going out to him [6]and were being baptized by him in the Jordan River as they acknowledged their sins.*

[7][e]When he saw many of the Pharisees and Sadducees* coming to his baptism, he said to them, "You brood of vipers! Who warned you

Judea around the Jordan River

to flee from the coming wrath? [8]Produce good fruit as evidence of your repentance. [9][f]And do not presume to say to yourselves, 'We have Abraham as our father.' For I tell you, God can raise up children to Abraham from these stones. [10]Even now the ax lies at the root of the trees. Therefore every tree that does not bear good fruit will be cut down and thrown into the fire. [11][g]I am baptizing you with water, for repentance, but the one who is coming after me is mightier than I.

I am not worthy to carry his sandals. He will baptize you with the holy Spirit and fire.* [12]*[h]His winnowing fan is in his hand. He will clear his threshing floor and gather his wheat into his barn, but the chaff he will burn with unquenchable fire."

The Baptism of Jesus

[13]*[i]Then Jesus came from Galilee to John at the Jordan to be baptized by him. [14]*John tried to prevent him, saying, "I need to be baptized by you, and yet you are coming to me?" [15]Jesus said to him in reply, "Allow it now, for thus it is fitting for us to fulfill all

---

3:4 The clothing of John recalls the austere dress of the prophet Elijah (2 Kgs 1:8). The expectation of the return of Elijah from heaven to prepare Israel for the final manifestation of God's kingdom was widespread, and according to Matthew this expectation was fulfilled in the Baptist's ministry (11:14; 17:11-13).

3:6 Ritual washing was practiced by various groups in Palestine between 150 B.C. and A.D. 250. John's baptism may have been related to the purificatory washings of the Essenes at Qumran.

3:7 Pharisees and Sadducees: the former were marked by devotion to the law, written and oral, and the scribes, experts in the law, belonged predominantly to this group. The Sadducees were the priestly aristocratic party, centered in Jerusalem. They accepted as scripture only the first five books of the Old Testament, followed only the letter of the law, rejected the oral legal traditions, and were opposed to teachings not found in the Pentateuch, such as the resurrection of the dead. Matthew links both of these groups together as enemies of Jesus (16:1, 6, 11, 12; cf. Mk 8:11-13, 15). The threatening words that follow are addressed to them rather than to "the crowds" as in Luke 3:7. **The coming wrath**: the judgment that will bring about the destruction of unrepentant sinners.

3:11 Baptize you with the holy Spirit and fire: the water baptism of John will be followed by an "immersion" of the repentant in the cleansing power of the Spirit of God, and of the unrepentant in

the destroying power of God's judgment. However, some see **the holy Spirit** and **fire** as synonymous, and the effect of this "baptism" as either purification or destruction. See the note on Luke 3:16.

3:12 The discrimination between the good and the bad is compared to the procedure by which a farmer separates wheat and chaff. The **winnowing fan** was a forklike shovel with which the threshed wheat was thrown into the air. The kernels fell to the ground; the light chaff, blown off by the wind, was gathered and burned up.

3:13-17 The baptism of Jesus is the occasion on which he is equipped for his ministry by the holy Spirit and proclaimed to be the Son of God.

3:14-15 This dialogue, peculiar to Matthew, reveals John's awareness of Jesus' superiority to him as the mightier one who is coming and who will baptize with the holy Spirit (3:11). His reluctance to admit Jesus among the sinners whom he is baptizing with water is overcome by Jesus' response. **To fulfill all righteousness**: in this gospel to **fulfill** usually refers to fulfillment of prophecy, and **righteousness** to moral conduct in conformity with God's will. Here, however, as in Matthew 5:6; 6:33, **righteousness** seems to mean the saving activity of God. **To fulfill all righteousness** is to submit to the plan of God for the salvation of the human race. This involves Jesus' identification with sinners; hence the propriety of his accepting John's baptism.

righteousness." Then he allowed him. [16]*[j]After Jesus was baptized, he came up from the water and behold, the heavens were opened [for him], and he saw the Spirit of God descending like a dove [and] coming upon him. [17][k]And a voice came from the heavens, saying, "This is my beloved Son,* with whom I am well pleased."

The Temptation of Jesus

4 [1]*[a]Then Jesus was led by the Spirit into the desert to be tempted by the devil. [2][b]He fasted for forty days and forty nights,* and afterwards he was hungry. [3][c]The tempter approached and said to him, "If you are the Son of God, command that these stones become loaves of bread." [4]*He said in reply, "It is written:

'One does not live by bread alone,
  but by every word that comes forth from the mouth of God.'"

j
Is 42:1

k
12:18; 17:5;
Gn 22:2;
Ps 2:7; Is 42:1

a
Mk 1:12-13;
Lk 4:1-13

b
Ex 24:18;
Dt 8:2

c
Dt 8:3

Getting It Right . . . Demons and Devils

The Bible speaks of numerous supernatural figures of evil. Although they are generally identified with one another, they actually have long, complex histories and are sometimes distinct.

Designation	Description	Key References
Satan	A Persian title that crept into the Bible; originally designated not an evil power but a kind of prosecuting attorney, part of God's heavenly retinue, whose job was to ensure good faith on earth; later is identified with the devil	Jb 1:6–2:7; Zec 3:1-2; Mt 4:10; Mk 1:13; 4:15; Lk 22:3; Jn 13:27; Acts 5:3
Beelzebul (NT) Baal-zebub (OT)	Literally, "the lord of the flies"; the name of a Philistine god; becomes explicitly identified with Satan as the prince of evil and master of demons (Mk 3:22-23)	Mt 12:24-27; Mk 3:22; Lk 11:15-19; cf. 2 Kgs 1:2-16
The devil	Term used to translate Hebrew *satan* in LXX (the Septuagint); is explicitly (Rev 12:9; 20:2) and implicitly (cf. Mt 4:1 and 10) identified with Satan, God's supernatural enemy; the embodiment of evil and the tempter who tests people and can lead them astray; is sometimes contrasted with the archangel Michael	Mt 4:1-11; Lk 4:1-13; Jn 8:44; 13:2; 1 Pt 5:8; Jude 1:9
Demons	Minor spiritual beings who are lesser minions of the devil; they can cause illness, disease, and possession; later Jewish tradition identified them as fallen angels; they were thought to dwell in the desert and wilderness	Tb 6–8; Mt 8:28-33; Lk 4:41; 8:26-39; cf. Mk 1:13

3:16 The Spirit . . . coming upon him: cf. Isaiah 42:1.

3:17 This is my beloved Son: the Marcan address to Jesus (Mk 1:11) is changed into a proclamation. The Father's voice speaks in terms that reflect Isaiah 42:1; Psalm 2:7; Genesis 22:2.

4:1-11 Jesus, proclaimed Son of God at his baptism, is subjected to a triple temptation. Obedience to the Father is a characteristic of true sonship, and Jesus is tempted by the devil to rebel against God, overtly in the third case, more subtly in the first two. Each refusal of Jesus is expressed in language taken from the Book of Deuteronomy (Dt 8:3; 6:13, 16). The testings of Jesus resemble those of Israel during the wandering in the desert and later in Canaan, and the victory of Jesus, the true Israel and the true Son, contrasts with the failure of the ancient and disobedient "son," the old Israel. In the temptation account Matthew is almost identical with Luke; both seem to have drawn upon the same source.

4:2 Forty days and forty nights: the same time as that during which Moses remained on Sinai (Ex 24:18). The time reference, however, seems primarily intended to recall the forty years during which Israel was tempted in the desert (Dt 8:2).

4:4 Cf. Deuteronomy 8:3. Jesus refuses to use his power for his own benefit and accepts whatever God wills.

<table>
<tr><td>

d
Ps 91:11-12

e
Dt 6:16

f
16:23; Dt 6:13

g
Mk 1:14-15;
Lk 4:14, 31

h
Jn 2:12

i
Is 8:23 LXX;
9:1

j
Lk 1:79

k
3:2

</td></tr>
</table>

5*Then the devil took him to the holy city, and made him stand on the parapet of the temple, 6dand said to him, "If you are the Son of God, throw yourself down. For it is written:

'He will command his angels concerning you
    and 'with their hands they will support you,
lest you dash your foot against a stone.'"

7eJesus answered him, "Again it is written, 'You shall not put the Lord, your God, to the test.'" 8Then the devil took him up to a very high mountain, and showed him all the kingdoms of the world in their magnificence, 9and he said to him, "All these I shall give to you, if you will prostrate yourself and worship me."* 10fAt this, Jesus said to him, "Get away, Satan! It is written:

'The Lord, your God, shall you worship
    and him alone shall you serve.'"

11Then the devil left him and, behold, angels came and ministered to him.

The Beginning of the Galilean Ministry

12*gWhen he heard that John had been arrested, he withdrew to Galilee. 13hHe left Nazareth and went to live in Capernaum by the sea, in the region of Zebulun and Naphtali, 14that what had been said through Isaiah the prophet might be fulfilled:

15i"Land of Zebulun and land of Naphtali,
    the way to the sea, beyond the Jordan,
    Galilee of the Gentiles,
16jthe people who sit in darkness
    have seen a great light,
on those dwelling in a land overshadowed by death
    light has arisen."

17*kFrom that time on, Jesus began to preach and say, "Repent, for the kingdom of heaven is at hand."

4:5-7 The devil supports his proposal by an appeal to the scriptures, Psalm 91:11a, 12. Unlike Israel (Dt 6:16), Jesus refuses to "test" God by demanding from him an extraordinary show of power.

4:9 The worship of Satan to which Jesus is tempted is probably intended to recall Israel's worship of false gods. His refusal is expressed in the words of Deuteronomy 6:13.

4:12-17 Isaiah's prophecy of the light rising upon Zebulun and Naphtali (Is 8:22–9:1) is fulfilled in Jesus' residence at Capernaum. The territory of these two tribes was the first to be devastated (733–32 B.C.) at the time of the Assyrian invasion. In order to accommodate Jesus' move to Capernaum to the prophecy, Matthew speaks of that town as being "in the region of Zebulun and Naphtali" (4:13), whereas it was only in the territory of the latter, and he understands the sea of the prophecy, the Mediterranean, as the sea of Galilee.

4:17 At the beginning of his preaching Jesus takes up the words of John the Baptist (3:2) although with a different meaning; in his ministry the kingdom of heaven has already begun to be present (12:28).

The section of Matthew from **4:23–9:38** is carefully structured in parallel fashion (a, b, b', a') to reinforce the portrait of Jesus as God's Son who has the authority to teach in WORD and in DEED.

(a) Summary statement of Jesus' teaching, preaching, and healing (4:23-25)

(b) The Sermon on the Mount, showing Jesus authoritatively teaching in WORD (5:1–7:29)

(b') Miracle stories and controversies, showing Jesus authoritatively healing in DEED (8:1–9:34)

(a') Summary statement of Jesus' teaching, preaching, and healing (9:35-38)

The Call of the First Disciples

[18]*[l]As he was walking by the Sea of Galilee, he saw two brothers, Simon who is called Peter, and his brother Andrew, casting a net into the sea; they were fishermen. [19]He said to them, "Come after me, and I will make you fishers of men." [20]*At once they left their nets and followed him. [21]He walked along from there and saw two other brothers, James, the son of Zebedee, and his brother John. They were in a boat, with their father Zebedee, mending their nets. He called them, [22]and immediately they left their boat and their father and followed him.

Ministering to a Great Multitude

[23]*[m]He went around all of Galilee, teaching in their synagogues,* proclaiming the gospel of the kingdom, and curing every disease and illness among the people. [24]*His fame spread to all of Syria, and they brought to him all who were sick with various diseases and racked with pain, those who were possessed, lunatics, and paralytics, and he cured them. [25][n]And great crowds from Galilee, the Decapolis,* Jerusalem, and Judea, and from beyond the Jordan followed him.

l
Mk 1:16-20;
Lk 5:1-11

m
9:35; Mk 1:39;
Lk 4:15, 44

n
Mk 3:7-8;
Lk 6:17-19

The origin of **synagogues** is obscure. They were places of assembly for Jews to worship and share a cultural heritage. They developed in the postexilic period in the wake of the absence of the Jerusalem temple that the Babylonians had destroyed (587 B.C.). The destruction of the second temple in A.D. 70 by the Romans further developed the synagogue into a place of reflection on the Torah and other Scriptures. By NT times the synagogue was a specific building that served Jews of the Diaspora ("scattering") in multiple ways for religious and cultural purposes. See more information about the Diaspora in Ezra (at 2:1).

Remains of the synagogue at Capernaum

4:18-22 The call of the first disciples promises them a share in Jesus' work and entails abandonment of family and former way of life. Three of the four, Simon, James, and John, are distinguished among the disciples by a closer relation with Jesus (17:1; 26:37).

4:20 Here and in Matthew 4:22, as in Mark (Mk 1:16-20) and unlike the Lucan account (Lk 5:1-11), the disciples' response is motivated only by Jesus' invitation, an element that emphasizes his mysterious power.

4:23-25 This summary of Jesus' ministry concludes the narrative part of the first book of Matthew's gospel (3–4). The activities of his ministry are teaching, proclaiming the gospel, and healing; cf. Matthew 9:35.

4:23 Their synagogues: Matthew usually designates the Jewish synagogues as **their synagogue(s)** (9:35; 10:17; 12:9; 13:54) or, in address to Jews, **your synagogues** (23:34), an indication that he wrote after the break between church and synagogue.

4:24 Syria: the Roman province to which Palestine belonged.

4:25 The Decapolis: a federation of Greek cities in Palestine, originally ten in number, all but one east of the Jordan.

a
Lk 6:20-23

b
Is 61:2-3;
Rev 21:4

c
Gn 13:15;
Ps 37:11

d
18:33; Jas 2:13

e
Pss 24:4-5;
73:1

The Sermon on the Mount

5 ¹*When he saw the crowds,* he went up the mountain, and after he had sat down, his disciples came to him. ²He began to teach them, saying:

The Beatitudes

³*ᵃ"Blessed are the poor in spirit,*
  for theirs is the kingdom of heaven.
⁴*ᵇBlessed are they who mourn,
  for they will be comforted.
⁵*ᶜBlessed are the meek,
  for they will inherit the land.
⁶Blessed are they who hunger and thirst for righteousness,*
  for they will be satisfied.
⁷ᵈBlessed are the merciful,
  for they will be shown mercy.
⁸*ᵉBlessed are the clean of heart,
  for they will see God.

Matthew favors the **mountain** as the site for divine revelation. Not only does the Sermon on the Mount take place on a mountain but also the transfiguration (17:1) and the Great Commission (28:16). Jesus also goes to the mountain to pray (14:23) and to heal (15:29). The Bible views mountains as holy sites, close to God. This Matthean theme recalls that the mountain (Horeb/Sinai) is where Moses received the Torah and also communed with God (Ex 24:12-18), thus showing continuity between Moses and Jesus.

The **Beatitudes** recorded in Matthew have an ageless quality that has fascinated every generation of Christians. The church has variously seen them as signs of the kingdom of God, ideals to be striven after, or unique virtues meant primarily for Jesus' followers. The *Catechism of the Catholic Church* calls the Beatitudes "the heart of Jesus' preaching" (1716).

5:1–7:29 The first of the five discourses that are a central part of this gospel. It is the discourse section of the first book and contains sayings of Jesus derived from Q and from M. The Lucan parallel is in that gospel's "Sermon on the Plain" (Lk 6:20-49), although some of the sayings in Matthew's "Sermon on the Mount" have their parallels in other parts of Luke. The careful topical arrangement of the sermon is probably not due only to Matthew's editing; he seems to have had a structured discourse of Jesus as one of his sources. The form of that source may have been as follows: four beatitudes (5:3-4, 6, 11-12), a section on the new righteousness with illustrations (5:17, 20-24, 27-28, 33-48), a section on good works (6:1-6, 16-18), and three warnings (7:1-2, 15-21, 24-27).

5:1-2 Unlike Luke's sermon, this is addressed not only to the disciples but to the crowds (see 7:28).

5:3-12 The form **Blessed are (is)** occurs frequently in the Old Testament in the Wisdom literature and in the Psalms. Although modified by Matthew, the first, second, fourth, and ninth beatitudes have Lucan parallels (Mt 5:3 // Lk 6:20; Mt 5:4 // Lk 6:21, 22; Mt 5:6 // Lk 6:21a; Mt 5:11-12 // Mt 5:22-23). The others were added by the evangelist and are probably his own composition. A few manuscripts, Western and Alexandrian, and many versions and patristic quotations give the second and third beatitudes in inverted order.

5:3 The poor in spirit: in the Old Testament, the poor (*ănāwîm*) are those who are without material possessions and whose confidence is in God (see Is 61:1; Zep 2:3; in the NAB the word is translated **lowly** and **humble**, respectively, in those texts). Matthew added **in spirit** in order either to indicate that only the devout poor were meant or to extend the beatitude to all, of whatever social rank, who recognized their complete dependence on God. The same phrase **poor in spirit** is found in the Qumran literature (1QM 14:7).

5:4 Cf. Isaiah 61:2 "(The Lord has sent me) . . . to comfort all who mourn." **They will be comforted**: here the passive is a "theological passive" equivalent to the active "God will comfort them"; so also in Matthew 5:6, 7.

5:5 Cf. Psalm 37:11, ". . . the meek shall possess the land." In the psalm "the land" means the land of Palestine; here it means the kingdom.

5:6 For righteousness: a Matthean addition. For the meaning of **righteousness** here, see the note on Matthew 3:14-15.

5:8 Cf. Psalm 24:4. Only one "whose heart is clean" can take part in the temple worship. To be with God in the temple is described in Psalm 42:2 as "beholding his face," but here the promise to **the clean of heart** is that they will **see God** not in the temple but in the coming kingdom.

⁹Blessed are the peacemakers,
>for they will be called children of God.
¹⁰ᶠBlessed are they who are persecuted for the sake of righteousness,*
>for theirs is the kingdom of heaven.

¹¹ᵍBlessed are you when they insult you and persecute you and utter every kind of evil against you [falsely] because of me. ¹²*ʰRejoice and be glad, for your reward will be great in heaven. Thus they persecuted the prophets who were before you.

f
1 Pt 2:20; 3:14; 4:14
g
10:22; Acts 5:41
h
2 Chr 36:16; Heb 11:32-38; Jas 5:10

A **beatitude** is an ancient literary form found in the Wisdom literature and Psalms of the OT (see, e.g., Ps 1:1). The opening word is usually translated "blessed" or "happy" and it expresses both a wish and a statement that God's blessing be upon the person or object. Matthew actually records nine beatitudes, eight of which are in the third person singular, with only the last one in the second person plural, directed to the disciples. See also Luke 6:20-26.

The Church of the Beatitudes near the Sea of Galilee

Applying the Beatitudes

The U.S. bishops noted the importance of the Beatitudes in implementing economic justice for all people in their pastoral letter on the topic:

We write to share our teaching, to raise questions, to challenge one another to live our faith in the world. We write as heirs of the biblical prophets who summon us "to do the right and to love goodness, and to walk humbly with your God" (Mi 6:8). We write as followers of Jesus who told us in the Sermon on the Mount: "Blessed are the poor in spirit . . . Blessed are the meek . . . Blessed are they who hunger and thirst for righteousness . . . You are the salt of the earth . . . You are the light of the world" (Mt 5:1-6, 13-14). These words challenge us not only as believers but also as consumers, citizens, workers, and owners. In the parable of the Last Judgment, Jesus said, "For I was hungry and you gave me food, I was thirsty and you gave me drink . . . As often as you did it for one of my least brothers, you did it for me" (Mt 25:35-40). The challenge for us is to discover in our own place and time what it means to be "poor in spirit" and "the salt of the earth" and what it means to serve "the least among us" and to "hunger and thirst for righteousness." (*EJ*, 4)

5:10 Righteousness here, as usually in Matthew, means conduct in conformity with God's will.

5:12 The prophets who were before you: the disciples of Jesus stand in the line of the persecuted prophets of Israel. Some would see the expression as indicating also that Matthew considered all Christian disciples as prophets.

i
Mk 9:50;
Lk 14:34-35

j
Jn 8:12

k
Mk 4:21;
Lk 8:16; 11:33

l
Jn 3:21

m
Lk 16:17

n
Ex 20:13;
Dt 5:17

The Similes of Salt and Light

13i"You are the salt of the earth. But if salt loses its taste, with what can it be seasoned? It is no longer good for anything but to be thrown out and trampled underfoot.* 14j*You are the light of the world. A city set on a mountain cannot be hidden. 15k*Nor do they light a lamp and then put it under a bushel basket; it is set on a lampstand, where it gives light to all in the house. 16l*Just so, your light must shine before others, that they may see your good deeds and glorify your heavenly Father.

"The law and the prophets" is Matthew's favorite expression for describing the whole of the OT (cf. 7:12; 22:40). For Matthew, Jesus does not come to abolish but to fulfill both the Law and the Prophets. This two-part division contrasts somewhat with Luke's threefold reference to the Law, the Prophets, and the Psalms (see Lk 24:44).

Teaching about the Law

17*"Do not think that I have come to abolish the law or the prophets. I have come not to abolish but to fulfill. 18m*Amen, I say to you, until heaven and earth pass away, not the smallest letter or the smallest part of a letter will pass from the law, until all things have taken place. 19*Therefore, whoever breaks one of the least of these commandments and teaches others to do so will be called least in the kingdom of heaven. But whoever obeys and teaches these commandments will be called greatest in the kingdom of heaven.* 20*I tell you, unless your righteousness surpasses that of the scribes and Pharisees, you will not enter into the kingdom of heaven.

Righteousness refers to the traditional Jewish concept of living an ethically upright life before God and humanity. Jesus nonetheless challenges his disciples to go beyond mere conformity to ethical standards to live the "greater righteousness," seen in forgiveness, love of enemies, etc., expressed in the antitheses of the Sermon on the Mount (Mt 5:21-48; "You have heard it said . . . but I say to you . . .").

Teaching about Anger

21n"You have heard that it was said to your ancestors, 'You shall not kill; and whoever kills will be liable to

---

5:13-16 By their deeds the disciples are to influence the world for good. They can no more escape notice than **a city set on a mountain.** If they fail in good works, they are as useless as flavorless salt or as a lamp whose light is concealed.

5:13 The unusual supposition of salt losing its flavor has led some to suppose that the saying refers to the salt of the Dead Sea that, because chemically impure, could lose its taste.

5:17-20 This statement of Jesus' position concerning the Mosaic law is composed of traditional material from Matthew's sermon documentation (see the note on 5:1–7:29), other Q material (cf. 18; Lk 16:17), and the evangelist's own editorial touches. **To fulfill** the law appears at first to mean a literal enforcement of the law in the least detail: **until heaven and earth pass away** nothing of the law **will pass** (5:18). Yet the "passing away" of heaven and earth is not necessarily the end of the world understood, as in much apocalyptic literature, as the dissolution of the existing universe. The "turning of the ages" comes with the apocalyptic event of Jesus' death and resurrection, and those to whom this gospel is addressed are living in the new and final age, prophesied by Isaiah as the time of "new

heavens and a new earth" (Is 65:17; 66:22). Meanwhile, during Jesus' ministry when the kingdom is already breaking in, his mission remains within the framework of the law, though with significant anticipation of the age to come, as the following antitheses (5:21-48) show.

5:19 Probably **these commandments** means those of the Mosaic law. But this is an interim ethic "until heaven and earth pass away."

5:21-48 Six examples of the conduct demanded of the Christian disciple. Each deals with a commandment of the law, introduced by **You have heard that it was said to your ancestors** or an equivalent formula, followed by Jesus' teaching in respect to that commandment, **But I say to you;** thus their designation as "antitheses." Three of them accept the Mosaic law but extend or deepen it (5:21-22; 27-28; 43-44); three reject it as a standard of conduct for the disciples (5:31-32; 33-37; 38-39).

5:21 Cf. Exodus 20:13; Deuteronomy 5:17. The second part of the verse is not an exact quotation from the Old Testament, but cf. Exodus 21:12.

judgment.'* [22]*[o]But I say to you, whoever is angry* with his brother will be liable to judgment, and whoever says to his brother, 'Raqa,' will be answerable to the Sanhedrin, and whoever says, 'You fool,' will be liable to fiery Gehenna. [23]*[p]Therefore, if you bring your gift to the altar, and there recall that your brother has anything against you, [24]leave your gift there at the altar, go first and be reconciled with your brother, and then come and offer your gift. [25]*[q]Settle with your opponent quickly while on the way to court with him. Otherwise your opponent will hand you over to the judge, and the judge will hand you over to the guard, and you will be thrown into prison. [26]Amen, I say to you, you will not be released until you have paid the last penny.

Teaching about Adultery

[27]*[r]"You have heard that it was said, 'You shall not commit adultery.' [28]But I say to you, everyone who looks at a woman with lust has already committed adultery with her in his heart. [29]*[s]If your right eye causes you to sin, tear it out and throw it away. It is better for you to lose one of your members than to have your whole body thrown into Gehenna. [30]And if your right hand causes you to sin, cut it off and throw it away. It is better for you to lose one of your members than to have your whole body go into Gehenna.

Teaching about Divorce

[31]*[t]"It was also said, 'Whoever divorces his wife must give her a bill of divorce.' [32]*[u]But I say to you, whoever divorces his wife (unless the marriage is unlawful) causes her to commit adultery, and whoever marries a divorced woman commits adultery.

Teaching about Oaths

[33]*[v]"Again you have heard that it was said to your ancestors, 'Do not take a false oath, but make good to the Lord all that you vow.' [34]*[w]But I say to you, do not swear at all;* not by heaven, for it is God's throne; [35]nor by the earth, for it is his footstool; nor

---

o
Jas 1:19-20

p
Mk 11:25

q
18:34-35;
Lk 12:58-59

r
Ex 20:14;
Dt 5:18

s
18:8-9;
Mk 9:43-47

t
19:3-9; Dt 24:1

u
Lk 16:18;
1 Cor 7:10-11

v
Lv 19:12;
Nm 30:3

w
Ps 48:3;
Sir 23:9;
Is 66:1;
Jas 5:12

5:22-26 Reconciliation with an offended brother is urged in the admonition of Matthew 5:23-24 and the parable of Matthew 5:25-26 (Lk 12:58-59). The severity of the judge in the parable is a warning of the fate of unrepentant sinners in the coming judgment by God.

5:22 Anger is the motive behind murder, as the insulting epithets are steps that may lead to it. They, as well as the deed, are all forbidden. **Raqa**: an Aramaic word *rēqāʾ* or *rēqâ* probably meaning "imbecile," "blockhead," a term of abuse. The ascending order of punishment, **judgment** (by a local council?), trial before **the Sanhedrin**, condemnation to **Gehenna**, points to a higher degree of seriousness in each of the offenses. Sanhedrin: the highest judicial body of Judaism. **Gehenna**: in Hebrew *gê-hinnōm*, "Valley of Hinnom," or *gê ben-hinnōm*, "Valley of the son of Hinnom," southwest of Jerusalem, the center of an idolatrous cult during the monarchy in which children were offered in sacrifice (see 2 Kgs 23:10; Jer 7:31). In Joshua 18:16 (Septuagint, Codex Vaticanus) the Hebrew is transliterated into Greek as *gaienna*, which appears in the New Testament as *geenna*. The concept of punishment of sinners by fire either after death or after the final judgment is found in Jewish apocalyptic literature (e.g., Enoch 90:26) but the name *geenna* is first given to the place of punishment in the New Testament.

5:27 See Exodus 20:14; Deuteronomy 5:18.

5:29-30 No sacrifice is too great to avoid total destruction in **Gehenna**.

5:31-32 See Deuteronomy 24:1-5. The Old Testament commandment that a bill of divorce be given to the woman assumes the le-

gitimacy of divorce itself. It is this that Jesus denies. **(Unless the marriage is unlawful)**: this "exceptive clause," as it is often called, occurs also in Matthew 19:9, where the Greek is slightly different. There are other sayings of Jesus about divorce that prohibit it absolutely (see Mk 10:11-12; Lk 16:18; cf. 1 Cor 7:10, 11b), and most scholars agree that they represent the stand of Jesus. Matthew's "exceptive clauses" are understood by some as a modification of the absolute prohibition. It seems, however, that the unlawfulness that Matthew gives as a reason why a marriage must be broken refers to a situation peculiar to his community: the violation of Mosaic law forbidding marriage between persons of certain blood and/ or legal relationship (Lv 18:6-18). Marriages of that sort were regarded as incest (*porneia*), but some rabbis allowed Gentile converts to Judaism who had contracted such marriages to remain in them. Matthew's "exceptive clause" is against such permissiveness for Gentile converts to Christianity; cf. the similar prohibition of *porneia* in Acts 15:20, 29. In this interpretation, the clause constitutes no exception to the absolute prohibition of divorce when the marriage is lawful.

5:33 This is not an exact quotation of any Old Testament text, but see Exodus 20:7; Deuteronomy 5:11; Leviticus 19:12. The purpose of an oath was to guarantee truthfulness by one's calling on God as witness.

5:34-36 The use of these oath formularies that avoid the divine name is in fact equivalent to swearing by it, for all the things sworn by are related to God.

x
Ex 21:24;
Lv 24:19-20

y
Lk 6:29-30

z
Lam 3:30

a
Dt 15:7-8

b
Lk 6:27, 32-36

c
Lv 19:18

d
Lv 11:44; 19:2;
Dt 18:13;
Jas 1:4;
1 Pt 1:16;
1 Jn 3:3

a
23:5

b
Jn 12:43

by Jerusalem, for it is the city of the great King. [36]Do not swear by your head, for you cannot make a single hair white or black. [37][*][x]Let your 'Yes' mean 'Yes,' and your 'No' mean 'No.' Anything more is from the evil one.

Teaching about Retaliation

[38][*][x]"You have heard that it was said, 'An eye for an eye and a tooth for a tooth.' [39][y]But I say to you, offer no resistance to one who is evil. When someone strikes you on [your] right cheek, turn the other one to him as well. [40]If anyone wants to go to law with you over your tunic, hand him your cloak as well. [41][z]Should anyone press you into service for one mile,[*] go with him for two miles. [42][a]Give to the one who asks of you, and do not turn your back on one who wants to borrow.

Love of Enemies

[43][*][b]"You have heard that it was said, 'You shall love your neighbor and hate your enemy.'[c] [44]But I say to you, love your enemies, and pray for those who persecute you, [45]that you may be children of your heavenly Father, for he makes his sun rise on the bad and the good, and causes rain to fall on the just and the unjust. [46]For if you love those who love you, what recompense will you have? Do not the tax collectors[*] do the same? [47]And if you greet your brothers only, what is unusual about that? Do not the pagans do the same?[*] [48][d]So be perfect,[*] just as your heavenly Father is perfect.

Teaching about Almsgiving

6 [1][*][a]"[But] take care not to perform righteous deeds in order that people may see them; otherwise, you will have no recompense from your heavenly Father. [2][b]When you give alms, do not blow a trumpet before you, as the hypocrites[*] do in the synagogues and in

---

5:37 Let your 'Yes' mean 'Yes,' and your 'No' mean 'No': literally, "let your speech be 'Yes, yes,' 'No, no.'" Some have understood this as a milder form of oath, permitted by Jesus. In view of Matthew 5:34, "Do not swear at all," that is unlikely. **From the evil one**: i.e., from the devil. Oath-taking presupposes a sinful weakness of the human race, namely, the tendency to lie. Jesus demands of his disciples a truthfulness that makes oaths unnecessary.

5:38-42 See Leviticus 24:20. The Old Testament commandment was meant to moderate vengeance; the punishment should not exceed the injury done. Jesus forbids even this proportionate retaliation. Of the five examples that follow, only the first deals directly with retaliation for evil; the others speak of liberality.

5:41 Roman garrisons in Palestine had the right to requisition the property and services of the native population.

5:43-48 See Leviticus 19:18. There is no Old Testament commandment demanding hatred of one's enemy, but the "neighbor" of the love commandment was understood as one's fellow countryman. Both in the Old Testament (Ps 139:19-22) and at Qumran (1QS 9:21) hatred of evil persons is assumed to be right. Jesus extends the love commandment to the enemy and the persecutor. His disciples, as children of God, must imitate the example of their Father, who grants his gifts of sun and rain to both the good and the bad.

5:46 Tax collectors: Jews who were engaged in the collection of indirect taxes such as tolls and customs. See the note on Mark 2:14.

5:47 Jesus' disciples must not be content with merely usual standards of conduct; see Matthew 5:20 where the verb "surpass" (Greek *perisseuō*) is cognate with the **unusual** (*perisson*) of this verse.

Being **"perfect"** does not mean being without fault, in the sense of a psychological perfectionism that impedes healthy, adult human behavior. Rather, it means being so oriented toward the values of God's kingdom that all else is secondary. It is goal oriented and is meant to entice "the greater righteousness."

5:48 Perfect: in the gospels this word occurs only in Matthew, here and in Matthew 19:21. The Lucan parallel (Lk 6:36) demands that the disciples be **merciful**.

6:1-18 The sermon continues with a warning against doing good in order to be seen and gives three examples, almsgiving (6:2-4), prayer (6:5-15), and fasting (6:16-18). In each, the conduct of the hypocrites (6:2) is contrasted with that demanded of the disciples. The sayings about reward found here and elsewhere (5:12, 46; 10:41-42) show that this is a genuine element of Christian moral exhortation. Possibly to underline the difference between the Christian idea of reward and that of the hypocrites, the evangelist uses two different Greek verbs to express the rewarding of the disciples and that of the hypocrites; in the latter case it is the verb *apechō*, a commercial term for giving a receipt for what has been paid in full (6:2, 5, 16).

6:2 The hypocrites: the scribes and Pharisees, see Matthew 23:13, 15, 23, 25, 27, 29. The designation reflects an attitude result-

the streets to win the praise of others. Amen, I say to you, they have received their reward. [3]But when you give alms, do not let your left hand know what your right is doing, [4]so that your almsgiving may be secret. And your Father who sees in secret will repay you.

Teaching about Prayer

[5]"When you pray, do not be like the hypocrites, who love to stand and pray in the synagogues and on street corners so that others may see them. Amen, I say to you, they have received their reward. [6]But when you pray, go to your inner room, close the door, and pray to your Father in secret. And your Father who sees in secret will repay you. [7]*In praying, do not babble like the pagans, who think that they will be heard because of their many words.* [8]Do not be like them. Your Father knows what you need before you ask him.

The Lord's Prayer

[9]*c"This is how you are to pray:*

> Our Father in heaven,
>   hallowed be your name,
> [10]dyour kingdom come,*
> your will be done,
>   on earth as in heaven.

Perhaps the most important part of prayer is the "sound of silence." All words fall away and we float in a lake of quiet surrender. It is in the spaces between the words that we hear God's voice.

The "Our Father"

The Lord's Prayer falls almost dead center in the Sermon on the Mount. It is the central prayer of all disciples of Jesus. Just as Jews pray the *Shema Israel* from memory as a hallmark of their identity and faith (Dt 6:4-5; "Hear O Israel! . . ."), so Christians pray the Our Father from memory. Although this prayer exists in two versions, in Matthew and in Luke, the Matthean version is the one that the church has prayed for centuries, most likely under the influence of consistent liturgical usage. In fact, it is always prayed in the Mass just prior to the communion rite. The chart below sets forth a comparison of the two versions. Scholars generally deem Luke's more streamlined version to be closer to the form that Jesus actually prayed. Matthew's version exhibits more liturgical influence.

Matthew's Version (6:9-15)	Luke's Version (11:2-4)
Our Father in heaven	Father
Hallowed be your name	Hallowed be your name
Your kingdom come	Your kingdom come
Your will be done on earth as in heaven	
Give us today our daily bread	Give us each day our daily bread
Forgive us our debts as we forgive our debtors	Forgive us our sins, for we forgive everyone in debt to us
Do not subject us to the test	Do not subject us to the final test
But deliver us from the evil one	

ing not only from the controversies at the time of Jesus' ministry but from the opposition between Pharisaic Judaism and the church of Matthew. **They have received their reward**: they desire praise and have received what they were looking for.

6:7-15 Matthew inserts into his basic traditional material an expansion of the material on prayer that includes the model prayer, the "Our Father." That prayer is found in Luke 11:2-4 in a different context and in a different form.

6:7 The example of what Christian prayer should be like contrasts it now not with the prayer of the hypocrites but with that of **the pagans**. Their babbling probably means their reciting a long list of divine names, hoping that one of them will force a response from the deity.

6:9-13 Matthew's form of the "Our Father" follows the liturgical tradition of his church. Luke's less developed form also represents the liturgical tradition known to him, but it is probably closer than Matthew's to the original words of Jesus.

6:9 Our Father in heaven: this invocation is found in many rabbinic prayers of the post–New Testament period. **Hallowed be your name**: though the "hallowing" of the divine name could be understood as reverence done to God by human praise and by obedience to his will, this is more probably a petition that God hallow his own name, i.e., that he manifest his glory by an act of power (cf. Ez 36:23), in this case, by the establishment of his kingdom in its fullness.

6:10 Your kingdom come: this petition sets the tone of the prayer, and inclines the balance toward divine rather than human

e
Prv 30:8-9

f
18:21-22;
Sir 28:2

g
Jn 17:15;
2 Thes 3:3

h
18:35;
Sir 28:1-5;
Mk 11:25

i
Jas 2:13

j
Jas 5:2-3

k
Lk 12:33-34

l
Lk 11:34-36

m
Lk 16:13

[11]*[e]Give us today our daily bread;
[12][f]and forgive us our debts,*
   as we forgive our debtors;
[13][g]and do not subject us to the final test,*
   but deliver us from the evil one.

[14]*[h]If you forgive others their transgressions, your heavenly Father will forgive you. [15][i]But if you do not forgive others, neither will your Father forgive your transgressions.

Teaching about Fasting

[16]"When you fast,* do not look gloomy like the hypocrites. They neglect their appearance, so that they may appear to others to be fasting. Amen, I say to you, they have received their reward. [17]But when you fast, anoint your head and wash your face, [18]so that you may not appear to be fasting, except to your Father who is hidden. And your Father who sees what is hidden will repay you.

Treasure in Heaven

[19]*[j]"Do not store up for yourselves treasures on earth, where moth and decay destroy, and thieves break in and steal. [20][k]But store up treasures in heaven, where neither moth nor decay destroys, nor thieves break in and steal. [21]For where your treasure is, there also will your heart be.

The Light of the Body

[22]*[l]"The lamp of the body is the eye. If your eye is sound, your whole body will be filled with light; [23]but if your eye is bad, your whole body will be in darkness. And if the light in you is darkness, how great will the darkness be.

God and Money

[24]*[m]"No one can serve two masters. He will either hate one and love the other, or be devoted to one and despise the other. You cannot serve God and mammon.

Prayer, fasting, and almsgiving are the great triumvirate of Lenten acts of penance practiced in the church for centuries. They exemplify the "righteous deeds" to which followers of Jesus should devote themselves regularly. Lent affords an opportunity to hone these skills and to do them more effectively.

---

action in the petitions that immediately precede and follow it. **Your will be done, on earth as in heaven**: a petition that the divine purpose to establish the kingdom, a purpose present now **in heaven**, be executed **on earth**.

6:11 Give us today our daily bread: the rare Greek word *epiousios*, here **daily**, occurs in the New Testament only here and in Luke 11:3. A single occurrence of the word outside of these texts and of literature dependent on them has been claimed, but the claim is highly doubtful. The word may mean **daily** or "future" (other meanings have also been proposed). The latter would conform better to the eschatological tone of the whole prayer. So understood, the petition would be for a speedy coming of the kingdom (today), which is often portrayed in both the Old Testament and the New under the image of a feast (Is 25:6; Mt 8:11; 22:1-10; Lk 13:29; 14:15-24).

6:12 Forgive us our debts: the word **debts** is used metaphorically of sins, "debts" owed to God (see Lk 11:4). The request is probably for forgiveness at the final judgment.

6:13 Jewish apocalyptic writings speak of a period of severe trial before the end of the age, sometimes called the "messianic woes." This petition asks that the disciples be spared that **final test**.

6:14-15 These verses reflect a set pattern called "Principles of Holy Law." Human action now will be met by a corresponding action of God at the final judgment.

6:16 The only fast prescribed in the Mosaic law was that of the Day of Atonement (Lv 16:31), but the practice of regular fasting was common in later Judaism; cf. *Didache* 9:1.

6:19-34 The remaining material of this chapter is taken almost entirely from Q. It deals principally with worldly possessions, and the controlling thought is summed up in Matthew 6:24, the disciple can serve only one master and must choose between God and wealth (**mammon**). See further the note on Luke 16:9.

6:22-23 In this context the parable probably points to the need for the disciple to be enlightened by Jesus' teaching on the transitory nature of earthly riches.

6:24 Mammon: an Aramaic word meaning wealth or property.

Dependence on God

25*n*"Therefore I tell you, do not worry about your life, what you will eat [or drink], or about your body, what you will wear. Is not life more than food and the body more than clothing? 26*o*Look at the birds in the sky; they do not sow or reap, they gather nothing into barns, yet your heavenly Father feeds them. Are not you more important than they? 27Can any of you by worrying add a single moment to your life-span?* 28Why are you anxious about clothes? Learn from the way the wild flowers grow. They do not work or spin. 29But I tell you that not even Solomon in all his splendor was clothed like one of them. 30*If God so clothes the grass of the field, which grows today and is thrown into the oven tomorrow, will he not much more provide for you, O you of little faith? 31So do not worry and say, 'What are we to eat?' or 'What are we to drink?' or 'What are we to wear?' 32All these things the pagans seek. Your heavenly Father knows that you need them all. 33But seek first the kingdom [of God] and his righteousness,* and all these things will be given you besides. 34Do not worry about tomorrow; tomorrow will take care of itself. Sufficient for a day is its own evil.

Judging Others*

7 1*a*"Stop judging, that you may not be judged.**b* 2*c*For as you judge, so will you be judged, and the measure with which you measure will be measured out to you. 3Why do you notice the splinter in your brother's eye, but do not perceive the wooden beam in your own eye? 4How can you say to your brother, 'Let me remove that splinter from your eye,' while the wooden beam is in your eye? 5You hypocrite,* remove the wooden beam from your eye first; then you will see clearly to remove the splinter from your brother's eye.

Pearls before Swine

6*d*"Do not give what is holy to dogs,* or throw your pearls before swine, lest they trample them underfoot, and turn and tear you to pieces.

The Answer to Prayers

7*e*"Ask and it will be given to you; seek and you will find; knock and the door will be opened to you.*f* 8*g*For everyone who asks, receives; and the one who seeks, finds;

"Little faith" is a favorite designation of Matthew's Jesus for his followers (cf. 8:26; 10:42; 14:31; 16:8; 17:20). Unlike Mark, who sees the disciples as lacking faith, Matthew portrays the insufficient faith of Jesus' disciples. Jesus challenges them to strengthen and expand their faith.

n
Lk 12:22-31

o
Pss 145:15-16; 147:9

a
Lk 6:37-38, 41-42

b
Rom 2:1-2; 1 Cor 4:5

c
Wis 12:22; Mk 4:24

d
Prv 23:9

e
Mk 11:24; Lk 11:9-13

f
18:19

g
Lk 18:1-8; Jn 14:13

6:25-34 Jesus does not deny the reality of human needs (6:32), but forbids making them the object of anxious care and, in effect, becoming their slave.

6:27 Life-span: the Greek word can also mean "stature." If it is taken in that sense, the word here translated **moment** (literally, "cubit") must be translated literally as a unit not of time but of spatial measure. The cubit is about eighteen inches.

6:30 Of little faith: except for the parallel in Luke 12:28, the word translated **of little faith** is found in the New Testament only in Matthew. It is used by him of those who are disciples of Jesus but whose faith in him is not as deep as it should be (see 8:26; 14:31; 16:8 and the cognate noun in 17:20).

6:33 Righteousness: see the note on Matthew 3:14-15.

7:1-12 In Matthew 7:1 Matthew returns to the basic traditional material of the sermon (Lk 6:37-38, 41-42). The governing thought is the correspondence between conduct toward one's fellows and

God's conduct toward the one so acting.

7:1 This is not a prohibition against recognizing the faults of others, which would be hardly compatible with Matthew 7:5, 6 but against passing judgment in a spirit of arrogance, forgetful of one's own faults.

7:5 Hypocrite: the designation previously given to the scribes and Pharisees is here given to the Christian disciple who is concerned with the faults of another and ignores his own more serious offenses.

7:6 Dogs and **swine** were Jewish terms of contempt for Gentiles. This saying may originally have derived from a Jewish Christian community opposed to preaching the gospel (**what is holy**, **pearls**) to Gentiles. In the light of Matthew 28:19 that can hardly be Matthew's meaning. He may have taken the saying as applying to a Christian dealing with an obstinately impenitent fellow Christian (18:17).

h
1 Jn 5:14-15

i
Lk 6:31

j
Lk 13:24

k
2 Pt 2:1

l
12:33;
Lk 6:43-44

m
3:10

n
Is 29:13;
Lk 6:46

o
Lk 13:26-27

p
25:11-12

q
Pss 5:5; 6:9

r
Lk 6:47-49

s
Prv 10:25

and to the one who knocks, the door will be opened. [9]Which one of you would hand his son a stone when he asks for a loaf of bread,* [10]or a snake when he asks for a fish? [11h]If you then, who are wicked, know how to give good gifts to your children, how much more will your heavenly Father give good things to those who ask him.

The Golden Rule

[12*i]"Do to others whatever you would have them do to you. This is the law and the prophets.

The Narrow Gate

[13j]"Enter through the narrow gate; for the gate is wide and the road broad that leads to destruction, and those who enter through it are many. [14]How narrow the gate and constricted the road that leads to life. And those who find it are few.

False Prophets

[15k]"Beware of false prophets, who come to you in sheep's clothing, but underneath are ravenous wolves. [16l]By their fruits you will know them. Do people pick grapes from thornbushes, or figs from thistles? [17]Just so, every good tree bears good fruit, and a rotten tree bears bad fruit. [18]A good tree cannot bear bad fruit, nor can a rotten tree bear good fruit. [19m]Every tree that does not bear good fruit will be cut down and thrown into the fire. [20]So by their fruits you will know them.

The True Disciple

[21n]"Not everyone who says to me, 'Lord, Lord,' will enter the kingdom of heaven,* but only the one who does the will of my Father in heaven. [22o]Many will say to me on that day, 'Lord, Lord, did we not prophesy in your name? Did we not drive out demons in your name? Did we not do mighty deeds in your name?'[p] [23q]Then I will declare to them solemnly, 'I never knew you.* Depart from me, you evildoers.'

The Two Foundations

[24*r]"Everyone who listens to these words of mine and acts on them will be like a wise man who built his house on rock. [25s]The rain fell, the floods came, and the winds blew and buffeted the house. But it did not collapse; it had been set solidly on rock. [26]And everyone who listens to these words of mine but does not act on them will be

---

7:9-10 There is a resemblance between a stone and a round loaf of bread and between a serpent and the scaleless fish called **barbut**.

7:12 See Luke 6:31. This saying, known since the eighteenth century as the "Golden Rule," is found in both positive and negative form in pagan and Jewish sources, both earlier and later than the gospel. **This is the law and the prophets** is an addition probably due to the evangelist.

7:13-28 The final section of the discourse is composed of a series of antitheses, contrasting two kinds of life within the Christian community, that of those who obey the words of Jesus and that of those who do not. Most of the sayings are from Q and are found also in Luke.

7:13-14 The metaphor of the "two ways" was common in pagan philosophy and in the Old Testament. In Christian literature it is found also in the *Didache* (1–6) and the **Epistle of Barnabas** (18–20).

7:15-20 Christian disciples who claimed to speak in the name of God are called **prophets** (7:15) in Matthew 10:41; Matthew 23:34.

They were presumably an important group within the church of Matthew. As in the case of the Old Testament prophets, there were both true and false ones, and for Matthew the difference could be recognized by the quality of their deeds, the **fruits** (7:16). The mention of **fruits** leads to the comparison with trees, some producing good fruit, others bad.

7:21-23 The attack on the false prophets is continued, but is broadened to include those disciples who perform works of healing and exorcism in the name of Jesus (**Lord**) but live evil lives. Entrance into the kingdom is only for those who do the will of the Father. On the day of judgment (**on that day**) the morally corrupt prophets and miracle workers will be rejected by Jesus.

7:23 I never knew you: cf. Matthew 10:33. **Depart from me, you evildoers**: cf. Psalm 6:8.

7:24-27 The conclusion of the discourse (cf. Lk 6:47-49). Here the relation is not between saying and doing as in Matthew 7:15-23 but between hearing and doing, and the words of Jesus are applied to every Christian (everyone who listens).

The **miracle stories** in the gospels generally share a familiar structure. Some thirty-five miracles are recorded in the gospels. Their form provides testimony to the oral tradition that helped to preserve them. There are often five parts to a miracle story:

(1) Description of a condition that needs healing
(2) Dialogue between Jesus and the one(s) needing to be healed
(3) The miracle effected through physical touch, prayer, or a gesture
(4) Testimony on the part of the one(s) healed, sometimes accompanied by Jesus' statement that the recipient's "faith" has effected the healing
(5) Reaction of bystanders and/or the one(s) healed

Besides healings, other categories of miracle stories include exorcisms (casting out demons) and nature miracles.

t
Mk 1:22;
Lk 4:32

a
Mk 1:40-44;
Lk 5:12-14

b
Lv 14:2-32;
Lk 17:14

like a fool who built his house on sand. ²⁷The rain fell, the floods came, and the winds blew and buffeted the house. And it collapsed and was completely ruined."

²⁸*When Jesus finished these words, the crowds were astonished at his teaching, ²⁹*ᵗfor he taught them as one having authority, and not as their scribes.

III: Ministry and Mission in Galilee

The Cleansing of a Leper

8 ¹*ᵃWhen Jesus came down from the mountain, great crowds followed him. ²And then a leper* approached, did him homage, and said, "Lord, if you wish, you can make me clean." ³He stretched out his hand, touched him, and said, "I will do it. Be made clean." His leprosy was cleansed immediately. ⁴*ᵇThen Jesus said to him, "See that you tell no one, but go show yourself to the priest, and offer the gift that Moses prescribed; that will be proof for them."

Leprosy was a mysterious and dreaded disease to ancient people. Its designation in the Bible, however, is not restricted to what modern medicine calls Hansen's disease. Rather the term designated virtually any skin blemish. The OT, in particular, cites the conditions that are to accompany imperfections of the skin (Lv 13–14). Contact with a person with such conditions rendered one ritually "unclean." The fact that Jesus heals lepers and does not shy away from them indicates the great extent of God's mercy and healing power.

7:28-29 When Jesus finished these words: this or a similar formula is used by Matthew to conclude each of the five great discourses of Jesus (cf. 11:1; 13:53; 19:1; 26:1).

7:29 Not as their scribes: scribal instruction was a faithful handing down of the traditions of earlier teachers; Jesus' teaching is based on his own authority. **Their scribes**: for the implications of **their**, see the note on Matthew 4:23.

8:1–9:38 This narrative section of the second book of the gospel is composed of nine miracle stories, most of which are found in Mark, although Matthew does not follow the Marcan order and abbreviates the stories radically. The stories are arranged in three groups of three, each group followed by a section composed principally of sayings of Jesus about discipleship.

Matthew 9:35 is an almost verbatim repetition of Matthew 4:23. Each speaks of Jesus' teaching, preaching, and healing. The teaching and preaching form the content of Matthew 5–7; the healing, that of Matthew 8–9. Some scholars speak of a portrayal of Jesus as "Messiah of the Word" in Matthew 5–7 and "Messiah of the Deed" in Matthew 8–9. That is accurate so far as it goes, but there is also a strong emphasis on discipleship in Matthew 8–9; these chapters have not only christological but ecclesiological import.

8:2 A leper: see the note on Mark 1:40.

8:4 Cf. Leviticus 14:2-9. **That will be proof for them**: the Greek can also mean "that will be proof against them." It is not clear whether **them** refers to the priests or the people.

MATTHEW

c
Lk 7:1-10;
Jn 4:46-53

d
13:42, 50;
22:13; 24:51;
25:30;
Lk 13:28-29

e
Mk 1:29-34;
Lk 4:38-41

f
9:25

g
Is 53:4

Detail of synagogue entrance in Capernaum

The Healing of a Centurion's Servant

⁵*ᶜWhen he entered Capernaum,* a centurion approached him and appealed to him, ⁶saying, "Lord, my servant is lying at home paralyzed, suffering dreadfully." ⁷He said to him, "I will come and cure him." ⁸The centurion said in reply,* "Lord, I am not worthy to have you enter under my roof; only say the word and my servant will be healed. ⁹For I too am a person subject to authority, with soldiers subject to me. And I say to one, 'Go,' and he goes; and to another, 'Come here,' and he comes; and to my slave, 'Do this,' and he does it." ¹⁰When Jesus heard this, he was amazed and said to those following him, "Amen, I say to you, in no one in Israel* have I found such faith. ¹¹ᵈI say to you,* many will come from the east and the west, and will recline with Abraham, Isaac, and Jacob at the banquet in the kingdom of heaven, ¹²but the children of the kingdom will be driven out into the outer darkness, where there will be wailing and grinding of teeth." ¹³And Jesus said to the centurion, "You may go; as you have believed, let it be done for you." And at that very hour [his] servant was healed.

The Cure of Peter's Mother-in-Law

¹⁴*ᵉJesus entered the house of Peter, and saw his mother-in-law lying in bed with a fever. ¹⁵ᶠHe touched her hand, the fever left her, and she rose and waited on him.

Other Healings

¹⁶When it was evening, they brought him many who were possessed by demons, and he drove out the spirits by a word* and cured all the sick, ¹⁷ᵍto fulfill what had been said by Isaiah the prophet:*

The **centurion's humble protest** of his unworthiness is enshrined in the Mass when, immediately prior to Communion, the entire congregation professes they are not worthy.

"He took away our infirmities
and bore our diseases."

8:5-13 This story comes from Q (see Lk 7:1-10) and is also reflected in John 4:46-54. The similarity between the Q story and the Johannine is due to a common oral tradition, not to a common literary source. As in the later story of the daughter of the Canaanite woman (15:21-28) Jesus here breaks with his usual procedure of ministering only to Israelites and anticipates the mission to the Gentiles.

8:5 A centurion: a military officer commanding a hundred men. He was probably in the service of Herod Antipas, tetrarch of Galilee; see the note on Matthew 14:1.

8:8-9 Acquainted by his position with the force of a command, the centurion expresses faith in the power of Jesus' mere word.

8:10 In no one in Israel: there is good textual attestation (e.g., Codex Sinaiticus) for a reading identical with that of Luke 7:9, "not even in Israel." But that seems to be due to a harmonization of Matthew with Luke.

8:11-12 Matthew inserts into the story a Q saying (see Lk 13:28-29) about the entrance of Gentiles into the kingdom and the exclusion of those Israelites who, though descended from the patriarchs and members of the chosen nation (**the children of the kingdom**), refused to believe in Jesus. **There will be wailing and grinding of teeth**: the first occurrence of a phrase used frequently in this gospel to describe final condemnation (13:42, 50; 22:13; 24:51; 25:30). It is found elsewhere in the New Testament only in Luke 13:28.

8:14-15 Cf. Mark 1:29-31. Unlike Mark, Matthew has no implied request by others for the woman's cure. Jesus acts on his own initiative, and the cured woman rises and waits not on "them" (Mk 1:31) but on **him**.

8:16 By a word: a Matthean addition to Mark 1:34; cf. 8:8.

8:17 This fulfillment citation from Isaiah 53:4 follows the MT, not the LXX. The prophet speaks of the Servant of the Lord who suffers vicariously for the sins ("infirmities") of others; Matthew takes the **infirmities** as physical afflictions.

The Would-be Followers of Jesus

[18][h]When Jesus saw a crowd around him, he gave orders to cross to the other side. [19][i]A scribe approached and said to him, "Teacher,* I will follow you wherever you go." [20]Jesus answered him, "Foxes have dens and birds of the sky have nests, but the Son of Man* has nowhere to rest his head." [21]Another of [his] disciples said to him, "Lord, let me go first and bury my father." [22]*But Jesus answered him, "Follow me, and let the dead bury their dead."

The Calming of the Storm at Sea

[23]*[j]He got into a boat and his disciples followed him. [24]Suddenly a violent storm* came up on the sea, so that the boat was being swamped by waves; but he was asleep. [25][k]They came and woke him, saying, "Lord, save us!* We are perishing!" [26]He said to them, "Why are you terrified, O you of little faith?"* Then he got up, rebuked the winds and the sea, and there was great calm. [27]The men were amazed and said, "What sort of man is this, whom even the winds and the sea obey?"

The Healing of the Gadarene Demoniacs

[28][l]When he came to the other side, to the territory of the Gadarenes,* two demoniacs who were coming from the tombs met him. They were so savage that no one could travel by that road. [29]They cried out, "What have you to do with us,* Son of God? Have you come here to torment us before the appointed time?" [30]Some distance away a herd of many swine was feeding.* [31][m]The demons pleaded with him, "If you drive us out, send us into the herd of swine." [32]And he said to them, "Go then!" They came out and entered the swine, and the whole herd rushed down the steep bank into the sea where they

h
Mk 4:35

i
Lk 9:57-60

j
Mk 4:35-40;
Lk 8:22-25

k
Ps 107:28-29

l
Mk 5:1-17;
Lk 8:26-37

m
Lk 4:34, 41

8:18-22 This passage between the first and second series of miracles about following Jesus is taken from Q (see Lk 9:57-62). The third of the three sayings found in the source is absent from Matthew.

8:18 The other side: i.e., of the Sea of Galilee.

8:19 Teacher: for Matthew, this designation of Jesus is true, for he has Jesus using it of himself (10:24, 25; 23:8; 26:18), yet when it is used of him by others they are either his opponents (9:11; 12:38; 17:24; 22:16, 24, 36) or, as here and in Matthew 19:16, well-disposed persons who cannot see more deeply. Thus it reveals an inadequate recognition of who Jesus is.

8:20 Son of Man: see the note on Mark 8:31. This is the first occurrence in Matthew of a term that appears in the New Testament only in sayings of Jesus, except for Acts 7:56 and possibly Matthew 9:6 (Mk 2:10; Lk 5:24). In Matthew it refers to Jesus in his ministry (seven times, as here), in his passion and resurrection (nine times, e.g., 17:22), and in his glorious coming at the end of the age (thirteen times, e.g., 24:30).

8:22 Let the dead bury their dead: the demand of Jesus overrides what both the Jewish and the Hellenistic world regarded as a filial obligation of the highest importance. See the note on Luke 9:60.

8:23 His disciples followed him: the first miracle in the second group (8:23–9:8) is introduced by a verse that links it with the preceding sayings by the catchword "follow." In Mark the initiative in entering the boat is taken by the disciples (Mk 4:35-41); here, Jesus enters first and the disciples follow.

8:24 Storm: literally, "earthquake," a word commonly used in apocalyptic literature for the shaking of the old world when God

brings in his kingdom. All the synoptics use it in depicting the events preceding the parousia of the Son of Man (24:7; Mk 13:8; Lk 21:11). Matthew has introduced it here and in his account of the death and resurrection of Jesus (27:51-54; 28:2).

8:25 The reverent plea of the disciples contrasts sharply with their reproach of Jesus in Mark 4:38.

8:26 You of little faith: see the note on Matthew 6:30. **Great calm**: Jesus' calming the sea may be meant to recall the Old Testament theme of God's control over the chaotic waters (Pss 65:8; 89:10; 93:3-4; 107:29).

8:28 Gadarenes: this is the reading of Codex Vaticanus, supported by other important textual witnesses. The original reading of Codex Sinaiticus was Gazarenes, later changed to Gergesenes, and a few versions have Gerasenes. Each of these readings points to a different territory connected, respectively, with the cities Gadara, Gergesa, and Gerasa (modern Jerash). There is the same confusion of readings in the parallel texts, Mark 5:1 and Luke 8:26; there the best reading seems to be "Gerasenes," whereas "Gadarenes" is probably the original reading in Matthew. The town of Gadara was about five miles southeast of the Sea of Galilee, and Josephus (*Life* 9:42) refers to it as possessing territory that lay on that sea. **Two demoniacs**: Mark (5:1-20) has one.

8:29 What have you to do with us?: see the note on John 2:4. **Before the appointed time**: the notion that evil spirits were allowed by God to afflict human beings until the time of the final judgment is found in Enoch 16:1 and Jubilees 10:7-10.

8:30 The tending of pigs, animals considered unclean by Mosaic law (Lv 11:6-7), indicates that the population was Gentile.

a
Mk 2:3-12;
Lk 5:18-26

b
Lk 7:48

c
Jn 5:27

d
Mk 2:14-17;
Lk 5:27-32

e
11:19;
Lk 15:1-2

f
12:7; Hos 6:6

g
Mk 2:18-22;
Lk 5:33-39

drowned. ³³The swineherds ran away, and when they came to the town they reported everything, including what had happened to the demoniacs. ³⁴Thereupon the whole town came out to meet Jesus, and when they saw him they begged him to leave their district.

The Healing of a Paralytic

9 ¹*ᵃHe entered a boat, made the crossing, and came into his own town. ²ᵇAnd there people brought to him a paralytic lying on a stretcher. When Jesus saw their faith, he said to the paralytic, "Courage, child, your sins are forgiven." ³At that, some of the scribes* said to themselves, "This man is blaspheming." ⁴Jesus knew what they were thinking, and said, "Why do you harbor evil thoughts? ⁵Which is easier, to say, 'Your sins are forgiven,' or to say, 'Rise and walk'? ⁶*ᶜBut that you may know that the Son of Man has authority on earth to forgive sins"—he then said to the paralytic, "Rise, pick up your stretcher, and go home." ⁷He rose and went home. ⁸*When the crowds saw this they were struck with awe and glorified God who had given such authority to human beings.

The Call of Matthew

⁹ᵈAs Jesus passed on from there, he saw a man named Matthew sitting at the customs post. He said to him, "Follow me." And he got up and followed him. ¹⁰ᵉWhile he was at table in his house,* many tax collectors and sinners came and sat with Jesus and his disciples. ¹¹The Pharisees saw this and said to his disciples, "Why does your teacher* eat with tax collectors and sinners?" ¹²He heard this and said, "Those who are well do not need a physician, but the sick do.* ¹³ᶠGo and learn the meaning of the words, 'I desire mercy, not sacrifice.'* I did not come to call the righteous but sinners."

The Question about Fasting

¹⁴ᵍThen the disciples of John approached him and said, "Why do we and the Pharisees fast [much], but your disciples do not fast?" ¹⁵Jesus answered them, "Can the wedding guests mourn as long as the bridegroom is with them? The days will come

---

9:1 His own town: Capernaum; see Matthew 4:13.

9:3 Scribes: see the note on Mark 2:6. Matthew omits the reason given in the Marcan story for the charge of blasphemy: "Who but God alone can forgive sins?" (Mk 2:7).

9:6 It is not clear whether "But that you may know . . . to forgive sins" is intended to be a continuation of the words of Jesus or a parenthetical comment of the evangelist to those who would hear or read this gospel. In any case, Matthew here follows the Marcan text.

9:8 Who had given such authority to human beings: a significant difference from Mark 2:12 ("They . . . glorified God, saying, 'We have never seen anything like this'"). Matthew's extension to **human beings** of the authority to forgive sins points to the belief that such authority was being claimed by Matthew's church.

9:9-17 In this section the order is the same as that of Mark 2:13-22.

9:9 A man named Matthew: Mark names this tax collector Levi (Mk 2:14). No such name appears in the four lists of the twelve who were the closest companions of Jesus (10:2-4; Mk 3:16-19; Lk 6:14-16; Acts 1:13 [eleven, because of the defection of Judas Iscariot]), whereas all four list a Matthew, designated in Matthew 10:3 as "the tax collector." The evangelist may have changed the "Levi" of his source to **Matthew** so that this man, whose call is given special notice, like that of the first four disciples (4:18-22), might be included among the twelve. Another reason for the change may be that the disciple Matthew was the source of traditions peculiar to the church for which the evangelist was writing.

9:10 His house: it is not clear whether **his** refers to Jesus or Matthew. **Tax collectors**: see the note on Matthew 5:46. Table association with such persons would cause ritual impurity.

9:11 Teacher: see the note on Matthew 8:19.

9:12 See the note on Mark 2:17.

9:13 Go and learn . . . not sacrifice: Matthew adds the prophetic statement of Hosea 6:6 to the Marcan account (see also 12:7). If mercy is superior to the temple sacrifices, how much more to the laws of ritual impurity.

9:15 Fasting is a sign of mourning and would be as inappropriate at this time of joy, when Jesus is proclaiming the kingdom, as it would be at a marriage feast. Yet the saying looks forward to the time when Jesus will no longer be with the disciples visibly, the time of Matthew's church. **Then they will fast**: see *Didache* 8:1.

when the bridegroom is taken away from them, and then they will fast.* [16]No one patches an old cloak with a piece of unshrunken cloth,* for its fullness pulls away from the cloak and the tear gets worse. [17]People do not put new wine into old wineskins. Otherwise the skins burst, the wine spills out, and the skins are ruined. Rather, they pour new wine into fresh wineskins, and both are preserved."

The Official's Daughter and the Woman with a Hemorrhage

[18]*[h]While he was saying these things to them, an official* came forward, knelt down before him, and said, "My daughter has just died. But come, lay your hand on her, and she will live." [19]Jesus rose and followed him, and so did his disciples. [20]A woman suffering hemorrhages for twelve years came up behind him and touched the tassel* on his cloak. [21][i]She said to herself, "If only I can touch his cloak, I shall be cured." [22]Jesus turned around and saw her, and said, "Courage, daughter! Your faith has saved you." And from that hour the woman was cured.

[23]When Jesus arrived at the official's house and saw the flute players and the crowd who were making a commotion, [24]he said, "Go away! The girl is not dead but sleeping."* And they ridiculed him. [25]When the crowd was put out, he came and took her by the hand, and the little girl arose. [26]And news of this spread throughout all that land.

The Healing of Two Blind Men

[27]*[j]And as Jesus passed on from there, two blind men followed [him], crying out, "Son of David,* have pity on us!"[k] [28]When he entered the house, the blind men approached him and Jesus said to them, "Do you believe that I can do this?" "Yes, Lord," they said to him. [29]Then he touched their eyes and said, "Let it be done for you according to your faith." [30]And their eyes were opened. Jesus warned them sternly, "See that no one knows about this." [31]But they went out and spread word of him through all that land.

The Healing of a Mute Person

[32][l]As they were going out,* a demoniac who could not speak was brought to him, [33][m]and when the demon was driven out the mute person spoke. The crowds were amazed

h
Mk 5:22-43;
Lk 8:41-56

i
14:36;
Nm 15:37

j
20:29-34

k
15:22

l
12:22-24;
Lk 11:14-15

m
Mk 2:12; 7:37

9:16-17 Each of these parables speaks of the unsuitability of attempting to combine the old and the new. Jesus' teaching is not a patching up of Judaism, nor can the gospel be contained within the limits of Mosaic law.

9:18-34 In this third group of miracles, the first (9:18-26) is clearly dependent on Mark (Mk 5:21-43). Though it tells of two miracles, the cure of the woman had already been included in the story of the raising of the official's daughter, so that the two were probably regarded as a single unit. The other miracles seem to have been derived from Mark and Q respectively, though there Matthew's own editing is much more evident.

9:18 Official: literally, "ruler." Mark calls him "one of the synagogue officials" (Mk 5:22). My daughter has just died: Matthew heightens the Marcan "my daughter is at the point of death" (Mk 5:23).

9:20 Tassel: possibly "fringe." The Mosaic law prescribed that tassels be worn on the corners of one's garment as a reminder to keep the commandments (see Nm 15:37-39; Dt 22:12).

9:24 Sleeping: sleep is a biblical metaphor for death (see Ps 87:6 LXX; Dn 12:2; 1 Thes 5:10). Jesus' statement is not a denial

of the child's real death, but an assurance that she will be roused from her sleep of death.

9:27-31 This story was probably composed by Matthew out of Mark's story of the healing of a blind man named Bartimaeus (Mk 10:46-52). Mark places the event late in Jesus' ministry, just before his entrance into Jerusalem, and Matthew has followed his Marcan source at that point in his gospel also (see 20:29-34). In each of the Matthean stories the single blind man of Mark becomes two. The reason why Matthew would have given a double version of the Marcan story and placed the earlier one here may be that he wished to add a story of Jesus' curing the blind at this point in order to prepare for Jesus' answer to the emissaries of the Baptist (11:4-6) in which Jesus, recounting his works, begins with his giving sight to the blind.

9:27 Son of David: this messianic title is connected once with the healing power of Jesus in Mark (Mk 10:47-48) and Luke (Lk 18:38-39) but more frequently in Matthew (see also 12:23; 15:22; 20:30-31).

9:32-34 The source of this story seems to be Q (see Lk 11:14-15). As in the preceding healing of the blind, Matthew has

n 10:25; Mk 3:22	
o 4:23; Lk 8:1	
p Nm 27:17; 1 Kgs 22:17; Jer 50:6; Ez 34:5; Mk 6:34	
q Lk 10:2; Jn 4:35	
a Mk 3:14-19; Lk 6:13-16; Acts 1:13	
b Mk 6:7-13; Lk 9:1-6	
c 15:24	
d 3:2; 4:17	

and said, "Nothing like this has ever been seen in Israel." [34]*[n]But the Pharisees said, "He drives out demons by the prince of demons."

The Compassion of Jesus

[35]*[o]Jesus went around to all the towns and villages, teaching in their synagogues, proclaiming the gospel of the kingdom, and curing every disease and illness. [36p]At the sight of the crowds, his heart was moved with pity for them because they were troubled and abandoned,* like sheep without a shepherd. [37]*[q]Then he said to his disciples, "The harvest is abundant but the laborers are few; [38]so ask the master of the harvest to send out laborers for his harvest."

If we look around the world with our far-seeing eyes we will observe a beautiful readiness for hearing the word of God residing in the people. Many hearts are eager for healing. So much good in our world needs to be harvested. *O God of the Harvest, send in your laborers. Let the harvest begin.*

The Mission of the Twelve

10 [1]*[a]Then he summoned his twelve disciples* and gave them authority over unclean spirits to drive them out and to cure every disease and every illness. [2]The names of the twelve apostles* are these: first, Simon called Peter, and his brother Andrew; James, the son of Zebedee, and his brother John; [3]Philip and Bartholomew, Thomas and Matthew the tax collector; James, the son of Alphaeus, and Thaddeus; [4]Simon the Cananean, and Judas Iscariot who betrayed him.

The Commissioning of the Twelve

[5b]Jesus sent out these twelve* after instructing them thus, "Do not go into pagan territory or enter a Samaritan town. [6c]Go rather to the lost sheep of the house of Israel. [7d]As you go, make this proclamation: 'The kingdom of heaven is at hand.' [8]*Cure the sick, raise the dead, cleanse lepers, drive out demons. Without cost you have received;

---

two versions of this healing, the later in Matthew 12:22-24 and the earlier here.

9:34 This spiteful accusation foreshadows the growing opposition to Jesus in Matthew 11; 12.

9:35 See the notes on Matthew 4:23-25; Matthew 8:1–9:38.

9:36 See Mark 6:34; Numbers 27:17; 1 Kings 22:17.

9:37-38 This Q saying (see Lk 10:2) is only imperfectly related to this context. It presupposes that only God (**the master of the harvest**) can take the initiative in sending out preachers of the gospel, whereas in Matthew's setting it leads into Matthew 10 where Jesus does so.

10:1–11:1 After an introductory narrative (10:1-4), the second of the discourses of the gospel. It deals with the mission now to be undertaken by the disciples (10:5-15), but the perspective broadens and includes the missionary activity of the church between the time of the resurrection and the parousia.

10:1 His twelve disciples: although, unlike Mark (Mk 3:13-14) and Luke (Lk 6:12-16), Matthew has no story of Jesus' choosing the Twelve, he assumes that the group is known to the reader. The earliest New Testament text to speak of it is 1 Corinthians 15:5. The number probably is meant to recall the twelve tribes of Israel and implies Jesus' authority to call all Israel into the kingdom. While Luke (Lk 6:13) and probably Mark (Mk 4:10, 34) distinguish between the Twelve and a larger group also termed

disciples, Matthew tends to identify the disciples and the Twelve. **Authority . . . every illness**: activities the same as those of Jesus; see Matthew 4:23; 9:35; 10:8. The Twelve also share in his proclamation of the kingdom (10:7). But although he teaches (4:23; 7:28; 9:35), they do not. Their commission to teach comes only after Jesus' resurrection, when they have been fully instructed by him (28:20).

10:2-4 Here, for the only time in Matthew, the Twelve are designated **apostles**. The word "apostle" means "one who is sent," and therefore fits the situation here described. In the Pauline letters, the place where the term occurs most frequently in the New Testament, it means primarily one who has seen the risen Lord and has been commissioned to proclaim the resurrection. With slight variants in Luke and Acts, the names of those who belong to this group are the same in the four lists given in the New Testament (see the note on 9:9). **Cananean:** this represents an Aramaic word meaning "zealot." The meaning of that designation is unclear (see the note on Lk 6:15).

10:5-6 Like Jesus (15:24), the Twelve are sent only to Israel. This saying may reflect an original Jewish Christian refusal of the mission to the Gentiles, but for Matthew it expresses rather the limitation that Jesus himself observed during his ministry.

10:8-11 The Twelve have received their own call and mission through God's gift, and the benefits they confer are likewise to

"The Twelve" in the Gospels

Curious as it may seem, the gospel tradition does not give a unified list of the twelve closest followers of Jesus known as the apostles. As the following list shows, there is some discrepancy as to exact names. These have sometimes been explained as dual names or nicknames for the same individual. Of the Twelve, only Peter, James and John, Philip, and Judas receive much explicit attention in the gospels and Acts. Only Luke-Acts restricts the expression "the twelve apostles" to the personal inner circle of Jesus. So important is the unity of the Twelve that Acts records the choice of Matthias as a substitute for Judas Iscariot, the betrayer (Acts 1:15-26).

Mt 10:2-4	Mk 3:13-14	Lk 6:12-16	John has no listing of the Twelve but mentions the unnamed "Beloved Disciple"
Simon = Peter	Simon = Peter	Simon = Peter	Andrew (1:40)
Andrew	James, son of Zebedee	Andrew	Simon Peter, called Kephas (1:40-42)
James, son of Zebedee	John, brother of James [these two = Boanerges, i.e., sons of thunder]	James	
John, son of Zebedee	Andrew	John	
Philip	Philip	Philip	Philip (1:43)
Bartholomew	Bartholomew	Bartholomew	Nathanael (1:45-49)
Thomas	Matthew	Matthew	
Matthew	Thomas	Thomas	
James, son of Alphaeus	James, son of Alphaeus	James, son of Alphaeus	
Thaddeus	Thaddeus	Simon the Zealot	
Simon the Cananaean	Simon the Cananaean	Judas, son of James	
Judas Iscariot	Judas Iscariot	Judas Iscariot	

without cost you are to give. [9][e]Do not take gold or silver or copper for your belts; [10][f]no sack for the journey, or a second tunic, or sandals, or walking stick. The laborer deserves his keep. [11][g]Whatever town or village you enter, look for a worthy person in it, and stay there until you leave. [12]As you enter a house, wish it peace. [13]If the house is worthy, let your peace come upon it; if not, let your peace return to you.[*] [14][h]Whoever will not receive you or listen to your words—go outside that house or town and shake the dust from your feet. [15][i]Amen, I say to you, it will be more tolerable for the land of Sodom and Gomorrah on the day of judgment than for that town.

Coming Persecutions

[16][j]"Behold, I am sending you like sheep in the midst of wolves; so be shrewd as serpents and simple as doves. [17][*][k]But beware of people, for they will hand you over to courts and scourge you in their synagogues,[l] [18]and you will be led before governors

e
Mk 6:8-9;
Lk 9:3; 10:4

f
Lk 10:7;
1 Cor 9:14;
2 Tm 5:18

g
Mk 6:10-11;
Lk 9:4-5;
10:5-12

h
Acts 13:51;
18:6

i
11:24;
Gn 19:1-29;
Jude 7

j Lk 10:3

k
Mk 13:9-13;
Lk 21:12-19

l
Acts 5:40

be given freely. They are not to take with them money, provisions, or unnecessary clothing; their lodging and food will be provided by those who receive them.

10:13 The greeting of peace is conceived of not merely as a salutation but as an effective word. If it finds no worthy recipient, it will return to the speaker.

10:14 Shake the dust from your feet: this gesture indicates a complete disassociation from such unbelievers.

10:17 The persecutions attendant upon the post-resurrection mission now begin to be spoken of. Here Matthew brings into the discourse sayings found in Mark 13, which deals with events preceding the parousia.

m
Ex 4:11-12;
Jer 1:6-10;
Lk 12:11-12

n
24:9, 13

o
Lk 6:40;
Jn 13:16;
15:20

p
Lk 12:2-9

q
Mk 4:22;
Lk 8:17;
1 Tm 5:25

r
Jas 4:12

s
Mk 8:38;
Lk 9:26;
2 Tm 2:12;
Rev 3:5

t
Lk 12:51-53

u
16:24-25;
Lk 14:26-27

and kings for my sake as a witness before them and the pagans. [19]*m*When they hand you over, do not worry about how you are to speak or what you are to say. You will be given at that moment what you are to say. [20]For it will not be you who speak but the Spirit of your Father speaking through you. [21]*n*Brother will hand over brother to death, and the father his child; children will rise up against parents and have them put to death. [22]You will be hated by all because of my name, but whoever endures to the end* will be saved. [23]When they persecute you in one town, flee to another. Amen, I say to you, you will not finish the towns of Israel before the Son of Man comes.* [24]*o*No disciple is above his teacher, no slave above his master. [25]It is enough for the disciple that he become like his teacher, for the slave that he become like his master. If they have called the master of the house Beelzebul,* how much more those of his household!

Courage under Persecution

[26]*p*"Therefore do not be afraid of them. Nothing is concealed that will not be revealed, nor secret that will not be known.*q [27]What I say to you in the darkness, speak in the light; what you hear whispered, proclaim on the housetops. [28]*r*And do not be afraid of those who kill the body but cannot kill the soul; rather, be afraid of the one who can destroy both soul and body in Gehenna. [29]Are not two sparrows sold for a small coin? Yet not one of them falls to the ground without your Father's knowledge. [30]Even all the hairs of your head are counted. [31]So do not be afraid; you are worth more than many sparrows. [32]*Everyone who acknowledges me before others I will acknowledge before my heavenly Father. [33]*s*But whoever denies me before others, I will deny before my heavenly Father.

Jesus: A Cause of Division

[34]*t*"Do not think that I have come to bring peace upon the earth. I have come to bring not peace but the sword. [35]For I have come to set

a man 'against his father,
 a daughter against her mother,
and a daughter-in-law against her mother-in-law;
  [36]and one's enemies will be those of his household.'

The Conditions of Discipleship

[37]*u*"Whoever loves father or mother more than me is not worthy of me, and whoever loves son or daughter more than me is not worthy of me; [38]and whoever does not take

---

10:21 See Micah 7:6 which is cited in Matthew 10:35, 36.

10:22 To the end: the original meaning was probably "until the parousia." But it is not likely that Matthew expected no missionary disciples to suffer death before then, since he envisages the martyrdom of other Christians (10:21). For him, **the end** is probably that of the individual's life (see 10:28).

10:23 Before the Son of Man comes: since the coming of the Son of Man at the end of the age had not taken place when this gospel was written, much less during the mission of the Twelve during Jesus' ministry, Matthew cannot have meant the coming to refer to the parousia. It is difficult to know what he understood it to be: perhaps the "proleptic parousia" of Matthew 28:16-20, or the destruction of the temple in A.D. 70, viewed as a coming of Jesus in judgment on unbelieving Israel.

10:25 Beelzebul: see Matthew 9:34 for the charge linking Jesus with "the prince of demons," who is named **Beelzebul** in Matthew 12:24. The meaning of the name is uncertain; possibly, "lord of the house."

10:26 The **concealed** and **secret** coming of the kingdom is to be proclaimed by them, and no fear must be allowed to deter them from that proclamation.

10:32-33 In the Q parallel (Lk 12:8-9), the Son of Man will acknowledge those who have acknowledged Jesus, and those who deny him will be denied (by the Son of Man) before the angels of God at the judgment. Here Jesus and the Son of Man are identified, and the acknowledgment or denial will be before his heavenly Father.

10:38 The first mention of the cross in Matthew, explicitly that of the disciple, but implicitly that of Jesus (and follow after me).

up his cross[*] and follow after me is not worthy of me. [39][*][v]Whoever finds his life will lose it, and whoever loses his life for my sake will find it.

Rewards

[40][w]"Whoever receives you receives me,[*] and whoever receives me receives the one who sent me. [41][*]Whoever receives a prophet because he is a prophet will receive a prophet's reward, and whoever receives a righteous man because he is righteous will receive a righteous man's reward. [42][x]And whoever gives only a cup of cold water to one of these little ones to drink because he is a disciple—amen, I say to you, he will surely not lose his reward."

11 [1]When Jesus finished giving these commands to his twelve disciples,[*] he went away from that place to teach and to preach in their towns.

IV: Opposition from Israel

The Messengers from John the Baptist

[2][*][a]When John heard in prison[*] of the works of the Messiah, he sent his disciples to him [3][*]with this question, "Are you the one who is to come, or should we look for another?" [4]Jesus said to them in reply, "Go and tell John what you hear and see: [5][*][b]the blind regain their sight, the lame walk, lepers are cleansed, the deaf hear, the dead are raised, and the poor have the good news proclaimed to them. [6]And blessed is the one who takes no offense at me."

Matthew clearly shows by **John the Baptist's attire and diet** (3:4) that he is to be identified with the OT figure of **Elijah** as the precursor of Jesus. Elijah is the only OT figure reputed to have been miraculously taken into heaven by a flaming chariot (2 Kgs 2:11). This ancient tradition gave rise among later generations of Jews to the expectation that Elijah would return one day immediately prior to the arrival of the Messiah (Mal 3:24). For Matthew, John and Jesus clearly fulfill these roles, respectively. Modern Jews still celebrate the expectation of Elijah in a tradition at Passover seder meals. A special cup of wine, designated "the Elijah cup," is set at a place at the table reserved for Elijah when he comes. During the ritual a door is opened to allow Elijah to enter and sip from his cup.

---

v
Mk 8:35;
Lk 9:24;
Jn 12:25

w
Lk 10:16;
Jn 12:44;
13:20

x
25:40; Mk 9:41

a
Lk 7:18-28

b
Is 26:19;
29:18-19;
35:5-6; 61:1

Crucifixion was a form of capital punishment used by the Romans for offenders who were not Roman citizens.

10:39 One who denies Jesus in order to save one's earthly life will be condemned to everlasting destruction; loss of earthly life for Jesus' sake will be rewarded by everlasting life in the kingdom.

10:40-42 All who receive the disciples of Jesus receive him, and God who sent them, and will be rewarded accordingly.

10:41 A prophet: one who speaks in the name of God; here, the Christian prophets who proclaim the gospel. **Righteous man:** since righteousness is demanded of all the disciples, it is difficult to take the **righteous man** of this verse and **one of these little ones** (10:42) as indicating different groups within the followers of Jesus. Probably all three designations are used here of Christian missionaries as such.

11:1 The closing formula of the discourse refers back to the original addressees, the Twelve.

11:2–12:50 The narrative section of the third book deals with the growing opposition to Jesus. It is largely devoted to disputes and attacks relating to faith and discipleship and thus contains much sayings-material, drawn in large part from Q.

11:2 In prison: see Matthew 4:12; 14:1-12. **The works of the Messiah:** the deeds of Matthew 8–9.

11:3 The question probably expresses a doubt of the Baptist that Jesus is **the one who is to come** (cf. Mal 3:1) because his mission has not been one of fiery judgment as John had expected (3:2).

11:5-6 Jesus' response is taken from passages of Isaiah (Is 26:19; 29:18-19; 35:5-6; 61:1) that picture the time of salvation as marked by deeds such as those that Jesus is doing. The beatitude is a warning to the Baptist not to disbelieve because his expectations have not been met.

c
3:3, 5

d
Ex 23:20;
Mal 3:1;
Mk 1:2;
Lk 1:76

e
Lk 16:16

f
17:10-13;
Mal 3:23;
Lk 1:17

g
Lk 7:31-35

h
Lk 1:15

i
9:10-11

j
Lk 10:12-15

k
Jl 4:4-7

l
Is 14:13-15

Jesus' Testimony to John

[7]*c*As they were going off, Jesus began to speak to the crowds about John, "What did you go out to the desert to see? A reed swayed by the wind? [8]Then what did you go out to see? Someone dressed in fine clothing? Those who wear fine clothing are in royal palaces. [9]Then why did you go out? To see a prophet?* Yes, I tell you, and more than a prophet. [10]*d*This is the one about whom it is written:

'Behold, I am sending my messenger ahead of you;
　　he will prepare your way before you.'

[11]Amen, I say to you, among those born of women there has been none greater than John the Baptist; yet the least in the kingdom of heaven is greater than he.* [12]*e*From the days of John the Baptist until now, the kingdom of heaven suffers violence,* and the violent are taking it by force. [13]All the prophets and the law* prophesied up to the time of John. [14]*f*And if you are willing to accept it, he is Elijah, the one who is to come. [15]Whoever has ears ought to hear.

[16]*g*"To what shall I compare this generation?* It is like children who sit in marketplaces and call to one another, [17]'We played the flute for you, but you did not dance, we sang a dirge but you did not mourn.' [18]*h*For John came neither eating nor drinking, and they said, 'He is possessed by a demon.' [19]*i*The Son of Man came eating and drinking and they said, 'Look, he is a glutton and a drunkard, a friend of tax collectors and sinners.' But wisdom is vindicated by her works."

Reproaches to Unrepentant Towns

[20]*j*Then he began to reproach the towns where most of his mighty deeds had been done, since they had not repented. [21]*k*"Woe to you, Chorazin! Woe to you, Bethsaida! For if the mighty deeds done in your midst had been done in Tyre and Sidon,* they would long ago have repented in sackcloth and ashes. [22]But I tell you, it will be more tolerable for Tyre and Sidon on the day of judgment than for you. [23]*l*And as for you, Capernaum:

11:7-19 Jesus' rebuke of John is counterbalanced by a reminder of the greatness of the Baptist's function (11:7-15) that is followed by a complaint about those who have heeded neither John nor Jesus (11:16-19).

11:9-10 In common Jewish belief there had been no prophecy in Israel since the last of the Old Testament prophets, Malachi. The coming of a new prophet was eagerly awaited, and Jesus agrees that John was such. Yet he was **more than a prophet**, for he was the precursor of the one who would bring in the new and final age. The Old Testament quotation is a combination of Malachi 3:1 and Exodus 23:20 with the significant change that the **before me** of Malachi becomes **before you**. The messenger now precedes not God, as in the original, but Jesus.

11:11 John's preeminent greatness lies in his function of announcing the imminence of the kingdom (3:1). But to be in the kingdom is so great a privilege that the least who has it is greater than the Baptist.

11:12 The meaning of this difficult saying is probably that the opponents of Jesus are trying to prevent people from accepting the kingdom and to snatch it away from those who have received it.

11:13 All the prophets and the law: Matthew inverts the usual order, "law and prophets," and says that both have **prophesied**.

This emphasis on the prophetic character of the law points to its fulfillment in the teaching of Jesus and to the transitory nature of some of its commandments (see the note on 5:17-20).

11:16-19 See Luke 7:31-35. The meaning of the parable (11:16-17) and its explanation (11:18-19b) is much disputed. A plausible view is that the **children** of the parable are two groups, one of which proposes different entertainments to the other that will not agree with either proposal. The first represents John, Jesus, and their disciples; the second those who reject John for his asceticism and Jesus for his table association with those despised by the religiously observant. Matthew 11:19c (**her works**) forms an inclusion with Matthew 11:2 ("the works of the Messiah"). The original form of the saying is better preserved in Luke 7:35, ". . . wisdom is vindicated by all her children." There John and Jesus are the children of Wisdom; here the works of Jesus the Messiah are those of divine Wisdom, of which he is the embodiment. Some important textual witnesses, however, have essentially the same reading as in Luke.

11:21 Tyre and Sidon were pagan cities denounced for their wickedness in the Old Testament; cf. Joel 3:4-7.

11:23 Capernaum's pride and punishment are described in language taken from the taunt song against the king of Babylon (Is 14:13-15).

'Will you be exalted to heaven?
You will go down to the netherworld.'

m
10:15

n
Lk 10:21-22

o
Jn 3:35; 6:46;
7:28; 10:15

For if the mighty deeds done in your midst had been done in Sodom, it would have remained until this day. [24m]But I tell you, it will be more tolerable for the land of Sodom on the day of judgment than for you."

The Praise of the Father

[25n]At that time Jesus said in reply,[*] "I give praise to you, Father, Lord of heaven and earth, for although you have hidden these things from the wise and the learned you have revealed them to the childlike. [26]Yes, Father, such has been your gracious will. [27o]All things have been handed over to me by my Father. No one knows the Son except the Father, and no one knows the Father except the Son and anyone to whom the Son wishes to reveal him.

Chorazin, Bethsaida, and Capernaum were three towns located near the northern shore of the Sea of Galilee. Each provided Jesus with a venue for his proclamation of the coming reign of God. While the gospels assert that Chorazin witnessed Jesus' miracles (Mt 11:21; Lk 10:13), no specific miracle is set in that town. Bethsaida was the hometown of three of Jesus' disciples: Philip, Peter, and Andrew (Jn 1:44; 12:21). Jesus preached and healed there and near its outskirts (Lk 9:10-11; Mk 8:22-26). Jesus, who made Capernaum the hub of his lakeside ministry (Mt 4:13), healed many people there (Mt 8:5; Mk 1:21-28; 2:1-12; Lk 7:1-10; Jn 4:46-54) and taught in its synagogue (Lk 4:31-38; Jn 6:22-59). Jesus, however, cursed all three towns because their people did not respond to his message (Mt 11:20-24; Lk 10:13-15).

All three sites have been the locus of intense archaeological work since the final decades of the twentieth century. Excavators have not found remains from the first-century village of Chorazin.

Though there is some debate about the location of Bethsaida, current excavations at et-Tell suggest that it is the site of first-century Bethsaida. The most thoroughly excavated site of the three is Capernaum. At one time, its well-preserved synagogue was thought to be the one in which Jesus preached, but recent excavations date the building to the fourth–fifth century A.D., though the excavators suggest that a synagogue from the first century lies below the later structure. Excavations have also revealed domestic architecture that was in use in the first century. Archaeologists have identified one house as belonging to Simon Peter (see Mt 8:14; 17:25; Mk 1:29; 2:1; 3:20; 9:33) because the first-century structure was modified to serve as a house church in the late first century and was radically restructured in the fourth century to accommodate pilgrims who believed it to be the site of "Peter's House." In the fifth century, an octagonal church was built over the site. Today, the modern church of St. Peter occupies the spot and contains a glass floor that reveals the excavations below.

11:25-27 This Q saying, identical with Luke 10:21-22 except for minor variations, introduces a joyous note into this section, so dominated by the theme of unbelief. **While the wise and the learned**, the scribes and Pharisees, have rejected Jesus' preaching and the significance of his mighty deeds, **the childlike** have accepted them. Acceptance depends upon the Father's revelation, but this is granted to those who are open to receive it and refused to the arrogant. Jesus can speak of all mysteries because he is **the Son** and there is perfect reciprocity of knowledge between him and the Father; what has been **handed over** to him is revealed only to those whom he wishes.

p
Sir 51:26;
Jer 6:16

a
Mk 2:23-28;
Lk 6:1-5

b
Dt 23:26

c
1 Sm 21:2-7

d
Lv 24:5-9

e
Lv 24:8;
Nm 28:9-10

f
Hos 6:6

g
Jn 5:16-17

h
Mk 3:1-6;
Lk 6:6-11

The Gentle Mastery of Christ

²⁸*"Come to me, all you who labor and are burdened,* and I will give you rest. ²⁹*ᵖTake my yoke upon you and learn from me, for I am meek and humble of heart; and you will find rest for yourselves. ³⁰For my yoke is easy, and my burden light."

We all need a place to go when life gets burdensome. When Jesus says, *"Come to me,"* one way to interpret that is to meet him in prayer. When we stop trying to work things out entirely on our own and take time to be with Jesus *in prayer* we find within ourselves answers we didn't know we possessed.

Picking Grain on the Sabbath

12 ¹*ᵃAt that time Jesus was going through a field of grain on the sabbath. His disciples were hungry and began to pick the heads* of grain and eat them.ᵇ ²When the Pharisees saw this, they said to him, "See, your disciples are doing what is unlawful to do on the sabbath." ³ᶜHe said to them,* "Have you not read what David did when he and his companions were hungry, ⁴ᵈhow he went into the house of God and ate the bread of offering, which neither he nor his companions but only the priests could lawfully eat? ⁵*ᵉOr have you not read in the law that on the sabbath the priests serving in the temple violate the sabbath and are innocent? ⁶I say to you, something greater than the temple is here. ⁷*ᶠIf you knew what this meant, 'I desire mercy, not sacrifice,' you would not have condemned these innocent men. ⁸*ᵍFor the Son of Man is Lord of the sabbath."

The Man with a Withered Hand

⁹ʰMoving on from there, he went into their synagogue. ¹⁰And behold, there was a man there who had a withered hand. They questioned him, "Is it lawful to cure on the sabbath?"* so that they might accuse him. ¹¹*He said to them, "Which one of you who has a sheep that falls into a pit on the sabbath will not take hold of it and lift it out? ¹²How much more valuable a person is than a sheep. So it is lawful to do good on the sabbath." ¹³Then he said to the man, "Stretch out your hand." He stretched it out, and

---

11:28-29 These verses are peculiar to Matthew and are similar to Ben Sirach's invitation to learn wisdom and submit to her yoke (Sir 51:23, 26).

11:28 Who labor and are burdened: burdened by the law as expounded by the scribes and Pharisees (23:4).

11:29 In place of the yoke of the law, complicated by scribal interpretation, Jesus invites the burdened to take the yoke of obedience to his word, under which they **will find rest**; cf. Jeremiah 6:16.

12:1-14 Matthew here returns to the Marcan order that he left in Matthew 9:18. The two stories depend on Mark 2:23-28 and 3:1-6, respectively, and are the only places in either gospel that deal explicitly with Jesus' attitude toward sabbath observance.

12:1-2 The picking of the heads of grain is here equated with reaping, which was forbidden on the sabbath (Ex 34:21).

12:3-4 See 1 Samuel 21:2-7. In the Marcan parallel (Mk 2:25-26) the high priest is called Abiathar, although in 1 Samuel this action is attributed to Ahimelech. The Old Testament story is not about a violation of the sabbath rest; its pertinence to this dispute is that a violation of the law was permissible because of David's men being without food.

12:5-6 This and the following argument (12:7) are peculiar to Matthew. The temple service seems to be the changing of the showbread on the sabbath (Lv 24:8) and the doubling on the sabbath of the usual daily holocausts (Nm 28:9-10). The argument is that the law itself requires work that breaks the sabbath rest, because of the higher duty of temple service. If temple duties outweigh sabbath law, how much more does the presence of Jesus, with his proclamation of the kingdom (**something greater than the temple**), justify the conduct of his disciples.

12:7 See the note on Matthew 9:13.

12:8 The ultimate justification for the disciples' violation of the sabbath rest is that Jesus, the Son of Man, has supreme authority over the law.

12:10 Rabbinic tradition later than the gospels allowed relief to be given to a sufferer on the sabbath if life was in danger. This may also have been the view of Jesus' Pharisaic contemporaries. But the case here is not about one in danger of death.

12:11 Matthew omits the question posed by Jesus in Mark 3:4 and substitutes one about rescuing a sheep on the sabbath, similar to that in Luke 14:5.

it was restored as sound as the other. [14][i]But the Pharisees* went out and took counsel against him to put him to death.

The Chosen Servant*

[15]When Jesus realized this, he withdrew from that place. Many [people] followed him, and he cured them all,* [16]but he warned them not to make him known. [17]This was to fulfill what had been spoken through Isaiah the prophet:

[18][j]"Behold, my servant whom I have chosen,
  my beloved in whom I delight;
I shall place my spirit upon him,
  and he will proclaim justice to the Gentiles.
[19]He will not contend* or cry out,
  nor will anyone hear his voice in the streets.
[20]A bruised reed he will not break,
  a smoldering wick he will not quench,
until he brings justice to victory.
  [21]And in his name the Gentiles will hope."*

Jesus and Beelzebul

[22]*[k]Then they brought to him a demoniac who was blind and mute. He cured the mute person so that he could speak and see. [23]*[l]All the crowd was astounded, and said, "Could this perhaps be the Son of David?" [24]*[m]But when the Pharisees heard this, they said, "This man drives out demons only by the power of Beelzebul, the prince of demons." [25][n]But he knew what they were thinking and said to them,* "Every kingdom divided against itself will be laid waste, and no town or house divided against itself will stand. [26]And if Satan drives out Satan, he is divided against himself; how, then, will his kingdom stand? [27]And if I drive out demons by Beelzebul, by whom do your own people* drive them out? Therefore they will be your judges. [28]*[o]But if it is by the Spirit of God that I drive out demons, then the kingdom of God has come upon you. [29]*How can anyone enter a strong man's house and steal his property, unless he first

i
Jn 5:18

j
Is 42:1-4

k
9:32-34;
Lk 11:14-15

l
9:27

m
10:25; Mk 3:22

n
Mk 3:23-27;
Lk 11:17-22

o
Lk 11:20

12:14 See Mark 3:6. Here the plan to bring about Jesus' death is attributed to the Pharisees only. This is probably due to the situation of Matthew's church, when the sole opponents were the Pharisees.

12:15-21 Matthew follows Mark 3:7-12 but summarizes his source in two verses (12:15, 16) that pick up the withdrawal, the healings, and the command for silence. To this he adds a fulfillment citation from the first Servant Song (Is 42:1-4) that does not correspond exactly to either the Hebrew or the LXX of that passage. It is the longest Old Testament citation in this gospel, emphasizing the meekness of Jesus, the Servant of the Lord, and foretelling the extension of his mission to the Gentiles.

12:15 Jesus' knowledge of the Pharisees' plot and his healing all are peculiar to Matthew.

12:19 The servant's not contending is seen as fulfilled in Jesus' withdrawal from the disputes narrated in Matthew 12:1-14.

12:21 Except for a minor detail, Matthew here follows the LXX, although the meaning of the Hebrew ("the coastlands will wait for his teaching") is similar.

12:22-32 For the exorcism, see the note on Matthew 9:32-34. The long discussion combines Marcan and Q material (Mk 3:22-30;

Lk 11:19-20, 23; 12:10). Mark 3:20-21 is omitted, with a consequent lessening of the sharpness of Matthew 12:48.

12:23 See the note on Matthew 9:27.

12:24 See the note on Matthew 10:25.

12:25-26 Jesus' first response to the Pharisees' charge is that if it were true, Satan would be destroying his own kingdom.

12:27 Besides pointing out the absurdity of the charge, Jesus asks how the work of Jewish exorcists (**your own people**) is to be interpreted. Are they, too, to be charged with collusion with Beelzebul? For an example of Jewish exorcism see Josephus, *Antiquities* 8, 2, 5, **42-49.

12:28 The Q parallel (Lk 11:20) speaks of the "finger" rather than of the "spirit" of God. While the difference is probably due to Matthew's editing, he retains **the kingdom of God** rather than changing it to his usual "kingdom of heaven." **Has come upon you**: see Matthew 4:17.

12:29 A short parable illustrates what Jesus is doing. The **strong man** is Satan, whom Jesus has tied up and whose **house** he is plundering. Jewish expectation was that Satan would be chained up in the last days (Rev 20:2); Jesus' exorcisms indicate that those days have begun.

p Lk 11:23
q Mk 3:28-30; Lk 12:10
r Lk 6:43-45
s 3:7; 23:33; 15:11-12; Lk 3:7
t Jas 3:1-2
u 16:1-4; Jon 2:1; 3:1-10; Mk 8:11-12; Lk 11:29-32
v 1 Kgs 10:1-10

ties up the strong man? Then he can plunder his house. [30*p]Whoever is not with me is against me, and whoever does not gather with me scatters. [31q]Therefore, I say to you, every sin and blasphemy will be forgiven people, but blasphemy against the Spirit* will not be forgiven. [32]And whoever speaks a word against the Son of Man will be forgiven; but whoever speaks against the holy Spirit will not be forgiven, either in this age or in the age to come.

A Tree and Its Fruits

[33r]"Either declare* the tree good and its fruit is good, or declare the tree rotten and its fruit is rotten, for a tree is known by its fruit. [34*s]You brood of vipers, how can you say good things when you are evil? For from the fullness of the heart the mouth speaks. [35]A good person brings forth good out of a store of goodness, but an evil person brings forth evil out of a store of evil. [36*t]I tell you, on the day of judgment people will render an account for every careless word they speak. [37]By your words you will be acquitted, and by your words you will be condemned."

The Demand for a Sign

[38*u]Then some of the scribes and Pharisees said to him, "Teacher,* we wish to see a sign from you." [39]He said to them in reply, "An evil and unfaithful* generation seeks a sign, but no sign will be given it except the sign of Jonah the prophet. [40]Just as Jonah was in the belly of the whale three days and three nights,* so will the Son of Man be in the heart of the earth three days and three nights. [41*]At the judgment, the men of Nineveh will arise with this generation and condemn it, because they repented at the preaching of Jonah; and there is something greater than Jonah here. [42v]At the judgment the queen of the south will arise with this generation and condemn it, because she came from the ends of the earth to hear the wisdom of Solomon; and there is something greater than Solomon here.

12:30 This saying, already attached to the preceding verses in Q (see Lk 11:23), warns that there can be no neutrality where Jesus is concerned. Its pertinence in a context where Jesus is addressing not the neutral but the bitterly opposed is not clear. The accusation of scattering, however, does fit the situation. Jesus is the shepherd of God's people (2:6), his mission is to the lost sheep of Israel (15:24); the Pharisees, who oppose him, are guilty of scattering the sheep.

12:31 Blasphemy against the Spirit: the sin of attributing to Satan (12:24) what is the work of the Spirit of God (12:28).

12:33 Declare: literally, "make." The meaning of this verse is obscure. Possibly it is a challenge to the Pharisees either to declare Jesus and his exorcisms good or both of them bad. A tree is known by its fruit; if the fruit is good, so must the tree be. If the driving out of demons is good, so must its source be.

12:34 The admission of Jesus' goodness cannot be made by the Pharisees, for they are evil, and the words that proceed from their evil hearts cannot be good.

12:36-37 If on the day of judgment people will be held accountable for even their **careless** words, the vicious accusations of the Pharisees will surely lead to their condemnation.

12:38-42 This section is mainly from Q (see Lk 11:29-32). Mark 8:11-12, which Matthew has followed in Matthew 16:1-4, has a similar demand for a sign. The scribes and Pharisees refuse to accept the exorcisms of Jesus as authentication of his claims and demand a sign that will end all possibility of doubt. Jesus' response is that no such sign will be given. Because his opponents are evil and see him as an agent of Satan, nothing will convince them.

12:38 Teacher: see the note on Matthew 8:19. In Matthew 16:1 the request is for a sign "from heaven" (Mk 8:11).

12:39 Unfaithful: literally, "adulterous." The covenant between God and Israel was portrayed as a marriage bond, and unfaithfulness to the covenant as adultery; cf. Hosea 2:4-15; Jeremiah 3:6-10.

12:40 See Jonah 2:1. While in Q the sign was simply Jonah's preaching to the Ninevites (Lk 11:30, 32), Matthew here adds Jonah's sojourn **in the belly of the whale** for **three days and three nights**, a prefigurement of Jesus' sojourn in the abode of the dead and, implicitly, of his resurrection.

12:41-42 The Ninevites who **repented** (see Jon 3:1-10) **and the queen of the south** (i.e., of Sheba; see 1 Kgs 10:1-13) were pagans who responded to lesser opportunities than have been offered to Israel in the ministry of Jesus, **something greater than Jonah** or **Solomon**. At the final judgment they will condemn the faithless **generation** that has rejected him.

The Return of the Unclean Spirit

w
Lk 11:24-26

x
Mk 3:31-35;
Lk 8:19-21

a
Mk 4:1-12;
Lk 8:4-10

[43]*w*"When an unclean spirit goes out of a person it roams through arid regions searching for rest but finds none. [44]Then it says, 'I will return to my home from which I came.' But upon returning, it finds it empty, swept clean, and put in order. [45]Then it goes and brings back with itself seven other spirits more evil than itself, and they move in and dwell there; and the last condition of that person is worse than the first. Thus it will be with this evil generation."

The True Family of Jesus

[46]*x*While he was still speaking to the crowds, his mother and his brothers appeared outside, wishing to speak with him. [47][Someone told him, "Your mother and your brothers are standing outside, asking to speak with you."]* [48]But he said in reply to the one who told him, "Who is my mother? Who are my brothers?" [49]And stretching out his hand toward his disciples, he said, "Here are my mother and my brothers. [50]For whoever does the will of my heavenly Father is my brother, and sister, and mother."

The Parable of the Sower

13 [1]*a*On that day, Jesus went out of the house and sat down by the sea. [2]Such large crowds gathered around him that he got into a boat and sat down, and the whole crowd stood along the shore. [3]*And he spoke to them at length in parables,* saying: "A sower went out to sow. [4]And as he sowed, some seed fell on the path, and birds came and ate it up. [5]Some fell on rocky ground, where it had little soil. It sprang up at once because the soil was not deep, [6]and when the sun rose it was scorched,

A **parable** is a short, pithy saying that provides a descriptive metaphor or analogy for the "kingdom of God" or imparts a moral perspective. Only Mark and Matthew have parable chapters, large collections of Jesus' parables joined into one long discourse. Scholars agree that Jesus used parables as a special teaching technique, but most of them would have been spoken as individual sayings given at different times and in different settings.

12:43-45 Another Q passage; cf. Matthew 11:24-26. Jesus' ministry has broken Satan's hold over Israel, but the refusal of **this evil generation** to accept him will lead to a worse situation than what preceded his coming.

12:46-50 See Mark 3:31-35. Matthew has omitted Mark 3:20-21 which is taken up in Mark 3:31 (see the note on Mt 12:22-23), yet the point of the story is the same in both gospels: natural kinship with Jesus counts for nothing; only one who **does the will** of **his heavenly Father** belongs to his true family.

12:47 This verse is omitted in some important textual witnesses, including Codex Sinaiticus (original reading) and Codex Vaticanus.

13:1-53 The discourse in parables is the third great discourse of Jesus in Matthew and constitutes the second part of the third book of the gospel. Matthew follows the Marcan outline (Mk 4:1-35) but has only two of Mark's parables, the five others being from Q and M. In addition to the seven parables, the discourse gives the reason why Jesus uses this type of speech (10-15), declares the blessedness of those who understand his teaching (16-17), explains the parable of the sower (18-23) and of the weeds (36-43), and ends with a concluding statement to the disciples (51-52).

13:3-8 Since in Palestine sowing often preceded ploughing, much is scattered on ground that is unsuitable. Yet while much is wasted, the seed that falls on good ground bears fruit in extraordinarily large measure. The point of the parable is that, in spite of some failure because of opposition and indifference, the message of Jesus about the coming of the kingdom will have enormous success.

13:3 In parables: the word "parable" (Greek *parabolē*) is used in the LXX to translate the Hebrew *māshāl*, a designation covering a wide variety of literary forms such as axioms, proverbs, similitudes, and allegories. In the New Testament the same breadth of meaning of the word is found, but there it primarily designates stories that are illustrative comparisons between Christian truths and events of everyday life. Sometimes the event has a strange element that is quite different from usual experience (e.g., in 13:33 the enormous amount of dough in the parable of the yeast); this is meant to sharpen the curiosity of the hearer. If each detail of such a story is given a figurative meaning, the story is an allegory. Those who maintain a sharp distinction between parable and allegory insist that a parable has only one point of comparison, and that while parables were characteristic of Jesus' teaching, to see allegorical details in them is to introduce meanings that go beyond their original intention and even falsify it. However, to exclude any allegorical elements from a parable is an excessively rigid mode of interpretation, now abandoned by many scholars.

b
25:29;
Mk 4:25;
Lk 8:18; 19:26

c
Jn 9:39

d
Is 6:9-10;
Jn 12:40;
Acts 28:26-27;
Rom 11:8

e
Lk 10:23-24;
1 Pt 1:10-12

f
Mk 4:13-20;
Lk 8:11-15

and it withered for lack of roots. [7]Some seed fell among thorns, and the thorns grew up and choked it. [8]But some seed fell on rich soil, and produced fruit, a hundred or sixty or thirtyfold. [9]Whoever has ears ought to hear."

The Purpose of Parables

[10]The disciples approached him and said, "Why do you speak to them in parables?" [11]*He said to them in reply, "Because knowledge of the mysteries of the kingdom of heaven has been granted to you, but to them it has not been granted. [12][b]To anyone who has, more will be given* and he will grow rich; from anyone who has not, even what he has will be taken away. [13]*[c]This is why I speak to them in parables, because 'they look but do not see and hear but do not listen or understand.' [14][d]Isaiah's prophecy is fulfilled in them, which says:

'You shall indeed hear but not understand
   you shall indeed look but never see.
[15]Gross is the heart of this people,
   they will hardly hear with their ears, they have closed their eyes, lest
      they see with their eyes
   and hear with their ears
and understand with their heart and be converted,
   and I heal them.'

The Privilege of Discipleship

[16]*[e]"But blessed are your eyes, because they see, and your ears, because they hear. [17]Amen, I say to you, many prophets and righteous people longed to see what you see but did not see it, and to hear what you hear but did not hear it.

The Explanation of the Parable of the Sower

[18]*[f]"Hear then the parable of the sower. [19]The seed sown on the path is the one who hears the word of the kingdom without understanding it, and the evil one comes and steals away what was sown in his heart. [20]The seed sown on rocky ground is the one who hears the word and receives it at once with joy. [21]But he has no root and lasts only

---

13:11 Since a parable is figurative speech that demands reflection for understanding, only those who are prepared to explore its meaning can come to know it. To understand is a gift of God, granted to the disciples but not to the crowds. In Semitic fashion, both the disciples' understanding and the crowd's obtuseness are attributed to God. The question of human responsibility for the obtuseness is not dealt with, although it is asserted in Matthew 13:13. **The mysteries**: as in Luke 8:10; Mark 4:11 has "the mystery." The word is used in Daniel 2:18, 19, 27 and in the Qumran literature (1QpHab 7:8; 1QS 3:23; 1QM 3:9) to designate a divine plan or decree affecting the course of history that can be known only when revealed. **Knowledge of the mysteries of the kingdom of heaven** means recognition that the kingdom has become present in the ministry of Jesus.

13:12 In the New Testament use of this axiom of practical "wisdom" (see 25:29; Mk 4:25; Lk 8:18; 19:26), the reference transcends the original level. God gives further understanding to one who accepts the revealed mystery; from the one who does not, he will take it away (note the "theological passive," **more will be given, what he has will be taken away**).

13:13 Because "they look . . . or understand": Matthew softens his Marcan source, which states that Jesus speaks in parables so that the crowds may not understand (Mk 4:12), and makes such speaking a punishment given **because** they have not accepted his previous clear teaching. However, his citation of Isaiah 6:9-10 in Matthew 13:14 supports the harsher Marcan view.

13:16-17 Unlike the unbelieving crowds, the disciples have seen that which the **prophets** and the **righteous** of the Old Testament **longed to see** without having their longing fulfilled.

13:18-23 See Mark 4:14-20; Luke 8:11-15. In this explanation of the parable the emphasis is on the various types of soil on which the seed falls, i.e., on the dispositions with which the preaching of Jesus is received. The second and third types particularly are explained in such a way as to support the view held by many scholars that the explanation derives not from Jesus but from early Christian reflection upon apostasy from the faith that was the consequence of persecution and worldliness respectively. Others, however, hold that the explanation may come basically from Jesus even though it was developed in the light of later Christian experience. The four

for a time. When some tribulation or persecution comes because of the word, he immediately falls away. [22]The seed sown among thorns is the one who hears the word, but then worldly anxiety and the lure of riches choke the word and it bears no fruit. [23]But the seed sown on rich soil is the one who hears the word and understands it, who indeed bears fruit and yields a hundred or sixty or thirtyfold."

The Parable of the Weeds among the Wheat

[24]He proposed another parable to them.* "The kingdom of heaven may be likened to a man who sowed good seed in his field. [25]While everyone was asleep his enemy came and sowed weeds* all through the wheat, and then went off. [26]When the crop grew and bore fruit, the weeds appeared as well. [27]The slaves of the householder came to him and said, 'Master, did you not sow good seed in your field? Where have the weeds come from?' [28]He answered, 'An enemy has done this.' His slaves said to him, 'Do you want us to go and pull them up?' [29]He replied, 'No, if you pull up the weeds you might uproot the wheat along with them. [30][g]Let them grow together until harvest;* then at harvest time I will say to the harvesters, "First collect the weeds and tie them in bundles for burning; but gather the wheat into my barn."'"

The Parable of the Mustard Seed

[31]*[h]He proposed another parable to them. "The kingdom of heaven is like a mustard seed that a person took and sowed in a field. [32]*[i]It is the smallest of all the seeds, yet when full-grown it is the largest of plants. It becomes a large bush, and the 'birds of the sky come and dwell in its branches.'"

The Parable of the Yeast

[33][j]He spoke to them another parable. "The kingdom of heaven is like yeast* that a woman took and mixed with three measures of wheat flour until the whole batch was leavened."

The Use of Parables

[34]*[k]All these things Jesus spoke to the crowds in parables. He spoke to them only in parables, [35][l]to fulfill what had been said through the prophet:*

---

g
3:12

h
Mk 4:30-32;
Lk 13:18-19

i
Ez 17:23; 31:6;
Dn 4:7-9, 17-19

j
Lk 13:20-21

k
Mk 4:33-34

l
Ps 78:2

---

types of persons envisaged are (1) those who never accept **the word of the kingdom** (13:19); (2) those who believe for a while but fall away because of **persecution** (13:20-21); (3) those who believe, but in whom **the word** is choked by **worldly anxiety** and the seduction of **riches** (13:22); (4) those who respond to **the word** and produce **fruit** abundantly (13:23).

13:24-30 This parable is peculiar to Matthew. The comparison in Matthew 13:24 does not mean that **the kingdom of heaven may be likened** simply to the person in question but to the situation narrated in the whole story. The refusal of the **householder** to allow his **slaves** to separate **the wheat** from **the weeds** while they are still growing is a warning to the disciples not to attempt to anticipate the final judgment of God by a definitive exclusion of sinners from the kingdom. In its present stage it is composed of the good and the bad. The judgment of God alone will eliminate the sinful. Until then there must be patience and the preaching of repentance.

13:25 Weeds: darnel, a poisonous weed that in its first stage of growth resembles wheat.

13:30 Harvest: a common biblical metaphor for the time of God's judgment; cf. Jeremiah 51:33; Joel 4:13; Hosea 6:11.

13:31-33 See Mark 4:30-32; Luke 13:18-21. The parables of the mustard seed and the yeast illustrate the same point: the amazing contrast between the small beginnings of the kingdom and its marvelous expansion.

13:32 See Daniel 4:7-9, 17-19 where the birds nesting in the tree represent the people of Nebuchadnezzar's kingdom. See also Ezekiel 17:23; 31:6.

13:33 Except in this Q parable and in Matthew 16:12, **yeast** (or "leaven") is, in New Testament usage, a symbol of corruption (see 16:6, 11-12; Mk 8:15; Lk 12:1; 1 Cor 5:6-8; Gal 5:9). **Three measures**: an enormous amount, enough to feed a hundred people. The exaggeration of this element of the parable points to the greatness of the kingdom's effect.

13:34 Only in parables: see Matthew 13:10-15.

13:35 The prophet: some textual witnesses read "Isaiah the prophet." The quotation is actually from Psalm 78:2; the first line corresponds to the LXX text of the psalm. The psalm's title ascribes

m
8:12; Rev 21:8

n
Dn 12:3

o
Prv 2:4; 4:7

"I will open my mouth in parables,
> I will announce what has lain hidden from the foundation [of the
> world]."

The Explanation of the Parable of the Weeds

[36]Then, dismissing the crowds,* he went into the house. His disciples approached him and said, "Explain to us the parable of the weeds in the field." [37]*He said in reply, "He who sows good seed is the Son of Man, [38]the field is the world,* the good seed the children of the kingdom. The weeds are the children of the evil one, [39]and the enemy who sows them is the devil. The harvest is the end of the age,* and the harvesters are angels. [40]Just as weeds are collected and burned [up] with fire, so will it be at the end of the age. [41]The Son of Man will send his angels, and they will collect out of his kingdom* all who cause others to sin and all evildoers. [42]*mThey will throw them into the fiery furnace, where there will be wailing and grinding of teeth. [43]*nThen the righteous will shine like the sun in the kingdom of their Father. Whoever has ears ought to hear.

More Parables

[44]*o"The kingdom of heaven is like a treasure buried in a field,* which a person finds and hides again, and out of joy goes and sells all that he has and buys that field. [45]Again, the kingdom of heaven is like a merchant searching for fine pearls. [46]When he finds a pearl of great price, he goes and sells all that he has and buys it. [47]Again, the kingdom of heaven is like a net thrown into the sea, which collects fish of every kind. [48]When it is full they haul it ashore and sit down to put what is good into buckets. What is bad they throw away. [49]Thus it will be at the end of the age. The angels will go out and separate the wicked from the righteous [50]and throw them into the fiery furnace, where there will be wailing and grinding of teeth.

Treasures New and Old

[51]"Do you understand* all these things?" They answered, "Yes." [52]*And he replied, "Then every scribe who has been instructed in the kingdom of heaven is like the head

---

it to Asaph, the founder of one of the guilds of temple musicians. He is called "the prophet" (NAB "the seer") in 2 Chronicles 29:30 but it is doubtful that Matthew averted to that; for him, any Old Testament text that could be seen as fulfilled in Jesus was prophetic.

13:36 Dismissing the crowds: the return of Jesus to the house marks a break with the crowds, who represent unbelieving Israel. From now on his attention is directed more and more to his disciples and to their instruction. The rest of the discourse is addressed to them alone.

13:37-43 In the explanation of the parable of the weeds emphasis lies on the fearful end of the wicked, whereas the parable itself concentrates on patience with them until judgment time.

13:38 The field is the world: this presupposes the resurrection of Jesus and the granting to him of "all power in heaven and on earth" (28:18).

13:39 The end of the age: this phrase is found only in Matthew (13:40, 49; 24:3; 28:20).

13:41 His kingdom: the **kingdom** of the **Son of Man** is distinguished from that of the Father (13:43); see 1 Corinthians 15:24-25.

The church is the place where Jesus' kingdom is manifested, but his royal authority embraces the entire world; see the note on Matthew 13:38.

13:43 See Daniel 12:3.

13:44-50 The first two of the last three parables of the discourse have the same point. The **person** who **finds** a buried **treasure** and the **merchant** who finds a **pearl of great price** sell **all** that they have to acquire these finds; similarly, the one who understands the supreme value of the kingdom gives up whatever he must to obtain it. The **joy** with which this is done is made explicit in the first parable, but it may be presumed in the second also. The concluding parable of the fishnet resembles the explanation of the parable of the weeds with its stress upon the final exclusion of evil persons from the kingdom.

13:44 In the unsettled conditions of Palestine in Jesus' time, it was not unusual to guard valuables by burying them in the ground.

13:51 Matthew typically speaks of the understanding of the disciples.

13:52 Since Matthew tends to identify the disciples and the Twelve (see the note on 10:1), this saying about the Christian **scribe** cannot

of a household who brings from his storeroom both the new and the old." [53]When Jesus finished these parables, he went away from there.

V: Jesus, the Kingdom, and the Church

The Rejection at Nazareth

[54]*[p]He came to his native place and taught the people in their synagogue. They were astonished* and said, "Where did this man get such wisdom and mighty deeds?[q] [55][r]Is he not the carpenter's son? Is not his mother named Mary and his brothers James, Joseph, Simon, and Judas? [56]Are not his sisters all with us? Where did this man get all this?" [57][s]And they took offense at him. But Jesus said to them, "A prophet is not without honor except in his native place and in his own house." [58]And he did not work many mighty deeds there because of their lack of faith.

p
Mk 6:1-6;
Lk 4:16-30

q
2:23; Jn 1:46;
7:15

r
12:46; 27:56;
Jn 6:42

s
Jn 4:44

Getting It Right . . . Which Mary?

As with other biblical names, the name Mary is quite common and can designate different individuals who may be confused with one another.

Name	Description	Main References
Mary, the mother of Jesus	Featured in all the gospels and mentioned in Acts; John alone never names her but calls her "the mother of Jesus"	Mt 1–2; Mk 3:31-35; 6:3; Lk 1–2; Jn 2:1-12; 19:25-27; Acts 1:14
Mary Magdalene	Recipient of Jesus' healing power; identified as the first to experience the risen Lord after the resurrection; often mistakenly identified with the anonymous woman who anointed Jesus (Mk 14:3-9) or with the anonymous woman caught in adultery (Jn 8:1-11)	Mt 27:56, 61; 28:1; Mk 15:40, 47; 16:1, 9-11; Lk 8:2; 24:10; Jn 19:25; 20:1, 11-18
Mary of Bethany, sister of Martha and Lazarus	Described as the one who sat at Jesus' feet to listen to him; also once identified as the one who anointed Jesus' feet	Lk 10:38-42; Jn 11:1-44
Mary, mother of James and Joseph (Joses)	One of those who witnessed the crucifixion and burial of Jesus and went to the empty tomb	Mt 27:56, 61; 28:1; Mk 15:40, 47; 16:1; Lk 24:10
Mary, wife of Clopas	Witness to the crucifixion along with other faithful women	Jn 19:25
Mary, mother of John Mark	Associated with the Jerusalem church	Acts 12:12
Mary of Rome	Worker in the church at Rome	Rom 16:6

---

be taken as applicable to all who accept the message of Jesus. While the Twelve are in many ways representative of all who believe in him, they are also distinguished from them in certain respects. The church of Matthew has leaders among whom are a group designated as "scribes" (23:34). Like the scribes of Israel, they are teachers. It is the Twelve and these their later counterparts to whom this verse applies. **The scribe . . . instructed in the kingdom** of heaven knows both the teaching of Jesus (**the new**) and the law and prophets (**the old**) and provides in his own teaching **both the new and the old** as interpreted and fulfilled by **the new**. On the translation **head of a household** (for the same Greek word translated **householder** in 13:27), see the note on Matthew 24:45-51.

13:54–17:27 This section is the narrative part of the fourth book of the gospel.

13:54 After the Sermon on the Mount the crowds are in admiring astonishment at Jesus' teaching (7:28); here the astonishment is of those who take **offense at him**. Familiarity with his background and family leads them to regard him as pretentious. Matthew modifies his Marcan source (6:1-6). Jesus is not the carpenter but **the carpenter's son** (13:55), "and among his own kin" is omitted (13:57), **he did not work many mighty deeds** in face of such unbelief (13:58) rather than the Marcan ". . . he was not able to perform any mighty deed there" (6:5), and there is no mention of his amazement at his townspeople's lack of faith.

a
Mk 6:14-29

b
Lk 9:7-9

c
Lk 3:1

d
Lk 3:19-20

e
Lv 18:16;
20:21

f
21:26

g
15:32-38;
Mk 6:32-44;
Lk 9:10-17;
Jn 6:1-13

Herod's Opinion of Jesus*

14 [1a]At that time Herod the tetrarch[b] heard of the reputation of Jesus*[c] [2]and said to his servants, "This man is John the Baptist. He has been raised from the dead; that is why mighty powers are at work in him."

The Death of John the Baptist

[3d]Now Herod had arrested John, bound [him], and put him in prison on account of Herodias,* the wife of his brother Philip, [4e]for John had said to him, "It is not lawful for you to have her." [5f]Although he wanted to kill him, he feared the people, for they regarded him as a prophet. [6]But at a birthday celebration for Herod, the daughter of Herodias performed a dance before the guests and delighted Herod [7]so much that he swore to give her whatever she might ask for. [8]Prompted by her mother, she said, "Give me here on a platter the head of John the Baptist." [9]The king was distressed, but because of his oaths and the guests who were present, he ordered that it be given, [10]and he had John beheaded in the prison. [11]His head was brought in on a platter and given to the girl, who took it to her mother. [12]His disciples came and took away the corpse and buried him; and they went and told Jesus.

The Return of the Twelve and the Feeding of the Five Thousand

[13*g]When Jesus heard of it, he withdrew in a boat to a deserted place by himself. The crowds heard of this and followed him on foot from their towns. [14]When he disembarked and saw the vast crowd, his heart was moved with pity for them, and he cured their sick. [15]When it was evening, the disciples approached him and said, "This is a deserted place and it is already late; dismiss the crowds so that they can go to the villages and buy food for themselves." [16][Jesus] said to them, "There is no need for them to go away; give them some food yourselves." [17]But they said to him, "Five loaves and two fish are all we have here." [18]Then he said, "Bring them here to me," [19]and he ordered the crowds to sit down on the grass. Taking* the five loaves and the two fish, and looking up to heaven, he said the blessing, broke the loaves, and gave them to the disciples, who in turn gave them to the crowds. [20]They all ate and were satisfied, and they picked

---

14:1-12 The murder of the Baptist by Herod Antipas prefigures the death of Jesus (see 17:12). The Marcan source (6:14-29) is much reduced and in some points changed. In Mark Herod reveres John as a holy man and the desire to kill him is attributed to Herodias (6:19, 20), whereas here that desire is Herod's from the beginning (14:5).

14:1 Herod the tetrarch: Herod Antipas, son of Herod the Great. When the latter died, his territory was divided among three of his surviving sons, Archelaus who received half of it (2:23), Herod Antipas who became ruler of Galilee and Perea, and Philip who became ruler of northern Transjordan. Since he received a quarter of his father's domain, Antipas is accurately designated **tetrarch** ("ruler of a fourth [part]"), although in Matthew 14:9 Matthew repeats the "king" of his Marcan source (6:26).

14:3 Herodias was not the wife of Herod's half-brother Philip but of another half-brother, Herod Boethus. The union was prohibited by Leviticus 18:16; 20:21. According to Josephus (*Antiquities* 18, 5, 2 **116–19**), Herod imprisoned and then executed John because he feared that the Baptist's influence over the people might enable him to lead a rebellion.

14:13-21 The feeding of the five thousand is the only miracle of Jesus that is recounted in all four gospels. The principal reason for that may be that it was seen as anticipating the Eucharist and the final banquet in the kingdom (8:11; 26:29), but it looks not only forward but backward, to the feeding of Israel with manna in the desert at the time of the Exodus (Ex 16), a miracle that in some contemporary Jewish expectation would be repeated in the messianic age (2 Bar 29:8). It may also be meant to recall Elisha's feeding a hundred men with small provisions (2 Kgs 4:42-44).

14:19 The **taking**, saying the blessing, breaking, and giving to the disciples correspond to the actions of Jesus over the bread at the Last Supper (26:26). Since they were usual at any Jewish meal, that correspondence does not necessarily indicate a eucharistic reference here. Matthew's silence about Jesus' dividing the fish among the people (Mk 6:41) is perhaps more significant in that regard.

14:20 The fragments left over: as in Elisha's miracle, food was left over after all had been fed. The word **fragments** (Greek *klasmata*) is used, in the singular, of the broken bread of the Eucharist in *Didache* 9:3-4.

up the fragments left over*—twelve wicker baskets full. ²¹Those who ate were about five thousand men, not counting women and children.

The Walking on the Water

²²*ʰThen he made the disciples get into the boat and precede him to the other side, while he dismissed the crowds. ²³ⁱAfter doing so, he went up on the mountain by himself to pray. When it was evening he was there alone. ²⁴Meanwhile the boat, already a few miles offshore, was being tossed about by the waves, for the wind was against it. ²⁵During the fourth watch of the night,* he came toward them, walking on the sea. ²⁶When the disciples saw him walking on the sea they were terrified. "It is a ghost," they said, and they cried out in fear. ²⁷At once [Jesus] spoke to them, "Take courage, it is I;* do not be afraid." ²⁸Peter said to him in reply, "Lord, if it is you, command me to come to you on the water." ²⁹He said, "Come." Peter got out of the boat and began to walk on the water toward Jesus. ³⁰ʲBut when he saw how [strong] the wind was he became frightened; and, beginning to sink, he cried out, "Lord, save me!" ³¹Immediately Jesus stretched out his hand and caught him, and said to him, "O you of little faith,* why did you doubt?" ³²After they got into the boat, the wind died down. ³³*ᵏThose who were in the boat did him homage, saying, "Truly, you are the Son of God."

The Healings at Gennesaret

³⁴ˡAfter making the crossing, they came to land at Gennesaret. ³⁵When the men of that place recognized him, they sent word to all the surrounding country. People brought to him all those who were sick ³⁶ᵐand begged him that they might touch only the tassel on his cloak, and as many as touched it were healed.

The Tradition of the Elders

15 ¹*ᵃThen Pharisees and scribes came to Jesus from Jerusalem and said, ²ᵇ"Why do your disciples break the tradition of the elders?* They do not wash [their]

h
Mk 6:45-52;
Jn 6:16-21

i
Mk 1:35;
Lk 5:16; 6:12

j
8:25-26

k
16:16

l
Mk 6:53-56

m
9:20-22

a
Mk 7:1-23

b
Lk 11:38

14:22-33 The disciples, laboring against the turbulent sea, are saved by Jesus. For his power over the waters, see the note on Matthew 8:26. Here that power is expressed also by his **walking on the sea** (14:25; cf. Ps 77:20; Jb 9:8). Matthew has inserted into the Marcan story (Mk 6:45-52) material that belongs to his special traditions on Peter (14:28-31).

14:25 The fourth watch of the night: between 3 a.m. and 6 a.m. The Romans divided the twelve hours between 6 p.m. and 6 a.m. into four equal parts called "watches."

14:27 It is I: see the note on Mark 6:50.

14:31 You of little faith: see the note on Matthew 6:30. **Why did you doubt?**: the verb is peculiar to Matthew and occurs elsewhere only in Matthew 28:17.

14:33 This confession is in striking contrast to the Marcan parallel (Mk 6:51) where the disciples are "completely astounded."

15:1-20 This dispute begins with the question of the Pharisees and scribes why Jesus' disciples are breaking **the tradition of the elders** about washing one's hands before eating (15:2). Jesus' counterquestion accuses his opponents of breaking **the commandment of God for the sake of** their **tradition** (15:3) and illustrates this by

their interpretation of the commandment of the Decalogue concerning parents (15:4-6). Denouncing them as hypocrites, he applies to them a derogatory prophecy of Isaiah (15:7-8). Then with a wider audience (**the crowd**, 15:10) he goes beyond the violation of tradition with which the dispute has started. The parable (15:11) is an attack on the Mosaic law concerning clean and unclean foods, similar to those antitheses that abrogate the law (5:31-32, 33-34, 38-39). After a warning to his disciples not to follow the moral guidance of the Pharisees (15:13-14), he explains the **parable** (15:15) to them, saying that defilement comes not from what **enters the mouth** (15:17) but from the evil thoughts and deeds that rise from within, **from the heart** (15:18-20). The last verse returns to the starting point of the dispute (eating **with unwashed hands**). Because of Matthew's omission of Mark 7:19b, some scholars think that Matthew has weakened the Marcan repudiation of the Mosaic food laws. But that half verse is ambiguous in the Greek, which may be the reason for its omission here.

15:2 The tradition of the elders: see the note on Mark 7:5. The purpose of the handwashing was to remove defilement caused by contact with what was ritually unclean.

c
Ex 20:12;
21:17; Lv 20:9;
Dt 5:16;
Prv 20:20

d
Is 29:13 LXX

e
Col 2:23

f
Mk 7:14

g
23:16, 19, 24;
Lk 6:39;
Jn 9:40

h
12:34

i
Mk 7:24-30

j
10:6

k
8:10

hands when they eat a meal." [3]He said to them in reply, "And why do you break the commandment of God* for the sake of your tradition? [4c]For God said, 'Honor your father and your mother,' and 'Whoever curses father or mother shall die.' [5*]But you say, 'Whoever says to father or mother, "Any support you might have had from me is dedicated to God," [6]need not honor his father.' You have nullified the word of God for the sake of your tradition. [7]Hypocrites, well did Isaiah prophesy about you when he said:

[8d]'This people honors me with their lips,*
  but their hearts are far from me;
[9e]in vain do they worship me,
  teaching as doctrines human precepts.'"

[10f]He summoned the crowd and said to them, "Hear and understand. [11]It is not what enters one's mouth that defiles that person; but what comes out of the mouth is what defiles one." [12]Then his disciples approached and said to him, "Do you know that the Pharisees took offense when they heard what you said?" [13]He said in reply,* "Every plant that my heavenly Father has not planted will be uprooted. [14g]Let them alone; they are blind guides [of the blind]. If a blind person leads a blind person, both will fall into a pit." [15]Then Peter* said to him in reply, "Explain [this] parable to us." [16]He said to them, "Are even you still without understanding? [17]Do you not realize that everything that enters the mouth passes into the stomach and is expelled into the latrine? [18h]But the things that come out of the mouth come from the heart, and they defile. [19*]For from the heart come evil thoughts, murder, adultery, unchastity, theft, false witness, blasphemy. [20]These are what defile a person, but to eat with unwashed hands does not defile."

The Canaanite Woman's Faith

[21*i]Then Jesus went from that place and withdrew to the region of Tyre and Sidon. [22]And behold, a Canaanite woman of that district came and called out, "Have pity on me, Lord, Son of David! My daughter is tormented by a demon." [23]But he did not say a word in answer to her. His disciples came and asked him, "Send her away, for she keeps calling out after us." [24*]He said in reply, "I was sent only to the lost sheep of the house of Israel." [25j]But the woman came and did him homage, saying, "Lord, help me." [26]He said in reply, "It is not right to take the food of the children* and throw it to the dogs." [27]She said, "Please, Lord, for even the dogs eat the scraps that fall from the table of their masters." [28k]Then Jesus said to her in reply, "O woman, great is your faith!* Let it be done for you as you wish." And her daughter was healed from that hour.

15:3-4 For the commandment see Exodus 20:12 (Dt 5:16); 21:17. The honoring of one's parents had to do with supporting them in their needs.

15:5 See the note on Mark 7:11.

15:8 The text of Isaiah 29:13 is quoted approximately according to the Septuagint.

15:13-14 Jesus leads his disciples away from the teaching authority of the Pharisees.

15:15 Matthew specifies **Peter** as the questioner, unlike Mark 7:17. Given his tendency to present the disciples as more understanding than in his Marcan source, it is noteworthy that here he retains the Marcan rebuke, although in a slightly milder form. This may be due to his wish to correct the Jewish Christians within his

church who still held to the food laws and thus separated themselves from Gentile Christians who did not observe them.

15:19 The Marcan list of thirteen things that defile (7:21-22) is here reduced to seven that partially cover the content of the Decalogue.

15:21-28 See the note on Matthew 8:5-13.

15:24 See the note on Matthew 10:5-6.

15:26 The children: the people of Israel. **Dogs**: see the note on Matthew 7:6.

15:28 As in the case of the cure of the centurion's servant (8:10), Matthew ascribes Jesus' granting the request to the woman's **great faith**, a point not made equally explicit in the Marcan parallel (7:24-30).

The Healing of Many People

[29]Moving on from there Jesus walked by the Sea of Galilee, went up on the mountain, and sat down there. [30l]Great crowds came to him, having with them the lame, the blind, the deformed, the mute, and many others. They placed them at his feet, and he cured them. [31]The crowds were amazed when they saw the mute speaking, the deformed made whole, the lame walking, and the blind able to see, and they glorified the God of Israel.

The Feeding of the Four Thousand

[32*m]Jesus summoned his disciples and said, "My heart is moved with pity for the crowd, for they have been with me now for three days and have nothing to eat. I do not want to send them away hungry, for fear they may collapse on the way." [33]The disciples said to him, "Where could we ever get enough bread in this deserted place to satisfy such a crowd?" [34]Jesus said to them, "How many loaves do you have?" "Seven," they replied, "and a few fish." [35]He ordered the crowd to sit down on the ground. [36]Then he took the seven loaves and the fish, gave thanks,* broke the loaves, and gave them to the disciples, who in turn gave them to the crowds. [37n]They all ate and were satisfied. They picked up the fragments left over—seven baskets full. [38]Those who ate were four thousand men, not counting women and children. [39]And when he had dismissed the crowds, he got into the boat and came to the district of Magadan.

The Demand for a Sign

16 [1*a]The Pharisees and Sadducees came and, to test him, asked him to show them a sign from heaven. [2*]He said to them in reply, "[In the evening you say, 'Tomorrow will be fair, for the sky is red'; [3b]and, in the morning, 'Today will be stormy, for the sky is red and threatening.' You know how to judge the appearance of the sky, but you cannot judge the signs of the times.] [4c]An evil and unfaithful generation seeks a sign, but no sign will be given it except the sign of Jonah."* Then he left them and went away.

The Leaven of the Pharisees and Sadducees

[5d]In coming to the other side of the sea,* the disciples had forgotten to bring bread. [6e]Jesus said to them, "Look out, and beware of the leaven* of the Pharisees and Sadducees." [7*]They concluded among themselves, saying, "It is because we have brought no bread." [8]When Jesus became aware of this he said, "You of little faith, why do you

---

l
Is 35:5-6

m
Mk 8:1-10

n
16:10

a
Mk 8:11-21

b
Lk 12:54-56

c
12:39; Jon 2:1

d
Mk 8:14-21

e
Lk 12:1

15:32-39 Most probably this story is a doublet of that of the feeding of the five thousand (14:13-21). It differs from it notably only in that Jesus takes the initiative, not the disciples (15:32), and in the numbers: the crowd has been with Jesus **three days** (15:32), **seven loaves** are multiplied (15:36), **seven baskets** of fragments remain after the feeding (15:37), and **four thousand** men are fed (15:38).

15:36 Gave thanks: see Matthew 14:19, "said the blessing." There is no difference in meaning. The thanksgiving was a blessing of God for his benefits.

16:1 A sign from heaven: see the note on Matthew 12:38-42.

16:2-3 The answer of Jesus in these verses is omitted in many important textual witnesses, and it is very uncertain that it is an original part of this gospel. It resembles Luke 12:54-56 and may have been inserted from there. It rebukes the Pharisees and Sadducees who are able to read indications of coming weather but not the indications of the coming kingdom in the signs that Jesus does offer, his mighty deeds and teaching.

16:4 See the notes on Matthew 12:39, 40.

16:5-12 Jesus' warning his disciples against **the teaching of the Pharisees and Sadducees** comes immediately before his promise to confer on Peter the authority to bind and to loose on earth (16:19), an authority that will be confirmed in heaven. Such authority most probably has to do, at least in part, with teaching. The rejection of the teaching authority of the Pharisees (see also 12:12-14) prepares for a new one derived from Jesus.

16:6 Leaven: see the note on Matthew 13:33. **Sadducees**: Matthew's Marcan source speaks rather of "the leaven of Herod" (8:15).

16:7-11 The disciples, men **of little faith**, misunderstand Jesus' metaphorical use of **leaven**, forgetting that, as the feeding of the crowds shows, he is not at a loss to provide them with bread.

f
14:17-21;
Jn 6:9

g
15:34-38

h
Mk 8:27-29;
Lk 9:18-20

i
14:2

j
Jn 6:69

k
Jn 1:42

conclude among yourselves that it is because you have no bread? ⁹*f*Do you not yet understand, and do you not remember the five loaves for the five thousand, and how many wicker baskets you took up? ¹⁰*g*Or the seven loaves for the four thousand, and how many baskets you took up? ¹¹How do you not comprehend that I was not speaking to you about bread? Beware of the leaven of the Pharisees and Sadducees." ¹²Then they understood* that he was not telling them to beware of the leaven of bread, but of the teaching of the Pharisees and Sadducees.

Peter's Confession about Jesus

¹³*ʰ*When Jesus went into the region of Caesarea Philippi* he asked his disciples, "Who do people say that the Son of Man is?" ¹⁴*ⁱ*They replied, "Some say John the Baptist,* others Elijah, still others Jeremiah or one of the prophets." ¹⁵He said to them, "But who do you say that I am?" ¹⁶*ʲ*Simon Peter said in reply, "You are the Messiah, the Son of the living God." ¹⁷Jesus said to him in reply, "Blessed are you, Simon son of Jonah. For flesh and blood* has not revealed this to you, but my heavenly Father. ¹⁸*ᵏ*And

---

16:12 After his rebuke, the disciples understand that by **leaven** he meant the corrupting influence of the **teaching of the Pharisees and Sadducees.** The evangelist probably understands this **teaching** as common to both groups. Since at the time of Jesus' ministry the two differed widely on points of **teaching,** e.g., the resurrection of the dead, and at the time of the evangelist the Sadducee party was no longer a force in Judaism, the supposed common **teaching** fits neither period. The disciples' eventual understanding of Jesus' warning contrasts with their continuing obtuseness in the Marcan parallel (8:14-21).

16:13-20 The Marcan confession of Jesus as Messiah, made by Peter as spokesman for the other disciples (8:27-29; cf. also Lk 9:18-20), is modified significantly here. The confession is of Jesus both as **Messiah** and as **Son of the living God** (16:16). Jesus' response, drawn principally from material peculiar to Matthew, attributes the confession to a divine revelation granted to Peter alone (16:17) and makes him the **rock** on which Jesus **will build** his **church** (16:18) and the disciple whose authority in the church **on earth** will be confirmed in **heaven,** i.e., by God (16:19).

16:13 Caesarea Philippi: situated about twenty miles north of the Sea of Galilee in the territory ruled by Philip, a son of Herod the Great, tetrarch from 4 B.C. until his death in A.D. 34 (see the note on 14:1). He rebuilt the town of Paneas, naming it **Caesarea** in honor of the emperor, and **Philippi** ("of Philip") to distinguish it from the seaport in Samaria that was also called Caesarea. **Who do people say that the Son of Man is?:** although the question differs from the Marcan parallel (Mk 8:27: "Who . . . that I am?"), the meaning is the same, for Jesus here refers to himself as **the Son of Man** (cf. 16:15).

16:14 John the Baptist: see Matthew 14:2. **Elijah:** cf. Malachi 3:19; Sirach 48:10; and see the note on Matthew 3:4. **Jeremiah:** an addition of Matthew to the Marcan source.

16:16 The Son of the living God: see Matthew 2:15; 3:17. The addition of this exalted title to the Marcan confession eliminates whatever ambiguity was attached to the title Messiah. This, among other things, supports the view proposed by many scholars that Matthew has here combined his source's confession with a post-resurrectional confession of faith in Jesus as **Son of the living**

Peter's confession of Jesus in its Matthean form is important for Roman Catholic tradition. The church interprets this passage as the founding of the church by Jesus. It is the only passage in the four gospels in which the word "church" (Greek, *ekklesia* = "assembly, those called") is used. The symbol of the keys given to Peter, the image of the "rock" as a firm foundation, and the promise that evil would never bring it down come together in a strong image of the church as the chosen people of God.

God that belonged to the appearance of the risen Jesus to Peter; cf. 1 Corinthians 15:5; Luke 24:34.

16:17 Flesh and blood: a Semitic expression for human beings, especially in their weakness. **Has not revealed this . . . but my heavenly Father:** that Peter's faith is spoken of as coming not through human means but through a revelation from God is similar to Paul's description of his recognition of who Jesus was; see Galatians 1:15-16, ". . . when he [God] . . . was pleased to reveal his Son to me. . . ."

16:18 You are Peter, and upon this rock I will build my church: the Aramaic word *kēpā'* meaning **rock** and transliterated into Greek as *Kēphas* is the name by which Peter is called in the Pauline letters (1 Cor 1:12; 3:22; 9:5; 15:4; Gal 1:18; 2:9, 11, 14) except in Galatians 2:7-8 (*Petros* ("Peter")) in John 1:42. The presumed original Aramaic of Jesus' statement would have been, in English, "You are the Rock (*Kēpā'*) and upon this rock (*kēpā'*) I will build my church." The Greek text probably means the same, for the difference in gender between the masculine noun *petros,* the disciple's new name, and the feminine noun *petra* (rock) may be due simply to the unsuitability of using a feminine noun as the proper name of a male. Although the two words were generally used with slightly different nuances, they were also used interchangeably with the same meaning, "rock." **Church:** this word (Greek *ekklēsia*) occurs in the gospels only here and in Mat-

so I say to you, you are Peter, and upon this rock I will build my church,[*] and the gates of the netherworld shall not prevail against it. [19]I will give you the keys to the kingdom of heaven.[*] Whatever you bind on earth shall be bound in heaven; and whatever you loose on earth shall be loosed in heaven." [20][*m]Then he strictly ordered his disciples to tell no one that he was the Messiah.

The First Prediction of the Passion

[21][*n]From that time on, Jesus began to show his disciples that he[*] must go to Jerusalem and suffer greatly from the elders, the chief priests, and the scribes, and be killed and on the third day be raised.[o] [22][*]Then Peter took him aside and began to rebuke him, "God forbid, Lord! No such thing shall ever happen to you." [23][p]He turned and said to Peter, "Get behind me, Satan! You are an obstacle to me. You are thinking not as God does, but as human beings do."

The Conditions of Discipleship

[24][*q]Then Jesus said to his disciples, "Whoever wishes to come after me must deny himself,[*] take up his cross, and follow me. [25][r]For whoever wishes to save his life will lose it, but whoever loses his life for my sake will find it.[*] [26]What profit would there be for one to gain the whole world and forfeit his life? Or what can one give in exchange

l
Is 22:22;
Rev 3:7

m
Mk 8:30;
Lk 9:21

n
Mk 8:31–9:1;
Lk 9:22-27

o
17:22-23;
20:17-19

p
4:10

q
Lk 14:27

r
Lk 17:33;
Jn 12:25

thew 18:17 (twice). There are several possibilities for an Aramaic original. Jesus' **church** means the community that he **will** gather and that, like a building, will have Peter as its solid foundation. That function of Peter consists in his being witness to Jesus as **the Messiah, the Son of the living God. The gates of the netherworld shall not prevail against it**: the netherworld (Greek *Hadēs*, the abode of the dead) is conceived of as a walled city whose **gates** will not close in upon the church of Jesus, i.e., it will not be overcome by the power of death.

16:19 The keys to the kingdom of heaven: the image of the keys is probably drawn from Isaiah 22:15-25 where Eliakim, who succeeds Shebnah as master of the palace, is given "the key of the house of David," which he authoritatively "opens" and "shuts" (22:22). **Whatever you bind . . . loosed in heaven**: there are many instances in rabbinic literature of the binding-loosing imagery. Of the several meanings given there to the metaphor, two are of special importance here: the giving of authoritative teaching, and the lifting or imposing of the ban of excommunication. It is disputed whether the image of **the keys** and that of binding and loosing are different metaphors meaning the same thing. In any case, the promise of **the keys** is given to Peter alone. In Matthew 18:18 all the disciples are given the power of binding and loosing, but the context of that verse suggests that there the power of excommunication alone is intended. That the keys are those to the **kingdom of heaven** and that Peter's exercise of authority in the church on earth will be confirmed **in heaven** show an intimate connection between, but not an identification of, the church and the **kingdom of heaven**.

16:20 Cf. Mark 8:30. Matthew makes explicit that the prohibition has to do with speaking of Jesus as **the Messiah**; see the note on Mark 8:27-30.

16:21-23 This first prediction of the passion follows Mark 8:31-33 in the main and serves as a corrective to an understanding of Jesus' messiahship as solely one of glory and triumph. By his addition of **from that time on** (16:21) Matthew has emphasized that Jesus' reve-

lation of his coming suffering and death marks a new phase of the gospel. Neither this nor the two later passion predictions (17:22-23; 20:17-19) can be taken as sayings that, as they stand, go back to Jesus himself. However, it is probable that he foresaw that his mission would entail suffering and perhaps death, but was confident that he would ultimately be vindicated by God (see 26:29).

16:21 He: the Marcan parallel (Mk 8:31) has "the Son of Man." Since Matthew has already designated Jesus by that title (13), its omission here is not significant. The Matthean prediction is equally about the sufferings of the Son of Man. **Must**: this necessity is part of the tradition of all the synoptics; cf. Mark 8:31; Luke 9:21. **The elders, the chief priests, and the scribes**: see the note on Mark 8:31. **On the third day**: so also Luke 9:22, against the Marcan "after three days" (Mk 8:31). Matthew's formulation is, in the Greek, almost identical with the pre-Pauline fragment of the kerygma in 1 Corinthians 15:4 and also with Hosea 6:2 which many take to be the Old Testament background to the confession that Jesus was raised **on the third day**. Josephus uses "after three days" and "on the third day" interchangeably (*Antiquities* 7, 11, 6 **280–81; 8, 8, 1–2 **214, 218) and there is probably no difference in meaning between the two phrases.

16:22-23 Peter's refusal to accept Jesus' predicted suffering and death is seen as a satanic attempt to deflect Jesus from his God-appointed course, and the disciple is addressed in terms that recall Jesus' dismissal of the devil in the temptation account (4:10: "Get away, Satan!"). Peter's satanic purpose is emphasized by Matthew's addition to the Marcan source of the words **You are an obstacle to me**.

16:24-28 A readiness to follow Jesus even to giving up one's life for him is the condition for true discipleship; this will be repaid by him at the final judgment.

16:24 Deny himself: to deny someone is to disown him (see 10:33; 26:34-35) and to deny oneself is to disown oneself as the center of one's existence.

16:25 See the notes on Matthew 10:38, 39.

s
25:31-33;
Jb 34:11;
Ps 62:13;
Jer 17:10;
2 Thes 1:7-8

a
Mk 9:2-8;
Lk 9:28-36

b
28:3; Dn 7:9;
10:6; Rev 4:4;
7:9; 19:14

c
3:17; Dt 18:15;
2 Pt 1:17

for his life? ²⁷*ˢFor the Son of Man will come with his angels in his Father's glory, and then he will repay everyone according to his conduct. ²⁸*Amen, I say to you, there are some standing here who will not taste death until they see the Son of Man coming in his kingdom."

The Transfiguration of Jesus*

17 ¹ᵃAfter six days Jesus took Peter, James, and John his brother, and led them up a high mountain by themselves.* ²*ᵇAnd he was transfigured before them; his face shone like the sun and his clothes became white as light. ³*And behold, Moses and Elijah appeared to them, conversing with him. ⁴Then Peter said to Jesus in reply, "Lord, it is good that we are here. If you wish, I will make three tents* here, one for you, one for Moses, and one for Elijah." ⁵ᶜWhile he was still speaking, behold, a bright cloud cast a shadow over them,* then from the cloud came a voice that said, "This is my beloved Son, with whom I am well pleased; listen to him." ⁶*When the disciples heard this, they fell prostrate and were very much afraid. ⁷But Jesus came and touched them, saying, "Rise, and do not be afraid." ⁸And when the disciples raised their eyes, they saw no one else but Jesus alone.

Basilica of the Transfiguration on Mount Tabor

16:27 The parousia and final judgment are described in Matthew 25:31 in terms almost identical with these.

16:28 Coming in his kingdom: since the **kingdom of the Son of Man** has been described as "the world" and Jesus' sovereignty precedes his final coming in glory (13:38, 41), the **coming** in this verse is not the parousia as in the preceding but the manifestation of Jesus' rule after his resurrection; see the notes on Matthew 13:38, 41.

17:1-8 The account of the transfiguration confirms that Jesus is the **Son** of God (17:5) and points to fulfillment of the prediction that he will come **in his Father's glory** at the end of the age (16:27). It has been explained by some as a resurrection appearance retrojected into the time of Jesus' ministry, but that is not probable since the account lacks many of the usual elements of the resurrection-appearance narratives. It draws upon motifs from the Old Testament and noncanonical Jewish apocalyptic literature that express the presence of the heavenly and the divine, e.g., brilliant light, white garments, and the overshadowing cloud.

17:1 These three disciples are also taken apart from the others by Jesus in Gethsemane (26:37). **A high mountain:** this has been identified with Tabor or Hermon, but probably no specific mountain was intended by the evangelist or by his Marcan source (9:2). Its meaning is theological rather than geographical, possibly recalling the revelation to Moses on Mount Sinai (Ex

24:12-18) and to Elijah at the same place (1 Kgs 19:8-18; Horeb = Sinai).

17:2 His face shone like the sun: this is a Matthean addition; cf. Daniel 10:6. **His clothes became white as light:** cf. Daniel 7:9 where the clothing of God appears "snow bright." For the **white** garments of other heavenly beings, see Revelation 4:4; 7:9; 19:14.

17:3 See the note on Mark 9:5.

17:4 Three tents: the booths in which the Israelites lived during the feast of Tabernacles (cf. Jn 7:2) were meant to recall their ancestors' dwelling in booths during the journey from Egypt to the promised land (Lv 23:39-42). The same Greek word, *skēnē*, here translated **tents**, is used in the LXX for the booths of that feast, and some scholars have suggested that there is an allusion here to that liturgical custom.

17:5 Cloud cast a shadow over them: see the note on Mark 9:7. **This is my beloved Son . . . listen to him:** cf. Matthew 3:17. The voice repeats the baptismal proclamation about Jesus, with the addition of the command **listen to him.** The latter is a reference to Deuteronomy 18:15 in which the Israelites are commanded to **listen to** the prophet like Moses whom God will raise up for them. The command to **listen** to Jesus is general, but in this context it probably applies particularly to the preceding predictions of his passion and resurrection (16:21) and of his coming (16:27, 28).

17:6-7 A Matthean addition; cf. Daniel 10:9-10, 18-19.

The Coming of Elijah

[9][d]As they were coming down from the mountain, Jesus charged them, "Do not tell the vision* to anyone until the Son of Man has been raised from the dead." [10][e]Then the disciples asked him, "Why do the scribes say that Elijah must come first?" [11][f]He said in reply,* "Elijah will indeed come and restore all things; [12][g]but I tell you that Elijah has already come, and they did not recognize him but did to him whatever they pleased. So also will the Son of Man suffer at their hands." [13]*Then the disciples understood that he was speaking to them of John the Baptist.

The Healing of a Boy with a Demon

[14]*[h]When they came to the crowd a man approached, knelt down before him, [15]and said, "Lord, have pity on my son, for he is a lunatic* and suffers severely; often he falls into fire, and often into water. [16]I brought him to your disciples, but they could not cure him." [17][i]Jesus said in reply, "O faithless and perverse* generation, how long will I be with you? How long will I endure you? Bring him here to me." [18]Jesus rebuked him and the demon came out of him,* and from that hour the boy was cured. [19]Then the disciples approached Jesus in private and said, "Why could we not drive it out?" [20]*[j]He said to them, "Because of your little faith. Amen, I say to you, if you have faith the size of a mustard seed, you will say to this mountain, 'Move from here to there,' and it will move. Nothing will be impossible for you." [[21]])*

The Second Prediction of the Passion

[22]*[k]As they were gathering in Galilee, Jesus said to them, "The Son of Man is to be handed over to men, [23]and they will kill him, and he will be raised on the third day." And they were overwhelmed with grief.

d
Mk 9:9-13

e
Mal 3:23-24

f
Lk 1:17

g
11:14

h
Mk 9:14-29;
Lk 9:37-43

i
Dt 32:5 LXX

j
21:21; Lk 17:6;
1 Cor 13:2

k
16:21;
20:18-19

17:9-13 In response to the disciples' question about the expected return of Elijah, Jesus interprets the mission of the Baptist as the fulfillment of that expectation. But that was not suspected by those who opposed and finally killed him, and Jesus predicts a similar fate for himself.

17:9 The vision: Matthew alone uses this word to describe the transfiguration. **Until the Son of Man has been raised from the dead**: only in the light of Jesus' resurrection can the meaning of his life and mission be truly understood; until then no testimony to **the vision** will lead people to faith.

17:10 See the notes on Matthew 3:4; 16:14.

17:11-12 The preceding question and this answer may reflect later controversy with Jews who objected to the Christian claims for Jesus that Elijah had not yet come.

17:13 See Matthew 11:14.

17:14-20 Matthew has greatly shortened the Marcan story (9:14-29). Leaving aside several details of the boy's illness, he concentrates on the need for faith, not so much on the part of the boy's father (as does Mark, for Matthew omits Mk 9:22b-24) but on that of his own disciples whose inability to drive out the demon is ascribed to their **little faith** (17:20).

17:15 A lunatic: this description of the boy is peculiar to Matthew. The word occurs in the New Testament only here and in Matthew 4:24 and means one affected or struck by the moon. The symptoms of the boy's illness point to epilepsy, and attacks of this were thought to be caused by phases of the moon.

17:17 Faithless and perverse: so Matthew and Luke (Lk 9:41) against Mark's **faithless** (Mt 9:19). The Greek word here translated **perverse** is the same as that in Deuteronomy 32:5 LXX, where

Moses speaks to his people. There is a problem in knowing to whom the reproach is addressed. Since the Matthean Jesus normally chides his disciples for their **little faith** (as in 17:20), it would appear that the charge of lack of faith could not be made against them and that the reproach is addressed to unbelievers among the Jews. However in Matthew 17:20b (**if you have faith the size of a mustard seed**), which is certainly addressed to the disciples, they appear to have not even the smallest faith; if they had, they would have been able to cure the boy. In the light of Matthew 17:20b the reproach of Matthew 17:17 could have applied to the disciples. There seems to be an inconsistency between the charge of **little faith** in Matthew 17:20a and that of not even a little in Matthew 17:20b.

17:18 The demon came out of him: not until this verse does Matthew indicate that the boy's illness is a case of demoniacal possession.

17:20 The entire verse is an addition of Matthew who (according to the better attested text) omits the reason given for the disciples' inability in Mark 9:29. **Little faith**: see the note on Matthew 6:30. **Faith the size of a mustard seed . . . and it will move**: a combination of a Q saying (cf. Lk 17:6) with a Marcan saying (cf. Mk 11:23).

17:21 Some manuscripts add, "But this kind does not come out except by prayer and fasting"; this is a variant of the better reading of Mark 9:29.

17:22-23 The second passion prediction (cf. 16:21-23) is the least detailed of the three and may be the earliest. In the Marcan parallel the disciples do not understand (9:32); here they understand and are **overwhelmed with grief** at the prospect of Jesus' death (17:23).

l
Ex 30:11-16;
Neh 10:33

a
Mk 9:36-37;
Lk 9:46-48

b
19:14;
Mk 10:15;
Lk 18:17

c
23:12

Payment of the Temple Tax

²⁴*ˡWhen they came to Capernaum, the collectors of the temple tax* approached Peter and said, "Doesn't your teacher pay the temple tax?" ²⁵"Yes," he said.* When he came into the house, before he had time to speak, Jesus asked him, "What is your opinion, Simon? From whom do the kings of the earth take tolls or census tax? From their subjects or from foreigners?" ²⁶*When he said, "From foreigners," Jesus said to him, "Then the subjects are exempt. ²⁷But that we may not offend them,* go to the sea, drop in a hook, and take the first fish that comes up. Open its mouth and you will find a coin worth twice the temple tax. Give that to them for me and for you."

Ruins of the synagogue at Capernaum

The Greatest in the Kingdom

18 ¹*ᵃAt that time the disciples* approached Jesus and said, "Who is the greatest in the kingdom of heaven?" ²He called a child over, placed it in their midst, ³ᵇand said, "Amen, I say to you, unless you turn and become like children,* you will not enter the kingdom of heaven. ⁴ᶜWhoever humbles himself like this child is the greatest in the kingdom of heaven. ⁵*And whoever receives one child such as this in my name receives me.

17:24-27 Like Matthew 14:28-31 and Matthew 16:16b-19, this episode comes from Matthew's special material on Peter. Although the question of **the collectors** concerns Jesus' payment of **the temple tax**, it is put to Peter. It is he who receives instruction from Jesus about freedom from the obligation of payment and yet why it should be made. The means of doing so is provided miraculously. The pericope deals with a problem of Matthew's church, whether its members should pay the temple tax, and the answer is given through a word of Jesus conveyed to Peter. Some scholars see here an example of the teaching authority of Peter exercised in the name of Jesus (see 16:19). The specific problem was a Jewish Christian one and may have arisen when the Matthean church was composed largely of that group.

17:24 The temple tax: before the destruction of the Jerusalem temple in A.D. 70 every male Jew above nineteen years of age was obliged to make an annual contribution to its upkeep (cf. Ex 30:11-16; Neh 10:33). After the destruction the Romans imposed upon Jews the obligation of paying that tax for the temple of Jupiter Capitolinus. There is disagreement about which period the story deals with.

17:25 From their subjects or from foreigners?: the Greek word here translated **subjects** literally means "sons."

17:26 Then the subjects are exempt: just as **subjects** are not bound by laws applying to **foreigners**, neither are Jesus and his disciples, who belong to the kingdom of heaven, bound by the duty of paying the temple tax imposed on those who are not of the kingdom. If the Greek is translated "sons," the freedom of Jesus, the Son of God, and of his disciples, children ("sons") of the kingdom (cf. 13:38), is even more clear.

17:27 That we may not offend them: though they are exempt (17:26), Jesus and his disciples are to avoid giving offense; therefore the tax is to be paid. **A coin worth twice the temple tax**: literally, "a stater," a Greek coin worth two double drachmas. Two double drachmas were equal to the Jewish shekel and the tax was a half-shekel. **For me and for you**: not only Jesus but Peter pays the tax, and this example serves as a standard for the conduct of all the disciples.

18:1-35 This discourse of the fourth book of the gospel is often called the "church order" discourse, but it lacks most of the considerations usually connected with church order, such as various offices in the church and the duties of each, and deals principally with the relations that must obtain among the members of the church. Beginning with the warning that greatness in the **kingdom of heaven** is measured not by rank or power but by childlikeness (18:1-5), it deals with the care that the disciples must take not to cause the **little ones to sin** or to neglect them if they stray from the community (18:6-14), the correction of members who sin (18:15-18), the efficacy of the prayer of the disciples because of the presence of Jesus (18:19-20), and the forgiveness that must be repeatedly extended to sinful members who repent (18:21-35).

18:1 The initiative is taken not by Jesus as in the Marcan parallel (Mk 9:33-34) but by the disciples. **Kingdom of heaven**: this may mean **the kingdom** in its fullness, i.e., after the parousia and the final judgment. But what follows about causes of sin, church discipline, and forgiveness, all dealing with the present age, suggests that the question has to do with rank also in the church, where **the kingdom** is manifested here and now, although only partially and by anticipation; see the notes on Matthew 3:2; 4:17.

18:3 Become like children: the child is held up as a model for the disciples not because of any supposed innocence of children but because of their complete dependence on, and trust in, their parents. So must the disciples be, in respect to God.

18:5 Cf. Matthew 10:40.

The designation **"little ones"** is a Matthean favorite term for Jesus' disciples. It simultaneously denotes their being subject to outside forces that often oppose them but also their status as servants rather than those who should "lord it over" others (Mk 10:42; cf. Mt 18:10, 14).

Temptations to Sin

[6d]"Whoever causes one of these little ones[*] who believe in me to sin, it would be better for him to have a great millstone hung around his neck and to be drowned in the depths of the sea. [7*]Woe to the world because of things that cause sin! Such things must come, but woe to the one through whom they come! [8e]If your hand or foot causes you to sin,[*] cut it off and throw it away. It is better for you to enter into life maimed or crippled than with two hands or two feet to be thrown into eternal fire. [9]And if your eye causes you to sin, tear it out and throw it away. It is better for you to enter into life with one eye than with two eyes to be thrown into fiery Gehenna.

The Parable of the Lost Sheep

[10*f]"See that you do not despise one of these little ones,[*] for I say to you that their angels in heaven always look upon the face of my heavenly Father. [[11]][*] [12g]What is your opinion? If a man has a hundred sheep and one of them goes astray, will he not leave the ninety-nine in the hills and go in search of the stray? [13]And if he finds it, amen, I say to you, he rejoices more over it than over the ninety-nine that did not stray. [14]In just the same way, it is not the will of your heavenly Father that one of these little ones be lost.

d
Mk 9:42;
Lk 17:1-2

e
5:29-30;
Mk 9:43-47

f
Ez 34:1-3, 16;
Lk 15:3-7

g
Lk 19:10

Shepherd and flock in modern Israel

18:6 One of these little ones: the thought passes from the child of Matthew 18:2-4 to the disciples, **little ones** because of their becoming **like children**. It is difficult to know whether this is a designation of all who are disciples or of those who are insignificant in contrast to others, e.g., the leaders of the community. Since apart from this chapter the designation **little ones** occurs in Matthew only in Matthew 10:42 where it means disciples as such, that is its more likely meaning here. **Who believe in me**: since discipleship is impossible without at least some degree of faith, this further specification seems superfluous. However, it serves to indicate that the warning against causing a **little one** to sin is principally directed against whatever would lead such a one to a weakening or loss of faith. The Greek verb *skandalizein*, here translated **causes . . . to sin**, means literally "causes to stumble"; what the stumbling is depends on the context. It is used of falling away from faith in Matthew 13:21. According to the better reading of Mark 9:42, **in me** is a Matthean addition to the Marcan source. **It would be better . . . depths of the sea**: cf. Mark 9:42.

18:7 This is a Q saying; cf. Luke 17:1. The inevitability of **things that cause sin** (literally, "scandals") does not take away the responsibility of **the one through whom they come**.

18:8 These verses are a doublet of Matthew 5:29-30. In that context they have to do with causes of sexual sin. As in the Marcan source from which they have been drawn (Mk 9:42-48), they differ from the first warning about scandal, which deals with causing

another person to sin, for they concern what **causes** oneself **to sin** and they do not seem to be related to another's loss of faith, as the first warning is. It is difficult to know how Matthew understood the logical connection between these verses and Matthew 18:6-7.

18:10-14 The first and last verses are peculiar to Matthew. The parable itself comes from Q; see Luke 15:3-7. In Luke it serves as justification for Jesus' table-companionship with sinners; here, it is an exhortation for the disciples to seek out fellow disciples who have gone **astray**. Not only must no one cause a fellow disciple to sin, but those who have strayed must be sought out and, if possible, brought back to the community. The joy of the shepherd on finding the sheep, though not absent in Matthew 18:13 is more emphasized in Luke. By his addition of Matthew 18:10, 14 Matthew has drawn out explicitly the application of the parable to the care of the **little ones**.

18:10 Their angels in heaven . . . my heavenly Father: for the Jewish belief in angels as guardians of nations and individuals, see Daniel 10:13, 20-21; Tobit 5:4-7; 1QH 5:20-22; as intercessors who present the prayers of human beings to God, see Tobit 13:12, 15. The high worth of the **little ones** is indicated by their being represented before God by these heavenly beings.

18:11 Some manuscripts add, "For the Son of Man has come to save what was lost"; cf. Matthew 9:13. This is practically identical with Luke 19:10 and is probably a copyist's addition from that source.

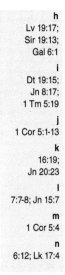

h
Lv 19:17;
Sir 19:13;
Gal 6:1

i
Dt 19:15;
Jn 8:17;
1 Tm 5:19

j
1 Cor 5:1-13

k
16:19;
Jn 20:23

l
7:7-8; Jn 15:7

m
1 Cor 5:4

n
6:12; Lk 17:4

A Brother Who Sins

15*h"If your brother* sins [against you], go and tell him his fault between you and him alone. If he listens to you, you have won over your brother. 16*i If he does not listen, take one or two others along with you, so that 'every fact may be established on the testimony of two or three witnesses.' 17If he refuses to listen to them, tell the church.* If he refuses to listen even to the church, then treat him as you would a Gentile or a tax collector. 18*k Amen, I say to you, whatever you bind on earth shall be bound in heaven, and whatever you loose on earth shall be loosed in heaven. 19*l Again, [amen,] I say to you, if two of you agree on earth about anything for which they are to pray, it shall be granted to them by my heavenly Father. 20*m For where two or three are gathered together in my name, there am I in the midst of them."

All prayer has power, but when prayer is united to the prayer of others, God promises to be present in a unique way. Do you ever ask others to pray with you? Who will you ask today?

The Parable of the Unforgiving Servant

21*n Then Peter approaching asked him, "Lord, if my brother sins against me, how often must I forgive him? As many as seven times?" 22*Jesus answered, "I say to you, not seven times

---

18:15-20 Passing from the duty of Christian disciples toward those who have strayed from their number, the discourse now turns to how they are to deal with one who sins and yet remains within the community. First there is to be private correction (18:15); if this is unsuccessful, further correction before **two or three witnesses** (18:16); if this fails, the matter is to be brought before the assembled community (**the church**), and if the sinner refuses to attend to the correction of **the church**, he is to be expelled (18:17). The church's judgment will be ratified **in heaven**, i.e., by God (18:18). This three-step process of correction corresponds, though not exactly, to the procedure of the Qumran community; see 1QS 5:25–6:1; 6:24–7:25; CD 9:2-8. The section ends with a saying about the favorable response of God to prayer, even to that of a very small number, for Jesus is in the midst of any gathering of his disciples, however small (18:19-20). Whether this prayer has anything to do with the preceding judgment is uncertain.

18:15 Your brother: a fellow disciple; see Matthew 23:8. The bracketed words, **against you**, are widely attested but they are not in the important codices Sinaiticus and Vaticanus or in some other textual witnesses. Their omission broadens the type of sin in question. **Won over**: literally, "gained."

18:16 Cf. Deuteronomy 19:15.

18:17 The church: the second of the only two instances of this word in the gospels; see the note on Matthew 16:18. Here it refers not to the entire **church** of Jesus, as in Matthew 16:18, but to the local congregation. **Treat him . . . a Gentile or a tax collector**: just as the observant Jew avoided the company of Gentiles and tax collectors, so must the congregation of Christian disciples separate itself from the arrogantly sinful member who refuses to repent even when convicted of his sin by the whole **church**. Such a one is to be set outside the fellowship of the community. The harsh language about **Gentile** and **tax collector** probably reflects a stage of the Matthean **church** when it was principally composed of Jewish Christians. That time had long since passed, but the principle of

exclusion for such a sinner remained. Paul makes a similar demand for excommunication in 1 Corinthians 5:1-13.

18:18 Except for the plural of the verbs **bind** and **loose**, this verse is practically identical with Matthew 16:19b and many scholars understand it as granting to all the disciples what was previously given to Peter alone. For a different view, based on the different contexts of the two verses, see the note on Matthew 16:19.

18:19-20 Some take these verses as applying to prayer on the occasion of the church's gathering to deal with the sinner of Matthew 18:17. Unless an *a fortiori* argument is supposed, this seems unlikely. God's answer to the prayer of **two or three** envisages a different situation from one that involves the entire congregation. In addition, the object of this prayer is expressed in most general terms as **anything for which they are to pray**.

18:20 For where two or three . . . midst of them: the presence of Jesus guarantees the efficacy of the prayer. This saying is similar to one attributed to a rabbi executed in A.D. 135 at the time of the second Jewish revolt: ". . . When two sit and there are between them the words of the Torah, the divine presence (Shekinah) rests upon them" (*Pirqê *'Abôt* 3:3).

18:21-35 The final section of the discourse deals with the forgiveness that the disciples are to give to their fellow disciples who sin against them. To the question of Peter how often forgiveness is to be granted (18:21), Jesus answers that it is to be given without limit (18:22) and illustrates this with the parable of the unmerciful servant (18:23-34), warning that his **heavenly Father** will give those who do not forgive the same treatment as that given to the unmerciful servant (18:35). Matthew 18:21-22 correspond to Luke 17:4; the parable and the final warning are peculiar to Matthew. That the parable did not originally belong to this context is suggested by the fact that it really does not deal with repeated forgiveness, which is the point of Peter's question and Jesus' reply.

18:22 Seventy-seven times: the Greek corresponds exactly to the LXX of Genesis 4:24. There is probably an allusion, by

but seventy-seven times. [23][o]That is why the kingdom of heaven may be likened to a
king who decided to settle accounts with his servants. [24]*When he began the accounting,
a debtor was brought before him who owed him a huge amount. [25]Since he had no way
of paying it back, his master ordered him to be sold, along with his wife, his children,
and all his property, in payment of the debt. [26]*At that, the servant fell down, did him
homage, and said, 'Be patient with me, and I will pay you back in full.' [27]Moved with
compassion the master of that servant let him go and forgave him the loan. [28]When that
servant had left, he found one of his fellow servants who owed him a much smaller
amount.* He seized him and started to choke him, demanding, 'Pay back what you
owe.' [29]Falling to his knees, his fellow servant begged him, 'Be patient with me, and
I will pay you back.' [30]But he refused. Instead, he had him put in prison until he paid
back the debt. [31]Now when his fellow servants saw what had happened, they were
deeply disturbed, and went to their master and reported the whole affair. [32]His master
summoned him and said to him, 'You wicked servant! I forgave you your entire debt
because you begged me to. [33][p]Should you not have had pity on your fellow servant, as
I had pity on you?' [34]Then in anger his master handed him over to the torturers until
he should pay back the whole debt.* [35]*[q]So will my heavenly Father do to you, unless
each of you forgives his brother from his heart."

o
25:19

p
Sir 28:4

q
6:15; Jas 2:13

VI: Ministry in Judea and Jerusalem

Marriage and Divorce

19 [1]*When Jesus* finished these words,* he left Galilee and went to the district
of Judea across the Jordan. [2]Great crowds followed him, and he cured them

---

contrast, to the limitless vengeance of Lamech in the Genesis text. In any case, what is demanded of the disciples is limitless forgiveness.

18:24 A huge amount: literally, "ten thousand talents." The talent was a unit of coinage of high but varying value depending on its metal (gold, silver, copper) and its place of origin. It is mentioned in the New Testament only here and in Matthew 25:14-30.

18:26 Pay you back in full: an empty promise, given the size of the debt.

18:28 A much smaller amount: literally, "a hundred denarii." A denarius was the normal daily wage of a laborer. The difference between the two debts is enormous and brings out the absurdity of the conduct of the Christian who has received the great forgiveness of God and yet refuses to forgive the relatively minor offenses done to him.

18:34 Since the debt is so great as to be unpayable, the punishment will be endless.

18:35 The Father's forgiveness, already given, will be withdrawn at the final judgment for those who have not imitated his forgiveness by their own.

19:1–23:39 The narrative section of the fifth book of the gospel. The first part (19:1–20:34) has for its setting the journey of Jesus from Galilee to Jerusalem; the second (21:1–23:39) deals with Jesus' ministry in Jerusalem up to the final great discourse of the gospel (24–25). Matthew follows the Marcan sequence of events, though adding material both special to this gospel and drawn from Q. The second part ends with the denunciation of the scribes and Pharisees (23:1-36) followed by Jesus' lament over Jerusalem (23:37-39). This long and important speech raises a problem for the view that Matthew is structured around five other discourses of Jesus (see Introduction) and that this one has no such function in the gospel. However, it is to be noted that this speech lacks the customary concluding formula that follows the five discourses (see the note on 7:28), and that those discourses are all addressed either exclusively (10; 18; 24; 25) or primarily (5-7; 13) to the disciples, whereas this is addressed primarily to the scribes and Pharisees (23:13-36). Consequently, it seems plausible to maintain that the evangelist did not intend to give it the structural importance of the five other discourses, and that, in spite of its being composed of sayings-material, it belongs to the narrative section of this book. In that regard, it is similar to the sayings-material of Matthew 11:7-30. Some have proposed that Matthew wished to regard it as part of the final discourse of Matthew 24–25, but the intervening material (24:1-4) and the change in matter and style of those chapters do not support that view.

19:1-12 In giving Jesus' teaching on divorce (19:3-9), Matthew here follows his Marcan source (Mk 10:2-12) as he does Q in Matthew 5:31-32 (cf. Lk 16:18). Matthew 19:10-12 are peculiar to Matthew.

19:1 When Jesus finished these words: see the note on Matthew 7:28-29. **The district of Judea across the Jordan**: an inexact designation of the territory. Judea did not extend **across the Jordan**; the territory east of the river was Perea. The route to Jerusalem by way of Perea avoided passage through Samaria.

a
Mk 10:2-12

b
Gn 1:27

c
Gn 2:24;
1 Cor 6:16;
Eph 5:31

d
Dt 24:1-4

e
5:32; Lk 16:18;
1 Cor 7:10-11

f
Mk 10:13-16;
Lk 18:15-17

g
18:3; Acts 8:36

h
Mk 10:17-31;
Lk 18:18-30

there. [3a]Some Pharisees approached him, and tested him,* saying, "Is it lawful for a man to divorce his wife for any cause whatever?" [4*b]He said in reply, "Have you not read that from the beginning the Creator 'made them male and female' [5c]and said, 'For this reason a man shall leave his father and mother and be joined to his wife, and the two shall become one flesh'? [6]So they are no longer two, but one flesh. Therefore, what God has joined together, no human being must separate." [7*d]They said to him, "Then why did Moses command that the man give the woman a bill of divorce and dismiss [her]?" [8]He said to them, "Because of the hardness of your hearts Moses allowed you to divorce your wives, but from the beginning it was not so. [9e]I say to you,* whoever divorces his wife (unless the marriage is unlawful) and marries another commits adultery." [10][His] disciples said to him, "If that is the case of a man with his wife, it is better not to marry." [11]He answered, "Not all can accept [this] word,* but only those to whom that is granted. [12]Some are incapable of marriage because they were born so; some, because they were made so by others; some, because they have renounced marriage* for the sake of the kingdom of heaven. Whoever can accept this ought to accept it."

Blessing of the Children

[13*f]Then children were brought to him that he might lay his hands on them and pray. The disciples rebuked them, [14g]but Jesus said, "Let the children come to me, and do not prevent them; for the kingdom of heaven belongs to such as these." [15]After he placed his hands on them, he went away.

The Rich Young Man*

[16h]Now someone approached him and said, "Teacher, what good must I do to gain

---

19:3 Tested him: the verb is used of attempts of Jesus' opponents to embarrass him by challenging him to do something they think impossible (16:1; Mk 8:11; Lk 11:16) or by having him say something that they can use against him (22:18, 35; Mk 10:2; 12:15). **For any cause whatever**: this is peculiar to Matthew and has been interpreted by some as meaning that Jesus was being asked to take sides in the dispute between the schools of Hillel and Shammai on the reasons for divorce, the latter holding a stricter position than the former. It is unlikely, however, that to ask Jesus' opinion about the differing views of two Jewish schools, both highly respected, could be described as "testing" him, for the reason indicated above.

19:4-6 Matthew recasts his Marcan source, omitting Jesus' question about Moses' command (Mk 10:3) and having him recall at once two Genesis texts that show the will and purpose of **the Creator** in making human beings **male and female** (Gn 1:27), namely, that a **man** may **be joined to his wife** in marriage in the intimacy of **one flesh** (Gn 2:24). **What God has** thus **joined** must not be separated by any **human being**. (The NAB translation of the Hebrew *bāśār* of Gn 2:24 as "body" rather than "flesh" obscures the reference of Matthew to that text.)

19:7 See Deuteronomy 24:1-4.

19:9 Moses' concession to human sinfulness (**the hardness of your hearts**, 19:8) is repudiated by Jesus, and the original will of the Creator is reaffirmed against that concession. (**Unless the marriage is unlawful**): see the note on Matthew 5:31-32. There is some evidence suggesting that Jesus' absolute prohibition of divorce was paralleled in the Qumran community (see 11QTemple 57:17-19; CD 4:12b–5:14). Matthew removes Mark's setting of this

verse as spoken to the disciples alone "in the house" (Mk 10:10) and also his extension of the divorce prohibition to the case of a woman's divorcing her husband (Mt 10:12), probably because in Palestine, unlike the places where Roman and Greek law prevailed, the woman was not allowed to initiate the divorce.

19:11 [This] word: probably the disciples' "**it is better not to marry**" (19:10). Jesus agrees but says that celibacy is not for all but only for those **to whom that is granted** by God.

19:12 Incapable of marriage: literally, "eunuchs." Three classes are mentioned, eunuchs from birth, eunuchs by castration, and those who have voluntarily **renounced marriage** (literally, "have made themselves eunuchs") **for the sake of the kingdom**, i.e., to devote themselves entirely to its service. Some scholars take the last class to be those who have been divorced by their spouses and have refused to enter another marriage. But it is more likely that it is rather those who have chosen never to marry, since that suits better the optional nature of the decision: **whoever can . . . ought to accept it**.

19:13-15 This account is understood by some as intended to justify the practice of infant baptism. That interpretation is based principally on the command not to **prevent** the children from coming, since that word sometimes has a baptismal connotation in the New Testament; see Acts 8:36.

19:16-30 Cf. Mark 10:17-31. This story does not set up a "two-tier" morality, that of those who seek (only) **eternal life** (19:16) and that of those who **wish to be perfect** (19:21). It speaks rather of the obstacle that riches constitute for the following of Jesus and of the impossibility, humanly speaking, for one who has **many possessions** (19:22) **to enter the kingdom** (19:24). Actual renunciation of

eternal life?"* [17]He answered him, "Why do you ask me about the good? There is only One who is good.* If you wish to enter into life, keep the commandments." [18]*[i]He asked him, "Which ones?" And Jesus replied, " 'You shall not kill; you shall not commit adultery; you shall not steal; you shall not bear false witness; [19]honor your father and your mother'; and 'you shall love your neighbor as yourself.'" [20]*The young man said to him, "All of these I have observed. What do I still lack?" [21][j]Jesus said to him, "If you wish to be perfect,* go, sell what you have and give to [the] poor, and you will have treasure in heaven. Then come, follow me." [22]When the young man heard this statement, he went away sad, for he had many possessions. [23]*Then Jesus said to his disciples, "Amen, I say to you, it will be hard for one who is rich to enter the kingdom of heaven. [24][k]Again I say to you, it is easier for a camel to pass through the eye of a needle than for one who is rich to enter the kingdom of God." [25]*When the disciples heard this, they were greatly astonished and said, "Who then can be saved?" [26][l]Jesus looked at them and said, "For human beings this is impossible, but for God all things are possible." [27][m]Then Peter said to him in reply, "We have given up everything and followed you. What will there be for us?" [28]*[n]Jesus said to them, "Amen, I say to you that you who have followed me, in the new age, when the Son of Man is seated on his throne of glory, will yourselves sit on twelve thrones, judging the twelve tribes of Israel. [29]And everyone who has given up houses or brothers or sisters or father or mother or children or lands for the sake of my name will receive a hundred times more, and will inherit eternal life. [30]*[o]But many who are first will be last, and the last will be first.

i
Ex 20:12-16;
Dt 5:16-20 /
Lv 19:18;
Rom 13:9

j
5:48; 6:20

k
7:14

l
Gn 18:14;
Jb 42:2;
Lk 1:37

m
4:20, 22

n
25:31; Dn 7:9,
22; Lk 22:30;
Rev 3:21; 20:4

o
20:16

---

riches is not demanded of all; Matthew counts the rich Joseph of Arimathea as a disciple of Jesus (27:57). But only the poor in spirit (5:3) can **enter the kingdom** and, as here, such poverty may entail the sacrifice of one's **possessions**. The Twelve, who **have given up everything** (19:27) to follow Jesus, will have as their reward a share in Jesus' (the Son of Man's) **judging the twelve tribes of Israel** (19:28), and all who have similarly sacrificed family or property for his sake **will inherit eternal life** (19:29).

19:16 Gain eternal life: this is equivalent to "entering into life" (19:17) and "being saved" (19:25); the **life** is that of the new age after the final judgment (see 25:46). It probably is also equivalent here to "entering the kingdom of heaven" (19:23) or "the kingdom of God" (19:24), but see the notes on Matthew 3:2; 4:17; 18:1 for the wider reference of **the kingdom** in Matthew.

19:17 By Matthew's reformulation of the Marcan question and reply (Mk 10:17-18) Jesus' repudiation of the term "good" for himself has been softened. Yet the Marcan assertion that "no one is good but God alone" stands, with only unimportant verbal modification.

19:18-19 The first five commandments cited are from the Decalogue (see Ex 20:12-16; Dt 5:16-20). Matthew omits Mark's "you shall not defraud" (10:19; see Dt 24:14) and adds Leviticus 19:18. This combination of commandments of the Decalogue with Leviticus 19:18 is partially the same as Paul's enumeration of the demands of Christian morality in Romans 13:9.

19:20 Young man: in Matthew alone of the synoptics the questioner is said to be a **young man**; thus the Marcan "from my youth" (10:20) is omitted.

19:21 If you wish to be perfect: **to be perfect** is demanded of all Christians; see Matthew 5:48. In the case of this man, it involves selling his possessions and giving to the poor; only so can he **follow Jesus**.

19:23-24 Riches are an obstacle to entering **the kingdom** that cannot be overcome by human power. The comparison with the impossibility of a camel's passing **through the eye of a needle** should not be mitigated by such suppositions as that **the eye of a needle** means a low or narrow gate. **The kingdom of God**: as in Matthew 12:28; 21:31, 43 instead of Matthew's usual **kingdom of heaven**.

19:25-26 See the note on Mark 10:23-27.

19:28 This saying, directed to the Twelve, is from Q; see Luke 22:29-30. **The new age**: the Greek word here translated "new age" occurs in the New Testament only here and in Titus 3:5. Literally, it means "rebirth" or "regeneration," and is used in Titus of spiritual rebirth through baptism. Here it means the "rebirth" effected by the coming of the kingdom. Since that coming has various stages (see the notes on 3:2; 4:17), the **new age** could be taken as referring to the time after the resurrection when the Twelve will govern the true Israel, i.e., the church of Jesus. (For "judge" in the sense of "govern," cf. Jgs 12:8, 9, 11; 15:20; 16:31; Ps 2:10). But since it is connected here with the time when the **Son of Man** will be **seated on his throne of glory**, language that Matthew uses in Matthew 25:31 for the time of final judgment, it is more likely that what the Twelve are promised is that they will be joined with Jesus then in judging the people of Israel.

19:30 Different interpretations have been given to this saying, which comes from Mark 10:31. In view of Matthew's associating it with the following parable (20:1-15) and substantially repeating it (in reverse order) at the end of that parable (20:16), it may be that his meaning is that all who respond to the call of Jesus, at whatever time (**first** or **last**), will be the same in respect to inheriting the benefits of the kingdom, which is the gift of God.

MATTHEW

a
Lv 19:13;
Dt 24:15

b
16:21;
17:22-23;
Mk 10:32-34;
Lk 18:31-33

The Workers in the Vineyard

20 [1]*"The kingdom of heaven is like a landowner who went out at dawn to hire laborers for his vineyard. [2]After agreeing with them for the usual daily wage, he sent them into his vineyard. [3]Going out about nine o'clock, he saw others standing idle in the marketplace, [4]*and he said to them, 'You too go into my vineyard, and I will give you what is just.' [5]So they went off. [And] he went out again around noon, and around three o'clock, and did likewise. [6]Going out about five o'clock, he found others standing around, and said to them, 'Why do you stand here idle all day?' [7]They answered, 'Because no one has hired us.' He said to them, 'You too go into my vineyard.' [8]*ᵃWhen it was evening the owner of the vineyard said to his foreman, 'Summon the laborers and give them their pay, beginning with the last and ending with the first.' [9]When those who had started about five o'clock came, each received the usual daily wage. [10]So when the first came, they thought that they would receive more, but each of them also got the usual wage. [11]And on receiving it they grumbled against the landowner, [12]saying, 'These last ones worked only one hour, and you have made them equal to us, who bore the day's burden and the heat.' [13]He said to one of them in reply, 'My friend, I am not cheating you.* Did you not agree with me for the usual daily wage? [14]*Take what is yours and go. What if I wish to give this last one the same as you? [15][Or] am I not free to do as I wish with my own money? Are you envious because I am generous?' [16]*Thus, the last will be first, and the first will be last."

The Third Prediction of the Passion

[17]*ᵇAs Jesus was going up to Jerusalem, he took the twelve [disciples] aside by themselves, and said to them on the way, [18]"Behold, we are going up to Jerusalem, and the Son of Man will be handed over to the chief priests and the scribes, and they will condemn him to death, [19]and hand him over to the Gentiles to be mocked and scourged and crucified, and he will be raised on the third day."

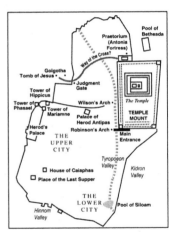

Jerusalem in the New Testament period

20:1-16 This parable is peculiar to Matthew. It is difficult to know whether the evangelist composed it or received it as part of his traditional material and, if the latter is the case, what its original reference was. In its present context its close association with Matthew 19:30 suggests that its teaching is the equality of all the disciples in the reward of inheriting eternal life.

20:4 What is just: although the wage is not stipulated as in the case of those first hired, it will be fair.

20:8 Beginning with the last . . . the first: this element of the parable has no other purpose than to show how **the first** knew what **the last** were given (20:12).

20:13 I am not cheating you: literally, "I am not treating you unjustly."

20:14-15 The owner's conduct involves no violation of justice (20:4, 13), and that all the workers receive the same wage is due only to his generosity to the latest arrivals; the resentment of the first comes from envy.

20:16 See the note on Matthew 19:30.

20:17-19 Cf. Mark 10:32-34. This is the third and the most detailed of the passion predictions (16:21-23; 17:22-23). It speaks of Jesus' **being "handed over to the Gentiles"** (27:2), his being **"mocked"** (27:27-30), **"scourged"** (27:26), and **"crucified"** (27:31, 35). In all but the last of these points Matthew agrees with his Marcan source, but whereas Mark speaks of Jesus' being killed (Mk 10:34), Matthew has the specific **"to be . . . crucified."**

The Request of James and John

20*ᶜThen the mother* of the sons of Zebedee approached him with her sons and did him homage, wishing to ask him for something. ²¹He said to her, "What do you wish?" She answered him, "Command that these two sons of mine sit, one at your right and the other at your left, in your kingdom." ²²Jesus said in reply, "You do not know what you are asking.* Can you drink the cup that I am going to drink?" They said to him, "We can." ²³He replied, "My cup you will indeed drink, but to sit at my right and at my left [, this] is not mine to give but is for those for whom it has been prepared by my Father." ²⁴ᵈWhen the ten heard this, they became indignant at the two brothers. ²⁵But Jesus summoned them and said, "You know that the rulers of the Gentiles lord it over them, and the great ones make their authority over them felt. ²⁶But it shall not be so among you. Rather, whoever wishes to be great among you shall be your servant; ²⁷ᵉwhoever wishes to be first among you shall be your slave. ²⁸ᶠJust so, the Son of Man did not come to be served but to serve and to give his life as a ransom* for many."

c
Mk 10:35-45

d
Lk 22:25-27

e
Mk 9:35

f
26:28;
Is 53:12;
Rom 5:6;
1 Tm 2:6

James and John, the sons of Zebedee, are part of the inner circle of the twelve apostles, along with Peter. They feature prominently in several passages of the NT, including the transfiguration story (Mt 17:1; Mk 9:2; Lk 9:28). Later Christian tradition identified this James as "the Greater." Interestingly, their mother—who is never named—features in several passages as well (Mt 20:20-21; 27:56).

The Sons of Zebedee

Some may associate the sons of Zebedee not with their father but with an overbearing mother who has high aspirations for her sons (cf. vv. 20-23). However, her sons do their own bidding in Mark's gospel account, and they are quite demanding. "Teacher, we want you to do for us *whatever* we ask of you . . . Grant that in your glory we may sit one at your right hand and the other at your left" (Mk 10:35-36).

James and John sound like spoiled children, used to getting their own way. After so much time with Jesus they show little awareness of Jesus' mission and certainly no understanding of what they are asking. Their self-centered desire to be in places of honor gives Jesus the opportunity to open their eyes, and ours. "Can you drink the cup that I drink or be baptized with the baptism with which I am to be baptized?" (Mt 10:38). Ironically, James and John will be unable to stay awake with Jesus as he approaches his hour of glory in the Garden of Gethsemane (Mt 26:36-46); however, their mother will be among the women at the cross who had ministered to Jesus.

The sons of Zebedee, in their desire for status and success, inadvertently discovered the deeper truth of suffering. We can sympathize with their desire for the "good life" of miracles and healings, honor, and glory. Perhaps God will use our desires to lead us where we could not go on our own.

20:20-28 Cf. Mark 10:35-45. The request of the sons of Zebedee, made through their mother, for the highest places of honor in the **kingdom**, and the indignation of **the** other **ten** disciples at this request, show that neither **the two brothers** nor the others have understood that what makes for greatness in the kingdom is not lordly power but humble service. Jesus gives the example, and his ministry of service will reach its highest point when he gives his life for the deliverance of the human race from sin.

20:20-21 The reason for Matthew's making **the mother** the petitioner (cf. Mk 10:35) is not clear. Possibly he intends an allusion to Bathsheba's seeking the kingdom for Solomon; see 1 Kings 1:11-21. **Your kingdom**: see the note on Matthew 16:28.

20:22 You do not know what you are asking: the Greek verbs are plural and, with the rest of the verse, indicate that the answer is addressed not to the woman but to her sons. **Drink the cup**: see the note on Mark 10:38-40. Matthew omits the Marcan "or be baptized with the baptism with which I am baptized" (10:38).

20:28 Ransom: this noun, which occurs in the New Testament only here and in the Marcan parallel (Mk 10:45) does not necessarily express the idea of liberation by payment of some price. The cognate verb is used frequently in the LXX of God's liberating Israel from Egypt or from Babylonia after the Exile; see Exodus 6:6; 15:13; Psalm 77:16 (76 LXX); Isaiah 43:1; 44:22. The liberation brought by Jesus' death will be **for many**; cf. Isaiah 53:12. **Many** does not mean that some are excluded, but is a Semitism designating the collectivity who benefit from the service of the one, and is equivalent to "all." While there are few verbal contacts between this saying and the fourth Servant Song (Is 52:13–53:12), the ideas of that passage are reflected here.

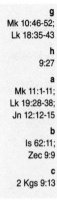

g
Mk 10:46-52;
Lk 18:35-43

h
9:27

a
Mk 11:1-11;
Lk 19:28-38;
Jn 12:12-15

b
Is 62:11;
Zec 9:9

c
2 Kgs 9:13

The Healing of Two Blind Men

[29]*[g]As they left Jericho, a great crowd followed him. [30][h]Two blind men were sitting by the roadside, and when they heard that Jesus was passing by, they cried out, "[Lord,]* Son of David, have pity on us!" [31]The crowd warned them to be silent, but they called out all the more, "Lord, Son of David, have pity on us!" [32]Jesus stopped and called them and said, "What do you want me to do for you?" [33]They answered him, "Lord, let our eyes be opened." [34]Moved with pity, Jesus touched their eyes. Immediately they received their sight, and followed him.

The Entry into Jerusalem

21 [1]*[a]When they drew near Jerusalem and came to Bethphage* on the Mount of Olives, Jesus sent two disciples, [2]saying to them, "Go into the village opposite you, and immediately you will find an ass tethered, and a colt with her.* Untie them and bring them here to me. [3]And if anyone should say anything to you, reply, 'The master has need of them.' Then he will send them at once." [4]*This happened so that what had been spoken through the prophet might be fulfilled:

[5][b]"Say to daughter Zion,
'Behold, your king comes to you,
meek and riding on an ass,
and on a colt, the foal of a beast of burden.'"

[6]The disciples went and did as Jesus had ordered them. [7]*They brought the ass and the colt and laid their cloaks over them, and he sat upon them. [8]*[c]The very large crowd spread their cloaks on the road,

Church of All Nations near the base of the Mount of Olives

20:29-34 The cure of the blind men is probably symbolic of what will happen to the disciples, now blind to the meaning of Jesus' passion and to the necessity of their sharing his suffering. As the men are given sight, so, after the resurrection, will the disciples come to see that to which they are now blind. Matthew has abbreviated his Marcan source (Mk 10:46-52) and has made Mark's one man two. Such doubling is characteristic of this gospel; see Matthew 8:28-34 (Mk 5:1-20) and the note on Matthew 9:27-31.

20:30 [Lord]: some important textual witnesses omit this, but that may be because copyists assimilated this verse to Matthew 9:27. **Son of David:** see the note on Matthew 9:27.

21:1-11 Jesus' coming to Jerusalem is in accordance with the divine will that he must go there (cf. 16:21) to suffer, die, and be raised. He prepares for his entry into the city in such a way as to make it a fulfillment of the prophecy of Zechariah 9:9 (21:2) that emphasizes the humility of the **king** who **comes** (21:5). That prophecy, absent from the Marcan parallel account (11:1-11) although found also in the Johannine account of the entry (12:15), is the center of the Matthean story. During the procession from Bethphage to Jerusalem, Jesus is acclaimed as the Davidic messianic king by the crowds who accompany him (21:9). On his arrival the **whole city was shaken**, and to the inquiry of the amazed populace about Jesus' identity the crowds with him reply that he is **the prophet, from Nazareth in Galilee** (21:10, 11).

21:1 Bethphage: a village that can no longer be certainly identified. Mark mentions it before Bethany (Mk 11:1), which suggests that it lay to the east of the latter. **The Mount of Olives:** the hill east of Jerusalem that is spoken of in Zechariah 14:4 as the place where the Lord will come to rescue Jerusalem from the enemy nations.

21:2 An ass tethered, and a colt with her: instead of the one animal of Mark 11:2, Matthew has two, as demanded by his understanding of Zechariah 9:9.

21:4-5 The prophet: this fulfillment citation is actually composed of two distinct Old Testament texts, Isaiah 62:11 (**Say to daughter Zion**) and Zechariah 9:9. The **ass** and the **colt** are the same animal in the prophecy, mentioned twice in different ways, the common Hebrew literary device of poetic parallelism. That Matthew takes them as two is one of the reasons why some scholars think that he was a Gentile rather than a Jewish Christian who would presumably not make that mistake (see Introduction).

21:7 Upon them: upon the two animals; an awkward picture resulting from Matthew's misunderstanding of the prophecy.

21:8 Spread . . . on the road: cf. 2 Kings 9:13. There is a similarity between the cutting and strewing of the **branches** and the festivities of Tabernacles (Lv 23:39-40); see also 2 Maccabees 10:5-8 where the celebration of the rededication of the temple is compared to that of Tabernacles.

At the time of Jesus, Judaism was a religion of **sacrifice**, which was inextricably linked to the temple in Jerusalem. The rituals were prescribed by ancient scriptural directives and controlled by the various categories of priests who worked at the temple. Sacrifices included foods from the harvest for certain feasts or various animals, such as birds, sheep, goats, and cattle, depending on the purpose of the request. Sacrifices helped to make God's presence concrete. They included peace offerings, purification rituals, or rituals for atonement and forgiveness. Later, after the destruction of the temple in A.D. 70, Judaism became a religion of the word with a strong ethical emphasis.

d
Ps 118:25-26

e
Mk 11:15-19;
Lk 19:45-48;
Jn 2:14-22

f
Lv 5:7

g
Is 56:7;
Jer 7:11

while others cut branches from the trees and strewed them on the road. [9][d]The crowds preceding him and those following kept crying out and saying:

> "Hosanna[*] to the Son of David;
> blessed is he who comes in the name of the Lord;
> hosanna in the highest."

[10]And when he entered Jerusalem the whole city was shaken[*] and asked, "Who is this?" [11]And the crowds replied, "This is Jesus the prophet,[*] from Nazareth in Galilee."

The Cleansing of the Temple[*]

[12][e]Jesus entered the temple area and drove out all those engaged in selling and buying there. He overturned the tables of the money changers and the seats of those who were selling doves.[*][f] [13][g]And he said to them, "It is written:

> 'My house shall be a house of
>   prayer,'[*]
> but you are making it a den of
>   thieves."

Model of ancient Jerusalem at the Holy Land Hotel in Jerusalem

---

21:9 Hosanna: the Hebrew means "(O LORD) grant salvation"; see Psalm 118:25, but that invocation had become an acclamation of jubilation and welcome. **Blessed is he . . . in the name of the Lord**: see Psalm 118:26 and the note on John 12:13. **In the highest**: probably only an intensification of the acclamation, although **Hosanna in the highest** could be taken as a prayer, "May God save (him)."

21:10 Was shaken: in the gospels this verb is peculiar to Matthew where it is used also of the earthquake at the time of the crucifixion (27:51) and of the terror of the guards of Jesus' tomb at the appearance of the angel (28:4). For Matthew's use of the cognate noun, see the note on Matthew 8:24.

21:11 The prophet: see Matthew 16:14 ("one of the prophets") and 21:46.

21:12-17 Matthew changes the order of Mark (11:11, 12, 15) and places the cleansing of the temple on the same day as the entry into Jerusalem, immediately after it. The activities going on in **the temple area** were not secular but connected with the temple worship. Thus Jesus' attack on those so engaged and his charge that they were **making** God's **house of prayer a den of thieves** (21:12-13) consti-

tuted a claim to authority over the religious practices of Israel and were a challenge to the priestly authorities. Matthew 21:14-17 are peculiar to Matthew. Jesus' healings and his countenancing the children's cries of praise rouse the indignation of **the chief priests and the scribes** (21:15). These two groups appear in the infancy narrative (2:4) and have been mentioned in the first and third passion predictions (16:21; 20:18). Now, as the passion approaches, they come on the scene again, exhibiting their hostility to Jesus.

21:12 These activities were carried on in the court of the Gentiles, the outermost court of **the temple area**. Animals for sacrifice were sold; the **doves** were for those who could not afford a more expensive offering; see Leviticus 5:7. **Tables of the money changers**: only the coinage of Tyre could be used for the purchases; other money had to be exchanged for that.

21:13 'My house . . . prayer': cf. Isaiah 56:7. Matthew omits the final words of the quotation, "for all peoples" ("all nations"), possibly because for him the worship of the God of Israel by all nations belongs to the time after the resurrection; see Matthew 28:19. **A den of thieves**: the phrase is taken from Jeremiah 7:11.

h
2 Sm 5:8 LXX

i
Ps 8:2 LXX;
Wis 10:21

j
Mk 11:12-14,
20-24

k
Jer 8:13;
Lk 13:6-9

l
17:20; Lk 17:6

m
7:7; 1 Jn 3:22

n
Mk 11:27-33;
Lk 20:1-8

o
Jn 2:18

p
14:5

[14h]The blind and the lame[*] approached him in the temple area, and he cured them. [15]When the chief priests and the scribes saw the wondrous things[*] he was doing, and the children crying out in the temple area, "Hosanna to the Son of David," they were indignant [16*i]and said to him, "Do you hear what they are saying?" Jesus said to them, "Yes; and have you never read the text, 'Out of the mouths of infants and nurslings you have brought forth praise'?" [17]And leaving them, he went out of the city to Bethany, and there he spent the night.

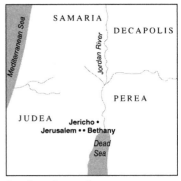

Jerusalem and surrounding towns

The Cursing of the Fig Tree

[18*j]When he was going back to the city in the morning, he was hungry. [19k]Seeing a fig tree by the road, he went over to it, but found nothing on it except leaves. And he said to it, "May no fruit ever come from you again." And immediately the fig tree withered. [20]When the disciples saw this, they were amazed and said, "How was it that the fig tree withered immediately?" [21*l]Jesus said to them in reply, "Amen, I say to you, if you have faith and do not waver, not only will you do what has been done to the fig tree, but even if you say to this mountain, 'Be lifted up and thrown into the sea,' it will be done. [22m]Whatever you ask for in prayer with faith, you will receive."

The Authority of Jesus Questioned

[23*n]When he had come into the temple area, the chief priests and the elders of the people approached him as he was teaching and said, "By what authority are you doing these things?[*] And who gave you this authority?"[o] [24]Jesus said to them in reply, "I shall ask you one question,[*] and if you answer it for me, then I shall tell you by what authority I do these things. [25]Where was John's baptism from? Was it of heavenly or of human origin?" They discussed this among themselves and said, "If we say 'Of heavenly origin,' he will say to us, 'Then why did you not believe him?' [26*p]But if we say, 'Of human origin,' we fear the crowd, for they all regard John as a prophet." [27]So they said to Jesus in reply, "We do not know." He himself said to them, "Neither shall I tell you by what authority I do these things.[*]

21:14 The blind and the lame: according to 2 Samuel 5:8 (LXX) **the blind and the lame** were forbidden to enter "the house of the Lord," the temple. These are the last of Jesus' healings in Matthew.

21:15 The wondrous things: the healings.

21:16 'Out of the mouths . . . praise': cf. Psalm 8:3 (LXX).

21:18-22 In Mark the effect of Jesus' cursing the fig tree is not immediate; see Mark 11:14, 20. By making it so, Matthew has heightened the miracle. Jesus' act seems arbitrary and ill-tempered, but it is a prophetic action similar to those of Old Testament prophets that vividly symbolize some part of their preaching; see, e.g., Ezekiel 12:1-20. It is a sign of the judgment that is to come upon the Israel that with all its apparent piety lacks the fruit of good deeds (3:10) and will soon bear the punishment of its fruitlessness (21:43). Some scholars propose that this story is the development in tradition of a parable of Jesus about the destiny of a fruitless tree, such as Luke 13:6-9. Jesus' answer to the question of the amazed dis-

ciples (21:20) makes the miracle an example of the power of prayer made with unwavering **faith** (21:21-22).

21:21 See Matthew 17:20.

21:23-27 Cf. Mark 11:27-33. This is the first of five controversies between Jesus and the religious authorities of Judaism in Matthew 21:23–22:46, presented in the form of questions and answers.

21:23 These things: probably his entry into the city, his cleansing of the temple, and his healings there.

21:24 To reply by counterquestion was common in rabbinical debate.

21:26 We fear . . . as a prophet: cf. Matthew 14:5.

21:27 Since through embarrassment on the one hand and fear on the other the religious authorities claim ignorance of the origin of John's baptism, they show themselves incapable of speaking with authority; hence Jesus refuses to discuss with them the grounds of his authority.

The Parable of the Two Sons

28*"What is your opinion? A man had two sons. He came to the first and said, 'Son, go out and work in the vineyard today.' 29He said in reply, 'I will not,' but afterwards he changed his mind and went. 30The man came to the other son and gave the same order. He said in reply, 'Yes, sir,' but did not go. 31*Which of the two did his father's will?" They answered, "The first." Jesus said to them, "Amen, I say to you, tax collectors and prostitutes are entering the kingdom of God before you. 32*qWhen John came to you in the way of righteousness, you did not believe him; but tax collectors and prostitutes did. Yet even when you saw that, you did not later change your minds and believe him.

The Parable of the Tenants

33*r"Hear another parable. There was a landowner who planted a vineyard,* put a hedge around it, dug a wine press in it, and built a tower. Then he leased it to tenants and went on a journey.s 34When vintage time drew near, he sent his servants* to the tenants to obtain his produce. 35But the tenants seized the servants and one they beat, another they killed, and a third they stoned. 36Again he sent other servants, more numerous than the first ones, but they

q
Lk 7:29-30

r
Mk 12:1-12;
Lk 20:9-19

s
Is 5:1-2, 7

The **vineyard** was an image from daily life in biblical times that possessed rich symbolic value in the OT as well as the NT. Isaiah uses it as a metaphor for Israel itself (Is 5:1-7). A well-tended and fertilized vineyard will produce plentiful ripe fruit; a poorly tended vineyard will produce nothing of value. Readers are thus urged to take proper care of the vineyard, which is ultimately a gift from God. Matthew's version of Jesus' vineyard story is highly allegorized to show the one-to-one correspondences between Israel and aspects of Jesus' own life and death. In Matthew's view, the failure of the Jewish leaders to care for the "vineyard" (God's kingdom) results in its being given to another people, that is, the Gentiles. See "Getting It Right . . . Anti-Semitism in the Gospels" (at Mt 23).

21:28-32 The series of controversies is interrupted by three parables on the judgment of Israel (21:28–22:14) of which this, peculiar to Matthew, is the first. The second (21:33-46) comes from Mark (12:1-12), and the third (22:1-14) from Q; see Luke 14:15-24. This interruption of the controversies is similar to that in Mark, although Mark has only one parable between the first and second controversy. As regards Matthew's first parable, Matthew 21:28-30 if taken by themselves could point simply to the difference between saying and doing, a theme of much importance in this gospel (cf. 7:21; 12:50); that may have been the parable's original reference. However, it is given a more specific application by the addition of Matthew 21:31-32. The two sons represent, respectively, the religious leaders and the religious outcasts who followed John's call to repentance. By the answer they give to Jesus' question (21:31) the leaders condemn themselves. There is much confusion in the textual tradition of the parable. Of the three different forms of the text given by important textual witnesses, one has the leaders answer that the son who agreed to go but did not was the one who did the father's will. Although some scholars accept that as the original reading, their arguments in favor of it seem unconvincing. The choice probably lies only between a reading that puts the son who agrees and then disobeys before the son who at first refuses and then obeys, and the reading followed in the present translation. The witnesses to the latter reading are slightly better than those that support the other.

21:31 Entering . . . before you: this probably means "they enter; you do not."

21:32 Cf. Luke 7:29-30. Although the thought is similar to that of the Lucan text, the formulation is so different that it is improbable that the saying comes from Q. **Came to you . . . way of righteous-**

ness: several meanings are possible: that John himself was righteous, that he taught righteousness to others, or that he had an important place in God's plan of salvation. For the last, see the note on Matthew 3:14-15.

21:33-46 Cf. Mark 12:1-12. In this parable there is a close correspondence between most of the details of the story and the situation that it illustrates, the dealings of God with his people. Because of that heavy allegorizing, some scholars think that it does not in any way go back to Jesus, but represents the theology of the later church. That judgment applies to the Marcan parallel as well, although the allegorizing has gone farther in Matthew. There are others who believe that while many of the allegorical elements are due to church sources, they have been added to a basic parable spoken by Jesus. This view is now supported by the Gospel of Thomas, #65, where a less allegorized and probably more primitive form of the parable is found.

21:33 Planted a vineyard . . . a tower: cf. Isaiah 5:1-2. The **vineyard** is defined in Isaiah 5:7 as "the house of Israel."

21:34-35 His servants: Matthew has two sendings of **servants** as against Mark's three sendings of a single servant (Mk 11:2-5a) followed by a statement about the sending of "many others" (Mk 11:2, 5b). That these servants stand for the prophets sent by God to Israel is clearly implied but not made explicit here, but see Matthew 23:37. **His produce**: cf. Mark 12:2 "some of the produce." The **produce** is the good works demanded by God, and his claim to them is total.

t
Heb 13:12

u
Ps 118:22-23;
Is 28:16;
Acts 4:11;
1 Pt 2:7

a
Lk 14:15-24

b
21:35

treated them in the same way. ³⁷Finally, he sent his son to them, thinking, 'They will respect my son.' ³⁸*But when the tenants saw the son, they said to one another, 'This is the heir. Come, let us kill him and acquire his inheritance.' ³⁹*ᵗThey seized him, threw him out of the vineyard, and killed him. ⁴⁰What will the owner of the vineyard do to those tenants when he comes?" ⁴¹They answered* him, "He will put those wretched men to a wretched death and lease his vineyard to other tenants who will give him the produce at the proper times." ⁴²*ᵘJesus said to them, "Did you never read in the scriptures:

'The stone that the builders rejected
    has become the cornerstone;
by the Lord has this been done,
    and it is wonderful in our eyes'?

⁴³*Therefore, I say to you, the kingdom of God will be taken away from you and given to a people that will produce its fruit. ⁴⁴[*The one who falls on this stone will be dashed to pieces; and it will crush anyone on whom it falls.]" ⁴⁵When the chief priests and the Pharisees* heard his parables, they knew that he was speaking about them. ⁴⁶And although they were attempting to arrest him, they feared the crowds, for they regarded him as a prophet.

The Parable of the Wedding Feast

22 ¹*ᵃJesus again in reply spoke to them in parables, saying, ²"The kingdom of heaven may be likened to a king who gave a wedding feast* for his son. ³*He dispatched his servants to summon the invited guests to the feast, but they refused to come. ⁴A second time he sent other servants, saying, 'Tell those invited: "Behold, I have prepared my banquet, my calves and fattened cattle are killed, and everything is ready; come to the feast."' ⁵Some ignored the invitation and went away, one to his farm, another to his business. ⁶ᵇThe rest laid hold of his servants, mistreated them, and killed

---

21:38 Acquire his inheritance: if a Jewish proselyte died without heir, the tenants of his land would have final claim on it.

21:39 Threw him out . . . and killed him: the change in the Marcan order where the son is killed and his corpse then thrown out (12:8) was probably made because of the tradition that Jesus died outside the city of Jerusalem; see John 19:17; Hebrews 13:12.

21:41 They answered: in Mark 12:9 the question is answered by Jesus himself; here the leaders answer and so condemn themselves; cf. Matthew 21:31. Matthew adds that the new **tenants** to whom the vineyard will be transferred **will give** the owner **the produce at the proper times.**

21:42 Cf. Psalm 118:22-23. The psalm was used in the early church as a prophecy of Jesus' resurrection; see Acts 4:11; 1 Peter 2:7. If, as some think, the original parable ended at Matthew 21:39 it was thought necessary to complete it by a reference to Jesus' vindication by God.

21:43 Peculiar to Matthew. **Kingdom of God**: see the note on Matthew 19:23-24. Its presence here instead of Matthew's usual "kingdom of heaven" may indicate that the saying came from Matthew's own traditional material. **A people that will produce its fruit**: believing Israelites and Gentiles, the church of Jesus.

21:44 The majority of textual witnesses omit this verse. It is probably an early addition to Matthew from Luke 20:18 with which it is practically identical.

21:45 The Pharisees: Matthew inserts into the group of Jewish leaders (21:23) those who represented the Judaism of his own time.

22:1-14 This parable is from Q; see Luke 14:15-24. It has been given many allegorical traits by Matthew, e.g., the burning of the **city** of the guests who refused the invitation (22:7), which corresponds to the destruction of Jerusalem by the Romans in A.D. 70. It has similarities with the preceding parable of the tenants: the sending of two groups of **servants** (22:3, 4), the murder of the **servants** (22:6) the punishment of the **murderers** (22:7), and the entrance of a new group into a privileged situation of which the others had proved themselves unworthy (22:8-10). The parable ends with a section that is peculiar to Matthew (22:11-14), which some take as a distinct parable. Matthew presents the **kingdom** in its double aspect, already present and something that can be entered here and now (22:1-10), and something that will be possessed only by those present members who can stand the scrutiny of the final judgment (22:11-14). The parable is not only a statement of God's judgment on Israel but a warning to Matthew's church.

22:2 Wedding feast: the Old Testament's portrayal of final salvation under the image of a banquet (Is 25:6) is taken up also in Matthew 8:11; cf. Luke 13:15.

22:3-4 Servants . . . other servants: probably Christian missionaries in both instances; cf. Matthew 23:34.

them. [7*]The king was enraged and sent his troops, destroyed those murderers, and burned their city. [8]Then he said to his servants, 'The feast is ready, but those who were invited were not worthy to come. [9]Go out, therefore, into the main roads and invite to the feast whomever you find.' [10]The servants went out into the streets and gathered all they found, bad and good alike,[*] and the hall was filled with guests. [11*]But when the king came in to meet the guests he saw a man there not dressed in a wedding garment. [12]He said to him, 'My friend, how is it that you came in here without a wedding garment?' But he was reduced to silence. [13*c]Then the king said to his attendants, 'Bind his hands and feet, and cast him into the darkness outside, where there will be wailing and grinding of teeth.' [14]Many are invited, but few are chosen."

Paying Taxes to the Emperor

[15*d]Then the Pharisees[*] went off and plotted how they might entrap him in speech. [16]They sent their disciples to him, with the Herodians,[*] saying, "Teacher, we know that you are a truthful man and that you teach the way of God in accordance with the truth. And you are not concerned with anyone's opinion, for you do not regard a person's status. [17*]Tell us, then, what is your opinion: Is it lawful to pay the census tax to Caesar or not?" [18]Knowing their malice, Jesus said, "Why are you testing me, you hypocrites? [19*]Show me the coin that pays the census tax." Then they handed him the Roman coin.

c
8:12; 25:30
d
Mk 12:13-17;
Lk 20:20-26

Coinage in New Testament Times

Matthew's gospel uses the most diverse terminology for money. The first-century monetary system had numerous denomina-tions of coins that appear in the gospels, beyond the mention of silver, gold, and copper. The most common are listed below.

Coin	Description	References
lepton	Very small copper coin worth ca. 1/8 cent, identified as "the widow's mite"	Mk 12:42
quadrans	Small Roman copper coin worth ca. 1/4 cent	Mt 5:26; Mk 12:42
assarion	Roman copper coin worth ca. 1 cent	Mt 10:29; Lk 12:6
denarius	Large Roman silver coin almost equivalent to the Greek drachma, worth ca. 18 cents; a typical day's wage for laborers	Mt 18:28; 20:2; Mk 6:37; 12:15; 14:5; Lk 7:41; Jn 12:5
didrachmon	Greek coin worth ca. 36 cents; also used for the annual temple tax	Mt 17:24 required of each Jew
stater	Greek silver coin worth ca. 80 cents	Mt 17:27
talent	Large Greek-Roman sum worth ca. 1,080 dollars	Mt 18:24; 25:14-30

22:7 See the note on Matthew 22:1-14.

22:10 Bad and good alike: cf. Matthew 13:47.

22:11 A wedding garment: the repentance, change of heart and mind, that is the condition for entrance into the kingdom (3:2; 4:17) must be continued in a life of good deeds (7:21-23).

22:13 Wailing and grinding of teeth: the Christian who lacks the wedding garment of good deeds will suffer the same fate as those Jews who have rejected Jesus; see the note on Matthew 8:11-12.

22:15-22 The series of controversies between Jesus and the representatives of Judaism (see the note on 21:23-27) is resumed. As in the first (21:23-27), here and in the following disputes Matthew follows his Marcan source with few modifications.

22:15 The Pharisees: while Matthew retains the Marcan union of Pharisees and Herodians in this account, he clearly emphasizes the Pharisees' part. They alone are mentioned here, and the Herodi-ans are joined with them only in a prepositional phrase of Matthew 22:16. **Entrap him in speech**: the question that they will pose is intended to force Jesus to take either a position contrary to that held by the majority of the people or one that will bring him into conflict with the Roman authorities.

22:16 Herodians: see the note on Mark 3:6. They would favor payment of the tax; the Pharisees did not.

22:17 Is it lawful: the law to which they refer is the law of God.

22:19 They handed him the Roman coin: their readiness in producing the money implies their use of it and their acceptance of the financial advantages of the Roman administration in Palestine.

e
Rom 13:7

f
Mk 12:18-27;
Lk 20:27-40

g
Gn 38:8;
Dt 25:5-6

h
Ex 3:6

i
Mk 12:28-34;
Lk 10:25-28

²⁰He said to them, "Whose image is this and whose inscription?" ²¹ᵉThey replied, "Caesar's."* At that he said to them, "Then repay to Caesar what belongs to Caesar and to God what belongs to God." ²²When they heard this they were amazed, and leaving him they went away.

The Question about the Resurrection

²³*ᶠOn that day Sadducees approached him, saying that there is no resurrection.* They put this question to him, ²⁴ᵍsaying, "Teacher, Moses said, 'If a man dies* without children, his brother shall marry his wife and raise up descendants for his brother.' ²⁵Now there were seven brothers among us. The first married and died and, having no descendants, left his wife to his brother. ²⁶The same happened with the second and the third, through all seven. ²⁷Finally the woman died. ²⁸Now at the resurrection, of the seven, whose wife will she be? For they all had been married to her." ²⁹*Jesus said to them in reply, "You are misled because you do not know the scriptures or the power of God. ³⁰At the resurrection they neither marry nor are given in marriage but are like the angels in heaven. ³¹And concerning the resurrection of the dead, have you not read what was said to you* by God, ³²ʰ'I am the God of Abraham, the God of Isaac, and the God of Jacob'? He is not the God of the dead but of the living." ³³When the crowds heard this, they were astonished at his teaching.

The Greatest Commandment

³⁴*ⁱWhen the Pharisees heard that he had silenced the Sadducees, they gathered together, ³⁵and one of them [a scholar of the law]* tested him by asking, ³⁶"Teacher,*

22:21 Caesar's: the emperor Tiberius (A.D. 14–37). **Repay to Caesar what belongs to Caesar**: those who willingly use the coin that is Caesar's should **repay** him in kind. The answer avoids taking sides in the question of the lawfulness of the tax. **To God what belongs to God**: Jesus raises the debate to a new level. Those who have hypocritically asked about tax in respect to its relation to the law of **God** should be concerned rather with repaying God with the good deeds that are his due; cf. Matthew 21:41, 43.

22:23-33 Here Jesus' opponents are the **Sadducees**, members of the powerful priestly party of his time; see the note on Matthew 3:7. Denying the resurrection of the dead, a teaching of relatively late origin in Judaism (cf. Dn 12:2), they appeal to a law of the Pentateuch (Dt 25:5-10) and present a case based on it that would make resurrection from the dead ridiculous (22:24-28). Jesus chides them for knowing neither **the scriptures** nor **the power of God** (22:29). His argument in respect to God's power contradicts the notion, held even by many proponents as well as by opponents of the teaching, that the life of those raised from the dead would be essentially a continuation of the type of life they had had before death (22:30). His argument based on the scriptures (22:31-32) is of a sort that was accepted as valid among Jews of the time.

22:23 Saying that there is no resurrection: in the Marcan parallel (12, 18) the Sadducees are correctly defined as those "who say there is no resurrection"; see also Luke 20:27. Matthew's rewording of Mark can mean that these particular Sadducees deny the resurrection, which would imply that he was not aware that the denial was characteristic of the party. For some scholars this is an indication of his being a Gentile Christian; see the note on Matthew 21:4-5.

22:24 "If a man dies . . . his brother': this is known as the "law of the levirate," from the Latin *levir*, "brother-in-law." Its purpose was to continue the family line of the deceased brother (Dt 25:6).

22:29 The sexual relationships of this world will be transcended; the risen body will be the work of the creative **power of God**.

22:31-32 Cf. Exodus 3:6. In the Pentateuch, which the Sadducees accepted as normative for Jewish belief and practice, God speaks even now (**to you**) of himself as the God of the patriarchs who died centuries ago. He identifies himself in relation to them, and because of their relation to him, the living God, they too are alive. This might appear no argument for the resurrection, but simply for life after death as conceived in Wisdom 3:1-3. But the general thought of early first-century Judaism was not influenced by that conception; for it human immortality was connected with the existence of the body.

22:34-40 The Marcan parallel (Mk 12:28-34) is an exchange between Jesus and a scribe who is impressed by the way in which Jesus has conducted himself in the previous controversy (Mk 12:28), who compliments him for the answer he gives him (Mk 12:32), and who is said by Jesus to be "not far from the kingdom of God" (Mk 12:34). Matthew has sharpened that scene. The questioner, as the representative of other Pharisees, tests Jesus by his question (22:34-35), and both his reaction to Jesus' reply and Jesus' commendation of him are lacking.

22:35 [A scholar of the law]: meaning "scribe." Although this reading is supported by the vast majority of textual witnesses, it is the only time that the Greek word so translated occurs in Matthew. It is relatively frequent in Luke, and there is reason to think that it may have been added here by a copyist since it occurs in the Lucan parallel (Lk 10:25-28). **Tested**: see the note on Matthew 19:3.

22:36 For the devout Jew all the commandments were to be kept with equal care, but there is evidence of preoccupation in Jewish sources with the question put to Jesus.

which commandment in the law is the greatest?" [37j]He said to him,[*] "You shall love the Lord, your God, with all your heart, with all your soul, and with all your mind. [38]This is the greatest and the first commandment. [39k]The second is like it:[*] You shall love your neighbor as yourself. [40*l]The whole law and the prophets depend on these two commandments."

The Question about David's Son[*]

[41m]While the Pharisees were gathered together, Jesus questioned them,[*] [42*]saying, "What is your opinion about the Messiah? Whose son is he?" They replied, "David's." [43]He said to them, "How, then, does David, inspired by the Spirit, call him 'lord,' saying:

[44n]'The Lord said to my lord,
"Sit at my right hand
until I place your enemies under your feet"'?

[45*]If David calls him 'lord,' how can he be his son?" [46o]No one was able to answer him a word, nor from that day on did anyone dare to ask him any more questions.

Denunciation of the Scribes and Pharisees

23 [1*a]Then Jesus spoke to the crowds and to his disciples, [2*]saying, "The scribes and the Pharisees have taken their seat on the chair of Moses. [3]Therefore, do

j
Dt 6:5

k
Lv 19:18;
Jas 2:8

l
Rom 13:8-10;
Gal 5:14

m
Mk 12:35-37;
Lk 20:41-44

n
Ps 110:1;
Acts 2:35;
Heb 1:13

o
Lk 20:40

a
Mk 12:38-39;
Lk 11:37-52;
13:34-35

22:37-38 Cf. Deuteronomy 6:5. Matthew omits the first part of Mark's fuller quotation (Mk 12:29; Dt 6:4-5), probably because he considered its monotheistic emphasis needless for his church. The love of God must engage the total person (**heart, soul, mind**).

22:39 Jesus goes beyond the extent of the question put to him and joins to **the greatest and the first commandment** a **second**, that of **love** of **neighbor**, Leviticus 19:18; see the note on Matthew 19:18-19. This combination of the two commandments may already have been made in Judaism.

22:40 The double commandment is the source from which **the whole law and the prophets** are derived.

22:41-46 Having answered the questions of his opponents in the preceding three controversies, Jesus now puts a question to them about the sonship of the Messiah. Their easy response (22:43a) is countered by his quoting a verse of Psalm 110 that raises a problem for their response (43b-45). They are unable to solve it and **from that day on** their questioning of him is ended.

22:41 The Pharisees . . . questioned them: Mark is not specific about who are questioned (Mk 12:35).

22:42-44 David's: this view of the Pharisees was based on such Old Testament texts as Isaiah 11:1-9; Jeremiah 23:5; and Ezekiel 34:23; see also the extrabiblical Psalms of Solomon 17:21. **How, then . . . saying**: Jesus cites Psalm 110:1 accepting the Davidic authorship of the psalm, a common view of his time. The psalm was probably composed for the enthronement of a Davidic king of Judah. Matthew assumes that the Pharisees interpret it as referring to the Messiah, although there is no clear evidence that it was so interpreted in the Judaism of Jesus' time. It was widely used in the early church as referring to the exaltation of the risen Jesus. **My lord**: understood as the Messiah.

22:45 Since Matthew presents Jesus both as Messiah (16:16) and as Son of David (1:1; see also the note on 9:27), the question is not meant to imply Jesus' denial of Davidic sonship. It probably means that although he is the Son of David, he is someone greater,

Son of Man and Son of God, and recognized as greater by David who calls him my **'lord.'**

23:1-39 The final section of the narrative part of the fifth book of the gospel is a denunciation by Jesus of the scribes and the Pharisees (see the note on 3:7). It depends in part on Mark and Q (cf. Mk 12:38-39; Lk 11:37-52; 13:34-35), but in the main it is peculiar to Matthew. (For the reasons against considering this extensive body of sayings-material either as one of the structural discourses of this gospel or as part of the one that follows in Matthew 24–25, see the note on 19:1–23:39.) While the tradition of a deep opposition between Jesus and the Pharisees is well founded, this speech reflects an opposition that goes beyond that of Jesus' ministry and must be seen as expressing the bitter conflict between Pharisaic Judaism and the church of Matthew at the time when the gospel was composed. The complaint often made that the speech ignores the positive qualities of Pharisaism and of its better representatives is true, but the complaint overlooks the circumstances that gave rise to the invective. Nor is the speech purely anti-Pharisaic. The evangelist discerns in his church many of the same faults that he finds in its opponents and warns his fellow Christians to look to their own conduct and attitudes.

23:2-3 Have taken their seat . . . Moses: it is uncertain whether this is simply a metaphor for Mosaic teaching authority or refers to an actual **chair** on which the teacher sat. It has been proved that there was a seat so designated in synagogues of a later period than that of this gospel. **Do and observe . . . they tell you**: since the Matthean Jesus abrogates Mosaic law (5:31-42), warns his disciples against the teaching of the Pharisees (14:1-12), and, in this speech, denounces the Pharisees as blind guides in respect to their teaching on oaths (16–22), this commandment **to observe all things whatsoever they** (the scribes and Pharisees) **tell you** cannot be taken as the evangelist's understanding of the proper standard of conduct for his church. The saying may reflect a period when the Matthean

b
Lk 11:46

c
6:1-6;
Ex 13:9, 16;
Nm 15:38-39;
Dt 6:8; 11:18

d
Mk 12:38-39;
Lk 11:43;
20:46

e
20:26

f
Lk 14:11; 18:14

g
Lk 11:52

and observe all things whatsoever they tell you, but do not follow their example. For they preach but they do not practice. [4b]They tie up heavy burdens* [hard to carry] and lay them on people's shoulders, but they will not lift a finger to move them. [5*c]All their works are performed to be seen. They widen their phylacteries and lengthen their tassels. [6*d]They love places of honor at banquets, seats of honor in synagogues, [7]greetings in marketplaces, and the salutation 'Rabbi.' [8*]As for you, do not be called 'Rabbi.' You have but one teacher, and you are all brothers. [9]Call no one on earth your father; you have but one Father in heaven. [10]Do not be called 'Master'; you have but one master, the Messiah. [11e]The greatest among you must be your servant. [12f]Whoever exalts himself will be humbled; but whoever humbles himself will be exalted.

[13*g]"Woe to you, scribes and Pharisees, you hypocrites. You lock the kingdom of heaven* before human beings. You do not enter yourselves, nor do you allow entrance to those trying to enter. [[14]]*

Getting It Right . . .
Anti-Semitism in the Gospels

Matthew 23 is the most virulent section of the NT with regard to its attitude toward the Jewish leaders in the first century. An unfortunate byproduct of Christian history is that such passages have wrongly been used to promote anti-Semitic actions that contradict the Gospel of Jesus Christ. Such passages do not provide a perspective on Jews as a people or on Jewish people in modern times. Rather, they reflect a period of NT history when those Jews who believed in Jesus as the Messiah were caught up in internal Jewish disputes with those who did not accept him. Matthew's gospel in particular reflects this situation. It is not anti-Semitic in perspective, since the evangelist and many in his community were most likely Jews themselves. It does reflect a time of turmoil, which eventually led to an exit from the synagogue and the gradual formation of a new religion, namely, Christianity. Modern readers of the NT must take care not to misinterpret these passages or use them to promote anti-Semitic words or actions.

community was largely Jewish Christian and was still seeking to avoid a complete break with the synagogue. Matthew has incorporated this traditional material into the speech in accordance with his view of the course of salvation history, in which he portrays the time of Jesus' ministry as marked by the fidelity to the law, although with significant pointers to the new situation that would exist after his death and resurrection (see the note on 5:17-20). The crowds and the disciples (23:1) are exhorted not to **follow** the **example** of the Jewish leaders, whose deeds do not conform to their teaching (23:3).

23:4 Tie up heavy burdens: see the note on Matthew 11:28.

23:5 To the charge of preaching but not practicing (23:3), Jesus adds that of acting in order to earn praise. The disciples have already been warned against this same fault (see the note on 6:1-18). **Phylacteries**: the Mosaic law required that during prayer small boxes containing parchments on which verses of scripture were written be worn on the left forearm and the forehead (see Ex 13:9, 16; Dt 6:8; 11:18). **Tassels**: see the note on Matthew 9:20. The widening of **phylacteries** and the lengthening of **tassels** were for the purpose of making these evidences of piety more noticeable.

23:6 Cf. Mark 12:38-39. '**Rabbi**': literally, "my great one," a title of respect for teachers and leaders.

23:8-12 These verses, warning against the use of various titles, are addressed to the disciples alone. While only the title '**Rabbi**' has been said to be used in addressing the scribes and Pharisees (23:7), the implication is that **Father** and '**Master**' also were. The prohibition of these titles to the disciples suggests that their use was present in Matthew's church. The Matthean Jesus forbids not only the titles but the spirit of superiority and pride that is shown by their acceptance. **Whoever exalts . . . will be exalted**: cf. Luke 14:11.

23:13-36 This series of seven "woes," directed against the **scribes and Pharisees** and addressed to them, is the heart of the speech. The phrase **woe to** occurs often in the prophetic and apocalyptic literature, expressing horror of a sin and punishment for those who commit it. **Hypocrites**: see the note on Matthew 6:2. The hypocrisy of the **scribes and Pharisees** consists in the difference between their speech and action (23:3) and in demonstrations of piety that have no other purpose than to enhance their reputation as religious persons (23:5).

23:13 You lock the kingdom of heaven: cf. Matthew 16:19 where Jesus tells Peter that he will give him the keys to **the kingdom of heaven**. The purpose of the authority expressed by that metaphor is to give entrance into the kingdom (the kingdom is closed only to those who reject the authority); here the charge is made that the authority of the **scribes and Pharisees** is exercised in such a way as to be an obstacle to entrance. Cf. Luke 11:52 where the accusation against the "scholars of the law" (Matthew's **scribes**) is that they "have taken away the key of knowledge."

23:14 Some manuscripts add a verse here or after Matthew 23:12 "Woe to you, scribes and Pharisees, you hypocrites. You devour the houses of widows and, as a pretext, recite lengthy prayers. Because of this, you will receive a very severe condemnation." Cf. Mark 12:40; Luke 20:47. This "woe" is almost identical with Mark 12:40 and seems to be an interpolation derived from that text.

The designation **"hypocrite"** stems from ancient Greek theater in which players wore masks that portrayed an emotion or attitude illustrative of characters in the play. The root notion, then, is to mask something that covers the true reality. Matthew uses this term frequently with regard to the enemies of Jesus, emphasizing their falsehood (cf. 6:2; 23:15, 23, 25, 27, 29).

¹⁵*"Woe to you, scribes and Pharisees, you hypocrites. You traverse sea and land to make one convert, and when that happens you make him a child of Gehenna twice as much as yourselves.

¹⁶*ʰ"Woe to you, blind guides, who say, 'If one swears by the temple, it means nothing, but if one swears by the gold of the temple, one is obligated.' ¹⁷Blind fools, which is greater, the gold, or the temple that made the gold sacred? ¹⁸And you say, 'If one swears by the altar, it means nothing, but if one swears by the gift on the altar, one is obligated.' ¹⁹You blind ones, which is greater, the gift, or the altar that makes the gift sacred? ²⁰ⁱOne who swears by the altar swears by it and all that is upon it; ²¹one who swears by the temple swears by it and by him who dwells in it; ²²one who swears by heaven swears by the throne of God and by him who is seated on it.

²³ʲ"Woe to you, scribes and Pharisees, you hypocrites. You pay tithes* of mint and dill and cummin, and have neglected the weightier things of the law: judgment and mercy and fidelity. [But] these you should have done, without neglecting the others. ²⁴*ᵏBlind guides, who strain out the gnat and swallow the camel!

²⁵*ˡ"Woe to you, scribes and Pharisees, you hypocrites. You cleanse the outside of cup and dish, but inside they are full of plunder and self-indulgence. ²⁶Blind Pharisee, cleanse first the inside of the cup, so that the outside also may be clean.

²⁷*"Woe to you, scribes and Pharisees, you hypocrites. You are like whitewashed tombs, which appear beautiful on the outside, but inside are full of dead men's bones and every kind of filth. ²⁸ᵐEven so, on the outside you appear righteous, but inside you are filled with hypocrisy and evildoing.

h
15:14

i
5:34-35

j
Lv 27:30;
Dt 14:22;
Lk 11:42

k
Lv 11:41-45

l
Mk 7:4;
Lk 11:39

m
Lk 16:15; 18:9

23:15 In the first century A.D. until the First Jewish Revolt against Rome (A.D. 66–70), many Pharisees conducted a vigorous missionary campaign among Gentiles. **Convert:** literally, "proselyte," a Gentile who accepted Judaism fully by submitting to circumcision and all other requirements of Mosaic law. **Child of Gehenna:** worthy of everlasting punishment; for **Gehenna**, see the note on Matthew 5:22. **Twice as much as yourselves:** possibly this refers simply to the zeal of the **convert**, surpassing that of the one who converted him.

23:16–22 An attack on the casuistry that declared some oaths binding (**one is obligated**) and others not (**it means nothing**) and held the binding oath to be the one made by something of lesser value (**the gold; the gift on the altar**). Such teaching, which inverts the order of values, reveals the teachers to be **blind guides**; cf. Matthew 15:14. Since the Matthean Jesus forbids all oaths to his disciples (5:33-37), this **woe** does not set up a standard for Christian moral conduct, but ridicules the Pharisees on their own terms.

23:23 The Mosaic law ordered tithing of the produce of the land (Lv 27:30; Dt 14:22-23), and the scribal tradition is said here to have extended this law to even the smallest herbs. The practice is criticized not in itself but because it shows the Pharisees' preoccupation with matters of less importance while they neglect **the weightier things of the law**.

23:24 Cf. Leviticus 11:41-45 that forbids the eating of any "swarming creature." The Pharisees' scrupulosity about minor matters and neglect of greater ones (23:23) is further brought out by this contrast between straining liquids that might contain a tiny "swarming creature" and yet swallowing **the camel**. The latter was one of the unclean animals forbidden by the law (Lv 11:4), but it is hardly possible that the scribes and Pharisees are being denounced as guilty of so gross a violation of the food laws. To **swallow the camel** is only a hyperbolic way of speaking of their neglect of what is important.

23:25–26 The ritual washing of utensils for dining (cf. Mk 7:4) is turned into a metaphor illustrating a concern for appearances while inner purity is ignored. The **scribes and Pharisees** are compared to cups carefully washed on the outside but filthy within. **Self-indulgence:** the Greek word here translated means lack of self-control, whether in drinking or in sexual conduct.

23:27–28 The sixth **woe**, like the preceding one, deals with concern for externals and neglect of what is **inside**. Since contact with dead bodies, even when one was unaware of it, caused ritual impurity (Nm 19:11-22), tombs were whitewashed so that no one would contract such impurity inadvertently.

n
Lk 11:47

o
Acts 7:52

p
3:7; 12:34

q
5:12; Gn 4:8;
2 Chr 24:20-22;
Zec 1:1;
Lk 11:49-51;
Rev 18:24

r
Lk 13:34-35;
19:41-44

s
21:35

t
Jer 12:7

u
Ps 118:26

a
Mk 13:1-37;
Lk 21:5-36

[29]*"Woe to you, scribes and Pharisees,* you hypocrites. You build the tombs of the prophets and adorn the memorials of the righteous, [30]*n*and you say, 'If we had lived in the days of our ancestors, we would not have joined them in shedding the prophets' blood.' [31]*o*Thus you bear witness against yourselves that you are the children of those who murdered the prophets; [32]now fill up what your ancestors measured out! [33]*p*You serpents, you brood of vipers, how can you flee from the judgment of Gehenna? [34]*q*Therefore, behold, I send to you prophets and wise men and scribes; some of them you will kill and crucify, some of them you will scourge in your synagogues and pursue from town to town, [35]so that there may come upon you all the righteous blood shed upon earth, from the righteous blood of Abel to the blood of Zechariah, the son of Barachiah, whom you murdered between the sanctuary and the altar. [36]Amen, I say to you, all these things will come upon this generation.

The Lament over Jerusalem

[37]*r*"Jerusalem, Jerusalem, you who kill the prophets and stone those sent to you, how many times I yearned to gather your children together, as a hen gathers her young under her wings, but you were unwilling! [38]*t*Behold, your house will be abandoned, desolate. [39]*u*I tell you, you will not see me again until you say, 'Blessed is he who comes in the name of the Lord.'"

The Destruction of the Temple Foretold

24 [1]*a*Jesus left the temple area and was going away, when his disciples ap-

Model of Herod the Great's reconstructed temple

23:29-36 The final **woe** is the most serious indictment of all. It portrays the **scribes and Pharisees** as standing in the same line as their **ancestors** who murdered **the prophets** and **the righteous**.

23:29-32 In spite of honoring the slain dead by building their **tombs** and adorning their **memorials**, and claiming that they would not have joined in their ancestors' crimes if they **had lived in** their **days**, the **scribes and Pharisees** are true children of their ancestors and are defiantly ordered by Jesus to **fill up** what those **ancestors measured out**. This order reflects the Jewish notion that there was an allotted measure of suffering that had to be completed before God's final judgment would take place.

23:34-36 There are important differences between the Matthean and the Lucan form of this Q material; cf. Luke 11:49-51. In Luke the one who sends the emissaries is the "wisdom of God." If, as many scholars think, that is the original wording of Q, Matthew, by making Jesus the sender, has presented him as the personified divine wisdom. In Luke, wisdom's emissaries are the Old Testament "prophets" and the Christian "apostles." Matthew's **prophets and wise men and scribes** are probably Christian disciples alone; cf. Matthew 10:41 and see the note on Matthew 13:52. **You will kill**: see Matthew 24:9. **Scourge in your synagogues . . . town to town**: see Matthew 10:17, 23 and the note on Matthew 10:17. **All the righteous blood shed upon the earth**: the slaying of the disciples is in continuity with all the shedding of **righteous blood** beginning with that of Abel. The persecution of Jesus' disciples by **this generation**

involves the persecutors in the guilt of their murderous ancestors. **The blood of Zechariah**: see the note on Luke 11:51. By identifying him as **the son of Barachiah** Matthew understands him to be Zechariah the Old Testament minor prophet; see Zechariah 1:1.

23:37-39 Cf. Luke 13:34-35. The denunciation of Pharisaic Judaism ends with this lament over **Jerusalem**, which has repeatedly rejected and murdered those whom God has **sent** to her. **How many times**: this may refer to various visits of Jesus to the city, an aspect of his ministry found in John but otherwise not in the synoptics. **As a hen . . . under her wings**: for imagery similar to this, see Psalm 17:8; 91:4. **Your house . . . desolate**: probably an allusion to the destruction of the temple in A.D. 70. **You will not see me . . . in the name of the Lord**: Israel will not see Jesus again until he comes in glory for the final judgment. The acclamation has been interpreted in contrasting ways, as an indication that Israel will at last accept Jesus at that time, and as its troubled recognition of him as its dreaded judge who will pronounce its condemnation; in support of the latter view see Matthew 24:30.

24:1–25:46 The discourse of the fifth book, the last of the five around which the gospel is structured. It is called the "eschatological" discourse since it deals with the coming of the new age (the *eschaton*) in its fullness, with events that will precede it, and with how the disciples are to conduct themselves while awaiting an event that is as certain as its exact time is unknown to all but the Father (24:36). The discourse may be divided into two parts, Matthew 24:1-44 and Matthew 24:45–25:46. In the first, Matthew follows

proached him to point out the temple buildings. [2*]He said to them in reply, "You see all these things, do you not? Amen, I say to you, there will not be left here a stone upon another stone that will not be thrown down."

The Beginning of Calamities

[3]As he was sitting on the Mount of Olives,[*] the disciples approached him privately and said, "Tell us, when will this happen, and what sign will there be of your coming, and of the end of the age?" [4*]Jesus said to them in reply, "See that no one deceives you. [5]For many will come in my name, saying, 'I am the Messiah,' and they will deceive many. [6b]You will hear of wars[*] and reports of wars; see that you are not alarmed, for these things must happen, but it will not yet be the end. [7c]Nation will rise against nation, and kingdom against kingdom; there will be famines and earthquakes from place to place. [8*]All these are the beginning of the labor pains. [9*d]Then they will hand you over to persecution, and they will kill you. You will be hated by all nations because of my name. [10]And then many will be led into sin; they will betray and hate one another. [11]Many false prophets will arise and deceive many; [12]and because of the increase of evildoing, the love of many will grow cold. [13e]But the one who perseveres to the end will be saved. [14f]And this gospel of the kingdom will be preached throughout the world as a witness to all nations,[*] and then the end will come.

b
Dn 2:28 LXX

c
Is 19:2

d
10:17

e
10:22

f
28:19;
Rom 10:18

---

his Marcan source (Mk 13:1-37) closely. The second is drawn from Q and from the evangelist's own traditional material. Both parts show Matthew's editing of his sources by deletions, additions, and modifications. The vigilant waiting that is emphasized in the second part does not mean a cessation of ordinary activity and concentration only on what is to come, but a faithful accomplishment of duties at hand, with awareness that the end, for which the disciples must always be ready, will entail the great judgment by which the everlasting destiny of all will be determined.

24:2 As in Mark, Jesus predicts the destruction of the temple. By omitting the Marcan story of the widow's contribution (Mk 12:41-44) that immediately precedes the prediction in that gospel, Matthew has established a close connection between it and Matthew 23:38, ". . . your house will be abandoned desolate."

24:3 The Mount of Olives: see the note on Matthew 21:1. The disciples: cf. Mark 13:3-4 where only Peter, James, John, and Andrew put the question that is answered by the discourse. In both gospels, however, the question is put privately: the ensuing discourse is only for those who are disciples of Jesus. When will this happen . . . end of the age?: Matthew distinguishes carefully between the destruction of the temple (this) and the coming of Jesus that will bring the end of the age. In Mark the two events are more closely connected, a fact that may be explained by Mark's believing that the one would immediately succeed the other. Coming: this translates the Greek word parousia, which is used in the gospels only here and in Matthew 24:27, 37, 39. It designated the official visit of a ruler to a city or the manifestation of a saving deity, and it was used by Christians to refer to the final coming of Jesus in glory, a term first found in the New Testament with that meaning in 1 Thessalonians 2:19. The end of the age: see the note on Matthew 13:39.

24:4-14 This section of the discourse deals with calamities in the world (24:6-7) and in the church (24:9-12). The former must happen before the end comes (24:6), but they are only the beginning of the labor pains (24:8). (It may be noted that the Greek word translated the end in Matthew 24:6 and in Matthew 24:13-14 is not the same as the phrase "the end of the age" in Matthew 24:3 although the meaning is the same.) The latter are sufferings of the church, both from within and without, that will last until the gospel is preached . . . to all nations. Then the end will come and those who have endured the sufferings with fidelity will be saved (24:13-14).

24:6-7 The disturbances mentioned here are a commonplace of apocalyptic language, as is the assurance that they must happen (see Dn 2:28 LXX), for that is the plan of God. Kingdom against kingdom: see Isaiah 19:2.

24:8 The labor pains: the tribulations leading up to the end of the age are compared to the pains of a woman about to give birth. There is much attestation for rabbinic use of the phrase "the woes (or birth pains) of the Messiah" after the New Testament period, but in at least one instance it is attributed to a rabbi who lived in the late first century A.D. In this Jewish usage it meant the distress of the time preceding the coming of the Messiah; here, the labor pains precede the coming of the Son of Man in glory.

24:9-12 Matthew has used Mark 13:9-12 in his missionary discourse (10:17-21) and omits it here. Besides the sufferings, including death, and the hatred of all nations that the disciples will have to endure, there will be worse affliction within the church itself. This is described in Matthew 24:10-12, which are peculiar to Matthew. Will be led into sin: literally, "will be scandalized," probably meaning that they will become apostates; see Matthew 13:21 where "fall away" translates the same Greek word as here. Betray: in the Greek this is the same word as the hand over of Matthew 24:9. The handing over to persecution and hatred from outside will have their counterpart within the church. False prophets: these are Christians; see the note on Matthew 7:15-20. Evildoing: see Matthew 7:23. Because of the apocalyptic nature of much of this discourse, the literal meaning of this description of the church should not be pressed too hard. However, there is reason to think that Matthew's addition of these verses reflects in some measure the condition of his community.

24:14 Except for the last part (and then the end will come), this verse substantially repeats Mark 13:10. The Matthean addition

g	Dn 9:27; 11:31; 12:11; Mk 13:14
h	Lk 17:31
i	Dn 12:1
j	Lk 17:23
k	Lk 17:24, 37
l	Is 13:10, 13; Ez 32:7; Am 8:9

The Great Tribulation

¹⁵*ᵍ"When you see the desolating abomination* spoken of through Daniel the prophet standing in the holy place (let the reader understand), ¹⁶then those in Judea must flee* to the mountains, ¹⁷*ʰa person on the housetop must not go down to get things out of his house, ¹⁸a person in the field must not return to get his cloak. ¹⁹Woe to pregnant women and nursing mothers in those days. ²⁰*Pray that your flight not be in winter or on the sabbath, ²¹*ⁱfor at that time there will be great tribulation, such as has not been since the beginning of the world until now, nor ever will be. ²²And if those days had not been shortened, no one would be saved; but for the sake of the elect they will be shortened. ²³ʲIf anyone says to you then, 'Look, here is the Messiah!' or, 'There he is!' do not believe it. ²⁴False messiahs and false prophets will arise, and they will perform signs and wonders so great as to deceive, if that were possible, even the elect. ²⁵Behold, I have told it to you beforehand. ²⁶So if they say to you, 'He is in the desert,' do not go out there; if they say, 'He is in the inner rooms,' do not believe it.* ²⁷ᵏFor just as lightning comes from the east and is seen as far as the west, so will the coming of the Son of Man be. ²⁸Wherever the corpse is, there the vultures will gather.

The Coming of the Son of Man

²⁹*ˡ"Immediately after the tribulation of those days,

the sun will be darkened,
and the moon will not give its light,
and the stars will fall from the sky,
and the powers of the heavens will be shaken.

---

raises a problem since what follows in Matthew 24:15-23 refers to the horrors of the First Jewish Revolt including the destruction of the temple, and Matthew, writing after that time, knew that the parousia of Jesus was still in the future. A solution may be that the evangelist saw the events of those verses as foreshadowing the cosmic disturbances that he associates with the parousia (24:29) so that the period in which the former took place could be understood as belonging to **the end.**

24:15-28 Cf. Mark 13:14-23; Luke 17:23-24, 37. A further stage in the tribulations that will precede the coming of the Son of Man, and an answer to the question of Matthew 24:3a, "when will this (the destruction of the temple) happen?"

24:15 The desolating abomination: in 167 B.C. the Syrian king Antiochus IV Epiphanes desecrated the temple by setting up in it a statue of Zeus Olympios (see 1 Mc 1:54). That event is referred to in Daniel 12:11 LXX as the "desolating abomination" (NAB "horrible abomination") and the same Greek term is used here; cf. also Daniel 9:27; 11:31. Although the desecration had taken place before Daniel was written, it is presented there as a future event, and Matthew sees that "prophecy" fulfilled in the desecration of the temple by the Romans. **In the holy place**: the temple; more precise than Mark's **where he should not** (Mk 13:14). **Let the reader understand**: this parenthetical remark, taken from Mark 13:14 invites **the reader** to realize the meaning of Daniel's "prophecy."

24:16 The tradition that the Christians of Jerusalem fled from that city to Pella, a city of Transjordan, at the time of the First Jewish Revolt is found in Eusebius (*Ecclesiastical History*, 3, 5, 3), who attributes the flight to "a certain oracle given by revelation before the war." The tradition is not improbable but the Matthean command,

derived from its Marcan source, is vague in respect to the place of flight (**to the mountains**), although some scholars see it as applicable to the flight to Pella.

24:17-19 Haste is essential, and the journey will be particularly difficult for women who are burdened with unborn or infant children.

24:20 On the sabbath: this addition to **in winter** (cf. Mk 13:18) has been understood as an indication that Matthew was addressed to a church still observing the Mosaic law of sabbath rest and the scribal limitations upon the length of journeys that might lawfully be made on that day. That interpretation conflicts with Matthew's view on sabbath observance (cf. 12:1-14). The meaning of the addition may be that those undertaking on the sabbath a journey such as the one here ordered would be offending the sensibilities of law-observant Jews and would incur their hostility.

24:21 For the unparalleled distress of that time, see Daniel 12:1.

24:26-28 Claims that the Messiah is to be found in some distant or secret place must be ignored. **The coming of the Son of Man** will be as clear as **lightning** is to all and as **the corpse** of an animal is to **vultures**; cf. Luke 17:24, 37. Here there is clear identification of the **Son of Man** and the Messiah; cf. Matthew 24:23.

24:29 The answer to the question of Matthew 24:3b "What will be the sign of your coming?" **Immediately after . . . those days**: the shortening of time between the preceding **tribulation** and the parousia has been explained as Matthew's use of a supposed device of Old Testament prophecy whereby certainty that a predicted event will occur is expressed by depicting it as imminent. While it is questionable that that is an acceptable understanding of the Old Testament predictions, it may be applicable here, for Matthew knew that the parousia had not come **immediately after** the fall of Jerusalem,

A fig tree in summer

[30] [m]"And then the sign of the Son of Man[*] will appear in heaven, and all the tribes of the earth will mourn, and they will see the Son of Man coming upon the clouds of heaven with power and great glory. [31] [n]And he will send out his angels[*] with a trumpet blast, and they will gather his elect from the four winds, from one end of the heavens to the other.

The Lesson of the Fig Tree

[32] [*]"Learn a lesson from the fig tree. When its branch becomes tender and sprouts leaves, you know that summer is near. [33]In the same way, when you see all these things, know that he is near, at the gates. [34]Amen, I say to you, this generation[*] will not pass away until all these things have taken place. [35] [o]Heaven and earth will pass away, but my words will not pass away.

The Unknown Day and Hour

[36] [*][p]"But of that day and hour no one knows, neither the angels of heaven, nor the Son,[*] but the Father alone. [37] [*][q]For as it was in the days of Noah, so it will be at the coming of the Son of Man. [38]In [those] days before the flood, they were eating and drinking, marrying and giving in marriage, up to the day that Noah entered the ark. [39]They did not know until the flood came and carried them all away. So will it be [also] at the coming of the Son of Man. [40] [*][r]Two men will be out in the field; one will be taken, and one will be left. [41]Two women will be grinding at the mill; one will be taken, and one will be left. [42] [*][s]Therefore, stay awake! For you do not know on which day your Lord will come. [43] [t]Be sure of this: if the master of the house had known the hour of night when the thief was coming, he would have stayed awake and not let his house be broken into. [44]So too, you also must be prepared, for at an hour you do not expect, the Son of Man will come.

m
Dn 7:13;
Zec 12:12-14;
Rev 1:7

n
Is 27:13;
1 Cor 15:52;
1 Thes 4:16

o
Is 40:8

p
Acts 1:7

q
Gn 6:5–7:23;
Lk 17:26-27;
2 Pt 3:6

r
Lk 17:34-35

s
25:13;
Lk 12:39-40

t
1 Thes 5:2

---

and it is unlikely that he is attributing a mistaken calculation of time to Jesus. **The sun . . . be shaken**: cf. Isaiah 13:10, 13.

24:30 The sign of the Son of Man: perhaps this means **the sign** that is the glorious appearance **of the Son of Man**; cf. Matthew 12:39-40 where "the sign of Jonah" is Jonah's being in the "belly of the whale." **Tribes of the earth will mourn**: peculiar to Matthew; cf. Zechariah 12:12-14. **Coming upon the clouds . . . glory**: cf. Daniel 7:13, although there the "one like a son of man" comes to God to receive kingship; here **the Son of Man** comes from heaven for judgment.

24:31 Send out his angels: cf. Matthew 13:41 where they are sent out to collect the wicked for punishment. **Trumpet blast**: cf. Isaiah 27:13; 1 Thessalonians 4:16.

24:32-35 Cf. Mark 13:28-31.

24:34 The difficulty raised by this verse cannot be satisfactorily removed by the supposition that **this generation** means the Jewish people throughout the course of their history, much less the entire human race. Perhaps for Matthew it means the **generation** to which he and his community belonged.

24:36-44 The statement of Matthew 24:34 is now counterbalanced by one that declares that the exact time of the parousia is

known only to **the Father** (24:36), and the disciples are warned to be always ready for it. This section is drawn from Mark and Q (cf. Lk 17:26-27, 34-35; 12:39-40).

24:36 Many textual witnesses omit **nor the Son**, which follows Mark 13:32. Since its omission can be explained by reluctance to attribute this ignorance to **the Son**, the reading that includes it is probably original.

24:37-39 Cf. Luke 17:26-27. **In the days of Noah**: the Old Testament account of the flood lays no emphasis upon what is central for Matthew, i.e., the unexpected coming of the flood upon those who were unprepared for it.

24:40-41 Cf. Luke 17:34-35. **Taken . . . left**: the former probably means **taken** into the kingdom; the latter, **left** for destruction. People in the same situation will be dealt with in opposite ways. In this context, the discrimination between them will be based on their readiness for the coming of the Son of Man.

24:42-44 Cf. Luke 12:39-40. The theme of vigilance and readiness is continued with the bold comparison of the Son of Man to a thief who comes to break into a house.

MATTHEW

u
Lk 12:41-46

v
13:42; 25:30

a
7:21, 23;
Lk 13:25-27

b
24:42;
Mk 13:33

c
Lk 19:12-27

The Faithful or the Unfaithful Servant*

[45u]"Who, then, is the faithful and prudent servant, whom the master has put in charge of his household to distribute to them their food at the proper time?* [46]Blessed is that servant whom his master on his arrival finds doing so. [47]Amen, I say to you, he will put him in charge of all his property. [48*]But if that wicked servant says to himself, 'My master is long delayed,' [49]and begins to beat his fellow servants, and eat and drink with drunkards, [50]the servant's master will come on an unexpected day and at an unknown hour [51v]and will punish him severely* and assign him a place with the hypocrites, where there will be wailing and grinding of teeth.

The Parable of the Ten Virgins

25 [1*]"Then* the kingdom of heaven will be like ten virgins who took their lamps and went out to meet the bridegroom. [2*]Five of them were foolish and five were wise. [3]The foolish ones, when taking their lamps, brought no oil with them, [4]but the wise brought flasks of oil with their lamps. [5]Since the bridegroom was long delayed, they all became drowsy and fell asleep. [6]At midnight, there was a cry, 'Behold, the bridegroom! Come out to meet him!' [7]Then all those virgins got up and trimmed their lamps. [8]The foolish ones said to the wise, 'Give us some of your oil, for our lamps are going out.' [9]But the wise ones replied, 'No, for there may not be enough for us and you. Go instead to the merchants and buy some for yourselves.' [10]While they went off to buy it, the bridegroom came and those who were ready went into the wedding feast with him. Then the door was locked. [11*a]Afterwards the other virgins came and said, 'Lord, Lord, open the door for us!' [12]But he said in reply, 'Amen, I say to you, I do not know you.' [13b]Therefore, stay awake,* for you know neither the day nor the hour.

The Parable of the Talents

[14*c]"It will be as when a man who was going on a journey* called in his servants and entrusted his possessions to them. [15]To one he gave five talents;* to another, two; to a third, one—to each according to his ability. Then he went away. Immediately [16]the one who received five talents went and traded with them, and made another five.

24:45-51 The second part of the discourse (see the note on 24:1–25:46) begins with this parable of **the faithful** or unfaithful **servant**; cf. Luke 12:41-46. It is addressed to the leaders of Matthew's church; **the servant has** been **put in charge** of his master's **household** (24:45) even though that household is composed of those who are his **fellow servants** (24:49).

24:45 To distribute . . . proper time: readiness for the master's return means a vigilance that is accompanied by faithful performance of the duty assigned.

24:48 My master . . . delayed: the note of delay is found also in the other parables of this section; cf. Matthew 25:5, 19.

24:51 Punish him severely: the Greek verb, found in the New Testament only here and in the Lucan parallel (Lk 12:46), means, literally, "cut in two." With the hypocrites: see the note on Matthew 6:2. Matthew classes the unfaithful Christian leader with the unbelieving leaders of Judaism. Wailing and grinding of teeth: see the note on Matthew 8:11-12.

25:1-13 Peculiar to Matthew.

25:1 Then: at the time of the parousia. Kingdom . . . will be like: see the note on Matthew 13:24-30.

25:2-4 Foolish . . . wise: cf. the contrasted "wise man" and "fool" of Matthew 7:24, 26 where the two are distinguished by good deeds and lack of them, and such deeds may be signified by the oil of this parable.

25:11-12 Lord, Lord: cf. Matthew 7:21. I do not know you: cf. Matthew 7:23 where the Greek verb is different but synonymous.

25:13 Stay awake: some scholars see this command as an addition to the original parable of Matthew's traditional material, since in Matthew 25:5 all the virgins, wise and foolish, fall asleep. But the wise virgins are adequately equipped for their task, and stay awake may mean no more than to be prepared; cf. Matthew 24:42, 44.

25:14-30 Cf. Luke 19:12-27.

25:14 It will be as when . . . journey: literally, "For just as a man who was going on a journey." Although the comparison is not completed, the sense is clear; the kingdom of heaven is like the situation here described. Faithful use of one's gifts will lead to participation in the fullness of the kingdom, lazy inactivity to exclusion from it.

25:15 Talents: see the note on Matthew 18:24.

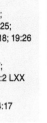

¹⁷Likewise, the one who received two made another two. ¹⁸*But the man who received one went off and dug a hole in the ground and buried his master's money. ¹⁹After a long time the master of those servants came back and settled accounts with them. ²⁰The one who had received five talents came forward bringing the additional five.* He said, 'Master, you gave me five talents. See, I have made five more.' ²¹ᵈHis master said to him, 'Well done, my good and faithful servant. Since you were faithful in small matters, I will give you great responsibilities. Come, share your master's joy.' ²²[Then] the one who had received two talents also came forward and said, 'Master, you gave me two talents. See, I have made two more.' ²³His master said to him, 'Well done, my good and faithful servant. Since you were faithful in small matters, I will give you great responsibilities. Come, share your master's joy.' ²⁴Then the one who had received the one talent came forward and said, 'Master, I knew you were a demanding person, harvesting where you did not plant and gathering where you did not scatter; ²⁵so out of fear I went off and buried your talent in the ground. Here it is back.' ²⁶His master said to him in reply, 'You wicked, lazy servant!* So you knew that I harvest where I did not plant and gather where I did not scatter? ²⁷Should you not then have put my money in the bank so that I could have got it back with interest on my return? ²⁸Now then! Take the talent from him and give it to the one with ten. ²⁹*ᵉFor to everyone who has, more will be given and he will grow rich; but from the one who has not, even what he has will be taken away. ³⁰*And throw this useless servant into the darkness outside, where there will be wailing and grinding of teeth.'

The Judgment of the Nations

³¹*ᶠ'When the Son of Man comes in his glory, and all the angels with him, he will sit upon his glorious throne, ³²ᵍand all the nations* will be assembled

d
Lk 16:10

e
13:12;
Mk 4:25;
Lk 8:18; 19:26

f
16:27;
Dt 33:2 LXX

g
Ez 34:17

Matthew's famous judgment scene of the sheep and goats evokes the church's tradition of the **corporal works of mercy**. For Jesus there is an intimate connection between love of God and love of neighbor (Mt 22:37-40). One cannot profess to love God and then not respond to the needs of other human beings. In church tradition the corporal works of mercy are concrete actions that put love of God into practice: "feeding the hungry, sheltering the homeless, clothing the naked, visiting the sick and imprisoned, and burying the dead" (CCC, 2447).

25:18 Buried his master's money: see the note on Matthew 13:44.

25:20-23 Although the first two servants have received and doubled large sums, their faithful trading is regarded by the master as fidelity **in small matters** only, compared with **the great responsibilities** now to be given to them. The latter are unspecified. **Share your master's joy**: probably the joy of the banquet of the kingdom; cf. Matthew 8:11.

25:26-28 Wicked, lazy servant: this man's inactivity is not negligible but seriously culpable. As punishment, he loses the gift he had received, that is now given to the first servant, whose possessions are already great.

25:29 See the note on Matthew 13:12 where there is a similar application of this maxim.

25:30 See the note on Matthew 8:11-12.

25:31-46 The conclusion of the discourse, which is peculiar to Matthew, portrays the final judgment that will accompany the parousia. Although often called a "parable," it is not really such, for the only parabolic elements are the depiction of **the Son of Man** as a **shepherd** and of **the righteous** and the wicked as sheep and goats respectively (25:32-33). The criterion of judgment

will be the deeds of mercy that have been done for the **least** of Jesus' **brothers** (25:40). A difficult and important question is the identification of these **least brothers**. Are they all people who have suffered hunger, thirst, etc. (25:35, 36) or a particular group of such sufferers? Scholars are divided in their response and arguments can be made for either side. But leaving aside the problem of what the traditional material that Matthew edited may have meant, it seems that a stronger case can be made for the view that in the evangelist's sense the sufferers are Christians, probably Christian missionaries whose sufferings were brought upon them by their preaching of the gospel. The criterion of judgment for **all the nations** is their treatment of those who have borne to the world the message of Jesus, and this means ultimately their acceptance or rejection of Jesus himself; cf. Matthew 10:40, "Whoever receives you, receives me." 25:31

25:31 See the note on Matthew 16:27.

25:32 All the nations: before the end the gospel will have been preached throughout the world (24:14); thus the Gentiles will be judged on their response to it. But the phrase **all the nations** includes the Jews also, for at the judgment "the Son of Man . . . will repay everyone according to his conduct" (16:27).

h
Is 58:7;
Ez 18:7
i
10:40, 42
j
7:23; Lk 13:27
k
Jb 22:7;
Jas 2:15-16
l
Dn 12:2
a
Mk 14:1-2;
Lk 22:1-2
b
Jn 11:47-53
c
Mk 14:3-9;
Jn 12:1-8

before him. And he will separate them one from another, as a shepherd separates the sheep from the goats. [33]He will place the sheep on his right and the goats on his left. [34]Then the king will say to those on his right, 'Come, you who are blessed by my Father. Inherit the kingdom prepared for you from the foundation of the world. [35h]For I was hungry and you gave me food, I was thirsty and you gave me drink, a stranger and you welcomed me, [36]naked and you clothed me, ill and you cared for me, in prison and you visited me.' [37]Then the righteous* will answer him and say, 'Lord, when did we see you hungry and feed you, or thirsty and give you drink? [38]When did we see you a stranger and welcome you, or naked and clothe you? [39]When did we see you ill or in prison, and visit you?' [40i]And the king will say to them in reply, 'Amen, I say to you, whatever you did for one of these least brothers of mine, you did for me.' [41*j]Then he will say to those on his left, 'Depart from me, you accursed, into the eternal fire prepared for the devil and his angels. [42k]For I was hungry and you gave me no food, I was thirsty and you gave me no drink, [43]a stranger and you gave me no welcome, naked and you gave me no clothing, ill and in prison, and you did not care for me.' [44*]Then they will answer and say, 'Lord, when did we see you hungry or thirsty or a stranger or naked or ill or in prison, and not minister to your needs?' [45]He will answer them, 'Amen, I say to you, what you did not do for one of these least ones, you did not do for me.' [46l]And these will go off to eternal punishment, but the righteous to eternal life."

VII: The Passion and Resurrection

The Conspiracy against Jesus

26 [1*]When Jesus finished all these words,* he said to his disciples, [2a]"You know that in two days' time it will be Passover, and the Son of Man will be handed over to be crucified." [3*]Then the chief priests and the elders of the people assembled in the palace of the high priest, who was called Caiaphas, [4b]and they consulted together to arrest Jesus by treachery and put him to death. [5]But they said, "Not during the festival,* that there may not be a riot among the people."

The Anointing at Bethany

[6*c]Now when Jesus was in Bethany in the house of Simon the leper, [7]a woman came up to him with an alabaster jar of costly perfumed oil, and poured it on his head while

---

25:37-40 The righteous will be astonished that in caring for the needs of the sufferers they were ministering to the **Lord** himself. **One of these least brothers of mine**: cf. Matthew 10:42.

25:41 Fire prepared . . . his angels: cf. 1 Enoch 10, 13 where it is said of the evil angels and Semyaza, their leader, "In those days they will lead them into the bottom of the fire—and in torment—in the prison (where) they will be locked up forever."

25:44-45 The **accursed** (25:41) will be likewise astonished that their neglect of the sufferers was neglect of the **Lord** and will receive from him a similar answer.

26:1–28:20 The five books with alternating narrative and discourse (3:1–25:46) that give this gospel its distinctive structure lead up to the climactic events that are the center of Christian belief and the origin of the Christian church, the passion and resurrection of Jesus. In his passion narrative (chaps. 26–27) Matthew follows his Marcan source closely but with omissions (e.g., Mk 14:51-52) and additions (e.g., 27:3-10, 19). Some of the additions indicate that he

utilized traditions that he had received from elsewhere; others are due to his own theological insight (e.g., 26:28 ". . . for the forgiveness of sins"; 27:52). In his editing Matthew also altered Mark in some minor details. But there is no need to suppose that he knew any passion narrative other than Mark's.

26:1-2 When Jesus finished all these words: see the note on Matthew 7:28-29. **"You know . . . crucified"**: Matthew turns Mark's statement of the time (Mk 14:1) into Jesus' final prediction of his passion. **Passover**: see the note on Mark 14:1.

26:3 Caiaphas was high priest from A.D. 18 to 36.

26:5 Not during the festival: the plan to delay Jesus' arrest and execution until after the **festival** was not carried out, for according to the synoptics he was arrested on the night of Nisan 14 and put to death the following day. No reason is given why the plan was changed.

26:6-13 See the notes on Mark 14:3-9 and John 12:1-8.

he was reclining at table. [8]When the disciples saw this, they were indignant and said, "Why this waste? [9]It could have been sold for much, and the money given to the poor." [10]Since Jesus knew this, he said to them, "Why do you make trouble for the woman? She has done a good thing for me. [11][d]The poor you will always have with you; but you will not always have me. [12]*In pouring this perfume oil upon my body, she did it to prepare me for burial. [13]Amen, I say to you, wherever this gospel is proclaimed in the whole world, what she has done will be spoken of, in memory of her."

The Betrayal by Judas

[14][e]Then one of the Twelve, who was called Judas Iscariot,* went to the chief priests [15]*[f]and said, "What are you willing to give me if I hand him over to you?" They paid him thirty pieces of silver, [16]and from that time on he looked for an opportunity to hand him over.

Preparations for the Passover

[17][g]On the first day of the Feast of Unleavened Bread,* the disciples approached Jesus and said, "Where do you want us to prepare for you to eat the Passover?"[h] [18]*He said, "Go into the city to a certain man and tell him, 'The teacher says, "My appointed time draws near; in your house I shall celebrate the Passover with my disciples."'" [19]The disciples then did as Jesus had ordered, and prepared the Passover.

The Betrayer

[20]When it was evening, he reclined at table with the Twelve. [21]And while they were eating, he said, "Amen, I say to you, one of you will betray me."* [22]Deeply distressed at this, they began to say to him one after another, "Surely it is not I, Lord?" [23]He said in reply, "He who has dipped his hand into the dish with me is the one who will betray me. [24]*[i]The Son of Man indeed goes, as it is written of him, but woe to that man by whom the Son of Man is betrayed. It would be better for that man if he had never been born." [25]*Then Judas, his betrayer, said in reply, "Surely it is not I, Rabbi?" He answered, "You have said so."

d
Dt 15:11

e
Mk 14:10-11;
Lk 22:3-6

f
Zec 11:12

g
Mk 14:12-21;
Lk 22:7-23

h
Ex 12:14-20

i
Is 53:8-10

26:12 To prepare me for burial: cf. Mark 14:8. In accordance with the interpretation of this act as Jesus' **burial** anointing, Matthew, more consistent than Mark, changes the purpose of the visit of the women to Jesus' tomb; they do not go to anoint him (Mk 16:1) but "to see the tomb" (28:1).

26:14 Iscariot: see the note on Luke 6:16.

26:15 The motive of avarice is introduced by Judas's question about the price for betrayal, which is absent in the Marcan source (Mk 14:10-11). **Hand him over**: the same Greek verb is used to express the saving purpose of God by which Jesus is handed over to death (cf. 17:22; 20:18; 26:2) and the human malice that hands him over. **Thirty pieces of silver**: the price of the betrayal is found only in Matthew. It is derived from Zechariah 11:12 where it is the wages paid to the rejected shepherd, a cheap price (Zec 11:13). That amount is also the compensation paid to one whose slave has been gored by an ox (Ex 21:32).

26:17 The first day of the Feast of Unleavened Bread: see the note on Mark 14:1. Matthew omits Mark's "when they sacrificed the Passover lamb."

26:18 By omitting much of Mark 14:13-15, adding **My appointed time draws near**, and turning the question into a statement, **in your house I shall celebrate the Passover**, Matthew has given this passage a solemnity and majesty greater than that of his source.

26:21 Given Matthew's interest in the fulfillment of the Old Testament, it is curious that he omits the Marcan designation of Jesus' betrayer as "one who is eating with me" (Mk 14:18), since that is probably an allusion to Psalm 41:10. However, the shocking fact that the betrayer is one who shares table fellowship with Jesus is emphasized in Matthew 26:23.

26:24 It would be better . . . born: the enormity of the deed is such that it would be better not to exist than to do it.

26:25 Peculiar to Matthew. **You have said so**: cf. Matthew 26:64; 27:11. This is a half-affirmative. Emphasis is laid on the pronoun and the answer implies that the statement would not have been made if the question had not been asked.

j
Mk 14:22-26;
Lk 22:14-23;
1 Cor 11:23-25

k
1 Cor 10:16

l
Ex 24:8;
Is 53:12

m
Mk 14:7-31

n
Zec 13:7;
Jn 16:32

o
Lk 22:33-34;
Jn 13:37-38

p
26:69-75

q
Mk 14:32-42;
Lk 22:39-46

The Lord's Supper*

²⁶*j*While they were eating, Jesus took bread, said the blessing, broke it, and giving it to his disciples said, "Take and eat; this is my body."*^k ²⁷Then he took a cup, gave thanks,* and gave it to them, saying, "Drink from it, all of you, ²⁸*l*for this is my blood of the covenant, which will be shed on behalf of many for the forgiveness of sins. ²⁹*I tell you, from now on I shall not drink this fruit of the vine until the day when I drink it with you new in the kingdom of my Father." ³⁰*Then, after singing a hymn, they went out to the Mount of Olives.

Peter's Denial Foretold

³¹*m*Then Jesus said to them, "This night all of you will have your faith in me shaken,* for it is written:ⁿ

'I will strike the shepherd,
   and the sheep of the flock will be dispersed';

³²but after I have been raised up, I shall go before you to Galilee." ³³Peter said to him in reply, "Though all may have their faith in you shaken, mine will never be." ³⁴*oJesus said to him, "Amen, I say to you, this very night before the cock crows, you will deny me three times."^p ³⁵Peter said to him, "Even though I should have to die with you, I will not deny you." And all the disciples spoke likewise.

The Agony in the Garden

³⁶*qThen Jesus came with them to a place called Gethsemane,* and he said to his

---

26:26-29 See the note on Mark 14:22-24. The Marcan-Matthean is one of the two major New Testament traditions of the words of Jesus when instituting the Eucharist. The other (and earlier) is the Pauline-Lucan (1 Cor 11:23-25; Lk 22:19-20). Each shows the influence of Christian liturgical usage, but the Marcan-Matthean is more developed in that regard than the Pauline-Lucan. The words over the bread and cup succeed each other without the intervening meal mentioned in 1 Corinthians 11:25; Luke 22:20; and there is parallelism between the consecratory words (**this is my body . . . this is my blood**). Matthew follows Mark closely but with some changes.

26:26 See the note on Matthew 14:19. **Said the blessing**: a prayer blessing God. **Take and eat**: literally, **Take, eat**. Eat is an addition to Mark's "take it" (literally, "take"; Mk 14:22). **This is my body**: the bread is identified with Jesus himself.

26:27-28 Gave thanks: see the note on Mark 15:36. **Gave it to them . . . all of you**: cf. Mark 14:23-24. In the Marcan sequence the disciples drink and then Jesus says the interpretative words. Matthew has changed this into a command to **drink** followed by those words. **My blood**: see Leviticus 17:11 for the concept that the **blood** is "the seat of life" and that when placed on the altar it "makes atonement." **Which will be shed**: the present participle, "being shed" or "going to be shed," is future in relation to the Last Supper. **On behalf of**: Greek *peri*; see the note on Mark 14:24. **Many**: see the note on Matthew 20:28. **For the forgiveness of sins**: a Matthean addition. The same phrase occurs in Mark 1:4 in connection with John's baptism but Matthew avoids it there (3:11). He places it here probably because he wishes to emphasize that it is the sacrificial death of Jesus that brings **forgiveness of sins**.

26:29 Although his death will interrupt the table fellowship he has had with the disciples, Jesus confidently predicts his vindication

by God and a new table fellowship with them at the banquet of the kingdom.

26:30 See the note on Mark 14:26.

26:31 Will have . . . shaken: literally, "will be scandalized in me"; see the note on Matthew 24:9-12. **I will strike . . . dispersed**: cf. Zechariah 13:7.

26:34 Before the cock crows: see the note on Matthew 14:25. The third watch of the night was called "cockcrow." **Deny me**: see the note on Matthew 16:24.

26:36-56 Cf. Mark 14:32-52. The account of Jesus in Gethsemane is divided between that of his agony (26:36-46) and that of his betrayal and arrest (26:47-56). Jesus' **sorrow and distress** (26:37) in face of death is unrelieved by the presence of his three disciples who, though urged to **watch with him** (26:38, 41), fall asleep (26:40, 43). He prays that **if . . . possible** his death may be avoided (26:39) but that his Father's will be done (26:39, 42, 44). Knowing then that his death must take place, he announces to his companions that **the hour** for his being **handed over** has come (26:45). Judas arrives with an armed band provided by the Sanhedrin and greets Jesus with a kiss, the prearranged sign for his identification (26:47-49). After his arrest, he rebukes a disciple who has attacked **the high priest's servant** with a **sword** (26:51-54), and chides those who have come out to seize him with **swords and clubs** as if he were a **robber** (26:55-56). In both rebukes Jesus declares that the treatment he is how receiving is the fulfillment of the scriptures (26:55, 56). The subsequent flight of **all the disciples** is itself the fulfillment of his own prediction (cf. 31). In this episode, Matthew follows Mark with a few alterations.

26:36 Gethsemane: the Hebrew name means "oil press" and designates an olive orchard on the western slope of the Mount of

disciples, "Sit here while I go over there and pray."[r] [37s]He took along Peter and the two sons of Zebedee,* and began to feel sorrow and distress. [38t] Then he said to them, "My soul is sorrowful even to death.* Remain here and keep watch with me." [39u]He advanced a little and fell prostrate in prayer, saying, "My Father,* if it is possible, let this cup pass from me; yet, not as I will, but as you will." [40]When he returned to his disciples he found them asleep. He said to Peter, "So you could not keep watch with me for one hour? [41]Watch and pray that you may not undergo the test.* The spirit is willing, but the flesh is weak." [42*v]Withdrawing a second time, he prayed again, "My Father, if it is not possible that this cup pass without my drinking it, your will be done!" [43]Then he returned once more and found them asleep, for they could not keep their eyes open. [44]He left them and withdrew again and prayed a third time, saying the same thing again. [45w]Then he returned to his disciples and said to them, "Are you still sleeping and taking your rest? Behold, the hour is at hand when the Son of Man is to be handed over to sinners. [46]Get up, let us go. Look, my betrayer is at hand."

The Betrayal and Arrest of Jesus

[47x]While he was still speaking, Judas, one of the Twelve, arrived, accompanied by a large crowd, with swords and clubs, who had come from the chief priests and the elders of the people. [48]His betrayer had arranged a sign with them, saying, "The man I shall kiss is the one; arrest him." [49]Immediately he went over to Jesus and said, "Hail, Rabbi!"* and he kissed him. [50]Jesus answered him, "Friend, do what you have come for." Then stepping forward they laid hands on Jesus and arrested him. [51]And behold, one of those who accompanied Jesus put his hand to his sword, drew it, and struck the high priest's servant, cutting off his ear. [52]Then Jesus said to him, "Put your sword back into its sheath, for all who take the sword will perish by the sword. [53]Do you think that I cannot call upon my Father and he will not provide me at this moment with more than twelve legions of angels? [54]But then how would the scriptures be fulfilled which say that it must come to pass in this way?" [55*]At that hour Jesus said to the crowds, "Have you come out as against a robber, with swords and clubs to seize me? Day after day I sat teaching in the temple area, yet you did not arrest me. [56y]But all this has come to pass that the writings of the prophets may be fulfilled." Then all the disciples left him and fled.

---

r
Jn 18:1

s
Heb 5:7

t
Ps 42:6, 12;
Jon 4:9

u
Jn 4:34; 6:38;
Phil 2:8

v
6:10; Heb 10:9

w
Jn 12:23; 13:1;
17:1

x
Mk 14:43-50;
Lk 22:47-53;
Jn 18:3-11

y
26:31

Olives; see the note on Matthew 21:1. The name appears only in Matthew and Mark. The place is called a "garden" in John 18:1.

26:37 Peter and the two sons of Zebedee: cf. Matthew 17:1.

26:38 Cf. Psalm 42:6, 12. In the Septuagint (Ps 41:5, 12) the same Greek word for **sorrowful** is used as here. **To death:** i.e., "enough to die"; cf. Jonah 4:9.

26:39 My Father: see the note on Mark 14:36. Matthew omits the Aramaic ʾabbāʾ and adds the qualifier *my*. **This cup:** see the note on Mark 10:38-40.

26:41 Undergo the test: see the note on Matthew 6:13. In that verse "the final test" translates the same Greek word as is here translated **the test**, and these are the only instances of the use of that word in Matthew. It is possible that the passion of Jesus is seen here as an anticipation of the great tribulation that will precede the parousia (see the notes on 24:8; 24:21) to which Matthew 6:13 refers, and that just as Jesus prays to be delivered from death

(26:39), so he exhorts the disciples to pray that they will not have to **undergo the** great **test** that his passion would be for them. Some scholars, however, understand **not undergo** (literally, "not enter") **the test** as meaning not that the disciples may be spared **the test** but that they may not yield to the temptation of falling away from Jesus because of his passion even though they will have to endure it.

26:42 Your will be done: cf. Matthew 6:10.

26:49 Rabbi: see the note on Matthew 23:6-7. Jesus is so addressed twice in Matthew (26:25), both times by Judas. For the significance of the closely related address "teacher" in Matthew, see the note on Matthew 8:19.

26:55 Day after day . . . arrest me: cf. Mark 14:49. This suggests that Jesus had taught for a relatively long period in Jerusalem, whereas Matthew 21:1-11 puts his coming to the city for the first time only a few days before.

z	Mk 14:53-65; Lk 22:54-55, 63-71; Jn 18:12-14, 19-24
a	Dt 19:15; Jn 2:19; Acts 6:14
b	Is 53:7
c	Ps 110:1; Dn 7:13
d	Wis 2:19; Is 50:6

Jesus before the Sanhedrin

[57][z]Those who had arrested Jesus led him away to Caiaphas* the high priest, where the scribes and the elders were assembled. [58]Peter was following him at a distance as far as the high priest's courtyard, and going inside he sat down with the servants to see the outcome. [59]The chief priests and the entire Sanhedrin* kept trying to obtain false testimony against Jesus in order to put him to death, [60][a]but they found none, though many false witnesses came forward. Finally two* came forward [61]who stated, "This man said, 'I can destroy the temple of God and within three days rebuild it.'" [62]The high priest rose and addressed him, "Have you no answer? What are these men testifying against you?" [63][b]But Jesus was silent.* Then the high priest said to him, "I order you to tell us under oath before the living God whether you are the Messiah, the Son of God." [64][c]Jesus said to him in reply, "You have said so.* But I tell you:

From now on you will see 'the Son of Man
  seated at the right hand of the Power'
  and 'coming on the clouds of heaven.'"

[65]Then the high priest tore his robes and said, "He has blasphemed!* What further need have we of witnesses? You have now heard the blasphemy; [66]what is your opinion?" They said in reply, "He deserves to die!" [67][d]Then they spat in his face and struck him, while some slapped him, [68]saying, "Prophesy for us, Messiah: who is it that struck you?"

26:57-68 Following Mark 14:53-65 Matthew presents the night-time appearance of Jesus before the **Sanhedrin** as a real trial. After **many false witnesses** bring charges against him that do not suffice for the death sentence (26:60), **two came forward** who charge him with claiming to be able to **destroy the temple . . . and within three days** to **rebuild it** (26:60-61). Jesus makes no answer even when challenged to do so by **the high priest**, who then orders him to declare **under oath . . . whether** he is the **Messiah, the Son of God** (26:62-63). Matthew changes Mark's clear affirmative response (Mk 14:62) to the same one as that given to Judas (26:25), but follows Mark almost verbatim in Jesus' predicting that his judges will see him **(the Son of Man) seated at the right hand of** God **and coming on the clouds of heaven** (26:64). **The high priest** then charges him with blasphemy (26:65), a charge with which the other members of **the Sanhedrin** agree by declaring that **he deserves to die** (26:66). They then attack him (26:67) and mockingly demand that he **prophesy** (26:68). This account contains elements that are contrary to the judicial procedures prescribed in the Mishnah, the Jewish code of law that dates in written form from ca. A.D. 200, e.g., trial on a feast day, a night session of the court, pronouncement of a verdict of condemnation at the same session at which testimony was received. Consequently, some scholars regard the account entirely as a creation of the early Christians without historical value. However, it is disputable whether the norms found in the Mishnah were in force at the time of Jesus. More to the point is the question whether the Matthean-Marcan night trial derives from a combination of two separate incidents, a nighttime preliminary investigation (cf. Jn 18:13, 19-24) and a formal trial on the following morning (cf. Lk 22:66-71).

26:57 Caiaphas: see the note on Matthew 26:3.

26:59 Sanhedrin: see the note on Luke 22:66.

26:60-61 Two: cf. Deuteronomy 19:15. **I can destroy . . . rebuild it**: there are significant differences from the Marcan parallel (Mk 14:58). Matthew omits "made with hands" and "not made with hands" and changes Mark's "will destroy" and "will build another" to **can destroy** and (can) **rebuild**. The charge is probably based on Jesus' prediction of the temple's destruction; see the notes on Matthew 23:37-39; 24:2; and John 2:19. A similar prediction by Jeremiah was considered as deserving death; cf. Jeremiah 7:1-15; 26:1-8.

26:63 Silent: possibly an allusion to Isaiah 53:7. **I order you . . . living God**: peculiar to Matthew; cf. Mark 14:61.

26:64 You have said so: see the note on Matthew 26:25. **From now on . . . heaven**: the Son of Man who is to be crucified (cf. 20:19) will be seen in glorious majesty (cf. Ps 110:1) and **coming on the clouds of heaven** (cf. Dn 7:13). **The Power**: see the note on Mark 14:61-62.

26:65 Blasphemed: the punishment for **blasphemy** was death by stoning (see Lv 24:10-16). According to the Mishnah, to be guilty of **blasphemy** one had to pronounce "the Name itself," i.e. Yahweh; cf. **Sanhedrin** 7, 4.5. Those who judge the gospel accounts of Jesus' trial by the later Mishnah standards point out that Jesus uses the surrogate "the Power," and hence no Jewish court would have regarded him as guilty of blasphemy; others hold that the Mishnah's narrow understanding of **blasphemy** was a later development.

26:67-68 The physical abuse, apparently done to Jesus by the members of the Sanhedrin themselves, recalls the sufferings of the Isaian Servant of the Lord; cf. Isaiah 50:6. The mocking challenge to **prophesy** is probably motivated by Jesus' prediction of his future glory (26:64).

Peter's Denial of Jesus

⁶⁹ᵉNow Peter was sitting outside in the courtyard. One of the maids came over to him and said, "You too were with Jesus the Galilean." ⁷⁰*But he denied it in front of everyone, saying, "I do not know what you are talking about!" ⁷¹As he went out to the gate, another girl saw him and said to those who were there, "This man was with Jesus the Nazorean." ⁷²Again he denied it with an oath, "I do not know the man!" ⁷³*A little later the bystanders came over and said to Peter, "Surely you too are one of them; even your speech gives you away." ⁷⁴At that he began to curse and to swear, "I do not know the man." And immediately a cock crowed. ⁷⁵ᶠThen Peter remembered the word that Jesus had spoken: "Before the cock crows you will deny me three times." He went out and began to weep bitterly.

e
Mk 14:66-72;
Lk 22:56-62;
Jn 18:17-18,
25-27

f
26:34

Peter

Peter is the most important of the original twelve apostles. The NT shows his prominence in several ways, especially by means of his role as the primary voice of the apostles. Peter uniformly appears first in the lists of the Twelve (Mt 10:2 and par.), he confessed Jesus as the Messiah (Mk 8:29 and par.), and he is among the first to encounter the risen Jesus (1 Cor 15:5). While his preeminence is clear, he is also a complex figure whose limitations the NT does not hide. Essentially, Peter is both saint and sinner.

"Peter" is actually a nickname for the apostle Simon, whose brother was Andrew. They, along with Philip, were natives of Bethsaida and fishermen on the Sea of Galilee (Jn 1:44; Mk 1:16). Jesus bestowed the name "Peter" on Simon, making a pun in reference to his steadfastness in faith (Mt 16:18; Mk 3:16; Acts 10:5). The pun appears in Greek (*petros*) and Aramaic (*kephas*), for both words mean "rock." The NT occasionally refers to Peter as Kephas (Gal 1:18; 2:9; "Cephas"). Jesus promised to build his church on this "rock" so that it would withstand the inevitable trials and tribulations of the ages (Mt 16:18).

How did this simple fisherman become so central a figure to the church? The NT portrays Peter as sometimes impulsive and unpredictable, as when he jumped into the sea with his clothes on in his excitement to see the risen Lord (Jn 21:7) or when Peter brashly says that his faith will never falter, shortly before he denies that he even knows Jesus (Mk 14:29, 68). Mark unrelentingly shows Peter, along with the other disciples, as somewhat obtuse in his understanding of Jesus' ministry. Just after his proper confession of Jesus' identity, Peter shows that he does not grasp the necessity of Jesus' suffering and death. Jesus goes so far as

to call him "Satan," a human stumbling block (Greek, *skandalon*) to God's plan fulfilled in Jesus (Mk 8:33).

Yet the faith of this man endured. Emboldened by the Holy Spirit at Pentecost, Peter appears in Acts as the primary evangelist among the apostles. Indeed, if the second half of Acts (chs. 16–28) is almost exclusively devoted to Paul, the first half focuses primarily on Peter (chs. 2–15). Peter gives bold and effective speeches, performs great miracles, and is frequently imprisoned or persecuted for the sake of the faith (e.g., Acts 2:17-41; 3:1-10; 5:18). His ordinary working-class background yields to a boundless evangelical spirit to carry forth Jesus' message to the world (Acts 4:13).

Perhaps the most serious flaw in this saint is the fact that he denied the Lord, not once but three times (Lk 22:54-62 and par.). That the NT proclaims this embarrassing scene boldly is sufficient proof of its historicity. John's gospel shows the most poignant scene of Peter's reconciliation, however, through the story of Peter's encounter with the risen Lord. Just as Peter had denied Jesus three times, so the risen Jesus asks him three times if he "loves" him (Jn 21:15-17). Peter's threefold positive response leads to a commission to shepherd the flock.

Peter is the source of the Petrine ministry in the church, which Roman Catholics identify with the papacy. Although in the early church Peter was not the only prominent leader among the apostles (remember James the brother of the Lord, Paul, Barnabas, the Beloved Disciple, etc.), he nonetheless became the most prominent of the apostles over time. He is especially identified with the early Christian community in the imperial city of Rome. Ancient tradition holds that he was martyred and buried there in the early 60s.

26:70 Denied it in front of everyone: see Matthew 10:33. Peter's repentance (26:75) saves him from the fearful destiny of which Jesus speaks there.

26:73 Your speech . . . away: Matthew explicates Mark's "you too are a Galilean" (Mk 14:70).

a
Mk 15:1;
Lk 23:1;
Jn 18:28

b
Acts 1:18-19

c
26:15

d
Zec 11:12-13

e
Mk 15:2-5;
Lk 23:2-3;
Jn 18:29-38

Jesus before Pilate*

27 [1a]When it was morning, all the chief priests and the elders of the people took counsel against Jesus to put him to death.* [2]They bound him, led him away, and handed him over to Pilate, the governor.

The Death of Judas

[3b]Then Judas, his betrayer, seeing that Jesus had been condemned, deeply regretted what he had done. He returned the thirty pieces of silver* to the chief priests and elders,[c] [4]saying, "I have sinned in betraying innocent blood." They said, "What is that to us? Look to it yourself." [5*]Flinging the money into the temple, he departed and went off and hanged himself. [6]The chief priests gathered up the money, but said, "It is not lawful to deposit this in the temple treasury, for it is the price of blood." [7]After consultation, they used it to buy the potter's field as a burial place for foreigners. [8]That is why that field even today is called the Field of Blood. [9]Then was fulfilled what had been said through Jeremiah the prophet,* "And they took the thirty pieces of silver, the value of a man with a price on his head, a price set by some of the Israelites, [10d]and they paid it out for the potter's field just as the Lord had commanded me."

Jesus Questioned by Pilate

[11e]Now Jesus stood before the governor, and he questioned him, "Are you

The title **"King of the Jews"** is curious in that it represents an "outsider's" perspective. The normal title for a Davidic king is "King of Israel." But Alexander Jannaeus (103–76 B.C.) and Herod the Great (37–4 B.C.), neither of whom was Davidic, both possessed the title "King of the Jews" when they ruled Palestine. An archaeological find in 1996 confirmed the title for Herod the Great when an inscription was discovered on a clay wine jug at a 2000-year-old garbage dump at Masada in Israel. This fact makes the passion narratives of the gospels all the more comprehensible. Jesus may have been crucified for political reasons as a threat to Roman authority for trying, in their view, to reestablish a Jewish monarchy.

27:1-31 Cf. Mark 15:1-20. Matthew's account of the Roman trial before **Pilate** is introduced by a consultation of the Sanhedrin after which Jesus is **handed over to . . . the governor** (27:1-2). Matthew follows his Marcan source closely but adds some material that is peculiar to him, the death of **Judas** (27:3-10), possibly the name **Jesus** as the name of **Barabbas** also (27:16-17), the intervention of Pilate's **wife** (27:19), Pilate's washing **his hands** in token of his disclaiming responsibility for Jesus' death (27:24), and the assuming of that responsibility by **the whole people** (27:25).

27:1-2 There is scholarly disagreement about the meaning of the Sanhedrin's taking **counsel** (*symboulion elabon*; cf. 12:14; 22:15; 27:7; 28:12); see the note on Mark 15:1. Some understand it as a discussion about the strategy for putting their death sentence against **Jesus** into effect since they lacked the right to do so themselves. Others see it as the occasion for their passing that sentence, holding that Matthew, unlike Mark (Mk 14:64), does not consider that it had been passed in the night session (26:66). Even in the latter interpretation, their handing **him over to Pilate** is best explained on the hypothesis that they did not have competence to put their sentence into effect, as is stated in John 18:31.

27:3 The thirty pieces of silver: see Matthew 26:15.

27:5-8 For another tradition about the death of Judas, cf. Acts 1:18-19. The two traditions agree only in the purchase of a **field** with **the money** paid to Judas for his betrayal of Jesus and the name given to the **field, the Field of Blood**. In Acts Judas himself buys the field and its name comes from his own blood shed in his fatal accident on it. **The potter's field**: this designation of the field is based on the fulfillment citation in Matthew 27:10.

27:9-10 Cf. Matthew 26:15. Matthew's attributing this text to Jeremiah is puzzling, for there is no such text in that book, and **the thirty pieces of silver** thrown by Judas "into the temple" (27:5) recall rather Zechariah 11:12-13. It is usually said that the attribution of the text to Jeremiah is due to Matthew's combining the Zechariah text with texts from Jeremiah that speak of a **potter** (Jer 18:2-3), the buying of a **field** (Jer 32:6-9), or the breaking of a potter's flask at Topheth in the valley of Ben-Hinnom with the prediction that it will become a burial place (Jer 19:1-13).

27:11 King of the Jews: this title is used of Jesus only by pagans. The Matthean instances are, besides this verse, Matthew 2:2; 27:29, 37. Matthew equates it with "Messiah"; cf. Matthew 2:2, 4 and 27:17, 22 where he has changed "the king of the Jews" of his Marcan source (Mk 15:9, 12) to "(Jesus) called Messiah." The normal

the king of the Jews?"* Jesus said, "You say so." [12]*f*And when he was accused by the chief priests and elders,* he made no answer. [13]Then Pilate said to him, "Do you not hear how many things they are testifying against you?" [14]But he did not answer him one word, so that the governor was greatly amazed.

The Sentence of Death

[15]*g*Now on the occasion of the feast the governor was accustomed to release to the crowd one prisoner whom they wished. [16]*And at that time they had a notorious prisoner called [Jesus] Barabbas. [17]So when they had assembled, Pilate said to them, "Which one do you want me to release to you, [Jesus] Barabbas, or Jesus called Messiah?" [18]*For he knew that it was out of envy that they had handed him over. [19]*While he was still seated on the bench, his wife sent him a message, "Have nothing to do with that righteous man. I suffered much in a dream today because of him." [20]*h*The chief priests and the elders persuaded the crowds to ask for Barabbas but to destroy Jesus. [21]The governor said to them in reply, "Which of the two do you want me to release to you?" They answered, "Barabbas!" [22]*Pilate said to them, "Then what shall I do with Jesus called Messiah?" They all said, "Let him be crucified!" [23]But he said, "Why? What evil has he done?" They only shouted the louder, "Let him be crucified!" [24]*i*When Pilate saw that he was not succeeding at all, but that a riot was breaking out instead, he took water and washed his hands in the sight of the crowd, saying, "I am innocent of this man's blood. Look to it yourselves." [25]And the whole people said in reply, "His blood be upon us and upon our children." [26]Then he released Barabbas to them, but after he had Jesus scourged,* he handed him over to be crucified.

f
Is 53:7

g
Mk 15:6-15;
Lk 23:17-25;
Jn 18:39–
19:16

h
Acts 3:14

i
Dt 21:1-8

---

political connotation of both titles would be of concern to the Roman **governor**. **You say so**: see the note on Matthew 26:25. An unqualified affirmative response is not made because Jesus' kingship is not what Pilate would understand it to be.

27:12-14 Cf. Matthew 26:62-63. As in the trial before the Sanhedrin, Jesus' silence may be meant to recall Isaiah 53:7. **Greatly amazed**: possibly an allusion to Isaiah 52:14-15.

27:15-26 The choice that Pilate offers **the crowd** between **Barabbas** and **Jesus** is said to be in accordance with a custom of releasing at the Passover feast **one prisoner** chosen by **the crowd** (27:15). This custom is mentioned also in Mark 15:6 and John 18:39 but not in Luke; see the note on Luke 23:17. Outside of the gospels there is no direct attestation of it, and scholars are divided in their judgment of the historical reliability of the claim that there was such a practice.

27:16-17 [Jesus] Barabbas: it is possible that the double name is the original reading; **Jesus** was a common Jewish name; see the note on Matthew 1:21. This reading is found in only a few textual witnesses, although its absence in the majority can be explained as an omission of **Jesus** made for reverential reasons. That name is bracketed because of its uncertain textual attestation. The Aramaic name **Barabbas** means "son of the father"; the irony of the choice offered between him and Jesus, the true son of the Father, would be evident to those addressees of Matthew who knew that.

27:18 Cf. Mark 14:10. This is an example of the tendency, found in varying degree in all the gospels, to present Pilate in a relatively favorable light and emphasize the hostility of the Jewish authorities and eventually of the people.

27:19 Jesus' innocence is declared by a Gentile woman. **In a dream**: in Matthew's infancy narrative, dreams are the means of divine communication; cf. Matthew 1:20; 2:12, 13, 19, 22.

27:22 Let him be crucified: incited by the chief priests and elders (27:20), the crowds demand that Jesus be executed by crucifixion, a peculiarly horrible form of Roman capital punishment. The Marcan parallel, "Crucify him" (Mk 15:3), addressed to Pilate, is changed by Matthew to the passive, probably to emphasize the responsibility of the crowds.

27:24-25 Peculiar to Matthew. **Took water . . . blood**: cf. Deuteronomy 21:1-8, the handwashing prescribed in the case of a murder when the killer is unknown. The elders of the city nearest to where the corpse is found must wash their hands, declaring, "Our hands did not shed this blood." **Look to it yourselves**: cf. Matthew 27:4. **The whole people**: Matthew sees in those who speak these words **the entire people** (Greek *laos*) of Israel. **His blood . . . and upon our children**: cf. Jeremiah 26:15. The responsibility for Jesus' death is accepted by the nation that was God's special possession (Ex 19:5), his own **people** (Hos 2:25), and they thereby lose that high privilege; see Matthew 21:43 and the note on that verse. The controversy between Matthew's church and Pharisaic Judaism about which was the true people of God is reflected here. As the Second Vatican Council has pointed out, guilt for Jesus' death is not attributable to all the Jews of his time or to any Jews of later times.

27:26 He had Jesus scourged: the usual preliminary to crucifixion.

j
Mk 15:16-20;
Jn 19:2-3

k
27:11

l
Is 50:6

m
Mk 15:21;
Lk 23:26

n
Mk 15:22-32;
Lk 23:32-38;
Jn 19:17-19,
23-24

o
Ps 69:21

p
Ps 22:19

q
Ps 22:8

r
4:3, 6; 26:61

Mockery by the Soldiers

[27]*j*Then the soldiers of the governor took Jesus inside the praetorium* and gathered the whole cohort around him. [28]They stripped off his clothes and threw a scarlet military cloak* about him. [29]*k*Weaving a crown out of thorns,* they placed it on his head, and a reed in his right hand. And kneeling before him, they mocked him, saying, "Hail, King of the Jews!" [30]*l*They spat upon him* and took the reed and kept striking him on the head. [31]And when they had mocked him, they stripped him of the cloak, dressed him in his own clothes, and led him off to crucify him.

The Way of the Cross

[32]*m*As they were going out, they met a Cyrenian named Simon; this man they pressed into service to carry his cross.

The Crucifixion

[33]*n*And when they came to a place called Golgotha (which means Place of the Skull), [34]*o*they gave Jesus wine to drink mixed with gall.* But when he had tasted it, he refused

Jesus crowned with thorns

to drink. [35]*p*After they had crucified him, they divided his garments* by casting lots; [36]then they sat down and kept watch over him there. [37]And they placed over his head the written charge* against him: This is Jesus, the King of the Jews. [38]Two revolutionaries* were crucified with him, one on his right and the other on his left. [39]*q*Those passing by reviled him, shaking their heads [40]*r*and saying, "You who would destroy the temple and rebuild it in three days, save yourself, if you are the Son of God, [and] come down from the cross!" [41]Likewise the chief priests with the scribes and elders mocked him and said,

---

27:27 The praetorium: the residence of the Roman governor. His usual place of residence was at Caesarea Maritima on the Mediterranean coast, but he went to Jerusalem during the great feasts, when the influx of pilgrims posed the danger of a nationalistic riot. It is disputed whether **the praetorium** in Jerusalem was the old palace of Herod in the west of the city or the fortress of Antonia northwest of the temple area. **The whole cohort**: normally six hundred soldiers.

27:28 Scarlet military cloak: so Matthew as against the royal purple of Mark 15:17 and John 19:2.

27:29 Crown out of thorns: probably of long **thorns** that stood upright so that it resembled the "radiant" **crown**, a diadem with spikes worn by Hellenistic kings. The soldiers' purpose was mockery, not torture. **A reed**: peculiar to Matthew; a mock scepter.

27:30 Spat upon him: cf. Matthew 26:67 where there also is a possible allusion to Isaiah 50:6.

27:32 See the note on Mark 15:21. **Cyrenian named Simon**: Cyrenaica was a Roman province on the north coast of Africa and Cyrene was its capital city. The city had a large population of Greek-speaking Jews. **Simon** may have been living in Palestine or have come there for the Passover as a pilgrim. **Pressed into service**: see the note on Matthew 5:41.

27:34 Wine . . . mixed with gall: cf. Mark 15:23 where the drink is "wine drugged with myrrh," a narcotic. Matthew's text is probably an inexact allusion to Psalm 69:22. That psalm belongs to the class called the individual lament, in which a persecuted just man prays for deliverance in the midst of great suffering and also expresses confidence that his prayer will be heard. That theme of the suffering Just One is frequently applied to the sufferings of Jesus in the passion narratives.

27:35 The clothing of an executed criminal went to his executioner(s), but the description of that procedure in the case of Jesus, found in all the gospels, is plainly inspired by Psalm 22:19. However, that psalm verse is quoted only in John 19:24.

27:37 The offense of a person condemned to death by crucifixion was written on a tablet that was displayed on his cross. The **charge** against **Jesus** was that he had claimed to be **the King of the Jews** (cf. 27:11), i.e., the Messiah (cf. 27:17, 22).

27:38 Revolutionaries: see the note on John 18:40 where the same Greek word as that found here is used for Barabbas.

27:39-40 Reviled him . . . heads: cf. Psalm 22:8. **You who would destroy . . . three days**; cf. Matthew 26:61. **If you are the Son of God**: the same words as those of the devil in the temptation of Jesus; cf. Matthew 4:3, 6.

42"He saved others; he cannot save himself. So he is the king of Israel!* Let him come down from the cross now, and we will believe in him. 43*ˢHe trusted in God; let him deliver him now if he wants him. For he said, 'I am the Son of God.'" 44The revolutionaries who were crucified with him also kept abusing him in the same way.

The Death of Jesus

45*ᵗFrom noon onward, darkness came over the whole land until three in the afternoon.ᵘ 46ᵛAnd about three o'clock Jesus cried out in a loud voice, "*Eli, Eli, lema sabachthani?*"* which means, "My God, my God, why have you forsaken me?" 47*Some of the bystanders who heard it said, "This one is calling for Elijah." 48ʷImmediately one of them ran to get a sponge; he soaked it in wine, and putting it on a reed, gave it to him to drink. 49But the rest said, "Wait, let us see if Elijah comes to save him." 50*But Jesus cried out again in a loud voice, and gave up his spirit. 51ˣAnd behold, the veil of the sanctuary was torn in two from top to bottom.* The earth quaked, rocks were split, 52ʸtombs were opened, and the bodies of many saints who had fallen asleep were raised. 53And coming forth from their tombs after his resurrection, they entered the holy city and appeared to many. 54*The centurion and the men with him who were keeping watch over Jesus feared greatly when they saw the earthquake and all that was happening, and they said, "Truly, this was the Son of God!" 55There were many women

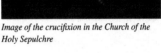

Image of the crucifixion in the Church of the Holy Sepulchre

s
Ps 22:9;
Wis 2:12-20

t
Mk 15:33-41;
Lk 23:44-49;
Jn 19:28-30

u
Am 8:9

v
Ps 22:2

w
Ps 69:21

x
Ex 26:31-36;
Pss 68:9;
77:19

y
Dn 12:1-3

27:42 King of Israel: in their mocking of Jesus the members of the Sanhedrin call themselves and their people not "the Jews" but **Israel**.

27:43 Peculiar to Matthew. **He trusted in God . . . wants him**: cf. Psalm 22:9. **He said . . . of God**: probably an allusion to Wisdom 2:12-20 where the theme of the suffering Just One appears.

27:45 Cf. Amos 8:9 where on the day of the Lord "the sun will set at midday."

27:46 Eli, Eli, lema sabachthani?: Jesus cries out in the words of Psalm 22:2, a psalm of lament that is the Old Testament passage most frequently drawn upon in this narrative. In Mark the verse is cited entirely in Aramaic, which Matthew partially retains but changes the invocation of God to the Hebrew *Eli*, possibly because that is more easily related to the statement of the following verse about Jesus' calling for Elijah.

27:47 Elijah: see the note on Matthew 3:4. This prophet, taken up into heaven (2 Kgs 2:11), was believed to come to the help of those in distress, but the evidences of that belief are all later than the gospels.

27:50 Gave up his spirit: cf. the Marcan parallel (Mk 15:37), "breathed his last." Matthew's alteration expresses both Jesus' control over his destiny and his obedient giving up of his life to God.

27:51-53 Veil of the sanctuary . . . bottom: cf. Mark 15:38; Luke 23:45. Luke puts this event immediately before the death of Jesus. There are two veils in the Mosaic tabernacle on the model of which the temple was constructed, the outer one before the entrance of the Holy Place and the inner one before the Holy of Holies

(see Ex 26:31-36). Only the high priest could pass through the latter and that only on the Day of Atonement (see Lv 16:1-18). Probably the **torn veil** of the gospels is the inner one. The meaning of the scene may be that now, because of Jesus' death, all people have access to the presence of God, or that the temple, its holiest part standing exposed, is now profaned and will soon be destroyed. **The earth quaked . . . appeared to many**: peculiar to Matthew. The earthquake, the splitting of the **rocks**, and especially the resurrection of the dead **saints** indicate the coming of the final age. In the Old Testament the coming of God is frequently portrayed with the imagery of an earthquake (see Pss 68:9; 77:19), and Jesus speaks of the earthquakes that will accompany the "labor pains" that signify the beginning of the dissolution of the old world (24:7-8). For the expectation of the resurrection of the dead at the coming of the new and final age, see Daniel 12:1-3. Matthew knows that the end of the old age has not yet come (28:20), but the new age has broken in with the death (and resurrection; cf. the earthquake in 28:2) of Jesus; see the note on Matthew 16:28. **After his resurrection**: this qualification seems to be due to Matthew's wish to assert the primacy of Jesus' **resurrection** even though he has placed the resurrection of the dead **saints** immediately after Jesus' death.

27:54 Cf. Mark 15:39. The Christian confession of faith is made by Gentiles, not only **the centurion**, as in Mark, but the other soldiers **who were keeping watch over Jesus** (cf. 27:36).

27:55-56 Looking on from a distance: cf. Psalm 38:12. **Mary Magdalene . . . Joseph**: these two women are mentioned again in Matthew 27:61 and 28:1 and are important as witnesses of the

95

z	13:55
a	Mk 15:42-47; Lk 23:50-56; Jn 19:38-42
b	Is 53:9
c	12:40; 16:21; 17:23; 20:19

there, looking on from a distance,* who had followed Jesus from Galilee, ministering to him. [56z]Among them were Mary Magdalene and Mary the mother of James and Joseph, and the mother of the sons of Zebedee.

The Burial of Jesus

[57*a]When it was evening, there came a rich man from Arimathea named Joseph, who was himself a disciple of Jesus.[b] [58]He went to Pilate and asked for the body of Jesus; then Pilate ordered it to be handed over. [59]Taking the body, Joseph wrapped it [in] clean linen [60]and laid it in his new tomb that he had hewn in the rock. Then he rolled a huge stone across the entrance to the tomb and departed. [61]But Mary Magdalene and the other Mary remained sitting there, facing the tomb.

The Guard at the Tomb

[62]*The next day, the one following the day of preparation,* the chief priests and the Pharisees gathered before Pilate [63c]and said, "Sir, we remember that this impostor while still alive said, 'After three days I will be raised up.' [64]Give orders, then, that the grave

Joseph of Arimathea

Toward the end of all four gospels, one person is named explicitly in relation to the burial of Jesus: Joseph of Arimathea. Burial was a necessity of Jewish law that opened Joseph to ritual impurity. Who was Joseph? And how is his role described in each gospel account?

Mark 15:42-46: The earliest gospel calls Joseph "a distinguished member of the council" (presumably the Sanhedrin) who was "awaiting the kingdom of God." Mark, known for describing discipleship as carrying the cross, notes Joseph's courage in asking Pilate for the body of one crucified.

Matthew 27:57-60: Noting that Joseph was a "rich man," Matthew identifies him as a disciple of Jesus. In this account, Joseph uses his own tomb for Jesus, emphasizing personal generosity.

Luke 23:50-54: Here Joseph is identified as "virtuous and righteous." Though a member of the

council, Joseph apparently did not go along with their plans about Jesus. In this account, Joseph buries Jesus in a rock-hewn tomb that is unused by anyone else.

John 19:38-42: The final gospel writer notes that Joseph was "secretly a disciple of Jesus for fear of the Jews" and that he was accompanied by Nicodemus when they buried Jesus in a new tomb. Recall that Nicodemus had earlier come to Jesus under cover of darkness (Jn 3:1-21), perhaps also fearful.

It appears that Joseph's secret devotion to Jesus was made public at the cross and tomb. His care of Jesus' body foreshadows the care every disciple of Jesus must have for the Body of Christ. His witness of courage in spite of fear, virtue in the face of injustice, and personal generosity model for us the way to follow the risen Christ.

---

reality of the empty tomb. A **James** and **Joseph** are referred to in Matthew 13:55 as brothers of Jesus.

27:57-61 Cf. Mark 15:42-47. Matthew drops Mark's designation of **Joseph** of **Arimathea** as "a distinguished member of the council" (the Sanhedrin), and makes him **a rich man** and **a disciple of Jesus**. The former may be an allusion to Isaiah 53:9 (the Hebrew reading of that text is disputed and the one followed in the NAB OT has nothing about the rich, but they are mentioned in the LXX version). That the tomb was the **new tomb** of **a rich man** and that it was seen by the women are indications of an apologetic intent of Matthew; there could be no question about the identity of Jesus' burial place. **The other Mary**: the mother of James and Joseph (56).

27:62-66 Peculiar to Matthew. The story prepares for Matthew 28:11-15 and the Jewish charge that the tomb was empty because the disciples had stolen the body of Jesus (28:13, 15).

27:62 The next day . . . preparation: the sabbath. According to the synoptic chronology, in that year **the day of preparation** (for the sabbath) was the Passover; cf. Mark 15:42. **The Pharisees**: the principal opponents of Jesus during his ministry and, in Matthew's time, of the Christian church, join with **the chief priests** to guarantee against a possible attempt of Jesus' **disciples** to steal his body.

27:64 This last imposture . . . the first: the claim that Jesus **has been raised from the dead** is clearly the **last imposture; the first** may be either his claim that he would **be raised up** (63) or his

be secured until the third day, lest his disciples come and steal him and say to the people, 'He has been raised from the dead.' This last imposture would be worse than the first."* ⁶⁵Pilate said to them, "The guard is yours;* go secure it as best you can." ⁶⁶So they went and secured the tomb by fixing a seal to the stone and setting the guard.

The Resurrection of Jesus

28 ¹*ᵃAfter the sabbath, as the first day of the week was dawning,* Mary Magdalene and the other Mary came to see the tomb. ²*ᵇAnd behold, there was a great earthquake; for an angel of the Lord descended from heaven, approached, rolled back the stone, and sat upon it. ³ᶜHis appearance was like lightning and his clothing was white as snow. ⁴The guards were shaken with fear of him and became like dead men. ⁵Then the angel said to the women in reply, "Do not be afraid! I know that you are seeking Jesus the crucified. ⁶*He is not here, for he has been raised just as he said. Come and see the place where he lay. ⁷ᵈThen go quickly and tell his disciples, 'He has been raised from the dead, and he is going before you to Galilee; there you will see him.' Behold, I have told you." ⁸Then they went away quickly from the tomb, fearful yet overjoyed, and ran to announce* this to his disciples. ⁹*ᵉAnd behold, Jesus met them on their way and greeted them. They approached, embraced his feet, and did him homage. ¹⁰Then Jesus said to them, "Do not be afraid. Go tell my brothers to go to Galilee, and there they will see me."

The church reads this **account of Jesus' resurrection** at the Easter Vigil of Year A. It is one of the most detailed accounts of the resurrection in the NT.

---

a Mk 16:1-8; Lk 24:1-12; Jn 20:1-10

b 25:51

c 17:2

d 26:32

e Jn 20:17

---

claim that he was the one with whose ministry the kingdom of God had come (see 12:28).

27:65 The guard is yours: literally, "have a guard" or "you have a guard." Either the imperative or the indicative could mean that Pilate granted the petitioners some Roman soldiers as guards, which is the sense of the present translation. However, if the verb is taken as an indicative it could also mean that Pilate told them to use their own Jewish guards.

28:1-20 Except for Matthew 28:1-8 based on Mark 16:1-8, the material of this final chapter is peculiar to Matthew. Even where he follows Mark, Matthew has altered his source so greatly that a very different impression is given from that of the Marcan account. The two points that are common to the resurrection testimony of all the gospels are that the tomb of Jesus had been found empty and that the risen Jesus had appeared to certain persons, or, in the original form of Mark, that such an appearance was promised as soon to take place (see Mk 16:7). On this central and all-important basis, Matthew has constructed an account that interprets the resurrection as the turning of the ages (28:2-4), shows the Jewish opposition to Jesus as continuing **to the present** in the claim that the resurrection is a deception perpetrated by the **disciples** who stole his body from the tomb (28:11-15), and marks a new stage in the mission of **the disciples** once limited to Israel (10:5-6); now they are to **make disciples of all nations**. In this work they will be strengthened by the presence of the exalted Son of Man, who will be with them **until** the kingdom comes in fullness at **the end of the age** (28:16-20).

28:1 After the sabbath . . . dawning: since the sabbath ended at sunset, this could mean in the early evening, for **dawning** can refer to the appearance of the evening star; cf. Luke 23:54. However, it is probable that Matthew means the morning dawn of the day after the sabbath, as in the similar though slightly different text of Mark, "when the sun had risen" (Mk 16:2). **Mary Magdalene and**

the other Mary: see the notes on Matthew 27:55-56; 57-61. **To see the tomb**: cf. Mark 16:1-2 where the purpose of the women's visit is to anoint Jesus' body.

28:2-4 Peculiar to Matthew. **A great earthquake**: see the note on Matthew 27:51-53. **Descended from heaven**: this trait is peculiar to Matthew, although his interpretation of the "young man" of his Marcan source (Mk 16:5) as an **angel** is probably true to Mark's intention; cf. Luke 24:23 where the "two men" of Luke 24:4 are said to be "angels." **Rolled back the stone . . . upon it**: not to allow the risen Jesus to leave the tomb but to make evident that the tomb is empty (see 28:6). Unlike the apocryphal Gospel of Peter (9:35–11:44), the New Testament does not describe the resurrection of Jesus, nor is there anyone who sees it. **His appearance was like lightning . . . snow**: see the note on Matthew 17:2.

28:6-7 Cf. Mark 16:6-7. **Just as he said**: a Matthean addition referring to Jesus' predictions of his resurrection, e.g., Matthew 16:21; 17:23; 20:19. **Tell his disciples**: like the angel of the Lord of the infancy narrative, the angel interprets a fact and gives a commandment about what is to be done; cf. Matthew 1:20-21. Matthew omits Mark's "and Peter" (Mk 16:7); considering his interest in Peter, this omission is curious. Perhaps the reason is that the Marcan text may allude to a first appearance of Jesus to Peter alone (cf. 1 Cor 15:5; Lk 24:34) which Matthew has already incorporated into his account of Peter's confession at Caesarea Philippi; see the note on Matthew 16:16. **He is going . . . Galilee**: like Mark 16:7, a reference to Jesus' prediction at the Last Supper (26:32; Mk 14:28). Matthew changes Mark's "as he told you" to a declaration of the angel.

28:8 Contrast Mark 16:8 where the women in their fear "said nothing to anyone."

28:9-10 Although these verses are peculiar to Matthew, there are similarities between them and John's account of the appearance of Jesus to Mary Magdalene (Jn 20:17). In both there is a

f
Mk 16:14-16;
Lk 24:36-49;
Jn 20:19-23

g
Dn 7:14 LXX

h
Acts 1:8

i
1:23; 13:39;
24:3

The Report of the Guard

[11]*While they were going, some of the guard went into the city and told the chief priests all that had happened. [12]They assembled with the elders and took counsel; then they gave a large sum of money to the soldiers, [13]telling them, "You are to say, 'His disciples came by night and stole him while we were asleep.' [14]And if this gets to the ears of the governor, we will satisfy [him] and keep you out of trouble." [15]The soldiers took the money and did as they were instructed. And this story has circulated among the Jews to the present [day].

The Commissioning of the Disciples

[16]*[f]The eleven* disciples went to Galilee, to the mountain to which Jesus had ordered them. [17]*When they saw him, they worshiped, but they doubted. [18]*[g]Then Jesus approached and said to them, "All power in heaven and on earth has been given to me. [19][h]Go, therefore,* and make disciples of all nations, baptizing them in the name of the Father, and of the Son, and of the holy Spirit, [20][i]teaching them to observe all that I have commanded you.* And behold, I am with you always, until the end of the age."

---

touching of Jesus' body, and a command of Jesus to bear a message to his disciples, designated as his **brothers**. Matthew may have drawn upon a tradition that appears in a different form in John. Jesus' words to the women are mainly a repetition of those of the angel (28:5a, 7b).

28:11-15 This account indicates that the dispute between Christians and Jews about the empty tomb was not whether the tomb was empty but why.

28:16-20 This climactic scene has been called a "proleptic parousia," for it gives a foretaste of the final glorious coming of the Son of Man (26:64). Then his triumph will be manifest to all; now it is revealed only to **the disciples**, who are commissioned to announce it to **all nations** and bring them to belief in Jesus and obedience to his commandments.

28:16 The eleven: the number recalls the tragic defection of Judas Iscariot. **To the mountain . . . ordered them**: since the message to **the disciples** was simply that they were to go to Galilee (28:10), some think that **the mountain** comes from a tradition of the message known to Matthew and alluded to here. For the significance of **the mountain**, see the note on Matthew 17:1.

28:17 But they doubted: the Greek can also be translated, "but some doubted." The verb occurs elsewhere in the New Testament only in Matthew 14:31 where it is associated with Peter's being of "little faith." For the meaning of that designation, see the note on Matthew 6:30.

28:18 All power . . . me: the Greek word here translated power is the same as that found in the LXX translation of Daniel 7:13-14 where one "like a son of man" is given **power** and an everlasting kingdom by God. The risen Jesus here claims universal power, i.e., **in heaven and on earth**.

28:19 Therefore: since universal power belongs to the risen Jesus (28:18), he gives the eleven a mission that is universal. They are to **make disciples of all nations**. While **all nations** is understood by some scholars as referring only to all Gentiles, it is prob-

Matthew's scene of **Jesus commissioning the disciples** is one of the most powerful in the NT. It emphasizes the worldwide task of evangelization, carrying forth the Good News (Gospel) of Jesus Christ. In 1990, Pope John Paul II called for a new evangelization: "I wish to invite the Church to renew her missionary commitment . . . For missionary activity renews the Church, revitalizes faith and Christian identity, and offers fresh enthusiasm and new incentive. Faith is strengthened when it is given to others! It is in commitment to the Church's universal mission that the new evangelization of Christian peoples will find inspiration and support" (*RM*, 2).

able that it included the Jews as well. **Baptizing them**: baptism is the means of entrance into the community of the risen one, the Church. **In the name of the Father . . . holy Spirit**: this is perhaps the clearest expression in the New Testament of trinitarian belief. It may have been the baptismal formula of Matthew's church, but primarily it designates the effect of baptism, the union of the one baptized with the Father, Son, and holy Spirit.

28:20 All that I have commanded you: the moral teaching found in this gospel, preeminently that of the Sermon on the Mount (5–7). The commandments of Jesus are the standard of Christian conduct, not the Mosaic law as such, even though some of the Mosaic commandments have now been invested with the authority of Jesus. **Behold, I am with you always**: the promise of Jesus' real though invisible presence echoes the name Emmanuel given to him in the infancy narrative; see the note on Matthew 1:23. **End of the age**: see the notes on Matthew 13:39 and 24:3.

This shortest of all New Testament gospels is likely the first to have been written, yet it often tells of Jesus' ministry in more detail than either Matthew or Luke (for example, the miracle stories at 5:1-20 or 9:14-29). It recounts what Jesus did in a vivid style, where one incident follows directly upon another. In this almost breathless narrative, Mark stresses Jesus' message about the kingdom of God now breaking into human life as good news (1:14-15) and Jesus himself as the gospel of God (1:1; 8:35; 10:29). Jesus is the Son whom God has sent to rescue humanity by serving and by sacrificing his life (10:45).

The opening verse about good news in Mark (1:1) serves as a title for the entire book. The action begins with the appearance of John the Baptist, a messenger of God attested by scripture. But John points to a mightier one, Jesus, at whose baptism God speaks from heaven, declaring Jesus his Son. The Spirit descends upon Jesus, who eventually, it is promised, will baptize "with the holy Spirit." This presentation of who Jesus really is (1:1-13) is rounded out with a brief reference to the temptation of Jesus and how Satan's attack fails. Jesus as Son of God will be victorious, a point to be remembered as one reads of Jesus' death and the enigmatic ending to Mark's Gospel.

The key verses at Mark 1:14-15, which are programmatic, summarize what Jesus proclaims as gospel: fulfillment, the nearness of the kingdom, and therefore the need for repentance and for faith. After the call of the first four disciples, all fishermen (1:16-20), we see Jesus engaged in teaching

SUMMARY

Mark recounts the story of Jesus of Nazareth, emphasizing his identity as Son of God and powerful miracle worker. The gospel begins with John the Baptist's preaching and extends through Jesus' public ministry of miracles and teaching, concluding with his passion, death, and resurrection, and the discovery of the empty tomb.

Author: Unknown, but ancient tradition calls him "Mark" and identifies him with John Mark (Acts 12:12), a cousin of Barnabas, and sometime interpreter for the apostle Peter.

Date: Shortly before A.D. 70.

Content: John the Baptist's announcement of Jesus' coming; Jesus' baptism by John; many miracle stories; Peter's confession of faith; the transfiguration; the passion, death, and resurrection of Jesus; story of the empty tomb.

Main Characters: Jesus of Nazareth, John the Baptist, Peter, Andrew, James and John (the sons of Zebedee), some Jewish leaders opposed to Jesus, Judas Iscariot, Pontius Pilate.

(1:21, 22, 27), preaching (1:38, 39), and healing (1:29-31, 34, 40-45), and exorcising demons (1:22-27, 34, 39). The content of Jesus' teaching is only rarely stated, and then chiefly in parables (chap. 4) about the kingdom. His cures, especially on the sabbath (3:1-5); his claim, like God, to forgive sins (2:3-12); his table fellowship with tax collectors and sinners (2:14-17); and the statement that his followers need not now fast but should rejoice while Jesus is present (2:18-22), all stir up opposition that will lead to Jesus' death (3:6).

In Mark, Jesus is portrayed as immensely popular with the people in Galilee during his ministry (2:2; 3:7; 4:1). He appoints twelve disciples to help preach and drive out demons, just as he does (3:13-19). He continues to work many miracles; the blocks Mark 4:35–6:44 and 6:45–7:10 are cycles of stories about healings, miracles at the Sea of Galilee, and marvelous feedings of the crowds. Jesus' teaching in Mark 7 exalts the word of God over "the tradition of the elders" and sees defilement as a matter of the heart, not of unclean foods. Yet opposition mounts. Scribes charge that Jesus is possessed by Beelzebul (3:22). His relatives think him "out of his mind" (3:21). Jesus' kinship is with those who do the will of God, in a new eschatological family, not even with mother, brothers, or sisters by blood ties (3:31-35; cf. 6:1-6). But all too often his own disciples do not understand Jesus (4:13, 40; 6:52; 8:17-21). The fate of John the Baptist (6:17-29) hints ominously at Jesus' own passion (9:13; cf. 8:31).

A breakthrough seemingly comes with Peter's confession that Jesus is the Christ (Messiah; 8:27-30). But Jesus himself emphasizes his passion (8:31; 9:31; 10:33-34), not glory in the kingdom (10:35-45). Momentarily he is glimpsed in his true identity when he is transfigured before three of the disciples (9:2-8), but by and large Jesus is depicted in Mark as moving obediently along the way to his cross in Jerusalem. Occasionally there are miracles (9:17-27; 10:46-52; 11:12-14, 20-21, the only such account in Jerusalem), sometimes teachings (10:2-11, 23-31), but the greatest concern is with discipleship (8:34–9:1; 9:33-50). For the disciples do not grasp the mystery being revealed (9:32;

10:32, 38). One of them will betray him, Judas (14:10-11, 43-45); one will deny him, Peter (14:27, 31, 54, 66-72); all eleven men will desert Jesus (14:27, 50).

The passion account, with its condemnation of Jesus by the Sanhedrin (14:53, 55-65; 15:1a) and sentencing by Pilate (15:1b-15), is prefaced with the entry into Jerusalem (11:1-11), ministry and controversies there (11:15–12:44), Jesus' Last Supper with the disciples (14:1-26), and his arrest at Gethsemane (14:32-52). A chapter of apocalyptic tone about the destruction of the temple (13:1-2, 14-23) and the coming of the Son of Man (13:24-27), a discourse filled with promises (13:11, 31) and admonitions to be watchful (13:2, 23, 37), is significant for Mark's Gospel, for it helps one see that God, in Jesus, will be victorious after the cross and at the end of history.

The Gospel of Mark ends in the most ancient manuscripts with an abrupt scene at Jesus' tomb, which the women find empty (16:1-8). His own prophecy of Mark 14:28 is reiterated, that Jesus goes before the disciples into Galilee; "there you will see him." These words may imply resurrection appearances there, or Jesus' parousia there, or the start of Christian mission, or a return to the roots depicted in Mark 1:9, 14-15 in Galilee. Other hands have attached additional endings after Mark 16:8; see the note on Mark 16:9-20.

The framework of Mark's Gospel is partly geographical: Galilee (1:14–9:49), through the area "across the Jordan" (10:1) and through Jericho (10:46-52), to Jerusalem (11:1–16:8). Only rarely does Jesus go into Gentile territory (5:1-20; 7:24-37), but those who acknowledge him there and the centurion who confesses Jesus at the cross (15:39) presage the gospel's expansion into the world beyond Palestine.

Mark's Gospel is even more oriented to christology. Jesus is the Son of God (1:11; 9:7; 15:39; cf. 1:1; 14:61). He is the Messiah, the anointed king of Davidic descent (12:35; 15:32), the Greek for which, *Christos*, has, by the time Mark wrote, become in effect a proper name (1:1; 9:41). Jesus is also seen as Son of Man, a term used in Mark not simply as a substitute for "I" or for humanity in

general (cf. 2:10, 27-28; 14:21) or with reference to a mighty figure who is to come (13:26; 14:62), but also in connection with Jesus' predestined, necessary path of suffering and vindication (8:31; 10:45).

The unfolding of Mark's story about Jesus is sometimes viewed by interpreters as centered around the term "mystery." The word is employed just once, at Mark 4:11, in the singular, and its content there is the kingdom, the open secret that God's reign is now breaking into human life with its reversal of human values. There is a related sense in which Jesus' real identity remained a secret during his lifetime, according to Mark, although demons and demoniacs knew it (1:24; 3:11; 5:7); Jesus warned against telling of his mighty deeds and revealing his identity (1:44; 3:12; 5:43; 7:36; 8:26, 30), an injunction sometimes broken (1:45; cf. 5:19-20). Further, Jesus teaches by parables, according to Mark, in such a way that those "outside" the kingdom do not understand, but only those to whom the mystery has been granted by God.

Mark thus shares with Paul, as well as with other parts of the New Testament, an emphasis on election (13:20, 22) and upon the gospel as Christ and his cross (cf. 1 Cor 1:23). Yet in Mark the person of Jesus is also depicted with an unaffected naturalness. He reacts to events with authentic human emotion: pity (1:44), anger (3:5), triumph (4:40), sympathy (5:36; 6:34), surprise (6:9), admiration (7:29; 10:21), sadness (14:33-34), and indignation (14:48-49).

Although the book is anonymous, apart from the ancient heading "According to Mark" in manuscripts, it has traditionally been assigned to John Mark, in whose mother's house (at Jerusalem) Christians assembled (Acts 12:12). This Mark was a cousin of Barnabas (Col 4:10) and accompanied Barnabas and Paul on a missionary journey (Acts 12:25; 13:3; 15:36-39). He appears in Pauline letters (2 Tm 4:11; Phlm 1:24) and with Peter (1 Pt 5:13). Papias (ca. A.D. 135) described Mark as Peter's "interpreter," a view found in other patristic writers. Petrine influence should not, however, be exaggerated. The evangelist has put together various oral and possibly written sources—miracle stories, parables, sayings, stories of controversies, and the passion—so as to speak of the crucified Messiah for Mark's own day.

Traditionally, the gospel is said to have been written shortly before A.D. 70 in Rome, at a time of impending persecution and when destruction loomed over Jerusalem. Its audience seems to have been Gentile, unfamiliar with Jewish customs (hence 7:3-4, 11). The book aimed to equip such Christians to stand faithful in the face of persecution (13:9-13), while going on with the proclamation of the gospel begun in Galilee (13:10; 14:9). Modern research often proposes as the author an unknown Hellenistic Jewish Christian, possibly in Syria, and perhaps shortly after the year 70.

The principal divisions of the Gospel according to Mark are the following:

I. The Preparation for the Public Ministry of Jesus (1:1-13)

II. The Mystery of Jesus (1:14–8:26)

III. The Mystery Begins to Be Revealed (8:27–9:32)

IV. The Full Revelation of the Mystery (9:33–16:8)
The Longer Ending (16:9-20)
The Shorter Ending
The Freer Logion (in the note on 16:9-20)

a
Mt 3:1-11;
Lk 3:2-16

b
Mal 3:1

c
Is 40:3;
Jn 1:23

d
Jn 1:27;
Acts 1:5; 11:16

e
Mt 3:13-17;
Lk 3:21-23;
Jn 1:32-33

f
Ps 2:7

g
Mt 4:1-11;
Lk 4:1-13

I: The Preparation for the Public Ministry of Jesus

1 ¹*The beginning of the gospel of Jesus Christ [the Son of God].*

The Preaching of John the Baptist

²*a*As it is written in Isaiah the prophet:*ᵇ

"Behold, I am sending my messenger ahead of you;
  he will prepare your way.
³*c*A voice of one crying out in the desert:
  'Prepare the way of the Lord,
  make straight his paths.'"

⁴John [the] Baptist appeared in the desert proclaiming a baptism of repentance for the forgiveness of sins. ⁵People of the whole Judean countryside and all the inhabitants of Jerusalem were going out to him and were being baptized by him in the Jordan River as they acknowledged their sins. ⁶John was clothed in camel's hair, with a leather belt around his waist.* He fed on locusts and wild honey. ⁷And this is what he proclaimed: "One mightier than I is coming after me. I am not worthy to stoop and loosen the thongs of his sandals. ⁸*d*I have baptized you with water; he will baptize you with the holy Spirit."

The Baptism of Jesus

⁹*e*It happened in those days that Jesus came from Nazareth of Galilee and was baptized in the Jordan by John. ¹⁰On coming up out of the water he saw the heavens being torn open and the Spirit, like a dove, descending upon him.* ¹¹*f*And a voice came from the heavens, "You are my beloved Son; with you I am well pleased."

The Temptation of Jesus

¹²*g*At once the Spirit drove him out into the desert, ¹³and he remained in the desert for forty days, tempted by Satan. He was among wild beasts, and the angels ministered to him.

1:1-13 The prologue of the Gospel according to Mark begins with the title (1:1) followed by three events preparatory to Jesus' preaching: (1) the appearance in the Judean wilderness of John, baptizer, preacher of repentance, and precursor of Jesus (1:2-8); (2) the baptism of Jesus, at which a voice from heaven acknowledges Jesus to be God's Son, and the holy Spirit descends on him (1:9-11); (3) the temptation of Jesus by Satan (1:12-13).

1:1 The gospel of Jesus Christ [the Son of God]: the "good news" of salvation in and through Jesus, crucified and risen, acknowledged by the Christian community as Messiah (8:29; 14:61-62) and Son of God (1:11; 9:7; 15:39), although some important manuscripts here omit **the Son of God**.

1:2-3 Although Mark attributes the prophecy to Isaiah, the text is a combination of Malachi 3:1; Isaiah 40:3; Exodus 23:20; cf. Matthew 11:10; Luke 7:27. John's ministry is seen as God's prelude to the saving mission of his Son. **The way of the Lord**: this prophecy of Deutero-Isaiah concerning the end of the Babylonian exile is here applied to the coming of Jesus; John the Baptist is to prepare the way for him.

1:6 **Clothed in camel's hair . . . waist**: the Baptist's garb recalls that of Elijah in 2 Kings 1:8. Jesus speaks of the Baptist as Elijah who has already come (9:11-13; Mt 17:10-12; cf. Mal 3:19; Lk 1:17).

1:8-9 Through the life-giving baptism with the holy Spirit (1:8), Jesus will create a new people of God. But first he identifies himself with the people of Israel in submitting to John's baptism of repentance and in bearing on their behalf the burden of God's decisive judgment (1:9; cf. 1:4). As in the desert of Sinai, so here in the wilderness of Judea, Israel's sonship with God is to be renewed.

1:10-11 **He saw the heavens . . . and the Spirit . . . upon him**: indicating divine intervention in fulfillment of promise. Here the descent of the Spirit on Jesus is meant, anointing him for his ministry; cf. Isaiah 11:2; 42:1; 61:1; 63:9. **A voice . . . with you I am well pleased**: God's acknowledgment of Jesus as his unique Son, the object of his love. His approval of Jesus is the assurance that Jesus will fulfill his messianic mission of salvation.

1:12-13 The same Spirit who descended on Jesus in his baptism now drives him into the desert for forty days. The result is

II: *The Mystery of Jesus*

The Beginning of the Galilean Ministry

^{14h}After John had been arrested,* Jesus came to Galilee proclaiming the gospel of God: ¹⁵ⁱ"This is the time of fulfillment. The kingdom of God is at hand. Repent, and believe in the gospel."

h
Mt 4:12-17;
Lk 4:14-15

i
Mt 3:2

John the Baptist

All four gospels feature John, but only the Synoptics call him "the Baptist" (because of his activity of baptizing for the forgiveness of sins). In his writings, Josephus, the first-century Jewish historian, describes John and his ministry of baptism. John was a relative of Jesus, the son of Zechariah the priest, and Elizabeth, who was related to Mary, mother of Jesus.

Luke alone in the NT provides detailed background of John, indicating that his parents were devout Jews associated with the temple in Jerusalem (Lk 1:5-17). The story is replete with OT imagery, which helps to flesh out John's identity as a prophet. In fulfillment of God's will, John is dedicated to the service of God and becomes destined to be a great leader who will turn the people back to God.

John was an ascetic who lived a simple life in wilderness settings. Exactly how John came to exercise his ministry of repentance by baptizing with water at the Jordan River is uncertain. Scholars suggest that he may have been associated with the Qumran community near the Dead Sea. Those living there, the Essenes, used ritual bathing as a sign of spiritual cleansing. Archaeologists have unearthed some pools used for these rites. They lived an ascetical life, believing that they were preserving the authentic Jewish faith.

Regardless of John's possible connection with Qumran, John had disciples of his own (Jn 3:25) who likely identified him as the Messiah. Some of these disciples later became Jesus' disciples (Jn 1:35-37). The Synoptic Gospels also narrate John's baptism of Jesus, albeit each with different details. The fact of Jesus' baptism clearly caused some anxiety among early Christians, as baptism was associated with cleansing from sin. Since Jesus was considered born sinless, they viewed his baptism as unnecessary (cf. Mt 4:14-15). The gospels, however, associate Jesus' baptism primarily not with washing sin away but with the inauguration of Jesus' mission of preaching, teaching, and healing.

John's intense ministry resulted in conflict with both religious and political authorities. The Jewish leaders allied to the temple were afraid of him, and Herod Antipas, tetrarch of Galilee and Perea, had John beheaded because he dared oppose his marriage to his half-brother's wife (Mt 14:3-12; Mk 6:17-29). This intriguing story has been celebrated in art and even in music (e.g., Richard Strauss' opera *Salome*).

From the NT perspective, John's primary significance is as the forerunner of Jesus. Matthew explicitly identifies him with Elijah (17:11-13), the OT prophet who was expected to precede the Messiah in the apocalyptic time of trials and tribulations. John's gospel, which does not emphasize John's baptismal activity but his preaching and his identification of Jesus as the "Lamb of God," portrays John as a minor lamp who prepares for the coming of "the light of the world" and gives testimony about him (Jn 1:1-30). In a sense, the NT portrait of John makes him a transitional figure who embodies the essence of OT prophecy, on the one hand, but prepares for the totally new ways of Jesus the Messiah, on the other.

---

radical confrontation and temptation by Satan who attempts to frustrate the work of God. The presence of wild beasts may indicate the horror and danger of the desert regarded as the abode of demons or may reflect the paradise motif of harmony among all creatures; cf. Isaiah 11:6-9. The presence of ministering angels to sustain Jesus recalls the angel who guided the Israelites in the desert in the first Exodus (Ex 14:19; 23:20) and the angel who supplied nourishment to Elijah in the wilderness (1 Kgs 19:5-7). The combined forces of good and evil were present to Jesus in the desert. His sustained obedience brings forth the new Israel of God there where Israel's rebellion had brought death and alienation.

1:14-15 After John had been arrested: in the plan of God, Jesus was not to proclaim the good news of salvation prior to the termination of the Baptist's active mission. In the Marcan account, scene of the major part of Jesus' public ministry before his arrest and condemnation. **The gospel of God**: not only the good news from God but about God at work in Jesus Christ. **This is the time of fulfillment**: i.e., of God's promises. **The kingdom of God . . . repent**: see the note on Matthew 3:2.

j
Mt 4:18-22;
Lk 5:2-11

k
Lk 4:31-37

l
Mt 7:28-29

m
Mt 8:14-16;
Lk 4:38-41

MARK

The Call of the First Disciples

[16]*[j]As he passed by the Sea of Galilee, he saw Simon and his brother Andrew casting their nets into the sea; they were fishermen. [17]Jesus said to them, "Come after me, and I will make you fishers of men." [18]Then they abandoned their nets and followed him. [19]He walked along a little farther and saw James, the son of Zebedee, and his brother John. They too were in a boat mending their nets. [20]Then he called them. So they left their father Zebedee in the boat along with the hired men and followed him.

The Cure of a Demoniac

[21]*[k]Then they came to Capernaum, and on the sabbath he entered the synagogue and taught. [22][l]The people were astonished at his teaching, for he taught them as one having authority and not as the scribes. [23]*In their synagogue was a man with an unclean spirit; [24]*he cried out, "What have you to do with us,* Jesus of Nazareth? Have you come to destroy us? I know who you are—the Holy One of God!" [25]Jesus rebuked him and said, "Quiet! Come out of him!" [26]The unclean spirit convulsed him and with a loud cry came out of him. [27]All were amazed and asked one another, "What is this? A new teaching with authority. He commands even the unclean spirits and they obey him." [28]His fame spread everywhere throughout the whole region of Galilee.

First-century fishing boat mosaic at Magdala

The Cure of Simon's Mother-in-Law

[29][m]On leaving the synagogue he entered the house of Simon and Andrew with James and John. [30]Simon's mother-in-law lay sick with a fever. They immediately told him about her. [31]He approached, grasped her hand, and helped her up. Then the fever left her and she waited on them.

Other Healings

[32]When it was evening, after sunset, they brought to him all who were ill or possessed by demons. [33]The whole town was gathered at the door. [34]He cured many who were sick with various diseases, and he drove out many demons, not permitting them to speak because they knew him.

Sunset on the Sea of Galilee

1:16-20 These verses narrate the call of the first Disciples. See the notes on Matthew 4:18-22 and 4:20.

1:21-45 The account of a single day's ministry of Jesus on a sabbath in and outside the synagogue of Capernaum (1:21-31) combines teaching and miracles of exorcism and healing. Mention is not made of the content of the teaching but of the effect of astonishment and alarm on the people. Jesus' teaching with authority, making an absolute claim on the hearer, was in the best tradition of the ancient prophets, not of the scribes. The narrative continues with events that evening (1:32-34; see the notes on Mt 8:14-17)

and the next day (1:35-39). The cleansing in Mark 1:40-45 stands as an isolated story.

1:23 An unclean spirit: so called because of the spirit's resistance to the holiness of God. The spirit knows and fears the power of Jesus to destroy his influence; cf. Mark 1:32, 34; 3:11; 6:13.

1:24-25 The Holy One of God: not a confession but an attempt to ward off Jesus' power, reflecting the notion that use of the precise name of an opposing spirit would guarantee mastery over him. Jesus silenced the cry of the unclean spirit and drove him out of the man.

1:24 What have you to do with us?: see the note on John 2:4.

Jesus Leaves Capernaum

[35]nRising very early before dawn, he left and went off to a deserted place, where he prayed. [36]Simon and those who were with him pursued him [37]and on finding him said, "Everyone is looking for you." [38]He told them, "Let us go on to the nearby villages that I may preach there also. For this purpose have I come." [39]So he went into their synagogues, preaching and driving out demons throughout the whole of Galilee.

The Cleansing of a Leper

[40]oA leper* came to him [and kneeling down] begged him and said, "If you wish, you can make me clean." [41]pMoved with pity, he stretched out his hand, touched him, and said to him, "I do will it. Be made clean." [42]qThe leprosy left him immediately, and he was made clean. [43]Then, warning him sternly, he dismissed him at once. [44]rThen he said to him, "See that you tell no one anything, but go, show yourself to the priest and offer for your cleansing what Moses prescribed; that will be proof for them." [45]The man went away and began to publicize the whole matter. He spread the report abroad so that it was impossible for Jesus to enter a town openly. He remained outside in deserted places, and people kept coming to him from everywhere.

The Healing of a Paralytic

2 [1]*aWhen Jesus returned to Capernaum after some days, it became known that he was at home.* [2]Many gathered together so that there was no longer room for them, not even around the door, and he preached the word to them. [3]They came bringing to him a paralytic carried by four men. [4]Unable to get near Jesus because of the crowd, they opened up the roof above him. After they had broken through, they let down the mat on which the paralytic was lying. [5]*When Jesus saw their faith, he said to the paralytic, "Child, your sins are forgiven." [6]*Now some of the scribes were sitting there asking themselves, [7]b"Why does this man speak that way?* He is blaspheming. Who but God alone can forgive sins?" [8]Jesus immediately knew in his mind what

n
Lk 4:42-44

o
Mt 8:2-4;
Lk 5:12-14

p
5:30

q
Lk 17:14

r
Lv 14:2-32

a
Mt 9:2-8;
Lk 5:18-26

b
Is 43:25

Mark exhibits a curious feature that scholars have dubbed **"the messianic secret,"** or perhaps more accurately, "the secret of Jesus' identity." After many miracles, Jesus instructs the recipient(s) not to tell anyone; they abruptly ignore the command and spread the news of Jesus' miraculous ministry! This may be a literary technique to show how the characters in the story fail to comprehend fully the true goal of Jesus' ministry. He is destined to suffer and die on the cross for the sake of "ransoming" sinful humanity. Christian readers understand this meaning, but the centurion standing at the cross is the only human character in Mark to exclaim, "Truly this man was the Son of God!" (15:39). The "secret" is finally revealed (by a Gentile!) who watches Jesus' death.

1:40 A leper: for the various forms of skin disease, see Leviticus 13:1-50 and the note on Leviticus 13:2-4. There are only two instances in the Old Testament in which God is shown to have cured a leper (Nm 12:10-15; 2 Kgs 5:1-14). The law of Moses provided for the ritual purification of a leper. In curing the leper, Jesus assumes that the priests will reinstate the cured man into the religious community. See also the note on Luke 5:14.

2:1–3:6 This section relates a series of conflicts between Jesus and the scribes and Pharisees in which the growing opposition of the latter leads to their plot to put Jesus to death (3:6).

2:1-2 He was at home: to the crowds that gathered in and outside the house Jesus **preached the word**, i.e., the gospel concerning the nearness of the kingdom and the necessity of repentance and faith (1:14).

2:5 It was the faith of the paralytic and those who carried him that moved Jesus to heal the sick man. Accounts of other miracles of Jesus reveal more and more his emphasis on faith as the requisite for exercising his healing powers (5:34; 9:23-24; 10:52).

2:6 Scribes: trained in oral interpretation of the written law; in Mark's gospel, adversaries of Jesus, with one exception (12:28, 34).

2:7 He is blaspheming: an accusation made here and repeated during the trial of Jesus (14:60-64).

c
4:1

d
Mt 9:9-13;
Lk 5:27-32

they were thinking to themselves, so he said, "Why are you thinking such things in your hearts? ⁹Which is easier, to say to the paralytic, 'Your sins are forgiven,' or to say, 'Rise, pick up your mat and walk'? ¹⁰*But that you may know that the Son of Man has authority to forgive sins on earth"— ¹¹he said to the paralytic, "I say to you, rise, pick up your mat, and go home." ¹²He rose, picked up his mat at once, and went away in the sight of everyone. They were all astounded and glorified God, saying, "We have never seen anything like this."

The Call of Levi

¹³*ᶜOnce again he went out along the sea. All the crowd came to him and he taught them. ¹⁴ᵈAs he passed by,* he saw Levi, son of Alphaeus, sitting at the customs post. He said to him, "Follow me." And he got up and followed him. ¹⁵While he was at table in his house,* many tax collectors and sinners sat with Jesus and his disciples; for there were many who followed him. ¹⁶*Some scribes who were Pharisees saw that he was eating with sinners and tax collectors and said to his disciples, "Why does he eat with tax collectors and sinners?" ¹⁷Jesus heard this and said to them [that], "Those who are well do not need a physician,* but the sick do. I did not come to call the righteous but sinners."

Levi, the Hospitable Tax Collector

Tax collectors in the ancient world did not have the best reputations. They were known for extortion and were often ostracized socially and religiously. When Jesus spoke with Levi, and not because of some tax obligation, Levi responded in two ways: he followed him, and he provided a meal for him.

Sharing a meal is an intrinsically social thing to do. Food is given as a gift; time is involved in preparation and in the meal-time itself; conversation is a natural part of the backdrop. Jesus was often criticized for eating with sinners and tax collectors, those who were on the fringes of society, not because of the food but because of the social connections it indicated.

And maybe that all began with one tax collector who was addressed as a person rather than as a social outcast: one tax collector who hosted a meal where Jesus was a guest and sinners were welcome at the table.

2:10 But that you may know that the Son of Man . . . on earth: although Mark 2:8-9 are addressed to the scribes, the sudden interruption of thought and structure in Mark 2:10 seems not addressed to them nor to the paralytic. Moreover, the early public use of the designation "Son of Man" to unbelieving scribes is most unlikely. The most probable explanation is that Mark's insertion of Mark 2:10 is a commentary addressed to Christians for whom he recalls this miracle and who already accept in faith that Jesus is Messiah and Son of God.

2:13 He taught them: see the note on Mark 1:21-45.

2:14 As he passed by: see the note on Mark 1:16-20. **Levi, son of Alphaeus**: see the note on Matthew 9:9. **Customs post**: such tax collectors paid a fixed sum for the right to collect customs duties within their districts. Since whatever they could collect above this amount constituted their profit, the abuse of extortion was wide-

spread among them. Hence, Jewish customs officials were regarded as sinners (2:16), outcasts of society, and disgraced along with their families. **He got up and followed him**: i.e., became a disciple of Jesus.

2:15 In his house: cf. Mark 2:1; Matthew 9:10. Luke 5:29 clearly calls it Levi's house.

2:16-17 This and the following conflict stories reflect a similar pattern: a statement of fact, a question of protest, and a reply by Jesus.

2:17 Do not need a physician: this maxim of Jesus with its implied irony was uttered to silence his adversaries who objected that he ate with **tax collectors and sinners** (2:16). Because the scribes and Pharisees were self-righteous, they were not capable of responding to Jesus' call to repentance and faith in the gospel.

MARK

The Question about Fasting

[18]*[e]The disciples of John and of the Pharisees were accustomed to fast. People came to him and objected, "Why do the disciples of John and the disciples of the Pharisees fast, but your disciples do not fast?" [19]Jesus answered them, "Can the wedding guests fast* while the bridegroom is with them? As long as they have the bridegroom with them they cannot fast. [20]But the days will come when the bridegroom is taken away from them, and then they will fast on that day. [21]No one sews a piece of unshrunken cloth on an old cloak. If he does, its fullness pulls away, the new from the old, and the tear gets worse. [22]Likewise, no one pours new wine into old wineskins. Otherwise, the wine will burst the skins, and both the wine and the skins are ruined. Rather, new wine is poured into fresh wineskins."

The Disciples and the Sabbath

[23]*[f]As he was passing through a field of grain on the sabbath, his disciples began to make a path while picking the heads of grain. [24][g]At this the Pharisees said to him, "Look, why are they doing what is unlawful on the sabbath?" [25]He said to them, "Have you never read what David did* when he was in need and he and his companions were hungry? [26][h]How he went into the house of God when Abiathar was high priest and ate the bread of offering that only the priests could lawfully eat, and shared it with his companions?" [27][i]Then he said to them, "The sabbath was made for man,* not man for the sabbath. [28]*That is why the Son of Man is lord even of the sabbath."

A Man with a Withered Hand

3 [1]*[a]Again he entered the synagogue. There was a man there who had a withered hand. [2]They watched him closely to see if he would cure him on the sabbath so that they might accuse him. [3]He said to the man with the withered hand, "Come up here before us." [4]Then he said to them, "Is it lawful to do good on the sabbath rather than to do evil, to save life rather than to destroy it?" But they remained silent. [5][b]Looking around at them with anger and grieved at their hardness of heart, he said to the man, "Stretch out your hand." He stretched it out and his hand was restored. [6]*The Pharisees went out and immediately took counsel with the Herodians against him to put him to death.

Side references

[e] Mt 9:14-17; Lk 5:33-39
[f] Mt 12:1-8; Lk 6:1-5
[g] Dt 23:25
[h] 1 Sm 21:2-7 / Lv 24:5-9
[i] 2 Mc 5:19
[a] Mt 12:9-14; Lk 6:6-11
[b] Lk 14:4

MARK

On the **Herodians** and **Pharisees**, see the chart of Jewish leaders in "Background to the Gospels," pp. 4–5.

2:18-22 This conflict over the question of fasting has the same pattern as Mark 2:16-17; see the notes on Matthew 9:15; 9:16-17.

2:19 Can the wedding guests fast?: the bridal metaphor expresses a new relationship of love between God and his people in the person and mission of Jesus to his disciples. It is the inauguration of the new and joyful messianic time of fulfillment and the passing of the old. Any attempt at assimilating the Pharisaic practice of fasting, or of extending the preparatory discipline of John's disciples beyond the arrival of the bridegroom, would be as futile as sewing **a piece of unshrunken cloth on an old cloak** or pouring **new wine into old wineskins** with the resulting destruction of both cloth and wine (2:21-22). Fasting is rendered superfluous during the earthly ministry of Jesus; cf. Mark 2:20.

2:23-28 This conflict regarding the sabbath follows the same pattern as in Mark 2:18-22.

2:25-26 Have you never read what David did?: Jesus defends the action of his disciples on the basis of 1 Samuel 21:2-7 in which an exception is made to the regulation of Leviticus 24:9 because of the extreme hunger of David and his men. According to 1 Samuel,

the priest who gave the bread to David was Ahimelech, father of Abiathar.

2:27 The sabbath was made for man: a reaffirmation of the divine intent of the sabbath to benefit Israel as contrasted with the restrictive Pharisaic tradition added to the law.

2:28 The Son of Man is lord even of the sabbath: Mark's comment on the theological meaning of the incident is to benefit his Christian readers; see the note on Mark 2:10.

3:1-5 Here Jesus is again depicted in conflict with his adversaries over the question of sabbath-day observance. His opponents were already ill disposed toward him because they regarded Jesus as a violator of the sabbath. Jesus' question **Is it lawful to do good on the sabbath rather than to do evil?** places the matter in the broader theological context outside the casuistry of the scribes. The answer is obvious. Jesus heals the man with the withered hand in the sight of all and reduces his opponents to silence; cf. John 5:17-18.

3:6 In reporting the plot of the Pharisees and Herodians to put Jesus to death after this series of conflicts in Galilee, Mark uses a pattern that recurs in his account of later controversies in Jerusalem

c
Mt 4:23-25;
12:15;
Lk 6:17-19

d
5:30

e
1:34; Lk 4:41

f
Mt 10:1-4;
Lk 6:12-16

g
6:7

h
Mt 16:18;
Jn 1:42

i
2:2

j
Jn 10:20

k
Mt 12:24-32;
Lk 11:15-22;
12:10

MARK

The Mercy of Jesus

[7]*[c]Jesus withdrew toward the sea with his disciples. A large number of people [followed] from Galilee and from Judea. [8]Hearing what he was doing, a large number of people came to him also from Jerusalem, from Idumea, from beyond the Jordan, and from the neighborhood of Tyre and Sidon. [9]He told his disciples to have a boat ready for him because of the crowd, so that they would not crush him. [10][d]He had cured many and, as a result, those who had diseases were pressing upon him to touch him. [11]*[e]And whenever unclean spirits saw him they would fall down before him and shout, "You are the Son of God." [12]He warned them sternly not to make him known.

The Mission of the Twelve

[13][f]He went up the mountain* and summoned those whom he wanted and they came to him. [14][g]He appointed twelve [whom he also named apostles] that they might be with him* and he might send them forth to preach [15]and to have authority to drive out demons: [16]*[he appointed the twelve:] Simon, whom he named Peter; [17][h]James, son of Zebedee, and John the brother of James, whom he named Boanerges, that is, sons of thunder; [18]Andrew, Philip, Bartholomew, Matthew, Thomas, James the son of Alphaeus; Thaddeus, Simon the Cananean, [19]and Judas Iscariot who betrayed him.

Blasphemy of the Scribes

[20]*[i]He came home. Again [the] crowd gathered, making it impossible for them even to eat.* [21][j]When his relatives heard of this they set out to seize him, for they said, "He is out of his mind." [22][k]The scribes who had come from Jerusalem said, "He is possessed by Beelzebul,"* and "By the prince of demons he drives out demons."

Jesus and Beelzebul

[23]Summoning them, he began to speak to them in parables, "How can Satan drive out Satan? [24]If a kingdom is divided against itself, that kingdom cannot stand. [25]And if a house is divided against itself, that house will not be able to stand. [26]And if Satan

On **Beelzebul** see "Getting It Right . . . Demons and Devils" (at Mt 4).

(11:17-18; 12:13-17). The help of the Herodians, supporters of Herod Antipas, tetrarch of Galilee and Perea, is needed to take action against Jesus. Both series of conflicts point to their gravity and to the impending passion of Jesus.

3:7-19 This overview of the Galilean ministry manifests the power of Jesus to draw people to himself through his teaching and deeds of power. The crowds from many regions surround Jesus (3:7-12). This phenomenon prepares the way for creating a new people of Israel. The choice and mission of the Twelve is the prelude (3:13-19).

3:11-12 See the note on Mark 1:24-25.

3:13 He went up the mountain: here and elsewhere the mountain is associated with solemn moments and acts in the mission and self-revelation of Jesus (6:46; 9:2-8; 13:3). Jesus acts with authority as he **summoned those whom he wanted and they came to him**.

3:14-15 He appointed twelve [whom he also named apostles] that they might be with him: literally, "he made," i.e., instituted them as apostles to extend his messianic mission through them (6:7-13). See the notes on Matthew 10:1 and 10:2-4.

3:16 Simon, whom he named Peter: Mark indicates that Simon's name was changed on this occasion. Peter is first in all lists of the apostles (Mt 10:2; Lk 6:14; Acts 1:13; cf. 1 Cor 15:5-8).

3:20-35 Within the narrative of the coming of Jesus' relatives (3:20-21) is inserted the account of the unbelieving scribes from Jerusalem who attributed Jesus' power over demons to Beelzebul (3:22-30); see the note on Mark 5:21-43. There were those even among the relatives of Jesus who disbelieved and regarded Jesus as **out of his mind** (3:21). Against this background, Jesus is informed of the arrival of his mother and brothers [and sisters] (3:32). He responds by showing that not family ties but doing God's will (3:35) is decisive in the kingdom; cf. the note on Matthew 12:46-50.

3:20 He came home: cf. Mark 2:1-2 and see the note on Mark 2:15.

3:22 By Beelzebul: see the note on Matthew 10:25. Two accusations are leveled against Jesus: (1) that **he is possessed** by an unclean spirit, and (2) **by the prince of demons he drives out demons**. Jesus answers the second charge by a parable (3:24-27) and responds to the first charge in Mark 3:28-29.

has risen up against himself and is divided, he cannot stand; that is the end of him. ²⁷But no one can enter a strong man's house to plunder his property unless he first ties up the strong man. Then he can plunder his house. ²⁸ˡAmen, I say to you, all sins and all blasphemies that people utter will be forgiven them. ²⁹But whoever blasphemes against the holy Spirit* will never have forgiveness, but is guilty of an everlasting sin." ³⁰For they had said, "He has an unclean spirit."

Jesus and His Family

³¹ᵐHis mother and his brothers arrived. Standing outside they sent word to him and called him. ³²A crowd seated around him told him, "Your mother and your brothers* [and your sisters] are outside asking for you." ³³But he said to them in reply, "Who are my mother and [my] brothers?" ³⁴And looking around at those seated in the circle he said, "Here are my mother and my brothers. ³⁵[For] whoever does the will of God is my brother and sister and mother."

The Parable of the Sower

4 ¹*ᵃOn another occasion he began to teach by the sea.* A very large crowd gathered around him so that he got into a boat on the sea and sat down. And the whole crowd was beside the sea on land.ᵇ ²And he taught them at length in parables, and in the course of his instruction he said to them, ³*"Hear this! A sower went out to sow. ⁴And as he sowed, some seed fell on the path, and the birds came and ate it up. ⁵Other seed fell on rocky ground where it had little soil. It sprang up at once because the soil was not deep. ⁶And when the sun rose, it was scorched and it withered for lack of roots. ⁷Some seed fell among thorns, and the thorns grew up and choked it and it produced no grain. ⁸And some seed fell on rich soil and produced fruit. It came up and grew and yielded thirty, sixty, and a hundredfold." ⁹He added, "Whoever has ears to hear ought to hear."

The Purpose of the Parables

¹⁰And when he was alone, those present along with the Twelve questioned him about the parables. ¹¹*He answered them, "The mystery of the kingdom of God has been granted to you. But to those outside everything comes in parables, ¹²ᶜso that

l Lk 12:10

m Mt 12:46-50; Lk 8:19-21

a Mt 13:1-13; Lk 8:4-10

b 2:13; Lk 5:1

c Is 6:9; Jn 12:40; Acts 28:26; Rom 11:8

On **parables**, see definition in Matthew (at 13:3).

3:29 Whoever blasphemes against the holy Spirit: this sin is called **an everlasting sin** because it attributes to Satan, who is the power of evil, what is actually the work of the holy Spirit, namely, victory over the demons.

3:32 Your brothers: see the note on Mark 6:3.

4:1-34 In parables (4:2): see the note on Matthew 13:3. The use of parables is typical of Jesus' enigmatic method of teaching the crowds (4:2-9, 12) as compared with the interpretation of the parables he gives to his disciples (4:10-25, 33-34) to each group according to its capacity to understand (4:9-11). The key feature of the parable at hand is the sowing of the seed (4:3), representing the breakthrough of the kingdom of God into the world. The various types of soil refer to the diversity of response accorded the word of God (4:4-7). The climax of the parable is the harvest of thirty, sixty, and a hundredfold (4:8). Thus both the present and the future action of God, from

the initiation to the fulfillment of the kingdom, is presented through this and other parables (4:26-29, 30-32).

4:1 By the sea: the shore of the Sea of Galilee or a boat near the shore (2:13; 3:7-8) is the place where Mark depicts Jesus teaching the crowds. By contrast the mountain is the scene of Jesus at prayer (6:46) or in the process of forming his disciples (3:13; 9:2).

4:3-8 See the note on Matthew 13:3-8.

4:11-12 These verses are to be viewed against their background in Mark 3:6, 22 concerning the unbelief and opposition Jesus encountered in his ministry. It is against this background that the distinction in Jesus' method becomes clear of presenting the kingdom to the disbelieving crowd in one manner and to the disciples in another. To the former it is presented in parables and the truth remains hidden; for the latter the parable is interpreted and the mystery is partially revealed because of their faith; see the notes on Matthew 13:11 and 13:13.

d
Mt 13:18-23;
Lk 8:11-15

e
Lk 8:16-18

f
Mt 5:15;
Lk 11:33

g
Mt 10:26;
Lk 12:2

h
Mt 7:2; Lk 6:38

i
Mt 13:12;
Lk 19:26

j
Jas 5:7

k
Mt 13:31-32;
Lk 13:18-19

l
Mt 13:34

'they may look and see but not perceive,
> and hear and listen but not understand,
> in order that they may not be converted and be forgiven.'"

[13]*[d]Jesus said to them, "Do you not understand this parable? Then how will you understand any of the parables? [14]The sower sows the word. [15]These are the ones on the path where the word is sown. As soon as they hear, Satan comes at once and takes away the word sown in them. [16]And these are the ones sown on rocky ground who, when they hear the word, receive it at once with joy. [17]But they have no root; they last only for a time. Then when tribulation or persecution comes because of the word, they quickly fall away. [18]Those sown among thorns are another sort. They are the people who hear the word, [19]but worldly anxiety, the lure of riches, and the craving for other things intrude and choke the word, and it bears no fruit. [20]But those sown on rich soil are the ones who hear the word and accept it and bear fruit thirty and sixty and a hundredfold."

Parable of the Lamp

[21]*[e]He said to them, "Is a lamp brought in to be placed under a bushel basket or under a bed, and not to be placed on a lampstand?[f] [22]*[g]For there is nothing hidden except to be made visible; nothing is secret except to come to light. [23]Anyone who has ears to hear ought to hear." [24]*[h]He also told them, "Take care what you hear. The measure with which you measure will be measured out to you, and still more will be given to you. [25]*[i]To the one who has, more will be given; from the one who has not, even what he has will be taken away."

Seed Grows of Itself

[26]*[j]He said, "This is how it is with the kingdom of God;* it is as if a man were to scatter seed on the land [27]and would sleep and rise night and day and the seed would sprout and grow, he knows not how. [28]Of its own accord the land yields fruit, first the blade, then the ear, then the full grain in the ear. [29]And when the grain is ripe, he wields the sickle at once, for the harvest has come."

The Mustard Seed

[30]*[k]He said, "To what shall we compare the kingdom of God, or what parable can we use for it? [31]It is like a mustard seed that, when it is sown in the ground, is the smallest of all the seeds on the earth. [32]*But once it is sown, it springs up and becomes the largest of plants and puts forth large branches, so that the birds of the sky can dwell in its shade." [33]*[l]With many such parables he spoke the word to them as they were able to understand it. [34]Without parables he did not speak to them, but to his own disciples he explained everything in private.

4:13-20 See the note on Matthew 13:18-23.

4:26-29 Only Mark records the parable of the seed's growth. Sower and harvester are the same. The emphasis is on the power of the seed to grow of itself without human intervention (4:27). Mysteriously it produces **blade** and **ear** and **full grain** (4:28). Thus the kingdom of God initiated by Jesus in proclaiming the word develops quietly yet powerfully until it is fully established by him at the final judgment (4:29); cf. Revelation 14:15.

4:32 The universality of the kingdom of God is indicated here; cf. Ezekiel 17:23; 31:6; Daniel 4:17-19.

The Calming of a Storm at Sea

[35]*[m]On that day, as evening drew on, he said to them, "Let us cross to the other side." [36]Leaving the crowd, they took him with them in the boat just as he was. And other boats were with him. [37]A violent squall came up and waves were breaking over the boat, so that it was already filling up. [38]Jesus was in the stern, asleep on a cushion. They woke him and said to him, "Teacher, do you not care that we are perishing?" [39]He woke up, rebuked the wind, and said to the sea, "Quiet! Be still!"* The wind ceased and there was great calm. [40]Then he asked them, "Why are you terrified? Do you not yet have faith?" [41]*[n]They were filled with great awe and said to one another, "Who then is this whom even wind and sea obey?"

The Healing of the Gerasene Demoniac

5 [1]*[a]They came to the other side of the sea, to the territory of the Gerasenes. [2]When he got out of the boat, at once a man* from the tombs who had an unclean spirit met him. [3]The man had been dwelling among the tombs, and no one could restrain him any longer, even with a chain. [4]In fact, he had frequently been bound with shackles and chains, but the chains had been pulled apart by him and the shackles smashed, and no one was strong enough to subdue him. [5]Night and day among the tombs and on the hillsides he was always crying out and bruising himself with stones. [6]Catching sight of Jesus from a distance, he ran up and prostrated himself before him, [7]crying out in a loud voice, "What have you to do with me,* Jesus, Son of the Most High God? I adjure you by God, do not torment me!" [8](He had been saying to him, "Unclean spirit, come out of the man!") [9]*[b]He asked him, "What is your name?" He replied, "Legion is my name. There are many of us." [10]And he pleaded earnestly with him not to drive them away from that territory.

[11]Now a large herd of swine* was feeding there on the hillside. [12]And they pleaded with him, "Send us into the swine. Let us enter them." [13]And he let them, and the unclean spirits came out and entered the swine. The herd of about two thousand rushed down a steep bank into the sea, where they were drowned. [14]The swineherds ran away and reported the incident in the town and throughout the countryside. And people came out to see what had happened. [15]As they approached Jesus, they caught sight of the man who had been possessed by Legion, sitting there clothed and in his right mind. And they were seized with fear. [16]Those who witnessed the incident explained to them what had happened to the possessed man and to the swine. [17]Then they began to beg

m
Mt 8:18, 23-37;
Lk 8:22-25

n
1:27

a
Mt 8:28-34;
Lk 8:26-39

b
Mt 12:45;
Lk 8:2; 11:26

4:35–5:43 After the chapter on parables, Mark narrates four miracle stories: Mark 4:35-41; 5:1-20; and two joined together in Mark 5:21-43. See also the notes on Matthew 8:23-34 and 9:8-26.

4:39 Quiet! Be still!: as in the case of silencing a demon (1:25), Jesus rebukes the wind and subdues the turbulence of the sea by a mere word; see the note on Matthew 8:26.

4:41 Jesus is here depicted as exercising power over wind and sea. In the Christian community this event was seen as a sign of Jesus' saving presence amid persecutions that threatened its existence.

5:1 The territory of the Gerasenes: the reference is to pagan territory; cf. Isaiah 65:1. Another reading is "Gadarenes"; see the note on Matthew 8:28.

5:2-6 The man was an outcast from society, dominated by unclean spirits (5:8, 13), living among the tombs. The prostration before Jesus (5:6) indicates Jesus' power over evil spirits.

5:7 What have you to do with me?: cf. Mark 1:24 and see the note on John 2:4.

5:9 Legion is my name: the demons were numerous and the condition of the possessed man was extremely serious; cf. Matthew 12:45.

5:11 Herd of swine: see the note on Matthew 8:30.

c
2:13

d
Mt 9:18-26;
Lk 8:41-56

him to leave their district. [18]As he was getting into the boat, the man who had been possessed pleaded to remain with him. [19]But he would not permit him but told him instead, "Go home* to your family and announce to them all that the Lord in his pity has done for you." [20]Then the man went off and began to proclaim in the Decapolis what Jesus had done for him; and all were amazed.

Jairus's Daughter and the Woman with a Hemorrhage

[21]*cWhen Jesus had crossed again [in the boat] to the other side, a large crowd gathered around him, and he stayed close to the sea. [22]dOne of the synagogue officials, named Jairus, came forward. Seeing him he fell at his feet [23]and pleaded earnestly with him, saying, "My daughter is at the point of death. Please, come lay your hands on her* that she may get well and live." [24]He went off with him, and a large crowd followed him and pressed upon him.

[25]There was a woman afflicted with hemorrhages for twelve years. [26]She had suffered greatly at the hands of many doctors and had spent all that she had. Yet she was not helped but only grew worse. [27]She had heard about Jesus and came up behind him in the crowd and touched his cloak. [28]*She said, "If I but touch his clothes, I shall be cured." [29]Immediately her flow of blood dried up. She felt in her body that she was healed of her affliction. [30]Jesus, aware at once that power had gone out from him, turned around in the crowd and asked, "Who has touched my clothes?" [31]But his disciples said to him, "You see how the

---

Vestiges of **Aramaic** and **Hebrew** occur in the NT, although the text is entirely written in Koine (common) Greek (the language of the Roman Empire at the time of Jesus). Aramaic was the spoken language used by Jews in daily life, while Hebrew was the formal language of the written Scriptures and used in liturgical services. In addition to place names (Gehenna, Golgotha, etc.) and the liturgical word *amen* ("so be it"), the main Aramaic-Hebrew expressions include:

Talitha koum (Little girl, arise!) Mk 5:41
Qorban (dedicated to God) Mk 7:11
Ephphatha (Be opened!) Mk 7:34
Abba (dearest father) Mk 14:36; Rom 8:15; Gal 4:6
Raqa (evil) Mt 5:22
Eloi, Eloi, lema sabachthani? Mk 15:34 and par. (My God, my God, why have you forsaken me?)

Scholars have reconstructed the Our Father (Mt 6:9b-13; Lk 11:2b-4) into an Aramaic version possibly spoken by Jesus, but only the Greek translation remains in the NT. Other Semitic influences appear occasionally in the style of writing.

5:19 Go home: Jesus did not accept the man's request **to remain with him** as a disciple (Mt 5:18), yet invited him to announce to his own people what the Lord had done for him, i.e., proclaim the gospel message to his pagan family; cf. Mark 1:14, 39; 3:14; 13:10.

5:21-43 The story of the raising to life of Jairus's daughter is divided into two parts: Mark 5:21-24; 5:35-43. Between these two separated parts the account of the cure of the hemorrhage victim (5:25-34) is interposed. This technique of intercalating or sandwiching one story within another occurs several times in Mark 3:19b-21;

3:22-30; 3:31-35; 6:6b-13; 6:14-29; 6:30; 11:12-14; 11:15-19; 11:20-25; 14:53; 14:54; 14:55-65; 14:66-73.

5:23 Lay your hands on her: this act for the purpose of healing is frequent in Mark 6:5; 7:32-35; 8:23-25; 16:18 and is also found in Matthew 9:18; Luke 4:40; 13:13; Acts 9:17; 28:8.

5:28 Both in the case of Jairus and his daughter (5:23) and in the case of the hemorrhage victim, the inner conviction that physical contact (5:30) accompanied by faith in Jesus' saving power could effect a cure was rewarded.

crowd is pressing upon you, and yet you ask, 'Who touched me?'" ³²And he looked around to see who had done it. ³³The woman, realizing what had happened to her, approached in fear and trembling. She fell down before Jesus and told him the whole truth. ³⁴ᵉHe said to her, "Daughter, your faith has saved you. Go in peace and be cured of your affliction."

³⁵*While he was still speaking, people from the synagogue official's house arrived and said, "Your daughter has died; why trouble the teacher any longer?" ³⁶Disregarding the message that was reported, Jesus said to the synagogue official, "Do not be afraid; just have faith." ³⁷He did not allow anyone to accompany him inside except Peter, James, and John, the brother of James. ³⁸When they arrived at the house of the synagogue official, he caught sight of a commotion, people weeping and wailing loudly. ³⁹*ᶠSo he went in and said to them, "Why this commotion and weeping? The child is not dead but asleep." ⁴⁰And they ridiculed him. Then he put them all out. He took along the child's father and mother and those who were with him and entered the room where the child was. ⁴¹*He took the child by the hand and said to her, "*Talitha koum*," which means, "Little girl, I say to you, arise!" ⁴²The girl, a child of twelve, arose immediately and walked around. [At that] they were utterly astounded. ⁴³He gave strict orders that no one should know this and said that she should be given something to eat.

The Rejection at Nazareth

6 ¹ᵃHe departed from there and came to his native place,* accompanied by his disciples. ²*When the sabbath came he began to teach in the synagogue, and many who heard him were astonished. They said, "Where did this man get all this? What kind of wisdom has been given him? What mighty deeds are wrought by his hands! ³ᵇIs he not the carpenter,* the son of Mary, and the brother of James and Joses and Judas and Simon? And are not his sisters here with us?" And they took offense at him. ⁴*ᶜJesus said to them, "A prophet is not without honor except in his native place and among his own

e
Lk 7:30

f
Acts 9:40

a
Mt 13:54-58;
Lk 4:16-30

b
15:40;
Mt 12:46;
Jn 6:42

c
Jn 4:44

Nazareth in relation to Jerusalem

5:35 The faith of Jairus was put to a twofold test: (1) that his daughter might be cured and, now that she had died, (2) that she might be restored to life. His faith contrasts with the lack of faith of the crowd.

5:39 Not dead but asleep: the New Testament often refers to death as sleep (Mt 27:52; Jn 11:11; 1 Cor 15:6; 1 Thes 4:13-15); see the note on Matthew 9:24.

5:41 Arise: the Greek verb *egeirein* is the verb generally used to express resurrection from death (6:14, 16; Mt 11:5; Lk 7:14) and Jesus' own resurrection (16:6; Mt 28:6; Lk 24:6).

6:1 His native place: the Greek word *patris* here refers to Nazareth (cf. 1:9; Lk 4:16, 23-24) though it can also mean native land.

6:2-6 See the note on Matthew 13:54-58.

6:3 Is he not the carpenter?: no other gospel calls Jesus a carpenter. Some witnesses have "the carpenter's son," as in Matthew 13:55. **Son of Mary:** contrary to Jewish custom, which calls a man the son of his father, this expression may reflect Mark's own faith that God is the Father of Jesus (1:1, 11; 8:38; 13:32; 14:36). **The brother of James . . . Simon:** in Semitic usage, the terms "brother," "sister" are applied not only to children of the same par-

ents, but to nephews, nieces, cousins, half-brothers, and half-sisters; cf. Genesis 14:16; 29:15; Leviticus 10:4. While one cannot suppose that the meaning of a Greek word should be sought in the first place from Semitic usage, the Septuagint often translates the Hebrew 'āḥ by the Greek word *adelphos*, "brother," as in the cited passages, a fact that may argue for a similar breadth of meaning in some New Testament passages. For instance, there is no doubt that in v. 17, "brother" is used of Philip, who was actually the half-brother of Herod Antipas. On the other hand, Mark may have understood the terms literally; see also Matthew 3:31-32; 12:46; 13:55-56; Luke 8:19; John 7:3, 5. The question of meaning here would not have arisen but for the faith of the church in Mary's perpetual virginity.

6:4 A prophet is not without honor except . . . in his own house: a saying that finds parallels in other literatures, especially Jewish and Greek, but without reference to a prophet. Comparing himself to previous Hebrew prophets whom the people rejected, Jesus intimates his own eventual rejection by the nation especially in view of the dishonor his own relatives had shown him (3:21) and now his townspeople as well.

113

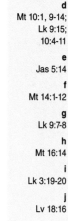

d
Mt 10:1, 9-14;
Lk 9:15;
10:4-11

e
Jas 5:14

f
Mt 14:1-12

g
Lk 9:7-8

h
Mt 16:14

i
Lk 3:19-20

j
Lv 18:16

kin and in his own house." ⁵So he was not able to perform any mighty deed there,* apart from curing a few sick people by laying his hands on them. ⁶He was amazed at their lack of faith.

The Mission of the Twelve

He went around to the villages in the vicinity teaching. ⁷ᵈHe summoned the Twelve* and began to send them out two by two and gave them authority over unclean spirits. ⁸*He instructed them to take nothing for the journey but a walking stick—no food, no sack, no money in their belts. ⁹They were, however, to wear sandals but not a second tunic. ¹⁰*He said to them, "Wherever you enter a house, stay there until you leave from there. ¹¹Whatever place does not welcome you or listen to you, leave there and shake the dust off your feet in testimony against them." ¹²So they went off and preached repentance. ¹³*ᵉThey drove out many demons, and they anointed with oil many who were sick and cured them.

Herod's Opinion of Jesus

¹⁴*ᶠKing Herod* heard about it, for his fame had become widespread, and people were saying, "John the Baptist has been raised from the dead; that is why mighty powers are at work in him."ᵍ ¹⁵ʰOthers were saying, "He is Elijah"; still others, "He is a prophet like any of the prophets." ¹⁶But when Herod learned of it, he said, "It is John whom I beheaded. He has been raised up."

> On **Herod Antipas**, see "Getting It Right . . . Which Herod?" (at Mt 2:1).

The Death of John the Baptist

¹⁷*ⁱHerod was the one who had John arrested and bound in prison on account of Herodias, the wife of his brother Philip, whom he had married. ¹⁸ʲJohn had said to Herod, "It is not lawful for you to have your brother's wife." ¹⁹Herodias* harbored a grudge against him and wanted to kill him but was unable to do so. ²⁰Herod feared John, knowing him to be a righteous and holy man, and kept him in custody. When he heard him speak he was very much perplexed, yet he liked to listen to him. ²¹She had an opportunity one day when Herod, on his birthday, gave a banquet for his courtiers,

---

6:5 He was not able to perform any mighty deed there: according to Mark, Jesus' power could not take effect because of a person's lack of faith.

6:7-13 The preparation for the mission of the Twelve is seen in the call (1) of the first disciples to be fishers of men (1:16-20), (2) then of the Twelve set apart to be with Jesus and to receive authority to preach and expel demons (3:13-19). Now they are given the specific mission to exercise that authority in word and power as representatives of Jesus during the time of their formation.

6:8-9 In Mark the use of a **walking stick** (6:8) and **sandals** (6:9) is permitted, but not in Matthew 10:10 nor in Luke 10:4. Mark does not mention any prohibition to visit pagan territory and to enter Samaritan towns. These differences indicate a certain adaptation to conditions in and outside of Palestine and suggest in Mark's account a later activity in the church. For the rest, Jesus required of his apostles a total dependence on God for food and shelter; cf. Mark 6:35-44; 8:1-9.

6:10-11 Remaining in the same house as a guest (6:10) rather than moving to another offering greater comfort avoided any impression of seeking advantage for oneself and prevented dishonor to one's host. Shaking the dust off one's feet served as testimony against those who rejected the call to repentance.

6:13 Anointed with oil . . . cured them: a common medicinal remedy, but seen here as a vehicle of divine power for healing.

6:14-16 The various opinions about Jesus anticipate the theme of his identity that reaches its climax in Mark 8:27-30.

6:14 King Herod: see the note on Matthew 14:1.

6:17-29 Similarities are to be noted between Mark's account of the imprisonment and death of John the Baptist in this pericope, and that of the passion of Jesus (15:1-47). Herod and Pilate, each in turn, acknowledges the holiness of life of one over whom he unjustly exercises the power of condemnation and death (6:26-27; 15:9-10, 14-15). The hatred of Herodias toward John parallels that of the Jewish leaders toward Jesus. After the deaths of John and of Jesus, well-disposed persons request the bodies of the victims of Herod and of Pilate in turn to give them respectful burial (6:29; 15:45-46).

6:19 Herodias: see the note on Matthew 14:3.

his military officers, and the leading men of Galilee. [22]Herodias's own daughter came in and performed a dance that delighted Herod and his guests. The king said to the girl, "Ask of me whatever you wish and I will grant it to you." [23k]He even swore [many things] to her, "I will grant you whatever you ask of me, even to half of my kingdom." [24]She went out and said to her mother, "What shall I ask for?" She replied, "The head of John the Baptist." [25]The girl hurried back to the king's presence and made her request, "I want you to give me at once on a platter the head of John the Baptist." [26]The king was deeply distressed, but because of his oaths and the guests he did not wish to break his word to her. [27l]So he promptly dispatched an executioner with orders to bring back his head. He went off and beheaded him in the prison. [28]He brought in the head on a platter and gave it to the girl. The girl in turn gave it to her mother. [29]When his disciples heard about it, they came and took his body and laid it in a tomb.

The Return of the Twelve

[30m]The apostles* gathered together with Jesus and reported all they had done and taught. [31*n]He said to them, "Come away by yourselves to a deserted place and rest a while." People were coming and going in great numbers, and they had no opportunity even to eat. [32o]So they went off in the boat by themselves to a deserted place. [33]People saw them leaving and many came to know about it. They hastened there on foot from all the towns and arrived at the place before them.

The Feeding of the Five Thousand

[34]When he disembarked and saw the vast crowd, his heart was moved with pity for them, for they were like sheep without a shepherd; and he began to teach them many things. [35*]By now it was already late and his disciples approached him and said, "This is a deserted place and it is already very late. [36]Dismiss them so that they can go to the surrounding farms and villages and buy themselves something to eat." [37]He said to them in reply, "Give them some food yourselves." But they said to him, "Are we to buy two hundred days' wages worth of food and give it to them to eat?" [38]He asked them, "How many loaves do you have? Go and see." And when they had found out they said, "Five loaves and two fish." [39]So he gave orders to have them sit down in groups on the green grass. [40*]The people took their places in rows by hundreds and by fifties. [41]Then, taking the five loaves and the two fish and looking up to heaven, he said the blessing,

k
Est 5:3

l
Lk 9:9

m
Lk 9:10

n
3:20; Mt 14:13; Lk 9:10

o
Mt 14:13-21; Lk 9:10-17; Jn 6:1-13

6:30 Apostles: here, and in some manuscripts at Mark 3:14, Mark calls apostles (i.e., those sent forth) the Twelve whom Jesus sends as his emissaries, empowering them to preach, to expel demons, and to cure the sick (6:13). Only after Pentecost is the title used in the technical sense.

6:31-34 The withdrawal of Jesus with his disciples to a desert place to rest attracts a great number of people to follow them. Toward this people of the new exodus Jesus is moved with pity; he satisfies their spiritual hunger by teaching them many things, thus gradually showing himself the faithful shepherd of a new Israel; cf. Numbers 27:17; Ezekiel 34:15.

6:35 See the note on Matthew 14:13-21. Compare this section with Mark 8:1-9. The various accounts of the multiplication of loaves and fishes, two each in Mark and in Matthew and one each in Luke and in John, indicate the wide interest of the early church in their eucharistic gatherings; see, e.g., Mark 6:41; 8:6; 14:22; and recall also the sign of bread in Exodus 16; Deuteronomy 8:3-16; Psalms 78:24-25; 105:40; Wisdom 16:20-21.

6:40 The people . . . in rows by hundreds and by fifties: reminiscent of the groupings of Israelites encamped in the desert (Ex 18:21-25) and of the wilderness tradition of the prophets depicting the transformation of the wasteland into pastures where the true shepherd feeds his flock (Ez 34:25-26) and makes his people beneficiaries of messianic grace.

p
Mt 14:22-32;
Jn 6:15-21

broke the loaves, and gave them to [his] disciples to set before the people; he also divided the two fish among them all.* ⁴²They all ate and were satisfied. ⁴³And they picked up twelve wicker baskets full of fragments and what was left of the fish. ⁴⁴Those who ate [of the loaves] were five thousand men.

The Walking on the Water

⁴⁵*ᵖThen he made his disciples get into the boat and precede him to the other side toward Bethsaida,* while he dismissed the crowd. ⁴⁶*And when he had taken leave of them, he went off to the mountain to pray. ⁴⁷When it was evening, the boat was far out

The **multiplication of the loaves** is the only NT miracle story recorded in multiple versions in all four gospels. In Mark, its existence in two different versions may point to a meaning applied to both Jewish and Gentile settings, thus indicating Jesus' ministry to both audiences. For John, Jesus' personal ministry and the overabundance of food highlight Jesus as the "bread of life." In all the versions, however, the eucharistic symbolism is unmistakable. Scholars believe the story may have originated with one tale of a miraculous feeding, which was preserved in numerous versions. The chart highlights some similarities and differences in details.

Mt 14:13-21	Mt 15:32-38	Mk 6:31-44	Mk 8:1-10	Lk 9:12-17	Jn 6:1-13
Feeding 5000 men, not counting women and children	Feeding 4000 men, not counting women and children	Feeding 5000 men	Feeding 4000 people	Feeding 5000 men	Feeding a large crowd, about 5000 men
5 loaves + 2 fish	7 loaves + a few fish	5 loaves + 2 fish	7 loaves + a few fish	5 loaves + 2 fish	5 barley loaves + 2 fish
Jesus looked to heaven, said a blessing, broke the loaves, gave them to the disciples who in turn gave them to the crowd	Jesus took the loaves, gave thanks, broke them, gave them to the disciples who in turn gave them to the crowd	Jesus looked to heaven, said a blessing, broke the loaves, gave them to the disciples to set out	Jesus took the loaves, gave thanks, broke them, gave them to his disciples to distribute	Jesus looked to heaven, blessed the loaves and fish, broke them, gave them to the disciples to set out	Jesus took the bread, gave thanks, and distributed it himself
All ate and were satisfied	All ate and were satisfied	All ate and were satisfied	They ate and were satisfied	All ate and were satisfied	They had their fill and more than they could eat
12 baskets left over	7 baskets left over	12 baskets left over	7 baskets left over	12 baskets left over	12 baskets left over
	Warning against the "leaven" of Pharisees and Sadducees; reminder of feeding the 5000 and 4000; Jesus asks about their understanding, then they understand		Warning against the "leaven" of Pharisees and Sadducees; reminder of feeding the 5000; Jesus bemoans disciples' lack of understanding		They declare Jesus "the Prophet"; followed by discourse on the bread of life

---

6:41 On the language of this verse as eucharistic (cf. 14:22), see the notes on Matthew 14:19, 20. Jesus observed the Jewish table ritual of blessing God before partaking of food.

6:45-52 See the note on Matthew 14:22-33.

6:45 **To the other side toward Bethsaida:** a village at the northeastern shore of the Sea of Galilee.

6:46 **He went off to the mountain to pray:** see Mark 1:35-38. In John 6:15 Jesus withdrew to evade any involvement in the false messianic hopes of the multitude.

on the sea and he was alone on shore. [48]Then he saw that they were tossed about while rowing, for the wind was against them. About the fourth watch of the night, he came toward them walking on the sea.* He meant to pass by them. [49]But when they saw him walking on the sea, they thought it was a ghost and cried out. [50]*They had all seen him and were terrified. But at once he spoke with them, "Take courage, it is I, do not be afraid!" [51]He got into the boat with them and the wind died down. They were [completely] astounded. [52][q]They had not understood the incident of the loaves.* On the contrary, their hearts were hardened.

q
4:13

r
Mt 14:34-36

s
5:27-28;
Acts 5:15

a
Mt 15:1-20

b
Is 29:13

MARK

The Healings at Gennesaret

[53][r]After making the crossing, they came to land at Gennesaret and tied up there. [54]As they were leaving the boat, people immediately recognized him. [55]They scurried about the surrounding country and began to bring in the sick on mats to wherever they heard he was. [56][s]Whatever villages or towns or countryside he entered, they laid the sick in the marketplaces and begged him that they might touch only the tassel on his cloak; and as many as touched it were healed.

The Tradition of the Elders

7 [1]*[a]Now when the Pharisees with some scribes who had come from Jerusalem gathered around him, [2]they observed that some of his disciples ate their meals with unclean, that is, unwashed, hands. [3](For the Pharisees and, in fact, all Jews, do not eat without carefully washing their hands,* keeping the tradition of the elders. [4]And on coming from the marketplace they do not eat without purifying themselves. And there are many other things that they have traditionally observed, the purification of cups and jugs and kettles [and beds].) [5]So the Pharisees and scribes questioned him, "Why do your disciples not follow the tradition of the elders* but instead eat a meal with unclean hands?" [6][b]He responded, "Well did Isaiah prophesy about you hypocrites, as it is written:

On the **scribes**, see the chart of Jewish leaders in "Background to the Gospels," p. 5.

When it comes to prayer, lip service is not enough. You must bring your whole being to God when you pray. Enter into the words with reverent awareness. Leap into your prayer with a lover's passion.

'This people honors me with their lips,
     but their hearts are far from me;
[7]In vain do they worship me,
     teaching as doctrines human precepts.'

6:48 Walking on the sea: see the notes on Matthew 14:22-33 and on John 6:19.

6:50 It is I, do not be afraid!: literally, "I am." This may reflect the divine revelatory formula of Exodus 3:14; Isaiah 41:4, 10, 14; 43:1-3, 10, 13. Mark implies the hidden identity of Jesus as Son of God.

6:52 They had not understood . . . the loaves: the revelatory character of this sign and that of the walking on the sea completely escaped the disciples. **Their hearts were hardened**: in Mark 3:5-6 hardness of heart was attributed to those who did not accept Jesus and plotted his death. Here the same disposition prevents the disciples from comprehending Jesus' self-revelation through signs; cf. Mark 8:17.

7:1-23 See the note on Matthew 15:1-20. Against the Pharisees' narrow, legalistic, and external practices of piety in matters of pu-

rification (7:2-5), external worship (7:6-7), and observance of commandments, Jesus sets in opposition the true moral intent of the divine law (7:8-13). But he goes beyond contrasting the law and Pharisaic interpretation of it. The parable of Mark 7:14-15 in effect sets aside the law itself in respect to clean and unclean food. He thereby opens the way for unity between Jew and Gentile in the kingdom of God, intimated by Jesus' departure for pagan territory beyond Galilee. For similar contrast see Mark 2:1–3:6; 3:20-35; 6:1-6.

7:3 Carefully washing their hands: refers to ritual purification.

7:5 Tradition of the elders: the body of detailed, unwritten, human laws regarded by the scribes and Pharisees to have the same binding force as that of the Mosaic law; cf. Galatians 1:14. 117

c
Ex 21:17;
Lv 20:9;
Dt 5:16;
Eph 6:2

d
Mt 15:10-20

e
4:10, 13

f
Acts 10:15

g
Jer 17:9

h
Mt 15:21-28

i
Mt 8:29

[8]You disregard God's commandment but cling to human tradition." [9]He went on to say, "How well you have set aside the commandment of God in order to uphold your tradition! [10c]For Moses said, 'Honor your father and your mother,' and 'Whoever curses father or mother shall die.' [11]Yet you say, 'If a person says to father or mother, "Any support you might have had from me is *qorban*"'* (meaning, dedicated to God), [12]you allow him to do nothing more for his father or mother. [13]You nullify the word of God in favor of your tradition that you have handed on. And you do many such things." [14d]He summoned the crowd again and said to them, "Hear me, all of you, and understand. [15]Nothing that enters one from outside can defile that person; but the things that come out from within are what defile." [[16]]*

[17*e]When he got home away from the crowd his disciples questioned him about the parable. [18]He said to them, "Are even you likewise without understanding? Do you not realize that everything that goes into a person from outside cannot defile, [19*f]since it enters not the heart but the stomach and passes out into the latrine?" (Thus he declared all foods clean.) [20]"But what comes out of a person, that is what defiles. [21g]From within people, from their hearts, come evil thoughts, unchastity, theft, murder, [22]adultery, greed, malice, deceit, licentiousness, envy, blasphemy, arrogance, folly. [23]All these evils come from within and they defile."

The Syrophoenician Woman's Faith

[24h]From that place he went off to the district of Tyre.* He entered a house and wanted no one to know about it, but he could not escape notice. [25]Soon a woman whose daughter had an unclean spirit heard about him. She came and fell at his feet. [26i]The woman was a Greek, a Syrophoenician by birth, and she begged him to drive the demon out of her daughter. [27]He said to her, "Let the children be fed first.* For it is not right to take the food of the children and throw it to the dogs." [28]She replied and said to him, "Lord, even the dogs under the table eat the children's scraps." [29]Then he said to her, "For saying this, you may go. The demon has gone out of your daughter." [30]When the woman went home, she found the child lying in bed and the demon gone.

The region of Tyre

The **Decapolis** was a Gentile district of ten towns. The title is a collective one; the NT does not list the towns themselves (cf. Mk 5:20; Mt 4:25), but they included the cities of Damascus, Scythopolis, Gadara, Gerasa, Hippos, Dion, Pella, Philadelphia, Raphana, and Canatha in the region of southern Syria and northern Jordan. These Hellenistic cities had an economic alliance that fostered their common association.

The Healing of a Deaf Man

³¹ʲAgain he left the district of Tyre and went by way of Sidon to the Sea of Galilee, into the district of the Decapolis. ³²And people brought to him a deaf man who had a speech impediment and begged him to lay his hand on him. ³³He took him off by himself away from the crowd. He put his finger into the man's ears and, spitting, touched his tongue; ³⁴then he looked up to heaven and groaned, and said to him, "*Ephphatha!*" (that is, "Be opened!") ³⁵And [immediately] the man's ears were opened, his speech impediment was removed, and he spoke plainly. ³⁶*He ordered them not to tell anyone. But the more he ordered them not to, the more they proclaimed it. ³⁷ᵏThey were exceedingly astonished and they said, "He has done all things well. He makes the deaf hear and [the] mute speak."

j
Mt 15:29-31

k
Mt 15:31

a
6:34-44;
Mt 15:32-39

MARK

The Feeding of Four Thousand

8 ¹*ᵃIn those days when there again was a great crowd without anything to eat, he summoned the disciples and said, ²"My heart is moved with pity for the crowd, because they have been with me now for three days and have nothing to eat. ³If I send them away hungry to their homes, they will collapse on the way, and some of them have come a great distance." ⁴His disciples answered him, "Where can anyone get enough bread to satisfy them here in this deserted place?" ⁵Still he asked them, "How many loaves

The Syrophoenician Woman, A Questioning Presence

A parent might do all kinds of things, stoop to all sorts of indignities, to save a child. When this Canaanite woman approaches Jesus, every generation can hear her desperation and recognize that she is literally begging for his attention to her daughter's condition. But she is a woman, and she is not a Jew, and so the scene surprisingly exposes a prejudice within this Jewish man of the time.

Jesus not only refuses to help her but uses insulting language to make his point. Brilliantly the woman turns his metaphor around and reminds him that even dogs are entitled to scraps from the table. She turns an insult into an opportunity, and the mission of Jesus is opened wider than expected.

The Syrophoenician woman stands in the gospel as a kind of question mark. We might hear her asking whether our communities and families are more like those seated at table or more like those begging for scraps. And then her presence asks us to become sensitive to needs that draw us beyond familiar boundaries. She might also ask whether we are willing to make fools of ourselves to obtain what we need, or to speak out for what others need.

7:36 The more they proclaimed it: the same verb **proclaim** attributed here to the crowd in relation to the miracles of Jesus is elsewhere used in Mark for the preaching of the gospel on the part of Jesus, of his disciples, and of the Christian community (1:14; 13:10; 14:9). Implied in the action of the crowd is a recognition of the salvific mission of Jesus; see the note on Matthew 11:5-6.

8:1-10 The two accounts of the multiplication of loaves and fishes (8:1-10; 6:31-44) have eucharistic significance. Their similarity of structure and themes but dissimilarity of detail are considered by many to refer to a single event that, however, developed in two distinct traditions, one Jewish Christian and the other Gentile Christian, since Jesus in Mark's presentation (7:24-37) has extended his saving mission to the Gentiles.

b
Mt 12:38-39;
16:1-4

c
Lk 11:16

d
Mt 16:5-12;
Lk 12:1

e
4:13

f
Jer 5:21;
Ez 12:2

g
7:33; Jn 9:6

Loaves and fishes mosaic at Tabgha, south of Capernaum

do you have?" "Seven," they replied. [6]*He ordered the crowd to sit down on the ground. Then, taking the seven loaves he gave thanks, broke them, and gave them to his disciples to distribute, and they distributed them to the crowd. [7]They also had a few fish. He said the blessing over them and ordered them distributed also. [8]They ate and were satisfied. They picked up the fragments left over—seven baskets. [9]There were about four thousand people.

He dismissed them [10]and got into the boat with his disciples and came to the region of Dalmanutha.

The Demand for a Sign

[11]*[b]The Pharisees came forward and began to argue with him, seeking from him a sign from heaven to test him.[c] [12]He sighed from the depth of his spirit and said, "Why does this generation seek a sign? Amen, I say to you, no sign will be given to this generation." [13]Then he left them, got into the boat again, and went off to the other shore.

The Leaven of the Pharisees

[14][d]They had forgotten to bring bread, and they had only one loaf with them in the boat. [15]*He enjoined them, "Watch out, guard against the leaven of the Pharisees and the leaven of Herod." [16]They concluded among themselves that it was because they had no bread. [17][e]When he became aware of this he said to them, "Why do you conclude that it is because you have no bread? Do you not yet understand or comprehend? Are your hearts hardened? [18][f]Do you have eyes and not see, ears and not hear? And do you not remember, [19]when I broke the five loaves for the five thousand, how many wicker baskets full of fragments you picked up?" They answered him, "Twelve." [20]"When I broke the seven loaves for the four thousand, how many full baskets of fragments did you pick up?" They answered [him], "Seven." [21]He said to them, "Do you still not understand?"

The Blind Man of Bethsaida

[22]*When they arrived at Bethsaida, they brought to him a blind man and begged him to touch him. [23][g]He took the blind man by the hand and led him outside the village. Putting spittle on his eyes he laid his hands on him and asked, "Do you see anything?" [24]Looking up he replied, "I

Bethsaida in the region of Galilee

8:6 See the note on Mark 6:41.

8:11-12 The objection of the Pharisees that Jesus' miracles are unsatisfactory for proving the arrival of God's kingdom is comparable to the request of the crowd for a sign in John 6:30-31. Jesus' response shows that a sign originating in human demand will not be provided; cf. Numbers 14:11, 22.

8:15 The leaven of the Pharisees . . . of Herod: the corruptive action of leaven (1 Cor 5:6-8; Gal 5:9) was an apt symbol of the evil

dispositions both of the Pharisees (8:11-13; 7:5-13) and of Herod (6:14-29) toward Jesus. The disciples of Jesus are warned against sharing such rebellious attitudes toward Jesus; cf. Mark 8:17, 21.

8:22-26 Jesus' actions and the gradual cure of the blind man probably have the same purpose as in the case of the deaf man (7:31-37). Some commentators regard the cure as an intended symbol of the gradual enlightenment of the disciples concerning Jesus' messiahship.

see people looking like trees and walking." ²⁵Then he laid hands on his eyes a second time and he saw clearly; his sight was restored and he could see everything distinctly. ²⁶Then he sent him home and said, "Do not even go into the village."

III: The Mystery Begins to Be Revealed

Peter's Confession about Jesus

²⁷*ʰNow Jesus and his disciples set out for the villages of Caesarea Philippi. Along the way he asked his disciples, "Who do people say that I am?" ²⁸They said in reply, "John the Baptist, others Elijah, still others one of the prophets." ²⁹And he asked them, "But who do you say that I am?" Peter said to him in reply, "You are the Messiah." ³⁰Then he warned them not to tell anyone about him.

The First Prediction of the Passion

³¹ⁱHe began to teach them that the Son of Man* must suffer greatly and be rejected by the elders, the chief priests, and the scribes, and be killed, and rise after three days. ³²He spoke this openly. Then Peter took him aside and began to rebuke him. ³³At this he turned around and, looking at his disciples, rebuked Peter and said, "Get behind me, Satan. You are thinking not as God does, but as human beings do."

The Conditions of Discipleship

³⁴ʲHe summoned the crowd with his disciples and said* to them, "Whoever wishes to come after me must deny himself, take up his cross, and follow me. ³⁵ᵏFor whoever wishes to save his life will lose it, but whoever loses his life for my sake and that of the gospel* will save it. ³⁶What profit is there for one to gain the whole world and forfeit his life? ³⁷What could one give in exchange for his life? ³⁸ˡWhoever is ashamed of me and of my words in this faithless and sinful generation, the Son of Man will be ashamed of when he comes in his Father's glory with the holy angels."

> The section between Mark 8:22 and 10:52 is a large narrative devoted to the theme of **discipleship**. It is framed by two stories of blind men whose faith contrasts with that of the disciples (8:22-26; 10:46-52). Whereas they learn to "see," Jesus' disciples remain "blind" to Jesus' true mission as the suffering Son of Man, the Messiah.

h
Mt 16:13-20;
Lk 9:18-21

i
Mt 16:21-27;
Lk 9:22-26

j
Mt 10:38-39;
16:24-27;
Lk 14:26-27

k
Jn 12:25

l
Mt 10:33;
Lk 12:8

8:27-30 This episode is the turning point in Mark's account of Jesus in his public ministry. Popular opinions concur in regarding him as a prophet. The disciples by contrast believe him to be the Messiah. Jesus acknowledges this identification but prohibits them from making his messianic office known to avoid confusing it with ambiguous contemporary ideas on the nature of that office. See further the notes on Matthew 16:13-20.

8:31 Son of Man: an enigmatic title. It is used in Daniel 7:13-14 as a symbol of "the saints of the Most High," the faithful Israelites who receive the everlasting kingdom from the Ancient One (God). They are represented by a human figure that contrasts with the various beasts who represent the previous kingdoms of the earth. In the Jewish apocryphal books of 1 Enoch and 4 Ezra the "Son of Man" is not, as in Daniel, a group, but a unique figure of extraordinary spiritual endowments, who will be revealed as the one through whom the everlasting kingdom decreed by God will be established. It is possible though doubtful that this individualization of the Son of Man figure had been made in Jesus' time, and therefore his use of the title in that sense is questionable. Of itself, this expression means simply a human being, or, indefinitely, someone, and there

are evidences of this use in pre-Christian times. Its use in the New Testament is probably due to Jesus' speaking of himself in that way, "a human being," and the later church's taking this in the sense of the Jewish apocrypha and applying it to him with that meaning. **Rejected by the elders, the chief priests, and the scribes**: the supreme council called the Sanhedrin was made up of seventy-one members of these three groups and presided over by the high priest. It exercised authority over the Jews in religious matters. See the note on Matthew 8:20.

8:34-35 This utterance of Jesus challenges all believers to authentic discipleship and total commitment to himself through self-renunciation and acceptance of the cross of suffering, even to the sacrifice of life itself. **Whoever wishes to save his life will lose it . . . will save it**: an expression of the ambivalence of life and its contrasting destiny. Life seen as mere self-centered earthly existence and lived in denial of Christ ends in destruction, but when lived in loyalty to Christ, despite earthly death, it arrives at fullness of life.

8:35 For my sake and that of the gospel: Mark here, as at Mark 10:29 equates Jesus with the gospel.

a
Mt 16:28;
Lk 9:27

b
Mt 17:1-13;
Lk 9:28-36

c
8:31

d
Is 53:3;
Mal 3:23

e
1 Kgs 19:2-10

f
Mt 17:14-21;
Lk 9:37-43

9 ¹*ᵃHe also said to them, "Amen, I say to you, there are some standing here who will not taste death until they see that the kingdom of God has come in power."

The Transfiguration of Jesus

²*ᵇAfter six days Jesus took Peter, James, and John and led them up a high mountain apart by themselves. And he was transfigured before them, ³and his clothes became dazzling white, such as no fuller on earth could bleach them. ⁴Then Elijah appeared to them along with Moses, and they were conversing

Mosaic in the apse of the Basilica of the Transfiguration on Mount Tabor

with Jesus. ⁵*Then Peter said to Jesus in reply, "Rabbi, it is good that we are here! Let us make three tents: one for you, one for Moses, and one for Elijah." ⁶He hardly knew what to say, they were so terrified. ⁷Then a cloud came, casting a shadow over them;* then from the cloud came a voice, "This is my beloved Son. Listen to him." ⁸Suddenly, looking around, they no longer saw anyone but Jesus alone with them.

The Coming of Elijah

⁹*ᶜAs they were coming down from the mountain, he charged them not to relate what they had seen to anyone, except when the Son of Man had risen from the dead. ¹⁰So they kept the matter to themselves, questioning what rising from the dead meant. ¹¹ᵈThen they asked him, "Why do the scribes say that Elijah must come first?" ¹²He told them, "Elijah will indeed come first and restore all things, yet how is it written regarding the Son of Man that he must suffer greatly and be treated with contempt? ¹³ᵉBut I tell you that Elijah has come and they did to him whatever they pleased, as it is written of him."

The Healing of a Boy with a Demon

¹⁴*ᶠWhen they came to the disciples, they saw a large crowd around them and scribes arguing with them. ¹⁵Immediately on seeing him, the whole crowd was utterly amazed.

9:1 There are some standing . . . come in power: understood by some to refer to the establishment by God's power of his kingdom on earth in and through the church; more likely, as understood by others, a reference to the imminent parousia.

9:2-8 Mark and Matthew 17:1 place the transfiguration of Jesus six days after the first prediction of his passion and death and his instruction to the disciples on the doctrine of the cross; Luke 9:28 has "about eight days." Thus the transfiguration counterbalances the prediction of the passion by affording certain of the disciples insight into the divine glory that Jesus possessed. His glory will overcome his death and that of his disciples; cf. 2 Corinthians 3:18; 2 Peter 1:16-19. The heavenly voice (9:7) prepares the disciples to understand that in the divine plan Jesus must die ignominiously before his messianic glory is made manifest; cf. Luke 24:25-27. See further the note on Matthew 17:1-8.

9:5 Moses and Elijah represent respectively law and prophecy in the Old Testament and are linked to Mount Sinai; cf. Exodus 19:16–20:17; 1 Kings 19:2, 8-14. They now appear with Jesus as witnesses to the fulfillment of the law and the prophets taking place in the person of Jesus as he appears in glory.

9:7 A cloud came, casting a shadow over them: even the disciples enter into the mystery of his glorification. In the Old Testament the cloud covered the meeting tent, indicating the Lord's presence in the midst of his people (Ex 40:34-35) and came to rest upon the temple in Jerusalem at the time of its dedication (1 Kgs 8:10).

9:9-13 At the transfiguration of Jesus his disciples had seen Elijah. They were perplexed because, according to the rabbinical interpretation of Malachi 3:23-24, Elijah was to come first. Jesus' response shows that Elijah has come, in the person of John the Baptist, to prepare for the day of the Lord. Jesus **must suffer greatly and be treated with contempt** (9:12) like the Baptist (9:13); cf. Mark 6:17-29.

9:14-29 The disciples' failure to effect a cure seems to reflect unfavorably on Jesus (9:14-18, 22). In response Jesus exposes their lack of trust in God (4:19) and scores their lack of prayer (4:29), i.e., of conscious reliance on God's power when acting in Jesus' name. For Matthew, see the note on Matthew 17:14-20. Luke 9:37-43 centers attention on Jesus' sovereign power.

They ran up to him and greeted him. [16]He asked them, "What are you arguing about with them?" [17]Someone from the crowd answered him, "Teacher, I have brought to you my son possessed by a mute spirit. [18]Wherever it seizes him, it throws him down; he foams at the mouth, grinds his teeth, and becomes rigid. I asked your disciples to drive it out, but they were unable to do so." [19]He said to them in reply, "O faithless generation, how long will I be with you? How long will I endure you? Bring him to me." [20]They brought the boy to him. And when he saw him, the spirit immediately threw the boy into convulsions. As he fell to the ground, he began to roll around and foam at the mouth. [21]Then he questioned his father, "How long has this been happening to him?" He replied, "Since childhood. [22]It has often thrown him into fire and into water to kill him. But if you can do anything, have compassion on us and help us." [23]Jesus said to him, "'If you can!' Everything is possible to one who has faith." [24]Then the boy's father cried out, "I do believe, help my unbelief!" [25]Jesus, on seeing a crowd rapidly gathering, rebuked the unclean spirit and said to it, "Mute and deaf spirit, I command you: come out of him and never enter him again!" [26]Shouting and throwing the boy into convulsions, it came out. He became like a corpse, which caused many to say, "He is dead!" [27]But Jesus took him by the hand, raised him, and he stood up. [28]When he entered the house, his disciples asked him in private, "Why could we not drive it out?" [29]*He said to them, "This kind can only come out through prayer."

The Second Prediction of the Passion

[30g]They left from there and began a journey through Galilee, but he did not wish anyone to know about it.[h] [31]He was teaching his disciples and telling them, "The Son of Man is to be handed over to men and they will kill him, and three days after his death he will rise." [32]But they did not understand the saying, and they were afraid to question him.

IV: The Full Revelation of the Mystery

The Greatest in the Kingdom

[33*i]They came to Capernaum and, once inside the house, he began to ask them, "What were you arguing about on the way?" [34]But they remained silent. They had been discussing among themselves on the way who was the greatest. [35j]Then he sat down, called the Twelve, and said to them, "If anyone wishes to be first, he shall be the last of all and the servant of all." [36]Taking a child he placed it in their midst, and putting his arms around it he said to them, [37k]"Whoever receives one child such as this in my name, receives me; and whoever receives me, receives not me but the One who sent me."

g
8:31;
Mt 17:22-23;
Lk 9:43-45

h
Jn 7:1

i
Mt 18:1-5;
Lk 9:46-48

j
Mt 20:27

k
Mt 10:40; 18:5;
Jn 13:20

An **exorcism** is a type of miracle story that relates the driving out of a demon from someone who is possessed (cf. also Mk 1:23-26, 34; 5:1-13). Jesus' reputation for being an exorcist caused some to accuse him of being allied to demons or to the devil (Beelzebul), which Jesus denied (Mk 3:22-27 and par.).

Capernaum in Galilee

9:29 **This kind can only come out through prayer**: a variant reading adds "and through fasting."

9:33-37 Mark probably intends this incident and the sayings that follow as commentary on the disciples' lack of understanding (9:32).

Their role in Jesus' work is one of service, especially to the poor and lowly. Children were the symbol Jesus used for the *ănăwîm*, the poor in spirit, the lowly in the Christian community.

MARK

Another Exorcist

[38*l]John said to him, "Teacher, we saw someone driving out demons in your name, and we tried to prevent him because he does not follow us." [39]Jesus replied, "Do not prevent him. There is no one who performs a mighty deed in my name who can at the same time speak ill of me. [40m]For whoever is not against us is for us. [41n]Anyone who gives you a cup of water to drink because you belong to Christ, amen, I say to you, will surely not lose his reward.

Temptations to Sin

[42o]"Whoever causes one of these little ones who believe [in me] to sin, it would be better for him if a great millstone were put around his neck and he were thrown into the sea. [43]If your hand causes you to sin, cut it off. It is better for you to enter into life maimed than with two hands to go into Gehenna,* into the unquenchable fire. [44]* [45]And if your foot causes you to sin, cut it off. It is better for you to enter into life crippled than with two feet to be thrown into Gehenna. [46] [47]And if your eye causes you to sin, pluck it out. Better for you to enter into the kingdom of God with one eye than with two eyes to be thrown into Gehenna, [48p]where 'their worm does not die, and the fire is not quenched.'

The Simile of Salt

[49*]"Everyone will be salted with fire. [50q]Salt is good, but if salt becomes insipid, with what will you restore its flavor? Keep salt in yourselves and you will have peace with one another."

Marriage and Divorce

10 [1]He set out from there and went into the district of Judea [and] across the Jordan. Again crowds gathered around him and, as was his custom, he again taught them. [2*a]The Pharisees approached and asked, "Is it lawful for a husband to divorce his wife?" They were testing him. [3]He said to them in reply, "What did Moses command you?" [4b]They replied, "Moses permitted him to write a bill of divorce and dismiss her." [5]But Jesus told them, "Because of the hardness of your hearts he wrote you this commandment. [6c]But from the beginning of creation, 'God made them male and female. [7d]For this reason a man shall leave his father and mother [and be joined to his wife], [8]and the two shall become one flesh.' So they are no longer two but one flesh. [9]Therefore what God has joined together, no human being must separate." [10]In the house the disciples again questioned him about this. [11e]He said to them, "Whoever

l Nm 11:28; Lk 9:49-50; 1 Cor 12:3
m Mt 12:30
n Mt 10:42; 1 Cor 3:23
o Mt 5:29-30; 18:6-9; Lk 17:1-2
p Is 66:24
q Lv 2:13; Mt 5:13; Lk 14:34-35; Col 4:6
a Mt 19:3-9
b Dt 24:1-4
c Gn 1:27
d Gn 2:24; 1 Cor 6:16; Eph 5:31
e Mt 5:32; Lk 16:18; 1 Cor 7:10-11

9:38-41 Jesus warns against jealousy and intolerance toward others, such as exorcists who do **not follow us**. The saying in Mark 9:40 is a broad principle of the divine tolerance. Even the smallest courtesies shown to those who teach in Jesus' name do not go unrewarded.

9:43, 45, 47 Gehenna: see the note on Matthew 5:22.

9:44, 46 These verses, lacking in some important early manuscripts, are here omitted as scribal additions. They simply repeat Mark 9:48, itself a modified citation of Isaiah 66:24.

9:49 Everyone will be salted with fire: so the better manuscripts. Some add "every sacrifice will be salted with salt." The purifying and preservative use of salt in food (Lv 2:13) and the refinement effected through fire refer here to comparable effects in the spiritual life of the disciples of Jesus.

10:2-9 In the dialogue between Jesus and the Pharisees on the subject of divorce, Jesus declares that the law of Moses permitted divorce (Dt 24:1) only **because of the hardness of your hearts** (10:4-5). In citing Genesis 1:27 and 2:24 Jesus proclaims permanence to be the divine intent from the beginning concerning human marriage (10:6-8). He reaffirms this with the declaration that **what God has joined together, no human being must separate** (10:9). See further the notes on Matthew 5:31-32; 19:3-9.

divorces his wife and marries another commits adultery against her; [12]and if she divorces her husband and marries another, she commits adultery."

Blessing of the Children

[13f]And people were bringing children to him that he might touch them, but the disciples rebuked them.[g] [14]When Jesus saw this he became indignant and said to them, "Let the children come to me; do not prevent them, for the kingdom of God belongs to such as these. [15h]Amen, I say to you, whoever does not accept the kingdom of God like a child* will not enter it." [16]Then he embraced them and blessed them, placing his hands on them.

The Rich Man

[17i]As he was setting out on a journey, a man ran up, knelt down before him, and asked him, "Good teacher, what must I do to inherit eternal life?" [18]Jesus answered him, "Why do you call me good?* No one is good but God alone. [19j]You know the commandments: 'You shall not kill; you shall not commit adultery; you shall not steal; you shall not bear false witness; you shall not defraud; honor your father and your mother.'" [20]He replied and said to him, "Teacher, all of these I have observed from my youth." [21]Jesus, looking at him, loved him and said to him, "You are lacking in one thing. Go, sell what you have, and give to [the] poor and you will have treasure in heaven; then come, follow me." [22]At that statement his face fell, and he went away sad, for he had many possessions.

[23*k]Jesus looked around and said to his disciples, "How hard it is for those who have wealth to enter the kingdom of God!" [24]The disciples were amazed at his words. So Jesus again said to them in reply, "Children, how hard it is to enter the kingdom of God! [25]It is easier for a camel to pass through [the] eye of [a] needle than for one who is rich to enter the kingdom of God." [26]They were exceedingly astonished and said among themselves, "Then who can be saved?" [27]Jesus looked at them and said, "For human beings it is impossible, but not for God. All things are possible for God." [28]Peter began to say to him, "We have given up everything and followed you." [29]Jesus said, "Amen, I say to you, there is no one who has given up house or brothers or sisters or mother or father or children or lands for my sake and for the sake of the gospel [30]who will not receive a hundred times more now in this present age: houses and brothers and sisters and mothers and children and lands, with persecutions, and eternal life in the age to come. [31l]But many that are first will be last, and [the] last will be first."

The Third Prediction of the Passion

[32m]They were on the way, going up to Jerusalem, and Jesus went ahead of them. They were amazed, and those who followed were afraid. Taking the Twelve aside again,

f
Mt 19:13-15;
Lk 18:15-17

g
Lk 9:47

h
Mt 18:3

i
Mt 19:16-30;
Lk 18:18-30

j
Ex 20:12-16;
Dt 5:16-21

k
Prv 11:28

l
Mt 19:30;
Lk 13:30

m
8:31; Mt
20:17-19;
Lk 18:31-33

MARK

10:15 Whoever does not accept the kingdom of God like a child: i.e., in total dependence upon and obedience to the gospel; cf. Matthew 18:3-4.

10:18 Why do you call me good?: Jesus repudiates the term "good" for himself and directs it to God, the source of all goodness who alone can grant the gift of eternal life; cf. Matthew 19:16-17.

10:23-27 In the Old Testament wealth and material goods are considered a sign of God's favor (Jb 1:10; Ps 128:1-2; Is 3:10). The words of Jesus in Mark 10:23-25 provoke astonishment among the disciples because of their apparent contradiction of the Old Testament concept (10:24, 26). Since wealth, power, and merit generate false security, Jesus rejects them utterly as a claim to enter the kingdom. Achievement of salvation is beyond human capability and depends solely on the goodness of God who offers it as a gift (10:27).

n Mt 20:20-28
o Lk 12:50
p Lk 22:25-27
q Mt 20:29-34; Lk 18:35-43

he began to tell them what was going to happen
to him. 33"Behold, we are going up to Jerusalem, and the Son of Man will be handed over
to the chief priests and the scribes, and they will
condemn him to death and hand him over to the
Gentiles 34who will mock him, spit upon him,
scourge him, and put him to death, but after
three days he will rise."

> Jesus made it very clear to his disciples that their importance arises not out of their greatness but out of their service; and their service must flow out of their humility, their willingness to *stand beside* rather than *lord it over* someone.

Ambition of James and John

35nThen James and John, the sons of Zebedee,
came to him and said to him, "Teacher, we want you to do for us whatever we ask of
you." 36He replied, "What do you wish [me] to do for you?" 37They answered him,
"Grant that in your glory we may sit one at your right and the other at your left." 38*oJesus
said to them, "You do not know what you are asking. Can you drink the cup that I drink
or be baptized with the baptism with which I am baptized?" 39They said to him, "We
can." Jesus said to them, "The cup that I drink, you will drink, and with the baptism
with which I am baptized, you will be baptized; 40but to sit at my right or at my left is
not mine to give but is for those for whom it has been prepared." 41When the ten heard
this, they became indignant at James and John. 42*pJesus summoned them and said to
them, "You know that those who are recognized as rulers over the Gentiles lord it over
them, and their great ones make their authority over them felt. 43But it shall not be so
among you. Rather, whoever wishes to be great among you will be your servant; 44who-
ever wishes to be first among you will be the slave of all. 45For the Son of Man did not
come to be served but to serve and to give his life as a ransom for many."

The Blind Bartimaeus

46*qThey came to Jericho. And as he was leaving Jericho with his disciples and a
sizable crowd, Bartimaeus, a blind man, the son of Timaeus, sat by the roadside begging. 47On hearing that it was Jesus of Nazareth, he began to cry out and say, "Jesus,
son of David, have pity on me." 48And many rebuked him, telling him to be silent. But
he kept calling out all the more, "Son of David, have pity on me." 49Jesus stopped and
said, "Call him." So they called the blind man, saying to him, "Take courage; get up,
he is calling you." 50He threw aside his cloak, sprang up, and came to Jesus. 51Jesus
said to him in reply, "What do you want me to do for you?" The blind man replied to
him, "Master, I want to see." 52Jesus told him, "Go your way; your faith has saved you."
Immediately he received his sight and followed him on the way.

10:38-40 Can you drink the cup . . . I am baptized?: the metaphor of drinking the cup is used in the Old Testament to refer to acceptance of the destiny assigned by God; see the note on Psalm 11:6. In Jesus' case, this involves divine judgment on sin that Jesus the innocent one is to expiate on behalf of the guilty (14:24; Is 53:5). His baptism is to be his crucifixion and death for the salvation of the human race; cf. Luke 12:50. The request of James and John for a share in the glory (10:35-37) must of necessity involve a share in Jesus' sufferings, the endurance of tribulation and suffering for the gospel (10:39). The authority of assigning places of honor in the kingdom is reserved to God (10:40).

10:42-45 Whatever authority is to be exercised by the disciples must, like that of Jesus, be rendered as service to others (10:45) rather than for personal aggrandizement (10:42-44). The service of Jesus is his passion and death for the sins of the human race (10:45); cf. Mark 14:24; Isaiah 53:11-12; Matthew 26:28; Luke 22:19-20.

10:46 See the notes on Matthew 9:27-31 and 20:29-34.

The Entry into Jerusalem

11 [1]*ᵃWhen they drew near to Jerusalem, to Bethphage and Bethany at the Mount of Olives, he sent two of his disciples [2]and said to them, "Go into the village opposite you, and immediately on entering it, you will find a colt tethered on which no one has ever sat. Untie it and bring it here. [3]If anyone should say to you, 'Why are you doing this?' reply, 'The Master has need of it and will send it back here at once.'" [4]So they went off and found a colt tethered at a gate outside on the street, and they untied it. [5]Some of the bystanders said to them, "What are you doing, untying the colt?" [6]They answered them just as Jesus had told them to, and they permitted them to do it. [7]So they brought the colt to Jesus and put their cloaks over it. And he sat on it. [8]Many people spread their cloaks on the road, and others spread leafy branches that they had cut from the fields. [9]ᵇThose preceding him as well as those following kept crying out:

Bethphage, Bethany, Mount of Olives

a
Mt 21:1-9;
Lk 19:29-38;
Jn 12:12-15

b
2 Sm 7:16;
Ps 118:26

c
Mt 21:10, 17

d
Mt 21:18-20;
Lk 13:6-9

> "Hosanna!
>> Blessed is he who comes in the name of the Lord!
>> [10]Blessed is the kingdom of our father David that
>>> is to come!
> Hosanna in the highest!"

[11]ᶜHe entered Jerusalem and went into the temple area. He looked around at everything and, since it was already late, went out to Bethany with the Twelve.

The church has incorporated these **verses of praise** (11:10) into the liturgy at the end of the preface, immediately before the beginning of the eucharistic prayer. They provide a fitting hymn to Jesus as triumphant Messiah.

Jesus Curses a Fig Tree

[12]*ᵈThe next day as they were leaving Bethany he was hungry. [13]Seeing from a distance a fig tree in leaf, he went over to see if he could find anything on it. When he reached it he found nothing but leaves; it was not the time for figs. [14]And he said to it in reply, "May no one ever eat of your fruit again!" And his disciples heard it.

Fig tree

11:1-11 In Mark's account Jesus takes the initiative in ordering the preparation for his entry into Jerusalem (11:1-6) even as he later orders the preparation of his last Passover Supper (14:12-16). In Mark 11:9-10 the greeting Jesus receives stops short of proclaiming him Messiah. He is greeted rather as the prophet of the coming messianic kingdom. Contrast Matthew 21:9.

11:12-14 Jesus' search for fruit on the fig tree recalls the prophets' earlier use of this image to designate Israel; cf. Jeremiah 8:13; 29:17; Joel 1:7; Hosea 9:10, 16. Cursing the fig tree is a parable in action representing Jesus' judgment (11:20) on barren Israel and the fate of Jerusalem for failing to receive his teaching; cf. Isaiah 34:4; Hosea 2:14; Luke 13:6-9.

MARK

e
Mt 21:12-13;
Lk 19:45-46;
Jn 2:14-16

f
Is 56:7;
Jer 7:11

g
Lk 21:37

h
Mt 21:20-22

i
Mt 17:20-21;
Lk 17:6

j
Mt 7:7;
Jn 11:22; 14:13

k
Mt 6:14; 18:35

l
Mt 21:23-27;
Lk 20:1-8

Cleansing of the Temple

[15]*[e]They came to Jerusalem, and on entering the temple area he began to drive out those selling and buying there. He overturned the tables of the money changers and the seats of those who were selling doves. [16]He did not permit anyone to carry anything through the temple area. [17][f]Then he taught them saying, "Is it not written:

'My house shall be called a house of prayer for all peoples'?
But you have made it a den of thieves."

[18]The chief priests and the scribes came to hear of it and were seeking a way to put him to death, yet they feared him because the whole crowd was astonished at his teaching. [19][g]When evening came, they went out of the city.

The Withered Fig Tree

[20][h]Early in the morning, as they were walking along, they saw the fig tree withered to its roots. [21]Peter remembered and said to him, "Rabbi, look! The fig tree that you cursed has withered." [22]Jesus said to them in reply, "Have faith in God. [23][i]Amen, I say to you, whoever says to this mountain, 'Be lifted up and thrown into the sea,' and does not doubt in his heart but believes that what he says will happen, it shall be done for him. [24][j]Therefore I tell you, all that you ask for in prayer, believe that you will receive it and it shall be yours. [25][k]When you stand to pray, forgive anyone against whom you have a grievance, so that your heavenly Father may in turn forgive you your transgressions." [26]*

Could it be that sometimes our prayer is not as effective because we come to prayer with an unforgiving spirit? When you begin to pray, cleanse your heart. Make of your heart a pure container of receptive love. Embellish it with forgiveness.

The Authority of Jesus Questioned

[27]*[l]They returned once more to Jerusalem. As he was walking in the temple area, the chief priests, the scribes, and the elders approached him [28]and said to him, "By what authority are you doing these things? Or who gave you this authority to do them?" [29]Jesus said to them, "I shall ask you one question. Answer me, and I will tell you by what authority I do these things. [30]Was John's baptism of heavenly or of human origin? Answer

In Jesus the world is reconciled with God; in Jesus all people are reconciled and forgiven: "Because the walls of hostility between God and humankind were broken down in the life and death of the true, perfect servant, union and well-being between God and the world were finally fully possible" (*The Challenge of Peace* 51; see also Eph 2:13-22 and Gal 3:28). This central Christian truth is the basis for the Christian forgiveness of one another (see Mt 6:14-15; Lk 6:37; 11:4; 17:3-4).

11:15-19 See the note on Matthew 21:12-17.

11:26 This verse, which reads, "But if you do not forgive, neither will your heavenly Father forgive your transgressions," is omitted in the best manuscripts. It was probably added by copyists under the influence of Matthew 6:15.

11:27-33 The mounting hostility toward Jesus came from the chief priests, the scribes, and the elders (11:27); the Herodians and the Pharisees (12:13); and the Sadducees (12:18). By their rejection of God's messengers, John the Baptist and Jesus, they incurred the divine judgment implied in Mark 11:27-33 and confirmed in the parable of the vineyard tenants (12:1-12).

me." [31]They discussed this among themselves and said, "If we say, 'Of heavenly origin,' he will say, '[Then] why did you not believe him?' [32]But shall we say, 'Of human origin'?"—they feared the crowd, for they all thought John really was a prophet. [33]So they said to Jesus in reply, "We do not know." Then Jesus said to them, "Neither shall I tell you by what authority I do these things."

Parable of the Tenants

12[1][*][a]He began to speak to them in parables. "A man planted a vineyard, put a hedge around it, dug a wine press, and built a tower. Then he leased it to tenant farmers and left on a journey.[b] [2]At the proper time he sent a servant to the tenants to obtain from them some of the produce of the vineyard. [3]But they seized him, beat him, and sent him away empty-handed. [4]Again he sent them another servant. And that one they beat over the head and treated shamefully. [5]He sent yet another whom they killed. So, too, many others; some they beat, others they killed. [6]He had one other to send, a beloved son. He sent him to them last of all, thinking, 'They will respect my son.' [7]But those tenants said to one another, 'This is the heir. Come, let us kill him, and the inheritance will be ours.' [8]So they seized him and killed him, and threw him out of the vineyard. [9]What [then] will the owner of the vineyard do? He will come, put the tenants to death, and give the vineyard to others. [10][c]Have you not read this scripture passage:

'The stone that the builders rejected
  has become the cornerstone;
[11]by the Lord has this been done,
  and it is wonderful in our eyes'?"

[12]They were seeking to arrest him, but they feared the crowd, for they realized that he had addressed the parable to them. So they left him and went away.

Paying Taxes to the Emperor

[13][*][d] They sent some Pharisees and Herodians to him to ensnare him in his speech.[*][e] [14]They came and said to him, "Teacher, we know that you are a truthful man and that you are not concerned with anyone's opinion. You do not regard a person's status but teach the way of God in accordance with the truth. Is it lawful to pay the census tax to Caesar or not? Should we pay or should we not pay?" [15]Knowing their hypocrisy he said to them, "Why are you testing me? Bring me a denarius to look at." [16]They brought one to him and he said to them, "Whose image and inscription is this?" They replied to him, "Caesar's." [17][f]So Jesus said to them, "Repay to

---

a
Mt 21:33-46;
Lk 20:9-19

b
Is 5:1-7;
Jer 2:21

c
Ps 118:22-23;
Is 28:16

d
Mt 22:15-33;
Lk 20:20-39

e
3:6

f
Rom 13:7

The NT quotes the words of Psalm 118:22-23 several times in reference to **Jesus as the "rejected stone"** who paradoxically becomes the cornerstone (cf. Mt 21:42; Lk 20:17; Acts 4:11; 1 Pt 2:7).

How easy it is to overlook, and even reject, wondrous treasures that have been sent for our healing. We suffer from poor eyesight. We must learn to see with the heart. How sad it would be to send something or someone away that was intended to rise up and bless us.

12:1-12 The vineyard denotes Israel (Is 5:1-7). The tenant farmers are the religious leaders of Israel. God is the owner of the vineyard. His servants are his messengers, the prophets. The beloved son is Jesus (1:11; 9:7; Mt 3:17; 17:5; Lk 3:22; 9:35). The punishment of the tenants refers to the religious leaders, and the transfer of the vineyard to others refers to the people of the new Israel.

12:13-34 In the ensuing conflicts (cf. also 2:1–3:6) Jesus vanquishes his adversaries by his responses to their questions and reduces them to silence (12:34).
12:13-17 See the note on Matthew 22:15-22.

MARK

g
Dt 25:5

h
Ex 3:6

i
Mt 22:34-40;
Lk 10:25-28

j
Dt 6:4-5

k
Lv 19:18;
Rom 13:9;
Gal 5:14;
Jas 2:8

l
Dt 6:4;
Ps 40:7-9

m
Mt 22:46;
Lk 20:40

n
Mt 22:41-45;
Lk 20:41-44

o
Ps 110:1

On **Sadducees,** see the chart on Jewish leaders in "Background to the Gospels," p. 4.

Caesar what belongs to Caesar and to God what belongs to God." They were utterly amazed at him.

The Question about the Resurrection

[18]*Some Sadducees, who say there is no resurrection, came to him and put this question to him, [19g]saying, "Teacher, Moses wrote for us, 'If someone's brother dies, leaving a wife but no child, his brother must take the wife and raise up descendants for his brother.' [20]Now there were seven brothers. The first married a woman and died, leaving no descendants. [21]So the second married her and died, leaving no descendants, and the third likewise. [22]And the seven left no descendants. Last of all the woman also died. [23]At the resurrection [when they arise] whose wife will she be? For all seven had been married to her." [24]Jesus said to them, "Are you not misled because you do not know the scriptures or the power of God? [25]When they rise from the dead, they neither marry nor are given in marriage, but they are like the angels in heaven. [26h]As for the dead being raised, have you not read in the Book of Moses, in the passage about the bush, how God told him, 'I am the God of Abraham, [the] God of Isaac, and [the] God of Jacob'? [27]He is not God of the dead but of the living. You are greatly misled."

The Greatest Commandment

[28*i]One of the scribes, when he came forward and heard them disputing and saw how well he had answered them, asked him, "Which is the first of all the commandments?" [29]Jesus replied, "The first is this: 'Hear, O Israel! The Lord our God is Lord alone! [30j]You shall love the Lord your God with all your heart, with all your soul, with all your mind, and with all your strength.' [31k]The second is this: 'You shall love your neighbor as yourself.' There is no other commandment greater than these." [32]The scribe said to him, "Well said, teacher. You are right in saying, 'He is One and there is no other than he.' [33l]And 'to love him with all your heart, with all your understanding, with all your strength, and to love your neighbor as yourself' is worth more than all burnt offerings and sacrifices." [34m]And when Jesus saw that [he] answered with understanding, he said to him, "You are not far from the kingdom of God." And no one dared to ask him any more questions.

The Question about David's Son

[35*n]As Jesus was teaching in the temple area he said, "How do the scribes claim that the Messiah is the son of David? [36o]David himself, inspired by the holy Spirit, said:

'The Lord said to my lord,
"Sit at my right hand
until I place your enemies under your feet."'

[37]David himself calls him 'lord'; so how is he his son?" [The] great crowd heard this with delight.

12:18-27 See the note on Matthew 22:23-33.
12:28-34 See the note on Matthew 22:34-40.
12:35-37 Jesus questions the claim of the scribes about the Davidic descent of the Messiah, not to deny it (Mt 1:1; Acts 2:20, 34; Rom 1:3; 2 Tm 2:8) but to imply that he is more than this. His superiority derives from his transcendent origin, to which David himself attested when he spoke of the Messiah with the name "Lord" (Ps 110:1). See also the note on Matthew 22:41-46.

Denunciation of the Scribes

[38]*[p]In the course of his teaching he said, "Beware of the scribes, who like to go around in long robes and accept greetings in the marketplaces, [39]seats of honor in synagogues, and places of honor at banquets. [40]They devour the houses of widows and, as a pretext, recite lengthy prayers. They will receive a very severe condemnation."

p
Mt 23:1-7;
Lk 11:43;
20:45-47

q
Lk 21:1-4

a
Mt 24:1-2;
Lk 21:5-6

The Generous Widow

This well-known story of the widow who gave more than she could afford has often been used in praise of generosity. After all, those who gave large sums are not the object of praise; their gifts were from their surplus. But the widow gave "from her poverty."

The story of the widow, however, occurs right in the middle of high criticism being leveled against the scribes and Pharisees. Jesus has lambasted the leaders of his faith tradition for "devouring the houses of widows" (Mk 12:40) and now tells the story of a widow who gave her all. Could it be that the story is meant to illustrate just what he has criticized? Giving to the temple collection was a religious requirement; using the temple collection for the needy was the intention. Instead, the temple leaders are accused of spending the funds on their own desires for long robes and banquets.

Widows were entirely dependent on male relatives or others in the community to provide for their needs. To give from one's needs could be seen indeed as generosity, but this was more likely meant to illustrate something about the abuse of position and power that the leading class possessed.

The widow's generosity can serve as a beautiful reminder to trust in God, even for life's essentials. But on another level, the widow reminds us of the responsibilities of leadership and the danger of abusing one's power.

The Poor Widow's Contribution

[41]*[q]He sat down opposite the treasury and observed how the crowd put money into the treasury. Many rich people put in large sums. [42]A poor widow also came and put in two small coins worth a few cents. [43]Calling his disciples to himself, he said to them, "Amen, I say to you, this poor widow put in more than all the other contributors to the treasury. [44]For they have all contributed from their surplus wealth, but she, from her poverty, has contributed all she had, her whole livelihood."

The Destruction of the Temple Foretold

13 [1]*[a]As he was making his way out of the temple area one of his disciples said to him, "Look, teacher, what stones and what buildings!" [2]Jesus said to him, "Do you see these great buildings? There will not be one stone left upon another that will not be thrown down."

12:38-40 See the notes on Mark 7:1-23 and Matthew 23:1-39.
12:41-44 See the note on Luke 21:1-4.
13:1-2 The reconstructed temple with its precincts, begun under Herod the Great ca. 20 B.C., was completed only some seven years before it was destroyed by fire in A.D. 70 at the hands of the Romans; cf. Jeremiah 26:18; Matthew 24:1-2. For the dating of the reconstruction of the temple, see further the note on John 2:20.

The Signs of the End

³*ᵇAs he was sitting on the Mount of Olives opposite the temple area, Peter, James, John, and Andrew asked him privately, ⁴"Tell us, when will this happen, and what sign will there be when all these things are about to come to an end?" ⁵ᶜJesus began to say to them, "See that no one deceives you. ⁶Many will come in my name saying, 'I am he,' and they will deceive many. ⁷When you hear of wars and reports of wars do not be alarmed; such things must happen, but it will not yet be the end. ⁸Nation will rise against nation and kingdom against kingdom. There will be earthquakes from place to place and there will be famines. These are the beginnings of the labor pains.

The Coming Persecution

⁹ᵈ"Watch out for yourselves. They will hand you over to the courts. You will be beaten in synagogues. You will be arraigned before governors and kings because of me, as a witness before them. ¹⁰But the gospel must first be preached to all nations.* ¹¹ᵉWhen they lead you away and hand you over, do not worry beforehand about what you are to say. But say whatever will be given to you at that hour. For it will not be you who are speaking but the holy Spirit. ¹²Brother will hand over brother to death, and the father his child; children will rise up against parents and have them put to death. ¹³You will be hated by all because of my name. But the one who perseveres to the end will be saved.

The Great Tribulation

¹⁴ᶠ"When you see the desolating abomination standing* where he should not (let the reader understand), then those in Judea must flee to the mountains,ᵍ ¹⁵ʰ[and] a person on a housetop must not go down or enter to get anything out of his house, ¹⁶and a person in a field must not return to get his cloak. ¹⁷Woe to pregnant women and nursing mothers in those days. ¹⁸Pray that this does not happen in winter. ¹⁹ⁱFor those times will

The **desolating abomination** refers back to the OT event of the defiling of the temple by Antiochus Epiphanes IV, the Seleucid king in 167 B.C. (Dn 9:27; cf. 11:31; 12:11; 1 Mc 1:54; 6:7). Here it refers to a similar dramatic sacrilege in the future, a bad omen of the destruction that will befall Jerusalem.

The wall of Jerusalem as seen from the Mount of Olives

13:3-37 Jesus' prediction of the destruction of the temple (13:2) provoked questions that the four named disciples put to him in private regarding the time and the sign when all **these things are about to come to an end** (13:3-4). The response to their questions was Jesus' eschatological discourse prior to his imminent death. It contained instruction and consolation exhorting the disciples and the church to faith and obedience through the trials that would confront them (13:5-13). The sign is the presence of **the desolating abomination** (13:14; see Dn 9:27), i.e., of the Roman power profaning the temple. Flight from Jerusalem is urged rather than defense of the city through misguided messianic hope

(13:14-23). Intervention will occur only after destruction (13:24-27), which will happen before the end of the first Christian generation (13:28-31). No one but the Father knows the precise time, or that of the parousia (13:32); hence the necessity of constant vigilance (13:33-37). Luke sets the parousia at a later date, after "the time of the Gentiles" (Lk 21:24). See also the notes on Matthew 24:1–25:46.

13:10 The gospel . . . to all nations: the period of the Christian mission.

13:14 The participle **standing** is masculine, in contrast to the neuter at Matthew 24:15.

have tribulation such as has not been since the beginning of God's creation until now, nor ever will be. [20]If the Lord had not shortened those days, no one would be saved; but for the sake of the elect whom he chose, he did shorten the days. [21]If anyone says to you then, 'Look, here is the Messiah! Look, there he is!' do not believe it. [22]False messiahs and false prophets will arise and will perform signs and wonders in order to mislead, if that were possible, the elect. [23]Be watchful! I have told it all to you beforehand.

The Coming of the Son of Man

[24][j]"But in those days after that tribulation[k]

the sun will be darkened,
and the moon will not give its light,
[25]and the stars will be falling from the sky,
and the powers in the heavens will be shaken.

[26][*][l]And then they will see 'the Son of Man coming in the clouds' with great power and glory, [27]and then he will send out the angels and gather [his] elect from the four winds, from the end of the earth to the end of the sky.

The Lesson of the Fig Tree

[28][m]"Learn a lesson from the fig tree. When its branch becomes tender and sprouts leaves, you know that summer is near. [29]In the same way, when you see these things happening, know that he is near, at the gates. [30]Amen, I say to you, this generation will not pass away until all these things have taken place. [31]Heaven and earth will pass away, but my words will not pass away.

Need for Watchfulness

[32]"But of that day or hour, no one knows, neither the angels in heaven, nor the Son, but only the Father. [33][n]Be watchful! Be alert! You do not know when the time will come. [34][o]It is like a man traveling abroad. He leaves home and places his servants in charge, each with his work, and orders the gatekeeper to be on the watch. [35]Watch, therefore; you do not know when the lord of the house is coming, whether in the evening, or at midnight, or at cockcrow, or in the morning. [36]May he not come suddenly and find you sleeping. [37]What I say to you, I say to all: 'Watch!'"

Jews and Romans reckoned **time** in different categories. Whereas the Jewish day began at sundown (see Gn 1:5), the Roman day began at sunrise. The Romans divided the day and night into two periods of twelve hours each, subdivided into three-hour segments. The length of "hours," however, varied between summer and winter seasons to ensure uniformity. The Jewish day generally had three periods (Ps 55:18; cf. Neh 9:3, which lists a fourth), while the Roman day had four (first, third, sixth, ninth hours). The Jewish night was divided into three "watches" while the Roman night was divided into four, which are mentioned in this passage: evening, midnight, cockcrow, and early morning.

j
Mt 24:29-31;
Lk 21:25-27

k
Is 13:10;
Ez 32:7;
Jl 2:10

l
14:62;
Dn 7:13-14

m
Mt 24:32-36;
Lk 21:29-33

n
Mt 24:42;
25:13-15

o
Mt 25:14-30;
Lk 19:12-27

MARK

13:26 Son of Man . . . with great power and glory: Jesus cites this text from Daniel 7:13 in his response to the high priest, **Are you the Messiah?** (14:61). In Exodus 34:5; Leviticus 16:2; and Numbers 11:25 the clouds indicate the presence of the divinity. Thus in his role of Son of Man, Jesus is a heavenly being who will come in power and glory.

a
Mt 26:2-5;
Lk 22:1-2;
Jn 11:45-53

b
Mt 26:6-13;
Jn 12:1-8

c
Mt 26:14-16;
Lk 22:3-6

d
Mt 26:17-19;
Lk 22:7-13

MARK

The Conspiracy against Jesus*

14 [1]*[a]The Passover and the Feast of Unleavened Bread were to take place in two days' time. So the chief priests and the scribes were seeking a way to arrest him by treachery and put him to death. [2]They said, "Not during the festival, for fear that there may be a riot among the people."

The Anointing at Bethany

[3]*[b]When he was in Bethany reclining at table in the house of Simon the leper, a woman came with an alabaster jar of perfumed oil, costly genuine spikenard. She broke the alabaster jar and poured it on his head. [4]There were some who were indignant. "Why has there been this waste of perfumed oil? [5]It could have been sold for more than three hundred days' wages and the money given to the poor." They were infuriated with her. [6]Jesus said, "Let her alone. Why do you make trouble for her? She has done a good thing for me. [7]The poor you will always have with you, and whenever you wish you can do good to them, but you will not always have me. [8]She has done what she could. She has anticipated anointing my body for burial. [9]Amen, I say to you, wherever the gospel is proclaimed to the whole world, what she has done will be told in memory of her."

The Betrayal by Judas

[10][c]Then Judas Iscariot, one of the Twelve, went off to the chief priests to hand him over to them. [11]When they heard him they were pleased and promised to pay him money. Then he looked for an opportunity to hand him over.

Preparations for the Passover

[12][d]On the first day of the Feast of Unleavened Bread, when they sacrificed the Passover lamb,* his disciples said to him, "Where do you want us to go and prepare for you to eat the Passover?" [13]He sent two of his disciples and said to them, "Go into the city and a man will

This site in Jerusalem is traditionally associated with the Upper Room

---

14:1–16:8 In the movement of Mark's gospel the cross is depicted as Jesus' way to glory in accordance with the divine will. Thus the passion narrative is seen as the climax of Jesus' ministry.

14:1 The Passover and the Feast of Unleavened Bread: the connection between the two festivals is reflected in Exodus 12:3-20; 34:18; Leviticus 23:4-8; Numbers 9:2-14; 28:16-17; Deuteronomy 16:1-8. The Passover commemorated the redemption from slavery and the departure of the Israelites from Egypt by night. It began at sundown after the Passover lamb was sacrificed in the temple in the afternoon of the fourteenth day of the month of Nisan. With the Passover supper on the same evening was associated the eating of unleavened bread. The latter was continued through Nisan 21, a reminder of the affliction of the Israelites and of the haste surrounding their departure. Praise and thanks to God for his goodness in the past were combined at this dual festival with the hope of future salvation. **The chief**

priests . . . to death: the intent to put Jesus to death was plotted for a long time but delayed for fear of the crowd (3:6; 11:18; 12:12).

14:3-9 At Bethany on the Mount of Olives, a few miles from Jerusalem, in **the house of Simon the leper,** Jesus defends a woman's loving action of anointing his head with perfumed oil in view of his impending death and burial as a criminal, in which case his body would not be anointed. See further the note on John 12:7. He assures the woman of the remembrance of her deed in the worldwide preaching of the good news.

14:12 The first day of the Feast of Unleavened Bread . . . the Passover lamb: a less precise designation of the day for sacrificing the Passover lamb as evidenced by some rabbinical literature. For a more exact designation, see the note on Mark 14:1. It was actually Nisan 14.

14:13 A man . . . carrying a jar of water: perhaps a prearranged signal, for only women ordinarily carried water in jars. The

meet you, carrying a jar of water.* Follow him. [14]Wherever he enters, say to the master of the house, 'The Teacher says, "Where is my guest room where I may eat the Passover with my disciples?"' [15]Then he will show you a large upper room furnished and ready. Make the preparations for us there." [16]The disciples then went off, entered the city, and found it just as he had told them; and they prepared the Passover.

The Betrayer

[17][e]When it was evening, he came with the Twelve. [18]*And as they reclined at table and were eating, Jesus said, "Amen, I say to you, one of you will betray me, one who is eating with me." [19]They began to be distressed and to say to him, one by one, "Surely it is not I?" [20]He said to them, "One of the Twelve, the one who dips with me into the dish. [21]For the Son of Man indeed goes, as it is written of him,* but woe to that man by whom the Son of Man is betrayed. It would be better for that man if he had never been born."

The Lord's Supper

[22]*[f]While they were eating, he took bread, said the blessing, broke it, and gave it to them, and said, "Take it; this is my body." [23]Then he took a cup, gave thanks, and gave it to them, and they all drank from it. [24]He said to them, "This is my blood of the covenant, which will be shed* for many. [25]Amen, I say to you, I shall not drink again the fruit of the vine until the day when I drink it new in the kingdom of God." [26][g]Then, after singing a hymn,* they went out to the Mount of Olives.

Peter's Denial Foretold

[27]*[h]Then Jesus said to them, "All of you will have your faith shaken, for it is written:

'I will strike the shepherd,
    and the sheep will be dispersed.'

[28]But after I have been raised up, I shall go before you to Galilee." [29]Peter said to him, "Even though all should have their faith shaken, mine will not be." [30]Then Jesus said to him, "Amen, I say to you, this very night before the cock crows twice you will deny me three times." [31]But he vehemently replied, "Even though I should have to die with you, I will not deny you." And they all spoke similarly.

e
Mt 26:20-24;
Lk 22:21-23;
Jn 13:21-26

f
Mt 26:26-30;
Lk 22:19-20;
1 Cor 11:23-25

g
Mt 26:30-35;
Lk 22:34, 39;
Jn 13:36-38

h
Zec 13:7;
Jn 16:32

MARK

Greek word used here, however, implies simply a person and not necessarily a male.

14:18 One of you will betray me, one who is eating with me: contrasts the intimacy of table fellowship at the Passover meal with the treachery of the traitor; cf. Psalm 41:10.

14:21 The Son of Man indeed goes, as it is written of him: a reference to Psalm 41:10 cited by Jesus concerning Judas at the Last Supper; cf. John 13:18-19.

14:22-24 The actions and words of Jesus express within the framework of the Passover meal and the transition to a new covenant the sacrifice of himself through the offering of his body and blood in anticipation of his passion and death. His **blood of the covenant** both alludes to the ancient rite of Exodus 24:4-8 and indicates the new community that the sacrifice of Jesus will bring into being (Mt 26:26-28; Lk 22:19-20; 1 Cor 11:23-25).

14:24 Which will be shed: see the note on Matthew 26:27-28. **For many**: the Greek preposition *hyper* is a different one from that at Matthew 26:28 but the same as that found at Luke 22:19, 20 and 1 Corinthians 11:24. The sense of both words is vicarious, and it is difficult in Hellenistic Greek to distinguish between them. For **many** in the sense of "all," see the note on Matthew 20:28.

14:26 After singing a hymn: Psalms 114–118, thanksgiving songs concluding the Passover meal.

14:27-31 Jesus predicted that the Twelve would waver in their faith, even abandon him, despite their protestations to the contrary. Yet he reassured them that after his resurrection he would regather them in Galilee (16:7; cf. Mt 26:32; 28:7, 10, 16; Jn 21), where he first summoned them to be his followers as he began to preach the good news (1:14-20).

i
Mt 26:36-46;
Lk 22:40-46

j
Jn 18:1

k
Rom 7:5

l
Mt 26:47-56;
Lk 22:47-53;
Jn 18:3-11

MARK

The Agony in the Garden

³²*ⁱThen they came to a place named Gethsemane, and he said to his disciples, "Sit here while I pray."ʲ ³³He took with him Peter, James, and John, and began to be troubled and distressed. ³⁴Then he said to them, "My soul is sorrowful even to death. Remain here and keep watch." ³⁵He advanced a little and fell to the ground and prayed that if it were possible the hour might pass by him; ³⁶he said, "Abba, Father,* all things are possible to you. Take this cup away from me, but not what I will but what you will." ³⁷When he returned he found them asleep. He said to

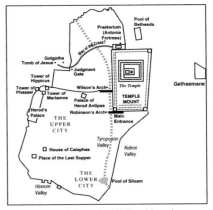

Gethsemane in relation to the Old City of Jerusalem

Peter, "Simon, are you asleep? Could you not keep watch for one hour? ³⁸*ᵏWatch and pray that you may not undergo the test. The spirit is willing but the flesh is weak." ³⁹Withdrawing again, he prayed, saying the same thing. ⁴⁰Then he returned once more and found them asleep, for they could not keep their eyes open and did not know what to answer him. ⁴¹He returned a third time and said to them, "Are you still sleeping and taking your rest? It is enough. The hour has come. Behold, the Son of Man is to be handed over to sinners. ⁴²Get up, let us go. See, my betrayer is at hand."

The Betrayal and Arrest of Jesus

⁴³ˡThen, while he was still speaking, Judas, one of the Twelve, arrived, accompanied by a crowd with swords and clubs who had come from the chief priests, the scribes, and the elders. ⁴⁴His betrayer had arranged a signal with them, saying, "The man I shall kiss is the one; arrest him and lead him away securely." ⁴⁵He came and immediately went over to him and said, "Rabbi." And he kissed him. ⁴⁶At this they laid hands on him and arrested him. ⁴⁷One of the bystanders drew his sword, struck the high priest's servant, and cut off his ear. ⁴⁸Jesus said to them in reply, "Have you come out as against a robber, with swords and clubs, to seize me? ⁴⁹Day after day I was with you teaching in the temple area, yet you did not arrest me; but that the scriptures may be fulfilled." ⁵⁰And they all left him and fled. ⁵¹Now a young man followed him wearing nothing but a linen cloth about his body. They seized him, ⁵²but he left the cloth behind and ran off naked.

14:32-34 The disciples who had witnessed the raising to life of the daughter of Jairus (5:37) and the transfiguration of their Master (9:2) were now invited to witness his degradation and agony and to watch and pray with him.

14:36 Abba, Father: an Aramaic term, here also translated by Mark, Jesus' special way of addressing God with filial intimacy. The word ʾabbāʾ seems not to have been used in earlier or contemporaneous Jewish sources to address God without some qualifier. Cf. Romans 8:15 and Galatians 4:6 for other occurrences of the Ara-

maic word in the Greek New Testament. **Not what I will but what you will**: note the complete obedient surrender of the human will of Jesus to the divine will of the Father; cf. John 4:34; 8:29; Romans 5:19; Philippians 2:8; Hebrews 5:8.

14:38 The spirit is willing but the flesh is weak: the spirit is drawn to what is good yet found in conflict with the flesh, inclined to sin; cf. Psalm 51:7, 12. Everyone is faced with this struggle, the full force of which Jesus accepted on our behalf and, through his bitter passion and death, achieved the victory.

Jesus before the Sanhedrin

[53]*[m]They led Jesus away to the high priest, and all the chief priests and the elders and the scribes came together. [54]Peter followed him at a distance into the high priest's courtyard and was seated with the guards, warming himself at the fire. [55]The chief priests and the entire Sanhedrin kept trying to obtain testimony against Jesus in order to put him to death, but they found none. [56]Many gave false witness against him, but their testimony did not agree. [57]*Some took the stand and testified falsely against him, alleging, [58][n]"We heard him say, 'I will destroy this temple made with hands and within three days I will build another not made with hands.'" [59]Even so their testimony did not agree. [60]The high priest rose before the assembly and questioned Jesus, saying, "Have you no answer? What are these men testifying against you?" [61]*But he was silent and answered nothing. Again the high priest asked him and said to him, "Are you the Messiah, the son of the Blessed One?" [62][o]Then Jesus answered, "I am; and

> 'you will see the Son of Man
> > seated at the right hand of the Power
> > and coming with the clouds of heaven.'"

m
Mt 26:57-68;
Lk 22:54-55,
63-65, 67-71;
Jn 18:12-13

n
15:29;
2 Cor 5:1

o
13:26;
Ps 110:1;
Dn 7:13;
Mt 24:30

On the **chief priests** and **high priest**, see the chart on Jewish leaders in "Background to the Gospels," p. 5.

An Unnamed Follower

The unnamed young follower of Jesus who appears in this climactic scene is not an accidental figure. In such a compact gospel as that of Mark, there is little room for incidentals.

But what does he bring to the story? What does he represent to the reader?

Those present at the arrest of Jesus included not only those followers we have come to know by name but also some whose identities are never known. Jesus touched many who apparently followed him without fanfare. It happened then and it happens now.

What are we to make of the simple linen cloth worn by this man? Is this a literary technique included only to give drama to the story, or is it intended to prefigure the linen cloth that will wrap Jesus in death? Does he leave it behind in personal terror or does he leave it behind in anticipation of Jesus' eventual need for it?

And what are we to make of the young man running off? The scene is somewhat reminiscent of the rich man who went away sad when told that to inherit eternal life he is to sell all his possessions (Mk 10:17-22). Is this young follower who literally left everything behind as he departed an intentional "counter-reminder" of that rich man whose fate we never know? Is the young man at least to be praised for staying on the scene longer than the named disciples of Jesus who fled immediately?

Discipleship requires everything of us: following without recognition or fanfare, being present with Jesus and his followers even in the dark hours, simplicity of life, and the willingness to stay the course rather than flee the unexpected.

14:53 They led Jesus away . . . came together: Mark presents a formal assembly of the whole Sanhedrin (chief priests, elders, and scribes) at night, leading to the condemnation of Jesus (14:64), in contrast to Luke 22:66, 71 where Jesus is condemned in a daytime meeting of the council; see also John 18:13, 19-24.

14:57-58 See the notes on Matthew 26:60-61 and John 2:19.

14:61-62 The Blessed One: a surrogate for the divine name, which Jews did not pronounce. **I am**: indicates Jesus' acknowledgment that he is the Messiah and Son of God; cf. Mark 1:1. Contrast Matthew 26:64 and Luke 22:67-70, in which Jesus leaves his interrogators to answer their own question. **You will see the Son of Man . . . with the clouds of heaven**: an allusion to Daniel 7:13 and Psalm 110:1, portending the enthronement of Jesus as judge in the transcendent glory of God's kingdom. **The Power**: another surrogate for the name of God.

MARK

p
Lk 22:63-65

q
Mt 26:69-75;
Lk 22:56-62;
Jn 18:16-18,
25-27

r
Jn 13:38

[63]At that the high priest tore his garments and said, "What further need have we of witnesses? [64]You have heard the blasphemy. What do you think?" They all condemned him as deserving to die. [65p]Some began to spit on him. They blindfolded him and struck him and said to him, "Prophesy!" And the guards greeted him with blows.

Peter's Denial of Jesus

[66q]While Peter was below in the courtyard, one of the high priest's maids came along. [67]Seeing Peter warming himself, she looked intently at him and said, "You too were with the Nazarene, Jesus." [68*]But he denied it saying, "I neither know nor understand what you are talking about." So he went out into the outer court. [Then the cock crowed.] [69]The maid saw him and began again to say to the bystanders, "This man is one of them." [70]Once again he denied it. A little later the bystanders said to Peter once more, "Surely you are one of them; for you too are a Galilean." [71]He began to curse and to swear, "I do not know this man about whom you are talking." [72r]And immediately a cock crowed

Pontius Pilate

There are two ways to evaluate the figure of Pilate. One is from the perspective of the gospels, which portray him in relatively benign terms. The gospels generally show a man caught in the middle, who recognized Jesus' innocence but felt pressured by the Jewish authorities to convict him of political intrigue.

The other perspective is from sources outside the NT, especially the Jewish writers Philo and Josephus. These sources portray a man much more cruel and ineffectual. Since the gospels may well have had apologetic interests in mind, so as not to offend the Roman authorities, their portrait of Pilate may be softened. Luke, however, records one instance, otherwise unknown in any source, that is consistent with a harsh ruler (Lk 13:1).

Pilate was appointed prefect of Judea in A.D. 26 or 27. As the governor of this Roman province, his primary duty was to protect Roman interests and to maintain order. He had command over a number of troops and also held reserved powers for capital punishment. Philo and Josephus assert that Pilate regularly clashed with his Jewish subjects (see NAB footnote on Lk 13:1). On one occasion he confiscated funds from the temple in Jerusalem to be used for construction of an aqueduct. On another occasion he introduced Roman military standards into Jerusalem, a strict violation of the Jewish prohibition of idols in the holy city. Pilate also harshly subdued a number of rebellious Samaritans at Mount Gerizim, killing many of them. This last incident proved to be disastrous. By A.D. 37, Pilate's rule had become so troublesome that he was recalled to Rome and removed from office.

Whatever the final assessment of the man, Pilate's role in the passion and death of Jesus must be acknowledged. The passion narratives of the gospels clearly acknowledge Pilate's condemnation of Jesus to crucifixion, a Roman form of execution often used for political criminals. Matthew's story of the intervention of Pilate's wife, proclaiming Jesus' innocence because of a dream (27:19), fits with Matthew's story of how God ultimately directed the fate of Jesus, even while he suffered wrongly at the hands of wicked people. It does not compensate for Pilate's final decision. His action of "washing his hands" of guilt has become a standard gesture of assuming no responsibility for the consequences of one's decisions.

Paradoxically, among Ethiopic and Coptic Christians, Pilate's role in condemning Jesus to death earned him sainthood, because he fulfilled God's plan of salvation history by having Jesus die for sinful humanity. Sadly, the Christian tendency to lessen Pilate's responsibility has been accompanied by increased emphasis on Jewish responsibility for the death of Jesus, something not justified by the historical evidence.

In 1961 an important archaeological reference to Pilate was unearthed in Caesarea Maritima that confirmed Pilate's governorship of Judea. The "Pilate stone," as it is called, notes that Pilate was "prefect" (a military term, as compared with the secular term "procurator") of Judea. See further explanation at John 18:33.

14:68 [Then the cock crowed]: found in most manuscripts, perhaps in view of Mark 14:30 and 72, but omitted in others.

a second time. Then Peter remembered the word that Jesus had said to him, "Before the cock crows twice you will deny me three times." He broke down and wept.

Jesus before Pilate

15 ¹ᵃAs soon as morning came, the chief priests with the elders and the scribes, that is, the whole Sanhedrin, held a council.* They bound Jesus, led him away, and handed him over to Pilate.ᵇ ²Pilate questioned him, "Are you the king of the Jews?"* He said to him in reply, "You say so." ³The chief priests accused him of many things. ⁴Again Pilate questioned him, "Have you no answer? See how many things they accuse you of." ⁵Jesus gave him no further answer, so that Pilate was amazed.

The Sentence of Death

⁶*ᶜNow on the occasion of the feast he used to release to them one prisoner whom they requested. ⁷A man called Barabbas* was then in prison along with the rebels who had committed murder in a rebellion. ⁸The crowd came forward and began to ask him to do for them as he was accustomed. ⁹Pilate answered, "Do you want me to release to you the king of the Jews?" ¹⁰For he knew that it was out of envy that the chief priests had handed him over. ¹¹But the chief priests stirred up the crowd to have him release Barabbas for them instead. ¹²Pilate again said to them in reply, "Then what [do you want] me to do with [the man you call] the king of the Jews?" ¹³*They shouted again, "Crucify him." ¹⁴Pilate said to them, "Why? What evil has he done?" They only shouted the louder, "Crucify him." ¹⁵*So Pilate, wishing to satisfy the crowd, released Barabbas to them and, after he had Jesus scourged, handed him over to be crucified.

Mockery by the Soldiers

¹⁶*ᵈThe soldiers led him away inside the palace, that is, the praetorium, and assembled the whole cohort. ¹⁷They clothed him in purple and, weaving a crown of thorns, placed it on him. ¹⁸They began to salute him with, "Hail, King of the Jews!" ¹⁹and kept striking his head with a reed and spitting upon him. They knelt before him in homage. ²⁰And when they had mocked him, they stripped him of the purple cloak, dressed him in his own clothes, and led him out to crucify him.

The Way of the Cross

²¹ᵉThey pressed into service a passer-by, Simon, a Cyrenian,* who was coming in from the country, the father of Alexander and Rufus, to carry his cross.

a
Mt 27:1-2, 11-14;
Lk 23:1-3

b
Jn 18:28

c
Mt 27:15-26;
Lk 23:17-25;
Jn 18:39-40

d
Mt 27:27-31;
Jn 19:2-3

e
Mt 27:32;
Lk 23:26

MARK

15:1 Held a council: the verb here, *poieō*, can mean either "convene a council" or "take counsel." This reading is preferred to a variant "reached a decision" (cf. 3:6), which Mark 14:64 describes as having happened at the night trial; see the note on Matthew 27:1-2. **Handed him over to Pilate**: lacking authority to execute their sentence of condemnation (14:64), the Sanhedrin had recourse to Pilate to have Jesus tried and put to death (15:15); cf. John 18:31.

15:2 The king of the Jews: in the accounts of the evangelists a certain irony surrounds the use of this title as an accusation against Jesus (see the note on 15:26). While Pilate uses this term (15:2, 9, 12), he is aware of the evil motivation of the chief priests who handed Jesus over for trial and condemnation (15:10; Lk 23:14-16, 20; Mt 27:18, 24; Jn 18:38; 19:4, 6, 12).

15:6-15 See the note on Matthew 27:15-26.
15:7 Barabbas: see the note on Matthew 27:16-17.
15:13 Crucify him: see the note on Matthew 27:22.
15:15 See the note on Matthew 27:26.
15:16 Praetorium: see the note on Matthew 27:27.
15:21 They pressed into service . . . Simon, a Cyrenian: a condemned person was constrained to bear his own instrument of torture, at least the crossbeam. The precise naming of Simon and his sons is probably due to their being known among early Christian believers to whom Mark addressed his gospel. See also the notes on Matthew 27:32; Luke 23:26-32.

f
Mt 27:33-51;
Lk 23:32-46;
Jn 19:17-30

g
Ps 22:18

h
Lk 23:33

i
Jn 2:19

j
Lk 23:39

k
Ps 22:2

l
Mt 27:54-56;
Lk 23:47-49

The Crucifixion

^{22f}They brought him to the place of Golgotha (which is translated Place of the Skull). ²³They gave him wine drugged with myrrh, but he did not take it. ^{24*g}Then they crucified him and divided his garments by casting lots for them to see what each should take. ²⁵It was nine o'clock in the morning* when they crucified him. ^{26*}The inscription of the charge against him read, "The King of the Jews." ^{27h}With him they crucified two revolutionaries, one on his right and one on his left. [²⁸]* ^{29*i}Those passing by reviled him, shaking their heads and saying, "Aha! You who would destroy the temple and rebuild it in three days, ³⁰save yourself by coming down from the cross." ³¹Likewise the chief priests, with the scribes, mocked him among themselves and said, "He saved others; he cannot save himself. ^{32j}Let the Messiah, the King of Israel, come down now from the cross that we may see and believe." Those who were crucified with him also kept abusing him.

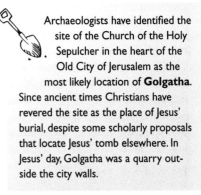

Archaeologists have identified the site of the Church of the Holy Sepulcher in the heart of the Old City of Jerusalem as the most likely location of **Golgatha**. Since ancient times Christians have revered the site as the place of Jesus' burial, despite some scholarly proposals that locate Jesus' tomb elsewhere. In Jesus' day, Golgatha was a quarry outside the city walls.

The Death of Jesus

³³At noon darkness came over the whole land until three in the afternoon. ^{34k}And at three o'clock Jesus cried out in a loud voice, "*Eloi, Eloi, lema sabachthani?*"* which is translated, "My God, my God, why have you forsaken me?" ^{35*}Some of the bystanders who heard it said, "Look, he is calling Elijah." ³⁶One of them ran, soaked a sponge with wine, put it on a reed, and gave it to him to drink, saying, "Wait, let us see if Elijah comes to take him down." ³⁷Jesus gave a loud cry and breathed his last. ^{38*}The veil of the sanctuary was torn in two from top to bottom. ^{39*l}When

Jesus, I can hardly imagine the abandonment you must have felt on the cross. As I look at our war-torn countries around the world I see many whose loved ones have been tragically killed or maimed. I hear them echo your cry of abandonment. Reveal to us how to reach out to those who feel forsaken by God.

15:24 See the notes on Matthew 27:35 and John 19:23-25a.

15:25 It was nine o'clock in the morning: literally, "the third hour," thus between 9 a.m. and 12 noon. Cf. Mark 15:33, 34, 42 for Mark's chronological sequence, which may reflect liturgical or catechetical considerations rather than the precise historical sequence of events; contrast the different chronologies in the other gospels, especially John 19:14.

15:26 The inscription . . . the King of the Jews: the political reason for the death penalty falsely charged by the enemies of Jesus. See further the notes on Matthew 27:37 and John 19:19.

15:28 This verse, "And the scripture was fulfilled that says, 'And he was counted among the wicked,'" is omitted in the earliest and best manuscripts. It contains a citation from Isaiah 53:12 and was probably introduced from Luke 22:37.

15:29 See the note on Matthew 27:39-40.

15:34 An Aramaic rendering of Psalm 22:2. See also the note on Matthew 27:46.

15:35 Elijah: a verbal link with *Eloi* (15:34). See the note on Mark 9:9-13; cf. Malachi 3:23-24. See also the note on Matthew 27:47.

15:38 See the note on Matthew 27:51-53.

15:39 The closing portion of Mark's gospel returns to the theme of its beginning in the Gentile centurion's climactic declaration of belief that Jesus **was the Son of God**. It indicates the fulfillment of the good news announced in the prologue (1:1) and may be regarded as the firstfruit of the passion and death of Jesus.

the centurion who stood facing him saw how he breathed his last he said, "Truly this man was the Son of God!" [40]*[m]There were also women looking on from a distance. Among them were Mary Magdalene, Mary the mother of the younger James and of Joses, and Salome. [41]These women had followed him when he was in Galilee and ministered to him. There were also many other women who had come up with him to Jerusalem.

Example of first-century rock slab tombs similar to the tomb in which Jesus would have been buried

m
6:3; Lk 8:2-3

n
Mt 27:57-61;
Lk 23:50-56;
Jn 19:38-42

The Burial of Jesus

[42][n]When it was already evening, since it was the day of preparation, the day before the sabbath, [43]Joseph of Arimathea,* a distinguished member of the council, who was himself awaiting the kingdom of God, came and courageously went to Pilate and asked for the body of Jesus. [44]Pilate was amazed that he was already dead. He summoned the centurion and asked him if Jesus had already died. [45]And when he learned of it from the centurion, he gave the body to Joseph. [46]Having bought a linen cloth, he took him down, wrapped him in the linen cloth and laid him in a tomb that had been hewn out of the rock. Then he rolled a stone against the entrance to the tomb. [47]Mary Magdalene and Mary the mother of Joses watched where he was laid.

Faithful Women Followers

That the gospels make mention of women followers of Jesus, some of them by name, is just one more indication of the barriers that Jesus overcame as he proclaimed the kingdom of God. Class, race, culture, and gender were seemingly unimportant among the followers of Jesus. We hear of tax collectors, sinners, a member of the Sanhedrin, single women and groups of women, young and old men, the blind and lame, and the hale and hearty—an unheard of combination in any social institution of the time.

The faithfulness of the women is noted or described on more than one occasion. They are with Jesus at his crucifixion when by most accounts his disciples have fled (here, and cf. Mt 27:55-56; Lk 23:48-49; Jn 19:25). Earlier, women are known to have traveled with Jesus and the Twelve and even used their resources to provide for their needs (cf. Lk 8:1-3). Finally, women are among the first to witness the reality of the risen Jesus.

Their faithfulness placed them near Jesus in all circumstances and challenges us to find ourselves with him too.

15:40-41 See the note on Matthew 27:55-56.
15:43 Joseph of Arimathea: see the note on Matthew 27:57-61.

a
Mt 28:1-8;
Lk 24:1-10;
Jn 20:1-10
b
Mt 28:1;
Lk 23:56
c
Jn 20:12
d
14:28

The Resurrection of Jesus

16 [1]*[a]When the sabbath was over, Mary Magdalene, Mary, the mother of James, and Salome bought spices so that they might go and anoint him.[b] [2]Very early when the sun had risen, on the first day of the week, they came to the tomb. [3]They were saying to one another, "Who will roll back the stone for us from the entrance to the tomb?" [4]When they looked up, they saw that the stone had been rolled back; it was very large. [5c]On entering the tomb they saw a young man sitting on the right side, clothed in a white robe, and they were utterly amazed. [6]He said to them, "Do not be amazed! You seek Jesus of Nazareth, the crucified. He has been raised; he is not here. Behold the place where they laid him. [7d]But go and tell his disciples and Peter, 'He is going before you to Galilee; there you will see him, as he told you.'" [8]Then they went out and fled from the tomb, seized with trembling and bewilderment. They said nothing to anyone, for they were afraid.

An Interactive Ending?

Scholars have long debated whether Mark originally ended at 16:8. The existence of several alternative endings indicates that the problem is an ancient one. On the one hand, the verse seems an odd way to end a gospel. Why conclude on a negative note that the women said nothing of their experience? On the other hand, the alternative endings show signs of being formed from other NT materials that were clearly not part of the original Gospel of Mark. While no solution is totally adequate, there is a possible explanation for concluding the gospel with v. 8. It invites Christian readers, who know well the message of the resurrection, to take up the story of Jesus and his disciples in their own lives.

Capstone of a pillar with scenes from the Gospel of Mark

16:1-8 The purpose of this narrative is to show that the tomb is empty and that Jesus **has been raised** (16:6) and is **going before you to Galilee** (16:7) in fulfillment of Mark 14:28. The women find the tomb empty, and an angel stationed there announces to them what has happened. They are told to proclaim the news to Peter and the disciples in order to prepare them for a reunion with him. Mark's composition of the gospel ends at Mark 16:8 with the women telling no one, because they were afraid. This abrupt termination causes some to believe that the original ending of this gospel may have been lost. See the following note.

The Longer Ending

The Appearance to Mary Magdalene

[9][e][*When he had risen, early on the first day of the week, he appeared first to Mary Magdalene, out of whom he had driven seven demons. [10][f]She went and told his companions who were mourning and weeping. [11]When they heard that he was alive and had been seen by her, they did not believe.

The Appearance to Two Disciples

[12][g]After this he appeared in another form to two of them walking along on their way to the country. [13]They returned and told the others; but they did not believe them either.

The Commissioning of the Eleven

[14][h][But] later, as the eleven were at table, he appeared to them and rebuked them for their unbelief and hardness of heart because they had not believed those who saw him after he had been raised. [15][i]He said to them, "Go into the whole world and proclaim the gospel to every creature. [16]Whoever believes and is baptized will be saved; whoever does not believe will be condemned. [17]These signs will accompany those who believe: in my name they will drive out demons, they will speak new languages. [18][j]They will pick up serpents [with their hands], and if they drink any deadly thing, it will not harm them. They will lay hands on the sick, and they will recover."

The Ascension of Jesus

[19][k]So then the Lord Jesus, after he spoke to them, was taken up into heaven and took his seat at the right hand of God. [20][l]But they went forth and preached everywhere, while the Lord worked with them and confirmed the word through accompanying signs.]*

The Shorter Ending

[And they reported all the instructions briefly to Peter's companions. Afterwards Jesus himself, through them, sent forth from east to west the sacred and imperishable proclamation of eternal salvation. Amen.]

---

e
Mt 28:1-10;
Jn 20:11-18

f
Lk 24:10-11;
Jn 20:18

g
Lk 24:13-35

h
Lk 24:36-49;
1 Cor 15:5

i
13:10;
Mt 28:18-20;
Lk 24:47;
Jn 20:21

j
Mt 10:1;
Lk 10:19;
Acts 28:3-6

k
Lk 24:50-53

l
1 Tm 3:16

16:9-20 This passage, termed the Longer Ending to the Marcan gospel by comparison with a much briefer conclusion found in some less important manuscripts, has traditionally been accepted as a canonical part of the gospel and was defined as such by the Council of Trent. Early citations of it by the Fathers indicate that it was composed by the second century, although vocabulary and style indicate that it was written by someone other than Mark. It is a general resume of the material concerning the appearances of the risen Jesus, reflecting, in particular, traditions found in Luke 24 and John 20.

The Shorter Ending: Found after Mark 16:8 before the Longer Ending in four seventh-to-ninth-century Greek manuscripts as well as in one Old Latin version, where it appears alone without the Longer Ending.

The Freer Logion: Found after v. 14 in a fourth-fifth century manuscript preserved in the Freer Gallery of Art, Washington, DC, this ending was known to Jerome in the fourth century. It reads: "And they excused themselves, saying, 'This age of lawlessness and unbelief is under Satan, who does not allow the truth and power of God to prevail over the unclean things dominated by the spirits [or, does not allow the unclean things dominated by the spirits to grasp the truth and power of God]. Therefore reveal your righteousness now.' They spoke to Christ. And Christ responded to them, 'The limit of the years of Satan's power is completed, but other terrible things draw near. And for those who sinned I was handed over to death, that they might return to the truth and no longer sin, in order that they might inherit the spiritual and incorruptible heavenly glory of righteousness. But . . . .'"

The Gospel according to Luke is the first part of a two-volume work that continues the biblical history of God's dealings with humanity found in the Old Testament, showing how God's promises to Israel have been fulfilled in Jesus and how the salvation promised to Israel and accomplished by Jesus has been extended to the Gentiles. The stated purpose of the two volumes is to provide Theophilus and others like him with certainty—assurance—about earlier instruction they have received (1:4). To accomplish his purpose, Luke shows that the preaching and teaching of the representatives of the early church are grounded in the preaching and teaching of Jesus, who during his historical ministry (Acts 1:21-22) prepared his specially chosen followers and commissioned them to be witnesses to his resurrection and to all else that he did (Acts 10:37-42). This continuity between the historical ministry of Jesus and the ministry of the apostles is Luke's way of guaranteeing the fidelity of the church's teaching to the teaching of Jesus.

Luke's story of Jesus and the church is dominated by a historical perspective. This history is first of all salvation history. God's divine plan for human salvation was accomplished during the period of Jesus, who through the events of his life (22:22) fulfilled the Old Testament prophecies (4:21; 18:31; 22:37; 24:26-27, 44), and this salvation is now extended to all humanity in the period of the church (Acts 4:12). This salvation history, moreover, is a

SUMMARY

Luke tells the story of Jesus of Nazareth as a mighty prophet and Savior of the world in fulfillment of OT expectations. He begins with Jesus' virginal conception and birth, and follows Jesus through his public ministry to his passion, death, resurrection, and ascension into heaven—all under the guidance of the Holy Spirit.

Author: Unknown, but ancient tradition calls him "Luke" and identifies him as a companion of Paul (Col 4:14; 2 Tm 4:11; Phlm 24).

Date: After A.D. 70 and perhaps between A.D. 80–90.

Content: Virginal conception of Jesus; the Sermon on the Plain; Peter's confession of faith; the transfiguration; the passion, death, and resurrection of Jesus; resurrection appearances in and around Jerusalem; the ascension of Jesus.

Main Characters: Holy Spirit, Mary the mother of Jesus, Jesus of Nazareth, John the Baptist, Peter, James and John (the sons of Zebedee), some Jewish leaders opposed to Jesus, Judas Iscariot, Pontius Pilate.

part of human history. Luke relates the story of Jesus and the church to events in contemporary Palestinian (1:5; 3:1-2; Acts 4:6) and Roman (2:1-2; 3:1; Acts 11:28; 18:2, 12) history for, as Paul says in Acts 26:26, "this was not done in a corner." Finally, Luke relates the story of Jesus and the church to contemporaneous church history. Luke is concerned with presenting Christianity as a legitimate form of worship in the Roman world, a religion that is capable of meeting the spiritual needs of a world empire like that of Rome. To this end, Luke depicts the Roman governor Pilate declaring Jesus innocent of any wrongdoing three times (Acts 23:29; 25:25; 26:31-32). At the same time Luke argues in Acts that Christianity is the logical development and proper fulfillment of Judaism and is therefore deserving of the same toleration and freedom traditionally accorded Judaism by Rome (Acts 13:16-41; 23:6-9; 24:10-21; 26:2-23).

The prominence given to the period of the church in the story has important consequences for Luke's interpretation of the teachings of Jesus. By presenting the time of the church as a distinct phase of salvation history, Luke accordingly shifts the early Christian emphasis away from the expectation of an imminent parousia to the day-to-day concerns of the Christian community in the world. He does this in the gospel by regularly emphasizing the words "each day" (9:23; cf. Mk 8:34; 11:3; 16:19; 19:47) in the sayings of Jesus. Although Luke still believes the parousia to be a reality that will come unexpectedly (12:38, 45-46), he is more concerned with presenting the words and deeds of Jesus as guides for the conduct of Christian disciples in the interim period between the ascension and the parousia and with presenting Jesus himself as the model of Christian life and piety.

Throughout the gospel, Luke calls upon the Christian disciple to identify with the master Jesus, who is caring and tender toward the poor and lowly, the outcast, the sinner, and the afflicted, toward all those who recognize their dependence on God (4:18; 6:20-23; 7:36-50; 14:12-14; 15:1-32; 16:19-31; 18:9-14; 19:1-10; 21:1-4), but who is severe toward the proud and self-righteous, and particularly toward those who place their material

wealth before the service of God and his people (6:24-26; 12:13-21; 16:13-15, 19-31; 18:9-14, 15-25; cf. 1:50-53). No gospel writer is more concerned than Luke with the mercy and compassion of Jesus (7:41-43; 10:29-37; 13:6-9; 15:11-32). No gospel writer is more concerned with the role of the Spirit in the life of Jesus and the Christian disciple (1:35, 41; 2:25-27; 4:1, 14, 18; 10:21; 11:13; 24:49), with the importance of prayer (3:21; 5:16; 6:12; 9:28; 11:1-13; 18:1-8), or with Jesus' concern for women (7:11-17, 36-50; 8:2-3; 10:38-42). While Jesus calls all humanity to repent (5:32; 10:13; 11:32; 13:1-5; 15:7-10; 16:30; 17:3-4; 24:47), he is particularly demanding of those who would be his disciples. Of them he demands absolute and total detachment from family and material possessions (9:57-62; 12:32-34; 14:25-35). To all who respond in faith and repentance to the word Jesus preaches, he brings salvation (2:30-32; 3:6; 7:50; 8:48, 50; 17:19; 19:9) and peace (2:14; 7:50; 8:48; 19:38, 42) and life (10:25-28; 18:26-30).

Early Christian tradition, from the late second century on, identifies the author of this gospel and of the Acts of the Apostles as Luke, a Syrian from Antioch, who is mentioned in the New Testament in Colossians 4:14, Philemon 1:24 and 2 Timothy 4:11. The prologue of the gospel makes it clear that Luke is not part of the first generation of Christian disciples but is himself dependent upon the traditions he received from those who were eyewitnesses and ministers of the word (1:2). His two-volume work marks him as someone who was highly literate both in the Old Testament traditions according to the Greek versions and in Hellenistic Greek writings.

Among the likely sources for the composition of this gospel (1:3) were the Gospel of Mark, a written collection of sayings of Jesus known also to the author of the Gospel of Matthew (Q; see Introduction to Matthew), and other special traditions that were used by Luke alone among the gospel writers. Some hold that Luke used Mark only as a complementary source for rounding out the material he took from other traditions. Because of its dependence on the Gospel of Mark and because details in Luke's Gospel (13:35a; 19:43-44; 21:20;

23:28-31) imply that the author was acquainted with the destruction of the city of Jerusalem by the Romans in A.D. 70, the Gospel of Luke is dated by most scholars after that date; many propose A.D. 80–90 as the time of composition.

Luke's consistent substitution of Greek names for the Aramaic or Hebrew names occurring in his sources (e.g., Lk 23:33 // Mk 15:22; Lk 18:41 // Mk 10:51), his omission from the gospel of specifically Jewish Christian concerns found in his sources (e.g., Mk 7:1-23), his interest in Gentile Christians (2:30-32; 3:6, 38; 4:16-30; 13:28-30; 14:15-24; 17:11-19; 24:47-48), and his incomplete knowledge of Palestinian geography, customs, and practices are among the characteristics of this gospel that suggest that Luke was a non-Palestinian writing to a non-Palestinian audience that was largely made up of Gentile Christians.

The principal divisions of the Gospel according to Luke are the following:

I. The Prologue (1:1-4)
II. The Infancy Narrative (1:5–2:52)
III. The Preparation for the Public Ministry (3:1–4:13)
IV. The Ministry in Galilee (4:14–9:50)
V. The Journey to Jerusalem: Luke's Travel Narrative (9:51–19:27)
VI. The Teaching Ministry in Jerusalem (19:28–21:38)
VII. The Passion Narrative (22:1–23:56)
VIII. The Resurrection Narrative (24:1-53)

a
Acts 1:1;
1 Cor 15:3

b
24:48;
Jn 15:27;
Acts 1:21-22

c
1 Chr 24:10

I: The Prologue

1 [1]*[a]Since many have undertaken to compile a narrative of the events that have been fulfilled among us, [2][b]just as those who were eyewitnesses from the beginning and ministers of the word have handed them down to us, [3]I too have decided, after investigating everything accurately anew, to write it down in an orderly sequence for you, most excellent Theophilus, [4]so that you may realize the certainty of the teachings you have received.

II: The Infancy Narrative

Announcement of the Birth of John

[5]*[c]In the days of Herod, King of Judea,* there was a priest named Zechariah of the priestly division of Abijah; his wife was from the daughters of Aaron, and her name was Elizabeth. [6]Both were righteous in the eyes of God, observing all the commandments and ordinances of

Luke has been **a favorite gospel** for many different people with diverse interests. Over time, Luke has thus earned numerous nicknames that describe certain thematic emphases found in the book, for example, "the Gospel of . . ." —you fill in the blank: "prayer," "social justice," "women," "God's mercy," "reconciliation," "joy," "festive dining," "salvation," "universalism," "healing," or perhaps another title of your own liking. Luke has an extremely broad appeal as a "favorite" among the canonical gospels.

On **Herod**, see "Getting It Right . . . Which Herod?" (at Mt 2:1).

1:1-4 The Gospel according to Luke is the only one of the synoptic gospels to begin with a literary prologue. Making use of a formal, literary construction and vocabulary, the author writes the prologue in imitation of Hellenistic Greek writers and, in so doing, relates his story about Jesus to contemporaneous Greek and Roman literature. Luke is not only interested in the words and deeds of Jesus, but also in the larger context of the birth, ministry, death, and resurrection of Jesus as the fulfillment of the promises of God in the Old Testament. As a second- or third-generation Christian, Luke acknowledges his debt to earlier **eyewitnesses** and **ministers of the word**, but claims that his contribution to this developing tradition is a complete and accurate account, told in an orderly manner, and intended to provide **Theophilus** ("friend of God," literally) and other readers with certainty about earlier teachings they have received.

1:5–2:52 Like the Gospel according to Matthew, this gospel opens with an infancy narrative, a collection of stories about the birth and childhood of Jesus. The narrative uses early Christian traditions about the birth of Jesus, traditions about the birth and circumcision of John the Baptist, and canticles such as the Magnificat (1:46-55) and Benedictus (1:67-79), composed of phrases drawn from the Greek Old Testament. It is largely, however, the composition of Luke who writes in imitation of Old Testament birth stories, combining historical and legendary details, literary ornamentation and interpretation of scripture, to answer in advance the question, "Who is Jesus Christ?" The focus of the narrative, therefore, is primarily christological. In this section Luke announces many of the themes that will become prominent in the rest of the gospel: the centrality of Jerusalem and the temple, the journey motif, the universality of salvation, joy and peace, concern for the lowly, the importance of women, the presentation of Jesus as savior, Spirit-guided revelation and prophecy, and the fulfillment of Old Testament promises. The account presents parallel scenes (diptychs) of angelic announcements of the birth of John the Baptist and of Jesus, and of the birth, circumcision, and presentation of John and Jesus. In this parallelism, the ascendency of Jesus over John is stressed: John is prophet of the Most High (1:76); Jesus is Son of the Most High (1:32). John is great in the sight of the Lord (1:15); Jesus will be Great (a LXX attribute, used absolutely, of God) (1:32). John will go before the Lord (1:16-17); Jesus will be Lord (1:43; 2:11).

1:5 In the days of Herod, King of Judea: Luke relates the story of salvation history to events in contemporary world history. Here and in Luke 3:1-2 he connects his narrative with events in Palestinian history; in Luke 2:1-2 and Luke 3:1, he casts the Jesus story in the light of events of Roman history. Herod the Great, the son of the Idumean Antipater, was declared "King of Judea" by the Roman Senate in 40 B.C., but became the undisputed ruler of Palestine only in 37 B.C. He continued as king until his death in 4 B.C. **Priestly division of Abijah:** a reference to the eighth of the twenty-four divisions of priests who, for a week at a time, twice a year, served in the Jerusalem temple.

Zechariah and Elizabeth, Righteous in the Eyes of God

In the ancient world, children were a gift from God, a way for the family name to be carried on, and a necessity for family financial security. Childlessness was often seen as divine punishment.

But Zechariah and Elizabeth are not childless because of their spiritual state—in fact, they are called "righteous in the eyes of God." They are in good company with Joseph, John the Baptist, Simeon, Joseph of Arimathea, Cornelius, and Jesus himself. In fact, in the NT Elizabeth is the only woman to be called righteous.

Righteousness can mean a number of things, among them innocence, moral conduct, justice or just judgment, and especially in the case of Jesus ("the Righteous One"; cf. Acts 3:14; 7:52; Jas 5:6; 1 Jn 2:1-2) all this is accompanied by victory and triumph.

The parents of John the Baptist were elderly and surely the subject of much whispering in their childless state. When pregnant past their prime, they must have caused even more gossip. But in the eyes of God they are righteous, and the triumph they experience comes in the form of a son who will one day follow in his mother's footsteps and reveal the identity of Jesus (Lk 1:42-43; 3:4-6, 16).

d
Gn 18:11;
Jgs 13:2-5;
1 Sm 1:5-6

e
Ex 30:7

f
1:57, 60, 63;
Mt 1:20-21

g
7:33;
Nm 6:1-21;
Jgs 13:4;
1 Sm 1:11 LXX

h
Sir 48:10;
Mal 3:1;
3:23-24;
Mt 11:14;
17:11-13

i
Dn 8:16; 9:21

LUKE

the Lord blamelessly. [7d]But they had no child,* because Elizabeth was barren and both were advanced in years. [8]Once when he was serving as priest in his division's turn before God, [9e]according to the practice of the priestly service, he was chosen by lot to enter the sanctuary of the Lord to burn incense. [10]Then, when the whole assembly of the people was praying outside at the hour of the incense offering, [11]the angel of the Lord appeared to him, standing at the right of the altar of incense. [12]Zechariah was troubled by what he saw, and fear came upon him. [13f]But the angel said to him, "Do not be afraid,* Zechariah, because your prayer has been heard. Your wife Elizabeth will bear you a son, and you shall name him John. [14]And you will have joy and gladness, and many will rejoice at his birth, [15g]for he will be great in the sight of [the] Lord. He will drink neither wine nor strong drink.* He will be filled with the holy Spirit even from his mother's womb, [16]and he will turn many of the children of Israel to the Lord their God. [17h]He will go before him in the spirit and power of Elijah* to turn the hearts of fathers toward children and the disobedient to the understanding of the righteous, to prepare a people fit for the Lord." [18]Then Zechariah said to the angel, "How shall I know this? For I am an old man, and my wife is advanced in years." [19i]And the angel

---

1:7 They had no child: though childlessness was looked upon in contemporaneous Judaism as a curse or punishment for sin, it is intended here to present Elizabeth in a situation similar to that of some of the great mothers of important Old Testament figures: Sarah (Gn 15:3; 16:1); Rebekah (Gn 25:21); Rachel (Gn 29:31; 30:1); the mother of Samson and wife of Manoah (Jgs 13:2-3); Hannah (1 Sm 1:2).

1:13 Do not be afraid: a stereotyped Old Testament phrase spoken to reassure the recipient of a heavenly vision (Gn 15:1; Jos 1:9; Dn 10:12, 19 and elsewhere in Lk 1:30; 2:10). **You shall name him John**: the name means "Yahweh has shown favor," an indication of John's role in salvation history.

1:15 He will drink neither wine nor strong drink: like Samson (Jgs 13:4-5) and Samuel (1 Sm 1:11 LXX and 4QSam[a]), John is to

be consecrated by Nazirite vow and set apart for the Lord's service.

1:17 He will go before him in the spirit and power of Elijah: John is to be the messenger sent before Yahweh, as described in Malachi 3:1-2. He is cast, moreover, in the role of the Old Testament fiery reformer, the prophet Elijah, who according to Malachi 3:23 (Lk 4:5) is sent before "the great and terrible day of the Lord comes."

1:19 I am Gabriel: "the angel of the Lord" is identified as Gabriel, the angel who in Daniel 9:20-25 announces the seventy weeks of years and the coming of an anointed one, a prince. By alluding to Old Testament themes in Luke 1:17, 19, such as the coming of the day of the Lord and the dawning of the messianic era, Luke is presenting his interpretation of the significance of the births of John and Jesus.

j
1:45

k
Gn 30:23

l
2:5;
Mt 1:16, 18

m
Jgs 6:12;
Ru 2:4;
Jdt 13:18

n
Gn 16:11;
Jgs 13:3;
Is 7:14;
Mt 1:21-23

o
2 Sm 7:12, 13,
16; Is 9:7

p
Dn 2:44; 7:14;
Mi 4:7;
Mt 28:18

q
Mt 1:20

said to him in reply, "I am Gabriel,* who stand before God. I was sent to speak to you and to announce to you this good news. 20jBut now you will be speechless and unable to talk* until the day these things take place, because you did not believe my words, which will be fulfilled at their proper time."

The angel **Gabriel** is an OT figure (Dn 8:16; 9:21-27) who is one of the heavenly messengers God uses to reveal special messages to human beings. In Daniel, his presence evokes terror; in this passage his message to Mary is likely interpreted as unsettling, although she accepts it with grace.

The Basilica of the Annunciation dominates the landscape of Nazareth

21Meanwhile the people were waiting for Zechariah and were amazed that he stayed so long in the sanctuary. 22But when he came out, he was unable to speak to them, and they realized that he had seen a vision in the sanctuary. He was gesturing to them but remained mute. 23Then, when his days of ministry were completed, he went home. 24After this time his wife Elizabeth conceived, and she went into seclusion for five months, saying, 25k"So has the Lord done for me at a time when he has seen fit to take away my disgrace before others."

Announcement of the Birth of Jesus

26*In the sixth month, the angel Gabriel was sent from God to a town of Galilee called Nazareth, 27lto a virgin betrothed to a man named Joseph, of the house of David, and the virgin's name was Mary. 28mAnd coming to her, he said, "Hail, favored one! The Lord is with you." 29But she was greatly troubled at what was said and pondered what sort of greeting this might be. 30Then the angel said to her, "Do not be afraid, Mary, for you have found favor with God. 31nBehold, you will conceive in your womb and bear a son, and you shall name him Jesus. 32oHe will be great and will be called Son of the Most High,* and the Lord God will give him the throne of David his father, 33pand he will rule over the house of Jacob forever, and of his kingdom there will be no end." 34But Mary said to the angel, "How can this be, since I have no relations with a man?"* 35qAnd the angel said to her in reply, "The holy Spirit will come upon you, and the power of the Most

---

1:20 You will be speechless and unable to talk: Zechariah's becoming mute is the sign given in response to his question in v. 18. When Mary asks a similar question in Luke 1:34, unlike Zechariah who was punished for his doubt, she, in spite of her doubt, is praised and reassured (1:35-37).

1:26-38 The announcement to Mary of the birth of Jesus is parallel to the announcement to Zechariah of the birth of John. In both the angel Gabriel appears to the parent who is troubled by the vision (1:11-12, 26-29) and then told by the angel not to fear (1:13, 30). After the announcement is made (1:14-17, 31-33) the parent objects (1:18, 34) and a sign is given to confirm the announcement (1:20, 36). The particular focus of the announcement of the birth

of Jesus is on his identity as Son of David (1:32-33) and Son of God (1:32, 35).

1:32 Son of the Most High: cf. Luke 1:76 where John is described as "prophet of the Most High." "Most High" is a title for God commonly used by Luke (1:35, 76; 6:35; 8:28; Acts 7:48; 16:17).

1:34 Mary's questioning response is a denial of sexual relations and is used by Luke to lead to the angel's declaration about the Spirit's role in the conception of this child (1:35). According to Luke, the virginal conception of Jesus takes place through the holy Spirit, the power of God, and therefore Jesus has a unique relationship to Yahweh: he is Son of God.

High will overshadow you. Therefore the child to be born will be called holy, the Son of God. [36]And behold, Elizabeth, your relative, has also conceived* a son in her old age, and this is the sixth month for her who was called barren; [37]for nothing will be impossible for God." [38r]Mary said, "Behold, I am the handmaid of the Lord. May it be done to me according to your word." Then the angel departed from her.

Mary Visits Elizabeth

[39]During those days Mary set out and traveled to the hill country in haste to a town of Judah, [40]where she entered the house of Zechariah and greeted Elizabeth. [41s]When Elizabeth heard Mary's greeting, the infant leaped in her womb, and Elizabeth, filled with the holy Spirit, [42t]cried out in a loud voice and said, "Most blessed are you among women, and blessed is the fruit of your womb. [43]And how does this happen to me, that the mother of my Lord* should come to me? [44]For at the moment the sound of your greeting reached my ears, the infant in my womb leaped for joy. [45u]Blessed are you who believed* that what was spoken to you by the Lord would be fulfilled."

The Canticle of Mary

[46v]And Mary said:*[w]

"My soul proclaims the greatness of the Lord;
  [47x]my spirit rejoices in God my savior.
[48y]For he has looked upon his handmaid's lowliness;
  behold, from now on will all ages call me blessed.
[49z]The Mighty One has done great things for me,
  and holy is his name.
[50a]His mercy is from age to age
  to those who fear him.
[51b]He has shown might with his arm,
  dispersed the arrogant of mind and
    heart.

The church uses the **Canticle of Mary** at Evening Prayer in the Liturgy of the Hours. It expresses a perfect model of surrender to God's will for every Christian, an attitude of surrender as the day begins to draw to a close.

r
Gn 18:14;
Jer 32:27;
Mt 19:26

s
1:15;
Gn 25:22 LXX

t
11:27-28;
Jgs 5:24;
Jdt 13:18;
Dt 28:4

u
1:20

v
1 Sm 2:1-10

w
Ps 35:9;
Is 61:10;
Heb 3:18

x
Ti 3:4; Jude 25

y
11:27;
1 Sm 1:11;
2 Sm 16:12;
2 Kgs 14:26;
Ps 113:7

z
Dt 10:21;
Pss 71:19;
111:9; 126:2-3

a
Pss 89:2;
103:13, 17

b
Pss 89:10;
118:15;
Jer 32:17
(39:17 LXX)

LUKE

1:36-37 The sign given to Mary in confirmation of the angel's announcement to her is the pregnancy of her aged relative Elizabeth. If a woman past the childbearing age could become pregnant, why, the angel implies, should there be doubt about Mary's pregnancy, for **nothing will be impossible for God**.

1:43 Even before his birth, Jesus is identified in Luke as the Lord.

1:45 Blessed are you who believed: Luke portrays Mary as a believer whose faith stands in contrast to the disbelief of Zechariah (1:20). Mary's role as believer in the infancy narrative should be seen in connection with the explicit mention of her presence among "those who believed" after the resurrection at the beginning of the Acts of the Apostles (Acts 1:14).

1:46-55 Although Mary is praised for being the mother of the Lord and because of her belief, she reacts as the servant in a psalm of praise, the Magnificat. Because there is no specific connection of the canticle to the context of Mary's pregnancy and her visit to Elizabeth, the Magnificat (with the possible exception of v. 48) may have been a Jewish Christian hymn that Luke found appropriate at this point in his story. Even if not composed by Luke, it fits in well with themes found elsewhere in Luke: joy and exultation in the Lord; the lowly being singled out for God's favor; the reversal of human fortunes; the fulfillment of Old Testament promises. The loose connection between the hymn and the context is further seen in the fact that a few Old Latin manuscripts identify the speaker of the hymn as Elizabeth, even though the overwhelming textual evidence makes Mary the speaker.

c
1 Sm 2:7;
2 Sm 22:28;
Jb 5:11; 12:19;
Ps 147:6;
Sir 10:14;
Jas 4:6;
1 Pt 5:5

d
1 Sm 2:5;
Ps 107:9

e
Ps 98:3;
Is 41:8-9

f
Gn 13:15; 17:7;
18:18;
22:17-18;
Mi 7:20

g
1:14

h
2:21;
Gn 17:10, 12;
Lv 12:3

i
1:13

j
1:20

k
7:16;
Pss 41:13;
72:18; 106:48;
111:9

l
Ps 18:3

m
Ps 106:10

[52]*c*He has thrown down the rulers from their thrones
 but lifted up the lowly.
[53]*d*The hungry he has filled with good things;
 the rich he has sent away empty.
[54]*e*He has helped Israel his servant,
 remembering his mercy,
[55]*f*according to his promise to our fathers,
 to Abraham and to his descendants forever."

[56]Mary remained with her about three months and then returned to her home.

The Birth of John

[57]*When the time arrived for Elizabeth to have her child she gave birth to a son. [58]*g*Her neighbors and relatives heard that the Lord had shown his great mercy toward her, and they rejoiced with her. [59]**h*When they came on the eighth day to circumcise the child, they were going to call him Zechariah after his father, [60]*i*but his mother said in reply, "No. He will be called John." [61]But they answered her, "There is no one among your relatives who has this name." [62]So they made signs, asking his father what he wished him to be called. [63]He asked for a tablet and wrote, "John is his name," and all were amazed. [64]*j*Immediately his mouth was opened, his tongue freed, and he spoke blessing God. [65]Then fear came upon all their neighbors, and all these matters were discussed throughout the hill country of Judea. [66]All who heard these things took them to heart, saying, "What, then, will this child be?" For surely the hand of the Lord was with him.

The Canticle of Zechariah

[67]Then Zechariah his father, filled with the holy Spirit, prophesied, saying:

[68]**k*"Blessed be the Lord, the God of Israel,
 for he has visited and brought redemption to his people.
[69]**l*He has raised up a horn for our salvation
 within the house of David his servant,
[70]even as he promised through the mouth of his holy prophets from of old:
[71]*m*salvation from our enemies and from the hand of all who hate us,

---

1:57-66 The birth and circumcision of John above all emphasize John's incorporation into the people of Israel by the sign of the covenant (Gn 17:1-12). The narrative of John's circumcision also prepares the way for the subsequent description of the circumcision of Jesus in Luke 2:21. At the beginning of his two-volume work Luke shows those who play crucial roles in the inauguration of Christianity to be wholly a part of the people of Israel. At the end of the Acts of the Apostles (Acts 21:20; 22:3; 23:6-9; 24:14-16; 26:2-8, 22-23) he will argue that Christianity is the direct descendant of Pharisaic Judaism.

1:59 The practice of Palestinian Judaism at this time was to name the child at birth; moreover, though naming a male child after the father is not completely unknown, the usual practice was to name the child after the grandfather (see 1:61). The naming of the child John and Zechariah's recovery from his loss of speech should be understood as fulfilling the angel's announcement to Zechariah in Luke 1:13, 20.

1:68-79 Like the canticle of Mary (1:46-55) the canticle of Zechariah is only loosely connected with its context. Apart from Luke 1:76-77, the hymn in speaking of **a horn for our salvation** (1:69) and **the daybreak from on high** (1:78) applies more closely to Jesus and his work than to John. Again like Mary's canticle, it is largely composed of phrases taken from the Greek Old Testament and may have been a Jewish Christian hymn of praise that Luke adapted to fit the present context by inserting Luke 1:76-77 to give Zechariah's reply to the question asked in Luke 1:66.

1:69 A horn for our salvation: the horn is a common Old Testament figure for strength (Pss 18:3; 75:5-6; 89:18; 112:9; 148:14). This description is applied to God in Psalm 18:2 and is here transferred to Jesus. The connection of the phrase with **the house of David** gives the title messianic overtones and may indicate an allusion to a phrase in Hannah's song of praise (1 Sm 2:10), "the horn of his anointed."

[72n]to show mercy to our fathers[o]

and to be mindful of his holy covenant

[73p]and of the oath he swore to Abraham our father,

and to grant us that,

[74]rescued from the hand of enemies,

without fear we might worship him

[75q]in holiness and righteousness

before him all our days.

[76r]And you, child, will be called prophet of the Most High,

for you will go before the Lord* to prepare his ways,

[77]to give his people knowledge of salvation

through the forgiveness of their sins,

[78s]because of the tender mercy of our God[t]

by which the daybreak from on high*
will visit us

[79]to shine on those who sit in darkness
and death's shadow,

to guide our feet into the path of peace."

The church uses the **Canticle of Zechariah** at Morning Prayer in the Liturgy of the Hours. It expresses God's awesome power to save all through Jesus Christ and is appropriate to beginning the day.

[80u]The child grew and became strong in spirit, and he was in the desert until the day of his manifestation to Israel.

n
Gn 17:7;
Lv 26:42;
Ps 105:8-9;
Mi 7:20

o
Ps 106:45-46

p
Gn 22:16-17

q
Ti 2:12

r
Is 40:3;
Mal 3:1;
Mt 3:3; 11:10

s
Is 60:1-2

t
Mal 3:20

u
2:40; Mt 3:1

a
Mi 5:2; Mt 2:6

b
1:27; Mt 1:18

LUKE

The Birth of Jesus

2 [1*]In those days a decree went out from Caesar Augustus* that the whole world should be enrolled. [2]This was the first enrollment, when Quirinius was governor of Syria. [3]So all went to be enrolled, each to his own town. [4a]And Joseph too went up from Galilee from the town of Nazareth to Judea, to the city of David that is called Bethlehem, because he was of the house and family of David, [5b]to be enrolled with

On the officials of Rome, see the chart in "Background to the Gospels," pp. **4–5.**

1:76 You will go before the Lord: here **the Lord** is most likely a reference to Jesus (contrast 1:15-17 where Yahweh is meant) and John is presented as the precursor of Jesus.

1:78 The daybreak from on high: three times in the LXX (Jer 23:5; Zec 3:8; 6:12), the Greek word used here for **daybreak** translates the Hebrew word for "scion, branch," an Old Testament messianic title.

2:1-2 Although universal registrations of Roman citizens are attested in 28 B.C., 8 B.C., and A.D. 14 and enrollments in individual provinces of those who are not Roman citizens are also attested, such a universal census of the Roman world under Caesar Augustus is unknown outside the New Testament. Moreover, there are notorious historical problems connected with Luke's dating of the census **when Quirinius was governor of Syria**, and the various attempts to resolve the difficulties have proved unsuccessful. P. Sulpicius Quirinius became legate of the province of Syria in A.D. 6–7 when Judea was annexed to the province of Syria. At that time, a provincial census of Judea was taken up. If Quirinius had been legate of Syria previously, it would have to have been before 10 B.C. because the various legates of Syria from 10 B.C. to 4 B.C. (the death of Herod) are known, and such a dating for an earlier

census under Quirinius would create additional problems for dating the beginning of Jesus' ministry (3:1, 23). A previous legateship after 4 B.C. (and before A.D. 6) would not fit with the dating of Jesus' birth in the days of Herod (1:5; Mt 2:1). Luke may simply be combining Jesus' birth in Bethlehem with his vague recollection of a census under Quirinius (see also Acts 5:37) to underline the significance of this birth for the whole Roman world: through this child born in Bethlehem peace and salvation come to the empire.

2:1 Caesar Augustus: the reign of the Roman emperor Caesar Augustus is usually dated from 27 B.C. to his death in A.D. 14. According to Greek inscriptions, Augustus was regarded in the Roman Empire as "savior" and "god," and he was credited with establishing a time of peace, the *pax Augusta*, throughout the Roman world during his long reign. It is not by chance that Luke relates the birth of Jesus to the time of Caesar Augustus: the real savior (2:11) and peace-bearer (2:14; see also 19:38) is the child born in Bethlehem. The great emperor is simply God's agent (like the Persian king Cyrus in Is 44:28–45:1) who provides the occasion for God's purposes to be accomplished. **The whole world**: that is, the whole Roman world: Rome, Italy, and the Roman provinces.

c
Mt 1:25

d
1:11, 26

e
Mt 1:21; 16:16;
Jn 4:42;
Acts 2:36;
5:31; Phil 2:11

f
19:38

Mary, his betrothed, who was with child. ⁶While they were there, the time came for her to have her child, ⁷ᶜand she gave birth to her firstborn son.* She wrapped him in swaddling clothes and laid him in a manger, because there was no room for them in the inn.

⁸*Now there were shepherds in that region living in the fields and keeping the night watch over their flock. ⁹ᵈThe angel of the Lord appeared to them and the glory of the Lord shone around them, and they were struck with great fear. ¹⁰The angel said to them, "Do not be afraid; for behold, I proclaim to you good news of great joy that will be for all the people. ¹¹ᵉFor today in the city of David a savior has been born for you who is Messiah and Lord. ¹²And this will be a sign for you: you will find an infant wrapped in swaddling clothes and lying in a manger." ¹³And suddenly there was a multitude of the heavenly host with the angel, praising God and saying:

On the title **"Savior,"** see the NAB footnote below.

¹⁴*ᶠ"Glory to God in the highest
    and on earth peace to those on whom his
    favor rests."

The hymn of the angels **"Glory to God . . ."** is used at Mass to begin the *Gloria,* an extended hymn of praise to God for all good things bestowed upon the earth.

The Visit of the Shepherds

¹⁵When the angels went away from them to heaven, the shepherds said to one another, "Let us go, then, to Bethlehem to see this thing that has taken place, which the Lord has made known to us." ¹⁶So they went in haste and found Mary and Joseph, and the infant lying in the manger. ¹⁷When they saw this, they made known the message that had been told them about this child. ¹⁸All who heard it were amazed by what had been told them by the shepherds. ¹⁹And Mary kept all these things, reflecting on them in her heart. ²⁰Then the shepherds returned, glorifying and praising God for all they had heard and seen, just as it had been told to them.

2:7 Firstborn son: the description of Jesus as **firstborn** son does not necessarily mean that Mary had other sons. It is a legal description indicating that Jesus possessed the rights and privileges of the firstborn son (Gn 27; Ex 13:2; Nm 3:12-13; 18:15-16; Dt 21:15-17). See the notes on Matthew 1:25; Mark 6:3. **Wrapped him in swaddling clothes:** there may be an allusion here to the birth of another descendant of David, his son Solomon, who though a great king was wrapped in swaddling clothes like any other infant (Wis 7:4-6). **Laid him in a manger:** a feeding trough for animals. A possible allusion to Isaiah 1:3 LXX.

2:8-20 The announcement of Jesus' birth to the shepherds is in keeping with Luke's theme that the lowly are singled out as the recipients of God's favors and blessings (see also 1:48, 52).

2:11 The basic message of the infancy narrative is contained in the angel's announcement: this child is **savior, Messiah,** and **Lord.** Luke is the only synoptic gospel writer to use the title **savior** for Jesus (2:11; Acts 5:31; 13:23; see also Lk 1:69; 19:9; Acts 4:12). As savior, Jesus is looked upon by Luke as the one who rescues humanity from sin and delivers humanity from the condition of alienation from God. The title *christos,* "Christ," is the Greek equivalent of the Hebrew *māšîaḥ,* "Messiah," "anointed one." Among certain groups in first-century Palestinian Judaism, the title was applied to an expected royal leader from the line of David who would restore the kingdom to Israel (see Acts 1:6). The political overtones of the title are played down in Luke and instead the Messiah of the Lord (2:26) or the Lord's anointed is the one who now brings salvation to all humanity, Jew and Gentile (2:29-32). Lord is the most frequently used title for Jesus in Luke and Acts. In the New Testament it is also applied to Yahweh, as it is in the Old Testament. When used of Jesus it points to his transcendence and dominion over humanity.

2:14 On earth peace to those on whom his favor rests: the peace that results from the Christ event is for those whom God has favored with his grace. This reading is found in the oldest representatives of the Western and Alexandrian text traditions and is the preferred one; the Byzantine text tradition, on the other hand, reads: "on earth peace, good will toward men." The peace of which Luke's gospel speaks (2:14; 7:50; 8:48; 10:5-6; 19:38, 42; 24:36) is more than the absence of war of the *pax Augusta;* it also includes the security and well-being characteristic of peace in the Old Testament.

The Circumcision and Naming of Jesus

²¹ᵍWhen eight days were completed for his circumcision,* he was named Jesus, the name given him by the angel before he was conceived in the womb.

The Presentation in the Temple

²²*ʰWhen the days were completed for their purification* according to the law of Moses, they took him up to Jerusalem to present him to the Lord, ²³ⁱjust as it is written

g
1:31;
Gn 17:12;
Mt 1:21

h
Lv 12:2-8

i
Ex 13:2, 12

Mary, Mother of Jesus

Surprisingly, the NT records very little about the details of Mary's background and life. The primary focus is on her relationship to her son Jesus. That her parents were named Joachim and Anna comes from a later apocryphal gospel (*Protoevangelium of James,* second century A.D.). We do not know when she was born or under what circumstances, but the church honors her above all other women for being the mother of Jesus, God's only begotten Son. Whereas the gospels hint that she was from a poor family in Nazareth, the apocryphal story asserts that she was born of wealthy parents in Jerusalem who served in the temple.

Of the gospels, Luke gives the most attention to Mary. Artists throughout history have portrayed poignant scenes from Luke's infancy narrative (chs. 1–2) such as the annunciation and the visitation. Mary takes center stage throughout the story as it unfolds and her destiny to be the mother of Jesus is revealed. Mary expresses her response to God's mysterious will in the Canticle of Mary (Lk 1:46-55). Filled with OT imagery, it shows that Mary acquiesces totally to God's will, even without understanding it fully.

All of the gospels feature Mary in some fashion, but John never names her. He refers to her only as "the mother of Jesus." Yet she figures prominently in John at the foot of the cross, where she becomes an icon of the church, entrusted to the care of the unnamed Beloved Disciple (Jn 19:26-27).

Matthew's story of Jesus' miraculous conception (chs. 1–2) emphasizes Joseph's role as the foster father of Jesus, whose Davidic lineage confirms that Jesus is the fulfillment of messianic expectations. In Matthew, Mary is seen primarily in a subservient role, humbly accepting God's will,

guided and protected by her betrothed's actions.

Mark does not include an infancy narrative, but Mary is located among Jesus' relatives. Jesus is called "son of Mary" (Mk 6:3), but she herself may be numbered among those relatives who think, because of his unusual ministry, he is "out of his mind" (Mk 3:21)!

Acts portrays Mary as a member of the early Christian community (1:14), but Paul makes almost no reference to her, except through the acknowledgment that Jesus was "born of a woman" (Gal 4:4).

The church's understanding of Mary's significance grew over time, beyond the testimony of the Bible, under the guidance of the Holy Spirit, and expressed through official church teachings. Most important, the church honors Mary for her role in salvation history. By saying "yes" to God's mysterious will, she enabled salvation to enter the world through the birth of her son.

The Roman Catholic Church has bestowed on Mary many honorific titles (Mother of God, Mother of the Church, the New Eve, Queen of Heaven, Star of the Sea, etc.) and has also proclaimed doctrines about her immaculate conception (1854) and assumption into heaven (1950). She is also identified with the unnamed woman "clothed with the sun" of the book of Revelation (12:1-18), an uncertain but ancient interpretation. After the Second Vatican Council, ecumenical dialogues promoted discussion among Roman Catholics and Protestants about Mary's significance, which led to a proliferation of books on Mary.

2:21 Just as John before him had been incorporated into the people of Israel through his circumcision, so too this child (see the note on 1:57-66).

2:22-40 The presentation of Jesus in the temple depicts the parents of Jesus as devout Jews, faithful observers of the law of the Lord (2:23-24, 39), i.e., the law of Moses. In this respect, they are described in a fashion similar to the parents of John (1:6) and Simeon (2:25) and Anna (2:36-37).

2:22 Their purification: syntactically, **their** must refer to Mary and Joseph, even though the Mosaic law never mentions the purification

Statue of a young Mary

j
3:6; Is 40:5
LXX; 52:10

k
Is 42:6; 46:13;
49:6; Acts
13:47; 26:23

l
12:51; Is 8:14;
Jn 9:39;
Rom 9:33;
1 Cor 1:23;
1 Pt 2:7-8

m
Is 52:9

n
Mt 2:23

o
1:80; 2:52

in the law of the Lord, "Every male that opens the womb shall be consecrated to the Lord," [24]and to offer the sacrifice of "a pair of turtledoves or two young pigeons," in accordance with the dictate in the law of the Lord.

[25]Now there was a man in Jerusalem whose name was Simeon. This man was righteous and devout, awaiting the consolation of Israel,* and the holy Spirit was upon him. [26]It had been revealed to him by the holy Spirit that he should not see death before he had seen the Messiah of the Lord. [27]He came in the Spirit into the temple; and when the parents brought in the child Jesus to perform the custom of the law in regard to him, [28]he took him into his arms and blessed God, saying:

> [29]"Now, Master, you may let your servant go
>   in peace, according to your word,
> [30]for my eyes have seen your salvation,
>   [31]which you prepared in sight of all the
>   peoples,
> [32k]a light for revelation to the Gentiles,
>   and glory for your people Israel."

The church uses the **Canticle of Simeon** at night prayer in the Liturgy of the Hours. It expresses a profound satisfaction at having witnessed God's saving action in Jesus Christ; thus we can retire in peace.

[33]The child's father and mother were amazed at what was said about him; [34l]and Simeon blessed them and said to Mary his mother, "Behold, this child is destined for the fall and rise of many in Israel, and to be a sign that will be contradicted [35](and you yourself a sword will pierce)* so that the thoughts of many hearts may be revealed." [36]There was also a prophetess, Anna, the daughter of Phanuel, of the tribe of Asher. She was advanced in years, having lived seven years with her husband after her marriage, [37]and then as a widow until she was eighty-four. She never left the temple, but worshiped night and day with fasting and prayer. [38m]And coming forward at that very time, she gave thanks to God and spoke about the child to all who were awaiting the redemption of Jerusalem.

The Return to Nazareth

[39n]When they had fulfilled all the prescriptions of the law of the Lord, they returned to Galilee, to their own town of Nazareth. [40o]The child grew and became strong, filled with wisdom; and the favor of God was upon him.

---

of the husband. Recognizing the problem, some Western scribes have altered the text to read "his purification," understanding the presentation of Jesus in the temple as a form of purification; the Vulgate version has a Latin form that could be either "his" or "her." According to the Mosaic law (Lv 12:2-8), the woman who gives birth to a boy is unable for forty days to touch anything sacred or to enter the temple area by reason of her legal impurity. At the end of this period she is required to offer a year-old lamb as a burnt offering and a turtledove or young pigeon as an expiation of sin. The woman who could not afford a lamb offered instead two turtledoves or two young pigeons, as Mary does here. **They took him up to Jerusalem to present him to the Lord**: as the firstborn son (2:7) Jesus was consecrated to the Lord as the law required (Ex 13:2, 12), but there was no requirement that this be done at the temple. The concept of a presentation at the temple is probably derived from 1 Samuel 1:24-28, where Hannah offers the child Samuel for sanctuary services. The law further stipulated (Nm 3:47-48) that the firstborn son should be redeemed by the parents through their payment of five shekels to a member of a priestly family. About this legal requirement Luke is silent.

2:25 Awaiting the consolation of Israel: Simeon here and later Anna who speak about the child to all who were awaiting the redemption of Jerusalem represent the hopes and expectations of faithful and devout Jews who at this time were looking forward to the restoration of God's rule in Israel. The birth of Jesus brings these hopes to fulfillment.

2:35 (And you yourself a sword will pierce): Mary herself will not be untouched by the various reactions to the role of Jesus (2:34). Her blessedness as mother of the Lord will be challenged by her son who describes true blessedness as "hearing the word of God and observing it" (11:27-28 and 8:20-21).

LUKE

Simeon and Anna and the Value in Waiting

If you have ever been promised something for which you had to wait a very long time, you might be able to appreciate the tenacity of Simeon and Anna. Schooled in the faithfulness of God throughout the history of their people, they anticipated God's action in some profound way.

It is not just their waiting that leads them to recognize that the child Jesus is the beginning of promises fulfilled. It is what they did with their waiting. Simeon is a man of prayer who experiences the Spirit and finds in the temple the sign he has been told to expect. Anna is a prophetess, in the long tradition of Israel's prophets, who reads the signs of the times and speaks for God. She spends her time at the temple in prayer and fasting.

Both Simeon and Anna illustrate that waiting involves action and contemplative listening. They go to the place where their faith finds its home and they are people of prayer. They were not simply in the right place at the right time; they were in the right space spiritually and recognized the time of God's action.

The Boy Jesus in the Temple

[41]*[p]Each year his parents went to Jerusalem for the feast of Passover, [42]and when he was twelve years old, they went up according to festival custom. [43]After they had completed its days, as they were returning, the boy Jesus remained behind in Jerusalem, but his parents did not know it. [44]Thinking that he was in the caravan, they journeyed for a day and looked for him among their relatives and acquaintances, [45]but not finding him, they returned to Jerusalem to look for him. [46]After three days they found him in the temple, sitting in the midst of the teachers, listening to them and asking them questions, [47]and all who heard him were astounded at his understanding and his answers. [48]When his parents saw him, they were astonished, and his mother said to him, "Son, why have you done this to us? Your father and I have been looking for you with great anxiety." [49]And he said to them, "Why were you looking for me? Did you not know that I must be in my Father's house?"* [50]But they did not understand what he said to them. [51][q]He went down with them and came to Nazareth, and was obedient to them; and his mother kept all these things in her heart. [52][r]And Jesus advanced [in] wisdom and age and favor before God and man.

III: The Preparation for the Public Ministry

The Preaching of John the Baptist

3 [1]*[a]In the fifteenth year of the reign of Tiberius Caesar, when Pontius Pilate was governor of Judea, and Herod was tetrarch of Galilee, and his brother Philip tetrarch

p
Ex 12:24-27; 23:15; Dt 16:1-8

q
2:19

r
1:80; 2:40; 1 Sm 2:26

a
Mt 3:1-12; Mk 1:1-8; Jn 1:19-28

2:41-52 This story's concern with an incident from Jesus' youth is unique in the canonical gospel tradition. It presents Jesus in the role of the faithful Jewish boy, raised in the traditions of Israel, and fulfilling all that the law requires. With this episode, the infancy narrative ends just as it began, in the setting of the Jerusalem temple.

2:49 I must be in my Father's house: this phrase can also be translated, "I must be about my Father's work." In either translation, Jesus refers to God as his Father. His divine sonship, and his obedience to his heavenly Father's will, take precedence over his ties to his family.

3:1-20 Although Luke is indebted in this section to his sources, the Gospel of Mark and a collection of sayings of John the Baptist, he has clearly marked this introduction to the ministry of Jesus with his own individual style. Just as the gospel began with a long periodic sentence (1:1-4), so too this section (3:1-2). He casts the call of John the Baptist in the form of an Old Testament prophetic call (3:2) and extends the quotation from Isaiah found in Mark 1:3 (Is 40:3) by the addition of Isaiah 40:4-5 in Luke 3:5-6. In doing so, he presents his theme of the universality of salvation, which he has announced earlier in the words of Simeon (2:30-32). Moreover, in describing the expectation of the people (3:15), Luke is characterizing the time of John's preaching in the same way as he had earlier described the situation of other devout Israelites in the infancy narrative (2:25-26, 37-38). In Luke 3:7-18 Luke presents the preaching of John the Baptist who urges the crowds to reform in view of **the coming wrath** (3:7, 9: eschatological preaching), and who offers the crowds certain standards for reforming social conduct (3:10-14: ethical preaching), and who 157

b
1:80

c
Acts 13:24;
19:4

d
Is 40:3-5

e
Jn 1:23

f
2:30-31

g
Mt 12:34

h
Jn 8:39

i
Mt 7:19;
Jn 15:6

j
7:29

of the region of Ituraea and Trachonitis, and Lysanias was tetrarch of Abilene,* [2b]during the high priesthood of Annas and Caiaphas,* the word of God came to John the son of Zechariah in the desert. [3]*[c]He went throughout [the] whole region of the Jordan, proclaiming a baptism of repentance for the forgiveness of sins, [4]*[d]as it is written in the book of the words of the prophet Isaiah:[e]

> "A voice of one crying out in the desert:
> 'Prepare the way of the Lord,
>   make straight his paths.
> [5]Every valley shall be filled
>   and every mountain and hill shall be made low.
> The winding roads shall be made straight,
>   and the rough ways made smooth,
> [6f]and all flesh shall see the salvation of God.'"

[7g]He said to the crowds who came out to be baptized by him, "You brood of vipers! Who warned you to flee from the coming wrath? [8h]Produce good fruits as evidence of your repentance; and do not begin to say to yourselves, 'We have Abraham as our father,' for I tell you, God can raise up children to Abraham from these stones. [9i]Even now the ax lies at the root of the trees. Therefore every tree that does not produce good fruit will be cut down and thrown into the fire."

[10]And the crowds asked him, "What then should we do?" [11]He said to them in reply, "Whoever has two cloaks should share with the person who has none. And whoever has food should do likewise." [12j]Even tax collectors came to be baptized and they said to him, "Teacher, what should we do?" [13]He answered them, "Stop collecting more than what is prescribed." [14]Soldiers also asked him, "And what is it that we should do?" He told them, "Do not practice extortion, do not falsely accuse anyone, and be satisfied with your wages."

---

announces to the crowds the coming of **one mightier than** he (3:15-18: messianic preaching).

3:1 Tiberius Caesar: Tiberius succeeded Augustus as emperor in A.D. 14 and reigned until A.D. 37. The fifteenth year of his reign, depending on the method of calculating his first regnal year, would have fallen between A.D. 27 and 29. **Pontius Pilate:** prefect of Judea from A.D. 26 to 36. The Jewish historian Josephus describes him as a greedy and ruthless prefect who had little regard for the local Jewish population and their religious practices (see 13:1). **Herod:** i.e., Herod Antipas, the son of Herod the Great. He ruled over Galilee and Perea from 4 B.C. to A.D. 39. His official title **tetrarch** means literally, "ruler of a quarter," but came to designate any subordinate prince. **Philip:** also a son of Herod the Great, tetrarch of the territory to the north and east of the Sea of Galilee from 4 B.C. to A.D. 34. Only two small areas of this territory are mentioned by Luke. **Lysanias:** nothing is known about this Lysanias who is said here to have been tetrarch of Abilene, a territory northwest of Damascus.

3:2 During the high priesthood of Annas and Caiaphas: after situating the call of John the Baptist in terms of the civil rulers of the period, Luke now mentions the religious leadership of Palestine (see the note on 1:5). Annas had been high priest A.D. 6–15. After being deposed by the Romans in A.D. 15 he was succeeded by various members of his family and eventually by his son-in-law, Caiaphas, who was high priest A.D. 18–36. Luke refers to Annas as high priest at this time (but see Jn 18:13, 19), possibly because of the continuing influence of Annas or because the title continued to be used for the ex-high priest. **The word of God came to John:** Luke is alone among the New Testament writers in associating the preaching of John with a call from God. Luke is thereby identifying John with the prophets whose ministries began with similar calls. In Luke 7:26 John will be described as "more than a prophet"; he is also the precursor of Jesus (7:27), a transitional figure inaugurating the period of the fulfillment of prophecy and promise.

3:3 See the note on Matthew 3:2.

3:4 The Essenes from Qumran used the same passage to explain why their community was in the desert studying and observing the law and the prophets (1QS 8:12-15).

^{15k}Now the people were filled with expectation, and all were asking in their hearts whether John might be the Messiah. ^{16*l}John answered them all, saying, "I am baptizing you with water, but one mightier than I is coming. I am not worthy to loosen the thongs of his sandals. He will baptize you with the holy Spirit and fire. ^{17m}His winnowing fan* is in his hand to clear his threshing floor and to gather the wheat into his barn, but the chaff he will burn with unquenchable fire." ¹⁸Exhorting them in many other ways, he preached good news to the people. ^{19*n}Now Herod the tetrarch, who had been censured by him because of Herodias, his brother's wife, and because of all the evil deeds Herod had committed, ²⁰added still another to these by [also] putting John in prison.

The Baptism of Jesus

^{21*o}After all the people had been baptized and Jesus also had been baptized and was praying, heaven was opened* ^{22*p}and the holy Spirit descended upon him in bodily form like a dove. And a voice came from heaven, "You are my beloved Son; with you I am well pleased."

The Genealogy of Jesus

^{23*q}When Jesus began his ministry he was about thirty years of age. He was the son, as was thought, of Joseph, the son of Heli,^r ²⁴the son of Matthat, the son of Levi, the son of Melchi, the son of Jannai, the son of Joseph, ²⁵the son of Mattathias, the son of Amos, the son of Nahum, the son of Esli, the son of Naggai, ²⁶the son of Maath, the son of Mattathias, the son of Semein, the son of Josech, the son of Joda, ^{27s}the son of Joanan, the son of Rhesa, the son of Zerubbabel, the son of Shealtiel, the son of Neri, ²⁸the son of Melchi, the son of Addi, the son of Cosam, the son of Elmadam, the son of Er, ²⁹the son of Joshua, the son of Eliezer, the son of Jorim, the son of Matthat, the son of Levi, ³⁰the son of Simeon, the son of Judah, the son of Joseph,

k
Acts 13:25

l
7:19-20;
Jn 1:27;
Acts 1:5; 11:16

m
Mt 3:12

n
Mt 14:3-4;
Mk 6:17-18

o
Mt 3:13-17;
Mk 1:9-11

p
9:35; Ps 2:7;
Is 42:1;
Mt 12:18; 17:5;
Mk 9:7;
Jn 1:32;
2 Pt 1:17

q
Mt 1:1-17

r
4:22; Jn 6:42

s
1 Chr 3:17;
Ez 3:2

3:16 He will baptize you with the holy Spirit and fire: in contrast to John's baptism with water, Jesus is said to baptize with the holy Spirit and with fire. From the point of view of the early Christian community, the Spirit and fire must have been understood in the light of the fire symbolism of the pouring out of the Spirit at Pentecost (Acts 2:1-4); but as part of John's preaching, the Spirit and fire should be related to their purifying and refining characteristics (Ez 36:25-27; Mal 3:2-3). See the note on Matthew 3:11.

3:17 Winnowing fan: see the note on Matthew 3:12.

3:19-20 Luke separates the ministry of John the Baptist from that of Jesus by reporting the imprisonment of John before the baptism of Jesus (3:21-22). Luke uses this literary device to serve his understanding of the periods of salvation history. With John the Baptist, the time of promise, the period of Israel, comes to an end; with the baptism of Jesus and the descent of the Spirit upon him, the time of fulfillment, the period of Jesus, begins. In his second volume, the Acts of the Apostles, Luke will introduce the third epoch in salvation history, the period of the church.

3:21-22 This episode in Luke focuses on the heavenly message identifying Jesus as Son and, through the allusion to Isaiah 42:1, as Servant of Yahweh. The relationship of Jesus to the Father has

already been announced in the infancy narrative (1:32, 35; 2:49); it occurs here at the beginning of Jesus' Galilean ministry and will reappear in Luke 9:35 before another major section of Luke's gospel, the travel narrative (9:51–19:27). Elsewhere in Luke's writings (4:18; Acts 10:38), this incident will be interpreted as a type of anointing of Jesus.

3:21 Was praying: Luke regularly presents Jesus at prayer at important points in his ministry: here at his baptism; at the choice of the Twelve (6:12); before Peter's confession (9:18); at the transfiguration (9:28); when he teaches his disciples to pray (11:1); at the Last Supper (22:32); on the Mount of Olives (22:41); on the cross (23:46).

3:22 You are my beloved Son; with you I am well pleased: this is the best attested reading in the Greek manuscripts. The Western reading, "You are my Son, this day I have begotten you," is derived from Psalm 2:7.

3:23-38 Whereas Matthew 1:2 begins the genealogy of Jesus with Abraham to emphasize Jesus' bonds with the people of Israel, Luke's universalism leads him to trace the descent of Jesus beyond Israel to Adam and beyond that to God (3:38) to stress again Jesus' divine sonship.

159

t
2 Sm 5:14

u
1 Sm 16:1, 18

v
Ru 4:17-22;
1 Chr 2:1-15

w
Gn 29:35;
38:29

x
Gn 21:3;
25:26;
1 Chr 1:34;
28:34

y
Gn 11:10-26;
1 Chr 1:24-27

z
Gn 4:25–5:32;
1 Chr 1:1-4

a
Mt 4:1-11;
Mk 1:12-13

b
Heb 4:15

Both Luke and Matthew include genealogies in their infancy narratives. They vary in ways that likely reveal the theological interests of each evangelist, respectively.

Matthew's Genealogy (1:1-17)	Luke's Genealogy (3:23-38)
Placed at the beginning of the gospel; alludes to a new "beginning" of salvation history in Jesus out of Israel's history	Placed between Jesus' baptism and temptation by the devil to emphasize Jesus as God's Son
Begins with Abraham, father of faith, and then structured in rough chronological order around three groups of fourteen kings each, with David as the central figure, emphasizing Jesus' Davidic heritage and the fulfillment of the Abrahamic covenant of becoming a "father of many nations"	Structured in reverse chronological order around significant figures (not kings) in Israel's history and concluding with Adam, "son of God," emphasizing the universalism of salvation achieved in Jesus, savior of all humankind
Interjects four female figures in the list (Tamar, Rahab, Ruth, the wife of Uriah the Hittite), perhaps emphasizing God's ability to write salvation history in extraordinary ways (all bore sons in unusual circumstances), thus prefiguring Mary's role as the bearer of Jesus, Emmanuel	Absence of women
Heightened role of Joseph in the infancy narrative as foster father and protector of Jesus	Heightened role of Mary in the infancy narrative as hearer and doer of God's word

the son of Jonam, the son of Eliakim, [31t]the son of Melea, the son of Menna, the son of Mattatha, the son of Nathan, the son of David,* [32u]the son of Jesse, the son of Obed, the son of Boaz, the son of Sala, the son of Nahshon,[v] [33w]the son of Amminadab, the son of Admin, the son of Arni, the son of Hezron, the son of Perez, the son of Judah, [34x]the son of Jacob, the son of Isaac, the son of Abraham, the son of Terah, the son of Nahor,[y] [35]the son of Serug, the son of Reu, the son of Peleg, the son of Eber, the son of Shelah, [36z]the son of Cainan, the son of Arphaxad, the son of Shem, the son of Noah, the son of Lamech, [37]the son of Methuselah, the son of Enoch, the son of Jared, the son of Mahalaleel, the son of Cainan, [38]the son of Enos, the son of Seth, the son of Adam, the son of God.

The Temptation of Jesus

4 [1*a]Filled with the holy Spirit,* Jesus returned from the Jordan and was led by the Spirit into the desert [2b]for forty days,* to be tempted by the devil. He ate nothing

---

3:31 The son of Nathan, the son of David: in keeping with Jesus' prophetic role in Luke and Acts (e.g., 7:16, 39; 9:8; 13:33; 24:19; Acts 3:22-23; 7:37) Luke traces Jesus' Davidic ancestry through the prophet Nathan (see 2 Sm 7:2) rather than through King Solomon, as Matthew 1:6-7.

4:1-13 See the note on Matthew 4:1-11.

4:1 Filled with the holy Spirit: as a result of the descent of the Spirit upon him at his baptism (3:21-22), Jesus is now

equipped to overcome the devil. Just as the Spirit is prominent at this early stage of Jesus' ministry (4:1, 14, 18), so too will it be at the beginning of the period of the church in Acts (Acts 1:4; 2:4, 17).

4:2 For forty days: the mention of forty days recalls the forty years of the wilderness wanderings of the Israelites during the Exodus (Dt 8:2).

during those days, and when they were over he was hungry. ³The devil said to him, "If you are the Son of God, command this stone to become bread." ⁴ᶜJesus answered him, "It is written, 'One does not live by bread alone.'" ⁵Then he took him up and showed him all the kingdoms of the world in a single instant. ⁶ᵈThe devil said to him, "I shall give to you all this power and their glory; for it has been handed over to me, and I may give it to whomever I wish. ⁷All this will be yours, if you worship me." ⁸ᵉJesus said to him in reply, "It is written:

> 'You shall worship the Lord, your God,
>> and him alone shall you serve.'"

⁹*Then he led him to Jerusalem, made him stand on the parapet of the temple, and said to him, "If you are the Son of God, throw yourself down from here, ¹⁰ᶠfor it is written:

> 'He will command his angels concerning you,
>> to guard you,'

¹¹ᵍand:

> 'With their hands they will support you,
>> lest you dash your foot against a stone.'"

¹²ʰJesus said to him in reply, "It also says, 'You shall not put the Lord, your God, to the test.'" ¹³*ⁱWhen the devil had finished every temptation, he departed from him for a time.

IV: The Ministry in Galilee

The Beginning of the Galilean Ministry

¹⁴ʲJesus returned to Galilee in the power of the Spirit, and news of him spread* throughout the whole region.ᵏ ¹⁵He taught in their synagogues and was praised by all.

The Rejection at Nazareth

¹⁶*ˡHe came to Nazareth, where he had grown up, and went according to his custom* into the synagogue on the sabbath day. He stood up to read ¹⁷and was handed a scroll of the prophet Isaiah. He unrolled the scroll and found the passage where it was written:

> ¹⁸ᵐ"The Spirit of the Lord is upon me,*
>> because he has anointed me
>>> to bring glad tidings to the poor.

---

c
Dt 8:3

d
Jer 27:5;
Mt 28:18

e
Dt 6:13

f
Ps 91:11

g
Ps 91:12

h
Dt 6:16;
1 Cor 10:9

i
22:3;
Jn 13:2, 27;
Heb 4:15

j
Mt 4:12-17;
Mk 1:14-15

k
5:15; Mt 3:16

l
Mt 13:53-58;
Mk 6:1-6

m
Is 61:1-2; 58:6

4:9 To Jerusalem: the Lucan order of the temptations concludes on the parapet of the temple in Jerusalem, the city of destiny in Luke-Acts. It is in Jerusalem that Jesus will ultimately face his destiny (9:51; 13:33).

4:13 For a time: the devil's opportune time will occur before the passion and death of Jesus (22:3, 31-32, 53).

4:14 News of him spread: a Lucan theme; see Luke 4:37; 5:15; 7:17.

4:16-30 Luke has transposed to the beginning of Jesus' ministry an incident from his Marcan source, which situated it near the end of the Galilean ministry (Mk 6:1-6a). In doing so, Luke turns the initial admiration (4:22) and subsequent rejection of Jesus (4:28-29)

into a foreshadowing of the whole future ministry of Jesus. Moreover, the rejection of Jesus in his own hometown hints at the greater rejection of him by Israel (Acts 13:46).

4:16 According to his custom: Jesus' practice of regularly attending synagogue is carried on by the early Christians' practice of meeting in the temple (Acts 2:46; 3:1; 5:12).

4:18 The Spirit of the Lord is upon me, because he has anointed me: see the note on Luke 3:21-22. As this incident develops, Jesus is portrayed as a prophet whose ministry is compared to that of the prophets Elijah and Elisha. Prophetic anointings are known in first-century Palestinian Judaism from the Qumran literature that speaks of prophets as God's anointed ones. **To bring glad tidings** 161

n
3:23; Jn 6:42

o
1 Kgs 17:1-7;
18:1; Jas 5:17

p
1 Kgs 17:9

q
2 Kgs 5:1-14

r
Mk 1:21-28

s
Mt 4:13;
Jn 2:12

t
Mt 7:28-29

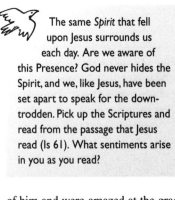

The same *Spirit* that fell upon Jesus surrounds us each day. Are we aware of this Presence? God never hides the Spirit, and we, like Jesus, have been set apart to speak for the downtrodden. Pick up the Scriptures and read from the passage that Jesus read (Is 61). What sentiments arise in you as you read?

He has sent me to proclaim liberty to captives
and recovery of sight to the blind,
to let the oppressed go free,
[19]and to proclaim a year acceptable to the Lord."

[20]Rolling up the scroll, he handed it back to the attendant and sat down, and the eyes of all in the synagogue looked intently at him. [21]He said to them, "Today this scripture passage is fulfilled in your hearing."* [22n]And all spoke highly of him and were amazed at the gracious words that came from his mouth. They also asked, "Isn't this the son of Joseph?" [23]He said to them, "Surely you will quote me this proverb, 'Physician, cure yourself,' and say, 'Do here in your native place the things that we heard were done in Capernaum.'"* [24]And he said, "Amen, I say to you, no prophet is accepted in his own native place. [25*o]Indeed, I tell you, there were many widows in Israel in the days of Elijah when the sky was closed for three and a half years and a severe famine spread over the entire land. [26*p]It was to none of these that Elijah was sent, but only to a widow in Zarephath in the land of Sidon. [27q]Again, there were many lepers in Israel during the time of Elisha the prophet; yet not one of them was cleansed, but only Naaman the Syrian." [28]When the people in the synagogue heard this, they were all filled with fury. [29]They rose up, drove him out of the town, and led him to the brow of the hill on which their town had been built, to hurl him down headlong. [30]But he passed through the midst of them and went away.

The Cure of a Demoniac

[31*r]Jesus then went down to Capernaum, a town of Galilee. He taught them on the sabbath,[s] [32t]and they were astonished at his teaching because he spoke with authority.

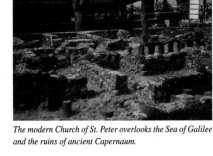

The modern Church of St. Peter overlooks the Sea of Galilee and the ruins of ancient Capernaum.

to the poor: more than any other gospel writer Luke is concerned with Jesus' attitude toward the economically and socially poor (see 6:20, 24; 12:16-21; 14:12-14; 16:19-26; 19:8). At times, the poor in Luke's gospel are associated with the downtrodden, the oppressed and afflicted, the forgotten and the neglected (4:18; 6:20-22; 7:22; 14:12-14), and it is they who accept Jesus' message of salvation.

4:21 Today this scripture passage is fulfilled in your hearing: this sermon inaugurates the time of fulfillment of Old Testament prophecy. Luke presents the ministry of Jesus as fulfilling Old Testament hopes and expectations (7:22); for Luke, even Jesus' suffering, death, and resurrection are done in fulfillment of the scriptures (24:25-27, 44-46; Acts 3:18).

4:23 The things that we heard were done in Capernaum: Luke's source for this incident reveals an awareness of an earlier ministry of Jesus in Capernaum that Luke has not yet made use of because of his transposition of this Nazareth episode to the beginning of Jesus' Galilean ministry. It is possible that by use of the future tense **you will quote me** . . . , Jesus is being portrayed as a prophet.

4:25-26 The references to Elijah and Elisha serve several purposes in this episode: they emphasize Luke's portrait of Jesus as a prophet like Elijah and Elisha; they help to explain why the initial admiration of the people turns to rejection; and they provide the scriptural justification for the future Christian mission to the Gentiles.

4:26 A widow in Zarephath in the land of Sidon: like Naaman the Syrian in Luke 4:27, a non-Israelite becomes the object of the prophet's ministry.

4:31-44 The next several incidents in Jesus' ministry take place in Capernaum and are based on Luke's source, Mark 1:21-39. To the previous portrait of Jesus as prophet (4:16-30) they now add a presentation of him as teacher (4:31-32), exorcist (4:32-37, 41), healer (4:38-40), and proclaimer of God's kingdom (4:43).

[33u]In the synagogue there was a man with the spirit of an unclean demon, and he cried out in a loud voice, [34v]"Ha! What have you to do with us, Jesus of Nazareth? Have you come to destroy us?* I know who you are—the Holy One of God!" [35]Jesus rebuked him and said, "Be quiet! Come out of him!" Then the demon threw the man down in front of them and came out of him without doing him any harm. [36]They were all amazed and said to one another, "What is there about his word? For with authority and power he commands the unclean spirits, and they come out." [37]And news of him spread everywhere in the surrounding region.

The Cure of Simon's Mother-in-Law

[38w]After he left the synagogue, he entered the house of Simon.* Simon's mother-in-law was afflicted with a severe fever, and they interceded with him about her. [39]He stood over her, rebuked the fever, and it left her. She got up immediately and waited on them.

Other Healings

[40x]At sunset, all who had people sick with various diseases brought them to him. He laid his hands on each of them and cured them. [41*y]And demons also came out from many, shouting, "You are the Son of God." But he rebuked them and did not allow them to speak because they knew that he was the Messiah.

Jesus Leaves Capernaum

[42*z]At daybreak, Jesus left and went to a deserted place. The crowds went looking for him, and when they came to him, they tried to prevent him from leaving them. [43a]But he said to them, "To the other towns also I must proclaim the good news of the kingdom of God, because for this purpose I have been sent." [44]And he was preaching in the synagogues of Judea.*

The Call of Simon the Fisherman

5 [1*a]While the crowd was pressing in on Jesus and listening to the word of God, he was standing by the Lake of Gennesaret.[b] [2]He saw two boats there alongside the

Cross references (right margin):

u
8:28; Mt 8:29;
Mk 1:23-24;
5:7

v
4:41; Jn 6:69

w
Mt 8:14-15;
Mk 1:29-31

x
Mt 8:16;
Mk 1:32-34

y
4:34; Mt 8:29;
Mk 3:11-12

z
Mk 1:35-39

a
8:1;
Mk 1:14-15

a
Mt 4:18-22;
Mk 1:16-20

b
Mt 13:1-2;
Mk 2:13;
3:9-10; 4:1-2

LUKE

4:34 What have you to do with us?: see the note on John 2:4. **Have you come to destroy us?:** the question reflects the current belief that before the day of the Lord control over humanity would be wrested from the evil spirits, evil destroyed, and God's authority over humanity reestablished. The synoptic gospel tradition presents Jesus carrying out this task.

4:38 The house of Simon: because of Luke's arrangement of material, the reader has not yet been introduced to Simon (cf. Mk 1:16-18, 29-31). Situated as it is before the call of Simon (5:1-11), it helps the reader to understand Simon's eagerness to do what Jesus says (5:5) and to follow him (5:11).

4:41 They knew that he was the Messiah: that is, the Christ (see the note on 2:11).

4:42 They tried to prevent him from leaving them: the reaction of these strangers in Capernaum is presented in contrast to the reactions of those in his hometown who rejected him (4:28-30).

4:44 In the synagogues of Judea: instead of **Judea**, which is the best reading of the manuscript tradition, the Byzantine text tradition and other manuscripts read "Galilee," a reading that harmonizes Luke with Matthew 4:23 and Mark 1:39. Up to this point Luke has spoken only of a ministry of Jesus in Galilee. Luke may

be using **Judea** to refer to the land of Israel, the territory of the Jews, and not to a specific portion of it.

5:1-11 This incident has been transposed from his source, Mark 1:16-20, which places it immediately after Jesus makes his appearance in Galilee. By this transposition Luke uses this example of Simon's acceptance of Jesus to counter the earlier rejection of him by his hometown people, and since several incidents dealing with Jesus' power and authority have already been narrated, Luke creates a plausible context for the acceptance of Jesus by Simon and his partners. Many commentators have noted the similarity between the wondrous catch of fish reported here (4:4-9) and the post-resurrectional appearance of Jesus in John 21:1-11. There are traces in Luke's story that the post-resurrectional context is the original one: in Luke 4:8 Simon addresses Jesus as **Lord** (a post-resurrectional title for Jesus—see 24:34; Acts 2:36—that has been read back into the historical ministry of Jesus) and recognizes himself as a sinner (an appropriate recognition for one who has denied knowing Jesus—22:54-62). As used by Luke, the incident looks forward to Peter's leadership in Luke-Acts (6:14; 9:20; 22:31-32; 24:34; Acts 1:15; 2:14-40; 10:11-18; 15:7-12) and symbolizes the future success of Peter as fisherman (Acts 2:41).

c
Jn 21:1-11
d
Jer 16:16
e
Mt 19:27
f
Mt 8:2-4;
Mk 1:40-45
g
8:56;
Lv 14:2-32;
Mk 7:36
h
Mk 1:35
i
Mt 9:1-8;
Mk 2:1-12
j
7:49; Is 43:25

LUKE

lake; the fishermen had disembarked and were washing their nets. [3]Getting into one of the boats, the one belonging to Simon, he asked him to put out a short distance from the shore. Then he sat down and taught the crowds from the boat. [4c]After he had finished speaking, he said to Simon, "Put out into deep water and lower your nets for a catch." [5]Simon said in reply, "Master, we have worked hard all night and have caught nothing, but at your command I will lower the nets." [6]When they had done this, they caught a great number of fish and their nets were tearing. [7]They signaled to their partners in the other boat to come to help them. They came and filled both boats so that they were in danger of sinking. [8]When Simon Peter saw this, he fell at the knees of Jesus and said, "Depart from me, Lord, for I am a sinful man." [9]For astonishment at the catch of fish they had made seized him and all those with him, [10d]and likewise James and John, the sons of Zebedee, who were partners of Simon. Jesus said to Simon, "Do not be afraid; from now on you will be catching men." [11e]When they brought their boats to the shore, they left everything* and followed him.

The Cleansing of a Leper

[12f]Now there was a man full of leprosy* in one of the towns where he was; and when he saw Jesus, he fell prostrate, pleaded with him, and said, "Lord, if you wish, you can make me clean." [13]Jesus stretched out his hand, touched him, and said, "I do will it. Be made clean." And the leprosy left him immediately. [14g]Then he ordered him not to tell anyone, but "Go, show yourself to the priest and offer for your cleansing what Moses prescribed;* that will be proof for them." [15]The report about him spread all the more, and great crowds assembled to listen to him and to be cured of their ailments, [16h]but he would withdraw to deserted places to pray.

The Healing of a Paralytic

[17*i]One day as Jesus was teaching, Pharisees and teachers of the law were sitting there who had come from every village of Galilee and Judea and Jerusalem, and the power of the Lord was with him for healing.* [18]And some men brought on a stretcher a man who was paralyzed; they were trying to bring him in and set [him] in his presence. [19]But not finding a way to bring him in because of the crowd, they went up on the roof and lowered him on the stretcher through the tiles* into the middle in front of Jesus. [20]When he saw their faith, he said, "As for you, your sins are forgiven."* [21j]Then the scribes* and Pharisees began to ask themselves, "Who is this who speaks blasphe-

---

5:11 **They left everything**: in Mark 1:16-20 and Matthew 4:18-22 the fishermen who follow Jesus leave their nets and their father; in Luke, they leave **everything** (see also 5:28; 12:33; 14:33; 18:22), an indication of Luke's theme of complete detachment from material possessions.

5:12 **Full of leprosy**: see the note on Mark 1:40.

5:14 **Show yourself to the priest . . . what Moses prescribed**: this is a reference to Leviticus 14:2-9 that gives detailed instructions for the purification of one who had been a victim of leprosy and thereby excluded from contact with others (see Lv 13:45-46, 49; Nm 5:2-3). **That will be proof for them**: see the note on Matthew 8:4.

5:17–6:11 From his Marcan source, Luke now introduces a series of controversies with Pharisees: controversy over Jesus' power to forgive sins (5:17-26); controversy over his eating and drinking with tax collectors and sinners (5:27-32); controversy over

not fasting (5:33-36); and finally two episodes narrating controversies over observance of the sabbath (5:1-11).

5:17 **Pharisees**: see the note on Matthew 3:7.

5:19 **Through the tiles**: Luke has adapted the story found in Mark to his non-Palestinian audience by changing "opened up the roof" (Mk 2:4 a reference to Palestinian straw and clay roofs) to **through the tiles**, a detail that reflects the Hellenistic Greco-Roman house with tiled roof.

5:20 **As for you, your sins are forgiven**: literally, "O man, your sins are forgiven you." The connection between the forgiveness of sins and the cure of the paralytic reflects the belief of first-century Palestine (based on the Old Testament: Ex 20:5; Dt 5:9) that sickness and infirmity are the result of sin, one's own or that of one's ancestors (see also 13:2; Jn 5:14; 9:2).

5:21 **The scribes**: see the note on Mark 2:6.

mies? Who but God alone can forgive sins?" [22k]Jesus knew their thoughts and said to them in reply, "What are you thinking in your hearts? [23]Which is easier, to say, 'Your sins are forgiven,' or to say, 'Rise and walk'? [24*l]But that you may know that the Son of Man has authority on earth to forgive sins"—he said to the man who was paralyzed, "I say to you, rise, pick up your stretcher, and go home." [25]He stood up immediately before them, picked up what he had been lying on, and went home, glorifying God. [26]Then astonishment seized them all and they glorified God, and, struck with awe, they said, "We have seen incredible things today."

The Call of Levi

[27m]After this he went out and saw a tax collector named Levi sitting at the customs post. He said to him, "Follow me." [28]And leaving everything behind,* he got up and followed him. [29n]Then Levi gave a great banquet for him in his house, and a large crowd of tax collectors and others were at table with them. [30]The Pharisees and their scribes complained to his disciples, saying, "Why do you eat and drink with tax collectors and sinners?" [31]Jesus said to them in reply, "Those who are healthy do not need a physician, but the sick do. [32]I have not come to call the righteous to repentance but sinners."

The Question about Fasting

[33o]And they said to him, "The disciples of John fast often and offer prayers, and the disciples of the Pharisees do the same; but yours eat and drink." [34*]Jesus answered them, "Can you make the wedding guests* fast while the bridegroom is with them? [35]But the days will come, and when the bridegroom is taken away from them, then they will fast in those days." [36*]And he also told them a parable. "No one tears a piece from a new cloak to patch an old one. Otherwise, he will tear the new and the piece from it will not match the old cloak. [37]Likewise, no one pours new wine into old wineskins. Otherwise, the new wine will burst the skins, and it will be spilled, and the skins will be ruined. [38]Rather, new wine must be poured into fresh wineskins. [39][And] no one who has been drinking old wine desires new, for he says, 'The old is good.'"*

Debates about the Sabbath

6 [1*a]While he was going through a field of grain on a sabbath, his disciples were picking the heads of grain, rubbing them in their hands, and eating them.[b] [2]Some Pharisees said, "Why are you doing what is unlawful on the sabbath?" [3c]Jesus said to them in reply, "Have you not read what David did when he and those [who were] with him were hungry? [4d][How] he went into the house of God, took the bread of offering,* which only the priests could lawfully eat, ate of it, and shared it with his companions." [5]Then he said to them, "The Son of Man is lord of the sabbath."

Cross-references (margin):

k — 6:8; 9:47
l — Jn 5:8-9, 27
m — Mt 9:9-13; Mk 2:13-17
n — 15:1-2
o — Mt 9:14-17; Mk 2:18-22
a — Mt 12:1-8; Mk 2:23-28
b — Dt 23:26
c — 1 Sm 21:1-6
d — Lv 24:5-9

LUKE

5:24 See the notes on Matthew 9:6 and Mark 2:10.

5:28 **Leaving everything behind**: see the note on Luke 5:11.

5:34-35 See the notes on Matthew 9:15 and Mark 2:19.

5:34 **Wedding guests**: literally, "sons of the bridal chamber."

5:36-39 See the notes on Matthew 9:16-17 and Mark 2:19.

5:39 **The old is good**: this saying is meant to be ironic and offers an explanation for the rejection by some of the new wine that Jesus offers: satisfaction with old forms will prevent one from sampling the new.

6:1-11 The two episodes recounted here deal with gathering grain and healing, both of which were forbidden on the sabbath. In his defense of his disciples' conduct and his own charitable deed, Jesus argues that satisfying human needs such as hunger and performing works of mercy take precedence even over the sacred sabbath rest. See also the notes on Matthew 12:1-14 and Mark 2:25-26.

6:4 **The bread of offering**: see the note on Matthew 12:5-6.

LUKE

e
Mt 12:9-14;
Mk 3:1-6

f
14:1

g
5:22; 9:47

h
Mt 10:1-4;
Mk 3:13-19

i
Acts 1:13

j
Mt 4:23-25;
Mk 3:7-10

k
Mt 5:1-12

⁶ᵉOn another sabbath he went into the synagogue and taught, and there was a man there whose right hand was withered. ⁷ᶠThe scribes and the Pharisees watched him closely to see if he would cure on the sabbath so that they might discover a reason to accuse him. ⁸ᵍBut he realized their intentions and said to the man with the withered hand, "Come up and stand before us." And he rose and stood there. ⁹Then Jesus said to them, "I ask you, is it lawful to do good on the sabbath rather than to do evil, to save life rather than to destroy it?" ¹⁰Looking around at them all, he then said to him, "Stretch out your hand." He did so and his hand was restored. ¹¹But they became enraged and discussed together what they might do to Jesus.

The Mission of the Twelve

¹²*ʰIn those days he departed to the mountain to pray, and he spent the night in prayer* to God. ¹³When day came, he called his disciples to himself, and from them he chose Twelve,* whom he also named apostles: ¹⁴ⁱSimon, whom he named Peter,* and his brother Andrew, James, John, Philip, Bartholomew, ¹⁵Matthew, Thomas, James the son of Alphaeus, Simon who was called a Zealot,* ¹⁶and Judas the son of James, and Judas Iscariot,* who became a traitor.

Ministering to a Great Multitude

¹⁷*ʲAnd he came down with them and stood on a stretch of level ground. A great crowd of his disciples and a large number of the people from all Judea and Jerusalem and the coastal region of Tyre and Sidon ¹⁸came to hear him and to be healed of their diseases; and even those who were tormented by unclean spirits were cured. ¹⁹Everyone in the crowd sought to touch him because power came forth from him and healed them all.

Sermon on the Plain

²⁰*ᵏAnd raising his eyes toward his disciples he said:*

6:12-16 See the notes on Matthew 10:1–11:1 and Mark 3:14-15.

6:12 Spent the night in prayer: see the note on Luke 3:21.

6:13 He chose Twelve: the identification of this group as the Twelve is a part of early Christian tradition (see 1 Cor 15:5), and in Matthew and Luke, the **Twelve** are associated with the twelve tribes of Israel (22:29-30; Mt 19:28). After the fall of Judas from his position among the Twelve, the need is felt on the part of the early community to reconstitute this group before the Christian mission begins at Pentecost (Acts 1:15-26). From Luke's perspective, they are an important group who because of their association with Jesus from the time of his baptism to his ascension (Acts 1:21-22) provide the continuity between the historical Jesus and the church of Luke's day and who as the original eyewitnesses guarantee the fidelity of the church's beliefs and practices to the teachings of Jesus (1:1-4). **Whom he also named apostles**: only Luke among the gospel writers attributes to Jesus the bestowal of the name **apostles** upon the Twelve. See the note on Matthew 10:2-4. "Apostle" becomes a technical term in early Christianity for a missionary sent out to preach the word of God. Although Luke seems to want to restrict the title to the Twelve (only in Acts 4:4, 14 are Paul and Barnabas termed apostles), other places in the New Testament show an awareness that the term was more widely applied (1 Cor 15:5-7; Gal 1:19; 1 Cor 1:1; 9:1; Rom 16:7).

6:14 Simon, whom he named Peter: see the note on Mark 3:16.

6:15 Simon who was called a Zealot: the Zealots were the instigators of the First Revolt of Palestinian Jews against Rome in A.D. 66–70. Because the existence of the Zealots as a distinct group during the lifetime of Jesus is the subject of debate, the meaning of the identification of Simon as a Zealot is unclear.

6:16 Judas Iscariot: the name **Iscariot** may mean "man from Kerioth."

6:17 The coastal region of Tyre and Sidon: not only Jews from Judea and Jerusalem, but even Gentiles from outside Palestine come to hear Jesus (see 2:31-32; 3:6; 4:24-27).

6:20-49 Luke's "Sermon on the Plain" is the counterpart to Matthew's "Sermon on the Mount" (Mt 5:1–7:27). It is addressed to the disciples of Jesus, and, like the sermon in Matthew, it begins with beatitudes (6:20-22) and ends with the parable of the two houses (6:46-49). Almost all the words of Jesus reported by Luke are found in Matthew's version, but because Matthew includes sayings that were related to specifically Jewish Christian problems (e.g., Mt 5:17-20; 6:1-8, 16-18) that Luke did not find appropriate for his predominantly Gentile Christian audience, the "Sermon on the Mount" is considerably longer. Luke's sermon may be outlined as follows: an introduction consisting of blessings and woes (6:20-26); the love of one's enemies (6:27-36); the demands of loving one's neighbor (6:37-42); good deeds as proof of one's goodness (6:43-45); a par-

"Blessed are you who are poor,
   for the kingdom of God is yours.
[21][l]Blessed are you who are now hungry,
   for you will be satisfied.
Blessed are you who are now weeping,
   for you will laugh.
[22][m]Blessed are you when people hate you,
   and when they exclude and insult you,
   and denounce your name as evil
   on account of the Son of Man.
[23][n]Rejoice and leap for joy on that day!
   Behold, your reward
   will be great in heaven.
   For their ancestors treated the prophets in the same way.
[24][o]But woe to you who are rich,
   for you have received your consolation.

l
Ps 126:5-6;
Is 61:3;
Jer 31:25;
Rev 7:16-17

m
Jn 15:19; 16:2;
1 Pt 4:14

n
11:47-48;
2 Chr 36:16;
Mt 23:30-31

o
Jas 5:1

LUKE

The **Beatitudes** in Luke differ from those in Matthew. Matthew has eight beatitudes poetically structured in the third person and one in the second person. In Luke, there are only four beatitudes accompanied by four woes, all in the second person. Both sets are well structured and written in parallel fashion but with different emphases. Many scholars believe Luke's version to be more original, but each has been shaped by the theological outlook of the respective evangelist. Matthew's are more spiritualized, while Luke's are concrete and emphasize the present time.

Matthew 5:3-12	Luke 6:20-26
Blessed are the poor in spirit . . .	Blessed are you . . . poor . . .
Blessed are the mourners . . .	Blessed are you . . . now hungry . . .
Blessed are the comforted . . .	Blessed are you . . . now weeping . . .
Blessed are the meek . . .	Blessed are you . . . hated and insulted . . .
Blessed are they who hunger and thirst for righteousness . . .	Woe to you . . . rich . . .
Blessed are the merciful . . .	Woe to you . . . now filled . . .
Blessed are the clean of heart . . .	Woe to you . . . now laughing . . .
Blessed are the peacemakers . . .	Woe to you . . . when all speak well of you . . . for so they treated the false prophets . . .
Blessed are you . . . when persecuted . . . for so they persecuted the prophets . . .	

able illustrating the result of listening to and acting on the words of Jesus (6:46-49). At the core of the sermon is Jesus' teaching on the love of one's enemies (6:27-36) that has as its source of motivation God's graciousness and compassion for all humanity (6:35-36) and Jesus' teaching on the love of one's neighbor (6:37-42) that is characterized by forgiveness and generosity.

6:20-26 The introductory portion of the sermon consists of blessings and woes that address the real economic and social conditions of humanity (the poor—the rich; the hungry—the satisfied; those grieving—those laughing; the outcast—the socially ac-ceptable). By contrast, Matthew emphasizes the religious and spiritual values of disciples in the kingdom inaugurated by Jesus ("poor in spirit," Mt 5:5; "hunger and thirst for righteousness," Mt 5:6). In the sermon, **blessed** extols the fortunate condition of persons who are favored with the blessings of God; the woes, addressed as they are to the disciples of Jesus, threaten God's profound displeasure on those so blinded by their present fortunate situation that they do not recognize and appreciate the real values of God's kingdom. In all the blessings and woes, the present condition of the persons addressed will be reversed in the future.

p
Is 65:13-14

q
Jas 4:4

r
Mt 5:38-48

s
Prv 25:21;
Rom 12:20-21

t
Rom 12:14;
1 Pt 3:9

u
Mt 7:12

v
Dt 15:7-8

w
Lv 25:35-36

x
Mt 7:1-5

y
Mt 6:14;
Jas 2:13

z
Mk 4:24

a
Mt 15:14;
23:16-17, 24

b
Mt 10:24-25;
Jn 13:16;
15:20

The **Beatitudes** are understood as the heart of Jesus' message. In Jesus, the poor and hungry are clearly situated among the citizens of God's city and reign. Matthew includes the peacemakers and those who thirst for justice to the membership list. As a result, we can only conclude along with *Justice in the World:* "Action on behalf of justice and participation in the transformation of the world fully appear to us as a constitutive dimension of the preaching of the Gospel, or, in other words, of the church's mission for the redemption of the human race and its liberation from every oppressive situation" (6).

^{25p}But woe to you who are filled now,
    for you will be hungry.
Woe to you who laugh now,
    for you will grieve and weep.
^{26q}Woe to you when all speak well of you,
    for their ancestors treated the false prophets in this way.

Love of Enemies

^{27*r}"But to you who hear I say, love your enemies, do good to those who hate you,^s ^{28t}bless those who curse you, pray for those who mistreat you. ²⁹To the person who strikes you on one cheek, offer the other one as well, and from the person who takes your cloak, do not withhold even your tunic. ³⁰Give to everyone who asks of you, and from the one who takes what is yours do not demand it back. ^{31u}Do to others as you would have them do to you. ³²For if you love those who love you, what credit is that to you? Even sinners love those who love them. ³³And if you do good to those who do good to you, what credit is that to you? Even sinners do the same. ^{34v}If you lend money to those from whom you expect repayment, what credit [is] that to you? Even sinners lend to sinners, and get back the same amount. ^{35w}But rather, love your enemies and do good to them, and lend expecting nothing back; then your reward will be great and you will be children of the Most High, for he himself is kind to the ungrateful and the wicked. ³⁶Be merciful, just as [also] your Father is merciful.

Judging Others

^{37*x}"Stop judging and you will not be judged. Stop condemning and you will not be condemned. Forgive and you will be forgiven.^y ^{38z}Give and gifts will be given to you; a good measure, packed together, shaken down, and overflowing, will be poured into your lap. For the measure with which you measure will in return be measured out to you." ^{39a}And he told them a parable, "Can a blind person guide a blind person? Will not both fall into a pit? ^{40b}No disciple is superior to the teacher; but when fully trained, every disciple will be like his teacher. ⁴¹Why do you notice the splinter in your brother's eye, but do not perceive the wooden beam in your own? ⁴²How can you say to your brother, 'Brother, let me remove that splinter in your eye,' when you do

---

6:27-36 See the notes on Matthew 5:43-48 and Matthew 5:48.
6:37-42 See the notes on Matthew 7:1-12; 7:1; 7:5.

not even notice the wooden beam in your own eye? You hypocrite! Remove the wooden beam from your eye first; then you will see clearly to remove the splinter in your brother's eye.

A Tree Known by Its Fruit

43*c"A good tree does not bear rotten fruit, nor does a rotten tree bear good fruit. 44For every tree is known by its own fruit. For people do not pick figs from thornbushes, nor do they gather grapes from brambles. 45A good person out of the store of goodness in his heart produces good, but an evil person out of a store of evil produces evil; for from the fullness of the heart the mouth speaks.

The Two Foundations

46d"Why do you call me, 'Lord, Lord,' but not do what I command? 47*e I will show you what someone is like who comes to me, listens to my words, and acts on them. 48That one is like a person building a house, who dug deeply and laid the foundation on rock; when the flood came, the river burst against that house but could not shake it because it had been well built. 49But the one who listens and does not act is like a person who built a house on the ground without a foundation. When the river burst against it, it collapsed at once and was completely destroyed."

The Healing of a Centurion's Slave

7 1*a When he had finished all his words to the people, he entered Capernaum.* 2A centurion* there had a slave who was ill and about to die, and he was valuable to him. 3When he heard about Jesus, he sent elders of the Jews to him, asking him to come and save the life of his slave. 4They approached Jesus and strongly urged him to come, saying, "He deserves to have you do this for him, 5for he loves our nation and he built the synagogue for us." 6And Jesus went with them, but when he was only a short distance from the house, the centurion sent friends to tell him, "Lord, do not trouble yourself, for I am not worthy to have you enter under my roof.* 7Therefore, I did not consider myself worthy to come to you; but say the word and let my servant be healed. 8For I too am a person subject to authority, with soldiers subject to me. And I say to one, 'Go,' and he goes; and to another, 'Come here,' and he comes; and to my slave, 'Do this,' and he does it." 9When Jesus heard this he was amazed at him and, turning, said to the crowd following him, "I tell you, not even in Israel have I found such faith." 10When the messengers returned to the house, they found the slave in good health.

---

c
Mt 7:16-20; 12:33, 35

d
Mt 7:21; Rom 2:13; Jas 1:22

e
Mt 7:24-27

a
Mt 8:5-13; Jn 4:43-54

6:43-46 See the notes on Matthew 7:15-20 and 12:33.

6:47-49 See the note on Matthew 7:24-27.

7:1–8:3 The episodes in this section present a series of reactions to the Galilean ministry of Jesus and reflect some of Luke's particular interests: the faith of a Gentile (7:1-10); the prophet Jesus' concern for a widowed mother (7:11-17); the ministry of Jesus directed to the afflicted and unfortunate of Isaiah 61:1 (7:18-23); the relation between John and Jesus and their role in God's plan for salvation (7:24-35); a forgiven sinner's manifestation of love (7:36-50); the association of women with the ministry of Jesus (8:1-3).

7:1-10 This story about the faith of the centurion, a Gentile who cherishes the Jewish nation (7:5), prepares for the story in Acts of the conversion by Peter of the Roman centurion Cornelius who is similarly described as one who is generous to the Jewish nation (Acts 10:2). See also Acts 10:34-35 in the speech of Peter: "God shows no partiality . . . the person who fears him and acts righteously is acceptable to him." See also the notes on Matthew 8:5-13 and John 4:43-54.

7:2 A centurion: see the note on Matthew 8:5.

7:6 I am not worthy to have you enter under my roof: to enter the house of a Gentile was considered unclean for a Jew; cf. Acts 10:28.

b
4:25-26;
1 Kgs 17:17-24

c
8:42;
1 Kgs 17:17

d
1 Kgs 17:23;
2 Kgs 4:36

e
1:68; 19:44

f
Mt 11:2-6

g
Mal 3:1;
Rev 1:4, 8; 4:8

h
4:18; Is 35:5-6;
61:1

i
Mt 11:7-15

j
1:76

k
Mal 3:1 /
Is 40:3

l
3:7, 12;
Mt 21:32

Raising of the Widow's Son

[11]*[b]Soon afterward he journeyed to a city called Nain, and his disciples and a large crowd accompanied him. [12c]As he drew near to the gate of the city, a man who had died was being carried out, the only son of his mother, and she was a widow. A large crowd from the city was with her. [13]When the Lord saw her, he was moved with pity for her and said to her, "Do not weep." [14]He stepped forward and touched the coffin; at this the bearers halted, and he said, "Young man, I tell you, arise!" [15d]The dead man sat up and began to speak, and Jesus gave him to his mother. [16e]Fear seized them all, and they glorified God, exclaiming, "A great prophet has arisen in our midst," and "God has visited his people." [17]This report about him spread through the whole of Judea and in all the surrounding region.

The Messengers from John the Baptist

[18]*[f]The disciples of John told him about all these things. John summoned two of his disciples [19g]and sent them to the Lord to ask, "Are you the one who is to come, or should we look for another?" [20]When the men came to him, they said, "John the Baptist has sent us to you to ask, 'Are you the one who is to come, or should we look for another?'" [21]At that time he cured many of their diseases, sufferings, and evil spirits; he also granted sight to many who were blind. [22h]And he said to them in reply, "Go and tell John what you have seen and heard: the blind regain their sight, the lame walk, lepers are cleansed, the deaf hear, the dead are raised, the poor have the good news proclaimed to them. [23]And blessed is the one who takes no offense at me."*

Jesus' Testimony to John

[24]*[i]When the messengers of John had left, Jesus began to speak to the crowds about John. "What did you go out to the desert to see—a reed swayed by the wind? [25]Then what did you go out to see? Someone dressed in fine garments? Those who dress luxuriously and live sumptuously are found in royal palaces. [26j]Then what did you go out to see? A prophet? Yes, I tell you, and more than a prophet. [27k]This is the one about whom scripture says:

'Behold, I am sending my messenger ahead of you,
  he will prepare your way before you.'

[28]I tell you, among those born of women, no one is greater than John; yet the least in the kingdom of God is greater than he." [29l](All the people who listened, including the tax collectors, and who were baptized with the baptism of John, acknowledged the righteousness of God; [30]but the Pharisees and scholars of the law, who were not baptized by him, rejected the plan of God for themselves.)

7:11-17 In the previous incident Jesus' power was displayed for a Gentile whose servant was dying; in this episode it is displayed toward a widowed mother whose only son has already died. Jesus' power over death prepares for his reply to John's disciples in Luke 7:22: "the dead are raised." This resuscitation in alluding to the prophet Elijah's resurrection of the only son of a widow of Zarephath (1 Kgs 7:8-24) leads to the reaction of the crowd: "A great prophet has arisen in our midst" (7:16).

7:18-23 In answer to John's question, **Are you the one who is to come?**—a probable reference to the return of the fiery prophet of reform, Elijah, "before the day of the Lord comes, the great and terrible day" (Mal 3:23)—Jesus responds that his role is rather to bring the blessings spoken of in Isaiah 61:1 to the oppressed and neglected of society (7:22; cf. 4:18).

7:23 Blessed is the one who takes no offense at me: this beatitude is pronounced on the person who recognizes Jesus' true identity in spite of previous expectations of what "the one who is to come" would be like.

7:24-30 In his testimony to John, Jesus reveals his understanding of the relationship between them: John is the precursor

LUKE

[31*m]"Then to what shall I compare the people of this generation? What are they like?
[32]They are like children who sit in the marketplace and call to one another,

'We played the flute for you, but you did not dance.
We sang a dirge, but you did not weep.'

[33]For John the Baptist came neither eating food nor drinking wine, and you said, 'He
is possessed by a demon.' [34n]The Son of Man came eating and drinking and you said,
'Look, he is a glutton and a drunkard, a friend of tax collectors and sinners.' [35]But
wisdom is vindicated by all her children."

The Pardon of the Sinful Woman

[36*o]A Pharisee invited him to dine with him, and he entered the Pharisee's house and
reclined at table.* [37p]Now there was a sinful woman in the city who learned that he was
at table in the house of the Pharisee. Bringing an alabaster flask of ointment,[q] [38]she stood
behind him at his feet weeping and began to bathe his feet with her tears. Then she wiped
them with her hair, kissed them, and anointed them with the ointment. [39]When the Pharisee
who had invited him saw this he said to himself, "If this man were a prophet, he would
know who and what sort of woman this is who is touching him, that she is a sinner."
[40]Jesus said to him in reply, "Simon, I have something to say to you." "Tell me, teacher,"
he said. [41]"Two people were in debt to a certain creditor; one owed five hundred days'
wages* and the other owed fifty. [42]Since they were unable to repay the debt, he forgave
it for both. Which of them will love him more?" [43]Simon said in reply, "The one, I suppose, whose larger debt was forgiven." He said to him, "You have judged rightly." [44]Then
he turned to the woman and said to Simon, "Do you see this woman? When I entered
your house, you did not give me water for my feet, but she has bathed them with her tears
and wiped them with her hair. [45]You did not give me a kiss, but she has not ceased kissing
my feet since the time I entered. [46]You did not anoint my head with oil, but she anointed
my feet with ointment. [47]So I tell you, her many sins have been forgiven; hence, she has
shown great love.* But the one to whom little is forgiven, loves little." [48r]He said to her,
"Your sins are forgiven." [49s]The others at table said to themselves, "Who is this who even
forgives sins?" [50]But he said to the woman, "Your faith has saved you; go in peace."

m Mt 11:16-19
n 15:2
o 11:37; 14:1
p Mt 26:7; Mk 14:3
q Jn 12:3
r 5:20; Mt 9:20; Mk 2:5
s 5:21

of Jesus (7:27); John is the messenger spoken of in Malachi 3:1 who in Malachi 3:23 is identified as Elijah. Taken with the previous episode, it can be seen that Jesus identifies John as precisely the person John envisioned Jesus to be: the Elijah who prepares the way for the coming of the day of the Lord.

7:31-35 See the note on Matthew 11:16-19.

7:36-50 In this story of the pardoning of the sinful woman Luke presents two different reactions to the ministry of Jesus. A Pharisee, suspecting Jesus to be a prophet, invites Jesus to a festive banquet in his house, but the Pharisee's self-righteousness leads to little forgiveness by God and consequently little love shown toward Jesus. The sinful woman, on the other hand, manifests a faith in God (7:50) that has led her to seek forgiveness for her sins, and because so much was forgiven, she now overwhelms Jesus with her display of love; cf. the similar contrast in attitudes in Luke 18:9-14. The whole episode is a powerful lesson on the relation between forgiveness and love.

7:36 Reclined at table: the normal posture of guests at a banquet. Other oriental banquet customs alluded to in this story include the reception by the host with a kiss (7:45), washing the feet of the guests (7:44), and the anointing of the guests' heads (7:46).

7:41 Days' wages: one denarius is the normal daily wage of a laborer.

7:47 Her many sins have been forgiven; hence, she has shown great love: literally, "her many sins have been forgiven, seeing that she has loved much." That the woman's sins have been forgiven is attested by the great love she shows toward Jesus. Her love is the consequence of her forgiveness. This is also the meaning demanded by the parable in Luke 7:41-43.

a
4:43

b
23:49; 24:10;
Mt 27:55-56;
Mk 15:40-41;
Jn 19:5

c
Mt 13:1-9;
Mk 4:1-9

d
14:35;
Mt 11:15;
13:43; Mk 4:23

e
Mt 13:10-13;
Mk 4:10-12

f
Is 6:9

g
Mt 13:18-23;
Mk 4:13-20

h
1 Pt 1:23

i
Mk 4:21-25

j
11:33; Mt 5:15

k
12:2; Mt 10:26

Galilean Women Follow Jesus

8 ¹*ᵃAfterward he journeyed from one town and village to another, preaching and proclaiming the good news of the kingdom of God. Accompanying him were the Twelve ²ᵇand some women who had been cured of evil spirits and infirmities, Mary, called Magdalene, from whom seven demons had gone out, ³Joanna, the wife of Herod's steward Chuza, Susanna, and many others who provided for them out of their resources.

The Parable of the Sower

⁴*ᶜWhen a large crowd gathered, with people from one town after another journeying to him, he spoke in a parable.* ⁵"A sower went out to sow his seed. And as he sowed, some seed fell on the path and was trampled, and the birds of the sky ate it up. ⁶Some seed fell on rocky ground, and when it grew, it withered for lack of moisture. ⁷Some seed fell among thorns, and the thorns grew with it and choked it. ⁸ᵈAnd some seed fell on good soil, and when it grew, it produced fruit a hundredfold." After saying this, he called out, "Whoever has ears to hear ought to hear."

The Purpose of the Parables

⁹ᵉThen his disciples asked him what the meaning of this parable might be. ¹⁰ᶠHe answered, "Knowledge of the mysteries of the kingdom of God has been granted to you; but to the rest, they are made known through parables so that 'they may look but not see, and hear but not understand.'

The Parable of the Sower Explained

¹¹*ᵍ"This is the meaning of the parable. The seed is the word of God.ʰ ¹²Those on the path are the ones who have heard, but the devil comes and takes away the word from their hearts that they may not believe and be saved. ¹³Those on rocky ground are the ones who, when they hear, receive the word with joy, but they have no root; they believe only for a time and fall away in time of trial. ¹⁴As for the seed that fell among thorns, they are the ones who have heard, but as they go along, they are choked by the anxieties and riches and pleasures of life, and they fail to produce mature fruit. ¹⁵But as for the seed that fell on rich soil, they are the ones who, when they have heard the word, embrace it with a generous and good heart, and bear fruit through perseverance.

The Parable of the Lamp

¹⁶*ⁱ"No one who lights a lamp conceals it with a vessel or sets it under a bed; rather, he places it on a lampstand so that those who enter may see the light.ʲ ¹⁷ᵏFor there is

---

8:1-3 Luke presents Jesus as an itinerant preacher traveling in the company of the Twelve and of the Galilean women who are sustaining them out of their means. These Galilean women will later accompany Jesus on his journey to Jerusalem and become witnesses to his death (23:49) and resurrection (24:9-11, where Mary Magdalene and Joanna are specifically mentioned; cf. also Acts 1:14). The association of women with the ministry of Jesus is most unusual in the light of the attitude of first-century Palestinian Judaism toward women. The more common attitude is expressed in John 4:27, and early rabbinic documents caution against speaking with women in public.

8:4-21 The focus in this section is on how one should hear the word of God and act on it. It includes the parable of the sower and its explanation (8:4-15), a collection of sayings on how one should

act on the word that is heard (8:16-18), and the identification of the mother and brothers of Jesus as the ones who hear the word and act on it (8:19-21). See also the notes on Matthew 13:1-53 and Mark 4:1-34.

8:4-8 See the note on Matthew 13:3-8.

8:11-15 On the interpretation of the parable of the sower, see the note on Matthew 13:18-23.

8:16-18 These sayings continue the theme of responding to the word of God. Those who hear the word must become a light to others (8:16); even the mysteries of the kingdom that have been made known to the disciples (8:9-10) must come to light (8:17); a generous and persevering response to the word of God leads to a still more perfect response to the word.

nothing hidden that will not become visible, and nothing secret that will not be known and come to light. [18l]Take care, then, how you hear. To anyone who has, more will be given, and from the one who has not, even what he seems to have will be taken away."

Jesus and His Family

[19m]Then his mother and his brothers[*] came to him but were unable to join him because of the crowd. [20n]He was told, "Your mother and your brothers are standing outside and they wish to see you." [21]He said to them in reply, "My mother and my brothers are those who hear the word of God and act on it."[*]

The Calming of a Storm at Sea

[22*o]One day he got into a boat with his disciples and said to them, "Let us cross to the other side of the lake." So they set sail, [23]and while they were sailing he fell asleep. A squall blew over the lake, and they were taking in water and were in danger. [24]They came and woke him saying, "Master, master, we are perishing!" He awakened, rebuked the wind and the waves, and they subsided and there was a calm. [25]Then he asked them, "Where is your faith?" But they were filled with awe and amazed and said to one another, "Who then is this, who commands even the winds and the sea, and they obey him?"

The Healing of the Gerasene Demoniac

[26p]Then they sailed to the territory of the Gerasenes,[*] which is opposite Galilee. [27]When he came ashore a man from the town who was possessed by demons met him. For a long time he had not worn clothes; he did not live in a house, but lived among the tombs. [28q]When he saw Jesus, he cried out and fell down before him; in a loud voice he shouted, "What have you to do with me, Jesus, son of the Most High God? I beg you, do not torment me!" [29]For he had ordered the unclean spirit to come out of the man. (It had taken hold of him many times, and he used to be bound with chains and shackles as a restraint, but he would break his bonds and be driven by the demon into deserted places.) [30]Then Jesus asked him, "What is your name?"[*] He replied, "Legion," because many demons had entered him. [31]And they pleaded with him not to order them to depart to the abyss.[*]

[32]A herd of many swine was feeding there on the hillside, and they pleaded with him to allow them to enter those swine; and he let them. [33]The demons came out of the man and entered the swine, and the herd rushed down the steep bank into the lake and

l
19:26;
Mt 13:12;
25:29

m
Mt 12:46-50;
Mk 3:31-35

n
11:27-28

o
Mt 8:18, 23-27;
Mk 4:35-41

p
Mt 8:28-34;
Mk 5:1-20

q
4:33-35;
Mt 8:29;
Mk 1:23-24

8:19 His brothers: see the note on Mark 6:3.

8:21 The family of Jesus is not constituted by physical relationship with him but by obedience to the word of God. In this, Luke agrees with the Marcan parallel (Mk 3:31-35), although by omitting Mark 3:33 and especially Mark 3:20-21 Luke has softened the Marcan picture of Jesus' natural family. Probably he did this because Mary has already been presented in Luke 1:38 as the obedient handmaid of the Lord who fulfills the requirement for belonging to the eschatological family of Jesus; cf. also Luke 11:27-28.

8:22-56 This section records four miracles of Jesus that manifest his power and authority: (1) the calming of a storm on the lake (8:22-25); (2) the exorcism of a demoniac (8:26-39); (3) the cure of a hemorrhaging woman (8:40-48); (4) the raising of Jairus's daughter to life (8:49-56). They parallel the same sequence of stories at Mark 4:35–5:43.

8:26 Gerasenes: other manuscripts read Gadarenes or Gergesenes. See also the note on Matthew 8:28. **Opposite Galilee**: probably Gentile territory (note the presence in the area of pigs—unclean animals to Jews) and an indication that the person who receives salvation (8:36) is a Gentile.

8:30 What is your name?: the question reflects the popular belief that knowledge of the spirit's name brought control over the spirit. **Legion**: to Jesus' question the demon replies with a Latin word transliterated into Greek. The Roman legion at this period consisted of 5,000 to 6,000 foot soldiers; hence the name implies a very large number of demons.

8:31 Abyss: the place of the dead (Rom 10:7) or the prison of Satan (Rev 20:3) or the subterranean "watery deep" that symbolizes the chaos before the order imposed by creation (Gn 1:2).

r
Mt 9:18-26;
Mk 5:21-43

s
6:19

t
7:50; 17:19;
18:42

u
7:13

was drowned. ³⁴When the swineherds saw what had happened, they ran away and reported the incident in the town and throughout the countryside. ³⁵People came out to see what had happened and, when they approached Jesus, they discovered the man from whom the demons had come out sitting at his feet.* He was clothed and in his right mind, and they were seized with fear. ³⁶Those who witnessed it told them how the possessed man had been saved. ³⁷The entire population of the region of the Gerasenes asked Jesus to leave them because they were seized with great fear. So he got into a boat and returned. ³⁸The man from whom the demons had come out begged to remain with him, but he sent him away, saying, ³⁹"Return home and recount what God has done for you." The man went off and proclaimed throughout the whole town what Jesus had done for him.

Jairus's Daughter and the Woman with a Hemorrhage

^{40*r}When Jesus returned, the crowd welcomed him, for they were all waiting for him. ⁴¹And a man named Jairus, an official of the synagogue, came forward. He fell at the feet of Jesus and begged him to come to his house, ⁴²because he had an only daughter,* about twelve years old, and she was dying. As he went, the crowds almost crushed him. ⁴³And a woman afflicted with hemorrhages for twelve years,* who [had spent her whole livelihood on doctors and] was unable to be cured by anyone, ⁴⁴came up behind him and touched the tassel on his cloak. Immediately her bleeding stopped. ⁴⁵Jesus then asked, "Who touched me?" While all were denying it, Peter said, "Master, the crowds are pushing and pressing in upon you." ^{46s}But Jesus said, "Someone has touched me; for I know that power has gone out from me." ⁴⁷When the woman realized that she had not escaped notice, she came forward trembling. Falling down before him, she explained in the presence of all the people why she had touched him and how she had been healed immediately. ^{48t}He said to her, "Daughter, your faith has saved you; go in peace."

⁴⁹While he was still speaking, someone from the synagogue official's house arrived and said, "Your daughter is dead; do not trouble the teacher any longer." ⁵⁰On hearing this, Jesus answered him, "Do not be afraid; just have faith and she will be saved." ⁵¹When he arrived at the house he allowed no one to enter with him except Peter and John and James, and the child's father and mother. ^{52*u}All were weeping and mourning for her, when he said, "Do not weep any longer, for she is not dead, but sleeping." ⁵³And they ridiculed him, because they knew that she was dead. ⁵⁴But he took her by the hand and called to her, "Child, arise!" ⁵⁵Her breath returned and she immediately arose. He then directed that she should be given something to eat. ⁵⁶Her parents were astounded, and he instructed them to tell no one what had happened.

8:35 Sitting at his feet: the former demoniac takes the position of a disciple before the master (10:39; Acts 22:3).

8:40-56 Two interwoven miracle stories, one a healing and the other a resuscitation, present Jesus as master over sickness and death. In the Lucan account, faith in Jesus is responsible for the cure (8:48) and for the raising to life (8:50).

8:42 An only daughter: cf. the son of the widow of Nain whom Luke describes as an "only" son (7:12; see also 9:38).

8:43 Afflicted with hemorrhages for twelve years: according to the Mosaic law (Lv 15:25-30) this condition would render the woman unclean and unfit for contact with other people.

8:52 Sleeping: her death is a temporary condition; cf. John 11:11-14.

The Mission of the Twelve

9 [1] *[a]*He summoned the Twelve and gave them power and authority over all demons and to cure diseases, [2]and he sent them to proclaim the kingdom of God and to heal [the sick]. [3]He said to them, "Take nothing for the journey,* neither walking stick, nor sack, nor food, nor money, and let no one take a second tunic. [4][b]Whatever house you enter, stay there and leave from there. [5][c]And as for those who do not welcome you, when you leave that town, shake the dust from your feet* in testimony against them." [6]Then they set out and went from village to village proclaiming the good news and curing diseases everywhere.

Herod's Opinion of Jesus

[7]*[d]Herod the tetrarch* heard about all that was happening, and he was greatly perplexed because some were saying, "John has been raised from the dead";[e] [8]others were saying, "Elijah has appeared"; still others, "One of the ancient prophets has arisen." [9]*[f]But Herod said, "John I beheaded. Who then is this about whom I hear such things?" And he kept trying to see him.

See the chart on the various accounts of the **multiplication of the loaves** (at Mk 6:34-44).

The Return of the Twelve and the Feeding of the Five Thousand

[10][g]When the apostles returned, they explained to him what they had done. He took them and withdrew in private to a town called Bethsaida. [11]The crowds, meanwhile, learned of this and followed him. He received them and spoke to them about the kingdom of God, and he healed those who needed to be cured. [12]As the day was drawing to a close, the Twelve approached him and said, "Dismiss the crowd so that they can go to the surrounding villages and farms and find lodging and provisions; for we are in a deserted place here." [13][h]He said to them, "Give them some food yourselves." They replied, "Five loaves and two fish are all we have, unless we ourselves go and buy food for all these people." [14]Now the men there numbered about five thousand. Then he said to his disciples, "Have them sit down in groups of [about] fifty." [15]They did so and made them all sit down. [16]*[i]Then taking* the five loaves and the two fish, and looking up to heaven, he said the blessing over them, broke them, and gave them to the disciples to set before the crowd. [17]They all ate and were satisfied. And when the leftover fragments were picked up, they filled twelve wicker baskets.

a
Mt 10:1, 5-15;
Mk 6:7-13

b
10:5-7

c
10:10-11;
Acts 13:51

d
Mt 14:1-12;
Mk 6:14-29

e
9:19; Mt 16:14;
Mk 8:28

f
23:8

g
Mt 14:13-21;
Mk 6:30-44;
Jn 6:1-14

h
2 Kgs 4:42-44

i
22:19;
24:30-31;
Acts 2:42;
20:11; 27:35

LUKE

9:1-6 Armed with the power and authority that Jesus himself has been displaying in the previous episodes, the Twelve are now sent out to continue the work that Jesus has been performing throughout his Galilean ministry: (1) proclaiming the kingdom (4:43; 8:1); (2) exorcising demons (4:33-37, 41; 8:26-39) and (3) healing the sick (4:38-40; 5:12-16, 17-26; 6:6-10; 7:1-10, 17, 22; 8:40-56).

9:3 Take nothing for the journey: the absolute detachment required of the disciple (14:33) leads to complete reliance on God (12:22-31).

9:5 Shake the dust from your feet: see the note on Matthew 10:14.

9:7-56 This section in which Luke gathers together incidents that focus on the identity of Jesus is introduced by a question that Herod is made to ask in this gospel: "Who then is this about whom I hear such things?" (9:9) In subsequent episodes, Luke reveals to the reader various answers to Herod's question: Jesus is one in whom God's power is present and who provides for the needs of God's people (9:10-17); Peter declares Jesus to be "the Messiah of God" (9:18-21); Jesus says he is the suffering Son of Man (9:22, 43-45); Jesus is the Master to be followed, even to death (9:23-27); Jesus is God's son, his Chosen One (9:28-36).

9:7 Herod the tetrarch: see the note on Luke 3:1.

9:9 And he kept trying to see him: this indication of Herod's interest in Jesus prepares for Luke 13:31-33 and for 23:8-12 where Herod's curiosity about Jesus' power to perform miracles remains unsatisfied.

9:16 Then taking . . .: the actions of Jesus recall the institution of the Eucharist in Luke 22:19; see also the note on Matthew 14:19.

j
Mt 16:13-20;
Mk 8:27-30

k
9:7-8

l
24:7, 26;
Mt 16:21;
20:18-19;
Mk 8:31;
10:33-34

m
Mt 16:24-28;
Mk 8:34–9:1

n
14:27;
Mt 10:38

o
17:33;
Mt 10:39;
Jn 12:25

p
12:9; Mt 10:33;
2 Tm 2:12

q
Mt 17:1-8;
Mk 9:2-8

r
9:22; 13:33

Peter's Confession about Jesus

[18]*[j]Once when Jesus was praying in solitude, and the disciples were with him, he asked them, "Who do the crowds say that I am?"* [19][k]They said in reply, "John the Baptist; others, Elijah; still others, 'One of the ancient prophets has arisen.'" [20]Then he said to them, "But who do you say that I am?" Peter said in reply, "The Messiah of God."* [21]He rebuked them and directed them not to tell this to anyone.

The First Prediction of the Passion

[22][l]He said, "The Son of Man must suffer greatly and be rejected by the elders, the chief priests, and the scribes, and be killed and on the third day be raised."

The Conditions of Discipleship

[23][m]Then he said to all, "If anyone wishes to come after me, he must deny himself and take up his cross daily* and follow me.[n] [24][o]For whoever wishes to save his life will lose it, but whoever loses his life for my sake will save it. [25]What profit is there for one to gain the whole world yet lose or forfeit himself? [26][p]Whoever is ashamed of me and of my words, the Son of Man will be ashamed of when he comes in his glory and in the glory of the Father and of the holy angels. [27]Truly I say to you, there are some standing here who will not taste death until they see the kingdom of God."

Have you given serious thought to what is required to be a disciple of Jesus in this age? What is the self you must deny? What is the life you must lose? What is the cross you must carry? Do you find the concept of *being a disciple* attractive?

The Transfiguration of Jesus

[28]*[q]About eight days after he said this, he took Peter, John, and James and went up the mountain to pray.* [29]While he was praying his face changed in appearance and his clothing became dazzling white. [30]And behold, two men were conversing with him, Moses and Elijah,* [31]*[r]who appeared in glory and spoke of his exodus that he was going

Location of Mount Tabor

9:18-22 This incident is based on Mark 8:27-33, but Luke has eliminated Peter's refusal to accept Jesus as suffering Son of Man (Mk 8:32) and the rebuke of Peter by Jesus (Mk 8:33). Elsewhere in the gospel, Luke softens the harsh portrait of Peter and the other apostles found in his Marcan source (cf. 22:39-46, which similarly lacks a rebuke of Peter that occurs in the source, Mk 14:37-38).

9:18 When Jesus was praying in solitude: see the note on Luke 3:21.

9:20 The Messiah of God: on the meaning of this title in first-century Palestinian Judaism, see the notes on Luke 2:11 and on Matthew 16:13-20 and Mark 8:27-30.

9:23 Daily: this is a Lucan addition to a saying of Jesus, removing the saying from a context that envisioned the imminent suffering and death of the disciple of Jesus (as does the saying in Mk 8:34-35) to one that focuses on the demands of daily Christian existence.

9:28-36 Situated shortly after the first announcement of the passion, death, and resurrection, this scene of Jesus' transfiguration provides the heavenly confirmation to Jesus' declaration that his suffering will end in glory (9:32); see also the notes on Matthew 17:1-8 and Mark 9:2-8.

9:28 Up the mountain to pray: the "mountain" is the regular place of prayer in Luke (see 6:12; 22:39-41).

9:30 Moses and Elijah: the two figures represent the Old Testament law and the prophets. At the end of this episode, the heavenly voice will identify Jesus as the one to be listened to now (9:35). See also the note on Mark 9:5.

9:31 His exodus that he was going to accomplish in Jerusalem: Luke identifies the subject of the conversation as the **exodus** of Jesus, a reference to the death, resurrection, and ascension of Jesus that will take place in Jerusalem, the city of destiny

to accomplish in Jerusalem. [32s]Peter and his companions had been overcome by sleep, but becoming fully awake, they saw his glory[*] and the two men standing with him. [33]As they were about to part from him, Peter said to Jesus, "Master, it is good that we are here; let us make three tents,[*] one for you, one for Moses, and one for Elijah." But he did not know what he was saying. [34*]While he was still speaking, a cloud came and cast a shadow over them, and they became frightened when they entered the cloud. [35*t]Then from the cloud came a voice that said, "This is my chosen Son; listen to him." [36]After the voice had spoken, Jesus was found alone. They fell silent and did not at that time[*] tell anyone what they had seen.

The Healing of a Boy with a Demon

[37*u]On the next day, when they came down from the mountain, a large crowd met him. [38]There was a man in the crowd who cried out, "Teacher, I beg you, look at my son; he is my only child. [39]For a spirit seizes him and he suddenly screams and it convulses him until he foams at the mouth; it releases him only with difficulty, wearing him out. [40]I begged your disciples to cast it out but they could not." [41]Jesus said in reply, "O faithless and perverse generation, how long will I be with you and endure you? Bring your son here." [42]As he was coming forward, the demon threw him to the ground in a convulsion; but Jesus rebuked the unclean spirit, healed the boy, and returned him to his father. [43v]And all were astonished by the majesty of God.

The Second Prediction of the Passion

While they were all amazed at his every deed, he said to his disciples, [44]"Pay attention to what I am telling you. The Son of Man is to be handed over to men." [45]But they did not understand this saying; its meaning was hidden from them so that they should not understand it, and they were afraid to ask him about this saying.

The Greatest in the Kingdom

[46*w]An argument arose among the disciples about which of them was the greatest.[x] [47]Jesus realized the intention of their hearts and took a child and placed it by his side [48y]and said to them, "Whoever receives this child in my name receives me, and whoever receives me receives the one who sent me. For the one who is least among all of you is the one who is the greatest."

Another Exorcist

[49z]Then John said in reply, "Master, we saw someone casting out demons in your name and we tried to prevent him because he does not follow in our company." [50]Jesus said to him, "Do not prevent him, for whoever is not against you is for you."

s
Jn 1:14;
2 Pt 1:16

t
3:22; Dt 18:15;
Ps 2:7; Is 42:1;
Mt 3:17; 12:18;
Mk 1:11;
2 Pt 1:17-18

u
Mt 17:14-18;
Mk 9:14-27

v
18:32-34;
Mt 17:22-23;
Mk 9:30-32

w
Mt 18:1-5;
Mk 9:33-37

x
22:24

y
10:16;
Mt 10:40;
Jn 13:20

z
Mk 9:38-40

LUKE

(see 9:51). The mention of **exodus**, however, also calls to mind the Israelite Exodus from Egypt to the promised land.

9:32 They saw his glory: the **glory** that is proper to God is here attributed to Jesus (see 24:26).

9:33 Let us make three tents: in a possible allusion to the feast of Tabernacles, Peter may be likening his joy on the occasion of the transfiguration to the joyful celebration of this harvest festival.

9:34 Over them: it is not clear whether **them** refers to Jesus, Moses, and Elijah, or to the disciples. For the cloud casting its shadow, see the note on Mark 9:7.

9:35 Like the heavenly voice that identified Jesus at his baptism prior to his undertaking the Galilean ministry (3:22), so too here before the journey to the city of destiny is begun (9:51) the heavenly voice again identifies Jesus as Son. Listen to him: the two representatives of Israel of old depart (9:33) and Jesus is left alone (9:36) as the teacher whose words must be heeded (see also Acts 3:22).

9:36 At that time: i.e., before the resurrection.

9:37-43a See the note on Mark 9:14-29.

9:46-50 These two incidents focus on attitudes that are opposed to Christian discipleship: rivalry and intolerance of outsiders.

a
9:53; 13:22,
33; 17:11;
18:31; 19:28;
24:51;
Acts 1:2, 9-11,
22
b
Mal 3:1
c
2 Kgs 1:10, 12
d
Mt 8:19-22

V: The Journey to Jerusalem: Luke's Travel Narrative*

Departure for Jerusalem; Samaritan Inhospitality

[51]*[a]When the days for his being taken up were fulfilled, he resolutely determined to journey to Jerusalem,* [52]*[b]and he sent messengers ahead of him. On the way they entered a Samaritan village to prepare for his reception there, [53]but they would not welcome him because the destination of his journey was Jerusalem. [54c]When the disciples James and John saw this they asked, "Lord, do you want us to call down fire from heaven to consume them?" [55]Jesus turned and rebuked them, [56]and they journeyed to another village.

The Would-be Followers of Jesus

[57]*[d]As they were proceeding on their journey someone said to him, "I will follow you wherever you go." [58]Jesus answered him, "Foxes have dens and birds of the sky have nests, but the Son of Man has nowhere to rest his head." [59]And to another he said, "Follow me." But he replied, "[Lord,] let me

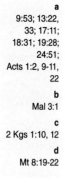

Only Luke has a **travel narrative** extending from 9:51 to 19:28, in which Jesus prophetically sets out for Jerusalem to embrace his fate. Along the way he performs his ministry of preaching, teaching, and healing.

Samaritans and Jews were bitter enemies because of a complex history. Although ethnically and religiously related, Jews considered Samaritans illegitimate "cousins" (cf. Jn 9:4). Samaria had been the capital of the northern kingdom (Israel) destroyed by the Assyrians in 721 B.C. As part of the destruction, the Assyrians imported pagan foreigners who eventually intermarried with the remnant Jews in that area, consequently tainting the bloodlines. Ever since, the Jews rejected Samaritans as fellow Jews. Over time, the Samaritans wrote their own Pentateuch (Torah) and established a separate temple on Mount Gerizim. For Jesus to use a "good Samaritan" as a model of a neighbor was religiously a bold move. See comment, "The Assyrian Captivity and Its Consequences" (at Hos 10).

9:51–18:14 The Galilean ministry of Jesus finishes with the previous episode and a new section of Luke's gospel begins, the journey to Jerusalem. This journey is based on Mark 10:1-52 but Luke uses his Marcan source only in Luke 18:15–19:27. Before that point he has inserted into his gospel a distinctive collection of sayings of Jesus and stories about him that he has drawn from Q, a collection of sayings of Jesus used also by Matthew, and from his own special traditions. All of the material collected in this section is loosely organized within the framework of a journey of Jesus to Jerusalem, the city of destiny, where his exodus (suffering, death, resurrection, ascension) is to take place (9:31), where salvation is accomplished, and from where the proclamation of God's saving word is to go forth (24:47; Acts 1:8). Much of the material in the Lucan travel narrative is teaching for the disciples. During the course of this journey Jesus is preparing his chosen Galilean witnesses for the role they will play after his exodus (9:31): they are to be his witnesses to the people (Acts 10:39; 13:31) and thereby provide certainty to the readers of Luke's gospel that the teachings they have received are rooted in the teachings of Jesus (1:1-4).

9:51-55 Just as the Galilean ministry began with a rejection of Jesus in his hometown, so too the travel narrative begins with the rejection of him by Samaritans. In this episode Jesus disassociates himself from the attitude expressed by his disciples that those who reject him are to be punished severely. The story alludes to 2 Kings 1:10, 12 where the prophet Elijah takes the course of action Jesus rejects, and Jesus thereby rejects the identification of himself with Elijah.

9:51 Days for his being taken up: like the reference to his exodus in Luke 9:31, this is probably a reference to all the events (suffering, death, resurrection, ascension) of his last days in Jerusalem. **He resolutely determined:** literally, "he set his face."

9:52 Samaritan: Samaria was the territory between Judea and Galilee west of the Jordan river. For ethnic and religious reasons, the Samaritans and the Jews were bitterly opposed to one another (see Jn 4:9).

9:57-62 In these sayings Jesus speaks of the severity and the unconditional nature of Christian discipleship. Even family ties and filial obligations, such as burying one's parents, cannot distract one no matter how briefly from proclaiming the kingdom of God. The

go first and bury my father." [60]But he answered him, "Let the dead bury their dead.* But you, go and proclaim the kingdom of God." [61e]And another said, "I will follow you, Lord, but first let me say farewell to my family at home." [62][To him] Jesus said, "No one who sets a hand to the plow and looks to what was left behind is fit for the kingdom of God."

The Mission of the Seventy-two

10 [1*a]After this the Lord appointed seventy [-two]* others whom he sent ahead of him in pairs to every town and place he intended to visit. [2b]He said to them, "The harvest is abundant but the laborers are few; so ask the master of the harvest to send out laborers for his harvest. [3c]Go on your way; behold, I am sending you like lambs among wolves. [4*d]Carry no money bag, no sack, no sandals; and greet no one along the way.[e] [5]Into whatever house you enter, first say, 'Peace to this household.'* [6]If a peaceful person* lives there, your peace will rest on him; but if not, it will return to you. [7]Stay in the same house and eat and drink what is offered to you, for the laborer deserves his payment. Do not move about from one house to another. [8g]Whatever town you enter and they welcome you, eat what is set before you, [9h]cure the sick in it and say to them, 'The kingdom of God is at hand for you.' [10i]Whatever town you enter and they do not receive you, go out into the streets and say, [11j]'The dust of your town that clings to our feet, even that we shake off against you.' Yet know this: the kingdom of God is at hand. [12k]I tell you, it will be more tolerable for Sodom on that day than for that town.

Reproaches to Unrepentant Towns

[13*l]"Woe to you, Chorazin! Woe to you, Bethsaida! For if the mighty deeds done in your midst had been done in Tyre and Sidon, they would long ago have repented, sitting in sackcloth and ashes.[m] [14]But it will be more tolerable for Tyre and Sidon at the judgment than for you. [15*n]And as for you, Capernaum, 'Will you be exalted to heaven? You will go down to the netherworld.'" [16o]Whoever listens to you listens to me. Whoever rejects you rejects me. And whoever rejects me rejects the one who sent me."

---

first two sayings are paralleled in Matthew 8:19-22; see also the notes there.

9:60 Let the dead bury their dead: i.e., let the spiritually dead (those who do not follow) bury their physically dead. See also the note on Matthew 8:22.

10:1-12 Only the Gospel of Luke contains two episodes in which Jesus sends out his followers on a mission: the first (Lk 9:1-6) is based on the mission in Mark 6:6b-13 and recounts the sending out of the Twelve; here in Luke 10:1-12 a similar report based on Q becomes the sending out of seventy-two in this gospel. The episode continues the theme of Jesus preparing witnesses to himself and his ministry. These witnesses include not only the Twelve but also the seventy-two who may represent the Christian mission in Luke's own day. Note that the instructions given to the Twelve and to the seventy-two are similar and that what is said to the seventy-two in Luke 10:4 is directed to the Twelve in Luke 22:35.

10:1 Seventy[-two]: important representatives of the Alexandrian and Caesarean text types read "seventy," while other important Alexandrian texts and Western readings have "seventy-two."

10:4 Carry no money bag . . . greet no one along the way: because of the urgency of the mission and the singlemindedness required of missionaries, attachment to material possessions should be avoided and even customary greetings should not distract from the fulfillment of the task.

Only Luke narrates the sending out of the **seventy [-two] disciples,** clearly a symbolic number. It is likely connected to Moses' choice of seventy elders to share his work with the community (Nm 11:16-17) or to the number of countries supposed to inhabit the earth, according to the OT (Gn 10).

10:5 First say, "Peace to this household': see the notes on Luke 2:14 and Matthew 10:13.

10:6 A peaceful person: literally, "a son of peace."

10:13-16 The call to repentance that is a part of the proclamation of the kingdom brings with it a severe judgment for those who hear it and reject it.

10:15 The netherworld: the underworld, the place of the dead (Acts 2:27, 31) here contrasted with heaven; see also the note on Matthew 11:23.

e
1 Kgs 19:20

a
Mk 6:7

b
Mt 9:37-38;
Jn 4:35

c
Mt 10:16

d
Mt 10:7-14

e
9:3; 2 Kgs 4:29

f
9:4; Mt 10:10;
1 Cor 9:6-14;
1 Tm 5:18

g
1 Cor 10:27

h
Mt 3:2; 4:17;
Mk 1:15

i
9:5

j
Acts 13:51;
18:6

k
Mt 10:15; 11:24

l
Mt 11:20-24

m
Is 23;
Ez 26–28;
Jl 3:4-8;
Am 1:1-10;
Zec 9:2-4

n
Is 14:13-15

o
Mt 10:40;
Jn 5:23; 13:20;
15:23

LUKE

p
Is 14:12;
Jn 12:31;
Rev 12:7-12

q
Ps 19:13;
Mk 16:18

r
Ex 32:32;
Dn 12:1;
Mt 7:22;
Phil 4:3;
Heb 12:23;
Rev 3:5; 21:27

s
Mt 11:25-27

t
1 Cor 1:26-28

u
Jn 3:35; 10:15

v
Mt 13:16-17

w
Mt 22:34-40;
Mk 12:28-34

x
18:18;
Mt 19:16;
Mk 10:17

y
Lv 19:18;
Dt 6:5; 10:12;
Jos 22:5;
Mt 19:19;
22:37-39;
Rom 13:9;
Gal 5:14;
Jas 2:8

z
Lv 18:5;
Prv 19:16;
Rom 10:5;
Gal 3:12

Return of the Seventy-two

[17]The seventy [-two] returned rejoicing, and said, "Lord, even the demons are subject to us because of your name." [18]*p*Jesus said, "I have observed Satan fall like lightning* from the sky. [19]*q*Behold, I have given you the power 'to tread upon serpents' and scorpions and upon the full force of the enemy and nothing will harm you. [20]*r*Nevertheless, do not rejoice because the spirits are subject to you, but rejoice because your names are written in heaven."

Praise of the Father

[21]*s*At that very moment he rejoiced [in] the holy Spirit and said, "I give you praise, Father, Lord of heaven and earth, for although you have hidden these things from the wise and the learned you have revealed them to the childlike.* Yes, Father, such has been your gracious will.[*t*] [22]"All things have been handed over to me by my Father. No one knows who the Son is except the Father, and who the Father is except the Son and anyone to whom the Son wishes to reveal him."

The Privileges of Discipleship

[23]*v*Turning to the disciples in private he said, "Blessed are the eyes that see what you see. [24]For I say to you, many prophets and kings desired to see what you see, but did not see it, and to hear what you hear, but did not hear it."

The Greatest Commandment

[25]**w*There was a scholar of the law* who stood up to test him and said, "Teacher, what must I do to inherit eternal life?"[*x*] [26]Jesus said to him, "What is written in the law? How do you read it?" [27]*y*He said in reply, "You shall love the Lord, your God, with all your heart, with all your being, with all your strength, and with all your mind, and your neighbor as yourself." [28]*z*He replied to him, "You have answered correctly; do this and you will live."

The Parable of the Good Samaritan

[29]But because he wished to justify himself, he said to Jesus, "And who is my neighbor?" [30]Jesus replied, "A man fell victim to robbers as he went down from Jerusalem to Jericho. They stripped and beat him and went off leaving him half-dead. [31]*A priest happened to be going down that road, but when he saw him, he passed by on the opposite side. [32]Likewise a Levite came to the place, and when he saw him, he passed by on the opposite side. [33]But a Samaritan traveler who came upon him was moved with compassion at the sight. [34]He approached the victim, poured oil and wine over his

---

10:18 I have observed Satan fall like lightning: the effect of the mission of the seventy-two is characterized by the Lucan Jesus as a symbolic fall of Satan. As the kingdom of God is gradually being established, evil in all its forms is being defeated; the dominion of Satan over humanity is at an end.

10:21 Revealed them to the childlike: a restatement of the theme announced in Luke 8:10: the mysteries of the kingdom are revealed to the disciples. See also the note on Matthew 11:25-27.

10:25-37 In response to a question from a Jewish legal expert about inheriting eternal life, Jesus illustrates the superiority of love over legalism through the story of the good Samaritan. The law of love proclaimed in the "Sermon on the Plain" (6:27-36) is exemplified by one whom the legal expert would have considered ritually impure (see Jn 4:9). Moreover, the identity of the "neighbor" requested by the legal expert (10:29) turns out to be a Samaritan, the enemy of the Jew (see the note on 9:52).

10:25 Scholar of the law: an expert in the Mosaic law, and probably a member of the group elsewhere identified as the scribes (5:21).

10:31-32 Priest . . . Levite: those religious representatives of Judaism who would have been expected to be models of "neighbor" to the victim pass him by.

wounds and bandaged them. Then he lifted him up on his own animal, took him to an inn and cared for him. ³⁵The next day he took out two silver coins and gave them to the innkeeper with the instruction, 'Take care of him. If you spend more than what I have given you, I shall repay you on my way back.' ³⁶Which of these three, in your opinion, was neighbor to the robbers' victim?" ³⁷He answered, "The one who treated him with mercy." Jesus said to him, "Go and do likewise."

a
Jn 11:1; 12:2-3

a
Mt 6:9-15

See the chart on the different persons named **Mary** (at Mt 13:55).

The **Good Samaritan** becomes a model for becoming neighbor of those in need: "Today, there is an inescapable duty to make ourselves the neighbor of every individual, without exception, and to take positive steps to help a neighbor whom we encounter, whether that neighbor be an elderly person abandoned by everyone, a foreign worker who suffers the injustice of being despised, a refugee, an illegitimate child wrongly suffering for a sin of which the child is innocent, or a starving human being who awakens our conscience by calling to mind the words of Christ: 'As you did it to one of the least of these my brothers or sisters, you did it to me' (Mt 25:40)" (GS 27).

Martha and Mary

³⁸*ᵃAs they continued their journey he entered a village where a woman whose name was Martha welcomed him. ³⁹*She had a sister named Mary [who] sat beside the Lord at his feet listening to him speak. ⁴⁰Martha, burdened with much serving, came to him and said, "Lord, do you not care that my sister has left me by myself to do the serving? Tell her to help me." ⁴¹The Lord said to her in reply, "Martha, Martha, you are anxious and worried about many things. ⁴²*There is need of only one thing. Mary has chosen the better part and it will not be taken from her."

The Lord's Prayer

11 ¹*ᵃHe was praying in a certain place, and when he had finished, one of his disciples said to him, "Lord, teach us to pray just as John taught his disciples."*
²*He said to them, "When you pray, say:

10:38-42 The story of Martha and Mary further illustrates the importance of hearing the words of the teacher and the concern with women in Luke.

10:39 Sat beside the Lord at his feet: it is remarkable for first-century Palestinian Judaism that a woman would assume the posture of a disciple at the master's feet (see also 8:35; Acts 22:3), and it reveals a characteristic attitude of Jesus toward women in this gospel (see 8:2-3).

10:42 There is need of only one thing: some ancient versions read, "there is need of few things"; another important, although probably inferior, reading found in some manuscripts is, "there is need of few things, or of one."

11:1-13 Luke presents three episodes concerned with prayer. The first (11:1-4) recounts Jesus teaching his disciples the Christian communal prayer, the "Our Father"; the second (11:5-8), the impor-

tance of persistence in prayer; the third (11:9-13), the effectiveness of prayer.

11:1-4 The Matthean form of the "Our Father" occurs in the "Sermon on the Mount" (Mt 6:9-15); the shorter Lucan version is presented while Jesus is at prayer (see the note on 3:21) and his disciples ask him to teach them to pray just as John taught his disciples to pray. In answer to their question, Jesus presents them with an example of a Christian communal prayer that stresses the fatherhood of God and acknowledges him as the one to whom the Christian disciple owes daily sustenance (11:3), forgiveness (11:4), and deliverance from the final trial (11:4). See also the notes on Matthew 6:9-13.

11:2 Your kingdom come: in place of this petition, some early church Fathers record: "May your holy Spirit come upon us and cleanse us," a petition that may reflect the use of the "Our Father" in a baptismal liturgy.

b
18:1-5

c
Mt 7:7-11

d
Mt 21:22;
Mk 11:24;
Jn 14:13; 15:7;
1 Jn 5:14-15

e
Mt 12:22-30;
Mk 3:20-27

f
Mt 9:34

g
Mt 12:38; 16:1;
Mk 8:11;
1 Cor 1:22

h
Ex 8:19

Father, hallowed be your name,
>your kingdom come.
>>[3]Give us each day our daily bread*
>>[4]and forgive us our sins
>for we ourselves forgive everyone in debt to us,
>and do not subject us to the final test."

On the **Our Father**, see the chart in Matthew (at 6:9).

Further Teachings on Prayer

[5b]And he said to them, "Suppose one of you has a friend to whom he goes at midnight and says, 'Friend, lend me three loaves of bread, [6]for a friend of mine has arrived at my house from a journey and I have nothing to offer him,' [7]and he says in reply from within, 'Do not bother me; the door has already been locked and my children and I are already in bed. I cannot get up to give you anything.' [8]I tell you, if he does not get up to give him the loaves because of their friendship, he will get up to give him whatever he needs because of his persistence.

The Answer to Prayer

[9c]"And I tell you, ask and you will receive; seek and you will find; knock and the door will be opened to you.[d] [10]For everyone who asks, receives; and the one who seeks, finds; and to the one who knocks, the door will be opened. [11]What father among you would hand his son a snake when he asks for a fish? [12]Or hand him a scorpion

If you take Jesus at his word today, about receiving whatever you ask for in prayer, what would you ask for? Where would your seeking lead you? Upon what door would you knock?

when he asks for an egg? [13]If you then, who are wicked, know how to give good gifts to your children, how much more will the Father in heaven give the holy Spirit* to those who ask him?"

Jesus and Beelzebul

[14e]He was driving out a demon [that was] mute, and when the demon had gone out, the mute person spoke and the crowds were amazed. [15f]Some of them said, "By the power of Beelzebul, the prince of demons, he drives out demons." [16g]Others, to test him, asked him for a sign from heaven. [17]But he knew their thoughts and said to them, "Every kingdom divided against itself will be laid waste and house will fall against house. [18]And if Satan is divided against himself, how will his kingdom stand? For you say that it is by Beelzebul that I drive out demons. [19]If I, then, drive out demons by Beelzebul, by whom do your own people* drive them out? Therefore they will be your judges. [20h]But if it is by the finger of God that [I] drive out demons, then the kingdom of God has come upon you. [21]When a strong man fully armed guards his palace, his possessions are safe. [22]But when one stronger* than he attacks and overcomes him, he

---

11:3-4 Daily bread: see the note on Matthew 6:11. **The final test:** see the note on Matthew 6:13.

11:13 The holy Spirit: this is a Lucan editorial alteration of a traditional saying of Jesus (see Mt 7:11). Luke presents the gift of the holy Spirit as the response of the Father to the prayer of the Christian disciple.

11:19 Your own people: the Greek reads "your sons." Other Jewish exorcists (see Acts 19:13-20), who recognize that the power of God is active in the exorcism, would themselves convict the accusers of Jesus. See also the note on Matthew 12:27.

11:22 One stronger: i.e., Jesus. Cf. Luke 3:16 where John the Baptist identifies Jesus as "more powerful than I."

takes away the armor on which he relied and distributes the spoils. [23i]Whoever is not with me is against me, and whoever does not gather with me scatters.

The Return of the Unclean Spirit

[24j]"When an unclean spirit goes out of someone, it roams through arid regions searching for rest but, finding none, it says, 'I shall return to my home from which I came.' [25]But upon returning, it finds it swept clean and put in order. [26k]Then it goes and brings back seven other spirits more wicked than itself who move in and dwell there, and the last condition of that person is worse than the first."

True Blessedness

[27*l]While he was speaking, a woman from the crowd called out and said to him, "Blessed is the womb that carried you and the breasts at which you nursed." [28]He replied, "Rather, blessed are those who hear the word of God and observe it."

The Demand for a Sign

[29*m]While still more people gathered in the crowd, he said to them, "This generation is an evil generation; it seeks a sign, but no sign will be given it, except the sign of Jonah.[n] [30]Just as Jonah became a sign to the Ninevites, so will the Son of Man be to this generation. [31o]At the judgment the queen of the south will rise with the men of this generation and she will condemn them, because she came from the ends of the earth to hear the wisdom of Solomon, and there is something greater than Solomon here. [32p]At the judgment the men of Nineveh will arise with this generation and condemn it, because at the preaching of Jonah they repented, and there is something greater than Jonah here.

The Simile of Light

[33q]"No one who lights a lamp hides it away or places it [under a bushel basket], but on a lampstand so that those who enter might see the light. [34r]The lamp of the body is your eye. When your eye is sound, then your whole body is filled with light, but when it is bad, then your body is in darkness. [35]Take care, then, that the light in you not become darkness. [36]If your whole body is full of light, and no part of it is in darkness, then it will be as full of light as a lamp illuminating you with its brightness."

Denunciation of the Pharisees and Scholars of the Law

[37*s]After he had spoken, a Pharisee invited him to dine at his home. He entered and reclined at table to eat.[t] [38u]The Pharisee was amazed to see that he did not observe the prescribed washing before the meal. [39v]The Lord said to him, "Oh you Pharisees! Although you cleanse the outside of the cup and the dish, inside you are filled with plunder

i
9:50; Mk 9:40

j
Mt 12:43-45

k
Jn 5:14

l
1:28, 42, 48

m
Mt 12:38-42;
Mk 8:12

n
Mt 16:1, 4;
Jn 6:30;
1 Cor 1:22

o
1 Kgs 10:1-10;
2 Chr 9:1-12

p
Jon 3:8, 10

q
8:16; Mt 5:15;
Mk 4:21

r
Mt 6:22-23

s
20:45-47;
Mt 23:1-36;
Mk 12:38-40

t
7:36; 14:1

u
Mt 15:2;
Mk 7:2-5

v
Mt 23:25-26

LUKE

11:27-28 The beatitude in Luke 11:28 should not be interpreted as a rebuke of the mother of Jesus; see the note on Luke 8:21. Rather, it emphasizes (like 2:35) that attentiveness to God's word is more important than biological relationship to Jesus.

11:29-32 The "sign of Jonah" in Luke is the preaching of the need for repentance by a prophet who comes from afar. Cf. Matthew 12:38-42 (and see the notes there) where the "sign of Jonah" is interpreted by Jesus as his death and resurrection.

11:37-54 This denunciation of the Pharisees (11:39-44) and the scholars of the law (11:45-52) is set by Luke in the context of Jesus' dining at the home of a Pharisee. Controversies with or reprimands of Pharisees are regularly set by Luke within the context of Jesus' eating with Pharisees (see 5:29-39; 7:36-50; 14:1-24). A different compilation of similar sayings is found in Matthew 23 (see also the notes there).

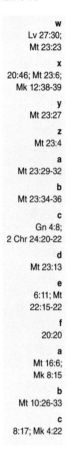

w
Lv 27:30;
Mt 23:23

x
20:46; Mt 23:6;
Mk 12:38-39

y
Mt 23:27

z
Mt 23:4

a
Mt 23:29-32

b
Mt 23:34-36

c
Gn 4:8;
2 Chr 24:20-22

d
Mt 23:13

e
6:11; Mt
22:15-22

f
20:20

a
Mt 16:6;
Mk 8:15

b
Mt 10:26-33

c
8:17; Mk 4:22

and evil. ⁴⁰You fools! Did not the maker of the outside also make the inside? ⁴¹But as to what is within, give alms, and behold, everything will be clean for you. ⁴²ʷWoe to you Pharisees! You pay tithes of mint and of rue and of every garden herb, but you pay no attention to judgment and to love for God. These you should have done, without overlooking the others. ⁴³ˣWoe to you Pharisees! You love the seat of honor in synagogues and greetings in marketplaces. ⁴⁴ʸWoe to you! You are like unseen graves* over which people unknowingly walk."

⁴⁵ᶻThen one of the scholars of the law* said to him in reply, "Teacher, by saying this you are insulting us too." ⁴⁶And he said, "Woe also to you scholars of the law! You impose on people burdens hard to carry, but you yourselves do not lift one finger to touch them. ⁴⁷ᵃWoe to you! You build the memorials of the prophets whom your ancestors killed. ⁴⁸Consequently, you bear witness and give consent to the deeds of your ancestors, for they killed them and you do the building. ⁴⁹ᵇTherefore, the wisdom of God said, 'I will send to them prophets and apostles;* some of them they will kill and persecute' ⁵⁰in order that this generation might be charged with the blood of all the prophets shed since the foundation of the world, ⁵¹ᶜfrom the blood of Abel to the blood of Zechariah* who died between the altar and the temple building. Yes, I tell you, this generation will be charged with their blood! ⁵²ᵈWoe to you, scholars of the law! You have taken away the key of knowledge. You yourselves did not enter and you stopped those trying to enter." ⁵³ᵉWhen he left, the scribes and Pharisees began to act with hostility toward him and to interrogate him about many things, ⁵⁴ᶠfor they were plotting to catch him at something he might say.

> On the **scholars of the law**, see the chart on the Jewish leaders in "Background to the Gospels," pp. 4–5.

The Leaven of the Pharisees

12 ¹*ᵃMeanwhile, so many people were crowding together that they were trampling one another underfoot. He began to speak, first to his disciples, "Beware of the leaven—that is, the hypocrisy—of the Pharisees.

Courage under Persecution

²*ᵇ"There is nothing concealed that will not be revealed, nor secret that will not be known.ᶜ ³Therefore whatever you have said in the darkness will be heard in the light, and what you have whispered behind closed doors will be proclaimed on the housetops. ⁴I tell you, my friends, do not be afraid of those who kill the body but after that can do no more. ⁵I shall show you whom to fear. Be afraid of the one who after killing has the power

---

11:44 Unseen graves: contact with the dead or with human bones or graves (see Nm 19:16) brought ritual impurity. Jesus presents the Pharisees as those who insidiously lead others astray through their seeming attention to the law.

11:45 Scholars of the law: see the note on Luke 10:25.

11:49 I will send to them prophets and apostles: Jesus connects the mission of the church (apostles) with the mission of the Old Testament prophets who often suffered the rebuke of their contemporaries.

11:51 From the blood of Abel to the blood of Zechariah: the murder of Abel is the first murder recounted in the Old Testament

(Gn 4:8). The Zechariah mentioned here may be the Zechariah whose murder is recounted in 2 Chronicles 24:20-22, the last murder presented in the Hebrew canon of the Old Testament.

12:1 See the notes on Mark 8:15 and Matthew 16:5-12.

12:2-9 Luke presents a collection of sayings of Jesus exhorting his followers to acknowledge him and his mission fearlessly and assuring them of God's protection even in times of persecution. They are paralleled in Matthew 10:26-33.

12:5 Gehenna: see the note on Matthew 5:22.

Blasphemy against the Holy Spirit has been the subject of many and varied interpretations in history. In the context of Luke-Acts, it constitutes resistance to the Spirit-empowered spread of the Gospel. To stand in the way of God's plan brings doom.

to cast into Gehenna;* yes, I tell you, be afraid of that one. [6]Are not five sparrows sold for two small coins?* Yet not one of them has escaped the notice of God. [7d]Even the hairs of your head have all been counted. Do not be afraid. You are worth more than many sparrows. [8]I tell you, everyone who acknowledges me before others the Son of Man will acknowledge before the angels of God. [9e]But whoever denies me before others will be denied before the angels of God.

Sayings about the Holy Spirit

[10*f]"Everyone who speaks a word against the Son of Man will be forgiven, but the one who blasphemes against the holy Spirit will not be forgiven. [11g]When they take you before synagogues and before rulers and authorities, do not worry about how or what your defense will be or about what you are to say. [12]For the holy Spirit will teach you at that moment what you should say."

Saying against Greed

[13*]Someone in the crowd said to him, "Teacher, tell my brother to share the inheritance with me." [14h]He replied to him, "Friend, who appointed me as your judge and arbitrator?" [15i]Then he said to the crowd, "Take care to guard against all greed, for though one may be rich, one's life does not consist of possessions."

Parable of the Rich Fool

[16]Then he told them a parable. "There was a rich man whose land produced a bountiful harvest. [17]He asked himself, 'What shall I do, for I do not have space to store my harvest?' [18]And he said, 'This is what I shall do: I shall tear down my barns and build larger ones. There I shall store all my grain and other goods [19j]and I shall say to myself, "Now as for you, you have so many good things stored up for many years, rest, eat, drink, be merry!"[k] [20]But God said to him, 'You fool, this night your life will be demanded of you; and the things you have prepared, to whom will they belong?' [21]Thus will it be for the one who stores up treasure for himself but is not rich in what matters to God."*

Dependence on God

[22l]He said to [his] disciples, "Therefore I tell you, do not worry about your life and what you will eat, or about your body and what you will wear. [23]For life is more than food and the body more than clothing. [24m]Notice the ravens: they do not sow or reap; they have neither storehouse nor barn, yet God feeds them. How much more important are you than

d
12:24; 21:18;
Acts 27:34

e
9:26; Mk 8:38;
2 Tm 2:12

f
Mt 12:31-32;
Mk 3:28-29

g
21:12-15;
Mt 10:17-20;
Mk 13:11

h
Ex 2:14;
Acts 7:27

i
1 Tm 6:9-10

j
Mt 6:19-21;
1 Tm 6:17

k
Sir 11:19

l
Mt 6:25-34

m
12:7

LUKE

12:6 Two small coins: the Roman copper coin, the assarion (Latin *as*), was worth about one-sixteenth of a denarius (see the note on 7:41).

12:10-12 The sayings about the holy Spirit are set in the context of fearlessness in the face of persecution (12:2-9; cf. Mt 12:31-32). The holy Spirit will be presented in Luke's second volume, the Acts of the Apostles, as the power responsible for the guidance of the Christian mission and the source of courage in the face of persecution.

12:13-34 Luke has joined together sayings contrasting those whose focus and trust in life is on material possessions, symbolized here by the rich fool of the parable (12:16-21), with those who recognize their complete dependence on God (12:21), those whose radical detachment from material possessions symbolizes their heavenly treasure (12:33-34).

12:21 Rich in what matters to God: literally, "rich for God."

n
1 Kgs 10:4-7;
2 Chr 9:3-6

o
22:29; Rev 1:6

p
18:22;
Mt 6:20-21;
Mk 10:21

q
Mt 24:45-51

r
Mt 25:1-13;
Mk 13:35-37

s
Mt 24:43-44;
1 Thes 5:2

t
Jas 4:17

u
Mk 10:38-39

birds! [25]Can any of you by worrying add a moment to your lifespan? [26]If even the smallest things are beyond your control, why are you anxious about the rest? [27n]Notice how the flowers grow. They do not toil or spin. But I tell you, not even Solomon in all his splendor was dressed like one of them. [28]If God so clothes the grass in the field that grows today and is thrown into the oven tomorrow, will he not much more provide for you, O you of little faith? [29]As for you, do not seek what you are to eat and what you are to drink, and do not worry anymore. [30]All the nations of the world seek for these things, and your Father knows that you need them. [31]Instead, seek his kingdom, and these other things will be given you besides. [32o]Do not be afraid any longer, little flock, for your Father is pleased to give you the kingdom. [33p]Sell your belongings and give alms. Provide money bags for yourselves that do not wear out, an inexhaustible treasure in heaven that no thief can reach nor moth destroy. [34]For where your treasure is, there also will your heart be.

Vigilant and Faithful Servants

[35*q]"Gird your loins and light your lamps [36r]and be like servants who await their master's return from a wedding, ready to open immediately when he comes and knocks. [37]Blessed are those servants whom the master finds vigilant on his arrival. Amen, I say to you, he will gird himself, have them recline at table, and proceed to wait on them. [38]And should he come in the second or third watch and find them prepared in this way, blessed are those servants. [39s]Be sure of this: if the master of the house had known the hour when the thief was coming, he would not have let his house be broken into. [40]You also must be prepared, for at an hour you do not expect, the Son of Man will come."

[41]Then Peter said, "Lord, is this parable meant for us or for everyone?" [42]And the Lord replied, "Who, then, is the faithful and prudent steward whom the master will put in charge of his servants to distribute [the] food allowance at the proper time? [43]Blessed is that servant whom his master on arrival finds doing so. [44]Truly, I say to you, he will put him in charge of all his property. [45]But if that servant says to himself, 'My master is delayed in coming,'* and begins to beat the menservants and the maidservants, to eat and drink and get drunk, [46]then that servant's master will come on an unexpected day and at an unknown hour and will punish him severely and assign him a place with the unfaithful. [47t]That servant who knew his master's will but did not make preparations nor act in accord with his will shall be beaten severely; [48]and the servant who was ignorant of his master's will but acted in a way deserving of a severe beating shall be beaten only lightly. Much will be required of the person entrusted with much, and still more will be demanded of the person entrusted with more.

Jesus: A Cause of Division

[49*]"I have come to set the earth on fire, and how I wish it were already blazing! [50*u]There is a baptism with which I must be baptized, and how great is my anguish until it is ac-

---

12:35-48 This collection of sayings relates to Luke's understanding of the end time and the return of Jesus. Luke emphasizes for his readers the importance of being faithful to the instructions of Jesus in the period before the parousia.
12:45 My master is delayed in coming: this statement indicates that early Christian expectations for the imminent return of Jesus had undergone some modification. Luke cautions his readers

against counting on such a delay and acting irresponsibly. Cf. the similar warning in Matthew 24:48.
12:49-53 Jesus' proclamation of the kingdom is a refining and purifying fire. His message that meets with acceptance or rejection will be a source of conflict and dissension even within families.
12:50 Baptism: i.e., his death.

complished! [51v]Do you think that I have come to establish peace on the earth? No, I tell you, but rather division.[w] [52]From now on a household of five will be divided, three against two and two against three; [53x]a father will be divided against his son and a son against his father, a mother against her daughter and a daughter against her mother, a mother-in-law against her daughter-in-law and a daughter-in-law against her mother-in-law."

Signs of the Times

[54y]He also said to the crowds, "When you see [a] cloud rising in the west you say immediately that it is going to rain—and so it does; [55]and when you notice that the wind is blowing from the south you say that it is going to be hot—and so it is. [56]You hypocrites! You know how to interpret the appearance of the earth and the sky; why do you not know how to interpret the present time?

Settlement with an Opponent

[57z]"Why do you not judge for yourselves what is right? [58]If you are to go with your opponent before a magistrate, make an effort to settle the matter on the way; otherwise your opponent will turn you over to the judge, and the judge hand you over to the constable, and the constable throw you into prison. [59]I say to you, you will not be released until you have paid the last penny.'"[*]

A Call to Repentance

13 [1*]At that time some people who were present there told him about the Galileans whose blood Pilate had mingled with the blood of their sacrifices.[*] [2a]He said to them in reply, "Do you think that because these Galileans suffered in this way they were greater sinners than all other Galileans? [3b]By no means! But I tell you, if you do not repent, you will all perish as they did! [4]Or those eighteen people who were killed when the tower at Siloam fell on them[*]—do you think they were more guilty than everyone else who lived in Jerusalem? [5]By no means! But I tell you, if you do not repent, you will all perish as they did!"

The Parable of the Barren Fig Tree

[6*c]And he told them this parable: "There once was a person who had a fig tree planted in his orchard, and when he came in search of fruit on it but found none, [7]he said to the gardener, 'For three years now I have come in search of fruit on this fig tree

---

v Mt 10:34-35

w 2:14

x Mi 7:6

y Mt 16:2-3

z Mt 5:25-26

a Jn 9:2

b Jn 8:24

c Jer 8:13; Heb 3:17; Mt 21:19; Mk 11:13

12:59 The last penny: Greek, *lepton*, a very small amount. Matthew 5:26 has for "the last penny" the Greek word *kodrantēs* (Latin *quadrans*, "farthing").

13:1-5 The death of the Galileans at the hands of Pilate (13:1) and the accidental death of those on whom the tower fell (13:4) are presented by the Lucan Jesus as timely reminders of the need for all to repent, for the victims of these tragedies should not be considered outstanding sinners who were singled out for punishment.

13:1 The slaughter of the Galileans by Pilate is unknown outside Luke; but from what is known about Pilate from the Jewish historian Josephus, such a slaughter would be in keeping with the character of

Pilate. Josephus reports that Pilate had disrupted a religious gathering of the Samaritans on Mt. Gerizim with a slaughter of the participants (*Antiquities* 18, 4, 1 **86-87), and that on another occasion Pilate had killed many Jews who had opposed him when he appropriated money from the temple treasury to build an aqueduct in Jerusalem (*Jewish War* 2, 9, 4 **175-77; *Antiquities* 18, 3, 2 **60-62).

13:4 Like the incident mentioned in Luke 13:1 nothing of this accident in Jerusalem is known outside Luke and the New Testament.

13:6-9 Following on the call to repentance in Luke 13:1-5, the parable of the barren fig tree presents a story about the continuing patience of God with those who have not yet given evidence of their

d
6:7; 14:3;
Ex 20:8-11;
Dt 5:12-15;
Mt 12:10;
Mk 3:2-4;
Jn 5:16; 7:23;
9:14, 16

e
14:5; Dt 22:4;
Mt 12:11

f
19:9

g
Mt 13:31-32;
Mk 4:30-32

h
Ez 17:23-24;
31:6

i
Mt 13:33

j
Mt 7:13-14,
21-23

but have found none. [So] cut it down. Why should it exhaust the soil?' [8]He said to him in reply, 'Sir, leave it for this year also, and I shall cultivate the ground around it and fertilize it; [9]it may bear fruit in the future. If not you can cut it down.'"

Cure of a Crippled Woman on the Sabbath

[10]*He was teaching in a synagogue on the sabbath. [11]And a woman was there who for eighteen years had been crippled by a spirit; she was bent over, completely incapable of standing erect. [12]When Jesus saw her, he called to her and said, "Woman, you are set free of your infirmity." [13]He laid his hands on her, and she at once stood up straight and glorified God. [14]dBut the leader of the synagogue, indignant that Jesus had cured on the sabbath, said to the crowd in reply, "There are six days when work should be done. Come on those days to be cured, not on the sabbath day." [15]*eThe Lord said to him in reply, "Hypocrites! Does not each one of you on the sabbath untie his ox or his ass from the manger and lead it out for watering? [16]*fThis daughter of Abraham, whom Satan has bound for eighteen years now, ought she not to have been set free on the sabbath day from this bondage?" [17]When he said this, all his adversaries were humiliated; and the whole crowd rejoiced at all the splendid deeds done by him.

The Parable of the Mustard Seed

[18]*gThen he said, "What is the kingdom of God like? To what can I compare it? [19]hIt is like a mustard seed that a person took and planted in the garden. When it was fully grown, it became a large bush and 'the birds of the sky dwelt in its branches.'"

The Parable of the Yeast

[20]iAgain he said, "To what shall I compare the kingdom of God? [21]It is like yeast that a woman took and mixed [in] with three measures of wheat flour until the whole batch of dough was leavened."

The Narrow Door; Salvation and Rejection

[22]*He passed through towns and villages, teaching as he went and making his way to Jerusalem. [23]Someone asked him, "Lord, will only a few people be saved?" He answered them, [24]j"Strive to enter through the narrow gate, for many, I tell you, will

repentance (see 3:8). The parable may also be alluding to the delay of the end time, when punishment will be meted out, and the importance of preparing for the end of the age because the delay will not be permanent (13:8-9).

13:10-17 The cure of the crippled woman on the sabbath and the controversy that results furnishes a parallel to an incident that will be reported by Luke in 14:1-6, the cure of the man with dropsy on the sabbath. A characteristic of Luke's style is the juxtaposition of an incident that reveals Jesus' concern for a man with an incident that reveals his concern for a woman; cf., e.g., Luke 7:11-17 and 8:49-56.

13:15-16 If the law as interpreted by Jewish tradition allowed for the untying of bound animals on the sabbath, how much more should this woman who has been bound by Satan's power be freed on the sabbath from her affliction.

13:16 Whom Satan has bound: affliction and infirmity are taken as evidence of Satan's hold on humanity. The healing ministry of

Jesus reveals the gradual wresting from Satan of control over humanity and the establishment of God's kingdom.

13:18-21 Two parables are used to illustrate the future proportions of the kingdom of God that will result from its deceptively small beginning in the preaching and healing ministry of Jesus. They are paralleled in Matthew 13:31-33 and Mark 4:30-32.

13:22-30 These sayings of Jesus follow in Luke upon the parables of the kingdom (13:18-21) and stress that great effort is required for entrance into the kingdom (13:24) and that there is an urgency to accept the present opportunity to enter because the narrow door will not remain open indefinitely (13:25). Lying behind the sayings is the rejection of Jesus and his message by his Jewish contemporaries (13:26) whose places at table in the kingdom will be taken by Gentiles from the four corners of the world (13:29). Those called last (the Gentiles) will precede those to whom the invitation to enter was first extended (the Jews). See also Luke 14:15-24.

attempt to enter but will not be strong enough.[k] [25][l]After the master of the house has arisen and locked the door, then will you stand outside knocking and saying, 'Lord, open the door for us.' He will say to you in reply, 'I do not know where you are from.' [26]And you will say, 'We ate and drank in your company and you taught in our streets.' [27][m]Then he will say to you, 'I do not know where [you] are from. Depart from me, all you evildoers!' [28][n]And there will be wailing and grinding of teeth when you see Abraham, Isaac, and Jacob and all the prophets in the kingdom of God and you yourselves cast out. [29][o]And people will come from the east and the west and from the north and the south and will recline at table in the kingdom of God. [30][p]For behold, some are last who will be first, and some are first who will be last."

Herod's Desire to Kill Jesus

[31]At that time some Pharisees came to him and said, "Go away, leave this area because Herod wants to kill you." [32]He replied, "Go and tell that fox, 'Behold, I cast out demons and I perform healings today and tomorrow, and on the third day I accomplish my purpose.* [33]*[q]Yet I must continue on my way today, tomorrow, and the following day, for it is impossible that a prophet should die outside of Jerusalem.'

The Lament over Jerusalem

[34][r]"Jerusalem, Jerusalem, you who kill the prophets and stone those sent to you, how many times I yearned to gather your children together as a hen gathers her brood under her wings, but you were unwilling! [35][s]Behold, your house will be abandoned. [But] I tell you, you will not see me until [the time comes when] you say, 'Blessed is he who comes in the name of the Lord.'"

Healing of the Man with Dropsy on the Sabbath

14 [1]*[a]On a sabbath he went to dine at the home of one of the leading Pharisees, and the people there were observing him carefully.[b] [2]In front of him there was a man suffering from dropsy.* [3][c]Jesus spoke to the scholars of the law and Pharisees in reply, asking, "Is it lawful to cure on the sabbath or not?" [4]But they kept silent; so he took the man and, after he had healed him, dismissed him. [5][d]Then he said to them, "Who among you, if your son or ox* falls into a cistern, would not immediately pull him out on the sabbath day?" [6][e]But they were unable to answer his question.

Conduct of Invited Guests and Hosts

[7]*[f]He told a parable to those who had been invited, noticing how they were choosing the places of honor at the table. [8][g]"When you are invited by someone to a wedding

k
Mk 10:25
l
Mt 25:10-12
m
Ps 6:9;
Mt 7:23; 25:41
n
Mt 8:11-12
o
Ps 107:2-3
p
Mt 19:20;
20:16;
Mk 10:31
q
2:38; Jn 6:30;
8:20
r
19:41-44;
Mt 23:37-39
s
19:38;
1 Kgs 9:7-8;
Ps 118:26;
Jer 7:4-7, 13-15;
12:7; 22:5
a
6:6-11;
13:10-17
b
11:37
c
6:9; Mk 3:4
d
13:15; Dt 22:4;
Mt 12:11
e
Mt 22:46
f
11:43; Mt 23:6;
Mk 12:38-39
g
Prv 25:6-7

13:32 Nothing, not even Herod's desire to kill Jesus, stands in the way of Jesus' role in fulfilling God's will and in establishing the kingdom through his exorcisms and healings.

13:33 It is impossible that a prophet should die outside of Jerusalem: Jerusalem is the city of destiny and the goal of the journey of the prophet Jesus. Only when he reaches the holy city will his work be accomplished.

14:1-6 See the note on Luke 13:10-17.

14:2 Dropsy: an abnormal swelling of the body because of the retention and accumulation of fluid.

14:5 Your son or ox: this is the reading of many of the oldest and most important New Testament manuscripts. Because of the strange collocation of **son** and **ox**, some copyists have altered it to "your ass or ox," on the model of the saying in Luke 13:15.

14:7-14 The banquet scene found only in Luke provides the opportunity for these teachings of Jesus on humility and presents a setting to display Luke's interest in Jesus' attitude toward the rich and the poor (see the notes on 4:18; 6:20-26; 12:13-34).

h
18:14

i
6:32-35

j
Jn 5:29

k
Mt 22:2-10

l
Mt 10:37-38

m
9:57-62; 18:29;
Jn 12:25

n
9:23; Mt 16:24;
Mk 8:34

banquet, do not recline at table in the place of honor. A more distinguished guest than you may have been invited by him, [9]and the host who invited both of you may approach you and say, 'Give your place to this man,' and then you would proceed with embarrassment to take the lowest place. [10]Rather, when you are invited, go and take the lowest place so that when the host comes to you he may say, 'My friend, move up to a higher position.' Then you will enjoy the esteem of your companions at the table. [11][h]For everyone who exalts himself will be humbled, but the one who humbles himself will be exalted." [12][i]Then he said to the host who invited him, "When you hold a lunch or a dinner, do not invite your friends or your brothers or your relatives or your wealthy neighbors, in case they may invite you back and you have repayment. [13]Rather, when you hold a banquet, invite the poor, the crippled, the lame, the blind; [14][j]blessed indeed will you be because of their inability to repay you. For you will be repaid at the resurrection of the righteous."

The Parable of the Great Feast

[15]*One of his fellow guests on hearing this said to him, "Blessed is the one who will dine in the kingdom of God." [16][k]He replied to him, "A man gave a great dinner to which he invited many. [17]When the time for the dinner came, he dispatched his servant to say to those invited, 'Come, everything is now ready.' [18]But one by one, they all began to excuse themselves. The first said to him, 'I have purchased a field and must go to examine it; I ask you, consider me excused.' [19]And another said, 'I have purchased five yoke of oxen and am on my way to evaluate them; I ask you, consider me excused.' [20]And another said, 'I have just married a woman, and therefore I cannot come.' [21]The servant went and reported this to his master. Then the master of the house in a rage commanded his servant, 'Go out quickly into the streets and alleys of the town and bring in here the poor and the crippled, the blind and the lame.' [22]The servant reported, 'Sir, your orders have been carried out and still there is room.' [23]The master then ordered the servant, 'Go out to the highways and hedgerows and make people come in that my home may be filled. [24]For, I tell you, none of those men who were invited will taste my dinner.' "

Sayings on Discipleship

[25]*Great crowds were traveling with him, and he turned and addressed them, [26][l]"If anyone comes to me without hating his father* and mother, wife and children, brothers and sisters, and even his own life, he cannot be my disciple.[m] [27][n]Whoever does not carry his own cross and come after me cannot be my disciple. [28]Which of you wishing to construct a tower does not first sit down and calculate the cost to see if there is enough for its completion? [29]Otherwise, after laying the foundation and finding himself unable to finish the work the onlookers should laugh at him [30]and say, 'This one began to build but did not have the resources to finish.' [31]Or what king marching into battle would not

---

14:15-24 The parable of the great dinner is a further illustration of the rejection by Israel, God's chosen people, of Jesus' invitation to share in the banquet in the kingdom and the extension of the invitation to other Jews whose identification as the poor, crippled, blind, and lame (14:21) classifies them among those who recognize their need for salvation, and to Gentiles (14:23). A similar parable is found in Matthew 22:1-10.

14:25-33 This collection of sayings, most of which are peculiar to Luke, focuses on the total dedication necessary for the disciple of Jesus. No attachment to family (14:26) or possessions (14:33) can stand in the way of the total commitment demanded of the disciple. Also, acceptance of the call to be a disciple demands readiness to accept persecution and suffering (14:27) and a realistic assessment of the hardships and costs (14:28-32).

14:26 Hating his father . . .: cf. the similar saying in Matthew 10:37. The disciple's family must take second place to the absolute dedication involved in following Jesus (see also 9:59-62).

first sit down and decide whether with ten thousand troops he can successfully oppose another king advancing upon him with twenty thousand troops? [32]But if not, while he is still far away, he will send a delegation to ask for peace terms. [33][o]In the same way, everyone of you who does not renounce all his possessions cannot be my disciple.

The Simile of Salt

[34][*][p]"Salt is good, but if salt itself loses its taste, with what can its flavor be restored? [35][q]It is fit neither for the soil nor for the manure pile; it is thrown out. Whoever has ears to hear ought to hear."

The Parable of the Lost Sheep

15 [1][*][a]The tax collectors and sinners were all drawing near to listen to him, [2][b]but the Pharisees and scribes began to complain, saying, "This man welcomes sinners and eats with them." [3]So to them he addressed this parable. [4][c]"What man among you having a hundred sheep and losing one of them would not leave the ninety-nine in the desert and go after the lost one[d] until he finds it?[e] [5]And when he does find it, he sets it on his shoulders with great joy [6]and, upon his arrival home, he calls together his friends and neighbors and says to them, 'Rejoice with me because I have found my lost sheep.' [7]I tell you, in just the same way there will be more joy in heaven over one sinner who repents than over ninety-nine righteous people who have no need of repentance.

The Parable of the Lost Coin

[8]"Or what woman having ten coins[*] and losing one would not light a lamp and sweep the house, searching carefully until she finds it? [9]And when she does find it, she calls together her friends and neighbors and says to them, 'Rejoice with me because I have found the coin that I lost.' [10]In just the same way, I tell you, there will be rejoicing among the angels of God over one sinner who repents."

The Parable of the Lost Son

[11]Then he said, "A man had two sons, [12]and the younger son said to his father, 'Father, give me the share of your estate that should come to me.' So the father divided the property between them. [13][g]After a few days, the younger son collected all his belongings and set off to a distant country where he squandered his inheritance on a life of dissipation. [14]When he had freely spent everything, a severe famine struck that country, and he found himself in dire need. [15]So he hired himself out to one of the local citizens who sent him to his farm to tend the swine. [16]And he longed to eat his fill of the pods on which the swine fed, but nobody gave him any. [17]Coming to his senses he thought, 'How many of my father's hired workers have more than enough food to eat, but here am I, dying from hunger. [18]I shall get up and go to my father and I shall say to him, "Father, I have sinned against heaven and against you. [19]I no longer deserve to be called your son; treat me as you would treat

o
5:11

p
Mt 5:13;
Mk 9:50

q
8:8; Mt 11:15;
13:9; Mk 4:9,
23

a
Mt 9:10-13

b
5:30; 19:7

c
Mt 18:12-14

d
19:10

e
Ez 34:11-12,
16

f
Ez 18:23

g
Prv 29:3

LUKE

14:34-35 The simile of salt follows the sayings of Jesus that demanded of the disciple total dedication and detachment from family and possessions and illustrates the condition of one who does not display this total commitment. The halfhearted disciple is like salt that cannot serve its intended purpose. See the simile of salt in Matthew 5:13 and the note there.

15:1-32 To the parable of the lost sheep (15:1-7) that Luke shares with Matthew (Mt 18:12-14), Luke adds two parables (the lost coin, 15:8-10; the prodigal son, 15:11-32) from his own special tradition to illustrate Jesus' particular concern for the lost and God's love for the repentant sinner.

15:8 Ten coins: literally, "ten drachmas." A drachma was a Greek silver coin.

a
Eph 5:8;
1 Thes 5:5

one of your hired workers.'" ²⁰So he got up and went back to his father. While he was still a long way off, his father caught sight of him, and was filled with compassion. He ran to his son, embraced him and kissed him. ²¹His son said to him, 'Father, I have sinned against heaven and against you; I no longer deserve to be called your son.' ²²But his father ordered his servants, 'Quickly bring the finest robe and put it on him; put a ring on his finger and sandals on his feet. ²³Take the fattened calf and slaughter it. Then let us celebrate with a feast, ²⁴because this son of mine was dead, and has come to life again; he was lost, and has been found.' Then the celebration began. ²⁵Now the older son had been out in the field and, on his way back, as he neared the house, he heard the sound of music and dancing. ²⁶He called one of the servants and asked what this might mean. ²⁷The servant said to him, 'Your brother has returned and your father has slaughtered the fattened calf because he has him back safe and sound.' ²⁸He became angry, and when he refused to enter the house, his father came out and pleaded with him. ²⁹He said to his father in reply, 'Look, all these years I served you and not once did I disobey your orders; yet you never gave me even a young goat to feast on with my friends. ³⁰But when your son returns who swallowed up your property with prostitutes, for him you slaughter the fattened calf.' ³¹He said to him, 'My son, you are here with me always; everything I have is yours. ³²But now we must celebrate and rejoice, because your brother was dead and has come to life again; he was lost and has been found.'"

The Parable of the Dishonest Steward

16 ¹*Then he also said to his disciples, "A rich man had a steward who was reported to him for squandering his property. ²He summoned him and said, 'What is this I hear about you? Prepare a full account of your stewardship, because you can no longer be my steward.' ³The steward said to himself, 'What shall I do, now that my master is taking the position of steward away from me? I am not strong enough to dig and I am ashamed to beg. ⁴I know what I shall do so that, when I am removed from the stewardship, they may welcome me into their homes.' ⁵He called in his master's debtors one by one. To the first he said, 'How much do you owe my master?' ⁶*He replied, 'One hundred measures of olive oil.' He said to him, 'Here is your promissory note. Sit down and quickly write one for fifty.' ⁷Then to another he said, 'And you, how much do you owe?' He replied, 'One hundred kors* of wheat.' He said to him, 'Here is your promissory note; write one for eighty.' ⁸*ᵃAnd the master commended that dishonest steward for acting prudently.*

16:1-8a The parable of the dishonest steward has to be understood in the light of the Palestinian custom of agents acting on behalf of their masters and the usurious practices common to such agents. The dishonesty of the steward consisted in the squandering of his master's property (16:1) and not in any subsequent graft. The master commends the dishonest steward who has forgone his own usurious commission on the business transaction by having the debtors write new notes that reflected only the real amount owed the master (i.e., minus the steward's profit). The dishonest steward acts in this way in order to ingratiate himself with the debtors because he knows he is being dismissed from his position (16:3). The parable, then, teaches the prudent use of one's material goods in light of an imminent crisis.

16:6 **One hundred measures**: literally, "one hundred baths." A bath is a Hebrew unit of liquid measurement equivalent to eight or nine gallons.

16:7 **One hundred kors**: a **kor** is a Hebrew unit of dry measure for grain or wheat equivalent to ten or twelve bushels.

16:8b-13 Several originally independent sayings of Jesus are gathered here by Luke to form the concluding application of the parable of the dishonest steward.

16:8b-9 The first conclusion recommends the prudent use of one's wealth (in the light of the coming of the end of the age) after the manner of the children of this world, represented in the parable by the dishonest steward.

Application of the Parable

"For the children of this world are more prudent in dealing with their own generation than are the children of light. [9b]I tell you, make friends for yourselves with dishonest wealth,[*] so that when it fails, you will be welcomed into eternal dwellings. [10*c]The person who is trustworthy in very small matters is also trustworthy in great ones; and the person who is dishonest in very small matters is also dishonest in great ones. [11]If, therefore, you are not trustworthy with dishonest wealth, who will trust you with true wealth? [12]If you are not trustworthy with what belongs to another, who will give you what is yours? [13d]No servant can serve two masters.[*] He will either hate one and love the other, or be devoted to one and despise the other. You cannot serve God and mammon."

A Saying against the Pharisees

[14*]The Pharisees, who loved money,[*] heard all these things and sneered at him. [15e]And he said to them, "You justify yourselves in the sight of others, but God knows your hearts; for what is of human esteem is an abomination in the sight of God.

Sayings about the Law

[16f]"The law and the prophets lasted until John;[*] but from then on the kingdom of God is proclaimed, and everyone who enters does so with violence. [17g]It is easier for heaven and earth to pass away than for the smallest part of a letter of the law to become invalid.

Sayings about Divorce

[18h]"Everyone who divorces his wife and marries another commits adultery, and the one who marries a woman divorced from her husband commits adultery.

The Parable of the Rich Man and Lazarus

[19*]"There was a rich man[*] who dressed in purple garments and fine linen and dined sumptuously each day. [20]And lying at his door was a poor man named Lazarus, covered with sores, [21i]who would gladly have eaten his fill of the scraps that fell from the rich man's table. Dogs even used to come and lick his sores. [22]When the poor man died, he was carried away by angels to the bosom of Abraham. The rich man also died and was buried, [23]and from the netherworld,[*] where he was in torment, he raised his eyes and saw Abraham

b
12:33

c
19:17;
Mt 25:20-23

d
Mt 6:24

e
18:9-14

f
Mt 11:12-13

g
Mt 5:18

h
Mt 5:32; 19:9;
Mk 10:11-12;
1 Cor 7:10-11

i
Mt 15:27;
Mk 7:28

LUKE

16:9 Dishonest wealth: literally, "mammon of iniquity." Mammon is the Greek transliteration of a Hebrew or Aramaic word that is usually explained as meaning "that in which one trusts." The characterization of this wealth as **dishonest** expresses a tendency of wealth to lead one to dishonesty. **Eternal dwellings:** or, "eternal tents," i.e., heaven.

16:10-12 The second conclusion recommends constant fidelity to those in positions of responsibility.

16:13 The third conclusion is a general statement about the incompatibility of serving God and being a slave to riches. To be dependent upon wealth is opposed to the teachings of Jesus who counseled complete dependence on the Father as one of the characteristics of the Christian disciple (12:22-39). **God and mammon:** see the note on Luke 16:9. Mammon is used here as if it were itself a god.

16:14-18 The two parables about the use of riches in chap. 16 are separated by several isolated sayings of Jesus on the hypocrisy of the Pharisees (16:14-15), on the law (16:16-17), and on divorce (16:18).

16:14-15 The Pharisees are here presented as examples of those who are slaves to wealth (see 16:13) and, consequently, they are unable to serve God.

16:16 John the Baptist is presented in Luke's gospel as a transitional figure between the period of Israel, the time of promise, and the period of Jesus, the time of fulfillment. With John, the fulfillment of the Old Testament promises has begun.

16:19-31 The parable of the rich man and Lazarus again illustrates Luke's concern with Jesus' attitude toward the rich and the poor. The reversal of the fates of the rich man and Lazarus (16:22-23) illustrates the teachings of Jesus in Luke's "Sermon on the Plain" (6:20-21, 24-25).

16:19 The oldest Greek manuscript of Luke dating from ca. A.D. 175–225 records the name of the rich man as an abbreviated form of "Nineveh," but there is very little textual support in other manuscripts for this reading. "Dives" of popular tradition is the Latin Vulgate's translation for "rich man."

16:23 The netherworld: see the note on Luke 10:15.

j
6:24-25

k
Jn 5:46-47;
11:44-48

a
Mt 18:6-7

b
Mt 18:15

c
Mt 6:14;
18:21-22, 35;
Mk 11:25

d
Mt 17:20;
21:21;
Mk 11:23

 The "rich man" of the parable stands in contrast to the **reverence for all human beings** taught by the Second Vatican Council. According to *Gaudium et Spes* "everyone should look upon his or her neighbor (without any exception) as another self, bearing in mind especially their neighbor's life and the means needed for a dignified way of life (27)." Catholic social teaching recognizes that the way societies are organized often makes it hard to treat one's neighbor with dignity and respect. Consequently believers are challenged to change laws, policies, procedures, and social attitudes, to promote the dignity and respect of every human being.

far off and Lazarus at his side. [24]And he cried out, 'Father Abraham, have pity on me. Send Lazarus to dip the tip of his finger in water and cool my tongue, for I am suffering torment in these flames.' [25j]Abraham replied, 'My child, remember that you received what was good during your lifetime while Lazarus likewise received what was bad; but now he is comforted here, whereas you are tormented. [26]Moreover, between us and you a great chasm is established to prevent anyone from crossing who might wish to go from our side to yours or from your side to ours.' [27]He said, 'Then I beg you, father, send him to my father's house, [28]for I have five brothers, so that he may warn them, lest they too come to this place of torment.' [29]But Abraham replied, 'They have Moses and the prophets. Let them listen to them.' [30*]He said, 'Oh no, father Abraham, but if someone from the dead goes to them, they will repent.' [31k]Then Abraham said, 'If they will not listen to Moses and the prophets, neither will they be persuaded if someone should rise from the dead.'"

Temptations to Sin

17 [1a]He said to his disciples, "Things that cause sin will inevitably occur, but woe to the person through whom they occur. [2]It would be better for him if a millstone were put around his neck and he be thrown into the sea than for him to cause one of these little ones to sin. [3b]Be on your guard!* If your brother sins, rebuke him; and if he repents, forgive him. [4c]And if he wrongs you seven times in one day and returns to you seven times saying, 'I am sorry,' you should forgive him."

Saying of Faith

[5]And the apostles said to the Lord, "Increase our faith." [6d]The Lord replied, "If you have faith the size of a mustard seed, you would say to [this] mulberry tree, 'Be uprooted and planted in the sea,' and it would obey you.

Attitude of a Servant

[7*]"Who among you would say to your servant who has just come in from plowing or tending sheep in the field, 'Come here immediately and take your place at table'?

16:30-31 A foreshadowing in Luke's gospel of the rejection of the call to repentance even after Jesus' resurrection.

17:3 Be on your guard: the translation takes Luke 17:3a as the conclusion to the saying on scandal in Luke 17:1-2. It is not impossible that it should be taken as the beginning of the saying on forgiveness in Luke 17:3b-4.

17:7-10 These sayings of Jesus, peculiar to Luke, which continue his response to the apostles' request to increase their faith (17:5-6), remind them that Christian disciples can make no claim on God's graciousness; in fulfilling the exacting demands of discipleship, they are only doing their duty.

[8]Would he not rather say to him, 'Prepare something for me to eat. Put on your apron and wait on me while I eat and drink. You may eat and drink when I am finished'? [9]Is he grateful to that servant because he did what was commanded? [10]So should it be with you. When you have done all you have been commanded, say, 'We are unprofitable servants; we have done what we were obliged to do.'"

The Cleansing of Ten Lepers

[11]*[e]As he continued his journey to Jerusalem, he traveled through Samaria and Galilee.* [12]As he was entering a village, ten lepers met [him]. They stood at a distance from him [13][f]and raised their voice, saying, "Jesus, Master! Have pity on us!" [14][g]And when he saw them, he said, "Go show yourselves to the priests."* As they were going they were cleansed. [15]And one of them, realizing he had been healed, returned, glorifying God in a loud voice; [16]and he fell at the feet of Jesus and thanked him. He was a Samaritan. [17]Jesus said in reply, "Ten were cleansed, were they not? Where are the other nine? [18]Has none but this foreigner returned to give thanks to God?" [19][h]Then he said to him, "Stand up and go; your faith has saved you."

e
9:51-53;
13:22, 33;
18:31; 19:28;
Jn 4:4

f
18:38; Mt 9:27;
15:22

g
5:14;
Lv 14:2-32;
Mt 8:4;
Mk 1:44

h
7:50; 18:42

The Grateful Samaritan

The story of the Good Samaritan is so much a part of our culture that we talk about "being a Good Samaritan" and we pass "Good Samaritan laws" to protect those who help others in an emergency. Maybe we can begin to bring another Samaritan into our consciousness—the *grateful* Samaritan.

When Jesus was met by ten lepers as he was passing through Samaria, we are told the lepers stood at a distance and "raised their voice . . .'Jesus, Master! Have pity on us!'" Collectively they asked for attention and mercy. Collectively they were cleansed. However, only one of them, a Samaritan, returned to thank Jesus. Why?

First, the Samaritan leper realized he had been healed. Perhaps we can think about times when we

suddenly felt stronger after a bout of the flu, or one day realized that some sadness had lifted. Gratitude begins when we become aware of what is happening in our lives and how we are being changed.

Second, the leper knew that his healing was not his own doing. If we fail to recognize that God is the source of our healing, cleansing, new spirit, or success, then we may miss the gift of felt gratitude. Gratitude is the natural response to a God who makes us whole.

Finally, the leper knew that he was shunned not only because of a skin condition but because he was a Samaritan. When Jesus took notice of him, it changed his perception of himself as an outsider. Gratitude flowed from his sense of worth and dignity as a person, restored to him by Jesus' acceptance.

17:11-19 This incident recounting the thankfulness of the cleansed Samaritan leper is narrated only in Luke's gospel and provides an instance of Jesus holding up a non-Jew (17:18) as an example to his Jewish contemporaries (cf. 10:33 where a similar purpose is achieved in the story of the good Samaritan). Moreover, it is the faith in Jesus manifested by the foreigner that has brought

him salvation (17:19; cf. the similar relationship between faith and salvation in 7:50; 8:48, 50).

17:11 Through Samaria and Galilee: or, "between Samaria and Galilee."

17:14 See the note on Luke 5:14.

i
Jn 3:3

j
17:23;
Mt 24:23;
Mk 13:21

k
17:21;
Mt 24:23, 26;
Mk 13:21

l
Mt 24:27

m
9:22; 18:32-33;
Mt 16:21;
17:22-23;
20:18-19;
Mk 8:31; 9:31;
10:33-34

n
Gn 6–8;
Mt 24:37-39

o
Gn 18:20-21;
19:1-29

p
Gn 19:17, 26

q
Mt 24:17-18;
Mk 13:15-16

r
9:24; Mt 10:39;
16:25;
Mk 8:35;
Jn 12:25

s
Mt 24:40-41

t
Jb 39:30;
Mt 24:28

The Coming of the Kingdom of God

[20]*[i]Asked by the Pharisees when the kingdom of God would come, he said in reply, "The coming of the kingdom of God cannot be observed, [21]*[j]and no one will announce, 'Look, here it is,' or, 'There it is.' For behold, the kingdom of God is among you."

The Day of the Son of Man

[22]Then he said to his disciples, "The days will come when you will long to see one of the days of the Son of Man, but you will not see it. [23][k]There will be those who will say to you, 'Look, there he is,' [or] 'Look, here he is.' Do not go off, do not run in pursuit. [24][l]For just as lightning flashes and lights up the sky from one side to the other, so will the Son of Man be [in his day]. [25][m]But first he must suffer greatly and be rejected by this generation. [26][n]As it was in the days of Noah, so it will be in the days of the Son of Man; [27]they were eating and drinking, marrying and giving in marriage up to the day that Noah entered the ark, and the flood came and destroyed them all. [28][o]Similarly, as it was in the days of Lot: they were eating, drinking, buying, selling, planting, building; [29]on the day when Lot left Sodom, fire and brimstone rained from the sky to destroy them all. [30]So it will be on the day the Son of Man is revealed. [31][p]On that day, a person who is on the housetop and whose belongings are in the house must not go down to get them, and likewise a person in the field must not return to what was left behind.[q] [32]Remember the wife of Lot. [33][r]Whoever seeks to preserve his life will lose it, but whoever loses it will save it. [34]I tell you, on that night there will be two people in one bed; one will be taken, the other left. [35][s]And there will be two women grinding meal together; one will be taken, the other left." [[36]]* [37][t]They said to him in reply, "Where, Lord?" He said to them, "Where the body is, there also the vultures will gather."

In every age let this be your comfort: *the kingdom of God is among you.* The work of God goes on in your midst every day. There are always faithful disciples of the Word who have invited God's Spirit into their hearts. Make yourself aware of all the good that is going on in our world. We have only to lift the veil that prevents us from seeing the kingdom of God trying to break through.

Jesus' death as a convicted criminal included the forgiveness of those involved in his execution. In death, Jesus made apparent—one more time—the mission to embody the love and reconciliation of God. The resurrection of Jesus gave God's own verdict, namely, that life, love, and peace are stronger than the forces of death, hatred, and violence. In light of this, Jesus' gives the **gifts of peace, forgiveness, and reconciliation** to the disciples who then possess the task of continuing the work that Jesus began. See *The Challenge of Peace* 49–51.

17:20-37 To the question of the Pharisees about the time of the coming of God's kingdom, Jesus replies that the kingdom is **among you** (17:20-21). The emphasis has thus been shifted from an imminent observable coming of the kingdom to something that is already present in Jesus' preaching and healing ministry. Luke has also appended further traditional sayings of Jesus about the unpredictable suddenness of the day of the Son of Man, and assures his readers that in spite of the delay of that day (12:45), it will bring judgment unexpectedly on those who do not continue to be vigilant.

17:21 Among you: the Greek preposition translated as **among** can also be translated as "within." In the light of other statements in Luke's gospel about the presence of the kingdom (see 10:9, 11; 11:20) "among" is to be preferred.

17:36 The inclusion of Luke 17:36, "There will be two men in the field; one will be taken, the other left behind," in some Western manuscripts appears to be a scribal assimilation to Matthew 24:40.

LUKE

The Parable of the Persistent Widow

18 ¹*ᵃThen he told them a parable about the necessity for them to pray always without becoming weary. He said, ²"There was a judge in a certain town who neither feared God nor respected any human being. ³And a widow in that town used to come to him and say, 'Render a just decision for me against my adversary.' ⁴For a long time the judge was unwilling, but eventually he thought, 'While it is true that I neither fear God nor respect any human being, ⁵*ᵇbecause this widow keeps bothering me I shall deliver a just decision for her lest she finally come and strike me.'" ⁶The Lord said, "Pay attention to what the dishonest judge says. ⁷Will not God then secure the rights of his chosen ones who call out to him day and night? Will he be slow to answer them? ⁸I tell you, he will see to it that justice is done for them speedily. But when the Son of Man comes, will he find faith on earth?"

The Parable of the Pharisee and the Tax Collector

⁹ᶜHe then addressed this parable to those who were convinced of their own righteousness and despised everyone else. ¹⁰"Two people went up to the temple area to pray; one was a Pharisee and the other was a tax collector. ¹¹The Pharisee took up his position and spoke this prayer to himself, 'O God, I thank you that I am not like the rest of humanity—greedy, dishonest, adulterous—or even like this tax collector. ¹²ᵈI fast twice a week, and I pay tithes on my whole income.' ¹³ᵉBut the tax collector stood off at a distance and would not even raise his eyes to heaven but beat his breast and prayed, 'O God, be merciful to me a sinner.' ¹⁴ᶠI tell you, the latter went home justified, not the former; for everyone who exalts himself will be humbled, and the one who humbles himself will be exalted."

Saying on Children and the Kingdom

¹⁵*ᵍPeople were bringing even infants to him that he might touch them, and when the disciples saw this, they rebuked them.* ¹⁶Jesus, however, called the children to himself and said, "Let the children come to me and do not prevent them; for the kingdom of God belongs to such as these. ¹⁷ʰAmen, I say to you, whoever does not accept the kingdom of God like a child will not enter it."

The Rich Official

¹⁸ⁱAn official asked him this question, "Good teacher, what must I do to inherit eternal life?"ʲ ¹⁹Jesus answered him, "Why do you call me good? No one is good but

---

a
Rom 12:12;
Col 4:2;
1 Thes 5:17

b
11:8

c
16:5;
Mt 23:25-28

d
Mt 23:23

e
Ps 51:3

f
14:11;
Mt 23:12

g
Mt 19:13-15;
Mk 10:13-16

h
Mt 18:3

i
Mt 19:16-30;
Mk 10:17-31

j
10:25

18:1-14 The particularly Lucan material in the travel narrative concludes with two parables on prayer. The first (18:1-8) teaches the disciples the need of persistent prayer so that they not fall victims to apostasy (18:8). The second (18:9-14) condemns the self-righteous, critical attitude of the Pharisee and teaches that the fundamental attitude of the Christian disciple must be the recognition of sinfulness and complete dependence on God's graciousness. The second parable recalls the story of the pardoning of the sinful woman (7:36-50) where a similar contrast is presented between the critical attitude of the Pharisee Simon and the love shown by the pardoned sinner.

18:5 Strike me: the Greek verb translated as **strike** means "to strike under the eye" and suggests the extreme situation to which the persistence of the widow might lead. It may, however, be used here in the much weaker sense of "to wear one out."

18:15–19:27 Luke here includes much of the material about the journey to Jerusalem found in his Marcan source (10:1-52) and adds to it the story of Zacchaeus (19:1-10) from his own particular tradition and the parable of the gold coins (minas) (19:11-27) from Q, the source common to Luke and Matthew.

18:15-17 The sayings on children furnish a contrast to the attitude of the Pharisee in the preceding episode (18:9-14) and that of the wealthy official in the following one (18:18-23) who think that they can lay claim to God's favor by their own merit. The attitude of the disciple should be marked by the receptivity and trustful dependence characteristic of the child.

k
Ex 20:12-16;
Dt 5:16-20

l
12:33;
Sir 29:11;
Mt 6:20

m
Mk 14:36

n
14:26

o
24:25-27, 44;
Mt 20:17-19;
Mk 10:32-34;
Acts 3:18

p
9:22, 44

q
Mk 9:32

r
Mt 20:29-34;
Mk 10:46-52

s
17:13;
Mt 9:27; 15:22

t
Mk 10:36

u
7:50; 17:19

God alone. [20k]You know the commandments, 'You shall not commit adultery; you shall not kill; you shall not steal; you shall not bear false witness; honor your father and your mother.'" [21]And he replied, "All of these I have observed from my youth." [22*l]When Jesus heard this he said to him, "There is still one thing left for you: sell all that you have and distribute it to the poor, and you will have a treasure in heaven. Then come, follow me." [23]But when he heard this he became quite sad, for he was very rich.

On Riches and Renunciation

[24]Jesus looked at him [now sad] and said, "How hard it is for those who have wealth to enter the kingdom of God! [25]For it is easier for a camel to pass through the eye of a needle than for a rich person to enter the kingdom of God." [26]Those who heard this said, "Then who can be saved?" [27m]And he said, "What is impossible for human beings is possible for God." [28]Then Peter said, "We have given up our possessions and followed you." [29n]He said to them, "Amen, I say to you, there is no one who has given up house or wife or brothers or parents or children for the sake of the kingdom of God [30]who will not receive [back] an overabundant return in this present age and eternal life in the age to come."

The Third Prediction of the Passion

[31*o]Then he took the Twelve aside and said to them, "Behold, we are going up to Jerusalem and everything written by the prophets about the Son of Man will be fulfilled.[*] [32p]He will be handed over to the Gentiles and he will be mocked and insulted and spat upon; [33]and after they have scourged him they will kill him, but on the third day he will rise." [34q]But they understood nothing of this; the word remained hidden from them and they failed to comprehend what he said.

The Healing of the Blind Beggar

[35r]Now as he approached Jericho a blind man was sitting by the roadside begging, [36]and hearing a crowd going by, he inquired what was happening. [37]They told him, "Jesus of Nazareth is passing by." [38s]He shouted, "Jesus, Son of David,[*] have pity on me!" [39]The people walking in front rebuked him, telling him to be silent, but he kept calling out all the more, "Son of David, have pity on me!" [40]Then Jesus stopped and ordered that he be brought to him; and when he came near, Jesus asked him, [41t]"What do you want me to do for you?" He replied, "Lord, please let me see." [42u]Jesus told him, "Have sight; your faith has saved you." [43]He immediately received his sight and followed him, giving glory to God. When they saw this, all the people gave praise to God.

Modern Jericho

18:22 Detachment from material possessions results in the total dependence on God demanded of one who would inherit eternal life. **Sell all that you have**: the original saying (cf. Mk 10:21) has characteristically been made more demanding by Luke's addition of "all."

18:31-33 The details included in this third announcement of Jesus' suffering and death suggest that the literary formulation of the announcement has been directed by the knowledge of the historical passion and death of Jesus.

18:31 Everything written by the prophets . . . will be fulfilled: this is a Lucan addition to the words of Jesus found in the Marcan source (Mk 10:32-34). Luke understands the events of Jesus' last days in Jerusalem to be the fulfillment of Old Testament prophecy, but, as is usually the case in Luke-Acts, the author does not specify which Old Testament prophets he has in mind; cf. Luke 24:25, 27, 44; Acts 3:8; 13:27; 26:22-23.

18:38 Son of David: the blind beggar identifies Jesus with a title that is related to Jesus' role as Messiah (see the note on 2:11). Through this Son of David, salvation comes to the blind man. Note the connection between salvation and house of David mentioned earlier in Zechariah's canticle (1:69). See also the note on Matthew 9:27.

LUKE

Zacchaeus the Tax Collector

19 [1]*He came to Jericho and intended to pass through the town. [2]Now a man there named Zacchaeus, who was a chief tax collector and also a wealthy man, [3]was seeking to see who Jesus was; but he could not see him because of the crowd, for he was short in stature. [4]So he ran ahead and climbed a sycamore tree in order to see Jesus, who was about to pass that way. [5]When he reached the place, Jesus looked up and said to him, "Zacchaeus, come down quickly, for today I must stay at your house." [6]And he came down quickly and received him with joy. [7]*aWhen they all saw this, they began to grumble, saying, "He has gone to stay at the house of a sinner." [8]*bBut Zacchaeus stood there and said to the Lord, "Behold, half of my possessions, Lord, I shall give to the poor, and if I have extorted anything from anyone I shall repay it four times over." [9]*cAnd Jesus said to him, "Today salvation has come to this house because this man too is a descendant of Abraham. [10]*dFor the Son of Man has come to seek and to save what was lost."

The Parable of the Ten Gold Coins

[11]*eWhile they were listening to him speak, he proceeded to tell a parable because he was near Jerusalem and they thought that the kingdom of God would appear there

a
5:30; 15:2

b
Ex 21:37;
Nm 5:6-7;
2 Sm 12:6

c
13:16;
Mt 21:31

d
15:4-10;
Ez 34:16

e
Mt 25:14-30

LUKE

 Blind Beggar at Jericho, Turning Needs to Abundance
Showing great courage in the face of rebuke, a blind man courageously answered Jesus' question, "What do you want me to do for you?" What does this man teach us today?

- To follow our curiosity, to ask what is going on around us
- To boldly proclaim who Jesus is in our lives
- To ask for help when we need it
- To persist in the face of misunderstanding
- To state our needs to the Lord directly and honestly
- That faith can save us in the very routine of our lives
- That restored sight is available to anyone who asks, whether the blindness is physical or spiritual

Parallel stories are found in Matthew 20:29-34 (the healing of two blind men) and Mark 10:46-52 (where the blind man is identified as Bartimaeus). In each account, the persons healed follow Jesus. Luke's version is unique in that the healed blind man glorifies God, which in turn causes others to praise God. Once a beggar, the man is now a generous giver to the God who heals and saves. His need has led to a great abundance.

19:1-10 The story of the tax collector Zacchaeus is unique to this gospel. While a rich man (19:2), Zacchaeus provides a contrast to the rich man of Luke 18:18-23 who cannot detach himself from his material possessions to become a follower of Jesus. Zacchaeus, according to Luke, exemplifies the proper attitude toward wealth: he promises to give half of his possessions to the poor (19:8) and consequently is the recipient of salvation (19:9-10).

19:9 A descendant of Abraham: literally, "a son of Abraham." The tax collector Zacchaeus, whose repentance is attested by his determination to amend his former ways, shows himself to be a true descendant of Abraham, the true heir to the promises of God in the Old Testament. Underlying Luke's depiction of Zacchaeus as a descendant of Abraham, the father of the Jews (1:73; 16:22-31), is his recognition of the central place occupied by Israel in the plan of salvation.

19:10 This verse sums up for Luke his depiction of the role of Jesus as savior in this gospel.

19:11-27 In this parable Luke has combined two originally distinct parables: (1) a parable about the conduct of faithful and productive servants (19:13, 15b-26) and (2) a parable about a rejected king (19:12, 14-15a, 27). The story about the conduct of servants occurs in another form in Matthew 25:14-20. The story about the rejected king may have originated with a contemporary historical event. After the death of Herod the Great, his son Archelaus traveled

f
Mk 13:34

g
16:10

h
8:18; Mt 13:12;
Mk 4:25

i
Mt 21:1-11;
Mk 11:1-11;
Jn 12:12-19

j
Zec 14:4

k
Nm 19:2;
Dt 21:3;
1 Sm 6:7;
Zec 9:9

l
22:13

m
2 Kgs 9:13

immediately. ¹²*So he said, "A nobleman went off to a distant country to obtain the kingship for himself and then to return. ¹³He called ten of his servants and gave them ten gold coins* and told them, 'Engage in trade with these until I return.' ¹⁴His fellow citizens, however, despised him and sent a delegation after him to announce, 'We do not want this man to be our king.' ¹⁵But when he returned after obtaining the kingship, he had the servants called, to whom he had given the money, to learn what they had gained by trading. ¹⁶The first came forward and said, 'Sir, your gold coin has earned ten additional ones.' ¹⁷*He replied, 'Well done, good servant! You have been faithful in this very small matter; take charge of ten cities.' ¹⁸Then the second came and reported, 'Your gold coin, sir, has earned five more.' ¹⁹And to this servant too he said, 'You, take charge of five cities.' ²⁰Then the other servant came and said, 'Sir, here is your gold coin; I kept it stored away in a handkerchief, ²¹for I was afraid of you, because you are a demanding person; you take up what you did not lay down and you harvest what you did not plant.' ²²He said to him, 'With your own words I shall condemn you, you wicked servant. You knew I was a demanding person, taking up what I did not lay down and harvesting what I did not plant; ²³why did you not put my money in a bank? Then on my return I would have collected it with interest.' ²⁴And to those standing by he said, 'Take the gold coin from him and give it to the servant who has ten.' ²⁵But they said to him, 'Sir, he has ten gold coins.' ²⁶*'I tell you, to everyone who has, more will be given, but from the one who has not, even what he has will be taken away. ²⁷Now as for those enemies of mine who did not want me as their king, bring them here and slay them before me.'"

VI: The Teaching Ministry in Jerusalem

The Entry into Jerusalem

²⁸*ᶦAfter he had said this, he proceeded on his journey up to Jerusalem. ²⁹ʲAs he drew near to Bethphage and Bethany at the place called the Mount of Olives, he sent two of his disciples. ³⁰ᵏHe said, "Go into the village opposite you, and as you enter it you will find a colt tethered on which no one has ever sat. Untie it and bring it here. ³¹And if anyone should ask you, 'Why are you untying it?' you will answer, 'The Master has need of it.'" ³²ˡSo those who had been sent went off and found everything just as he had told them. ³³And as they were untying the colt, its owners said to them, "Why are you untying this colt?" ³⁴They answered, "The Master has need of it." ³⁵*So they brought it to Jesus, threw their cloaks over the colt, and helped Jesus to mount. ³⁶As he rode along, the people were spreading their cloaks on the road; ³⁷and now as he was approaching

---

to Rome to receive the title of king. A delegation of Jews appeared in Rome before Caesar Augustus to oppose the request of Archelaus. Although not given the title of king, Archelaus was made ruler over Judea and Samaria. As the story is used by Luke, however, it furnishes a correction to the expectation of the imminent end of the age and of the establishment of the kingdom in Jerusalem (19:11). Jesus is not on his way to Jerusalem to receive the kingly power; for that, he must go away and only after returning from the distant country (a reference to the parousia) will reward and judgment take place.

19:13 Ten gold coins: literally, "ten minas." A mina was a monetary unit that in ancient Greece was the equivalent of one hundred drachmas.

19:28–21:38 With the royal entry of Jesus into Jerusalem, a new section of Luke's gospel begins, the ministry of Jesus in Jerusalem before his death and resurrection. Luke suggests that this was a lengthy ministry in Jerusalem (19:47; 20:1; 21:37-38; 22:53) and it is characterized by Jesus' daily teaching in the temple (21:37-38). For the story of the entry of Jesus into Jerusalem, see also Matthew 21:1-11; Mark 11:1-10; John 12:12-19 and the notes there.

the slope of the Mount of Olives, the whole multitude of his disciples began to praise God aloud with joy for all the mighty deeds they had seen. [38]*n*They proclaimed:

> "Blessed is the king who comes in the name of the Lord.*
> Peace in heaven and glory in the highest."

[39]Some of the Pharisees in the crowd said to him, "Teacher, rebuke your disciples."* [40]He said in reply, "I tell you, if they keep silent, the stones will cry out!"

The Lament for Jerusalem

[41]*o*As he drew near, he saw the city and wept over it,*p* [42]*q*saying, "If this day you only knew what makes for peace—but now it is hidden from your eyes. [43]*r*For the days are coming upon you when your enemies will raise a palisade against you; they will encircle you and hem you in on all sides. [44]*s*They will smash you to the ground and your children within you, and they will not leave one stone upon another within you because you did not recognize the time of your visitation."

The Cleansing of the Temple

[45]*t*Then Jesus entered the temple area* and proceeded to drive out those who were selling things,*u* [46]*v*saying to them, "It is written, 'My house shall be a house of prayer, but you have made it a den of thieves.'" [47]*w*And every day he was teaching in the temple area. The chief priests, the scribes, and the leaders of the people, meanwhile, were seeking to put him to death,*x* [48]but they could find no way to accomplish their purpose because all the people were hanging on his words.

The Authority of Jesus Questioned

20 [1]*a*One day as he was teaching the people in the temple area and proclaiming the good news, the chief priests and scribes, together with the elders, approached him [2]*b*and said to him, "Tell us, by what authority are you doing these things? Or who is the one who gave you this authority?" [3]He said to them in reply, "I shall ask you a question. Tell me, [4]*c*was John's baptism of heavenly or of human origin?" [5]*d*They

---

n
2:14;
Ps 118:26

o
13:34-35

p
2 Kgs 8:11-12;
Jer 14:17; 15:5

q
8:10; Is 6:9-10;
Mt 13:14;
Mk 4:12;
Acts 28:26-27;
Rom 11:8, 10

r
Is 29:3

s
1:68; 21:6;
Ps 137:9;
Mt 24:2;
Mk 13:2

t
Mt 21:12-13;
Mk 11:15-17;
Jn 2:13-17

u
Mal 3:1 /
Hos 9:15

v
Is 56:7;
Jer 7:11

w
20:19; 22:2;
Mt 21:46;
Mk 11:18;
12:12; 14:1-2;
Jn 5:18; 7:30

x
21:37; 22:53;
Jn 18:20

a
Mt 21:23-27;
Mk 11:27-33

b
Acts 4:7

c
3:3, 16

d
Mt 21:32

LUKE

19:38 Blessed is the king who comes in the name of the Lord: only in Luke is Jesus explicitly given the title **king** when he enters Jerusalem in triumph. Luke has inserted this title into the words of Psalm 118:26 that heralded the arrival of the pilgrims coming to the holy city and to the temple. Jesus is thereby acclaimed as **king** (see 1:32) and as the one **who comes** (see Mal 3:1; Lk 7:19). **Peace in heaven . . .**: the acclamation of the disciples of Jesus in Luke echoes the announcement of the angels at the birth of Jesus (2:14). The peace Jesus brings is associated with the salvation to be accomplished here in Jerusalem.

19:39 Rebuke your disciples: this command, found only in Luke, was given so that the Roman authorities would not interpret the acclamation of Jesus as king as an uprising against them; cf. Luke 23:2-3.

19:41-44 The lament for Jerusalem is found only in Luke. By not accepting Jesus (the one who mediates peace), Jerusalem will not find peace but will become the victim of devastation.

19:43-44 Luke may be describing the actual disaster that befell Jerusalem in A.D. 70 when it was destroyed by the Romans during the First Revolt.

19:45-46 Immediately upon entering the holy city, Jesus in a display of his authority enters the temple (see Mal 3:1-3) and lays claim to it after cleansing it that it might become a proper place for his teaching ministry in Jerusalem (19:47; 20:1; 21:37; 22:53). See Matthew 21:12-17; Mark 11:15-19; John 2:13-17 and the notes there.

20:1-47 The Jerusalem religious leaders or their representatives, in an attempt to incriminate Jesus with the Romans and to discredit him with the people, pose a number of questions to him (about his authority, 20:2; about payment of taxes, Luke 20:22; about the resurrection, 20:28-33).

e
Mt 21:33-46;
Mk 12:1-12

f
Is 5:1-7

g
2 Chr 36:15-16

h
3:22

i
Ps 118:22;
Is 28:16

j
19:47-48; 22:2;
Mt 21:46;
Mk 11:18;
12:12; 14:1-2;
Jn 5:18; 7:30

k
Mt 22:15-22;
Mk 12:13-17

l
11:54

m
Jn 3:2

discussed this among themselves, and said, "If we say, 'Of heavenly origin,' he will say, 'Why did you not believe him?' [6]But if we say, 'Of human origin,' then all the people will stone us, for they are convinced that John was a prophet." [7]So they answered that they did not know from where it came. [8]Then Jesus said to them, "Neither shall I tell you by what authority I do these things."

The Parable of the Tenant Farmers

[9]*[e]Then he proceeded to tell the people this parable. "[A] man planted a vineyard, leased it to tenant farmers, and then went on a journey for a long time.[f] [10][g]At harvest time he sent a servant to the tenant farmers to receive some of the produce of the vineyard. But they beat the servant and sent him away empty-handed. [11]So he proceeded to send another servant, but him also they beat and insulted and sent away empty-handed. [12]Then he proceeded to send a third, but this one too they wounded and threw out. [13][h]The owner of the vineyard said, 'What shall I do? I shall send my beloved son; maybe they will respect him.' [14]But when the tenant farmers saw him they said to one another, 'This is the heir. Let us kill him that the inheritance may become ours.' [15]So they threw him out of the vineyard and killed him.* What will the owner of the vineyard do to them? [16]He will come and put those tenant farmers to death and turn over the vineyard to others." When the people heard this, they exclaimed, "Let it not be so!" [17][i]But he looked at them and asked, "What then does this scripture passage mean:

> 'The stone which the builders rejected
> has become the cornerstone'?

[18]Everyone who falls on that stone will be dashed to pieces; and it will crush anyone on whom it falls." [19][j]The scribes and chief priests sought to lay their hands on him at that very hour, but they feared the people, for they knew that he had addressed this parable to them.

Paying Taxes to the Emperor

[20]*[k]They watched him closely and sent agents pretending to be righteous who were to trap him in speech, in order to hand him over to the authority and power of the governor.[l] [21][m]They posed this question to him, "Teacher, we know that what you say and teach is correct, and you show no partiality, but teach the way of God in accordance with the truth. [22]Is it lawful for us to pay tribute to Caesar or not?"* [23]Recognizing their craftiness he said to them, [24]"Show me a denarius;*

Ancient coin bearing Caesar's image

20:9-19 This parable about an absentee landlord and a tenant farmers' revolt reflects the social and economic conditions of rural Palestine in the first century. The synoptic gospel writers use the parable to describe how the rejection of the landlord's son becomes the occasion for the vineyard to be taken away from those to whom it was entrusted (the religious leadership of Judaism that rejects the teaching and preaching of Jesus; 20:19).

20:15 They threw him out of the vineyard and killed him: cf. Mark 12:8. Luke has altered his Marcan source and reports that the murder of the son takes place outside the vineyard to reflect the tradition of Jesus' death outside the walls of the city of Jerusalem (see Heb 13:12).

20:20 The governor: i.e., Pontius Pilate, the Roman administrator responsible for the collection of taxes and maintenance of order in Palestine.

20:22 Through their question the agents of the Jerusalem religious leadership hope to force Jesus to take sides on one of the sensitive political issues of first-century Palestine. The issue of nonpayment of taxes to Rome becomes one of the focal points of the First Jewish Revolt (A.D. 66–70) that resulted in the Roman destruction of Jerusalem and the temple. See also the note on Matthew 22:15-22.

20:24 Denarius: a Roman silver coin (see the note on 7:41).

whose image and name does it bear?" They replied, "Caesar's." [25n]So he said to them, "Then repay to Caesar what belongs to Caesar and to God what belongs to God." [26]They were unable to trap him by something he might say before the people, and so amazed were they at his reply that they fell silent.

The Question about the Resurrection

[27o]Some Sadducees,[*] those who deny that there is a resurrection, came forward and put this question to him,[p] [28*q]saying, "Teacher, Moses wrote for us, 'If someone's brother dies leaving a wife but no child, his brother must take the wife and raise up descendants for his brother.' [29]Now there were seven brothers; the first married a woman but died childless. [30]Then the second [31]and the third married her, and likewise all the seven died childless. [32]Finally the woman also died. [33]Now at the resurrection whose wife will that woman be? For all seven had been married to her." [34]Jesus said to them, "The children of this age marry and remarry; [35]but those who are deemed worthy to attain to the coming age and to the resurrection of the dead neither marry nor are given in marriage. [36]They can no longer die, for they are like angels; and they are the children of God because they are the ones who will rise.[*] [37r]That the dead will rise even Moses made known in the passage about the bush, when he called 'Lord' the God of Abraham, the God of Isaac, and the God of Jacob; [38s]and he is not God of the dead, but of the living, for to him all are alive." [39]Some of the scribes said in reply, "Teacher, you have answered well." [40t]And they no longer dared to ask him anything.

The Question about David's Son

[41*u]Then he said to them, "How do they claim that the Messiah is the Son of David? [42v]For David himself in the Book of Psalms says:

'The Lord said to my lord,
"Sit at my right hand
[43]till I make your enemies your footstool."'

[44]Now if David calls him 'lord,' how can he be his son?"

Denunciation of the Scribes

[45w]Then, within the hearing of all the people, he said to [his] disciples, [46x]"Be on guard against the scribes, who like to go around in long robes and love greetings in marketplaces, seats of honor in synagogues, and places of honor at banquets. [47]They devour the houses of widows and, as a pretext, recite lengthy prayers. They will receive a very severe condemnation."

---

n
Rom 13:6-7

o
Mt 22:23-33;
Mk 12:18-27

p
Acts 23:8

q
Gn 38:8;
Dt 25:5

r
Ex 3:2, 6,
15-16

s
Rom 14:8-9

t
Mt 22:46;
Mk 12:34

u
Mt 22:41-45;
Mk 12:35-37

v
Ps 110:1

w
11:37-54;
Mt 23:1-36;
Mk 12:38-40

x
14:7-11

20:27 Sadducees: see the note on Matthew 3:7.

20:28-33 The Sadducees' question, based on the law of levirate marriage recorded in Deuteronomy 25:5-10, ridicules the idea of the resurrection. Jesus rejects their naive understanding of the resurrection (20:35-36) and then argues on behalf of the resurrection of the dead on the basis of the written law (20:37-38) that the Sadducees accept. See also the notes on Matthew 22:23-33.

20:36 Because they are the ones who will rise: literally, "being sons of the resurrection."

20:41-44 After successfully answering the three questions of his opponents, Jesus now asks them a question. Their inability to respond implies that they have forfeited their position and authority as the religious leaders of the people because they do not understand the scriptures. This series of controversies between the religious leadership of Jerusalem and Jesus reveals Jesus as the authoritative teacher whose words are to be listened to (see 9:35). See also the notes on Matthew 22:41-46.

a
Mk 12:41-44

b
Mt 24:1-2;
Mk 13:1-2

c
19:44

d
Mt 24:3-14;
Mk 13:3-13

e
17:23;
Mk 13:5, 6, 21;
1 Jn 2:18

f
2 Chr 15:6;
Is 19:2

g
12:11-12;
Mt 10:17-20;
Mk 13:9-11

h
Jn 16:2;
Acts 25:24

i
Acts 6:10

j
Mt 10:21-22

k
12:52-53

l
12:7;
1 Sm 14:45;
Mt 10:30;
Acts 27:34

m
8:15

The Poor Widow's Contribution

21 [1]*^aWhen he looked up he saw some wealthy people putting their offerings into the treasury [2]and he noticed a poor widow putting in two small coins. [3]He said, "I tell you truly, this poor widow put in more than all the rest; [4]for those others have all made offerings from their surplus wealth, but she, from her poverty, has offered her whole livelihood."

The Destruction of the Temple Foretold

[5]*^bWhile some people were speaking about how the temple was adorned with costly stones and votive offerings, he said, [6]^c"All that you see here—the days will come when there will not be left a stone upon another stone that will not be thrown down."

The Sign of the End

[7]^dThen they asked him, "Teacher, when will this happen? And what sign will there be when all these things are about to happen?" [8]^eHe answered, "See that you not be deceived, for many will come in my name, saying, 'I am he,' and 'The time has come.'* Do not follow them! [9]When you hear of wars and insurrections, do not be terrified; for such things must happen first, but it will not immediately be the end." [10]^fThen he said to them, "Nation will rise against nation, and kingdom against kingdom. [11]There will be powerful earthquakes, famines, and plagues from place to place; and awesome sights and mighty signs will come from the sky.

The Coming Persecution

[12]^g"Before all this happens,* however, they will seize and persecute you, they will hand you over to the synagogues and to prisons, and they will have you led before kings and governors because of my name.^h [13]It will lead to your giving testimony. [14]Remember, you are not to prepare your defense beforehand, [15]ⁱfor I myself shall give you a wisdom in speaking* that all your adversaries will be powerless to resist or refute. [16]^jYou will even be handed over by parents, brothers, relatives, and friends, and they will put some of you to death.^k [17]You will be hated by all because of my name, [18]^lbut not a hair on your head will be destroyed. [19]^mBy your perseverance you will secure your lives.

21:1-4 The widow is another example of the poor ones in this gospel whose detachment from material possessions and dependence on God leads to their blessedness (6:20). Her simple offering provides a striking contrast to the pride and pretentiousness of the scribes denounced in the preceding section (20:45-47). The story is taken from Mark 12:41-44.

21:5-36 Jesus' eschatological discourse in Luke is inspired by Mark 13, but Luke has made some significant alterations to the words of Jesus found there. Luke maintains, though in a modified form, the belief in the early expectation of the end of the age (see 21:27, 28, 31, 32, 36), but, by focusing attention throughout the gospel on the importance of the day-to-day following of Jesus and by reinterpreting the meaning of some of the signs of the end from Mark 13, he has come to terms with what seemed to the early Christian community to be a delay of the parousia. Mark, for example, described the desecration of the Jerusalem temple by the Romans (Mk 13:14) as the apocalyptic symbol (see Dn 9:27; 12:11) accompanying the end of the age and the coming of the Son of Man. Luke (21:20-24), however, removes the apocalyptic setting and separates the historical destruction of Jerusalem from the signs of the coming of the Son of Man by a period that he refers to as "the times of the Gentiles" (21:24). See also the notes on Matthew 24:1-36 and Mark 13:1-37.

21:8 The time has come: in Luke, the proclamation of the imminent end of the age has itself become a false teaching.

21:12 Before all this happens . . .: to Luke and his community, some of the signs of the end just described (21:10-11) still lie in the future. Now in dealing with the persecution of the disciples (21:12-19) and the destruction of Jerusalem (21:20-24) Luke is pointing to eschatological signs that have already been fulfilled.

21:15 A wisdom in speaking: literally, "a mouth and wisdom."

The Great Tribulation

[20]*[n]"When you see Jerusalem surrounded by armies, know that its desolation is at hand.[o] [21][p]Then those in Judea must flee to the mountains. Let those within the city escape from it, and let those in the countryside not enter the city, [22]for these days are the time of punishment when all the scriptures are fulfilled. [23][q]Woe to pregnant women and nursing mothers in those days, for a terrible calamity will come upon the earth and a wrathful judgment upon this people. [24][r]They will fall by the edge of the sword and be taken as captives to all the Gentiles; and Jerusalem will be trampled underfoot by the Gentiles until the times of the Gentiles* are fulfilled.

The Coming of the Son of Man

[25][s]"There will be signs in the sun, the moon, and the stars, and on earth nations will be in dismay, perplexed by the roaring of the sea and the waves.[t] [26][u]People will die of fright in anticipation of what is coming upon the world, for the powers of the heavens* will be shaken. [27][v]And then they will see the Son of Man coming in a cloud with power and great glory. [28][w]But when these signs begin to happen, stand erect and raise your heads because your redemption is at hand."

The Lesson of the Fig Tree

[29][x]He taught them a lesson. "Consider the fig tree and all the other trees. [30]When their buds burst open, you see for yourselves and know that summer is now near; [31]in the same way, when you see these things happening, know that the kingdom of God is near. [32][y]Amen, I say to you, this generation will not pass away until all these things have taken place. [33][z]Heaven and earth will pass away, but my words will not pass away.

View of Jerusalem from a Jewish cemetery on the Mount of Olives

Exhortation to be Vigilant

[34][a]"Beware that your hearts do not become drowsy from carousing and drunkenness and the anxieties of daily life, and that day catch you by surprise [35]like a trap. For that day will assault everyone who lives on the face of the earth. [36][b]Be vigilant at all times and pray that you have the strength to escape the tribulations that are imminent and to stand before the Son of Man."

Ministry in Jerusalem

[37][c]During the day, Jesus was teaching in the temple area, but at night he would leave and stay at the place called the Mount of Olives. [38]And all the people would get up early each morning to listen to him in the temple area.

n Mt 24:15-21; Mk 13:14-19
o 19:41-44
p 17:31
q 1 Cor 7:26
r Tb 14:5; Ps 79:1; Is 63:18; Jer 21:7; Rom 11:25; Rev 11:2
s Mt 24:29-31; Mk 13:24-27
t Wis 5:22; Is 13:10; Ez 32:7; Jl 2:10; 3:3-4; 4:15; Rev 6:12-14
u Hg 2:6, 21
v Dn 7:13-14; Mt 26:64; Rev 1:7
w 2:38
x Mt 24:32-35; Mk 13:28-31
y 9:27; Mt 16:28
z 16:17
a 12:45-46; Mt 24:48-50; 1 Thes 5:3, 6-7
b Mk 13:33
c 19:47; 22:39

21:20-24 The actual destruction of Jerusalem by Rome in A.D. 70 upon which Luke and his community look back provides the assurance that, just as Jesus' prediction of Jerusalem's destruction was fulfilled, so too will be his announcement of their final redemption (21:27-28).

21:24 The times of the Gentiles: a period of indeterminate length separating the destruction of Jerusalem from the cosmic signs accompanying the coming of the Son of Man.

21:26 The powers of the heavens: the heavenly bodies mentioned in Luke 21:25 and thought of as cosmic armies.

VII: The Passion Narrative

The Conspiracy against Jesus

22 [1][*a]Now the feast of Unleavened Bread, called the Passover,[*] was drawing near, [2b]and the chief priests and the scribes were seeking a way to put him to death, for they were afraid of the people. [3c]Then Satan entered into Judas,[*] the one surnamed Iscariot, who was counted among the Twelve,[d] [4]and he went to the chief priests and temple guards to discuss a plan for handing him over to them. [5]They were pleased and agreed to pay him money. [6]He accepted their offer and sought a favorable opportunity to hand him over to them in the absence of a crowd.

Preparations for the Passover

[7e]When the day of the Feast of Unleavened Bread arrived, the day for sacrificing the Passover lamb,[f] [8]he sent out Peter and John, instructing them, "Go and make preparations for us to eat the Passover." [9]They asked him, "Where do you want us to make the preparations?" [10]And he answered them, "When you go into the city, a man will meet you carrying a jar of water.[*] Follow him into the house that he enters [11]and say to the master of the house, 'The teacher says to you, "Where is the guest room where I may eat the Passover with my disciples?"' [12]He will show you a large upper room that is furnished. Make the preparations there." [13g]Then they went off and found everything exactly as he had told them, and there they prepared the Passover.

The Last Supper

[14h]When the hour came, he took his place at table with the apostles. [15]He said to them, "I have eagerly desired to eat this Passover[*] with you before I suffer, [16i]for, I tell you, I shall not eat it [again] until there is fulfillment in the kingdom of God." [17]Then he took a cup,[*] gave thanks, and said, "Take this and share it among yourselves; [18]for I tell you [that] from this time on I shall not drink of the fruit of the vine until the kingdom of God comes." [19*j]Then he took the bread, said the blessing, broke it, and gave it to them, saying, "This is my body, which will be given for you; do this in memory of me." [20k]And likewise the cup after they had eaten, saying, "This cup is the new covenant in my blood, which will be shed for you.

22:1–23:56a The passion narrative. Luke is still dependent upon Mark for the composition of the passion narrative but has incorporated much of his own special tradition into the narrative. Among the distinctive sections in Luke are: (1) the tradition of the institution of the Eucharist (22:15-20); (2) Jesus' farewell discourse (22:21-38); (3) the mistreatment and interrogation of Jesus (22:63-71); (4) Jesus before Herod and his second appearance before Pilate (23:6-16); (5) words addressed to the women followers on the way to the crucifixion (23:27-32); (6) words to the penitent thief (23:39-41); (7) the death of Jesus (23:46, 47b-49). Luke stresses the innocence of Jesus (23:4, 14-15, 22) who is the victim of the powers of evil (22:3, 31, 53) and who goes to his death in fulfillment of his Father's will (22:42, 46). Throughout the narrative Luke emphasizes the mercy, compassion, and healing power of Jesus (22:51; 23:43) who does not go to death lonely and deserted, but is accompanied by others who follow him on the way of the cross (23:26-31, 49).

22:1 Feast of Unleavened Bread, called the Passover: see the note on Mark 14:1.

22:3 Satan entered into Judas: see the note on Luke 4:13.

22:10 A man will meet you carrying a jar of water: see the note on Mark 14:13.

22:15 This Passover: Luke clearly identifies this last supper of Jesus with the apostles as a Passover meal that commemorated the deliverance of the Israelites from slavery in Egypt. Jesus reinterprets the significance of the Passover by setting it in the context of the kingdom of God (22:16). The "deliverance" associated with the Passover finds its new meaning in the blood that will be shed (22:20).

22:17 Because of a textual problem in Luke 22:19-20 some commentators interpret this cup as the eucharistic cup.

22:19c-20 Which will be given . . . do this in memory of me: these words are omitted in some important Western text manuscripts and a few Syriac manuscripts. Other ancient text

The Betrayal Foretold

[21][l]"And yet behold, the hand of the one who is to betray me is with me on the table;
[22]for the Son of Man indeed goes as it has been determined; but woe to that man by
whom he is betrayed." [23]And they began to debate among themselves who among them
would do such a deed.

The Role of the Disciples

[24*][m]Then an argument broke out among them about which of them should be regarded as the greatest. [25*][n]He said to them, "The kings of the Gentiles lord it over them
and those in authority over them are addressed as 'Benefactors'; [26][o]but among you it
shall not be so. Rather, let the greatest among you be as the youngest, and the leader
as the servant. [27]For who is greater: the one seated at table or the one who serves? Is
it not the one seated at table? I am among you as the one who serves. [28]It is you who
have stood by me in my trials; [29][p]and I confer a kingdom on you, just as my Father has
conferred one on me, [30][q]that you may eat and drink at my table in my kingdom; and
you will sit on thrones judging the twelve tribes of Israel.

Peter's Denial Foretold

[31*][r]"Simon, Simon, behold Satan has demanded to sift all of you like wheat,[*][s] [32]but
I have prayed that your own faith may not fail; and once you have turned back, you
must strengthen your brothers." [33][t]He said to him, "Lord, I am prepared to go to prison
and to die with you." [34][u]But he replied, "I tell you, Peter, before the cock crows this
day, you will deny three times that you know me."

Instructions for the Time of Crisis

[35][v]He said to them, "When I sent you forth without a money bag or a sack or sandals,
were you in need of anything?" "No, nothing," they replied. [36][w]He said to them,[*] "But
now one who has a money bag should take it, and likewise a sack, and one who does
not have a sword should sell his cloak and buy one. [37][x]For I tell you that this scripture
must be fulfilled in me, namely, 'He was counted among the wicked'; and indeed what
is written about me is coming to fulfillment." [38]Then they said, "Lord, look, there are
two swords here." But he replied, "It is enough!"[*]

l Ps 41:10; Mt 26:21-25; Mk 14:18-21; Jn 13:21-30

m 9:46; Mt 18:1; Mk 9:34

n Mt 20:25-27; Mk 10:42-44; Jn 13:3-16

o Mt 23:11; Mk 9:35

p 12:32

q Mt 19:28

r Mt 26:33-35; Mk 14:29-31; Jn 13:37-38

s Jb 1:6-12; Am 9:9

t 22:54

u 22:54-62

v 9:3; 10:4; Mt 10:9-10; Mk 6:7-9

w 22:49

x Is 53:12

types, including the oldest papyrus manuscript of Luke dating from the late second or early third century, contain the longer reading presented here. The Lucan account of the words of institution of the Eucharist bears a close resemblance to the words of institution in the Pauline tradition (see 1 Cor 11:23-26). See also the notes on Matthew 26:26-29; 26:27-28; and Mark 14:22-24.

22:24-38 The Gospel of Luke presents a brief farewell discourse of Jesus; compare the lengthy farewell discourses and prayer in John 13–17.

22:25 'Benefactors': this word occurs as a title of rulers in the Hellenistic world.

22:31-32 Jesus' prayer for Simon's faith and the commission to strengthen his brothers anticipates the post-resurrectional prominence of Peter in the first half of Acts, where he appears as the spokesman for the Christian community and the one who begins the mission to the Gentiles (Acts 10–11).

22:31 All of you: literally, "you." The translation reflects the meaning of the Greek text that uses a second person plural pronoun here.

22:36 In contrast to the ministry of the Twelve and of the seventy-two during the period of Jesus (9:3; 10:4), in the future period of the church the missionaries must be prepared for the opposition they will face in a world hostile to their preaching.

22:38 It is enough!: the farewell discourse ends abruptly with these words of Jesus spoken to the disciples when they take literally what was intended as figurative language about being prepared to face the world's hostility.

y
Mt 26:30,
36-46;
Mk 14:26,
32-42;
Jn 18:1-2

z
22:46

a
Heb 5:7-8

b
Mt 6:10

c
22:40

d
Mt 26:47-56;
Mk 14:43-50;
Jn 18:3-4

e
22:36

f
Jn 18:26

g
22:37

h
19:47; 21:37;
Jn 7:30; 8:20;
Col 1:13

i
Mt 26:57-58,
69-75;
Mk 14:53-54,
66-72;
Jn 18:12-18,
25-27

j
22:33

View of Jerusalem from the Garden of Gethsemane

What is commonly called **"the agony in the garden"** is actually portrayed thus only in Luke's version. Luke calls the "garden" the Mount of Olives and uses the Greek word *agonia* ("anguish, intense struggle") to evoke the kind of preparation that athletes undergo before an athletic contest. Luke emphasizes the intensity by describing sweat "like drops of blood," but these lines (22:43-44) are missing from the oldest and best manuscripts. Nonetheless, Christian theology and art have interpreted Jesus' time of prayer on the Mount of Olives as an ultimate test of his willingness to accept his Father's will.

The Agony in the Garden

[39]yThen going out he went, as was his custom, to the Mount of Olives, and the disciples followed him. [40]zWhen he arrived at the place he said to them, "Pray that you may not undergo the test." [41]aAfter withdrawing about a stone's throw from them and kneeling, he prayed, [42]bsaying, "Father, if you are willing, take this cup away from me; still, not my will but yours be done." [43]*[And to strengthen him an angel from heaven appeared to him. [44]He was in such agony and he prayed so fervently that his sweat became like drops of blood falling on the ground.] [45]When he rose from prayer and returned to his disciples, he found them sleeping from grief. [46]cHe said to them, "Why are you sleeping? Get up and pray that you may not undergo the test."

The Betrayal and Arrest of Jesus

[47]dWhile he was still speaking, a crowd approached and in front was one of the Twelve, a man named Judas. He went up to Jesus to kiss him. [48]Jesus said to him, "Judas, are you betraying the Son of Man with a kiss?" [49]eHis disciples realized what was about to happen, and they asked, "Lord, shall we strike with a sword?" [50]fAnd one of them struck the high priest's servant and cut off his right ear. [51]*But Jesus said in reply, "Stop, no more of this!" Then he touched the servant's ear and healed him. [52]gAnd Jesus said to the chief priests and temple guards and elders who had come for him, "Have you come out as against a robber, with swords and clubs? [53]hDay after day I was with you in the temple area, and you did not seize me; but this is your hour, the time for the power of darkness."

Peter's Denial of Jesus

[54]iAfter arresting him they led him away and took him into the house of the high priest; Peter was following at a distance.j [55]They lit a fire in the middle of the courtyard and sat around it, and Peter sat down with them. [56]When a maid saw him seated in the light, she looked intently at him and said, "This man too was with him." [57]But he denied

---

22:43-44 These verses, though very ancient, were probably not part of the original text of Luke. They are absent from the oldest papyrus manuscripts of Luke and from manuscripts of wide geographical distribution.

22:51 And healed him: only Luke recounts this healing of the injured servant.

it saying, "Woman, I do not know him." [58]A short while later someone else saw him and said, "You too are one of them"; but Peter answered, "My friend, I am not." [59]About an hour later, still another insisted, "Assuredly, this man too was with him, for he also is a Galilean." [60]But Peter said, "My friend, I do not know what you are talking about." Just as he was saying this, the cock crowed, [61][k]and the Lord turned and looked at Peter;[*] and Peter remembered the word of the Lord, how he had said to him, "Before the cock crows today, you will deny me three times." [62]He went out and began to weep bitterly. [63][l]The men who held Jesus in custody were ridiculing and beating him. [64]They blindfolded him and questioned him, saying, "Prophesy! Who is it that struck you?" [65]And they reviled him in saying many other things against him.

Jesus before the Sanhedrin

[66][*][m]When day came the council of elders of the people met, both chief priests and scribes, and they brought him before their Sanhedrin.[*][n] [67][o]They said, "If you are the Messiah, tell us," but he replied to them, "If I tell you, you will not believe, [68]and if I question, you will not respond. [69][p]But from this time on the Son of Man will be seated at the right hand of the power of God." [70]They all asked, "Are you then the Son of God?" He replied to them, "You say that I am." [71]Then they said, "What further need have we for testimony? We have heard it from his own mouth."

Jesus before Pilate

23 [1][*][a]Then the whole assembly of them arose and brought him before Pilate. [2][b]They brought charges against him, saying, "We found this man misleading our people; he opposes the payment of taxes to Caesar and maintains that he is the Messiah, a king." [3][c]Pilate asked him, "Are you the king of the Jews?" He said to him in reply, "You say so." [4][d]Pilate then addressed the chief priests and the crowds, "I find this man not guilty." [5]But they were adamant and said, "He is inciting the people with his teaching throughout all Judea, from Galilee where he began even to here."

Jesus before Herod

[6][*]On hearing this Pilate asked if the man was a Galilean; [7][e]and upon learning that he was under Herod's jurisdiction, he sent him to Herod who was in Jerusalem at that time. [8][f]Herod was very glad to see Jesus; he had been wanting to see him for a long time, for he had heard about him and had been hoping to see him perform some sign.

k 22:34
l Mt 26:67-68; Mk 14:65
m Mt 26:59-66; Mk 14:55-64
n Mt 27:1; Mk 15:1
o Jn 3:12; 8:45; 10:24
p Ps 110:1; Dn 7:13-14; Acts 7:56
a Mt 27:1-2, 11-14; Mk 15:1-5; Jn 18:28-38
b 20:22-25; Acts 17:7; 24:5
c 22:70; 1 Tm 6:13
d 23:14, 22, 41; Mt 27:24; Jn 19:4, 6; Acts 13:28
e 3:1; 9:7
f 9:9; Acts 4:27-28

22:61 Only Luke recounts that **the Lord turned and looked at Peter.** This look of Jesus leads to Peter's weeping bitterly over his denial (22:62).

22:66-71 Luke recounts one daytime trial of Jesus (22:66-71) and hints at some type of preliminary nighttime investigation (22:54-65). Mark (and Matthew who follows Mark) has transferred incidents of this day into the nighttime interrogation with the result that there appear to be two Sanhedrin trials of Jesus in Mark (and Matthew); see the note on Mark 14:53.

22:66 Sanhedrin: the word is a Hebraized form of a Greek word meaning a "council," and refers to the elders, chief priests, and scribes who met under the high priest's leadership to decide religious and legal questions that did not pertain to Rome's interests.

Jewish sources are not clear on the competence of the Sanhedrin to sentence and to execute during this period.

23:1-5, 13-25 Twice Jesus is brought before Pilate in Luke's account, and each time Pilate explicitly declares Jesus innocent of any wrongdoing (23:4, 14, 22). This stress on the innocence of Jesus before the Roman authorities is also characteristic of John's gospel (Jn 18:38; 19:4, 6). Luke presents the Jerusalem Jewish leaders as the ones who force the hand of the Roman authorities (23:1-2, 5, 10, 13, 18, 21, 23-25).

23:6-12 The appearance of Jesus before Herod is found only in this gospel in Luke (9:7-9; 13:31-33) and has been presented as someone who has been curious about Jesus for a long time. His curiosity goes unrewarded. It

g
Mk 15:5

h
Mt 27:12;
Mk 15:3

i
Mt 27:28-30;
Mk 15:17-19;
Jn 19:2-3

j
23:4, 22, 41

k
23:22;
Jn 19:12-14

l
Mt 27:20-26;
Mk 15:6-7,
11-15;
Jn 18:38b-40;
19:14-16;
Acts 3:13-14

m
Mt 27:32, 38;
Mk 15:21, 27;
Jn 19:17

n
19:41-44;
21:23-24

o
Hos 10:8;
Rev 6:16

p
Mt 27:33-44;
Mk 15:22-32;
Jn 19:17-24

q
22:37; Is 53:12

r
Nm 15:27-31;
Ps 22:19;
Mt 5:44;
Acts 7:60

[9g]He questioned him at length, but he gave him no answer. [10h]The chief priests and scribes, meanwhile, stood by accusing him harshly. [11i][Even] Herod and his soldiers treated him contemptuously and mocked him, and after clothing him in resplendent garb, he sent him back to Pilate. [12]Herod and Pilate became friends that very day, even though they had been enemies formerly. [13]Pilate then summoned the chief priests, the rulers, and the people [14j]and said to them, "You brought this man to me and accused him of inciting the people to revolt. I have conducted my investigation in your presence and have not found this man guilty of the charges you have brought against him, [15]nor did Herod, for he sent him back to us. So no capital crime has been committed by him. [16k]Therefore I shall have him flogged and then release him." [[17]]*

The Sentence of Death

[18l]But all together they shouted out, "Away with this man! Release Barabbas to us." [19](Now Barabbas had been imprisoned for a rebellion that had taken place in the city and for murder.) [20]Again Pilate addressed them, still wishing to release Jesus, [21]but they continued their shouting, "Crucify him! Crucify him!" [22]Pilate addressed them a third time, "What evil has this man done? I found him guilty of no capital crime. Therefore I shall have him flogged and then release him." [23]With loud shouts, however, they persisted in calling for his crucifixion, and their voices prevailed. [24]The verdict of Pilate was that their demand should be granted. [25]So he released the man who had been imprisoned for rebellion and murder, for whom they asked, and he handed Jesus over to them to deal with as they wished.

The Way of the Cross

[26*m]As they led him away they took hold of a certain Simon, a Cyrenian, who was coming in from the country; and after laying the cross on him, they made him carry it behind Jesus. [27]A large crowd of people followed Jesus, including many women who mourned and lamented him. [28n]Jesus turned to them and said, "Daughters of Jerusalem, do not weep for me; weep instead for yourselves and for your children, [29]for indeed, the days are coming when people will say, 'Blessed are the barren, the wombs that never bore and the breasts that never nursed.' [30o]At that time people will say to the mountains, 'Fall upon us!' and to the hills, 'Cover us!' [31]for if these things are done when the wood is green what will happen when it is dry?" [32]Now two others, both criminals, were led away with him to be executed.

The Crucifixion

[33p]When they came to the place called the Skull, they crucified him and the criminals there, one on his right, the other on his left.[q] [34r][Then Jesus said, "Father, forgive them,

---

is faith in Jesus, not curiosity, that is rewarded (7:50; 8:48, 50; 17:19).

23:17 This verse, "He was obliged to release one prisoner for them at the festival," is not part of the original text of Luke. It is an explanatory gloss from Mark 15:6 (also Mt 27:15) and is not found in many early and important Greek manuscripts. On its historical background, see the notes on Matthew 27:15-26.

23:26-32 An important Lucan theme throughout the gospel has been the need for the Christian disciple to follow in the footsteps

of Jesus. Here this theme comes to the fore with the story of Simon of Cyrene who takes up the cross and follows Jesus (see 9:23; 14:27) and with the large crowd who likewise follow Jesus on the way of the cross. See also the note on Mark 15:21.

23:34 [Then Jesus said, "Father, forgive them, they know not what they do."]: this portion of Luke 23:34 does not occur in the oldest papyrus manuscript of Luke and in other early Greek manuscripts and ancient versions of wide geographical distribution.

they know not what they do."]* They divided his garments by casting lots. ³⁵ˢThe people stood by and watched; the rulers, meanwhile, sneered at him and said, "He saved others, let him save himself if he is the chosen one, the Messiah of God."ᵗ ³⁶ᵘEven the soldiers jeered at him. As they approached to offer him wine ³⁷they called out, "If you are King of the Jews, save yourself." ³⁸Above him there was an inscription that read, "This is the King of the Jews." ³⁹*Now one of the criminals hanging there reviled Jesus, saying, "Are you not the Messiah? Save yourself and us." ⁴⁰The other, however, rebuking him, said in reply, "Have you no fear of God, for you are subject to the same condemnation? ⁴¹ᵛAnd indeed, we have been condemned justly, for the sentence we received corresponds to our crimes, but this man has done nothing criminal." ⁴²ʷThen he said, "Jesus, remember me when you come into your kingdom." ⁴³ˣHe replied to him, "Amen, I say to you, today you will be with me in Paradise."

Paradise is a Persian loanword ("park" or "garden") that here does not mean the Garden of Eden (Gn 2:8) but is a synonym for heaven.

The Death of Jesus

⁴⁴*ʸIt was now about noon and darkness came over the whole land until three in the afternoonᶻ ⁴⁵ᵃbecause of an eclipse of the sun. Then the veil of the temple was torn down the middle. ⁴⁶ᵇJesus cried out in a loud voice, "Father, into your hands I commend my spirit"; and when he had said this he breathed his last. ⁴⁷The centurion who witnessed what had happened glorified God and said, "This man was innocent* beyond doubt." ⁴⁸ᶜWhen all the people who had gathered for this spectacle saw what had happened, they returned home beating their breasts; ⁴⁹ᵈbut all his acquaintances stood at a distance, including the women who had followed him from Galilee and saw these events.

The Burial of Jesus

⁵⁰ᵉNow there was a virtuous and righteous man named Joseph who, though he was a member of the council, ⁵¹ᶠhad not consented to their plan of action. He came from the Jewish town of Arimathea and was awaiting the kingdom of God. ⁵²He went to Pilate and asked for the body of Jesus. ⁵³ᵍAfter he had taken the body down, he wrapped it in a linen cloth and laid him in a rock-hewn tomb in which no one had yet been buried. ⁵⁴It was the day of preparation, and the sabbath was about to begin. ⁵⁵ʰThe women who had come from Galilee with him followed behind, and when they had seen the tomb and the way in which his body was laid in it, ⁵⁶ⁱthey returned and prepared spices and perfumed oils. Then they rested on the sabbath according to the commandment.

23:39–43 This episode is recounted only in this gospel. The penitent sinner receives salvation through the crucified Jesus. Jesus' words to the penitent thief reveal Luke's understanding that the destiny of the Christian is "to be with Jesus."

23:44 Noon . . . three in the afternoon: literally, the sixth and ninth hours. See the note on Mark 15:25.

23:47 This man was innocent: or, "This man was righteous."

s
Ps 22:8-9

t
4:23

u
Ps 69:22;
Mt 27:48;
Mk 15:36

v
23:4, 14, 22

w
9:27;
23:2, 3, 38

x
2 Cor 12:3;
Rev 2:7

y
Mt 27:45-56;
Mk 15:33-41;
Jn 19:25-30

z
Am 8:9

a
Ex 26:31-33;
36:35

b
Ps 31:6;
Acts 7:59

c
18:13;
Zec 12:10

d
8:1-3;
23:55-56;
24:10;
Ps 38:12

e
Mt 27:57-61;
Mk 15:42-47;
Jn 19:38-42;
Acts 13:29

f
2:25, 38

g
19:30;
Acts 13:29

h
8:2; 23:49;
24:10

i
Ex 12:16;
20:10; Dt 5:14

LUKE

a
Mt 28:1-8;
Mk 16:1-8;
Jn 20:1-17

b
2 Mc 3:26;
Acts 1:10

c
Acts 2:9

d
9:22, 44;
17:25;
18:32-33;
Mt 16:21;
17:22-23;
Mk 9:31;
Acts 17:3

e
Jn 2:22

f
Mk 16:10-11;
Jn 20:18

g
8:2-3; Mk 16:9

h
Jn 20:3-7

i
Mk 16:12-13

j
Jn 20:14; 21:4

k
Mt 2:23; 21:11;
Acts 2:22

l
1:54, 68; 2:38

VIII: The Resurrection Narrative

The Resurrection of Jesus

24 [1]*[a]But at daybreak on the first day of the week they took the spices they had prepared and went to the tomb. [2]They found the stone rolled away from the tomb; [3]but when they entered, they did not find the body of the Lord Jesus. [4][b]While they were puzzling over this, behold, two men in dazzling garments appeared to them. [5][c]They were terrified and bowed their faces to the ground. They said to them, "Why do you seek the living one among the dead? [6]He is not here, but he has been raised.* Remember what he said to you while he was still in Galilee, [7][d]that the Son of Man must be handed over to sinners and be crucified, and rise on the third day." [8][e]And they remembered his words. [9]*[f]Then they returned from the tomb and announced all these things to the eleven and to all the others. [10][g]The women were Mary Magdalene, Joanna, and Mary the mother of James; the others who accompanied them also told this to the apostles, [11]but their story seemed like nonsense and they did not believe them. [12]*[h]But Peter got up and ran to the tomb, bent down, and saw the burial cloths alone; then he went home amazed at what had happened.

The Appearance on the Road to Emmaus

[13]*[i]Now that very day two of them were going to a village seven miles from Jerusalem called Emmaus,* [14]and they were conversing about all the things that had occurred. [15]And it happened that while they were conversing and debating, Jesus himself drew near and walked with them, [16]*[j]but their eyes were prevented from recognizing him. [17]He asked them, "What are you discussing as you walk along?" They stopped, looking downcast. [18]One of them, named Cleopas, said to him in reply, "Are you the only visitor to Jerusalem who does not know of the things that have taken place there in these days?" [19][k]And he replied to them, "What sort of things?" They said to him, "The things that happened to Jesus the Nazarene, who was a prophet mighty in deed and word before God and all the people, [20]how our chief priests and rulers both handed him over to a sentence of death and crucified him. [21][l]But we were hoping that he would

---

24:1-53 The resurrection narrative in Luke consists of five sections: (1) the women at the empty tomb (23:56b–24:12); (2) the appearance to the two disciples on the way to Emmaus (24:13-35); (3) the appearance to the disciples in Jerusalem (24:36-43); (4) Jesus' final instructions (24:44-49); (5) the ascension (24:50-53). In Luke, all the resurrection appearances take place in and around Jerusalem; moreover, they are all recounted as having taken place on Easter Sunday. A consistent theme throughout the narrative is that the suffering, death, and resurrection of Jesus were accomplished in fulfillment of Old Testament promises and of Jewish hopes (24:19a, 21, 26-27, 44, 46). In his second volume, Acts, Luke will argue that Christianity is the fulfillment of the hopes of Pharisaic Judaism and its logical development (see Acts 24:10-21).

24:6 He is not here, but he has been raised: this part of the verse is omitted in important representatives of the Western text tradition, but its presence in other text types and the slight difference in wording from Matthew 28:6 and Mark 16:6 argue for its retention.

24:9 The women in this gospel do not flee from the tomb and tell no one, as in Mark 16:8, but return and tell the disciples about their experience. The initial reaction to the testimony of the women is disbelief (24:11).

24:12 This verse is missing from the Western textual tradition but is found in the best and oldest manuscripts of other text types.

24:13-35 This episode focuses on the interpretation of scripture by the risen Jesus and the recognition of him in the breaking of the bread. The references to the quotations of scripture and explanation of it (24:25-27), the kerygmatic proclamation (24:34), and the liturgical gesture (24:30) suggest that the episode is primarily catechetical and liturgical rather than apologetic.

24:13 Seven miles: literally, "sixty stades." A stade was 607 feet. Some manuscripts read "160 stades" or more than eighteen miles. The exact location of Emmaus is disputed.

24:16 A consistent feature of the resurrection stories is that the risen Jesus was different and initially unrecognizable (24:37; Mk 16:12; Jn 20:14; 21:4).

Lessons while Traveling

In one of the most beloved passages of Scripture we hear of disciples of Jesus who gradually shed their disappointment and fear to embrace the risen Lord. What happened to them as they traveled away from Jerusalem, no doubt intending to escape their dashed dreams and any possible dangers as followers of an executed criminal?

We know they talked. They *told stories* to each other, and to someone they believed to be a stranger traveling their direction. Their stories were a way of trying to make sense of what had happened, of trying to recover the meaning they felt in the presence of Jesus.

We know they attempted to *put the facts in order.* They retraced Jesus' ministry, his betrayal and gruesome death, and finally the report that Jesus' body was missing from the grave. Maybe they were searching for something they had missed or maybe they just wanted the stranger to know the facts before making a judgment.

We know they *listened to their fellow traveler.* They didn't argue with him when he expressed dismay and called them foolish, but in their listening they began to gain clarity.

We know they *offered hospitality.* Hospitality was a cardinal virtue in the ancient world and still is throughout the Middle East. Their generosity was a spontaneous and natural response to the relationship that had grown between them as they traveled.

We know they *saw with new eyes,* and in the breaking of the bread recognized Jesus in their midst.

Who knows what they learned as they traveled back to Jerusalem with lighter feet and the urgent message, "The Lord has truly been raised!"

LUKE

---

be the one to redeem Israel; and besides all this, it is now the third day since this took place. [22][m]Some women from our group, however, have astounded us: they were at the tomb early in the morning [23]and did not find his body; they came back and reported that they had indeed seen a vision of angels who announced that he was alive. [24][n]Then some of those with us went to the tomb and found things just as the women had described, but him they did not see." [25][o]And he said to them, "Oh, how foolish you are! How slow of heart to believe all that the prophets spoke! [26]Was it not necessary that the Messiah should suffer[*] these things and enter into his glory?" [27][p]Then beginning with Moses and all the prophets, he interpreted to them what referred to him in all the scriptures. [28]As they approached the village to which they were going, he gave the impression that he was going on farther. [29]But they urged him, "Stay with us, for it is nearly evening and the day is almost over." So he went in to stay with them. [30]And it happened that, while he was with them at table, he took bread, said the blessing, broke it, and gave it to them. [31]With that their eyes were opened and they recognized him, but he vanished from their sight. [32]Then they said to each other, "Were not our hearts burning [within us] while he spoke to us on the way and opened the scriptures to us?" [33]So they set out at once and returned to Jerusalem where they found gathered together the eleven and those with them [34][q]who were saying, "The Lord has truly been raised and has appeared to Simon!" [35]Then the two recounted what had taken place on the way and how he was made known to them in the breaking of the bread.

m
24:1-11;
Mt 28:1-8;
Mk 16:1-8

n
Jn 20:3-10

o
9:22; 18:31;
24:44;
Acts 3:24; 17:3

p
24:44;
Dt 18:25;
Ps 22:1-18;
Is 53;
1 Pt 1:10-11

q
1 Cor 15:4-5

24:26 That the Messiah should suffer . . .: Luke is the only New Testament writer to speak explicitly of a suffering Messiah (24:26, 46; Acts 3:18; 17:3; 26:23). The idea of a suffering Messiah is not found in the Old Testament or in other Jewish literature prior to the New Testament period, although the idea is hinted at in Mark 8:31-33. See the notes on Matthew 26:63 and 26:67-68.

r
Mk 16:14-19;
Jn 20:19-20

s
1 Cor 15:5

t
Mt 14:26

u
Jn 21:5, 9-10,
13

v
Acts 10:41

w
18:31; 24:27;
Mt 16:21;
Jn 5:39, 46

x
Jn 20:9

y
9:22; Is 53;
Hos 6:2

z
Mt 3:2;
28:19-20;
Mk 16:15-16;
Acts 10:41

a
Acts 1:8

b
Jn 14:26;
Acts 1:4; 2:3-4

c
Mk 16:19;
Acts 1:9-11

d
Acts 1:12

LUKE

The Appearance to the Disciples in Jerusalem

36*[r]While they were still speaking about this, he stood in their midst and said to them, "Peace be with you."[s] 37[t]But they were startled and terrified and thought that they were seeing a ghost. 38Then he said to them, "Why are you troubled? And why do questions arise in your hearts? 39*Look at my hands and my feet, that it is I myself. Touch me and see, because a ghost does not have flesh and bones as you can see I have." 40[u]And as he said this, he showed them his hands and his feet. 41While they were still incredulous for joy and were amazed, he asked them, "Have you anything here to eat?" 42They gave him a piece of baked fish; 43[v]he took it and ate it in front of them. 44[w]He said to them, "These are my words that I spoke to you while I was still with you, that everything written about me in the law of Moses and in the prophets and psalms must be fulfilled." 45[x]Then he opened their minds to understand the scriptures. 46*[y]And he said to them, "Thus it is written that the Messiah would suffer and rise from the dead on the third day 47[z]and that repentance, for the forgiveness of sins, would be preached in his name to all the nations, beginning from Jerusalem. 48[a]You are witnesses of these things. 49[b]And [behold] I am sending the promise of my Father* upon you; but stay in the city until you are clothed with power from on high."

The Ascension

50*[c]Then he led them [out] as far as Bethany, raised his hands, and blessed them. 51As he blessed them he parted from them and was taken up to heaven. 52[d]They did him homage and then returned to Jerusalem with great joy, 53and they were continually in the temple praising God.*

Luke's story of the **ascension** appears twice, here at the end of the gospel, and again at the beginning of Acts (1:6-12), although it is meant to be seen as one event. It provides continuity between the story of Jesus in the gospel and the story of the church in Acts. The ascension is Jesus' return to heaven in glory; it completes his "exodus" to the Father (Lk 9:31). He then sends the Holy Spirit, "the promise of the Father" (Lk 24:49; Acts 1:4), to accompany the church on its missionary journey.

24:36-43, 44-49 The Gospel of Luke, like each of the other gospels (Mt 28:16-20; Mk 16:14-15; Jn 20:19-23), focuses on an important appearance of Jesus to the Twelve in which they are commissioned for their future ministry. As in Luke 24:6, 12, so in 24:36, 40 there are omissions in the Western text.

24:39-42 The apologetic purpose of this story is evident in the concern with the physical details and the report that Jesus ate food.

24:46 See the note on Luke 24:26.

24:49 The promise of my Father: i.e., the gift of the holy Spirit.

24:50-53 Luke brings his story about the time of Jesus to a close with the report of the ascension. He will also begin the story of the time of the church with a recounting of the ascension. In the gospel, Luke recounts the ascension of Jesus on Easter Sunday night, thereby closely associating it with the resurrection. In Acts 1:3, 9-11 and 13:31 he historicizes the ascension by speaking of a forty-day period between the resurrection and the ascension. The Western text omits some phrases in Luke 24:51, 52 perhaps to avoid any chronological conflict with Acts 1 about the time of the ascension.

24:53 The Gospel of Luke ends as it began (1:9), in the Jerusalem temple.

The Gospel according to John is quite different in character from the three synoptic gospels. It is highly literary and symbolic. It does not follow the same order or reproduce the same stories as the synoptic gospels. To a much greater degree, it is the product of a developed theological reflection and grows out of a different circle and tradition. It was probably written in the 90s of the first century.

The Gospel of John begins with a magnificent prologue, which states many of the major themes and motifs of the gospel, much as an overture does for a musical work. The prologue proclaims Jesus as the preexistent and incarnate Word of God who has revealed the Father to us. The rest of the first chapter forms the introduction to the gospel proper and consists of the Baptist's testimony about Jesus (there is no baptism of Jesus in this gospel—John simply points him out as the Lamb of God), followed by stories of the call of the first disciples, in which various titles predicated of Jesus in the early church are presented.

The gospel narrative contains a series of "signs"—the gospel's word for the wondrous deeds of Jesus. The author is primarily interested in the significance of these deeds, and so interprets them for the reader by various reflections, narratives, and discourses. The first sign is the transformation

SUMMARY

John tells the life story of Jesus, the incarnate Word of God, from his heavenly existence to his descent into the world and his public ministry of "signs" that led to his passion, death, resurrection, and ultimate ascent to the "glory" of his heavenly Father.

Author: Unknown, but ancient tradition calls him "John" and identifies him with John, son of Zebedee, the "beloved disciple."

Date: Between A.D. 90–100.

Content: Descent of the Word made flesh; Jesus' multiple signs; wedding at Cana; various encounters between Jesus and individuals; multiple discourses by Jesus ("I AM" discourses, bread of life, vine and branches, etc.); passion, death, and resurrection of Jesus; resurrection appearances in Jerusalem and by the Sea of Galilee.

Main Characters: Jesus of Nazareth, John the Baptist, Nicodemus, Simon Peter and the "beloved disciple," Lazarus, Mary and Martha (siblings), the Samaritan woman, the man born blind, Mary Magdalene, Judas Iscariot, Caiaphas the High Priest, Pontius Pilate.

of water into wine at Cana (2:1-11); this represents the replacement of the Jewish ceremonial washings and symbolizes the entire creative and transforming work of Jesus. The second sign, the cure of the royal official's son (4:46-54) simply by the word of Jesus at a distance, signifies the power of Jesus' life-giving word. The same theme is further developed by other signs, probably for a total of seven. The third sign, the cure of the paralytic at the pool with five porticoes in chap. 5, continues the theme of water offering newness of life. In the preceding chapter, to the woman at the well in Samaria Jesus had offered living water springing up to eternal life, a symbol of the revelation that Jesus brings; here Jesus' life-giving word replaces the water of the pool that failed to bring life. John 6 contains two signs, the multiplication of loaves and the walking on the waters of the Sea of Galilee. These signs are connected much as the manna and the crossing of the Red Sea are in the Passover narrative and symbolize a new exodus. The multiplication of the loaves is interpreted for the reader by the discourse that follows, where the bread of life is used first as a figure for the revelation of God in Jesus and then for the Eucharist. After a series of dialogues reflecting Jesus' debates with the Jewish authorities at the Feast of Tabernacles in John 7 and 8, the sixth sign is presented in John 9, the sign of the young man born blind. This is a narrative illustration of the theme of conflict in the preceding two chapters; it proclaims the triumph of light over darkness, as Jesus is presented as the Light of the world. This is interpreted by a narrative of controversy between the Pharisees and the young man who had been given his sight by Jesus, ending with a discussion of spiritual blindness and spelling out the symbolic meaning of the cure. And finally, the seventh sign, the raising of Lazarus in chap. 11, is the climax of signs. Lazarus is presented as a token of the real life that Jesus, the Resurrection and the Life, who will now ironically be put to death because of his gift of life to Lazarus, will give to all who believe in him once he has been raised from the dead.

After the account of the seven signs, the "hour" of Jesus arrives, and the author passes from sign to reality, as he moves into the discourses in the upper room that interpret the meaning of the passion, death, and resurrection narratives that follow. The whole gospel of John is a progressive revelation of the glory of God's only Son, who comes to reveal the Father and then returns in glory to the Father. The author's purpose is clearly expressed in what must have been the original ending of the gospel at the end of John 20: "Now Jesus did many other signs in the presence of [his] disciples that are not written in this book. But these are written that you may [come to] believe that Jesus is the Messiah, the Son of God, and that through this belief you may have life in his name."

Critical analysis makes it difficult to accept the idea that the gospel as it now stands was written by one person. John 21 seems to have been added after the gospel was completed; it exhibits a Greek style somewhat different from that of the rest of the work. The prologue (1:1-18) apparently contains an independent hymn, subsequently adapted to serve as a preface to the gospel. Within the gospel itself there are also some inconsistencies, e.g., there are two endings of Jesus' discourse in the upper room (14:31; 18:1). To solve these problems, scholars have proposed various rearrangements that would produce a smoother order. However, most have come to the conclusion that the inconsistencies were probably produced by subsequent editing in which homogeneous materials were added to a shorter original.

Other difficulties for any theory of eyewitness authorship of the gospel in its present form are presented by its highly developed theology and by certain elements of its literary style. For instance, some of the wondrous deeds of Jesus have been worked into highly effective dramatic scenes (chap. 9); there has been a careful attempt to have these followed by discourses that explain them (chaps. 5 and 6); and the sayings of Jesus have been woven into long discourses of a quasi-poetic form resembling the speeches of personified Wisdom in the Old Testament.

The gospel contains many details about Jesus not found in the synoptic gospels, e.g., that Jesus engaged in a baptizing ministry (3:22) before he changed to one of preaching and signs; that Jesus' public ministry lasted for several years (see the note

on 2:13); that he traveled to Jerusalem for various festivals and met serious opposition long before his death (2:14-25; 5; 7–8); and that he was put to death on the day before Passover (18:28). These events are not always in chronological order because of the development and editing that took place. However, the accuracy of much of the detail of the fourth gospel constitutes a strong argument that the Johannine tradition rests upon the testimony of an eyewitness. Although tradition identified this person as John, the son of Zebedee, most modern scholars find that the evidence does not support this.

The fourth gospel is not simply history; the narrative has been organized and adapted to serve the evangelist's theological purposes as well. Among them are the opposition to the synagogue of the day and to John the Baptist's followers, who tried to exalt their master at Jesus' expense, the desire to show that Jesus was the Messiah, and the desire to convince Christians that their religious belief and practice must be rooted in Jesus. Such theological purposes have impelled the evangelist to emphasize motifs that were not so clear in the synoptic account of Jesus' ministry, e.g., the explicit emphasis on his divinity.

The polemic between synagogue and church produced bitter and harsh invective, especially regarding the hostility toward Jesus of the authorities—Pharisees and Sadducees—who are combined and referred to frequently as "the Jews" (see the note on 1:19). These opponents are even described in John 8:44 as springing from their father the devil, whose conduct they imitate in opposing God by rejecting Jesus, whom God has sent. On the other hand, the author of this gospel seems to take pains to show that women are not inferior to men in the Christian community: the woman at the well in Samaria (chap. 4) is presented as a prototype of a missionary (4:4-42), and the first witness of the resurrection is a woman (20:11-18).

The final editing of the gospel and arrangement in its present form probably dates from between A.D. 90 and 100. Traditionally, Ephesus has been favored as the place of composition, though many support a location in Syria, perhaps the city of Antioch, while some have suggested other places, including Alexandria.

The principal divisions of the Gospel according to John are the following:

I. Prologue (1:1-18)

II. The Book of Signs (1:19–12:50)

III. The Book of Glory (13:1–20:31)

IV. Epilogue: The Resurrection Appearance in Galilee (21:1-25)

I: Prologue

a
10:30;
Gn 1:1-5;
Jb 28:12-27;
Prv 8:22-25;
Wis 9:1-2;
1 Jn 1:1-2;
Col 1:1, 15;
Rev 3:14;
19:13

b
Ps 33:9;
Wis 9:1;
Sir 42:15;
1 Cor 8:6;
Col 1:16;
Heb 1:2;
Rev 3:14

c
5:26; 8:12;
1 Jn 1:2

d
3:19; 8:12; 9:5;
12:35, 46;
Wis 7:29-30;
1 Thes 5:4;
1 Jn 2:8

e
Mt 3:1; Mk 1:4;
Lk 3:2-3

f
1:19-34; 5:33

g
5:35

h
3:19; 8:12;
9:39; 12:46

1 [1]*[a]In the beginning was the Word,*
and the Word was with God,
and the Word was God. [2]He was in the beginning with God. [3]*[b]All things came to be through him,
and without him nothing came to be. What came to be [4][c]through him was life,
and this life was the light of the human race; [5]*[d]the light shines in the darkness,
and the darkness has not overcome it.

[6]*[e]A man named John was sent from God. [7][f]He came for testimony,* to testify to the light, so that all might believe through him. [8][g]He was not the light, but came to testify to the light. [9][h]The true light, which enlightens everyone, was coming into the world.

John has a **"high Christology"** that emphasizes the divine aspects of Jesus' identity, as compared with a "low Christology" that emphasizes the human aspects. To appreciate this gospel one must keep in mind its overall framework. John proposes that Jesus preexisted with God the Father who sent him down to earth for a time to testify to the truth and to bring people to faith. Then, in his passion, death, and resurrection, Jesus returned to his heavenly existence and glory. This descending-ascending movement is unique in the NT. One must also remember that Christian faith, as expressed in the Creeds, demands that the human and divine aspects of Jesus' identity are equal. Jesus Christ is fully God and fully human. One aspect cannot overshadow the other without leading to a heretical stance, something that has happened frequently in Christian history. John's gospel ultimately retains a balance by emphasizing both the human and the divine qualities of Jesus.

1:1-18 The prologue states the main themes of the gospel: life, light, truth, the world, testimony, and the preexistence of Jesus Christ, the incarnate **Logos**, who reveals God the Father. In origin, it was probably an early Christian hymn. Its closest parallel is in other christological hymns, Colossians 1:15-20 and Philippians 2:6-11. Its core (1:1-5, 10-11, 14) is poetic in structure, with short phrases linked by "staircase parallelism," in which the last word of one phrase becomes the first word of the next. Prose inserts (at least 1:6-8, 15) deal with John the Baptist.

1:1 In the beginning: also the first words of the Old Testament (Gn 1:1). **Was**: this verb is used three times with different meanings in this verse: existence, relationship, and predication. **The Word** (Greek *logos*): this term combines God's dynamic, creative word (Genesis), personified preexistent Wisdom as the instrument of God's creative activity (Proverbs), and the ultimate intelligibility of reality (Hellenistic philosophy). **With God**: the Greek preposition here connotes communication with another. **Was God**: lack of a definite article with "God" in Greek signifies predication rather than identification.

1:3 What came to be: while the oldest manuscripts have no punctuation here, the corrector of Bodmer Papyrus P[75], some manuscripts, and the Ante-Nicene Fathers take this phrase with what follows, as staircase parallelism. Connection with John 1:3 reflects fourth-century anti-Arianism.

1:5 The ethical dualism of light and darkness is paralleled in intertestamental literature and in the Dead Sea Scrolls. **Overcome**: "comprehend" is another possible translation, but cf. John 12:35; Wisdom 7:29-30.

1:6 John was **sent** just as Jesus was "sent" (4:34) in divine mission. Other references to John the Baptist in this gospel emphasize the differences between them and John's subordinate role.

1:7 Testimony: the testimony theme of John is introduced, which portrays Jesus as if on trial throughout his ministry. All testify to Jesus: John the Baptist, the Samaritan woman, scripture, his works, the crowds, the Spirit, and his disciples.

Dualism is characteristic of John's gospel in which opposites are contrasted to emphasize the choice that must be made to follow Jesus. John emphasizes the struggle between light and darkness, truth and falsehood, living water and still water, the descent and ascent of Christ, earthly and heavenly things, and so on. Some of this dualistic imagery is also found in the Dead Sea Scrolls, indicating that it might have been a feature of sectarian Judaism. Such dualism forces people to choose one side or the other: one lives by the light or one lives by darkness (cf. 1 Thes 5:4-8). There is no mediocrity with Jesus.

[10]He was in the world,
and the world came to be through him,
but the world did not know him.
[11]He came to what was his own,*
but his own people* did not accept him.

[12][i]But to those who did accept him he gave power to become children of God, to those who believe in his name, [13][*j]who were born not by natural generation nor by human choice nor by a man's decision but of God.

[14][k]And the Word became flesh*
and made his dwelling among us,
and we saw his glory,
the glory as of the Father's only Son,
full of grace and truth.

[15][*l]John testified to him and cried out, saying, "This was he of whom I said, 'The one who is coming after me ranks ahead of me because he existed before me.'" [16]From his fullness we have all received, grace in place of grace,* [17][m]because while the law was given through Moses, grace and truth came through Jesus Christ. [18][n]No one has ever seen God. The only Son, God,* who is at the Father's side, has revealed him.

i
3:11-12;
5:43-44;
12:46-50;
Gal 3:26;
4:6-7; Eph 1:5;
1 Jn 3:2

j
3:5-6

k
Ex 16:10;
24:17; 25:8-9;
33:22; 34:6;
Sir 24:4, 8;
Is 60:1;
Ez 43:7;
Jl 4:17;
Heb 2:14;
1 Jn 1:2; 4:2;
2 Jn 7

l
1:30; 3:27-30

m
7:19; Ex 31:18;
34:28

n
5:37; 6:46;
Ex 33:20;
Jgs 13:21-22;
1 Tm 6:16;
1 Jn 4:12

JOHN

1:11 What was his own . . . his own people: first a neuter, literally, "his own property/possession" (probably = Israel), then a masculine, "his own people" (the Israelites).

1:13 Believers in Jesus become children of God not through any of the three natural causes mentioned but through God who is the immediate cause of the new spiritual life. **Were born**: the Greek verb can mean "begotten" (by a male) or "born" (from a female or of parents). The variant "he who was begotten," asserting Jesus' virginal conception, is weakly attested in Old Latin and Syriac versions.

1:14 Flesh: the whole person, used probably against docetic tendencies (cf. 1 Jn 4:2; 2 Jn 1:7). **Made his dwelling**: literally, "pitched his tent/tabernacle." Cf. the tabernacle or tent of meeting that was the place of God's presence among his people (Ex 25:8-9). The incarnate Word is the new mode of God's presence among his people. The Greek verb has the same consonants as the Aramaic word for God's presence (Shekinah). **Glory**: God's visible manifestation of majesty in power, which once filled the tabernacle (Ex 40:34) and the temple (1 Kgs 8:10-11, 27), is now centered in Jesus.

Only Son: Greek, *monogenēs*, but see the note on John 1:18. **Grace and truth**: these words may represent two Old Testament terms describing Yahweh in covenant relationship with Israel (cf. Ex 34:6), thus God's "love" and "fidelity." The Word shares Yahweh's covenant qualities.

1:15 This verse, interrupting John 1:14, 16 seems drawn from John 1:30.

1:16 Grace in place of grace: replacement of the Old Covenant with the New (cf. 1:17). Other possible translations are "grace upon grace" (accumulation) and "grace for grace" (correspondence).

1:18 The only Son, God: while the vast majority of later textual witnesses have another reading, "the Son, the only one" or "the only Son," the translation above follows the best and earliest manuscripts, *monogenēs theos*, but takes the first term to mean not just "Only One" but to include a filial relationship with the Father, as at Luke 9:38 ("only child") or Hebrews 11:17 ("only son") and as translated at John 1:14. The Logos is thus "only Son" and God but not Father/God.

II: The Book of Signs

John the Baptist's Testimony to Himself

19*And this is the testimony of John. When the Jews from Jerusalem sent priests
and Levites [to him] to ask him, "Who are you?"* 20*ohe admitted and did not deny it,
but admitted, "I am not the Messiah." 21pSo they asked him, "What are you then? Are
you Elijah?"* And he said, "I am not." "Are you the Prophet?" He answered, "No."
22So they said to him, "Who are you, so we can give an answer to those who sent us?
What do you have to say for yourself?" 23qHe said:

> "I am 'the voice of one crying out in the desert,
> "Make straight the way of the Lord,"'*

as Isaiah the prophet said." 24Some Pharisees*
were also sent. 25rThey asked him, "Why then
do you baptize if you are not the Messiah or
Elijah or the Prophet?" 26sJohn answered them,
"I baptize with water;* but there is one among
you whom you do not recognize, 27the one who
is coming after me, whose sandal strap I am not
worthy to untie." 28This happened in Bethany
across the Jordan,* where John was baptizing.

John's acclamation, **"Behold the Lamb of God . . ."** is used at every Eucharist when the priest presents the consecrated host, the Body and Blood of Jesus Christ, to the assembly. It evokes an assent of faith in the one who saves the world from sin.

John the Baptist's Testimony to Jesus

29tThe next day he saw Jesus coming toward him and said, "Behold, the Lamb of
God,* who takes away the sin of the world. 30*uHe is the one of whom I said, 'A man
is coming after me who ranks ahead of me because he existed before me.' 31I did not

o 3:28; Lk 3:15; Acts 13:25
p Dt 18:15, 18; 2 Kgs 2:11; Sir 48:10; Mal 3:1, 23; Mt 11:14; 17:11-13; Mk 9:13; Acts 3:22
q Is 40:3; Mt 3:3; Mk 1:2; Lk 3:4
r Ez 36:25; Zec 13:1; Mt 16:14
s Mt 3:11; Mk 1:7-8; Lk 3:16; Acts 13:25
t 1:36; Ex 12; Is 53:7; Rev 5–7; 17:14
u 1:15; Mt 3:11; Mk 1:7; Lk 3:16

1:19-51 The testimony of John the Baptist about the Messiah and Jesus' self-revelation to the first disciples. This section constitutes the introduction to the gospel proper and is connected with the prose inserts in the prologue. It develops the major theme of testimony in four scenes: John's negative testimony about himself; his positive testimony about Jesus; the revelation of Jesus to Andrew and Peter; the revelation of Jesus to Philip and Nathanael.

1:19 The Jews: throughout most of the gospel, the "Jews" does not refer to the Jewish people as such but to the hostile authorities, both Pharisees and Sadducees, particularly in Jerusalem, who refuse to believe in Jesus. The usage reflects the atmosphere, at the end of the first century, of polemics between church and synagogue, or possibly it refers to Jews as representative of a hostile world (1:10-11).

1:20 Messiah: the anointed agent of Yahweh, usually considered to be of Davidic descent. See further the note on John 1:41.

1:21 Elijah: the Baptist did not claim to be Elijah returned to earth (cf. Mal 3:23; Mt 11:14). **The Prophet**: probably the prophet like Moses (Dt 18:15; cf. Acts 3:22).

1:23 This is a repunctuation and reinterpretation (as in the synoptic gospels and Septuagint) of the Hebrew text of Isaiah 40:3 which reads, "A voice cries out: In the desert prepare the way of the Lord."

1:24 Some Pharisees: other translations, such as "Now they had been sent from the Pharisees," misunderstand the grammatical construction. This is a different group from that in John 1:19; the priests and Levites would have been Sadducees, not Pharisees.

1:26 I baptize with water: the synoptics add "but he will baptize you with the holy Spirit" (Mk 1:8) or ". . . holy Spirit and fire" (Mt 3:11; Lk 3:16). John's emphasis is on purification and preparation for a better baptism.

1:28 Bethany across the Jordan: site unknown. Another reading is "Bethabara."

1:29 The Lamb of God: the background for this title may be the victorious apocalyptic lamb who would destroy evil in the world (Rev 5–7; 17:14); the paschal lamb, whose blood saved Israel (Ex 12); and/or the suffering servant led like a lamb to the slaughter as a sin-offering (Is 53:7, 10).

1:30 He existed before me: possibly as Elijah (to come, 1:27); for the evangelist and his audience, Jesus' preexistence would be implied (see the note on 1:1).

1:31 I did not know him: this gospel shows no knowledge of the tradition (Lk 1) about the kinship of Jesus and John the Baptist. **The reason why I came baptizing with water**: in this gospel, John's baptism is not connected with forgiveness of sins; its purpose is revelatory, that Jesus may be made known to Israel.

know him,* but the reason why I came baptizing with water was that he might be made known to Israel." [32v]John testified further, saying, "I saw the Spirit come down like a dove* from the sky and remain upon him. [33w]I did not know him, but the one who sent me to baptize with water told me, 'On whomever you see the Spirit come down and remain, he is the one who will baptize with the holy Spirit.' [34*x]Now I have seen and testified that he is the Son of God."

The First Disciples

[35y]The next day John was there again with two of his disciples, [36]and as he watched Jesus walk by, he said, "Behold, the Lamb of God."* [37]The two disciples* heard what he said and followed Jesus. [38]Jesus turned and saw them following him and said to them, "What are you looking for?" They said to him, "Rabbi" (which translated means Teacher), "where are you staying?" [39]He said to them, "Come, and you will see." So they went and saw where he was staying, and they stayed with him that day. It was about four in the afternoon.* [40]Andrew, the brother of Simon Peter, was one of the two who heard John and followed Jesus. [41z]He first found his own brother Simon and told him, "We have found the Messiah"* (which is translated Anointed). [42a]Then he brought him to Jesus. Jesus looked at him and said, "You are Simon the son of John;* you will be called Cephas" (which is translated Peter).

[43]The next day he* decided to go to Galilee, and he found Philip. And Jesus said to him, "Follow me." [44]Now Philip was from Bethsaida, the town of Andrew and Peter. [45b]Philip found Nathanael and told him, "We have found the one about whom Moses wrote in the law, and also the prophets, Jesus, son of Joseph, from Nazareth." [46]But Nathanael said to him, "Can anything good come from Nazareth?" Philip said to him, "Come and see." [47]Jesus saw Nathanael coming toward him and said of him, "Here is a true Israelite.* There is no duplicity in him." [48*c]Nathanael said to him, "How do you know me?" Jesus answered and said to him, "Before Philip called you, I saw you under

v
Sg 5:2; Is 11:2;
Hos 11:11;
Mt 3:16;
Mk 1:10;
Lk 3:21-22

w
Is 42:1;
Mt 3:11;
Mk 1:8;
Lk 3:16

x
Is 42:1;
Mt 3:17;
Mk 1:11;
Lk 9:35

y
Mt 4:18-22;
Mk 1:16-20;
Lk 5:1-11

z
4:25

a
Mt 16:18;
Mk 3:16

b
21:2

c
Mi 4:4;
Zec 3:10

JOHN

1:32 Like a dove: a symbol of the new creation (Gn 8:8) or the community of Israel (Hos 11:11). **Remain**: the first use of a favorite verb in John, emphasizing the permanency of the relationship between Father and Son (as here) and between the Son and the Christian. Jesus is the permanent bearer of the Spirit.

1:34 The Son of God: this reading is supported by good Greek manuscripts, including the Chester Beatty and Bodmer Papyri and the Vatican Codex, but is suspect because it harmonizes this passage with the synoptic version: "This is my beloved Son" (Mt 3:17; Mk 1:11; Lk 3:22). The poorly attested alternate reading, "God's chosen One," is probably a reference to the Servant of Yahweh (Is 42:1).

1:36 John the Baptist's testimony makes his disciples' following of Jesus plausible.

1:37 The two disciples: Andrew (1:40) and, traditionally, John, son of Zebedee (see the note on 13:23).

1:39 Four in the afternoon: literally, the tenth hour, from sunrise, in the Roman calculation of time. Some suggest that the next day, beginning at sunset, was the sabbath; they would have stayed with Jesus to avoid travel on it.

1:41 Messiah: the Hebrew word *māšîah*, "anointed one" (see the note on Lk 2:11), appears in Greek as the transliterated *messias* only here and in John 4:25. Elsewhere the Greek translation *christos* is used.

1:42 Simon, the son of John: in Matthew 16:17, Simon is called *Bariōna*, "son of Jonah," a different tradition for the name of Simon's father. *Kephas*: in Aramaic = the Rock; cf. Matthew 16:18. Neither the Greek equivalent *Petros* nor, with one isolated exception, *Kephas* is attested as a personal name before Christian times.

1:43 He: grammatically, could be Peter, but logically is probably Jesus.

1:47 A true Israelite. There is no duplicity in him: Jacob was the first to bear the name "Israel" (Gn 32:29), but Jacob was a man of duplicity (Gn 27:35-36).

1:48 Under the fig tree: a symbol of messianic peace (cf. Mi 4:4; Zec 3:10).

the fig tree." [49d]Nathanael answered him, "Rabbi, you are the Son of God;* you are the King of Israel." [50]Jesus answered and said to him, "Do you believe because I told you that I saw you under the fig tree?* You will see greater things than this." [51e]And he said to him, "Amen, amen,* I say to you, you will see the sky opened and the angels of God ascending and descending on the Son of Man."

On **Son of Man**, see the chart on christological titles in "Background to the Gospels," p. 2.

The Wedding at Cana

2 [1*a]On the third day there was a wedding* in Cana* in Galilee, and the mother of Jesus was there. [2]Jesus and his disciples were also invited to the wedding. [3]When the wine ran short, the mother of Jesus said to him, "They have no wine." [4*b][And] Jesus said to her, "Woman, how does your concern affect me? My hour has not yet come." [5c]His mother said to the servers, "Do whatever he tells you." [6*d]Now there were six stone water jars there for Jewish ceremonial washings, each holding twenty to thirty gallons. [7]Jesus told them, "Fill the jars with water." So they filled them to the brim. [8]Then he told them, "Draw some out now and take it to the headwaiter."* So they took it. [9]And when the headwaiter tasted the water that had become wine, without knowing where it came from (although the servers who had drawn the water knew), the headwaiter called the bridegroom [10]and

The expression **"Amen, amen"** is unique to John's gospel. It is a characteristic way in which the Johannine Jesus solemnly teaches or proclaims something. The Hebrew word *Amen* normally was used to *conclude* prayers. The Synoptic Gospels portray Jesus using it once at the *beginning* of solemn statements (Mt 5:18; Mk 8:12; Lk 12:37), an apparent characteristic of his teaching style. Only John records the double expression.

1:49 Son of God: this title is used in the Old Testament, among other ways, as a title of adoption for the Davidic king (2 Sm 7:14; Pss 2:7; 89:27), and thus here, with **King of Israel**, in a messianic sense. For the evangelist, Son of God also points to Jesus' divinity (cf. 20:28).

1:50 Possibly a statement: "You [singular] believe because I saw you under the fig tree."

1:51 The double "Amen" is characteristic of John. **You** is plural in Greek. The allusion is to Jacob's ladder (Gn 28:12).

2:1–6:71 Signs revealing Jesus as the Messiah to all Israel. "Sign" (*sēmeion*) is John's symbolic term for Jesus' wondrous deeds (see Introduction). The Old Testament background lies in the Exodus story (cf. Dt 11:3; 29:2). John is interested primarily in what the *sēmeia* signify: God's intervention in human history in a new way through Jesus.

2:1-11 The first sign. This story of replacement of Jewish ceremonial washings (2:6) presents the initial revelation about Jesus at the outset of his ministry. He manifests his glory; the disciples believe. There is no synoptic parallel.

2:1 Cana: unknown from the Old Testament. **The mother of Jesus**: she is never named in John.

2:4 This verse may seek to show that Jesus did not work miracles to help his family and friends, as in the apocryphal gospels. **Woman**: a normal, polite form of address, but unattested in reference to one's mother. Cf. also John 19:26. **How does your concern affect me?**: literally, "What is this to me and to you?"—a Hebrew expression of either hostility (Jgs 11:12; 2 Chr 35:21; 1 Kgs 17:18) or denial of common interest (Hos 14:9; 2 Kgs 3:13). Cf. Mark 1:24; 5:7, used by demons to Jesus. **My hour has not yet come**: the translation as a question ("Has not my hour now come?"), while preferable grammatically and supported by Greek Fathers, seems unlikely from a comparison with John 7:6, 30. The "hour" is that of Jesus' passion, death, resurrection, and ascension (13:1).

2:6 Twenty to thirty gallons: literally, "two or three measures"; the Attic liquid measure contained 39.39 liters. The vast quantity recalls prophecies of abundance in the last days; cf. Amos 9:13-14; Hosea 14:7; Jeremiah 31:12.

2:8 Headwaiter: used of the official who managed a banquet, but there is no evidence of such a functionary in Palestine. Perhaps here a friend of the family acted as master of ceremonies; cf. Sirach 32:1.

The Latin church at Cana—the site of Jesus' first miracle

John is the only NT book to use **"the Jews"** as a generic term for the opponents of Jesus. This is a delicate point, since some parts of the NT have wrongly been used throughout history to justify anti-Semitic actions against all Jews on the alleged role they had in crucifying Jesus. John, however, does not use the term "Jews" in that fashion. Rather, he uses the expression to represent a small group of Jewish leaders, mostly allied to the temple, who opposed Jesus and felt threatened by him. Nothing in the NT can rightly justify condemning the Jews as a people or a race for actions taken against Jesus.

said to him, "Everyone serves good wine first, and then when people have drunk freely, an inferior one; but you have kept the good wine until now." [11e]Jesus did this as the beginning of his signs* in Cana in Galilee and so revealed his glory, and his disciples began to believe in him.

[12*]After this, he and his mother, [his] brothers, and his disciples went down to Capernaum and stayed there only a few days.*

Cleansing of the Temple

[13*f]Since the Passover of the Jews was near, Jesus went up to Jerusalem.* [14*g]He found in the temple area those who sold oxen, sheep, and doves,* as well as the money-changers seated there. [15]He made a whip out of cords and drove them all out of the temple area, with the sheep and oxen, and spilled the coins of the money-changers and overturned their tables, [16h]and to those who sold doves he said, "Take these out of here, and stop making my Father's house a marketplace." [17*i]His disciples recalled the words of scripture, "Zeal for your house will consume me." [18j]At this the Jews answered and said to him, "What sign can you show us for doing this?" [19k]Jesus answered and said to them,* "Destroy this temple and in three days I will raise it up." [20]The Jews said, "This temple has been under construction for forty-six years,* and you will raise it up

e
4:54

f
Mt 21:12-13;
Mk 11:15-17;
Lk 19:45-46

g
Ex 30:11-16;
Lv 5:7

h
Zec 14:21

i
Ps 69:9

j
6:30

k
Mt 24:2; 26:61;
27:40;
Mk 13:2;
14:58; 15:29;
Lk 21:6;
Acts 6:14

2:11 The beginning of his signs: the first of seven (see Introduction).

2:12–3:21 The next three episodes take place in Jerusalem. Only the first is paralleled in the synoptic gospels.

2:12 This transitional verse may be a harmonization with the synoptic tradition in Luke 4:31 and Matthew 4:13. There are many textual variants. John depicts no extended ministry in Capernaum as do the synoptics.

2:13-22 This episode indicates the post-resurrectional replacement of the temple by the person of Jesus.

2:13 Passover: this is the first Passover mentioned in John; a second is mentioned in John 6:4, a third in John 13:1. Taken literally, they point to a ministry of at least two years.

2:14-22 The other gospels place the cleansing of the temple in the last days of Jesus' life (Matthew, on the day Jesus entered Jerusalem; Mark, on the next day). The order of events in the gospel narratives is often determined by theological motives rather than by chronological data.

2:14 Oxen, sheep, and doves: intended for sacrifice. The doves were the offerings of the poor (Lv 5:7). **Money-changers**: for a temple tax paid by every male Jew more than nineteen years of age, with a half-shekel coin (Ex 30:11-16), in Tyrian currency. See the note on Matthew 17:24.

2:17 Psalm 69:10, changed to future tense to apply to Jesus.

2:19 This saying about the destruction of the temple occurs in various forms (Mt 24:2; 27:40; Mk 13:2; 15:29; Lk 21:6; cf. Acts 6:14). Matthew 26:61 has: "I **can** destroy the temple of God . . ."; see the note there. In Mark 14:58, there is a metaphorical contrast with a new temple: "I will destroy this temple **made with hands** and within three days I will build another **not made with hands**." Here it is symbolic of Jesus' resurrection and the resulting community (see 2:21 and Rev 21:2). **In three days**: an Old Testament expression for a short, indefinite period of time; cf. Hosea 6:2.

2:20 Forty-six years: based on references in Josephus (Jewish Wars 1, 21, 1 #401; Antiquities 15, 11, 1 #380), possibly the spring of A.D. 28. Cf. the note on Luke 3:1.

in three days?" [21]But he was speaking about the temple of his body. [22l]Therefore, when he was raised from the dead, his disciples remembered that he had said this, and they came to believe the scripture and the word Jesus had spoken.

[23m]While he was in Jerusalem for the feast of Passover, many began to believe in his name when they saw the signs he was doing. [24]But Jesus would not trust himself to them because he knew them all, [25n]and did not need anyone to testify about human nature. He himself understood it well.

Nicodemus

3 [1*a]Now there was a Pharisee named Nicodemus, a ruler of the Jews.* [2b]He came to Jesus at night and said to him, "Rabbi, we know that you are a teacher who has come from God, for no one can do these signs that you are doing unless God is with him." [3]Jesus answered and said to him, "Amen, amen, I say to you, no one can see the kingdom of God without being born* from above." [4c]Nicodemus said to him, "How can a person once grown old be born again? Surely he cannot reenter his mother's womb and be born again, can he?" [5d]Jesus answered, "Amen, amen, I say to you, no one can enter the kingdom of God without being born of water and Spirit. [6e]What is born of flesh is flesh and what is born of spirit is spirit. [7]Do not be amazed that I told you, 'You must be born from above.' [8f]The wind* blows where it wills, and you can hear the sound it makes, but you do not know where it comes from or where it goes; so it is with everyone who is born of the Spirit." [9]Nicodemus answered and said to him, "How can this happen?" [10]Jesus answered and said to him, "You are the teacher of Israel and you do not understand this? [11g]Amen, amen, I say to you, we speak of what we know and we testify to what we have seen, but you people do not accept our testimony. [12h]If I tell you about earthly things and you do not believe, how will you believe if I tell you about heavenly things? [13i]No one has gone up to heaven except the one who has come down from heaven, the Son of Man. [14j]And just as Moses lifted up* the serpent in the desert, so must the Son of Man be lifted up, [15*]so that everyone who believes in him may have eternal life."

O gracious God, what you have done for the world, through Jesus, is another name for unconditional love. Make me always mindful of the ways you have saved me from the folly of my own deeds. As I discern that your dream for me is no less than eternal life gratitude rises in my heart like the sun on a winter's day.

3:1-21 Jesus instructs Nicodemus on the necessity of a new birth from above. This scene in Jerusalem at Passover exemplifies the faith engendered by signs (2:23). It continues the self-manifestation of Jesus in Jerusalem begun in John 2. This is the first of the Johannine discourses, shifting from dialogue to monologue (3:11-15) to reflection of the evangelist (3:16-21). The shift from singular through John 3:10 to plural in John 3:11 may reflect the early church's controversy with the Jews.

3:1 A ruler of the Jews: most likely a member of the Jewish council, the Sanhedrin; see the note on Mark 8:31.

3:3 Born: see the note on John 1:13. **From above**: the Greek adverb *anōthen* means both "from above"

and "again." Jesus means "from above" (see 3:31) but Nicodemus misunderstands it as "again." This misunderstanding serves as a springboard for further instruction.

3:8 Wind: the Greek word *pneuma* (as well as the Hebrew *rûah*) means both "wind" and "spirit." In the play on the double meaning, "wind" is primary.

3:14 Lifted up: in Numbers 21:9, Moses simply "mounted" a serpent upon a pole. John here substitutes a verb implying glorification. Jesus, exalted to glory at his cross and resurrection, represents healing for all.

3:15 Eternal life: used here for the first time in John, this term stresses quality of life rather than duration.

[16][k]For God so loved the world that he gave[*] his only Son, so that everyone who believes in him might not perish but might have eternal life. [17][l]For God did not send his Son into the world to condemn[*] the world, but that the world might be saved through him. [18][m]Whoever believes in him will not be condemned, but whoever does not believe has already been condemned, because he has not believed in the name of the only Son of God. [19][*][n]And this is the verdict, that the light came into the world, but people preferred darkness to light, because their works were evil. [20][o]For everyone who does wicked things hates the light and does not come toward the light, so that his works might not be exposed. [21][p]But whoever lives the truth comes to the light, so that his works may be clearly seen as done in God.

Final Witness of the Baptist

[22][*][q]After this, Jesus and his disciples went into the region of Judea, where he spent some time with them baptizing. [23]John was also baptizing in Aenon near Salim,[*] because there was an abundance of water there, and people came to be baptized, [24][r]for John had not yet been imprisoned. [25]Now a dispute arose between the disciples of John and a Jew[*] about ceremonial washings. [26][s]So they came to John and said to him, "Rabbi, the one who was with you across the Jordan, to whom you testified, here he is baptizing and everyone is coming to him." [27]John answered and said, "No one can receive anything except what has been given him from heaven. [28][u]You yourselves can testify that I said [that] I am not the Messiah, but that I was sent before him. [29][v]The one who has the bride is the bridegroom; the best man,[*] who stands and listens for him, rejoices greatly at the bridegroom's voice. So this joy of mine has been made complete. [30][w]He must increase; I must decrease."

The One from Heaven

[31][*][x]The one who comes from above is above all. The one who is of the earth is earthly and speaks of earthly things. But the one who comes from heaven [is above all]. [32][y]He testifies to what he has seen and heard, but no one accepts his testimony. [33][z]Whoever does accept his testimony certifies that God is trustworthy. [34]For the one

---

3:16 **Gave**: as a gift in the incarnation, and also "over to death" in the crucifixion; cf. Romans 8:32.

3:17-19 **Condemn**: the Greek root means both judgment and condemnation. Jesus' purpose is to save, but his coming provokes judgment; some condemn themselves by turning from the light.

3:19 Judgment is not only future but is partially realized here and now.

3:22-26 Jesus' ministry in Judea is only loosely connected with John 2:13–3:21; cf. John 1:19-36. Perhaps John the Baptist's further testimony was transposed here to give meaning to "water" in John 3:5. Jesus is depicted as baptizing (3:22); contrast John 4:2.

3:23 **Aenon near Salim**: site uncertain, either in the upper Jordan valley or in Samaria.

3:24 A remark probably intended to avoid objections based on a chronology like that of the synoptics (Mt 4:12; Mk 1:14).

3:25 **A Jew**: some think Jesus is meant. Many manuscripts read "Jews."

3:29 **The best man**: literally, "the friend of the groom," the *shoshben* of Jewish tradition, who arranged the wedding. Competition between him and the groom would be unthinkable.

3:31-36 It is uncertain whether these are words by the Baptist, Jesus, or the evangelist. They are reflections on the two preceding scenes.

3:34 **His gift**: of God or to Jesus, perhaps both. This verse echoes John 3:5, 8.

---

k
1 Jn 4:9

l
5:22, 30; 8:15-18; 12:47

m
5:24; Mk 16:16

n
1:5, 9-11; 8:12; 9:5

o
Jb 24:13-17

p
Gn 47:29 LXX; Jos 2:14 LXX; 2 Sm 2:6 LXX; 15:20 LXX; Tb 4:6 LXX; 13:6; Is 26:10 LXX; Mt 5:14-16

q
4:1-2

r
Mt 4:12; 14:3; Mk 1:14; 6:17; Lk 3:20

s
1:26, 32-34, 36

t
19:11; 1 Cor 4:7; 2 Cor 3:5; Heb 5:4

u
1:20-23; Lk 3:15

v
15:11; 17:13; Mt 9:15

w
2 Sm 3:1

x
8:23

y
3:11

z
8:26; 12:44-50; 1 Jn 5:10

JOHN

a
13:3; Mt 11:27;
28:18;
Lk 10:22

b
3:16; 1 Jn 5:13

a
Gn 33:18-19;
48:22;
Jos 24:32

b
Sir 50:25-26;
Mt 10:5

c
Sir 24:20-21;
Is 55:1;
Jer 2:13

d
8:53; Mt 12:41

e
6:35, 58;
7:37-39;
Is 44:3; 49:10;
Jl 4:18;
Rev 7:16; 21:6

whom God sent speaks the words of God. He does not ration his gift* of the Spirit. ^{35a}The Father loves the Son and has given everything over to him. ^{36b}Whoever believes in the Son has eternal life, but whoever disobeys the Son will not see life, but the wrath of God remains upon him.

4 ^{1*}Now when Jesus learned that the Pharisees had heard that Jesus was making and baptizing more disciples than John ²(although Jesus himself was not baptizing, just his disciples),* ³he left Judea and returned to Galilee.

The Samaritan Woman

⁴He had to* pass through Samaria. ^{5a}So he came to a town of Samaria called Sychar,* near the plot of land that Jacob had given to his son Joseph. ⁶Jacob's well was there. Jesus, tired from his journey, sat down there at the well. It was about noon.

⁷A woman of Samaria came to draw water. Jesus said to her, "Give me a drink." ⁸His disciples had gone into the town to buy food. ^{9*b}The Samaritan woman said to him, "How can you, a Jew, ask me, a Samaritan woman, for a drink?" (For Jews use nothing in common with Samaritans.) ^{10*c}Jesus answered and said to her, "If you knew the gift of God and who is saying to you, 'Give me a drink,' you would have asked him and he would have given you living water." ¹¹[The woman] said to him, "Sir,* you do not even have a bucket and the cistern is deep; where then can you get this living water? ^{12d}Are you greater than our father Jacob, who gave us this cistern and drank from it himself with his children and his flocks?" ¹³Jesus answered and said to her, "Everyone who drinks this water will be thirsty again; ^{14e}but whoever drinks the water I shall give will never thirst; the water I shall give will become in him a spring of water welling up to eternal life." ¹⁵The woman

Samaria in relation to Judea

Modern church at the site of Jacob's well

4:1–42 Jesus in Samaria. The self-revelation of Jesus continues with his second discourse, on his mission to "half-Jews." It continues the theme of replacement, here with regard to cult (4:21). Water (4:7-15) serves as a symbol (as at Cana and in the Nicodemus episode).

4:2 An editorial refinement of John 3:22, perhaps directed against followers of John the Baptist who claimed that Jesus imitated him.

4:4 He had to: a theological necessity; geographically, Jews often bypassed Samaria by taking a route across the Jordan.

4:5 Sychar: Jerome identifies this with Shechem, a reading found in Syriac manuscripts.

4:9 Samaritan women were regarded by Jews as ritually impure, and therefore Jews were forbidden to drink from any vessel they had handled.

4:10 Living water: the water of life, i.e., the revelation that Jesus brings; the woman thinks of "flowing water," so much more desirable than stagnant cistern water. On John's device of such misunderstanding, cf. the note on John 3:3.

4:11 Sir: the Greek *kyrios* means "master" or "lord," as a respectful mode of address for a human being or a deity; cf. John 4:19. It is also the word used in the Septuagint for the Hebrew *'ădônai*, substituted for the tetragrammaton YHWH.

said to him, "Sir, give me this water, so that I may not be thirsty or have to keep coming here to draw water."

[16]Jesus said to her, "Go call your husband and come back." [17]The woman answered and said to him, "I do not have a husband." Jesus answered her, "You are right in saying, 'I do not have a husband.' [18f]For you have had five husbands, and the one you have now is not your husband. What you have said is true." [19g]The woman said to him, "Sir, I can see that you are a prophet. [20h]Our ancestors worshiped on this mountain;* but you people say that the place to worship is in Jerusalem." [21]Jesus said to her, "Believe me, woman, the hour is coming when you will worship the Father neither on this mountain nor in Jerusalem. [22i]You people worship what you do not understand; we worship what we understand, because salvation is from the Jews. [23]But the hour is coming, and is now here, when true worshipers will worship the Father in Spirit and truth;* and indeed the Father seeks such people to worship him. [24j]God is Spirit, and those who worship him must worship in Spirit and truth." [25*k]The woman said to him, "I know that the Messiah is coming, the one called the Anointed; when he comes, he will tell us everything." [26l]Jesus said to her, "I am he,* the one who is speaking with you."

[27]At that moment his disciples returned, and were amazed that he was talking with a woman,* but still no one said, "What are you looking for?" or "Why are you talking with her?" [28]The woman left her water jar and went into the town and said to the people, [29]"Come see a man who told me everything I have done. Could he possibly be the Messiah?" [30]They went out of the town and came to him. [31]Meanwhile, the disciples urged him, "Rabbi, eat." [32]But he said to them, "I have food to eat of which you do not know." [33]So the disciples said to one another, "Could someone have brought him something to eat?" [34m]Jesus said to them, "My food is to do the will of the one who sent me and to finish his work. [35n]Do you not say, 'In four months* the harvest will be here'? I tell you, look up and see the fields ripe for the harvest. [36o]The reaper is already* receiving his payment and gathering crops for eternal life, so that the sower and reaper can rejoice together. [37p]For here the saying is verified that 'One sows and another reaps.' [38]I sent you to reap what you have not worked for; others have done the work, and you are sharing the fruits of their work."

f
2 Kgs 17:24-34

g
9:17; Hos 1:3

h
Dt 11:29; 27:4; Jos 8:33; Ps 122:1-5

i
2 Kgs 17:27; Ps 76:2-3

j
2 Cor 3:17

k
1:41

l
9:37

m
5:30, 36; 6:38; 9:4; 17:4

n
Mt 9:37-38; Lk 10:2; Rev 14:15

o
Ps 126:5-6; Am 9:13-14

p
Dt 20:6; 28:30; Jb 31:8; Mi 6:15

JOHN

The church uses three lengthy stories in John as the centerpiece of the Lenten regimen of preparing catechumens for baptism and reception into the church. These are: **the Samaritan woman** (4:1-42), **the man born blind** (9:1-41), and **the raising of Lazarus** (11:1-44). The themes in these simple but profound stories directly relate to the gift of faith in baptism. The church uses these readings from Year A on the second, third, and fourth Sundays of Lent even during the other liturgical years if there are catechumens being prepared for baptism. The three readings correspond to the three scrutinies.

4:20 This mountain: Gerizim, on which a temple was erected in the fourth century B.C. by Samaritans to rival Mount Zion in Jerusalem; cf. Deuteronomy 27:4 (Mount Ebal = the Jews' term for Gerizim).

4:23 In Spirit and truth: not a reference to an interior worship within one's own spirit. The Spirit is the spirit given by God that reveals truth and enables one to worship God appropriately (14:16-17). Cf. "born of water and Spirit" (3:5).

4:25 The expectations of the Samaritans are expressed here in Jewish terminology. They did not expect a messianic king of the house of David but a prophet like Moses (Dt 18:15).

4:26 I am he: it could also be translated "I am," an Old Testament self-designation of Yahweh (Is 43:3, etc.); cf. John 6:20; 8:24, 28, 58; 13:19; 18:5-6, 8. See the note on Mark 6:50.

4:27 Talking with a woman: a religious and social restriction that Jesus is pictured treating as unimportant.

4:35 'In four months . . .': probably a proverb; cf. Matthew 9:37-38.

4:36 Already: this word may go with the preceding verse rather than with John 4:36.

q
1 Jn 4:14

r
Mt 13:57;
Mk 6:4; Lk
4:24

s
2:1-11;
Mt 8:5-13;
15:21-28;
Mk 7:24-30;
Lk 7:1-10

t
2:18, 23;
Wis 8:8;
Mt 12:38;
1 Cor 1:22

u
1 Kgs 17:23

v
2:11

a
6:4

b
Neh 3:1, 32;
12:39

³⁹Many of the Samaritans of that town began to believe in him because of the word of the woman* who testified, "He told me everything I have done." ⁴⁰When the Samaritans came to him, they invited him to stay with them; and he stayed there two days. ⁴¹Many more began to believe in him because of his word, ^{42q}and they said to the woman, "We no longer believe because of your word; for we have heard for ourselves, and we know that this is truly the savior of the world."

Return to Galilee

⁴³*After the two days, he left there for Galilee. ^{44*r}For Jesus himself testified that a prophet has no honor in his native place. ⁴⁵When he came into Galilee, the Galileans welcomed him, since they had seen all he had done in Jerusalem at the feast; for they themselves had gone to the feast.

Second Sign at Cana

⁴⁶*sThen he returned to Cana in Galilee, where he had made the water wine. Now there was a royal official whose son was ill in Capernaum. ⁴⁷When he heard that Jesus had arrived in Galilee from Judea, he went to him and asked him to come down and heal his son, who was near death. ^{48t}Jesus said to him, "Unless you people see signs and wonders, you will not believe." ⁴⁹The royal official said to him, "Sir, come down before my child dies." ^{50u}Jesus said to him, "You may go; your son will live." The man believed what Jesus said to him and left. ⁵¹While he was on his way back, his slaves met him and told him that his boy would live. ⁵²He asked them when he began to recover. They told him, "The fever left him yesterday, about one in the afternoon." ⁵³The father realized that just at that time Jesus had said to him, "Your son will live," and he and his whole household came to believe. ^{54v}[Now] this was the second sign Jesus did when he came to Galilee from Judea.

Cure on a Sabbath

5 ¹*aAfter this, there was a feast of the Jews, and Jesus went up to Jerusalem.* ^{2b}Now there is in

Archaeological remains of the Pool of Bethesda

4:39 The woman is presented as a missionary, described in virtually the same words as the disciples are in Jesus' prayer (17:20).

4:43-54 Jesus' arrival in Cana in Galilee; the second sign. This section introduces another theme, that of the life-giving word of Jesus. It is explicitly linked to the first sign (2:11). The royal official believes (4:50). The natural life given his son is a sign of eternal life.

4:44 Probably a reminiscence of a tradition as in Mark 6:4. Cf. Gospel of Thomas 31: "No prophet is acceptable in his village, no physician heals those who know him."

4:46-54 The story of the cure of the royal official's son may be a third version of the cure of the centurion's son (Mt 8:5-13) or servant (Lk 7:1-10). Cf. also Matthew 15:21-28; Mark 7:24-30.

5:1-47 The self-revelation of Jesus continues in Jerusalem at a feast. The third sign (cf. 2:11; 4:54) is performed, the cure of a para-

lytic by Jesus' life-giving word. The water of the pool fails to bring life; Jesus' word does.

5:1 The reference in John 5:45-46 to Moses suggests that the feast was Pentecost. The connection of that feast with the giving of the law to Moses on Sinai, attested in later Judaism, may already have been made in the first century. The feast could also be Passover (cf. 6:4). John stresses that the day was a sabbath (5:9).

5:2 There is no noun with **Sheep**. "Gate" is supplied on the grounds that there must have been a gate in the NE wall of the temple area where animals for sacrifice were brought in; cf. Nehemiah 3:1, 32; 12:39. **Hebrew**: more precisely, Aramaic. **Bethesda**: preferred to variants "Be(th)zatha" and "Bethsaida"; *bêt-'ešdatayîn* is given as the name of a double pool northeast of the temple area in the Qumran Copper Roll. **Five porticoes**: a pool excavated in Jerusalem actually has five porticoes.

Jerusalem at the Sheep [Gate]* a pool called in Hebrew Bethesda, with five porticoes. ³In these lay a large number of ill, blind, lame, and crippled.* [⁴]* ⁵One man was there who had been ill for thirty-eight years. ⁶When Jesus saw him lying there and knew that he had been ill for a long time, he said to him, "Do you want to be well?" ⁷The sick man answered him, "Sir, I have no one to put me into the pool when the water is stirred up; while I am on my way, someone else gets down there before me." ⁸ᶜJesus said to him, "Rise, take up your mat, and walk." ⁹ᵈImmediately the man became well, took up his mat, and walked.

Now that day was a sabbath. ¹⁰ᵉSo the Jews said to the man who was cured, "It is the sabbath, and it is not lawful for you to carry your mat." ¹¹He answered them, "The man who made me well told me, 'Take up your mat and walk.'" ¹²They asked him, "Who is the man who told you, 'Take it up and walk'?" ¹³ᶠThe man who was healed did not know who it was, for Jesus had slipped away, since there was a crowd there. ¹⁴*ᵍAfter this Jesus found him in the temple area and said to him, "Look, you are well; do not sin any more, so that nothing worse may happen to you." ¹⁵The man went and told the Jews that Jesus was the one who had made him well. ¹⁶ʰTherefore, the Jews began to persecute Jesus because he did this on a sabbath. ¹⁷*ⁱBut Jesus answered them, "My Father is at work until now, so I am at work." ¹⁸ʲFor this reason the Jews tried all the more to kill him, because he not only broke the sabbath but he also called God his own father, making himself equal to God.

The Work of the Son

¹⁹*ᵏJesus answered and said to them, "Amen, amen, I say to you, a son cannot do anything on his own, but only what he sees his father doing; for what he does, his son will do also. ²⁰For the Father loves his Son and shows him everything that he himself does, and he will show him greater works than these, so that you may be amazed. ²¹ᵐFor just as the Father raises the dead and gives life,* so also does the Son give life to whomever he wishes. ²²ⁿNor does the Father judge anyone, but he has given all judgment* to his Son, ²³so that all may honor the Son just as they honor the Father. Whoever does not honor the Son does not honor the Father who sent him. ²⁴ᵒAmen, amen, I say

---

5:3 The Caesarean and Western recensions, followed by the Vulgate, add "waiting for the movement of the water." Apparently an intermittent spring in the pool bubbled up occasionally (see 5:7). This turbulence was believed to cure.

5:4 Toward the end of the second century in the West and among the fourth-century Greek Fathers, an additional verse was known: "For [from time to time] an angel of the Lord used to come down into the pool; and the water was stirred up, so the first one to get in [after the stirring of the water] was healed of whatever disease afflicted him." The angel was a popular explanation of the turbulence and the healing powers attributed to it. This verse is missing from all early Greek manuscripts and the earliest versions, including the original Vulgate. Its vocabulary is markedly non-Johannine.

5:14 While the cure of the paralytic in Mark 2:1-12 is associated with the forgiveness of sins, Jesus never drew a one-to-one connection between sin and suffering (cf. 9:3; Lk 12:1-5), as did Ezekiel 18:20.

5:17 Sabbath observance (10) was based on God's resting on the seventh day (cf. Gn 2:2-3; Ex 20:11). Philo and some rabbis insisted that God's providence remains active on the sabbath, keeping all things in existence, giving life in birth and taking it away in death. Other rabbis taught that God rested from creating, but not from judging (= ruling, governing). Jesus here claims the same authority to work as the Father, and, in the discourse that follows, the same divine prerogatives: power over life and death (5:21, 24-26) and judgment (5:22, 27).

5:19 This proverb or parable is taken from apprenticeship in a trade: the activity of a son is modeled on that of his father. Jesus' dependence on the Father is justification for doing what the Father does.

5:21 Gives life: in the Old Testament, a divine prerogative (Dt 32:39; 1 Sm 2:6; 2 Kgs 5:7; Tb 13:2; Is 26:19; Dn 12:2).

5:22 Judgment: another divine prerogative, often expressed as acquittal or condemnation (Dt 32:36; Ps 43:1).

---

c
Mt 9:6;
Mk 2:11;
Lk 5:24;
Acts 3:6

d
Mk 2:12;
Lk 5:25; 9:14

e
Ex 20:8;
Jer 17:21-27;
Mk 3:2;
Lk 13:10 / 14:1

f
Mt 8:18; 13:36;
Mk 4:36; 7:17

g
8:11; 9:2;
Ez 18:20

h
7:23; Mt 12:8

i
Ex 20:11

j
7:1, 25;
8:37, 40;
10:33, 36;
14:28;
Gn 3:5-6;
Wis 2:16;
Mt 26:4;
2 Thes 2:4

k
3:34; 8:26;
12:49; 9:4;
10:30

l
3:35

m
11:25;
Dt 32:39;
1 Sm 2:6;
2 Kgs 5:7;
Tb 13:2;
Wis 16:13;
Is 26:19;
Dn 7:10, 13;
12:2;
Rom 4:17;
2 Cor 1:9

n
Acts 10:42;
17:31

o
3:18; 8:51;
1 Jn 3:14

JOHN

p
5:28; 8:51;
11:25-26;
Eph 2:1; 5:14;
Rev 3:1

q
1:4; 1 Jn 5:11

r
5:22; Dn 7:13,
22; Mt 25:31;
Lk 21:36

s
11:43

t
Dn 12:2;
Mt 16:27;
25:46;
Acts 24:15;
2 Cor 5:10

u
6:38

v
8:13-14, 18

w
1:19-27;
Mt 11:10-11

x
1 Jn 5:9

y
1:8; Ps 132:17;
Sir 48:1

z
10:25

a
8:18; Dt 4:12,
15; 1 Jn 5:9

b
1 Jn 2:14

c
12:16; 19:28;
20:9; Lk 24:27,
44; 1 Pt 1:10

d
1 Jn 2:15

e
Mt 24:5, 24

f
12:43

g
Dt 31:26

h
5:39; Dt 18:15;
Lk 16:31;
24:44

to you, whoever hears my word and believes in the one who sent me has eternal life and will not come to condemnation, but has passed from death to life. [25p]Amen, amen, I say to you, the hour is coming and is now here when the dead will hear the voice of the Son of God, and those who hear will live. [26q]For just as the Father has life in himself, so also he gave to his Son the possession of life in himself. [27r]And he gave him power to exercise judgment, because he is the Son of Man. [28*s]Do not be amazed at this, because the hour is coming in which all who are in the tombs will hear his voice [29t]and will come out, those who have done good deeds to the resurrection of life, but those who have done wicked deeds to the resurrection of condemnation.

[30u]"I cannot do anything on my own; I judge as I hear, and my judgment is just, because I do not seek my own will but the will of the one who sent me.

Witnesses to Jesus

[31v]"If I testify on my own behalf, my testimony cannot be verified. [32]But there is another* who testifies on my behalf, and I know that the testimony he gives on my behalf is true. [33w]You sent emissaries to John, and he testified to the truth. [34x]I do not accept testimony from a human being, but I say this so that you may be saved. [35y]He was a burning and shining lamp,* and for a while you were content to rejoice in his light. [36z]But I have testimony greater than John's. The works that the Father gave me to accomplish, these works that I perform testify on my behalf that the Father has sent me. [37a]Moreover, the Father who sent me has testified on my behalf. But you have never heard his voice nor seen his form, [38b]and you do not have his word remaining in you, because you do not believe in the one whom he has sent. [39c]You search* the scriptures, because you think you have eternal life through them; even they testify on my behalf. [40]But you do not want to come to me to have life.

Unbelief of Jesus' Hearers

[41]"I do not accept human praise;* [42d]moreover, I know that you do not have the love of God in you. [43e]I came in the name of my Father, but you do not accept me; yet if another comes in his own name, you will accept him. [44f]How can you believe, when you accept praise from one another and do not seek the praise that comes from the only God? [45g]Do not think that I will accuse you before the Father: the one who will accuse you is Moses, in whom you have placed your hope. [46h]For if you had believed Moses, you would have believed me, because he wrote about me. [47]But if you do not believe his writings, how will you believe my words?"

5:28-29 While John 5:19-27 present realized eschatology, John 5:28-29 are future eschatology; cf. Daniel 12:2.

5:32 Another: likely the Father, who in four different ways gives testimony to Jesus, as indicated in the verse groupings John 5:33-34, 36, 37-38, 39-40.

5:35 Lamp: cf. Psalm 132:17—"I will place a lamp for my anointed (= David)," and possibly the description of Elijah in Sirach 48:1. But only **for a while**, indicating the temporary and subordinate nature of John's mission.

5:39 You search: this may be an imperative: "Search the scriptures, because you think that you have eternal life through them."

5:41 Praise: the same Greek word means "praise" or "honor" (from others) and "glory" (from God). There is a play on this in John 5:44.

JOHN

Multiplication of the Loaves

6 [1]*[a]After this, Jesus went across the Sea of Galilee [of Tiberias].* [2]A large crowd followed him, because they saw the signs he was performing on the sick. [3]Jesus went up on the mountain, and there he sat down with his disciples. [4][b]The Jewish feast of Passover was near. [5]*[c]When Jesus raised his eyes and saw that a large crowd was coming to him, he said to Philip, "Where can we buy enough food for them to eat?" [6]*He said this to

A view of the Sea of Galilee

test him, because he himself knew what he was going to do. [7][d]Philip answered him, "Two hundred days' wages* worth of food would not be enough for each of them to have a little [bit]." [8]One of his disciples, Andrew, the brother of Simon Peter, said to him, [9][e]"There is a boy here who has five barley loaves* and two fish; but what good are these for so many?" [10]Jesus said, "Have the people recline." Now there was a great deal of grass* in that place. So the men reclined, about five thousand in number. [11][g]Then Jesus took the loaves, gave thanks, and distributed them to those who were reclining, and also as much of the fish as they wanted. [12]When they had had their fill, he said to his disciples, "Gather the fragments left over, so that nothing will be wasted." [13]So they collected them, and filled twelve wicker baskets* with fragments from the five barley loaves that had been more than they could eat. [14][h]When the people saw the sign he had done, they said, "This is truly the Prophet,* the one who is to come into the world." [15][i]Since Jesus knew that they were going to come and carry him off to make him king, he withdrew again to the mountain alone.

Walking on the Water

[16]*[j]When it was evening, his disciples went down to the sea, [17]embarked in a boat, and went across the sea to Capernaum. It had already grown dark, and Jesus had not yet come to them. [18]The sea was stirred up because a strong wind was blowing. [19][k]When

a
Mt 14:13-21;
Mk 6:32-44;
Lk 9:10-17

b
2:13; 11:55

c
Nm 11:13

d
Mt 20:2

e
2 Kgs 4:42-44

f
Mt 14:21;
Mk 6:44

g
21:13

h
Dt 18:15, 18;
Mal 3:1, 23;
Acts 3:22

i
18:36

j
Mt 14:22-27;
Mk 6:45-52

k
Jb 9:8;
Pss 29:3-4;
77:20; Is 43:16

JOHN

6:1-15 This story of the multiplication of the loaves is the fourth sign (cf. the note on 5:1-47). It is the only miracle story found in all four gospels (occurring twice in Mark and Matthew). See the notes on Matthew 14:13-21; 15:32-39. John differs on the roles of Philip and Andrew, the proximity of Passover (6:4), and the allusion to Elisha (see 6:9). The story here symbolizes the food that is really available through Jesus. It connotes a new exodus and has eucharistic overtones.

6:1 [Of Tiberias]: the awkward apposition represents a later name of the Sea of Galilee. It was probably originally a marginal gloss.

6:5 Jesus takes the initiative (in the synoptics, the disciples do), possibly pictured as (cf. 6:14) the new Moses (cf. Nm 11:13).

6:6 Probably the evangelist's comment; in this gospel Jesus is never portrayed as ignorant of anything.

6:7 Days' wages: literally, "denarii"; a Roman denarius is a day's wage in Matthew 20:2.

6:9 Barley loaves: the food of the poor. There seems an allusion to the story of Elisha multiplying the barley bread in 2 Kings 4:42-44.

6:10 Grass: implies springtime, and therefore Passover. **Five thousand:** so Mark 6:39, 44 and parallels.

6:13 Baskets: the word describes the typically Palestinian wicker basket, as in Mark 6:43 and parallels.

6:14 The Prophet: probably the prophet like Moses (see the note on 1:21). **The one who is to come into the world:** probably Elijah; cf. Malachi 3:1, 23.

6:16-21 The fifth sign is a nature miracle, portraying Jesus sharing Yahweh's power. Cf. the parallel stories following the multiplication of the loaves in Mark 6:45-52 and Matthew 14:22-33.

6:19 Walking on the sea: although the Greek (cf. 6:16) could mean "on the seashore" or "by the sea" (cf. 21:1), the parallels, especially Matthew 14:25, make clear that Jesus walked upon the water. John may allude to Job 9:8: God "treads upon the crests of the sea."

l
6:50, 51, 54,
58

m
Mt 16:1-4;
Lk 11:29-30

n
Ex 16:4-5;
Nm 11:7-9;
Ps 78:24

o
Mt 6:11

p
4:15

q
Is 55:1-3;
Am 8:11-13

r
20:29

s
4:34; Mt 26:39;
Heb 10:9

t
10:28-29;
17:12; 18:9

u
1 Jn 2:25

v
Mt 13:54-57;
Mk 6:1-4;
Lk 4:22

w
Ex 16:2, 7, 8;
Lk 4:22

JOHN

they had rowed about three or four miles, they saw Jesus walking on the sea[*] and coming near the boat, and they began to be afraid. [20]But he said to them, "It is I.[*] Do not be afraid." [21]They wanted to take him into the boat, but the boat immediately arrived at the shore to which they were heading.

The Bread of Life Discourse

[22*]The next day, the crowd that remained across the sea saw that there had been only one boat there, and that Jesus had not gone along with his disciples in the boat, but only his disciples had left. [23*]Other boats came from Tiberias near the place where they had eaten the bread when the Lord gave thanks. [24]When the crowd saw that neither Jesus nor his disciples were there, they themselves got into boats and came to Capernaum looking for Jesus. [25]And when they found him across the sea they said to him, "Rabbi, when did you get here?" [26]Jesus answered them and said, "Amen, amen, I say to you, you are looking for me not because you saw signs but because you ate the loaves and were filled. [27l]Do not work for food that perishes but for the food that endures for eternal life,[*] which the Son of Man will give you. For on him the Father, God, has set his seal." [28]So they said to him, "What can we do to accomplish the works of God?" [29]Jesus answered and said to them, "This is the work of God, that you believe in the one he sent." [30m]So they said to him, "What sign can you do, that we may see and believe in you? What can you do? [31*n]Our ancestors ate manna in the desert, as it is written:

'He gave them bread from heaven to eat.'"

[32o]So Jesus said to them, "Amen, amen, I say to you, it was not Moses who gave the bread from heaven; my Father gives you the true bread from heaven. [33p]For the bread of God is that which comes down from heaven and gives life to the world."

[34q]So they said to him, "Sir, give us this bread always." [35*]Jesus said to them, "I am the bread of life; whoever comes to me will never hunger, and whoever believes in me will never thirst. [36r]But I told you that although you have seen [me], you do not believe. [37]Everything that the Father gives me will come to me, and I will not reject anyone who comes to me, [38s]because I came down from heaven not to do my own will but the will of the one who sent me. [39t]And this is the will of the one who sent me, that I should not lose anything of what he gave me, but that I should raise it [on] the last day. [40u]For this is the will of my Father, that everyone who sees the Son and believes in him may have eternal life, and I shall raise him [on] the last day."

[41]The Jews murmured about him because he said, "I am the bread that came down from heaven," [42v]and they said, "Is this not Jesus, the son of Joseph? Do we not know his father and mother? Then how can he say, 'I have come down from heaven'?" [43w]Jesus

---

6:20 It is I: literally, "I am." See also the notes on John 4:26 and Mark 6:50.

6:22–71 Discourse on the bread of life; replacement of the manna. John 6:22-34 serve as an introduction, John 6:35-59 constitute the discourse proper, John 6:60-71 portray the reaction of the disciples and Peter's confession.

6:23 Possibly a later interpolation, to explain how the crowd got to Capernaum.

6:27 The food that endures for eternal life: cf. John 4:14, on water "springing up to eternal life."

6:31 Bread from heaven: cf. Exodus 16:4, 15, 32-34 and the notes there; Psalm 78:24. The manna, thought to have been hidden by Jeremiah (2 Mc 2:5-8), was expected to reappear miraculously at Passover, in the last days.

6:35–59 Up to John 6:50, "bread of life" is a figure for God's revelation in Jesus; in John 6:51-58, the eucharistic theme comes to the fore. There may thus be a break between John 6:50 and 51.

6:43 Murmuring: the word may reflect the Greek of Exodus 16:2, 7-8.

answered and said to them, "Stop murmuring* among yourselves. ⁴⁴No one can come to me unless the Father who sent me draw him, and I will raise him on the last day. ⁴⁵ˣIt is written in the prophets:

'They shall all be taught by God.'

Everyone who listens to my Father and learns from him comes to me. ⁴⁶ʸNot that anyone has seen the Father except the one who is from God; he has seen the Father. ⁴⁷Amen, amen, I say to you, whoever believes has eternal life. ⁴⁸I am the bread of life. ⁴⁹ᶻYour ancestors ate the manna in the desert, but they died; ⁵⁰this is the bread that comes down from heaven so that one may eat it and not die. ⁵¹ᵃI am the living bread that came down from heaven; whoever eats this bread will live forever; and the bread that I will give is my flesh for the life of the world."

⁵²The Jews quarreled among themselves, saying, "How can this man give us [his] flesh to eat?" ⁵³Jesus said to them, "Amen, amen, I say to you, unless you eat the flesh of the Son of Man and drink his blood, you do not have life within you. ⁵⁴Whoever eats* my flesh and drinks my blood has eternal life, and I will raise him on the last day. ⁵⁵For my flesh is true food, and my blood is true drink. ⁵⁶Whoever eats my flesh and drinks my blood remains in me and I in him. ⁵⁷ᵇJust as the living Father sent me and I have life because of the Father, so also the one who feeds on me will have life because of me. ⁵⁸This is the bread that came down from heaven. Unlike your ancestors who ate and still died, whoever eats this bread will live forever." ⁵⁹These things he said while teaching in the synagogue in Capernaum.

The Words of Eternal Life

⁶⁰*Then many of his disciples who were listening said, "This saying is hard; who can accept it?" ⁶¹Since Jesus knew that his disciples were murmuring about this, he said to them, "Does this shock you? ⁶²What if you were to see the Son of Man ascending to where he was before?* ⁶³It is the spirit that gives life, while the flesh* is of no avail. The words I have spoken to you are spirit and life. ⁶⁴ᶜBut there are some of you who do not believe." Jesus knew from the beginning the ones who would not believe and the one who would betray him. ⁶⁵And he said, "For this reason I have told you that no one can come to me unless it is granted him by my Father."

⁶⁶As a result of this, many [of] his disciples returned to their former way of life and no longer accompanied him. ⁶⁷Jesus then said to the Twelve, "Do you also want to leave?" ⁶⁸Simon Peter answered him, "Master, to whom shall we go? You have the words of eternal life. ⁶⁹ᵈWe have come to believe and are convinced that you are the Holy One of God." ⁷⁰Jesus answered them, "Did I not choose you twelve? Yet is not one of you a devil?" ⁷¹ᵉHe was referring to Judas, son of Simon the Iscariot; it was he who would betray him, one of the Twelve.

---

x Is 54:13; Jer 31:33-34
y 1:18; 7:29; Ex 33:20
z 1 Cor 10:3, 5
a Mt 26:26-27; Lk 22:19
b 5:26
c 13:11
d 11:27; Mt 16:16; Mk 1:24; Lk 4:34
e 12:4; 13:2, 27

6:54-58 Eats: the verb used in these verses is not the classical Greek verb used of human eating, but that of animal eating: "munch," "gnaw." This may be part of John's emphasis on the reality of the flesh and blood of Jesus (cf. 6:55), but the same verb eventually became the ordinary verb in Greek meaning "eat."

6:60-71 These verses refer more to themes of John 6:35-50 than to those of John 6:51-58 and seem to be addressed to members of the Johannine community who found it difficult to accept the high christology reflected in the bread of life discourse.

6:62 This unfinished conditional sentence is obscure. Probably there is a reference to John 6:49-51. Jesus claims to be **the bread that comes down from heaven** (6:50); this claim provokes incredulity (6:60); and so Jesus is pictured as asking what his disciples will say when he goes up to heaven.

6:63 Spirit . . . flesh: probably not a reference to the eucharistic body of Jesus but to the supernatural and the natural, as in John 3:6. **Spirit and life:** all Jesus said about the bread of life is the revelation of the Spirit.

233

a
5:18; 8:37, 40

b
Ex 23:16;
Lv 23:34;
Nm 29:12;
Dt 16:13-16;
Zec 14:16-19

c
14:22

d
15:18

e
9:22; 19:38;
20:19

f
Lk 2:47

g
6:29

h
Acts 7:53

i
8:48-49; 10:20

j
5:1-9

k
Gn 17:10;
Lv 12:3

JOHN

The Feast of Tabernacles

7 [1]*[a]After this, Jesus moved about within Galilee; but he did not wish to travel in Judea, because the Jews were trying to kill him. [2][b]But the Jewish feast of Tabernacles was near. [3]So his brothers* said to him, "Leave here and go to Judea, so that your disciples also may see the works you are doing. [4][c]No one works in secret if he wants to be known publicly. If you do these things, manifest yourself to the world." [5]For his brothers did not believe in him. [6]*So Jesus said to them, "My time is not yet here, but the time is always right for you. [7][d]The world cannot hate you, but it hates me, because I testify to it that its works are evil. [8]You go up to the feast. I am not going up* to this feast, because my time has not yet been fulfilled." [9]After he had said this, he stayed on in Galilee.

[10]But when his brothers had gone up to the feast, he himself also went up, not openly but [as it were] in secret. [11]The Jews were looking for him at the feast and saying, "Where is he?" [12]And there was considerable murmuring about him in the crowds. Some said, "He is a good man," [while] others said, "No; on the contrary, he misleads the crowd." [13][e]Still, no one spoke openly about him because they were afraid of the Jews.

The First Dialogue

[14]*When the feast was already half over, Jesus went up into the temple area and began to teach. [15]*[f]The Jews were amazed and said, "How does he know scripture without having studied?" [16]Jesus answered them and said, "My teaching is not my own but is from the one who sent me. [17][g]Whoever chooses to do his will* shall know whether my teaching is from God or whether I speak on my own. [18]Whoever speaks on his own seeks his own glory, but whoever seeks the glory of the one who sent him is truthful, and there is no wrong in him. [19][h]Did not Moses give you the law? Yet none of you keeps the law. Why are you trying to kill me?" [20][i]The crowd answered, "You are possessed!* Who is trying to kill you?" [21][j]Jesus answered and said to them, "I performed one work* and all of you are amazed [22][k]because of it. Moses gave you circumcision—not that it came from Moses but rather from the patriarchs—and you circumcise a man on the

---

7:1-8 These chapters contain events about the feast of Tabernacles (Sukkoth, Ingathering: Ex 23:16; Tents, Booths: Dt 16:13-16), with its symbols of booths (originally built to shelter harvesters), rain (water from Siloam poured on the temple altar), and lights (illumination of the four torches in the Court of the Women). They continue the theme of the replacement of feasts (Passover, 2:13; 6:4; Hanukkah, 10:22; Pentecost, 5:1), here accomplished by Jesus as the Living Water. These chapters comprise seven miscellaneous controversies and dialogues. There is a literary inclusion with Jesus in hiding in John 7:4, 10; 8:59. There are frequent references to attempts on his life: John 7:1, 13, 19, 25, 30, 32, 44; 8:37, 40, 59.

7:3 Brothers: these relatives (cf. 2:12 and see the note on Mk 6:3) are never portrayed as disciples until after the resurrection (Acts 1:14). Matthew 13:55 and Mark 6:3 give the names of four of them. Jesus has already performed works/signs in Judea; cf. John 2:23; 3:2; 4:45; 5:8.

7:6 Time: the Greek word means "opportune time," here a synonym for Jesus' "hour" (see the note on 2:4), his death and resurrection. In the wordplay, any time is suitable for Jesus' brothers, because they are not dependent on God's will.

7:8 I am not going up: an early attested reading "not yet" seems a correction, since Jesus in the story does go up to the feast. "Go up," in a play on words, refers not only to going up to Jerusalem but also to exaltation at the cross, resurrection, and ascension; cf. John 3:14; 6:62; 20:17.

7:14-31 Jesus teaches in the temple; debate with the Jews.

7:15 Without having studied: literally, "How does he know letters without having learned?" Children were taught to read and write by means of the scriptures. But here more than Jesus' literacy is being discussed; the people are wondering how he can teach like a rabbi. Rabbis were trained by other rabbis and traditionally quoted their teachers.

7:17 To do his will: presumably a reference back to the "work" of John 6:29: belief in the one whom God has sent.

7:20 You are possessed: literally, "You have a demon." The insane were thought to be possessed by a demoniacal spirit.

7:21 One work: the cure of the paralytic (5:1-9) because of the reference to the sabbath (7:22; 5:9-10).

sabbath. [23l]If a man can receive circumcision on a sabbath so that the law of Moses may not be broken, are you angry with me because I made a whole person well on a sabbath? [24m]Stop judging by appearances, but judge justly."

[25]So some of the inhabitants of Jerusalem said, "Is he not the one they are trying to kill? [26]And look, he is speaking openly and they say nothing to him. Could the authorities* have realized that he is the Messiah? [27n]But we know where he is from. When the Messiah comes, no one will know where he is from." [28o]So Jesus cried out in the temple area as he was teaching and said, "You know me and also know where I am from. Yet I did not come on my own, but the one who sent me, whom you do not know, is true. [29p]I know him, because I am from him, and he sent me." [30q]So they tried to arrest him, but no one laid a hand upon him, because his hour had not yet come. [31r]But many of the crowd began to believe in him, and said, "When the Messiah comes, will he perform more signs than this man has done?"

Officers Sent to Arrest Jesus

[32*]The Pharisees heard the crowd murmuring about him to this effect, and the chief priests and the Pharisees sent guards to arrest him. [33s]So Jesus said, "I will be with you only a little while longer, and then I will go to the one who sent me. [34t]You will look for me but not find [me], and where I am you cannot come." [35]So the Jews said to one another, "Where is he going that we will not find him? Surely he is not going to the dispersion* among the Greeks to teach the Greeks, is he? [36]What is the meaning of his saying, 'You will look for me and not find [me], and where I am you cannot come'?"

Rivers of Living Water

[37*u]On the last and greatest day of the feast, Jesus stood up and exclaimed, "Let anyone who thirsts come to me and drink. [38v]Whoever believes in me, as scripture says:

'Rivers of living water* will flow from within him.'"

[39w]He said this in reference to the Spirit that those who came to believe in him were to receive. There was, of course, no Spirit yet,* because Jesus had not yet been glorified.

Discussion about the Origins of the Messiah

[40*x]Some in the crowd who heard these words said, "This is truly the Prophet." [41]Others said, "This is the Messiah." But others said, "The Messiah will not come from Galilee, will he? [42y]Does not scripture say that the Messiah will be of David's family and come from Bethlehem, the village where David lived?" [43]So a division occurred in the crowd because of him. [44]Some of them even wanted to arrest him, but no one laid hands on him.

l
5:2-9, 16;
Mt 12:11-12;
Lk 14:5

m
8:15; Lv 19:15;
Is 11:3-4

n
Heb 7:3

o
8:19

p
6:46; 8:55

q
7:44; 8:20;
Lk 4:29-30

r
2:11; 10:42;
11:45

s
13:33; 16:16

t
8:21; 12:36;
13:33, 36;
16:5; Dt 4:29;
Prv 1:28;
Is 55:6;
Hos 5:6

u
Rev 21:6

v
4:10, 14;
19:34; Is 12:3;
Ez 47:1

w
16:7

x
Dt 18:15, 18

y
2 Sm 7:12-14;
Pss 89:3-4;
132:11; Mi 5:1;
Mt 2:5-6

7:26 The authorities: the members of the Sanhedrin (same term as 3:1).

7:32-36 Jesus announces his approaching departure (cf. also 8:21; 12:36; 13:33) and complete control over his destiny.

7:35 Dispersion: or "diaspora": Jews living outside Palestine. **Greeks**: probably refers to the Gentiles in the Mediterranean area; cf. John 12:20.

7:37-39 Promise of living water through the Spirit.

7:38 Living water: not an exact quotation from any Old Testament passage; in the gospel context the gift of the Spirit is meant;

cf. John 3:5. **From within him**: either Jesus or the believer; if Jesus, it continues the Jesus-Moses motif (water from the rock, Ex 17:6; Nm 20:11) as well as Jesus as the new temple (cf. Ez 47:1). Grammatically, it goes better with the believer.

7:39 No Spirit yet: Codex Vaticanus and early Latin, Syriac, and Coptic versions add "given." In this gospel, the sending of the Spirit cannot take place until Jesus' glorification through his death, resurrection, and ascension; cf. John 20:22.

7:40-53 Discussion of the Davidic lineage of the Messiah.

z
12:42

a
3:1; 19:39

b
Dt 1:16-17

a
Lk 21:37-38

b
Lv 20:10;
Dt 22:22-29

c
Dt 17:7

d
Ez 33:11

e
5:14

f
1:4-5, 9; 12:46;
Ex 13:22;
Is 42:6;
Zec 14:8

g
5:31

⁴⁵So the guards went to the chief priests and Pharisees, who asked them, "Why did you not bring him?" ⁴⁶The guards answered, "Never before has anyone spoken like this one." ⁴⁷So the Pharisees answered them, "Have you also been deceived? ⁴⁸ᶻHave any of the authorities or the Pharisees believed in him? ⁴⁹But this crowd, which does not know the law, is accursed." ⁵⁰ᵃNicodemus, one of their members who had come to him earlier, said to them, ⁵¹ᵇ"Does our law condemn a person before it first hears him and finds out what he is doing?" ⁵²They answered and said to him, "You are not from Galilee also, are you? Look and see that no prophet arises from Galilee."

A Woman Caught in Adultery

⁵³*[Then each went to his own house,

8 ¹ᵃwhile Jesus went to the Mount of Olives.* ²But early in the morning he arrived again in the temple area, and all the people started coming to him, and he sat down and taught them. ³Then the scribes and the Pharisees brought a woman who had been caught in adultery and made her stand in the middle. ⁴They said to him, "Teacher, this woman was caught in the very act of committing adultery. ⁵ᵇNow in the law, Moses commanded us to stone such women.* So what do you say?" ⁶They said this to test him, so that they could have some charge to bring against him. Jesus bent down and began to write on the ground with his finger.* ⁷*ᶜBut when they continued asking him, he straightened up and said to them, "Let the one among you who is without sin be the first to throw a stone at her." ⁸Again he bent down and wrote on the ground. ⁹And in response, they went away one by one, beginning with the elders. So he was left alone with the woman before him. ¹⁰ᵈThen Jesus straightened up and said to her, "Woman, where are they? Has no one condemned you?" ¹¹ᵉShe replied, "No one, sir." Then Jesus said, "Neither do I condemn you. Go, [and] from now on do not sin any more."]

The Light of the World

¹²*ᶠJesus spoke to them again, saying, "I am the light of the world. Whoever follows me will not walk in darkness, but will have the light of life." ¹³So the Pharisees said to him, "You testify on your own behalf, so your testimony cannot be verified." ¹⁴ᵍJesus answered and said to them, "Even if I do testify on my own behalf, my testimony can be verified,* because I know where I came from and where I am going. But you do not

---

7:53–8:11 The story of the woman caught in adultery is a later insertion here, missing from all early Greek manuscripts. A Western text-type insertion, attested mainly in Old Latin translations, it is found in different places in different manuscripts: here, or after John 7:36, or at the end of this gospel, or after Luke 21:38, or at the end of that gospel. There are many non-Johannine features in the language, and there are also many doubtful readings within the passage. The style and motifs are similar to those of Luke, and it fits better with the general situation at the end of Luke 21, but it was probably inserted here because of the allusion to Jeremiah 17:13 (cf. the note on 8:6) and the statement, "I do not judge anyone," in John 8:15. The Catholic Church accepts this passage as canonical scripture.

8:1 Mount of Olives: not mentioned elsewhere in the gospel tradition outside of passion week.

8:5 Leviticus 20:10 and Deuteronomy 22:22 mention only death, but Deuteronomy 22:23-24 prescribes stoning for a betrothed virgin.

8:6 Cf. Jeremiah 17:13 (RSV): "Those who turn away from thee shall be written in the earth, for they have forsaken the Lᴏʀᴅ, the fountain of living water"; cf. John 7:38.

8:7 The first stones were to be thrown by the witnesses (Dt 17:7).

8:12-20 Jesus the light of the world. Jesus replaces the four torches of the illumination of the temple as the light of joy.

8:14 My testimony can be verified: this seems to contradict John 5:31 but the emphasis here is on Jesus' origin from the Father and his divine destiny. **Where I am going**: indicates Jesus' passion and glorification.

JOHN

know where I come from or where I am going. [15h]You judge by appearances,[*] but I do not judge anyone. [16i]And even if I should judge, my judgment is valid, because I am not alone, but it is I and the Father who sent me. [17j]Even in your law[*] it is written that the testimony of two men can be verified. [18k]I testify on my behalf and so does the Father who sent me." [19l]So they said to him, "Where is your father?" Jesus answered, "You know neither me nor my Father. If you knew me, you would know my Father also." [20m]He spoke these words while teaching in the treasury in the temple area. But no one arrested him, because his hour had not yet come.

Jesus, the Father's Ambassador

[21*n]He said to them again, "I am going away and you will look for me, but you will die in your sin. Where I am going you cannot come."[*] [22*]So the Jews said, "He is not going to kill himself, is he, because he said, 'Where I am going you cannot come'?" [23o]He said to them, "You belong to what is below, I belong to what is above. You belong to this world, but I do not belong to this world. [24p]That is why I told you that you will die in your sins. For if you do not believe that I AM,[*] you will die in your sins." [25*q]So

The expression **"I AM"** is of special importance in John's gospel. It is a way of translating the Hebrew name for God (YHWH), which means something like "I am who I am" or "I am who I will be present." Four times in John, Jesus uses this expression without any qualifiers. It is a bald statement of identification with God. At other times, the expression is accompanied by images that describe aspects of Jesus' special mission from the Father. See "Names of God" (at Ex 3:14).

I AM Sayings in John's Gospel	
8:24	For if you do not believe that I AM, you will die in your sins.
8:28	When you lift up the Son of Man, you will realize that I AM.
8:58	Amen, amen, I say to you, before Abraham came to be, I AM.
13:19	So that when it [fulfillment of Scripture] happens you may believe that I AM.
6:35	I am the bread of life.
6:51	I am the living bread that came down from heaven.
8:12	I am the light of the world (cf. 9:5).
10:7	I am the gate of the sheep (cf. 10:9).
10:11	I am the good shepherd (cf. 10:14).
11:25	I am the resurrection and the life.
14:6	I am the way and the truth and the life.
15:5	I am the vine, you are the branches (cf. 15:1).

h
12:47;
1 Sm 16:7

i
5:30

j
Dt 17:6; 19:15;
Nm 35:30

k
5:23, 37

l
7:28; 14:7;
15:21

m
7:30

n
7:34; 13:33

o
3:31; 17:14;
18:36

p
Ex 3:14;
Dt 32:39;
Is 43:10

q
10:24

JOHN

8:15 By appearances: literally, "according to the flesh." **I do not judge anyone**: superficial contradiction of John 5:22, 27, 30; here the emphasis is that the judgment is not by material standards.

8:17 Your law: a reflection of later controversy between church and synagogue.

8:21-30 He whose ambassador I am is with me. Jesus' origin is from God; he can reveal God.

8:21 You will die in your sin: i.e., of disbelief; cf. John 8:24. **Where I am going you cannot come**: except through faith in Jesus' passion-resurrection.

8:22 The Jews suspect that he is referring to his death. Johannine irony is apparent here; Jesus' death will not be self-inflicted but destined by God.

8:24, 28 I AM: an expression that late Jewish tradition understood as Yahweh's own self-designation (Is 43:10); see the note on John 4:26. Jesus is here placed on a par with Yahweh.

8:25 What I told you from the beginning: this verse seems textually corrupt, with several other possible translations: "(I am) what I say to you"; "Why do I speak to you at all?" The earliest attested reading (Bodmer Papyrus P[66]) has (in a second hand), "I

r
12:44-50

s
3:14; 12:32, 34

t
Is 42:7;
Gal 4:31

u
Mt 3:9

v
Rom 6:16-17

w
Gn 21:10;
Gal 4:30;
Heb 3:5-6

x
Gn 26:5;
Rom 4:11-17;
Jas 2:21-23

y
Mal 2:10

z
1 Jn 5:1

a
Gn 3:4;
Wis 1:13; 2:24;
Acts 13:10;
1 Jn 3:8-15

b
Heb 4:15;
1 Pt 2:22;
1 Jn 3:5

they said to him, "Who are you?" Jesus said to them, "What I told you from the beginning. ²⁶ʳI have much to say about you in condemnation. But the one who sent me is true, and what I heard from him I tell the world." ²⁷They did not realize that he was speaking to them of the Father. ²⁸ˢSo Jesus said [to them], "When you lift up the Son of Man, then you will realize that I AM, and that I do nothing on my own, but I say only what the Father taught me. ²⁹The one who sent me is with me. He has not left me alone, because I always do what is pleasing to him." ³⁰Because he spoke this way, many came to believe in him.

Jesus and Abraham

³¹*Jesus then said to those Jews who believed in him, "If you remain in my word, you will truly be my disciples,* ³²ᵗand you will know the truth, and the truth will set you free." ³³ᵘThey answered him, "We are descendants of Abraham and have never been enslaved to anyone.* How can you say, 'You will become free'?" ³⁴ᵛJesus answered them, "Amen, amen, I say to you, everyone who commits sin is a slave of sin. ³⁵ʷA slave does not remain in a household forever, but a son* always remains. ³⁶So if a son frees you, then you will truly be free. ³⁷I know that you are descendants of Abraham. But you are trying to kill me, because my word has no room among you. ³⁸*I tell you what I have seen in the Father's presence; then do what you have heard from the Father."

³⁹*ˣThey answered and said to him, "Our father is Abraham." Jesus said to them, "If you were Abraham's children, you would be doing the works of Abraham. ⁴⁰But now you are trying to kill me, a man who has told you the truth that I heard from God; Abraham did not do this. ⁴¹ʸYou are doing the works of your father!" [So] they said to him, "We are not illegitimate. We have one Father, God." ⁴²ᶻJesus said to them, "If God were your Father, you would love me, for I came from God and am here; I did not come on my own, but he sent me. ⁴³Why do you not understand what I am saying? Because you cannot bear to hear my word. ⁴⁴ᵃYou belong to your father the devil and you willingly carry out your father's desires. He was a murderer from the beginning and does not stand in truth, because there is no truth in him. When he tells a lie, he speaks in character, because he is a liar and the father of lies. ⁴⁵But because I speak the truth, you do not believe me. ⁴⁶ᵇCan any of you charge me with sin? If I am telling the truth,

We long for freedom yet we struggle with the gift that sets us free. It is the truth that sets us free. If we make the word of God our home, truth will become our daily attire. It will be the blessed robe we put on each morning. How can you remain in God's Word?

---

told you at the beginning what I am also telling you (now)." The answer here (cf. Prv 8:22) seems to hinge on a misunderstanding of John 8:24 "**that I AM**" as "**what** I am."

8:31-59 Jesus' origin ("before Abraham") and destiny are developed; the truth will free them from sin (8:34) and death (8:51).

8:31 Those Jews who believed in him: a rough editorial suture, since in John 8:37 they are described as trying to kill Jesus.

8:33 Have never been enslaved to anyone: since, historically, the Jews were enslaved almost continuously, this verse is probably Johannine irony, about slavery to sin.

8:35 A slave . . . a son: an allusion to Ishmael and Isaac (Gn 16; 21), or to the release of a slave after six years (Ex 21:2; Dt 15:12).

8:38 The Father: i.e., God. It is also possible, however, to understand the second part of the verse as a sarcastic reference to descent of the Jews from the devil (8:44), "You do what you have heard from [your] father."

8:39 The works of Abraham: Abraham believed; cf. Romans 4:11-17; James 2:21-23.

JOHN

why do you not believe me? [47c]Whoever belongs to God hears the words of God; for this reason you do not listen, because you do not belong to God."

[48]The Jews answered and said to him, "Are we not right in saying that you are a Samaritan* and are possessed?" [49]Jesus answered, "I am not possessed; I honor my Father, but you dishonor me. [50d]I do not seek my own glory; there is one who seeks it and he is the one who judges. [51e]Amen, amen, I say to you, whoever keeps my word will never see death." [52][So] the Jews said to him, "Now we are sure that you are possessed. Abraham died, as did the prophets, yet you say, 'Whoever keeps my word will never taste death.' [53f]Are you greater than our father Abraham,* who died? Or the prophets, who died? Who do you make yourself out to be?" [54]Jesus answered, "If I glorify myself, my glory is worth nothing; but it is my Father who glorifies me, of whom you say, 'He is our God.' [55g]You do not know him, but I know him. And if I should say that I do not know him, I would be like you a liar. But I do know him and I keep his word. [56h]Abraham your father rejoiced to see my day; he saw it* and was glad. [57]So the Jews said to him, "You are not yet fifty years old and you have seen Abraham?" [58*i]Jesus said to them, "Amen, amen, I say to you, before Abraham came to be, I AM." [59j]So they picked up stones to throw at him; but Jesus hid and went out of the temple area.

The Man Born Blind

9 [1*a]As he passed by he saw a man blind from birth. [2*b]His disciples asked him, "Rabbi, who sinned, this man or his parents, that he was born blind?" [3c]Jesus answered, "Neither he nor his parents sinned; it is so that the works of God might be made visible through him. [4d]We have to do the works of the one who sent me while it is day. Night is coming when no one can work. [5e]While I am in the world, I am the light of the world." [6f]When he had said this, he spat on the ground and made clay with the saliva, and smeared the clay on his eyes, [7g]and said to him, "Go wash* in the Pool of Siloam" (which means Sent). So he went and washed, and came back able to see.

The Pool of Siloam

[8]His neighbors and those who had seen him earlier as a beggar said, "Isn't this the one who used to sit and beg?" [9]Some said, "It is," but

Margin references:

c
10:26; 1 Jn 4:6

d
7:18

e
5:24-29; 6:40, 47; 11:25-26

f
4:12

g
7:28-29

h
Gn 17:17; Mt 13:17; Lk 17:22

i
1:30; 17:5

j
10:31, 39; 11:8; Lk 4:29-30

a
Is 42:7

b
Ex 20:5; Ez 18:20; Lk 13:2

c
5:14; 11:4

d
11:9-10; 12:35-36

e
8:12

f
5:11; Mk 7:33; 8:23

g
2 Kgs 5:10-14

JOHN

8:48 Samaritan: therefore interested in magical powers; cf. Acts 7:14-24.

8:53 Are you greater than our father Abraham?: cf. John 4:12.

8:56 He saw it: this seems a reference to the birth of Isaac (Gn 17:7; 21:6), the beginning of the fulfillment of promises about Abraham's seed.

8:57 The evidence of the third-century Bodmer Papyrus P[75] and the first hand of Codex Sinaiticus indicates that the text originally read: "How can Abraham have seen you?"

8:58 Came to be, I AM: the Greek word used for "came to be" is the one used of all creation in the prologue, while the word used for "am" is the one reserved for the Logos.

9:1–10:21 Sabbath healing of the man born blind. This fifth sign is introduced to illustrate the saying, "I am the light of the world" (8:12; 9:5). The narrative of conflict about Jesus contrasts Jesus (light) with the Jews (blindness, 9:39-41). The theme of water is reintroduced in the reference to the pool of Siloam. Ironically, Jesus is being judged by the Jews, yet the Jews are judged by the Light of the world; cf. John 3:19-21.

9:2 See the note on John 5:14, and Exodus 20:5, that parents' sins were visited upon their children. Jesus denies such a cause and emphasizes the purpose: the infirmity was providential.

9:7 Go wash: perhaps a test of faith; cf. 2 Kings 5:10-14. The water tunnel Siloam (= Sent) is used as a symbol of Jesus, sent by his Father.

h
5:9

i
3:2;
Mt 12:10-11;
Lk 13:10-11;
14:1-4

j
4:19

k
7:13; 12:42;
16:2; 19:38

l
12:42

m
Jos 7:19;
1 Sm 6:5 LXX

n
Ex 33:11

o
10:21;
Pss 34:16;
66:18;
Prv 15:29;
Is 1:15

p
3:2

q
4:26; Dn 7:13

r
Mt 13:33-35

JOHN

others said, "No, he just looks like him." He said, "I am." [10]So they said to him, "[So] how were your eyes opened?" [11]He replied, "The man called Jesus made clay and anointed my eyes and told me, 'Go to Siloam and wash.' So I went there and washed and was able to see." [12]And they said to him, "Where is he?" He said, "I don't know."

[13]They brought the one who was once blind to the Pharisees. [14h]Now Jesus had made clay* and opened his eyes on a sabbath. [15]So then the Pharisees also asked him how he was able to see. He said to them, "He put clay on my eyes, and I washed, and now I can see." [16i]So some of the Pharisees said, "This man is not from God, because he does not keep the sabbath." [But] others said, "How can a sinful man do such signs?" And there was a division among them. [17j]So they said to the blind man again, "What do you have to say about him, since he opened your eyes?" He said, "He is a prophet."

[18]Now the Jews did not believe that he had been blind and gained his sight until they summoned the parents of the one who had gained his sight. [19]They asked them, "Is this your son, who you say was born blind? How does he now see?" [20]His parents answered and said, "We know that this is our son and that he was born blind. [21]We do not know how he sees now, nor do we know who opened his eyes. Ask him, he is of age; he can speak for himself." [22k*]His parents said this because they were afraid of the Jews, for the Jews had already agreed that if anyone acknowledged him as the Messiah, he would be expelled from the synagogue. [23l]For this reason his parents said, "He is of age; question him."

[24m]So a second time they called the man who had been blind and said to him, "Give God the praise!* We know that this man is a sinner." [25]He replied, "If he is a sinner, I do not know. One thing I do know is that I was blind and now I see." [26]So they said to him, "What did he do to you? How did he open your eyes?" [27]He answered them, "I told you already and you did not listen. Why do you want to hear it again? Do you want to become his disciples, too?" [28]They ridiculed him and said, "You are that man's disciple; we are disciples of Moses! [29n]We know that God spoke to Moses, but we do not know where this one is from." [30]The man answered and said to them, "This is what is so amazing, that you do not know where he is from, yet he opened my eyes. [31o]We know that God does not listen to sinners, but if one is devout and does his will, he listens to him. [32]It is unheard of that anyone ever opened the eyes of a person born blind. [33p]If this man were not from God, he would not be able to do anything." [34]They answered and said to him, "You were born totally in sin, and are you trying to teach us?" Then they threw him out.

[35]When Jesus heard that they had thrown him out, he found him and said, "Do you believe in the Son of Man?" [36]He answered and said, "Who is he, sir, that I may believe in him?" [37q]Jesus said to him, "You have seen him and the one speaking with you is he." [38]He said, "I do believe, Lord," and he worshiped him. [39*r]Then Jesus said, "I came

---

9:14 In using spittle, kneading clay, and healing, Jesus had broken the sabbath rules laid down by Jewish tradition.

9:22 This comment of the evangelist (in terms used again in 12:42 and 16:2) envisages a situation after Jesus' ministry. Rejection/excommunication from the synagogue of Jews who confessed Jesus as Messiah seems to have begun ca. A.D. 85, when the curse against the *mînîm* or heretics was introduced into the "Eighteen Benedictions."

9:24 Give God the praise!: an Old Testament formula of adjuration to tell the truth; cf. Joshua 7:19; 1 Samuel 6:5 LXX. Cf. John 5:41.

9:32 A person born blind: the only Old Testament cure from blindness is found in Tobit (cf. Tb 7:7; 11:7-13; 14:1-2), but Tobit was not born blind.

9:39-41 These verses spell out the symbolic meaning of the cure; the Pharisees are not the innocent blind, willing to accept the testimony of others.

into this world for judgment, so that those who do not see might see, and those who do see might become blind."

⁴⁰ˢSome of the Pharisees who were with him heard this and said to him, "Surely we are not also blind, are we?" ⁴¹ᵗJesus said to them, "If you were blind, you would have no sin; but now you are saying, 'We see,' so your sin remains.

The Good Shepherd

10 ¹*ᵃ"Amen, amen, I say to you, whoever does not enter a sheepfold through the gate but climbs over elsewhere is a thief and a robber.* ²But whoever enters through the gate is the shepherd of the sheep. ³The gatekeeper opens it for him, and the sheep hear his voice, as he calls his own sheep by name and leads them out. ⁴*ᵇWhen he has driven out all his own, he walks ahead of them, and the sheep follow him, because they recognize his voice. ⁵But they will not follow a stranger; they will run away from him, because they do not recognize the voice of strangers." ⁶Although Jesus used this figure of speech,* they did not realize what he was trying to tell them.

Grazing sheep are a common sight on the hillsides of Israel

⁷*So Jesus said again, "Amen, amen, I say to you, I am the gate for the sheep. ⁸*All who came [before me] are thieves and robbers, but the sheep did not listen to them. ⁹I am the gate. Whoever enters through me will be saved, and will come in and go out and find pasture. ¹⁰A thief comes only to steal and slaughter and destroy; I came so that they might have life and have it more abundantly. ¹¹ᶜI am the good shepherd. A good shepherd lays down his life for the sheep. ¹²ᵈA hired man, who is not a shepherd and whose sheep are not his own, sees a wolf coming and leaves the sheep and runs away, and the wolf catches and scatters them. ¹³This is because he works for pay and has no concern for the sheep. ¹⁴I am the good shepherd, and I know mine and mine know me, ¹⁵ᵉjust as the Father knows me and I know the Father; and I will lay down my life for the sheep. ¹⁶ᶠI have other sheep* that do not belong to this fold. These also I must lead, and they will hear my voice, and there will be one flock, one shepherd. ¹⁷ᵍThis is why the Father loves me, because I lay down my life in order to take it up again. ¹⁸ʰNo one takes it from me, but I lay it down on my own. I have power to lay it down, and power to take it up again.* This command I have received from my Father."

s
Mt 15:14;
23:26;
Rom 2:19

t
15:22

a
Gn 48:15;
49:24;
Pss 23:1-4;
80:2;
Jer 23:1-4;
Ez 34:1-31;
Mi 7:14

b
Mi 2:12-13

c
Ps 23:1-4;
Is 40:11;
49:9-10;
Heb 13:20;
Rev 7:17

d
Zec 11:17

e
15:13;
1 Jn 3:16

f
11:52; Is 56:8;
Jer 23:3;
Ez 34:23;
37:24; Mi 2:12

g
Heb 10:10

h
19:11

JOHN

10:1-21 The good shepherd discourse continues the theme of attack on the Pharisees that ends John 9. The figure is allegorical: the hired hands are the Pharisees who excommunicated the cured blind man. It serves as a commentary on John 9. For the shepherd motif, used of Yahweh in the Old Testament, cf. Exodus 34; Genesis 48:15; 49:24; Micah 7:14; Psalms 23:1-4; 80:1.

10:1 **Sheepfold**: a low stone wall open to the sky.

10:4 **Recognize his voice**: the Pharisees do not recognize Jesus, but the people of God, symbolized by the blind man, do.

10:6 **Figure of speech**: John uses a different word for illustrative speech than the "parable" of the synoptics, but the idea is similar.

10:7-10 In John 10:7-8, the figure is of a gate for the shepherd to come to the sheep; in John 10:9-10, the figure is of a gate for the sheep to **come in and go out**.

10:8 **[Before me]**: these words are omitted in many good early manuscripts and versions.

10:16 **Other sheep**: the Gentiles, possibly a reference to "God's dispersed children" of John 11:52 destined to be gathered into one, or "apostolic Christians" at odds with the community of the beloved disciple.

10:18 **Power to take it up again**: contrast the role of the Father as the efficient cause of the resurrection in Acts 2:24; 4:10; etc.; 241

i
7:43; 9:16

j
7:20; 8:48

k
3:2

l
1 Mc 4:54, 59

m
Lk 22:67

n
8:25 / 5:36;
10:38

o
8:45, 47

p
Dt 32:39

q
Wis 3:1;
Is 43:13

r
1:1; 12:45;
14:9; 17:21

s
8:59

t
5:18; 19:7;
Lv 24:16

u
Ps 82:6

v
5:18

w
14:10-11, 20

x
1:28

[19]ⁱAgain there was a division among the Jews because of these words. [20]^jMany of them said, "He is possessed and out of his mind; why listen to him?" [21]^kOthers said, "These are not the words of one possessed; surely a demon cannot open the eyes of the blind, can he?"

Feast of the Dedication

[22]^lThe feast of the Dedication* was then taking place in Jerusalem. It was winter. [23]*And Jesus walked about in the temple area on the Portico of Solomon. [24]^mSo the Jews gathered around him and said to him, "How long are you going to keep us in suspense?* If you are the Messiah, tell us plainly." [25]ⁿJesus answered them, "I told you* and you do not believe. The works I do in my Father's name testify to me. [26]^oBut you do not believe, because you are not among my sheep. [27]My sheep hear my voice; I know them, and they follow me. [28]^pI give them eternal life, and they shall never perish. No one can take them out of my hand. [29]^qMy Father, who has given them to me, is greater than all,* and no one can take them out of the Father's hand. [30]*^rThe Father and I are one."

[31]^sThe Jews again picked up rocks to stone him. [32]Jesus answered them, "I have shown you many good works from my Father. For which of these are you trying to stone me?" [33]^tThe Jews answered him, "We are not stoning you for a good work but for blasphemy. You, a man, are making yourself God." [34]*^uJesus answered them, "Is it not written in your law, 'I said, "You are gods"'? [35]If it calls them gods to whom the word of God came, and scripture cannot be set aside, [36]^vcan you say that the one whom the Father has consecrated* and sent into the world blasphemes because I said, 'I am the Son of God'? [37]If I do not perform my Father's works, do not believe me; [38]^wbut if I perform them, even if you do not believe me, believe the works, so that you may realize [and understand] that the Father is in me and I am in the Father." [39][Then] they tried again to arrest him; but he escaped from their power.

[40]^xHe went back across the Jordan to the place where John first baptized, and there he remained.

The Jordan River valley

Romans 1:4; 4:24. Yet even here is added: **This command I have received from my Father**.

10:22 Feast of the Dedication: an eight-day festival of lights (Hebrew, Hanukkah) held in December, three months after the feast of Tabernacles (7:2), to celebrate the Maccabees' rededication of the altar and reconsecration of the temple in 164 B.C., after their desecration by Antiochus IV Epiphanes (Dn 8:13; 9:27; cf. 1 Mc 4:36-59; 2 Mc 1:18–2:19; 10:1-8).

10:23 Portico of Solomon: on the east side of the temple area, offering protection against the cold winds from the desert.

10:24 Keep us in suspense: literally, "How long will you take away our life?" Cf. John 11:48-50. **If you are the Messiah, tell us plainly**: cf. Luke 22:67. This is the climax of Jesus' encounters with the Jewish authorities. There has never yet been an open confession before them.

10:25 I told you: probably at John 8:25 which was an evasive answer.

10:29 The textual evidence for the first clause is very divided; it may also be translated: "As for the Father, what he has given me is greater than all," or "My Father is greater than all, in what he has given me."

10:30 This is justification for John 10:29; it asserts unity of power and reveals that the words and deeds of Jesus are the words and deeds of God.

10:34 This is a reference to the judges of Israel who, since they exercised the divine prerogative to judge (Dt 1:17), were called "gods"; cf. Exodus 21:6, besides Psalm 82:6 from which the quotation comes.

10:36 Consecrated: this may be a reference to the rededicated altar at the Hanukkah feast; see the note on John 10:22.

[41]Many came to him and said, "John performed no sign,* but everything John said about this man was true." [42y]And many there began to believe in him.

The Raising of Lazarus

11 [1*a]Now a man was ill, Lazarus from Bethany, the village of Mary and her sister Martha. [2]Mary was the one who had anointed the Lord with perfumed oil and dried his feet with her hair; it was her brother Lazarus who was ill. [3]So the sisters sent word to him, saying, "Master, the one you love is ill." [4b]When Jesus heard this he said, "This illness is not to end in death,* but is for the glory of God, that the Son of God may be glorified through it." [5]Now Jesus loved Martha and her sister and Lazarus. [6]So when he heard that he was ill, he remained for two days in the place where he was. [7]Then after this he said to his disciples, "Let us go back to Judea." [8c]The disciples said to him, "Rabbi, the Jews were just trying to stone you, and you want to go back there?" [9d]Jesus answered, "Are there not twelve hours in a day? If one walks during the day, he does not stumble, because he sees the light of this world.[e] [10]But if one walks at night, he stumbles, because the light is not in him."* [11]He said this, and then told them, "Our friend Lazarus is asleep, but I am going to awaken him." [12]So the disciples said to him, "Master, if he is asleep, he will be saved." [13f]But Jesus was talking about his death, while they thought that he meant ordinary sleep. [14]So then Jesus said to them clearly, "Lazarus has died. [15]And I am glad for you that I was not there, that you may believe. Let us go to him." [16g]So Thomas, called Didymus,* said to his fellow disciples, "Let us also go to die with him."

[17]When Jesus arrived, he found that Lazarus had already been in the tomb for four days. [18]Now Bethany was near Jerusalem, only about two miles* away. [19h]And many of the Jews had come to Martha and Mary to comfort them about their brother. [20]When Martha heard that Jesus was coming, she went to meet him; but Mary sat at home. [21i]Martha said to Jesus, "Lord, if you had been here, my brother would not have died. [22][But] even now I know that whatever you ask of God, God will give you." [23]Jesus said to her, "Your brother will rise." [24j]Martha said to him, "I know he will rise, in the resurrection on the last day." [25k]Jesus told her, "I am the resurrection and the life; whoever believes in me, even if he dies, will live, [26]and everyone who lives and believes in me will never die. Do you believe this?" [27*l]She said to him, "Yes, Lord. I have come to believe that you are the Messiah, the Son of God, the one who is coming into the world."

y
2:23; 7:31; 8:30

a
12:1-8; Lk 10:38-42; 16:19-31

b
9:3, 24

c
8:59; 10:31

d
12:35; 1 Jn 2:10

e
8:12; 9:4

f
Mt 9:24

g
14:5, 22

h
12:9, 17-18

i
11:32

j
5:29; 6:39-40, 44, 54; 12:48; Is 2:2; Mi 4:1; Acts 23:8; 24:15

k
5:24; 8:51; 14:6; Dn 12:2

l
1:9; 6:69

JOHN

10:41 Performed no sign: this is to stress the inferior role of John the Baptist. The Transjordan topography recalls the great witness of John the Baptist to Jesus, as opposed to the hostility of the authorities in Jerusalem.

11:1-44 The raising of Lazarus, the longest continuous narrative in John outside of the passion account, is the climax of the signs. It leads directly to the decision of the Sanhedrin to kill Jesus. The theme of life predominates. Lazarus is a token of the real life that Jesus dead and raised will give to all who believe in him. Johannine irony is found in the fact that Jesus' gift of life leads to his own death. The story is not found in the synoptics, but cf. Mark 5:21 and parallels; Luke 7:11-17. There are also parallels between this story and Luke's parable of the rich man and poor Lazarus (Lk 16:19-31). In both a man named Lazarus dies; in Luke, there is a request that he return to convince his contemporaries of the need for faith and repentance, while in John, Lazarus does return and some believe but others do not.

11:4 Not to end in death: this is misunderstood by the disciples as referring to physical death, but it is meant as spiritual death.

11:10 The light is not in him: the ancients apparently did not grasp clearly the entry of light **through** the eye; they seem to have thought of it as being **in** the eye; cf. Luke 11:34; Matthew 6:23.

11:16 Called Didymus: *Didymus* is the Greek word for twin. Thomas is derived from the Aramaic word for twin; in an ancient Syriac version and in the Gospel of Thomas (80:11-12) his given name, Judas, is supplied.

11:18 About two miles: literally, "about fifteen stades"; a stade was 607 feet.

11:27 The titles here are a summary of titles given to Jesus earlier in the gospel.

m
Lk 19:41

n
12:30

o
Lk 16:31

p
12:19;
Mt 26:3-5;
Lk 22:2;
Acts 4:16

q
18:13-14

r
5:18; 7:1;
Mt 12:14

[28]When she had said this, she went and called her sister Mary secretly, saying, "The teacher is here and is asking for you." [29]As soon as she heard this, she rose quickly and went to him. [30]For Jesus had not yet come into the village, but was still where Martha had met him. [31]So when the Jews who were with her in the house comforting her saw Mary get up quickly and go out, they followed her, presuming that she was going to the tomb to weep there. [32]When Mary came to where Jesus was and saw him, she fell at his feet and said to him, "Lord, if you had been here, my brother would not have died." [33]When Jesus saw her weeping and the Jews who had come with her weeping, he became perturbed[*] and deeply troubled, [34]and said, "Where have you laid him?" They said to him, "Sir, come and see." [35m]And Jesus wept. [36]So the Jews said, "See how he loved him." [37]But some of them said, "Could not the one who opened the eyes of the blind man have done something so that this man would not have died?"

[38]So Jesus, perturbed again, came to the tomb. It was a cave, and a stone lay across it. [39]Jesus said, "Take away the stone." Martha, the dead man's sister, said to him, "Lord, by now there will be a stench; he has been dead for four days." [40]Jesus said to her, "Did I not tell you that if you believe you will see the glory of God?" [41]So they took away the stone. And Jesus raised his eyes and said, "Father,[*] I thank you for hearing me. [42n]I know that you always hear me; but because of the crowd here I have said this, that they may believe that you sent me." [43]And when he had said this, he cried out in a loud voice,[*] "Lazarus, come out!" [44]The dead man came out, tied hand and foot with burial bands, and his face was wrapped in a cloth. So Jesus said to them, "Untie him and let him go."

Session of the Sanhedrin

[45o]Now many of the Jews who had come to Mary and seen what he had done began to believe in him. [46]But some of them went to the Pharisees and told them what Jesus had done. [47p]So the chief priests and the Pharisees convened the Sanhedrin and said, "What are we going to do? This man is performing many signs. [48]If we leave him alone, all will believe in him, and the Romans will come[*] and take away both our land and our nation." [49q]But one of them, Caiaphas, who was high priest that year,[*] said to them, "You know nothing, [50]nor do you consider that it is better for you that one man should die instead of the people, so that the whole nation may not perish." [51]He did not say this on his own, but since he was high priest for that year, he prophesied that Jesus was going to die for the nation, [52]and not only for the nation, but also to gather into one the dispersed children of God.[*] [53r]So from that day on they planned to kill him.

[54]So Jesus no longer walked about in public among the Jews, but he left for the region near the desert, to a town called Ephraim,[*] and there he remained with his disciples.

11:33 Became perturbed: a startling phrase in Greek, literally, "He snorted in spirit," perhaps in anger at the presence of evil (death).

11:41 Father: in Aramaic, *'abbā'*. See the note on Mark 14:36.

11:43 Cried out in a loud voice: a dramatization of John 5:28; "the hour is coming when all who are in the tombs will hear his voice."

11:48 The Romans will come: Johannine irony; this is precisely what happened after Jesus' death.

11:49 That year: emphasizes the conjunction of the office and the year. Actually, Caiaphas was high priest A.D. 18–36. The Jews attributed a gift of prophecy, sometimes unconscious, to the high priest.

11:52 Dispersed children of God: perhaps the "other sheep" of John 10:16.

11:54 Ephraim is usually located about twelve miles northeast of Jerusalem, where the mountains descend into the Jordan valley.

The Last Passover

[55s]Now the Passover of the Jews was near, and many went up from the country to Jerusalem before Passover to purify[*] themselves. [56]They looked for Jesus and said to one another as they were in the temple area, "What do you think? That he will not come to the feast?" [57]For the chief priests and the Pharisees had given orders that if anyone knew where he was, he should inform them, so that they might arrest him.

The Anointing at Bethany

12 [1*a]Six days before Passover Jesus came to Bethany, where Lazarus was, whom Jesus had raised from the dead.[b] [2c]They gave a dinner for him there, and Martha served, while Lazarus was one of those reclining at table with him. [3d]Mary took a liter of costly perfumed oil made from genuine aromatic nard and anointed the feet of Jesus[*] and dried them with her hair; the house was filled with the fragrance of the oil. [4]Then Judas the Iscariot, one [of] his disciples, and the one who would betray him, said, [5]"Why was this oil not sold for three hundred days' wages[*] and given to the poor?" [6e]He said this not because he cared about the poor but because he was a thief and held the money bag and used to steal the contributions. [7]So Jesus said, "Leave her alone. Let her keep this for the day of my burial.[*] [8f]You always have the poor with you, but you do not always have me."

[9g][The] large crowd of the Jews found out that he was there and came, not only because of Jesus, but also to see Lazarus, whom he had raised from the dead. [10]And the chief priests plotted to kill Lazarus too, [11h]because many of the Jews were turning away and believing in Jesus because of him.

The Entry into Jerusalem

[12*i]On the next day, when the great crowd that had come to the feast heard that Jesus was coming to Jerusalem, [13j]they took palm branches[*] and went out to meet him, and cried out:

"Hosanna!
Blessed is he who comes in the name of the Lord,
[even] the king of Israel."

[14]Jesus found an ass and sat upon it, as is written:

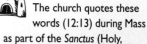

The church quotes these words (12:13) during Mass as part of the *Sanctus* (Holy, Holy), as a hymn of praise at the end of the preface. They honor Jesus as the Davidic Messiah.

s
2:13; 5:1;
6:4; 18:28;
Ex 19:10-11, 15;
Nm 9:6-14;
19:12; Dt 16:6;
2 Chr 30:1-3,
15-18

a
Mt 26:6-13;
Mk 14:3-9

b
11:1

c
Lk 10:38-42

d
11:2

e
13:29

f
Dt 15:11

g
11:19

h
11:45

i
Mt 21:1-16;
Mk 11:1-10;
Lk 19:28-40

j
1:49; Lv 23:40;
1 Mc 13:51;
2 Mc 10:7;
Rev 7:9

JOHN

11:55 Purify: prescriptions for purity were based on Exodus 19:10-11, 15; Numbers 9:6-14; 2 Chronicles 30:1-3, 15-18.

12:1-8 This is probably the same scene of anointing found in Mark 14:3-9 (see the note there) and Matthew 26:6-13. The anointing by a penitent woman in Luke 7:36-38 is different. Details from these various episodes have become interchanged.

12:3 The feet of Jesus: so Mark 14:3; but in Matthew 26:6, Mary anoints Jesus' head as a sign of regal, messianic anointing.

12:5 Days' wages: literally, "denarii." A denarius is a day's wage in Matthew 20:2; see the note on John 6:7.

12:7 Jesus' response reflects the rabbinical discussion of what was the greatest act of mercy, almsgiving or burying the dead. Those who favored proper burial of the dead thought it an essential condition for sharing in the resurrection.

12:12-19 In John, the entry into Jerusalem follows the anointing whereas in the synoptics it precedes. In John, the crowd, not the disciples, are responsible for the triumphal procession.

12:13 Palm branches: used to welcome great conquerors; cf. 1 Maccabees 13:51; 2 Maccabees 10:7. They may be related to the *lûlāb*, the twig bundles used at the feast of Tabernacles. **Hosanna**: see Psalm 118:25-26. The Hebrew word means: "(O Lord), grant salvation." **He who comes in the name of the Lord**: referred in Psalm 118:26 to a pilgrim entering the temple gates, but here a title for Jesus (see the notes on Mt 11:3 and Jn 6:14; 11:27). **The king of Israel**: perhaps from Zephaniah 3:14-15, in connection with the next quotation from Zechariah 9:9.

k
Is 40:9;
Zec 9:9

l
2:22

m
11:47-48

n
Acts 10:2

o
1:44

p
1:40

q
2:4

r
Is 53:10-12;
1 Cor 15:36

s
Mt 10:39;
16:25;
Mk 8:35;
Lk 9:24; 17:33

t
14:3; 17:24;
Mt 16:24;
Mk 8:34;
Lk 9:23

u
6:38; 18:11;
Mt 26:38-39;
Mk 14:34-36;
Lk 22:42;
Heb 5:7-8

v
2:11; 17:5;
Dn 4:31, 34

w
Ex 9:28;
2 Sm 22:14;
Jb 37:4;
Ps 29:3;
Lk 22:43;
Acts 23:9

[15k]"Fear no more, O daughter Zion;*
   see, your king comes, seated upon an ass's colt."

[16l]His disciples did not understand this at first, but when Jesus had been glorified they remembered that these things were written about him and that they had done this* for him. [17*]So the crowd that was with him when he called Lazarus from the tomb and raised him from death continued to testify. [18]This was [also] why the crowd went to meet him, because they heard that he had done this sign. [19m]So the Pharisees said to one another, "You see that you are gaining nothing. Look, the whole world* has gone after him."

The Coming of Jesus' Hour

[20*n]Now there were some Greeks* among those who had come up to worship at the feast. [21*o]They came to Philip, who was from Bethsaida in Galilee, and asked him, "Sir, we would like to see Jesus." [22p]Philip went and told Andrew; then Andrew and Philip went and told Jesus. [23*q]Jesus answered them, "The hour has come for the Son of Man to be glorified. [24*r]Amen, amen, I say to you, unless a grain of wheat falls to the ground and dies, it remains just a grain of wheat; but if it dies, it produces much fruit. [25s]Whoever loves his life* loses it, and whoever hates his life in this world will preserve it for eternal life. [26t]Whoever serves me must follow me, and where I am, there also will my servant be. The Father will honor whoever serves me.

[27u]"I am troubled* now. Yet what should I say? 'Father, save me from this hour'? But it was for this purpose that I came to this hour. [28v]Father, glorify your name." Then a voice came from heaven, "I have glorified it and will glorify it again." [29w]The

The seed falls into the ground, surrenders its seed-form, and new life emerges. Each day we make choices about what needs to die in the ground of our own beings so that our daily living might be enriched. Some day we will be asked to hand over the breath of life that is on loan to us from God. In our moment of letting go we will be breathed back into God. Meditate today on the fruit of dying.

12:15 Daughter Zion: Jerusalem. **Ass's colt:** symbol of peace, as opposed to the war horse.

12:16 They had done this: the antecedent of **they** is ambiguous.

12:17-18 There seem to be two different crowds in these verses. There are some good witnesses to the text that have another reading for John 12:17: "Then the crowd that was with him began to testify that he had called Lazarus out of the tomb and raised him from the dead."

12:19 The whole world: the sense is that everyone is following Jesus, but John has an ironic play on **world**; he alludes to the universality of salvation (3:17; 4:42).

12:20-36 This announcement of glorification by death is an illustration of "the whole world" (19) going after him.

12:20 Greeks: not used here in a nationalistic sense. These are probably Gentile proselytes to Judaism; cf. John 7:35.

12:21-22 Philip . . . Andrew: the approach is made through disciples who have distinctly Greek names, suggesting that access to Jesus was mediated to the Greek world through his disciples. Philip and Andrew were from Bethsaida (1:44); Galileans were mostly bilingual. **See:** here seems to mean "have an interview with."

12:23 Jesus' response suggests that only after the crucifixion could the gospel encompass both Jew and Gentile.

12:24 This verse implies that through his death Jesus will be accessible to all. **It remains just a grain of wheat:** this saying is found in the synoptic triple and double traditions (Mk 8:35 // Mt 16:25 // Lk 9:24; Mt 10:39 // Lk 17:33). John adds the phrases (12:25) **in this world** and **for eternal life**.

12:25 His life: the Greek word *psychē* refers to a person's natural life. It does not mean "soul," for Hebrew anthropology did not postulate body/soul dualism in the way that is familiar to us.

12:27 I am troubled: perhaps an allusion to the Gethsemane agony scene of the synoptics.

crowd there heard it and said it was thunder; but others said, "An angel has spoken to him." [30x]Jesus answered and said, "This voice did not come for my sake but for yours. [31y]Now is the time of judgment on this world; now the ruler of this world* will be driven out. [32z]And when I am lifted up from the earth, I will draw everyone to myself." [33]He said this indicating the kind of death he would die. [34a]So the crowd answered him, "We have heard from the law that the Messiah remains forever.* Then how can you say that the Son of Man must be lifted up? Who is this Son of Man?" [35b]Jesus said to them, "The light will be among you only a little while. Walk while you have the light, so that darkness may not overcome you. Whoever walks in the dark does not know where he is going. [36c]While you have the light, believe in the light, so that you may become children of the light."

Unbelief and Belief among the Jews

After he had said this, Jesus left and hid from them. [37*d]Although he had performed so many signs in their presence they did not believe in him, [38*e]in order that the word which Isaiah the prophet spoke might be fulfilled:

> "Lord, who has believed our preaching,
> to whom has the might of the Lord been revealed?"

[39]For this reason they could not believe, because again Isaiah said:

> [40fx]"He blinded their eyes
> and hardened their heart,
> so that they might not see with their eyes
> and understand with their heart and be converted,
> and I would heal them."

[41g]Isaiah said this because he saw his glory* and spoke about him. [42h]Nevertheless, many, even among the authorities, believed in him, but because of the Pharisees they did not acknowledge it openly in order not to be expelled from the synagogue. [43i]For they preferred human praise to the glory of God.

Recapitulation

[44j]Jesus cried out and said, "Whoever believes in me believes not only in me but also in the one who sent me, [45k]and whoever sees me sees the one who sent me. [46l]I came into the world as light, so that everyone who believes in me might not remain in darkness. [47m]And if anyone hears my words and does not observe them, I do not condemn him, for I did not come to condemn the world but to save the world. [48n]Whoever rejects me and does not accept my words has something to judge him: the word that I

x
11:42

y
16:11;
Lk 10:18;
Rev 12:9

z
3:14; 8:28;
Is 52:13

a
Pss 89:5;
110:4; Is 9:7;
Dn 7:13-14;
Rev 20:1-6

b
9:4; 11:10;
Jb 5:14

c
Eph 5:8

d
Dt 29:2-4;
Mk 4:11-12;
Rom 9–11

e
Is 53:1;
Rom 10:16

f
Is 6:9-10;
Mt 13:13-15;
Mk 4:12

g
5:39; Is 6:1, 4

h
9:22

i
5:44

j
13:20; 14:1

k
14:7-9

l
1:9; 8:12

m
3:17

n
Lk 10:16;
Heb 4:12

JOHN

12:31 Ruler of this world: Satan.

12:34 There is no passage in the Old Testament that states precisely that **the Messiah remains forever**. Perhaps the closest is Psalm 89:37.

12:37-50 These verses, on unbelief of the Jews, provide an epilogue to the Book of Signs.

12:38-41 John gives a historical explanation of the disbelief of the Jewish people, not a psychological one. The Old Testament had to be fulfilled; the disbelief that met Isaiah's message was a foreshadowing of the disbelief that Jesus encountered. In John 12:42 and also in John 3:20 we see that there is no negation of freedom.

12:41 His glory: Isaiah saw the glory of Yahweh enthroned in the heavenly temple, but in John the antecedent of **his** is Jesus.

o
14:10, 31;
Dt 18:18-19

a
2:4; 7:30; 8:20;
Mt 26:17, 45;
Mk 14:12, 41;
Lk 22:7

b
6:71; 17:12;
Mt 26:20-21;
Mk 14:17-18;
Lk 22:3

c
3:35

d
1 Sm 25:41

e
2 Sm 20:1

f
15:3

g
6:70

h
Mt 23:8, 10

JOHN

spoke, it will condemn him on the last day, [49]*o*because I did not speak on my own, but the Father who sent me commanded me what to say and speak. [50]And I know that his commandment is eternal life. So what I say, I say as the Father told me."

Washing of the feet

Jesus' washing the feet of his disciples is a profound action proclaimed and (almost always) ritualized every Holy Thursday during the Mass of the Lord's Supper to emphasize the nature of true service, ministry to others.

III: The Book of Glory[*]

The Washing of the Disciples' Feet

13 [1]*a*Before the feast of Passover, Jesus knew that his hour had come to pass from this world to the Father. He loved his own in the world and he loved them to the end.[*] [2]*b*The devil had already induced[*] Judas, son of Simon the Iscariot, to hand him over. So, during supper, [3]*c*fully aware that the Father had put everything into his power and that he had come from God and was returning to God, [4]he rose from supper and took off his outer garments. He took a towel and tied it around his waist. [5]*d*Then he poured water into a basin and began to wash the disciples' feet and dry them with the towel around his waist. [6]He came to Simon Peter, who said to him, "Master, are you going to wash my feet?" [7]Jesus answered and said to him, "What I am doing, you do not understand now, but you will understand later." [8]*e*Peter said to him, "You will never wash my feet." Jesus answered him, "Unless I wash you, you will have no inheritance with me." [9]Simon Peter said to him, "Master, then not only my feet, but my hands and head as well." [10]*f*Jesus said to him, "Whoever has bathed[*] has no need except to have his feet washed, for he is clean all over; so you are clean, but not all." [11]*g*For he knew who would betray him; for this reason, he said, "Not all of you are clean."

[12]So when he had washed their feet [and] put his garments back on and reclined at table again, he said to them, "Do you realize what I have done for you? [13]*h*You call me

---

13:1–19:42 The Book of Glory. There is a major break here; the word "sign" is used again only in John 20:30. In this phase of Jesus' return to the Father, the discourses (13–17) precede the traditional narrative of the passion (18–20) to interpret them for the Christian reader. This is the only extended example of esoteric teaching of disciples in John.

13:1-20 Washing of the disciples' feet. This episode occurs in John at the place of the narration of the institution of the Eucharist in the synoptics. It may be a dramatization of Luke 22:27—"I am your servant." It is presented as a "model" ("pattern") of the crucifixion. It symbolizes cleansing from sin by sacrificial death.

13:1 Before the feast of Passover: this would be Thursday evening, before the day of preparation; in the synoptics, the Last Supper is a Passover meal taking place, in John's chronology, on Friday evening. **To the end**: or, "completely."

13:2 Induced: literally, "The devil put into the heart that Judas should hand him over."

13:5 The act of washing another's feet was one that could not be required of the lowliest Jewish slave. It is an allusion to the humiliating death of the crucifixion.

13:10 Bathed: many have suggested that this passage is a symbolic reference to baptism. The Greek root involved is used in baptismal contexts in 1 Corinthians 6:11; Ephesians 5:26; Titus 3:5; Hebrews 10:22.

'teacher' and 'master,' and rightly so, for indeed I am. [14]If I, therefore, the master and teacher, have washed your feet, you ought to wash one another's feet. [15i]I have given you a model to follow, so that as I have done for you, you should also do. [16j]Amen, amen, I say to you, no slave is greater than his master nor any messenger[*] greater than the one who sent him. [17]If you understand this, blessed are you if you do it. [18k]I am not speaking of all of you. I know those whom I have chosen. But so that the scripture might be fulfilled, 'The one who ate my food has raised his heel against me.' [19]From now on I am telling you before it happens, so that when it happens you may believe that I AM. [20l]Amen, amen, I say to you, whoever receives the one I send receives me, and whoever receives me receives the one who sent me."

Announcement of Judas's Betrayal

[21m]When he had said this, Jesus was deeply troubled and testified, "Amen, amen, I say to you, one of you will betray me." [22]The disciples looked at one another, at a loss as to whom he meant. [23n]One of his disciples, the one whom Jesus loved,[*] was reclining at Jesus' side. [24]So Simon Peter nodded to him to find out whom he meant. [25o]He leaned back against Jesus' chest and said to him, "Master, who is it?" [26]Jesus answered, "It is the one to whom I hand the morsel[*] after I have dipped it." So he dipped the morsel and [took it and] handed it to Judas, son of Simon the Iscariot. [27p]After he took the morsel, Satan entered him. So Jesus said to him, "What you are going to do, do quickly." [28][Now] none of those reclining at table realized why he said this to him. [29q]Some thought that since Judas kept the money bag, Jesus had told him, "Buy what we need for the feast," or to give something to the poor. [30]So he took the morsel and left at once. And it was night.

Why does Jesus say he is giving us a *new* commandment of love when the old commandment also asked us to love? In this new command to love, is Jesus equating our love for one another with our love for God? If so, others will know we love God not just because we keep the rules but, rather, by the way we treat one another.

The New Commandment

[31*]When he had left, Jesus said, "Now is the Son of Man glorified, and God is glorified in him.[*] [32r][If God is glorified in him,] God will also glorify him in himself, and he will glorify him at once. [33s]My children, I will be with you only a little while longer. You will look for me, and as I told the Jews, 'Where I go you cannot come,' so now I say it to you. [34t]I give you a new commandment:[*] love one another. As I

i
Lk 22:27;
1 Pt 2:21

j
15:20;
Mt 10:24;
Lk 6:40

k
Ps 41:10

l
Mt 10:40;
Mk 9:37;
Lk 9:48

m
Mt 26:21-25;
Mk 14:18-21;
Lk 22:21-23

n
19:26; 20:2;
21:7, 20;
Mt 10:37

o
21:20

p
13:2; Lk 22:3

q
12:5-6

r
17:1-5

s
7:33; 8:21

t
15:12-13, 17;
Lv 19:18;
1 Thes 4:9;
1 Jn 2:7-10;
3:23; 2 Jn 5

JOHN

13:16 Messenger: the Greek has *apostolos*, the only occurrence of the term in John. It is not used in the technical sense here.

13:23 The one whom Jesus loved: also mentioned in John 19:26; 20:2; 21:7. A disciple, called "another disciple" or "the other disciple," is mentioned in John 18:15 and 20:2; in the latter reference he is identified with the disciple whom Jesus loved. There is also an unnamed disciple in John 1:35-40; see the note on John 1:37.

13:26 Morsel: probably the bitter herb dipped in salt water.

13:31–17:26 Two farewell discourses and a prayer. These seem to be Johannine compositions, including sayings of Jesus at the Last Supper and on other occasions, modeled on similar farewell

discourses in Greek literature and the Old Testament (of Moses, Joshua, David).

13:31-38 Introduction: departure and return. Terms of coming and going predominate. These verses form an introduction to the last discourse of Jesus, which extends through John 14–17. In it John has collected Jesus' words to **his own** (13:1). There are indications that several speeches have been fused together, e.g., in John 14:31 and 17:1.

13:34 I give you a new commandment: this puts Jesus on a par with Yahweh. The commandment itself is not new; cf. Leviticus 19:18 and the note there.

u
Mk 14:27;
Lk 22:23

v
18:27;
Mt 26:33-35;
Mk 14:29-31;
Lk 22:33-34

a
12:26; 17:24;
1 Jn 2:28

b
8:31-47

c
8:19; 12:45

d
Ex 24:9-10;
33:18

e
1:18; 10:30;
12:45;
2 Cor 4:4;
Col 1:15;
Heb 1:3

f
1:1; 10:37-38;
12:49

g
10:38

h
1:50; 5:20

i
15:7, 16;
16:23-24;
Mt 7:7-11

j
15:10;
Dt 6:4-9;
Ps 119;
Wis 6:18;
1 Jn 5:3;
2 Jn 6

k
15:26;
Lk 24:49;
1 Jn 2:1

have loved you, so you also should love one another. [35]This is how all will know that you are my disciples, if you have love for one another."

Peter's Denial Predicted

[36u]Simon Peter said to him, "Master, where are you going?" Jesus answered [him], "Where I am going, you cannot follow me now, though you will follow later." [37]Peter said to him, "Master, why can't I follow you now? I will lay down my life for you." [38v]Jesus answered, "Will you lay down your life for me? Amen, amen, I say to you, the cock will not crow before you deny me three times."

Last Supper Discourses

14 [1]*"Do not let your hearts be troubled. You have faith in God; have faith also in me.* [2]In my Father's house there are many dwelling places. If there were not, would I have told you that I am going to prepare a place for you? [3]*aAnd if I go and prepare a place for you, I will come back again and take you to myself, so that where I am you also may be. [4]Where [I] am going you know the way."* [5]Thomas said to him, "Master, we do not know where you are going; how can we know the way?" [6b]Jesus said to him, "I am the way and the truth* and the life. No one comes to the Father except through me. [7c]If you know me, then you will also know my Father.* From now on you do know him and have seen him." [8d]Philip said to him, "Master, show us the Father,* and that will be enough for us." [9e]Jesus said to him, "Have I been with you for so long a time and you still do not know me, Philip? Whoever has seen me has seen the Father. How can you say, 'Show us the Father'? [10f]Do you not believe that I am in the Father and the Father is in me? The words that I speak to you I do not speak on my own. The Father who dwells in me is doing his works. [11g]Believe me that I am in the Father and the Father is in me, or else, believe because of the works themselves. [12h]Amen, amen, I say to you, whoever believes in me will do the works that I do, and will do greater ones than these, because I am going to the Father. [13i]And whatever you ask in my name, I will do, so that the Father may be glorified in the Son. [14]If you ask anything of me in my name, I will do it.

The Advocate

[15j]"If you love me, you will keep my commandments. [16k]And I will ask the Father, and he will give you another Advocate* to be with you

You are the way to the Father. You are the path I explore when I want to know the truth. You are the life I breathe with every breath. You are my way, my truth, my life.

14:1-31 Jesus' departure and return. This section is a dialogue marked off by a literary inclusion in John 14:1, 27: "Do not let your hearts be troubled."

14:1 You have faith: could also be imperative: "Have faith."

14:3 Come back again: a rare Johannine reference to the parousia; cf. 1 John 2:28.

14:4 The way: here, of Jesus himself; also a designation of Christianity in Acts 9:2; 19:9, 23; 22:4; 24:14, 22.

14:6 The truth: in John, the divinely revealed reality of the Father manifested in the person and works of Jesus. The possession of truth confers knowledge and liberation from sin (8:32).

14:7 An alternative reading, "If you knew me, then you would have known my Father also," would be a rebuke, as in John 8:19.

14:8 Show us the Father: Philip is pictured asking for a theophany like Exodus 24:9-10; 33:18.

14:16 Another Advocate: Jesus is the first advocate (*paraclete*); see 1 John 2:1, where Jesus is an advocate in the sense of intercessor in heaven. The Greek term derives from legal terminology for an advocate or defense attorney, and can mean spokesman, mediator, intercessor, comforter, consoler, although none of these terms encompasses the meaning in John. The Paraclete in John is a teacher, a witness to Jesus, and a prosecutor of the world, who

The **Paraclete** is John's unique expression for the Holy Spirit. The Greek term *parakletos* is a masculine form. Here it means an advocate or counselor, in the sense of one who speaks on someone's behalf. Thus, the Holy Spirit is really a second advocate or counselor, since the word also applies to Jesus (14:16). The Paraclete abides with Jesus' followers and guides them in a variety of ways:

Passage	Duties of the Paraclete
14:15-17	He is "another Advocate" and the "Spirit of truth"; he will remain with believers always; the world will reject him (as it rejected Jesus)
14:26	He teaches and reminds the disciples of all Jesus said
15:26	The Father will send him to testify on behalf of Jesus
16:7-14	He will come only when Jesus leaves; he will convict the world; he will guide believers in the truth, will speak only what he hears, will declare things to come, and will glorify Jesus

always, [17l]the Spirit of truth,* which the world cannot accept, because it neither sees nor knows it. But you know it, because it remains with you, and will be in you. [18]I will not leave you orphans; I will come to you.* [19m]In a little while the world will no longer see me, but you will see me, because I live and you will live. [20n]On that day you will realize that I am in my Father and you are in me and I in you. [21o]Whoever has my commandments and observes them is the one who loves me. And whoever loves me will be loved by my Father, and I will love him and reveal myself to him." [22p]Judas, not the Iscariot,* said to him, "Master, [then] what happened that you will reveal yourself to us and not to the world?" [23q]Jesus answered and said to him, "Whoever loves me will keep my word, and my Father will love him, and we will come to him and make our dwelling with him. [24]Whoever does not love me does not keep my words; yet the word you hear is not mine but that of the Father who sent me.

[25]"I have told you this while I am with you. [26r]The Advocate, the holy Spirit that the Father will send in my name—he will teach you everything and remind you of all that [I] told you. [27s]Peace* I leave with you; my peace I give to you. Not as the world gives do I give it to you. Do not let your hearts be troubled or afraid. [28*t]You heard me tell you, 'I am going away and I will come back to you.' If you loved me, you would rejoice that I am going to the Father; for the Father is greater than I. [29u]And now I have

l
16:13;
Mt 28:20;
2 Jn 1–2

m
16:16

n
10:38; 17:21;
Is 2:17; 4:2-3

o
16:27;
1 Jn 2:5; 3:24

p
7:4;
Acts 10:40-41

q
Rev 3:20

r
15:26;
16:7, 13-14;
Ps 51:13;
Is 63:10

s
16:33;
Eph 2:14-18

t
8:40

u
13:19; 16:4

JOHN

---

represents the continued presence on earth of the Jesus who has returned to the Father.

14:17 The Spirit of truth: this term is also used at Qumran, where it is a moral force put into a person by God, as opposed to the spirit of perversity. It is more personal in John; it will teach the realities of the new order (14:26), and testify to the truth (14:6). While it has been customary to use masculine personal pronouns in English for the Advocate, the Greek word for "spirit" is neuter, and the Greek text and manuscript variants fluctuate between masculine and neuter pronouns.

14:18 I will come to you: indwelling, not parousia.

14:22 Judas, not the Iscariot: probably not the brother of Jesus in Mark 6:3 // Matthew 13:55 or the apostle named Jude in Luke 6:16, but Thomas (see the note on 11:16), although other readings have "Judas the Cananean."

14:27 Peace: the traditional Hebrew salutation *šālôm*; but Jesus' "Shalom" is a gift of salvation, connoting the bounty of messianic blessing.

14:28 The Father is greater than I: because he **sent, gave**, etc., and Jesus is "a man who has told you the truth that I heard from God" (8:40).

Cross-references (left column):

v 6:38

a Ps 80:9-17; Is 5:1-7; Jer 2:21; Ez 15:2; 17:5-10; 19:10

b 13:10

c Ez 15:6-7; 19:10-14

d 14:13; Mt 7:7; Mk 11:24; 1 Jn 5:14

e Mt 5:16

f 17:23

g 8:29; 14:15

h 16:22; 17:13

i 13:34

j Rom 5:6-8; 1 Jn 3:16

told you this before it happens, so that when it happens you may believe. [30]I will no longer speak much with you, for the ruler of the world* is coming. He has no power over me, [31][v]but the world must know that I love the Father and that I do just as the Father has commanded me. Get up, let us go.

The Vine and the Branches

15 [1][*][a]"I am the true vine, and my Father is the vine grower.* [2]He takes away every branch in me that does not bear fruit, and everyone that does he prunes* so that it bears more fruit. [3][b]You are already pruned because of the word that I spoke to you. [4]Remain in me, as I remain in you. Just as a branch cannot bear fruit on its own unless it remains on the vine, so neither can you unless you remain in me. [5]I am the vine, you are the branches. Whoever remains in me and I in him will bear much fruit, because without me you can do nothing. [6][*][c]Anyone who does not remain in me will be thrown out like a branch and wither; people will gather them and throw them into a fire and they will be burned. [7][d]If you remain in me and my words remain in you, ask for whatever you want and it will be done for you. [8][e]By this is my Father glorified, that you bear much fruit and become my disciples. [9][f]As the Father loves me, so I also love you. Remain in my love. [10][g]If you keep my commandments, you will remain in my love, just as I have kept my Father's commandments and remain in his love.

[11][h]"I have told you this so that my joy may be in you and your joy may be complete. [12][i]This is my commandment: love one another as I love you. [13][*][j]No one has greater love than this, to lay down one's life for one's friends. [14]You are my friends if you

Take your barren and fruitful branches to prayer. In regard to your barren branches perhaps, with a little pruning, there is still something that can be saved. Bring your fruitful branches to God for a blessing. They are blossoming because they have remained connected to the Source of Life. Both your barren and your fruitful branches can befriend you. Name them.

14:30 The ruler of the world: Satan; cf. John 12:31; 16:11.

15:1–16:4 Discourse on the union of Jesus with his disciples. His words become a monologue and go beyond the immediate crisis of the departure of Jesus.

15:1-17 Like John 10:1-5, this passage resembles a parable. Israel is spoken of as a vineyard at Isaiah 5:1-7; Matthew 21:33-46 and as a vine at Psalm 80:9-17; Jeremiah 2:21; Ezekiel 15:2; 17:5-10; 19:10; Hosea 10:1. The identification of the vine as the Son of Man in Psalm 80:15 and Wisdom's description of herself as a vine in Sirach 24:17 are further background for portrayal of Jesus by this figure. There may be secondary eucharistic symbolism here; cf. Mark 14:25, "the fruit of the vine."

15:2 Takes away . . . prunes: in Greek there is a play on two related verbs.

15:6 Branches were cut off and dried on the wall of the vineyard for later use as fuel.

15:13 For one's friends: or: "those whom one loves." In John 15:9-13a, the words for love are related to the Greek *agapaō*. In John 15:13b-15, the words for love are related to the Greek *phileō*. For John, the two roots seem synonymous and mean "to love"; cf. also John 21:15-17. The word *philos* is used here.

Vine and branches

do what I command you. [15k]"I no longer call you slaves, because a slave does not know what his master is doing. I have called you friends,* because I have told you everything I have heard from my Father. [16]"It was not you who chose me, but I who chose you and appointed you to go and bear fruit that will remain, so that whatever you ask the Father in my name he may give you. [17m]"This I command you: love one another.

The World's Hatred

[18*n]"If the world hates you, realize that it hated me first. [19o]"If you belonged to the world, the world would love its own; but because you do not belong to the world, and I have chosen you out of the world, the world hates you. [20p]"Remember the word I spoke to you,* 'No slave is greater than his master.' If they persecuted me, they will also persecute you. If they kept my word, they will also keep yours. [21q]"And they will do all these things to you on account of my name,* because they do not know the one who sent me. [22]"If I had not come and spoken* to them, they would have no sin; but as it is they have no excuse for their sin. [23s]"Whoever hates me also hates my Father. [24]"If I had not done works among them that no one else ever did, they would not have sin; but as it is, they have seen and hated both me and my Father. [25u]"But in order that the word written in their law* might be fulfilled, 'They hated me without cause.'

[26v]"When the Advocate comes whom I will send* you from the Father, the Spirit of truth that proceeds from the Father, he will testify to me. [27w]"And you also testify, because you have been with me from the beginning.

16 [1]"I have told you this so that you may not fall away. [2a]"They will expel you from the synagogues; in fact, the hour* is coming when everyone who kills you will think he is offering worship to God. [3b]"They will do this because they have not known either the Father or me. [4c]"I have told you this so that when their hour comes you may remember that I told you.*

k
Dt 34:5;
Jos 24:29;
2 Chr 20:7;
Ps 89:21;
Is 41:8;
Rom 8:15;
Gal 4:7;
Jas 2:23

l
14:13; Dt 7:6

m
13:34;
1 Jn 3:23; 4:21

n
7:7; 14:17;
Mt 10:22; 24:9;
Mk 13:13;
Lk 6:22;
1 Jn 3:13

o
17:14-16;
1 Jn 4:5

p
13:16;
Mt 10:24

q
8:19; 16:3

r
8:21, 24; 9:41

s
5:23; Lk 10:16;
1 Jn 2:23

t
3:2; 9:32;
Dt 4:32-33

u
Pss 35:19;
69:4

v
14:16, 26;
Mt 10:19-20

w
Lk 1:2;
Acts 1:8

a
9:22; 12:42;
Mt 10:17;
Lk 21:12;
Acts 26:11

b
15:21

c
13:19; 14:29

15:15 Slaves . . . friends: in the Old Testament, Moses (Dt 34:5), Joshua (Jos 24:29), and David (Ps 89:21) were called "servants" or "slaves of Yahweh"; only Abraham (Is 41:8; 2 Chr 20:7; cf. Jas 2:23) was called a "friend of God."

15:18–16:4 The hostile reaction of the world. There are synoptic parallels, predicting persecution, especially at Matthew 10:17-25; 24:9-10.

15:20 The word I spoke to you: a reference to John 13:16.

15:21 On account of my name: the idea of persecution for Jesus' name is frequent in the New Testament (Mt 10:22; 24:9; Acts 9:14). For John, association with Jesus' name implies union with Jesus.

15:22, 24 Jesus' words (**spoken**) and deeds (**works**) are the great motives of credibility. **They have seen and hated**: probably means that they have seen his works and still have hated; but the Greek can be read: "have seen both me and my Father and still have hated both me and my Father." **Works . . . that no one else ever did**: so Yahweh in Deuteronomy 4:32-33.

15:25 In their law: law is here used as a larger concept than the Pentateuch, for the reference is to Psalm 35:19 or Psalm 69:5. See the notes on John 10:34; 12:34. **Their** law reflects the argument of the church with the synagogue.

15:26 Whom I will send: in John 14:16, 26, the Paraclete is to be sent by the Father, at the request of Jesus. Here the Spirit comes from both Jesus and the Father in mission; there is no reference here to the eternal procession of the Spirit.

16:2 Hour: of persecution, not Jesus' "hour" (see the note on 2:4).

16:4b-33 A duplicate of John 14:1-31 on departure and return.

253

d
7:33; 13:36;
14:5

e
7:39;
14:16-17, 26;
15:26

f
8:21-24; 15:22

g
12:31

h
14:17, 26;
15:26;
Pss 25:5;
143:10;
1 Jn 2:27;
Rev 7:17

i
7:33; 14:19

j
Ps 126:6

k
Is 26:17-18;
Jer 31:13;
Mi 4:9

l
14:19; 15:11;
20:20

m
14:13

n
Mt 13:34-35

o
14:13

p
1:1

JOHN

Jesus' Departure; Coming of the Advocate

"I did not tell you this from the beginning, because I was with you. [5d]But now I am going to the one who sent me, and not one of you asks me,[*] 'Where are you going?' [6]But because I told you this, grief has filled your hearts. [7e]But I tell you the truth, it is better for you that I go. For if I do not go, the Advocate will not come to you. But if I go, I will send him to you. [8*]And when he comes he will convict the world in regard to sin and righteousness and condemnation: [9f]sin, because they do not believe in me; [10]righteousness, because I am going to the Father and you will no longer see me; [11g]condemnation, because the ruler of this world has been condemned.

[12]"I have much more to tell you, but you cannot bear it now. [13*h]But when he comes, the Spirit of truth, he will guide you to all truth. He will not speak on his own, but he will speak what he hears, and will declare to you the things that are coming. [14]He will glorify me, because he will take from what is mine and declare it to you. [15]Everything that the Father has is mine; for this reason I told you that he will take from what is mine and declare it to you.

[16i]"A little while and you will no longer see me, and again a little while later and you will see me." [17]So some of his disciples said to one another, "What does this mean that he is saying to us, 'A little while and you will not see me, and again a little while and you will see me,' and 'Because I am going to the Father'?" [18]So they said, "What is this 'little while' [of which he speaks]? We do not know what he means." [19]Jesus knew that they wanted to ask him, so he said to them, "Are you discussing with one another what I said, 'A little while and you will not see me, and again a little while and you will see me'? [20j]Amen, amen, I say to you, you will weep and mourn, while the world rejoices; you will grieve, but your grief will become joy. [21k]When a woman is in labor, she is in anguish because her hour has arrived; but when she has given birth to a child, she no longer remembers the pain because of her joy that a child has been born into the world. [22l]So you also are now in anguish. But I will see you again, and your hearts will rejoice, and no one will take your joy away from you. [23m]On that day you will not question me about anything. Amen, amen, I say to you, whatever you ask the Father in my name he will give you. [24]Until now you have not asked anything in my name; ask and you will receive, so that your joy may be complete.

[25*n]"I have told you this in figures of speech. The hour is coming when I will no longer speak to you in figures but I will tell you clearly about the Father. [26o]On that day you will ask in my name, and I do not tell you that I will ask the Father for you. [27]For the Father himself loves you, because you have loved me and have come to believe that I came from God. [28p]I came from the Father and have come into the world. Now I am leaving the world and going back to the Father." [29]His disciples said, "Now you

---

16:5 Not one of you asks me: the difficulty of reconciling this with Simon Peter's question in John 13:36 and Thomas's words in John 14:5 strengthens the supposition that the last discourse has been made up of several collections of Johannine material.

16:8-11 These verses illustrate the forensic character of the Paraclete's role: in the forum of the disciples' conscience he prosecutes the world. He leads believers to see (a) that the basic sin was and is refusal to believe in Jesus; (b) that, although Jesus was

found guilty and apparently died in disgrace, in reality righteousness has triumphed, for Jesus has returned to his Father; (c) finally, that it is the ruler of this world, Satan, who has been condemned through Jesus' death (12:32).

16:13 Declare to you the things that are coming: not a reference to new predictions about the future, but interpretation of what has already occurred or been said.

16:25 See the note on John 10:6. Here, possibly a reference to John 15:1-16 or 16:21.

are talking plainly, and not in any figure of speech. [30]Now we realize that you know everything and that you do not need to have anyone question you. Because of this we believe that you came from God."* [31]Jesus answered them, "Do you believe now? [32q]Behold, the hour is coming and has arrived when each of you will be scattered* to his own home and you will leave me alone. But I am not alone, because the Father is with me. [33r]I have told you this so that you might have peace in me. In the world you will have trouble, but take courage, I have conquered the world."

The Prayer of Jesus

17 [1*a]When Jesus had said this, he raised his eyes to heaven and said, "Father, the hour has come. Give glory to your son, so that your son may glorify you,* [2*b]just as you gave him authority over all people, so that he may give eternal life to all you gave him. [3*c]Now this is eternal life, that they should know you, the only true God, and the one whom you sent, Jesus Christ. [4]I glorified you on earth by accomplishing the work that you gave me to do. [5d]Now glorify me, Father, with you, with the glory that I had with you before the world began.

[6]"I revealed your name* to those whom you gave me out of the world. They belonged to you, and you gave them to me, and they have kept your word. [7]Now they know that everything you gave me is from you, [8]because the words you gave to me I have given to them, and they accepted them and truly understood that I came from you, and they have believed that you sent me. [9e]I pray for them. I do not pray for the world but for the ones you have given me, because they are yours, [10f]and everything of mine is yours and everything of yours is mine, and I have been glorified in them. [11]And now I will no longer be in the world, but they are in the world, while I am coming to you. Holy Father, keep them in your name that you have given me, so that they may be one just as we are. [12g]When I was with them I protected them in your name that you gave me, and I guarded them, and none of them was lost except the son of destruction, in order that the scripture might be fulfilled. [13h]But now I am coming to you. I speak this in the world so that they may share my joy completely. [14i]I gave them your word, and the world hated them, because they do not belong to the world any more than I belong to the world. [15*j]I do not ask that you take them out of the world but that you keep them from the evil one. [16]They do not belong to the world any more than I belong to the

q
8:29; Zec 13:7; Mt 26:31; Mk 14:27

r
14:27

a
13:31

b
3:35; Mt 28:18

c
1:17; Wis 14:7; 15:3; 1 Jn 5:20

d
1:1, 2; 12:28; Phil 2:6, 9-11

e
17:20

f
16:15; 2 Thes 1:10, 12

g
13:18; 18:9; Ps 41:10; Mt 26:24; Acts 1:16

h
15:11

i
15:19

j
Mt 6:13; 2 Thes 3:3; 1 Jn 5:18

JOHN

16:30 The reference is seemingly to the fact that Jesus could anticipate their question in John 16:19. The disciples naively think they have the full understanding that is the climax of "the hour" of Jesus' death, resurrection, and ascension (16:25), but the only part of the hour that is at hand for them is their share in the passion (16:32).

16:32 You will be scattered: cf. Mark 14:27 and Matthew 26:31, where both cite Zechariah 13:7 about the sheep being dispersed.

17:1-26 Climax of the last discourse(s). Since the sixteenth century, this chapter has been called the "high priestly prayer" of Jesus. He speaks as intercessor, with words addressed directly to the Father and not to the disciples, who supposedly only overhear. Yet the prayer is one of petition, for immediate (17:6-19) and future (17:20-21) disciples. Many phrases reminiscent of the Lord's Prayer occur. Although still in the world (17:13), Jesus looks on his earthly ministry as a thing of the past (17:4, 12). Whereas Jesus has up to this time stated that the disciples could follow him (13:33, 36), now he wishes them to be with him in union with the Father (17:12-14).

17:1 The action of looking up to heaven and the address **Father** are typical of Jesus at prayer; cf. John 11:41 and Luke 11:2.

17:2 Another possible interpretation is to treat the first line of the verse as parenthetical and the second as an appositive to the clause that ends v. 1: **so that your son may glorify you (just as . . . all people), so that he may give eternal life. . . .**

17:3 This verse was clearly added in the editing of the gospel as a reflection on the preceding verse; Jesus nowhere else refers to himself as Jesus Christ.

17:6 I revealed your name: perhaps the name **I AM**; cf. John 8:24, 28, 58; 13:19.

17:15 Note the resemblance to the petition of the Lord's Prayer, "deliver us from the evil one." Both probably refer to the devil rather than to abstract evil.

k
1 Pt 1:22

l
20:21-22

m
10:30;
14:10-11, 20

n
14:3;
1 Thes 4:17

o
1:10

a
2 Sm 15:23;
Mt 26:30, 36;
Mk 14:26, 32;
Lk 22:39

b
Mt 26:47-51;
Mk 14:43-44;
Lk 22:47

c
6:39; 10:28;
17:12

d
Mt 20:22;
26:39;
Mk 10:38;
Lk 22:42

e
Mt 26:57-58;
Mk 14:53-54;
Lk 22:54-55

f
Lk 3:2

world. [17][k]Consecrate them in the truth. Your word is truth. [18][l]As you sent me into the world, so I sent them into the world. [19]And I consecrate myself for them, so that they also may be consecrated in truth.

[20]"I pray not only for them, but also for those who will believe in me through their word, [21][m]so that they may all be one, as you, Father, are in me and I in you, that they also may be in us, that the world may believe that you sent me. [22]And I have given them the glory you gave me, so that they may be one, as we are one, [23]I in them and you in me, that they may be brought to perfection as one, that the world may know that you sent me, and that you loved them even as you loved me. [24][n]Father, they are your gift to me. I wish that where I am[*] they also may be with me, that they may see my glory that you gave me, because you loved me before the foundation of the world. [25][o]Righteous Father, the world also does not know you, but I know you, and they know that you sent me. [26]I made known to them your name and I will make it known,[*] that the love with which you loved me may be in them and I in them."

Jesus Arrested

18 [1][*][a]When he had said this, Jesus went out with his disciples across the Kidron valley to where there was a garden, into which he and his disciples entered.[*] [2]Judas his betrayer also knew the place, because Jesus had often met there with his disciples. [3][b]So Judas got a band of soldiers[*] and guards from the chief priests and the Pharisees and went there with lanterns, torches, and weapons. [4]Jesus, knowing everything that was going to happen to him, went out and said to them, "Whom are you looking for?" [5]They answered him, "Jesus the Nazorean."[*] He said to them, "I AM." Judas his betrayer was also with them. [6]When he said to them, "I AM," they turned away and fell to the ground. [7]So he again asked them, "Whom are you looking for?" They said, "Jesus the Nazorean." [8]Jesus answered, "I told you that I AM. So if you are looking for me, let these men go." [9][*][c]This was to fulfill what he had said, "I have not lost any of those you gave me." [10]Then Simon Peter, who had a sword, drew it, struck the high priest's slave, and cut off his right ear. The slave's name was Malchus.[*] [11][d]Jesus said to Peter, "Put your sword into its scabbard. Shall I not drink the cup[*] that the Father gave me?"

[12][e]So the band of soldiers, the tribune, and the Jewish guards seized Jesus, bound him, [13][f]and brought him to Annas[*] first. He was the father-in-law of Caiaphas, who was

---

17:24 Where I am: Jesus prays for the believers ultimately to join him in heaven. Then they will not see his glory as in a mirror but clearly (2 Cor 3:18; 1 Jn 3:2).

17:26 I will make it known: through the Advocate.

18:1-14 John does not mention the agony in the garden and the kiss of Judas, nor does he identify the place as Gethsemane or the Mount of Olives.

18:1 Jesus went out: see John 14:31 where it seems he is leaving the supper room. **Kidron valley**: literally, "the winter-flowing Kidron"; this wadi has water only during the winter rains.

18:3 Band of soldiers: seems to refer to Roman troops, either the full cohort of 600 men (1/10 of a legion), or more likely the maniple of 200 under their tribune (18:12). In this case, John is hinting at Roman collusion in the action against Jesus before he was brought to Pilate. The lanterns and torches may be symbolic of the hour of darkness.

18:5 Nazorean: the form found in Matthew 26:71 (see the note on Mt 2:23) is here used, not **Nazarene** of Mark. **I AM**: or "I am he," but probably intended by the evangelist as an expression of divinity (cf. their appropriate response in 18:6); see the note on John 8:24. John sets the confusion of the arresting party against the background of Jesus' divine majesty.

18:9 The citation may refer to John 6:39; 10:28; or 17:12.

18:10 Only John gives the names of the two antagonists; both John and Luke mention the right ear.

18:11 The theme of the cup is found in the synoptic account of the agony (Mk 14:36 and parallels).

18:13 Annas: only John mentions an inquiry before Annas; cf. John 18:16, 19-23; see the note on Luke 3:2. It is unlikely that this nighttime interrogation before Annas is the same as the trial before Caiaphas placed by Matthew and Mark at night and by Luke in the morning.

high priest that year. [14g]It was Caiaphas who had counseled the Jews that it was better that one man should die rather than the people.

Peter's First Denial

[15h]Simon Peter and another disciple* followed Jesus. Now the other disciple was known to the high priest, and he entered the courtyard of the high priest with Jesus. [16]But Peter stood at the gate outside. So the other disciple, the acquaintance of the high priest, went out and spoke to the gatekeeper and brought Peter in. [17]Then the maid who was the gatekeeper said to Peter, "You are not one of this man's disciples, are you?" He said, "I am not." [18]Now the slaves and the guards were standing around a charcoal fire that they had made, because it was cold, and were warming themselves. Peter was also standing there keeping warm.

The Inquiry before Annas

[19i]The high priest questioned Jesus about his disciples and about his doctrine. [20j]Jesus answered him, "I have spoken publicly to the world. I have always taught in a synagogue or in the temple area* where all the Jews gather, and in secret I have said nothing. [21]Why ask me? Ask those who heard me what I said to them. They know what I said." [22k]When he had said this, one of the temple guards standing there struck Jesus and said, "Is this the way you answer the high priest?" [23]Jesus answered him, "If I have spoken wrongly, testify to the wrong; but if I have spoken rightly, why do you strike me?" [24l]Then Annas sent him bound to Caiaphas* the high priest.

Peter Denies Jesus Again

[25m]Now Simon Peter was standing there keeping warm. And they said to him, "You are not one of his disciples, are you?" He denied it and said, "I am not." [26]One of the slaves of the high priest, a relative of the one whose ear Peter had cut off, said, "Didn't I see you in the garden with him?" [27]Again Peter denied it. And immediately the cock crowed.*

The Trial before Pilate

[28n]Then they brought Jesus from Caiaphas to the praetorium.* It was morning. And they themselves did not enter the praetorium, in order not to be defiled so that they could eat the Passover. [29]So Pilate came out to them and said, "What charge do you bring [against] this man?" [30]They answered and said to him, "If he were not a criminal, we would not have handed him over to you." [31]At this, Pilate said to them, "Take him yourselves, and judge him according to your law." The Jews answered him, "We do

---

g
11:49-50

h
Mt 26:58,
69-70;
Mk 14:54,
66-68;
Lk 22:54-57

i
Mt 26:59-66;
Mk 14:55-64;
Lk 22:66-71

j
6:59; 7:14, 26;
Is 48:16;
Mt 26:55;
Mk 4:23;
Lk 19:47;
22:53

k
Acts 23:2

l
Mt 26:57

m
Mt 26:71-75;
Mk 14:69-72;
Lk 22:58-62

n
Mt 27:1-2,
11-25;
Mk 15:1-5;
Lk 23:1-5

JOHN

On the **praetorium**, see the NAB footnote (at Mt 27:27).

---

o
3:14; 8:28;
12:32-33

p
1:11

q
1:10; 8:23

r
8:47;
1 Tm 6:13

s
Mt 27:15-26;
Mk 15:6-15;
Lk 23:18-25;
Acts 3:14

a
Mt 27:27-31;
Mk 15:16-20;
Lk 23:13-25

not have the right to execute anyone,"* [32]*[o]in order that the word of Jesus might be fulfilled that he said indicating the kind of death he would die. [33]So Pilate went back into the praetorium and summoned Jesus and said to him, "Are you the King of the Jews?" [34]Jesus answered, "Do you say this on your own or have others told you about me?" [35p]Pilate answered, "I am not a Jew, am I? Your own nation and the chief priests handed you over to me. What have you done?" [36q]Jesus answered, "My kingdom does not belong to this world. If my kingdom did belong to this world, my attendants [would] be fighting to keep me from being handed over to the Jews. But as it is, my kingdom is not here." [37r]So Pilate said to him, "Then you are a king?" Jesus answered, "You say I am a king.* For this I was born and for this I came into the world, to testify to the truth. Everyone who belongs to the truth listens to my voice." [38s]Pilate said to him, "What is truth?"

When he had said this, he again went out to the Jews and said to them, "I find no guilt in him. [39]But you have a custom that I release one prisoner to you at Passover.* Do you want me to release to you the King of the Jews?" [40]They cried out again, "Not this one but Barabbas!"* Now Barabbas was a revolutionary.

In 1961 archaeologists discovered a unique fragmentary limestone inscription that mentions **Pontius Pilate**. The block was used by ancient construction workers for a secondary project, thus marring the original inscription. The words are the remnant of a dedication given to the Emperor Tiberius Caesar from Pilate, who was then prefect of the Roman province of Judea. The fragmentary lines still visible (in Latin capital letters) read:

......S TIBERIEVM = (Temple?) Tiberieum
......NTIVS PILATVS = (Po)ntius Pilate
......ECTVS IUDAE = (Pr)efect of Judea

The original is now housed in the Israeli Museum in Jerusalem, although a replica remains at the site of its discovery in Caesarea Maritima.

The Pilate inscription, Caesarea Maritima

19 [1]*[a]Then Pilate took Jesus and had him scourged. [2]And the soldiers wove a crown out of thorns and placed it on his head, and clothed him in a purple cloak, [3]and they came to him and said, "Hail, King of the Jews!" And they struck him repeatedly.

18:32 The Jewish punishment for blasphemy was stoning (Lv 24:16). In coming to the Romans to ensure that Jesus would be crucified, the Jewish authorities fulfilled his prophecy that he would be **exalted** (3:14; 12:32-33). There is some historical evidence, however, for Jews crucifying Jews.

18:37 You say I am a king: see Matthew 26:64 for a similar response to the high priest. It is at best a reluctant affirmative.

18:39 See the note on Matthew 27:15.

18:40 Barabbas: see the note on Matthew 27:16-17. **Revolutionary:** a guerrilla warrior fighting for nationalistic aims, though the term can also denote a robber. See the note on Matthew 27:38.

19:1 Luke places the mockery of Jesus at the midpoint in the trial when Jesus was sent to Herod. Mark and Matthew place the scourging and mockery at the end of the trial after the sentence of death. Scourging was an integral part of the crucifixion penalty.

[4b]Once more Pilate went out and said to them, "Look, I am bringing him out to you, so that you may know that I find no guilt in him." [5c]So Jesus came out, wearing the crown of thorns and the purple cloak. And he said to them, "Behold, the man!" [6d]When the chief priests and the guards saw him they cried out, "Crucify him, crucify him!" Pilate said to them, "Take him yourselves and crucify him. I find no guilt in him." [7*e]The Jews answered, "We have a law, and according to that law he ought to die, because he made himself the Son of God." [8]Now when Pilate heard this statement, he became even more afraid, [9f]and went back into the praetorium and said to Jesus, "Where are you from?" Jesus did not answer him. [10]So Pilate said to him, "Do you not speak to me? Do you not know that I have power to release you and I have power to crucify you?" [11g]Jesus answered [him], "You would have no power over me if it had not been given to you from above. For this reason the one who handed me over to you has the greater sin." [12h]Consequently, Pilate tried to release him; but the Jews cried out, "If you release him, you are not a Friend of Caesar.* Everyone who makes himself a king opposes Caesar."

[13]When Pilate heard these words he brought Jesus out and seated him* on the judge's bench in the place called Stone Pavement, in Hebrew, Gabbatha. [14]It was preparation day for Passover, and it was about noon.* And he said to the Jews, "Behold, your king!"

Traditional site of the Ecce Homo Arch in Jerusalem

[15]They cried out, "Take him away, take him away! Crucify him!" Pilate said to them, "Shall I crucify your king?" The chief priests answered, "We have no king but Caesar." [16]Then he handed him over to them to be crucified.*

The Crucifixion of Jesus

So they took Jesus, [17i]and carrying the cross himself* he went out to what is called the Place of the Skull, in Hebrew, Golgotha. [18]There they crucified him, and with him two others, one on either side, with Jesus in the middle. [19*]Pilate also had an

Side references (right margin):

b
18:38

c
Is 52:14

d
18:31; 19:15

e
10:33-36;
Lv 24:16

f
7:28

g
3:27; 10:18;
Rom 13:1

h
Acts 17:7

i
Mt 27:32-37;
Mk 15:21-26;
Lk 23:26-35

JOHN

19:7 Made himself the Son of God: this question was not raised in John's account of the Jewish interrogations of Jesus as it was in the synoptic account. Nevertheless, see John 5:18; 8:53; 10:36.

19:12 Friend of Caesar: a Roman honorific title bestowed upon high-ranking officials for merit.

19:13 Seated him: others translate "(Pilate) sat down." In John's thought, Jesus is the real judge of the world, and John may here be portraying him seated on the judgment bench. **Stone pavement**: in Greek *lithostrotos*; under the fortress Antonia, one of the conjectured locations of the praetorium, a massive stone pavement has been excavated. **Gabbatha** (Aramaic rather than Hebrew) probably means "ridge, elevation."

19:14 Noon: Mark 15:25 has Jesus crucified "at the third hour," which means either 9 a.m. or the period from 9 to 12. Noon, the time when, according to John, Jesus was sentenced to death, was the hour at which the priests began to slaughter Passover lambs in the temple; see John 1:29.

19:16 He handed him over to them to be crucified: in context this would seem to mean "handed him over to the chief priests." Luke 23:25 has a similar ambiguity. There is a polemic tendency in the gospels to place the guilt of the crucifixion on the Jewish authorities and to exonerate the Romans from blame. But John later mentions the Roman soldiers (19:23), and it was to these soldiers that Pilate handed Jesus over.

19:17 Carrying the cross himself: a different picture from that of the synoptics, especially Luke 23:26 where Simon of Cyrene is made to carry the cross, walking behind Jesus. In John's theology, Jesus remained in complete control and master of his destiny (cf. 10:18). **Place of the Skull**: the Latin word for skull is *Calvaria*; hence "Calvary." **Golgotha** is actually an Aramaic rather than a Hebrew word.

19:19 The inscription differs with slightly different words in each of the four gospels. John's form is fullest and gives the equivalent of the Latin *INRI = Iesus Nazarenus Rex Iudaeorum*. Only John mentions its polyglot character (19:20) and Pilate's role in keeping the title unchanged (19:21-22).

j
18:33;
Lk 19:14

k
Mt 27:38-44;
Mk 15:27-32;
Lk 23:36-43

l
Ps 22:19;
Mt 27:35;
Mk 15:24;
Lk 23:34

m
Mt 27:55;
Mk 15:40-41;
Lk 8:2; 23:49

n
13:23

o
Mt 27:45-56;
Mk 15:33-41;
Lk 23:44-49

p
Pss 22:16;
69:22

q
4:34; 10:18;
17:4; Lk 23:46

inscription written and put on the cross. It read, "Jesus the Nazorean, the King of the Jews." [20]Now many of the Jews read this inscription, because the place where Jesus was crucified was near the city; and it was written in Hebrew, Latin, and Greek. [21j]So the chief priests of the Jews said to Pilate, "Do not write 'The King of the Jews,' but that he said, 'I am the King of the Jews.'" [22]Pilate answered, "What I have written, I have written."

[23k]When the soldiers had crucified Jesus, they took his clothes and divided them into four shares, a share for each soldier. They also took his tunic, but the tunic was seamless, woven in one piece from the top down.[l] [24]So they said to one another, "Let's not tear it, but cast lots for it to see whose it will be," in order that the passage of scripture might be fulfilled [that says]:

> "They divided my garments among them,
>   and for my vesture they cast lots."

This is what the soldiers did. [25*m]Standing by the cross of Jesus were his mother and his mother's sister, Mary the wife of Clopas, and Mary of Magdala. [26n]When Jesus saw his mother[*] and the disciple there whom he loved, he said to his mother, "Woman, behold, your son." [27]Then he said to the disciple, "Behold, your mother." And from that hour the disciple took her into his home.

John's gospel never reveals the identity of the **Beloved Disciple**. Ancient tradition identifies him with John, son of Zebedee, and presumed author of the gospel. Regardless of the accuracy of this identification, the "one whom Jesus loved" was an important authority in the Johannine community and the source of authentic witness for the gospel. He also provides a model for the readers, since he is the one who regularly comes to faith and understanding prior to the other disciples of Jesus, including Peter.

[28o]After this, aware that everything was now finished, in order that the scripture might be fulfilled,[*] Jesus said, "I thirst."[p] [29]There was a vessel filled with common wine.[*] So they put a sponge soaked in wine on a sprig of hyssop and put it up to his mouth. [30*q]When Jesus had taken the wine, he said, "It is finished." And bowing his head, he handed over the spirit.

19:23-25a While all four gospels describe the soldiers casting lots to divide Jesus' garments (see the note on Mt 27:35), only John quotes the underlying passage from Psalm 22:19, and only John sees each line of the poetic parallelism literally carried out in two separate actions (19:23-24).

19:25 It is not clear whether four women are meant, or three (i.e., **Mary the wife of Cl[e]opas** [cf. Lk 24:18] is in apposition with **his mother's sister**) or two (his mother and his mother's sister, i.e., Mary of Cl[e]opas and Mary of Magdala). Only John mentions the mother of Jesus here. The synoptics have a group of women looking on from a distance at the cross (Mk 15:40).

19:26-27 This scene has been interpreted literally, of Jesus' concern for his mother; and symbolically, e.g., in the light of the Cana story in John 2 (the presence of the mother of Jesus, the address **woman**, and the mention of the **hour**) and of the upper room in John 13 (the presence of the beloved disciple; the **hour**). Now that the hour has come (19:28), Mary (a symbol of the church?) is given a role as the mother of Christians (personified by the be-

loved disciple); or, as a representative of those seeking salvation, she is supported by the disciple who interprets Jesus' revelation; or Jewish and Gentile Christianity (or Israel and the Christian community) are reconciled.

19:28 The scripture . . . fulfilled: either in the scene of John 19:25-27, or in the **I thirst** of John 19:28. If the latter, Psalms 22:16; 69:22 deserve consideration.

19:29 Wine: John does not mention the drugged wine, a narcotic that Jesus refused as the crucifixion began (Mk 15:23), but only this final gesture of kindness at the end (Mk 15:36). **Hyssop**, a small plant, is scarcely suitable for carrying a sponge (Mark mentions a reed) and may be a symbolic reference to the hyssop used to daub the blood of the paschal lamb on the doorpost of the Hebrews (Ex 12:22).

19:30 Handed over the spirit: there is a double nuance of dying (giving up the last breath or spirit) and that of passing on the holy Spirit; see John 7:39, which connects the giving of the Spirit with Jesus' glorious return to the Father, and John 20:22 where the author portrays the conferral of the Spirit.

The Blood and Water

[31]"Now since it was preparation day, in order that the bodies might not remain on the cross on the sabbath, for the sabbath day of that week was a solemn one, the Jews asked Pilate that their legs be broken and they be taken down. [32]So the soldiers came and broke the legs of the first and then of the other one who was crucified with Jesus. [33]But when they came to Jesus and saw that he was already dead, they did not break his legs, [34]*but one soldier thrust his lance into his side, and immediately blood and water flowed out. [35]An eyewitness has testified, and his testimony is true; he knows* that he is speaking the truth, so that you also may [come to] believe. [36]For this happened so that the scripture passage might be fulfilled:

"Not a bone of it will be broken."

[37]And again another passage says:

"They will look upon him whom they have pierced."

The Burial of Jesus

[38]*After this, Joseph of Arimathea, secretly a disciple of Jesus for fear of the Jews, asked Pilate if he could remove the body of Jesus. And Pilate permitted it. So he came and took his body. [39]Nicodemus, the one who had first come to him at night, also came bringing a mixture of myrrh and aloes weighing about one hundred pounds. [40]They took the body of Jesus and bound it with burial cloths along with the spices, according to the Jewish burial custom. [41]Now in the place where he had been crucified there was a garden, and in the garden a new tomb, in which no one had yet been buried. [42]So they laid Jesus there because of the Jewish preparation day; for the tomb was close by.

The Empty Tomb

20 [1]*On the first day of the week,[a] Mary of Magdala came to the tomb early in the morning, while it was still dark, and saw the stone removed from the tomb.*[b] [2]So she ran* and went to Simon Peter and to the other disciple whom Jesus loved, and told them, "They have taken the Lord from the tomb, and we don't know where they put him." [3]*So Peter and the other disciple went out and came to the tomb. [4]They both ran, but the other disciple ran faster than Peter and arrived at the tomb first; [5]he bent down and saw the burial cloths there, but did not go in. [6]When Simon Peter

---

r
Ex 12:16;
Dt 21:23

s
Nm 20:11;
1 Jn 5:6

t
7:37-39; 21:24

u
Ex 12:46;
Nm 9:12;
Ps 34:21

v
Nm 21:9;
Zec 12:10;
Rev 1:7

w
Mt 27:57-60;
Mk 15:42-46;
Lk 23:50-54

x
3:1-2; 7:50;
Ps 45:9

a
Mt 28:1-10;
Mk 16:1-11;
Lk 24:1-12

b
19:25

c
Lk 24:12

JOHN

19:34-35 John probably emphasizes these verses to show the reality of Jesus' death, against the Docetist heretics. In the blood and water there may also be a symbolic reference to the Eucharist and baptism.

19:35 **He knows**: it is not certain from the Greek that this **he** is the **eyewitness** of the first part of the sentence. **May [come to] believe**: see the note on John 20:31.

19:38-42 In the first three gospels there is no anointing on Friday. In Matthew and Luke the women come to the tomb on Sunday morning precisely to anoint Jesus.

20:1-31 The risen Jesus reveals his glory and confers the Spirit. This story fulfills the basic need for testimony to the resurrection. What we have here is not a record but a series of single stories.

20:1-10 The story of the empty tomb is found in both the Matthean and the Lucan traditions; John's version seems to be a fusion of the two.

20:1 **Still dark**: according to Mark the sun had risen, Matthew describes it as "dawning," and Luke refers to early dawn. Mary sees the stone removed, not the empty tomb.

20:2 Mary runs away, not directed by an angel/young man as in the synoptic accounts. The plural "we" in the second part of her statement might reflect a tradition of more women going to the tomb.

20:3-10 The basic narrative is told of Peter alone in Luke 24:12, a verse missing in important manuscripts and which may be borrowed from tradition similar to John. Cf. also Luke 24:24.

20:6-8 Some special feature about the state of the burial cloths caused the beloved disciple to believe. Perhaps the details emphasized that the grave had not been robbed.

<table>
<tr><td>

d
11:44; 19:40

e
Acts 2:26-27;
1 Cor 15:4

f
Mk 16:9-11

g
21:4;
Mk 16:12;
Lk 24:16;
1 Cor 15:43-44

h
Mt 28:9-10

</td><td>

arrived after him, he went into the tomb and saw the burial cloths* there, [7d]and the cloth that had covered his head, not with the burial cloths but rolled up in a separate place. [8]Then the other disciple also went in, the one who had arrived at the tomb first, and he saw and believed. [9*e]For they did not yet understand the scripture that he had to rise from the dead. [10]Then the disciples returned home.

</td></tr>
</table>

The Appearance to Mary of Magdala

[11*f]But Mary stayed outside the tomb weeping. And as she wept, she bent over into the tomb [12]and saw two angels in white sitting there, one at the head and one at the feet where the body of Jesus had been. [13]And they said to her, "Woman, why are you weeping?" She said to them, "They have taken my Lord, and I don't know where they laid him." [14g]When she had said this, she turned around and saw Jesus there, but did not know it was Jesus. [15h]Jesus said to her, "Woman, why are you weeping? Whom are you looking for?" She thought it was the gardener and said to him, "Sir, if you carried him away, tell me where you laid him, and I will take him." [16]Jesus said to her, "Mary!"

Mary Magdalene

Mary of Magdala, the proper form of her name (Jn 19:25; 20:1), is one of the most prominent women in the NT. She is exclusively identified with the death and resurrection of Jesus in both the synoptic and Johannine traditions of the gospels.

Little is actually known of her history. Magdala was a fishing town on the western shore of the Sea of Galilee. Luke refers to Mary as the woman out of whom Jesus drove seven demons (Jn 8:2; also Mk 16:9, a later ending to Mark's gospel). She has been erroneously identified with the anonymous woman who anointed Jesus before his death (Mk 14:3-9; Mt 26:6-13), or the sinful woman who anointed Jesus in Simon the Pharisee's house (Lk 7:36-50), or with the woman caught in adultery (Jn 8:3-11; a passage that is likely misplaced). Nothing in the NT, however, actually makes these identifications securely. There is no evidence that she was a prostitute. Most likely, she was a wealthy woman of independent means who became an important follower of Jesus (see Lk 8:3).

More important, the NT testifies to Mary's presence during the death and burial of Jesus (Mk 15:40, 47; Mt 27:56, 61). She is part of the group of faithful women who witnessed Jesus being placed in the tomb and who went out early on Easter morning, ostensibly to anoint the body of Jesus (Mk 16:1; Mt 28:1; Lk 24:1, 10). Indeed, she is often listed first among the women, perhaps hinting at her prominence. A secondary ending to Mark's gospel states explicitly that Mary Magdalene is the first to receive an appearance of the risen Lord (Jn 16:9), an extraordinary claim given the cultural limitations of women in first-century Jewish society. Women generally did not count as reliable witnesses. Thus, to name her the first witness to the risen Jesus is a bold move and most likely is rooted in the earliest Christian memory of the resurrection.

John's gospel bolsters this assertion. John recounts Mary's encounter with the risen Lord on Easter morning (Jn 20:11-18). It is a most poignant scene in which Mary, at first, does not recognize the Lord; she thinks he is the gardener who may have displaced the body of Jesus for some reason. Only when Jesus tenderly speaks her name "Mary" does she recognize him, in fulfillment of the model shepherd who calls each sheep by name (Jn 10:3). Remarkably, John also testifies to Mary's subsequent announcement of her encounter with the risen Jesus (Jn 20:18), prefiguring the evangelism of all the disciples. This action earned her the designation of "the apostle to the apostles."

Mary's alleged checkered past, dating from at least the time of Gregory the Great (sixth century A.D.), has made her an intriguing figure in history. Her story led to many bizarre tales, especially about a possible sexual or marital relationship with Jesus. This has been exploited in many stories, books, and films throughout history, but there is no evidence whatsoever for these tales, inside or outside of the NT. Most likely, such stories arose to discredit early Christian claims for the resurrection of Jesus.

20:9 Probably a general reference to the scriptures is intended, as in Luke 24:26 and 1 Corinthians 15:4. Some individual Old Testament passages suggested are Psalm 16:10; Hosea 6:2; Jonah 2:1, 2, 11.

20:11-18 This appearance to Mary is found only in John, but cf. Matthew 28:8-10 and Mark 16:9-11.

20:16 Rabbouni: Hebrew or Aramaic for "my master."

She turned and said to him in Hebrew, "Rabbouni,"* which means Teacher. [17][i]Jesus said to her, "Stop holding on to me,* for I have not yet ascended to the Father. But go to my brothers and tell them, 'I am going to my Father and your Father, to my God and your God.'" [18]Mary of Magdala went and announced to the disciples, "I have seen the Lord," and what he told her.

Appearance to the Disciples

[19]*[j]On the evening of that first day of the week, when the doors were locked, where the disciples were, for fear of the Jews, Jesus came and stood in their midst and said to them, "Peace be with you."* [20][k]When he had said this, he showed them his hands and his side.* The disciples rejoiced when they saw the Lord. [21]*[l][Jesus] said to them again, "Peace be with you. As the Father has sent me, so I send you." [22]*[m]And when he had said this, he breathed on them and said to them, "Receive the holy Spirit. [23]*[n]Whose sins you forgive are forgiven them, and whose sins you retain are retained."

Thomas

[24]Thomas, called Didymus, one of the Twelve, was not with them when Jesus came. [25][o]So the other disciples said to him, "We have seen the Lord." But he said to them, "Unless I see the mark of the nails in his hands and put my finger into the nailmarks and put my hand into his side, I will not believe." [26][p]Now a week later his disciples were again inside and Thomas was with them. Jesus came, although the doors were locked, and stood in their midst and said, "Peace be with you." [27]Then he said to Thomas, "Put your finger here and see my hands, and bring your hand and put it into my side, and do not be unbelieving, but

"Peace be with you" is a profound greeting by the risen Lord to his disciples. The church has incorporated the greeting in the Mass when those assembled turn to one another and extend a sincere wish for *shalom*— the deep well-being and blessing that comes with life in Jesus. Bishops also use this greeting at the beginning of their Masses to extend Christ's deep gift of well-being to the assembly.

i
Acts 1:9

j
Mt 28:16-20;
Mk 16:14-18;
Lk 24:36-44

k
14:27

l
17:18;
Mt 28:19;
Mk 16:15;
Lk 24:47-48

m
Gn 2:7;
Ez 37:9;
1 Cor 15:45

n
Mt 16:19;
18:18

o
1 Jn 1:1

p
21:14

JOHN

20:17 Stop holding on to me: see Matthew 28:9, where the women take hold of his feet. **I have not yet ascended**: for John and many of the New Testament writers, the ascension in the theological sense of going to the Father to be glorified took place with the resurrection as one action. This scene in John dramatizes such an understanding, for by Easter night Jesus is glorified and can give the Spirit. Therefore his ascension takes place immediately after he has talked to Mary. In such a view, the ascension after forty days described in Acts 1:1-11 would be simply a termination of earthly appearances or, perhaps better, an introduction to the conferral of the Spirit upon the early church, modeled on Elisha's being able to have a (double) share in the spirit of Elijah if he saw him being taken up (same verb as ascending) into heaven (2 Kgs 2:9-12). **To my Father and your Father, to my God and your God**: this echoes Ruth 1:16: "Your people shall be my people, and your God my God." The Father of Jesus will now become the Father of the disciples because, once ascended, Jesus can give them the Spirit that comes from the Father and they can be reborn as God's children (3:5). That is why he calls them **my brothers**.

20:19-29 The appearances to the disciples, without or with Thomas (cf. 11:16; 14:5), have rough parallels in the other gospels only for John 20:19-23; cf. Luke 24:36-39; Mark 16:14-18.

20:19 The disciples: by implication from John 20:24 this means ten of the Twelve, presumably in Jerusalem. **Peace be with you**: although this could be an ordinary greeting, John intends here to echo John 14:27. The theme of rejoicing in John 20:20 echoes John 16:22.

20:20 Hands and . . . side: Luke 24:39-40 mentions "hands and feet," based on Psalm 22:17.

20:21 By means of this sending, the Eleven were made apostles, that is, "those sent" (cf. 17:18), though John does not use the noun in reference to them (see the note on 13:16). A solemn mission or "sending" is also the subject of the post-resurrection appearances to the Eleven in Matthew 28:19; Luke 24:47; Mark 16:15.

20:22 This action recalls Genesis 2:7, where God breathed on the first man and gave him life; just as Adam's life came from God, so now the disciples' new spiritual life comes from Jesus. Cf. also the revivification of the dry bones in Ezekiel 37. This is the author's version of Pentecost. Cf. also the note on John 19:30.

20:23 The Council of Trent defined that this power to forgive sins is exercised in the sacrament of penance. See Matthew 16:19 and 18:18.

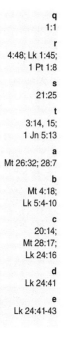

q	1:1
r	4:48; Lk 1:45; 1 Pt 1:8
s	21:25
t	3:14, 15; 1 Jn 5:13
a	Mt 26:32; 28:7
b	Mt 4:18; Lk 5:4-10
c	20:14; Mt 28:17; Lk 24:16
d	Lk 24:41
e	Lk 24:41-43

believe." ²⁸*^qThomas answered and said to him, "My Lord and my God!" ²⁹*^rJesus said to him, "Have you come to believe because you have seen me? Blessed are those who have not seen and have believed."

Conclusion

³⁰*^sNow Jesus did many other signs in the presence of [his] disciples that are not written in this book. ³¹^tBut these are written that you may [come to] believe that Jesus is the Messiah, the Son of God, and that through this belief you may have life in his name.

"My Lord and my God": Thomas' words express the most profound assent of faith that can be given to Jesus as God's Son and Savior of the world. Traditionally, Catholics were urged to say this exclamatory prayer whenever the consecrated host was elevated at Mass for the assembly to reverence.

IV: Epilogue: The Resurrection Appearance in Galilee

The Appearance to the Seven Disciples

21 ¹*^aAfter this, Jesus revealed himself again to his disciples at the Sea of Tiberias. He revealed himself in this way. ²Together were Simon Peter, Thomas called Didymus, Nathanael from Cana in Galilee, Zebedee's sons,* and two others of his disciples. ³*^bSimon Peter said to them, "I am going fishing." They said to him, "We also will come with you." So they went out and got into the boat, but that night they caught nothing. ⁴^cWhen it was already dawn, Jesus was standing on the shore; but the disciples did not realize that it was Jesus. ⁵^dJesus said to them, "Children, have you caught anything to eat?" They answered him, "No." ⁶So he said to them, "Cast the net over the right side of the boat and you will find something." So they cast it, and were not able to pull it in because of the number of fish. ⁷So the disciple whom Jesus loved said to Peter, "It is the Lord." When Simon Peter heard that it was the Lord, he tucked in his garment, for he was lightly clad, and jumped into the sea. ⁸The other disciples came in the boat, for they were not far from shore, only about a hundred yards, dragging the net with the fish. ⁹*^eWhen they climbed out on shore, they saw a charcoal fire with fish on it and bread. ¹⁰Jesus said to them, "Bring some of the fish you just caught."

20:28 My Lord and my God: this forms a literary inclusion with the first verse of the gospel: "and the Word was God."

20:29 This verse is a beatitude on future generations; faith, not sight, matters.

20:30-31 These verses are clearly a conclusion to the gospel and express its purpose. While many manuscripts read **come to believe**, possibly implying a missionary purpose for John's gospel, a small number of quite early ones read "continue to believe," suggesting that the audience consists of Christians whose faith is to be deepened by the book; cf. John 19:35.

21:1-23 There are many non-Johannine peculiarities in this chapter, some suggesting Lucan Greek style; yet this passage is closer to John than John 7:53–8:11. There are many Johannine features as well. Its closest parallels in the synoptic gospels are found in Luke 5:1-11 and Matthew 14:28-31. Perhaps the tradition was ultimately derived from John but preserved by some disciple other than the writer of the rest

of the gospel. The appearances narrated seem to be independent of those in John 20. Even if a later addition, the chapter was added before publication of the gospel, for it appears in all manuscripts.

21:2 Zebedee's sons: the only reference to James and John in this gospel (but see the note on 1:37). Perhaps the phrase was originally a gloss to identify, among the five, the **two others of his disciples**. The anonymity of the latter phrase is more Johannine (1:35). The total of seven may suggest the community of the disciples in its fullness.

21:3-6 This may be a variant of Luke's account of the catch of fish; see the note on Luke 5:1-11.

21:9, 12-13 It is strange that Jesus already has fish since none have yet been brought ashore. This meal may have had eucharistic significance for early Christians since John 21:13 recalls John 6:11 which uses the vocabulary of Jesus' action at the Last Supper; but see also the note on Matthew 14:19.

[11f]So Simon Peter went over and dragged the net ashore full of one hundred fifty-three[*] large fish. Even though there were so many, the net was not torn. [12]Jesus said to them, "Come, have breakfast." And none of the disciples dared to ask him,[*] "Who are you?" because they realized it was the Lord. [13g]Jesus came over and took the bread and gave it to them, and in like manner the fish. [14*h]This was now the third time Jesus was revealed to his disciples after being raised from the dead.

f
2 Chr 2:16

g
Lk 24:42

h
20:19, 26

i
13:37-38;
18:15-18,
25-27;
Mt 26:69-75;
Mk 14:66-72;
Lk 22:55-62

j
Acts 21:11, 14;
2 Pt 1:14

k
13:36

To reaffirm a love for someone you once betrayed is a bittersweet joy, a tender heartache. Become Peter for a day. Try to feel both the angst and the love that Peter must have experienced with Jesus' searing question, "Do you love me?" In his follow-up command, "feed my sheep," Jesus implies that if you love him your automatic response will be to care for others.

A modern statue depicts Peter's commissioning

JOHN

Jesus and Peter

[15*]When they had finished breakfast, Jesus said to Simon Peter,[*] "Simon, son of John, do you love me more than these?" He said to him, "Yes, Lord, you know that I love you."[*] He said to him, "Feed my lambs." [16]He then said to him a second time, "Simon, son of John, do you love me?" He said to him, "Yes, Lord, you know that I love you." He said to him, "Tend my sheep." [17i]He said to him the third time, "Simon, son of John, do you love me?" Peter was distressed that he had said to him a third time, "Do you love me?" and he said to him, "Lord, you know everything; you know that I love you." [Jesus] said to him, "Feed my sheep. [18*j]Amen, amen, I say to you, when you were younger, you used to dress yourself and go where you wanted; but when you grow old, you will stretch out your hands, and someone else will dress you and lead you where you do not want to go." [19k]He said this signifying by what kind of death he would glorify God. And when he had said this, he said to him, "Follow me."

21:11 The exact number 153 is probably meant to have a symbolic meaning in relation to the apostles' universal mission; Jerome claims that Greek zoologists catalogued 153 species of fish. Or 153 is the sum of the numbers from 1 to 17. Others invoke Ezekiel 47:10.

21:12 None . . . dared to ask him: is Jesus' appearance strange to them? Cf. Luke 24:16; Mark 16:12; John 20:14. The disciples do, however, recognize Jesus **before** the breaking of the bread (opposed to Lk 24:35).

21:14 This verse connects John 20 and 21; cf. John 20:19, 26.

21:15-23 This section constitutes Peter's rehabilitation and emphasizes his role in the church.

21:15-17 In these three verses there is a remarkable variety of synonyms: two different Greek verbs for **love** (see the note on 15:13); two verbs for **feed/tend**; two nouns for **sheep**; two verbs for **know**. But apparently there is no difference of meaning. The threefold confession of Peter is meant to counteract his earlier threefold denial (18:17, 25, 27). The First Vatican Council cited these verses in defining that Jesus after his resurrection gave Peter the jurisdiction of supreme shepherd and ruler over the whole flock.

21:15 More than these: probably "more than these disciples do" rather than "more than you love them" or "more than you love these things [fishing, etc.]."

21:18 Originally probably a proverb about old age, now used as a figurative reference to the crucifixion of Peter.

l
13:25

m
Mt 16:28

n
19:35

o
20:30

The Beloved Disciple

[20l]Peter turned and saw the disciple following whom Jesus loved, the one who had also reclined upon his chest during the supper and had said, "Master, who is the one who will betray you?" [21]When Peter saw him, he said to Jesus, "Lord, what about him?" [22m]Jesus said to him, "What if I want him to remain until I come?* What concern is it of yours? You follow me." [23*]So the word spread among the brothers that that disciple would not die. But Jesus had not told him that he would not die, just "What if I want him to remain until I come? [What concern is it of yours?]"

Conclusion

[24n]It is this disciple who testifies to these things and has written them,* and we know that his testimony is true. [25o]There are also many other things that Jesus did, but if these were to be described individually, I do not think the whole world would contain the books that would be written.

21:22 Until I come: a reference to the parousia.

21:23 This whole scene takes on more significance if the disciple is already dead. The death of the apostolic generation caused problems in the church because of a belief that Jesus was to have returned first. Loss of faith sometimes resulted; cf. 2 Peter 3:4.

21:24 Who . . . has written them: this does not necessarily mean he wrote them with his own hand. The same expression is used in John 19:22 of Pilate, who certainly would not have written the inscription himself. **We know**: i.e., the Christian community; cf. John 1:14, 16.

The Bible and Liturgy

Irene Nowell, O.S.B.

"From the earliest days of the church, the reading of Scripture has been an integral part of the Christian liturgy" (*IBC* 222). The Bible is read at the fundamental Christian celebration, the Eucharist. The Liturgy of the Hours, the daily prayer of the church, consists almost totally of psalms and Scripture readings. Every celebration of a sacrament is supported by biblical readings. Scripture is the central pillar for personal prayer. "The sacred Synod [of Vatican II] forcefully and specifically exhorts all the Christian faithful . . . to learn 'the surpassing knowledge of Jesus Christ' [Phil 3:8] by frequent reading of the divine Scriptures" (*DV* 25).

Biblical Readings in the Eucharist

Thus it is no wonder that the bishops of the Second Vatican Council initiated a reform of the Roman Lectionary by declaring: "The treasures of the Bible are to be opened up more lavishly so that richer fare may be provided for the faithful at the table of God's word" (*SC* 51). The practice of using a set table of readings, called a "lectionary," goes back to the traditions of the Jewish synagogue and of early Christian communities. The fruit of the bishops' instruction, the 1970 Roman Lectionary, with its revisions, has become such a part of Catholic life that most worshipers do not remember the pre–Vatican II Lectionary. A brief reminder is in order.

The pre–Vatican II Lectionary, based on Pius V's Missal of 1570, had only a single cycle repeated every year. On Sundays there were only two readings: one from the New Testament letters and one from a gospel. The only Old Testament reading in the Sunday cycle was on the feast of Epiphany. There was no daily lectionary except for weekdays during Lent, Easter week, and Pentecost week. The Sunday readings were repeated during the week unless there was a Mass for the Dead, the feast day of a saint, or another special occasion. The gift the bishops of Vatican II gave the church was the invitation to expand this minimal offering of biblical readings to a lavish banquet.

The Roman Lectionary of 1970

This banquet is represented by the Roman Lectionary that was published in 1970 and has been modestly revised twice (in 1981 and 1998). A three-year Sunday cycle replaces the old one-year cycle, and each Sunday's selection has been expanded to include three readings plus a responsorial psalm. During Ordinary Time the Sunday lectionary is designed to revolve around the gospels. In Year A the Gospel of Matthew is read, in Year B the Gospel of Mark, and in Year C the Gospel of Luke. Each of these gospels is read virtually from beginning to end, with adjustments made to fit the thirty-four Sundays of Ordinary Time (an arrangement called "semi-continuous reading"). The first reading for each Sunday of Ordinary Time is from the Old Testament. This reading is selected to complement the gospel: presenting the same theme, foreshadowing an occurrence in the life of Christ, or providing background information for a gospel story. The responsorial psalm for each Sunday, chosen with the first reading and the gospel in mind, is intended to allow the congregation to take hold of the other readings and to say, "Yes! This reading has something to say to me!" The second reading follows its own path and is not closely related to the other readings. These second readings are taken from the New Testament letters and are read in semi-continuous fashion.

During the major seasons of Advent-Christmas and Lent-Easter, the Sunday Lectionary has a slightly different pattern. All the readings are chosen to fit the theme of the season. For example, during Advent the gospel readings move from a focus on Christ's second coming to the events immediately preceding his birth. The Old Testament readings represent prophetic preaching about the Messiah and messianic age, and the second read- 267

ings instruct us to prepare for the Lord's coming (see table 1 below). During Lent the Old Testament readings lead us through the history of salvation. On the first two Lenten Sundays the gospel stories of the temptation and transfiguration are always read from the gospel of the year (see above). On the Third, Fourth, and Fifth Sundays of Lent, the Gospel of John is read in Year A (and optionally during Years B and C), with special attention to the Rite of Christian Initiation. The second readings are chosen to complement the other two readings. The Christmas and Easter seasons are similarly planned to emphasize appropriate themes. For those who are interested, the whole arrangement is described in chapters 4–5 of the introduction to the *Lectionary for Mass* (1998).

Table 1: Arrangement of Advent Sunday Readings

Note: *The following charts can be read several ways. Reading the columns downward shows the flow of the readings through the season. Reading the First Sundays of Years A, B, and C together shows the similarity in the three-year cycle. Reading the rows across shows the interplay of themes on each Sunday.*

Year A		First Reading	Second Reading	Gospel
	1st	Isaiah's vision of Jerusalem (Is 2:1-5)	The hour to wake from sleep (Rom 13:11-14)	The coming of the Son of Man (Mt 24:37-44)
	2nd	A shoot from the stump of Jesse (Is 11:1-10)	Welcome one another (Rom 15:4-9)	The voice of one crying in the desert (Mt 3:1-12)
	3rd	Those ransomed by the Lord will rejoice (Is 35:1-6a, 10)	Be patient until the coming of the Lord (Jas 5:7-10)	Are you the one who is to come? (Mt 11:2-11)
	4th	A virgin will conceive and bear a son (Is 7:10-14)	Called to proclaim the gospel of Jesus Christ (Rom 1:1-7)	She will bear a son; name him Jesus (Mt 1:18-24)
Year B		**First Reading**	**Second Reading**	**Gospel**
	1st	Rend the heavens and come (Is 63:16b-17, 19b; 64:2-7)	God keeps you firm to the end (1 Cor 1:3-9)	Watch! You do not know when he will come (Mk 13:33-37)
	2nd	Prepare the way (Is 40:1-5, 9-11)	We await new heavens and new earth (2 Pt 3:8-14)	John the Baptist appeared in the desert (Mk 1:1-8)
	3rd	In my God is the joy of my soul (Is 61:1-2a, 10-11)	May God make you perfectly holy (1 Thes 5:16-24)	There is one coming after me (Jn 1:6-8, 19-28)
	4th	Your kingdom shall endure forever (2 Sm 7:1-5, 8b-11, 16)	The mystery kept for ages is now manifested (Rom 16:25-27)	Behold you shall conceive and bear a son (Lk 1:26-38)
Year C		**First Reading**	**Second Reading**	**Gospel**
	1st	God will fulfill the promise to David (Jer 33:14-16)	The Lord will strengthen your hearts (1 Thes 3:12–4:2)	Signs show your redemption is near (Lk 21:25-28, 34-36)
	2nd	Up, Jerusalem! Rejoice (Bar 5:1-9)	May you be blameless for the day of Christ (Phil 1:4-6, 8-11)	John proclaimed a baptism of repentance (Lk 3:1-6)
	3rd	The Lord is in your midst (Zep 3:14-18a)	Rejoice! The Lord is near (Phil 4:4-7)	People asked if John might be the Christ (Lk 3:10-18)
	4th	The ruler of Israel shall come from Bethlehem (Mi 5:1-4a)	Behold, I come to do your will (Heb 10:5-10)	Blessed are you among women (Lk 1:39-45)

Table 2: Arrangement of Lenten Sunday Readings

Year A	First Reading	Second Reading	Gospel
1st	God creates human beings; they disobey (Gn 2:7-9; 3:1-7)	Sin came through Adam, life through Jesus (Rom 5:12-19)	Jesus was tempted by the devil (Mt 4:1-11)
2nd	Call of Abraham to become a blessing for all (Gn 12:1-4)	God saved us and called us to be holy (2 Tm 1:8b-10)	Jesus was transfigured before them (Mt 17:1-9)
3rd	Water in the desert (Ex 17:3-7)	The love of God has been poured into our hearts (Rom 5:1-2, 5-8)	The water I give will become a spring of eternal life (Jn 4:5-42)
4th	David is anointed king (1 Sm 16:1b, 6-7, 10-13a)	Awake and Christ will give you light (Eph 5:8-14)	Jesus cures the blind man (Jn 9:1-41)
5th	I will put my spirit in you and you will live (Ezek 37:12-14)	The Spirit of the One who raised Jesus lives in you (Rom 8:8-11)	Raising of Lazarus (Jn 11:1-45)
Year B	**First Reading**	**Second Reading**	**Gospel**
1st	God's covenant with Noah (Gn 9:8-15)	The waters of the flood prefigured baptism (1 Pt 3:18-22)	The Spirit drove Jesus into the desert where he was tempted (Mk 1:12-15)
2nd	God tests Abraham (Gn 22:1-2, 9a, 10-13, 15-18)	God did not spare his own Son (Rom 8:31b-34)	Jesus was transfigured before them (Mk 9:2-10)
3rd	Ten Commandments: Sinai covenant charter (Ex 20:1-17)	We proclaim Christ crucified (1 Cor 1:22-25)	Destroy this temple; I will raise it up (Jn 2:13-25)
4th	Cyrus allows the exiles to return home (2 Chr 36:14-16, 19-23)	God brought us to life with Christ (Eph 2:4-10)	God so loved the world that he sent his Son (Jn 3:14-21)
5th	I will make a new covenant (Jer 31:31-34)	Christ learned obedience through suffering (Heb 5:7-9)	The grain of wheat that dies produces much fruit (Jn 12:20-33)
Year C	**First Reading**	**Second Reading**	**Gospel**
1st	God brought us out of Egypt; I praise you (Dt 26:4-10)	All who call on the name of the Lord will be saved (Rom 10:8-13)	The Spirit led Jesus into the desert to be tempted (Lk 4:1-13)
2nd	God's covenant with Abraham (Gn 15:5-12, 17-18)	Christ will transform us into his image (Phil 3:17–4:1)	While Jesus was praying his appearance changed (Lk 9:28b-36)
3rd	I come to rescue my people from the Egyptians (Ex 3:1-8a, 13-15)	The events in the desert serve as an example for us (1 Cor 10:1-6, 10-12)	If you do not repent, you will perish (Lk 13:1-9)
4th	God's people enter the Promised Land (Jos 5:9a, 10-12)	God has given us the ministry of reconciliation (2 Cor 5:17-21)	The Prodigal Son (Lk 15:1-3, 11-32)
5th	I am doing something new (Is 43:16-21)	Everything is loss except Christ (Phil 3:8-14)	A woman taken in adultery (Jn 8:1-11)

269

The arrangement of readings for the three-year Sunday cycle certainly spreads the table richly for the church. A large portion of the first three gospels is read during Ordinary Time and most of the Gospel of John is read during the Lent-Easter season. The major New Testament letters are also read along with a sizeable portion of Revelation. The Acts of the Apostles is read during Easter time. The Old Testament is less thoroughly represented for two reasons: it is much too long to fit into a three-year cycle, and the books are not read in semi-continuous fashion but are chosen to complement the gospel. As a consequence readings from the prophets lead the list of selections and many important figures and events are underrepresented or omitted altogether, for example, Noah and the flood, Jacob and his family, and much of the story of David. Women too seem conspicuously absent: the midwives of the Exodus, Deborah, Ruth, Judith, Esther, and the heroic mother of seven martyred sons (2 Mc 7; see tables 3 and 4 below).

Thus some "treasures of the Bible" must be opened in other ways than through the Lectionary: for example, Bible study groups, personal prayerful reading, Liturgy of the Hours.

In addition to the Sunday cycle, the 1970 Lectionary also provided a two-year cycle for daily Eucharist. The daily fare consists of a reading from the Old or New Testaments, a responsorial psalm, and a gospel passage. The gospel selections remain the same for both years, beginning with a semi-continuous reading of Mark and moving through Matthew and Luke. The first reading is not chosen to complement the gospel; rather an attempt is made, through semi-continuous readings, to present representative texts from all the biblical books. The only books from which nothing is read are Judith and Obadiah. Daily readings during the seasons of Advent-Christmas and Lent-Easter are chosen to represent the themes appropriate to those seasons.

The goal of the Roman Lectionary is to provide the rich fare called for by the council fathers: "The prolonged use of this Order of Readings . . . will, it is hoped, prove to be an effective step toward achieving the objective stated repeatedly by the Second Vatican Council" (*Lectionary for Mass*, introduction, 58).

Implications of Sharing in this Banquet of the Word

"When the Sacred Scriptures are read in the Church, God himself speaks to his people, and Christ, present in his own word, proclaims the Gospel" (*GIRM* 9). This lavish table of Scripture nourishes us with the very word of God. God speaks to us today—every day—through this word. "Christ himself is present in the midst of the faithful through his word" (*GIRM* 55). What kind of people must we be, who participate in this banquet?

It is a truism that we are what we eat. We who are nourished by the word of God are called to honor that sacred word in prayer and to give flesh to the word in daily life. The gestures of worship show loving reverence to the Word made flesh. We stand for the gospel reading and honor the Book of the Gospels. "The Church has always venerated the divine Scriptures as she venerated the Body of the Lord" (*DV* 21). We listen to the readings with love and attention and those who are entrusted with the ministry of lector prepare with diligent care. We also express devotion to God's word in our personal prayer. Daily prayerful reading of Scripture flows from the rich table spread in the Eucharist and prepares us for the next celebration. Such reading also fills in the omissions in the Lectionary so that the whole of Scripture can nourish the faithful.

The constant nourishment of Scripture gives us the courage and wisdom to shape our daily lives by God's word. "The participation of the faithful in the Liturgy increases to the degree that, as they listen to the word of God proclaimed in the liturgy, they strive harder to commit themselves to the Word of God incarnate in Christ. Thus they endeavor to conform their way of life to what they celebrate in the Liturgy, and then in turn to bring to the celebration of the Liturgy all that they do in life" (*Lectionary for Mass*, introduction, 6).

The faithful reading of Scripture also has profound implications for the ecumenical movement. "The idea of the unity of God's people, which this [ecumenical] movement seeks to restore, is pro-

foundly based in Scripture" (*IBC* 235). In the area of biblical interpretation "a remarkable degree of progress has already been achieved" (*IBC* 237). Biblical scholars from many denominations work together to translate and interpret God's word. Also remarkable is the acceptance of the 1970 Roman Lectionary. Within a few years of its publication most of the Christian churches that use a fixed lectionary had adopted the Roman Lectionary, with adaptations to fit their particular biblical canon and tradition.

The effect of reading the same biblical texts year after year cannot be underestimated. "In the hearing of God's word the Church is built up and grows" (*Lectionary for Mass*, introduction, 7). The council fathers' goal, that "the treasures of the Bible are to be opened up more lavishly," is still in the process of fulfillment.

Table 3: Distribution of Old Testament Readings in Sunday Lectionary (including Solemnities and Feasts of the Lord)

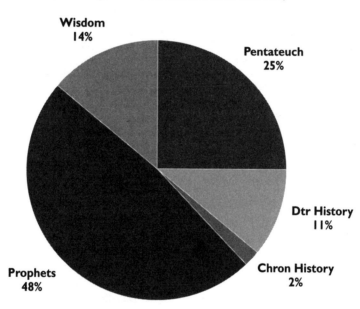

Biblical Area	# of Readings
Pentateuch	41
Deuteronomic History	19
Chronicler's History	3
Prophets	80
Wisdom	24

Table 4: Distribution of Prophetic Readings in Sunday Lectionary
(including Solemnities and Feasts of the Lord)

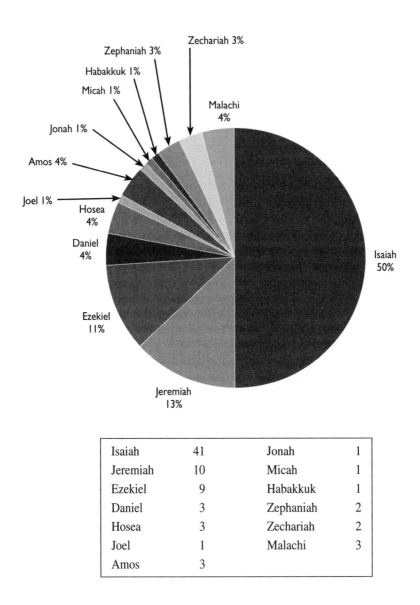

Isaiah	41	Jonah	1
Jeremiah	10	Micah	1
Ezekiel	9	Habakkuk	1
Daniel	3	Zephaniah	2
Hosea	3	Zechariah	2
Joel	1	Malachi	3
Amos	3		

Sunday Readings of Holy Scripture

	Year A	Year B	Year C
Advent Season			
1st Sunday of Advent			
1	Is 2:1-5	Is 63:16b-17, 19b; 64:2-7	Jer 33:14-16
2	Rom 13:11-14	1 Cor 1:3-9	1 Thes 3:12–4:2
3	Mt 24:37-44	Mk 13:33-37	Lk 21:25-28, 34-36
2nd Sunday of Advent			
1	Is 11:1-10	Is 40:1-5, 9-11	Bar 5:1-9
2	Rom 15:4-9	2 Pt 3:8-14	Phil 1:4-6, 8-11
3	Mt 3:1-12	Mk 1:1-8	Lk 3:1-6
3rd Sunday of Advent			
1	Is 35:1-6a, 10	Is 61:1-2a, 10-11	Zeph 3:14-18a
2	Jas 5:7-10	1 Thes 5:16-24	Phil 4:4-7
3	Mt 11:2-11	Jn 1:6-8, 19-28	Lk 3:10-18
4th Sunday of Advent			
1	Is 7:10-14	2 Sam 7:1-5, 8b-12, 14a, 16	Mic 5:1-4a
2	Rom 1:1-7	Rom 16:25-27	Heb 10:5-10
3	Mt 1:18-24	Lk 1:26-38	Lk 1:39-45
Christmas Season			
Christmas Vigil			
1	Is 62:1-5	Is 62:1-5	Is 62:1-5
2	Acts 13:16-17, 22-25	Acts 13:16-17, 22-25	Acts 13:16-17, 22-25
3	Mt 1:1-25 or 1:18-25	Mt 1:1-25 or 1:18-25	Mt 1:1-25 or 1:18-25
Christmas (Midnight)			
1	Is 9:1-6	Is 9:1-6	Is 9:1-6
2	Ti 2:11-14	Ti 2:11-14	Ti 2:11-14
3	Lk 2:1-14	Lk 2:1-14	Lk 2:1-14
Christmas (Dawn)			
1	Is 62:11-12	Is 62:11-12	Is 62:11-12
2	Ti 3:4-7	Ti 3:4-7	Ti 3:4-7
3	Lk 2:15-20	Lk 2:15-20	Lk 2:15-20
Christmas (During the Day)			
1	Is 52:7-10	Is 52:7-10	Is 52:7-10
2	Heb 1:1-6	Heb 1:1-6	Heb 1:1-6
3	Jn 1:1-18 or 1:1-5, 9-14	Jn 1:1-18 or 1:1-5, 9-14	Jn 1:1-18 or 1:1-5, 9-14

	Year A	Year B	Year C
Sunday after Christmas *(Holy Family)*			
1	Sir 3:2-7, 12-14	Sir 3:2-7, 12-14 or Gn 15:1-6; 21:1-3	Sir 3:2-7, 12-14 or 1 Sam 1:20-22, 24-28
2	Col 3:12-21 or 3:12-17	Col 3:12-21 or 3:12-17 or Heb 11:8, 11-12, 17-19	Col 3:12-21 or 3:12-17 or 1 Jn 3:1-2, 21-24
3	Mt 2:13-15, 19-23	Lk 2:22-40 or 2:22, 39-40	Lk 2:41-52
January 1 (Solemnity of Mary, Mother of God)			
1	Nm 6:22-27	Nm 6:22-27	Nm 6:22-27
2	Gal 4:4-7	Gal 4:4-7	Gal 4:4-7
3	Lk 2:16-21	Lk 2:16-21	Lk 2:16-21
2nd Sunday after Christmas			
1	Sir 24:1-2, 8-12	Sir 24:1-2, 8-12	Sir 24:1-2, 8-12
2	Eph 1:3-6, 15-18	Eph 1:3-6, 15-18	Eph 1:3-6, 15-18
3	Jn 1:1-18 or 1:1-5, 9-14	Jn 1:1-18 or 1:1-5, 9-14	Jn 1:1-18 or 1:1-5, 9-14
Epiphany			
1	Is 60:1-6	Is 60:1-6	Is 60:1-6
2	Eph 3:2-3a, 5-6	Eph 3:2-3a, 5-6	Eph 3:2-3a, 5-6
3	Mt 2:1-12	Mt 2:1-12	Mt 2:1-12
Sunday after Epiphany *(Baptism of the Lord)*			
1	Is 42:1-4, 6-7	Is 42:1-4, 6-7, or Is 55:1-11	Is 42:1-4, 6-7 or Is 40:1-5, 9-11
2	Acts 10:34-38	Acts 10:34-38 or 1 Jn 5:1-9	Acts 10:34-38 or Ti 2:11-14; 3:4-7
3	Mt 3:13-17	Mk 1:7-11	Lk 3:15-16, 21-22
Lenten Season			
1st Sunday of Lent			
1	Gn 2:7-9; 3:1-7	Gn 9:8-15	Dt 26:4-10
2	Rom 5:12-19 or 5:12, 17-19	1 Pt 3:18-22	Rom 10:8-13
3	Mt 4:1-11	Mk 1:12-15	Lk 4:1-13
2nd Sunday of Lent			
1	Gn 12:1-4a	Gn 22:1-2, 9a, 10-13, 15-18	Gn 15:5-12, 17-18
2	2 Tm 1:8b-10	Rom 8:31b-34	Phil 3:17–4:1 or 3:20–4:1
3	Mt 17:1-9	Mk 9:2-10	Lk 9:28b-36
3rd Sunday of Lent			
1	Ex 17:3-7	Ex 20:1-17 or 20:1-3, 7-8, 12-17	Ex 3:1-8a, 13-15

	Year A	Year B	Year C
2	Rom 5:1-2, 5-8	1 Cor 1:22-25	1 Cor 10:1-6, 10-12
3	Jn 4:5-42 or Jn 4:4-14, 19b-39a, 40-42	Jn 2:13-25	Lk 13:1-9

4th Sunday of Lent

	Year A	Year B	Year C
1	1 Sam 16:1b, 6-7, 10-13a	2 Chr 36:14-16, 19-23	Josh 5:9a, 10-12
2	Eph 5:8-14	Eph 2:4-10	2 Cor 5:17-21
3	Jn 9:1-41 or Jn 9:1, 6-9, 13-17, 34-38	Jn 3:14-21	Lk 15:1-3, 11-32

5th Sunday of Lent

	Year A	Year B	Year C
1	Ez 37:12-14	Jer 31:31-34	Is 43:16-21
2	Rom 8:8-11	Heb 5:7-9	Phil 3:8-14
3	Jn 11:1-45 or Jn 11:3-7, 17, 20-27, 33b-45	Jn 12:20-33	Jn 8:1-11

Passion Sunday
(Palm Sunday)

	Year A	Year B	Year C
Procession	Mt 21:1-11	Mk 11:1-10 or Jn 12:12-16	Lk 19:28-40
1	Is 50:4-7	Is 50:4-7	Is 50:4-7
2	Phil 2:6-11	Phil 2:6-11	Phil 2:6-11
3	Mt 26:14–27:66 or 27:11-54	Mk 14:1–15:47 or 15:1-39	Lk 22:14–23:56 or 23:1-49

Easter Triduum and Easter Season

Mass of the Lord's Supper

	Year A	Year B	Year C
1	Ex 12:1-8, 11-14	Ex 12:1-8, 11-14	Ex 12:1-8, 11-14
2	1 Cor 11:23-26	1 Cor 11:23-26	1 Cor 11:23-26
3	Jn 13:1-15	Jn 13:1-15	Jn 13:1-15

Good Friday

	Year A	Year B	Year C
1	Is 52:13–53:12	Is 52:13–53:12	Is 52:13–53:12
2	Heb 4:14-16; 5:7-9	Heb 4:14-16; 5:7-9	Heb 4:14-16; 5:7-9
3	Jn 18:1–19:42	Jn 18:1–19:42	Jn 18:1–19:42

Easter Vigil

	Year A	Year B	Year C
1	Gn 1:1–2:2 or 1:1, 26-31a	Gn 1:1–2:2 or 1:1, 26-31a	Gn 1:1–2:2 or 1:1, 26-31a
	Gn 22:1-18 or 22:1-2, 9a, 10-13, 15-18	Gn 22:1-18 or 22:1-2, 9a, 10-13, 15-18	Gn 22:1-18 or 22:1-2, 9a, 10-13, 15-18
	Ex 14:15–15:1	Ex 14:15–15:1	Ex 14:15–15:1
	Is 54:5-14	Is 54:5-14	Is 54:5-14
	Is 55:1-11	Is 55:1-11	Is 55:1-11
	Bar 3:9-15, 32–4:4	Bar 3:9-15, 32–4:4	Bar 3:9-15, 32–4:4
	Ez 36:16-17a, 18-28	Ez 36:16-17a, 18-28	Ez 36:16-17a, 18-28

	Year A	**Year B**	**Year C**
2	Rom 6:3-11	Rom 6:3-11	Rom 6:3-11
3	Mt 28:1-10	Mk 16:1-7	Lk 24:1-12
Easter Sunday			
1	Acts 10:34a, 37-43	Acts 10:34a, 37-43	Acts 10:34a, 37-43
2	2 Col 3:1-4 or	Col 3:1-4 or	Col 3:1-4 or
	1 Cor 5:6b-8	1 Cor 5:6b-8	1 Cor 5:6b-8
3	Jn 20:1-9 or Mt 28:1-10	Jn 20:1-9 or Mk 16:1-7 or	Jn 20:1-9 or Lk 24:1-12
	or Lk 24:13-35	Lk 24:13-35	or Lk 24:13-35
2nd Sunday of Easter			
1	Acts 2:42-47	Acts 4:32-35	Acts 5:12-16
2	1 Pt 1:3-9	1 Jn 5:1-6	Rev 1:9-11a, 12-13, 17-19
3	Jn 20:19-31	Jn 20:19-31	Jn 20:19-31
3rd Sunday of Easter			
1	Acts 2:14, 22-33	Acts 3:13-15, 17-19	Acts 5:27-32, 40b-41
2	1 Pt 1:17-21	1 Jn 2:1-5a	Rev 5:11-14
3	Lk 24:13-35	Lk 24:35-48	Jn 21:1-19 or 21:1-14
4th Sunday of Easter			
1	Acts 2:14a, 36-41	Acts 4:8-12	Acts 13:14, 43-52
2	1 Pt 2:20b-25	1 Jn 3:1-2	Rev 7:9, 14b-17
3	Jn 10:1-10	Jn 10:11-18	Jn 10:27-30
5th Sunday of Easter			
1	Acts 6:1-7	Acts 9:26-31	Acts 14:21-27
2	1 Pt 2:4-9	1 Jn 3:18-24	Rev 21:1-5a
3	Jn 14:1-12	Jn 15:1-8	Jn 13:31-33a, 34-35
6th Sunday of Easter			
1	Acts 8:5-8, 14-17	Acts 10:25-26, 34-35, 44-48	Acts 15:1-2, 22-29
2	1 Pt 3:15-18	1 Jn 4:7-10	Rev 21:10-14, 22-23
3	Jn 14:15-21	Jn 15:9-17	Jn 14:23-29
Ascension of the Lord			
1	Acts 1:1-11	Acts 1:1-11	Acts 1:1-11
2	Eph 1:17-23	Eph 1:17-23 or Eph 4:1-13 or 4:1-7, 11-13	Eph 1:17-23 or Heb 9:24-28; 10:19-23
3	Mt 28:16-20	Mk 16:15-20	Lk 24:46-53
7th Sunday of Easter			
1	Acts 1:12-14	Acts 1:15-17, 20a, 20c-26	Acts 7:55-60
2	1 Pt 4:13-16	1 Jn 4:11-16	Rev 22:12-14, 16-17, 20
3	Jn 17:1-11a	Jn 17:11b-19	Jn 17:20-26

	Year A	**Year B**	**Year C**
Pentecost Vigil			
1	Gn 11:1-9 or Ex 19:3-8a, 16-20b or Ez 37:1-14 or Jl 3:1-5	Gn 11:1-9 or Ex 19:3-8a, 16-20b or Ez 37:1-14 or Jl 3:1-5	Gn 11:1-9 or Ex 19:3-8a, 16-20b or Ez 37:1-14 or Jl 3:1-5
2	Rom 8:22-27	Rom 8:22-27	Rom 8:22-27
3	Jn 7:37-39	Jn 7:37-39	Jn 7:37-39
Pentecost			
1	Acts 2:1-11	Acts 2:1-11	Acts 2:1-11
2	1 Cor 12:3b-7, 12-13	1 Cor 12:3b-7, 12-13 or Gal 5:16-25	1 Cor 12:3b-7, 12-13 or Rom 8:8-17
3	Jn 20:19-23	Jn 20:19-23 or Jn 15:26-27; 16:12-15	Jn 20:19-23 or Jn 14:15-16, 23b-26

Ordinary Time

1st Sunday	(See *Baptism of the Lord,* above)		
2nd Sunday			
1	Is 49:3, 5-6	1 Sam 3:3b-10, 19	Is 62:1-5
2	1 Cor 1:1-3	1 Cor 6:13c-15a, 17-20	1 Cor 12:4-11
3	Jn 1:29-34	Jn 1:35-42	Jn 2:1-11
3rd Sunday			
1	Is 8:23–9:3	Jon 3:1-5, 10	Neh 8:2-4a, 5-6, 8-10
2	1 Cor 1:10-14, 17	1 Cor 7:29-31	1 Cor 12:12-30 or 12:12-14, 27
3	Mt 4:12-23 or 4:12-17	Mk 1:14-20	Lk 1:1-4; 4:14-21
4th Sunday			
1	Zeph 2:3, 3:12-13	Dt 18:15-20	Jer 1:4-5, 17-19
2	1 Cor 1:26-31	1 Cor 7:32-35	1 Cor 12:31–13:13 or 13:4-13
3	Mt 5:1-12a	Mk 1:21-28	Lk 4:21-30
5th Sunday			
1	Is 58:7-10	Jb 7:1-4, 6-7	Is 6:1-2a, 3-8
2	1 Cor 2:1-5	1 Cor 9:16-19, 22-23	1 Cor 15:1-11 or 1 Cor 15:3-8, 11
3	Mt 5:13-16	Mk 1:29-39	Lk 5:1-11
6th Sunday			
1	Sir 15:15-20	Lv 13:1-2, 44-46	Jer 17:5-8
2	1 Cor 2:6-10	1 Cor 10:31–11:1	1 Cor 15:12, 16-20
3	Mt 5:17-37 or Mt 5:20-22a, 27-28, 33-34a, 37	Mk 1:40-45	Lk 6:17, 20-26

	Year A	**Year B**	**Year C**
7th Sunday			
1	Lv 19:1-2, 17-18	Is 43:18-19, 21-22, 24b-25	1 Sam 26:2, 7-9, 12-13, 22-23
2	1 Cor 3:16-23	2 Cor 1:18-22	1 Cor 15:45-49
3	Mt 5:38-48	Mk 2:1-12	Lk 6:27-38
8th Sunday			
1	Is 49:14-15	Hos 2:16b, 17b, 21-22	Sir 27:4-7
2	1 Cor 4:1-5	2 Cor 3:1b-6	1 Cor 15:54-58
3	Mt 6:24-34	Mk 2:18-22	Lk 6:39-45
9th Sunday			
1	Dt 11:18, 26-28, 32	Dt 5:12-15	1 Kgs 8:41-43
2	Rom 3:21-25, 28	2 Cor 4:6-11	Gal 1:1-2, 6-10
3	Mt 7:21-27	Mk 2:23–3:6 or 2:23-28	Lk 7:1-10
10th Sunday			
1	Hos 6:3-6	Gn 3:9-15	1 Kgs 17:17-24
2	Rom 4:18-25	2 Cor 4:13–5:1	Gal 1:11-19
3	Mt 9:9-13	Mk 3:20-35	Lk 7:11-17
11th Sunday			
1	Ex 19:2-6a	Ez 17:22-24	2 Sam 12:7-10, 13
2	Rom 5:6-11	2 Cor 5:6-10	Gal 2:16, 19-21
3	Mt 9:36–10:8	Mk 4:26-34	Lk 7:36–8:3 or 7:36-50
12th Sunday			
1	Jer 20:10-13	Jb 38:1, 8-11	Zech 12:10-11; 13:1
2	Rom 5:12-15	2 Cor 5:14-17	Gal 3:26-29
3	Mt 10:26-33	Mk 4:35-41	Lk 9:18-24
13th Sunday			
1	2 Kgs 4:8-11, 14-16a	Wis 1:13-15; 2:23-24	1 Kgs 19:16b, 19-21
2	Rom 6:3-4, 8-11	2 Cor 8:7, 9, 13-15	Gal 5:1, 13-18
3	Mt 10:37-42	Mk 5:21-43 or 5:21-24, 35b-43	Lk 9:51-62
14th Sunday			
1	Zech 9:9-10	Ez 2:2-5	Is 66:10-14c
2	Rom 8:9, 11-13	2 Cor 12:7-10	Gal 6:14-18
3	Mt 11:25-30	Mk 6:1-6	Lk 10:1-12, 17-20 or 10:1-9
15th Sunday			
1	Is 55:10-11	Am 7:12-15	Dt 30:10-14
2	Rom 8:18-23	Eph 1:3-14 or 1:3-10	Col 1:15-20
3	Mt 13:1-23 or 13:1-9	Mk 6:7-13	Lk 10:25-37

	Year A	**Year B**	**Year C**
16th Sunday			
1	Wis 12:13, 16-19	Jer 23:1-6	Gn 18:1-10a
2	Rom 8:26-27	Eph 2:13-18	Col 1:24-28
3	Mt 13:24-43 or 13:24-30	Mk 6:30-34	Lk 10:38-42
17th Sunday			
1	1 Kgs 3:5, 7-12	2 Kgs 4:42-44	Gn 18:20-32
2	Rom 8:28-30	Eph 4:1-6	Col 2:12-14
3	Mt 13:44-52 or 13:44-46	Jn 6:1-15	Lk 11:1-13
18th Sunday			
1	Is 55:1-3	Ex 16:2-4, 12-15	Eccl 1:2; 2:21-23
2	Rom 8:35, 37-39	Eph 4:17, 20-24	Col 3:1-5, 9-11
3	Mt 14:13-21	Jn 6:24-35	Lk 12:13-21
19th Sunday			
1	1 Kgs 19:9a, 11-13a	1 Kgs 19:4-8	Wis 18:6-9
2	Rom 9:1-5	Eph 4:30–5:2	Heb 11:1-2, 8-19 or Heb 11:1-2, 8-12
3	Mt 14:22-33	Jn 6:41-51	Lk 12:32-48 or 12:35-40
20th Sunday			
1	Is 56:1, 6-7	Prov 9:1-6	Jer 38:4-6, 8-10
2	Rom 11:13-15, 29-32	Eph 5:15-20	Heb 12:1-4
3	Mt 15:21-28	Jn 6:51-58	Lk 12:49-53
21st Sunday			
1	Is 22:19-23	Josh 24:1-2a, 15-17, 18b	Is 66:18-21
2	Rom 11:33-36	Eph 5:21-32 or 5:2a, 25-32	Heb 12:5-7, 11-13
3	Mt 16:13-20	Jn 6:60-69	Lk 13:22-30
22nd Sunday			
1	Jer 20:7-9	Dt 4:1-2, 6-8	Sir 3:17-18, 20, 28-29
2	Rom 12:1-2	Jas 1:17-18, 21b-22, 27	Heb 12:18-19, 22-24a
3	Mt 16:21-27	Mk 7:1-8, 14-15, 21-23	Lk 14:1, 7-14
23rd Sunday			
1	Ez 33:7-9	Is 35:4-7a	Wis 9:13-18b
2	Rom 13:8-10	Jas 2:1-5	Phlm 9-10, 12-17
3	Mt 18:15-20	Mk 7:31-37	Lk 14:25-33
24th Sunday			
1	Sir 27:30–28:9	Is 50:5-9a	Ex 32:7-11, 13-14
2	Rom 14:7-9	Jas 2:14-18	1 Tm 1:12-17
3	Mt 18:21-35	Mk 8:27-35	Lk 15:1-32 or 15:1-10

	Year A	Year B	Year C
25th Sunday			
1	Is 55:6-9	Wis 2:12, 17-20	Amos 8:4-7
2	Phil 1:20c-24, 27a	Jas 3:16–4:3	1 Tm 2:1-8
3	Mt 20:1-16a	Mk 9:30-37	Lk 16:1-13 or 16:10-13
26th Sunday			
1	Ez 18:25-28	Nm 11:25-29	Amos 6:1a, 4-7
2	Phil 2:1-11 or 2:1-5	Jas 5:1-6	1 Tm 6:11-16
3	Mt 21:28-32	Mk 9:38-43, 45, 47-48	Lk 16:19-31
27th Sunday			
1	Is 5:1-7	Gn 2:18-24	Hab 1:2-3; 2:2-4
2	Phil 4:6-9	Heb 2:9-11	2 Tm 1:6-8, 13-14
3	Mt 21:33-43	Mk 10:2-16 or 10:2-12	Lk 17:5-10
28th Sunday			
1	Is 25:6-10a	Wis 7:7-11	2 Kgs 5:14-17
2	Phil 4:12-14, 19-20	Heb 4:12-13	2 Tm 2:8-13
3	Mt 22:1-14 or 22:1-10	Mk 10:17-30 or 10:17-27	Lk 17:11-19
29th Sunday			
1	Is 45:1, 4-6	Is 53:10-11	Ex 17:8-13
2	1 Thes 1:1-5b	Heb 4:14-16	2 Tm 3:14–4:2
3	Mt 22:15-21	Mk 10:35-45 or 10:42-45	Lk 18:1-8
30th Sunday			
1	Ex 22:20-26	Jer 31:7-9	Sir 35:12-14, 16-18
2	1 Thes 1:5c-10	Heb 5:1-6	2 Tm 4:6-8, 16-18
3	Mt 22:34-40	Mk 10:46-52	Lk 18:9-14
31st Sunday			
1	Mal 1:14b–2:2b, 8-10	Dt 6:2-6	Wis 11:22–12:2
2	1 Thes 2:7b-9, 13	Heb 7:23-28	2 Thes 1:11–2:2
3	Mt 23:1-12	Mk 12:28b-34	Lk 19:1-10
32nd Sunday			
1	Wis 6:12-16	1 Kgs 17:10-16	2 Macc 7:1-2, 9-14
2	1 Thes 4:13-18 or 4:13-14	Heb 9:24-28	2 Thes 2:16–3:5
3	Mt 25:1-13	Mk 12:38-44 or 12:41-44	Lk 20:27-38 or 20:27, 34-38
33rd Sunday			
1	Prov 31:10-13, 19-20, 30-31	Dan 12:1-3	Mal 3:19-20a
2	1 Thes 5:1-6	Heb 10:11-14, 18	2 Thes 3:7-12
3	Mt 25:14-30 or 25:14-15, 19-21	Mk 13:24-32	Lk 21:5-19

	Year A	Year B	Year C
34th Sunday *(Christ the King)*			
1	Ez 34:11-12, 15-17	Dan 7:13-14	2 Sam 5:1-3
2	1 Cor 15:20-26, 28	Rev 1:5-8	Col 1:12-20
3	Mt 25:31-46	Jn 18:33b-37	Lk 23:35-43

Solemnities of the Lord during Ordinary Time

	Year A	Year B	Year C
Trinity Sunday *(Sunday after Pentecost)*			
1	Ex 34:4b-6, 8-9	Dt 4:32-34, 39-40	Prov 8:22-31
2	2 Cor 13:11-13	Rom 8:14-17	Rom 5:1-5
3	Jn 3:16-18	Mt 28:16-20	Jn 16:12-15
Body and Blood of Christ			
1	Dt 8:2-3, 14b-16a	Ex 24:3-8	Gn 14:18-20
2	1 Cor 10:16-17	Heb 9:11-15	1 Cor 11:23-26
3	Jn 6:51-58	Mk 14:12-16, 22-26	Lk 9:11b-17
Sacred Heart of Jesus			
1	Dt 7:6-11	Hos 11:1, 3-4, 8c-9	Ez 34:11-16
2	1 Jn 4:7-16	Eph 3:8-12, 14-19	Rom 5:5b-11
3	Mt 11:25-30	Jn 19:31-37	Lk 15:3-7

Years A, B, C

Other Solemnities and Celebrations

	Years A, B, C
Chrism Mass	
1	Is 61:1-3ab, 6a, 8b-9
2	Rev 1:5-8
3	Lk 4:16-21
Easter Monday	
1	Acts 2:14, 22-33
2	Mt 28:8-15
Easter Tuesday	
1	Acts 2:36-41
2	Jn 20:11-18
Easter Wednesday	
1	Acts 3:1-10
2	Lk 24:13-35
Easter Thursday	
1	Acts 3:11-26
2	Lk 24:35-48

Years A, B, C

Easter Friday	
1	Acts 4:1-12
2	Jn 21:1-14
Easter Saturday	
1	Acts 4:13-21
2	Mk 16:9-15
Presentation of the Lord	
1	Mal 3:1-4
2	Heb 2:14-18
3	Lk 2:22-40 or 2:22-32
Joseph, Husband of Mary	
1	2 Sam 7:4-5a, 12-14a, 16
2	Rom 4:13, 16-18, 22
3	Mt 1:16, 18-21, 24a or Lk 2:41-51a
Annunciation of the Lord	
1	Is 7:10-14, 8:10
2	Heb 10:4-10
3	Lk 1:26-38
Birth of John the Baptist (Vigil)	
1	Jer 1:4-10
2	1 Pt 1:8-12
3	Lk 1:5-17
Birth of John the Baptist (During the Day)	
1	Is 49:1-6
2	Acts 13:22-26
3	Lk 1:57-66, 80
Saints Peter and Paul (Vigil)	
1	Acts 3:1-10
2	Gal 1:11-20
3	Jn 21:15-19
Saints Peter and Paul (During the Day)	
1	Acts 12:1-11
2	2 Tm 4:6-8, 17-18
3	Mt 16:13-19
Transfiguration of the Lord	
1	Dn 7:9-10, 13-14
2	2 Pt 1:16-19
3	A Mt 17:1-9, B Mk 9:2-10, C Lk 9:28b-36

Years A, B, C

Assumption of the Blessed Virgin (Vigil)

1	1 Chr 15:3-4, 15-16; 16:1-2
2	1 Cor 15:54b-57
3	Lk 11:27-28

Assumption of the Blessed Virgin (During the Day)

1	Rev 11:19a; 12:1-6a, 10ab
2	1 Cor 15:20-27
3	Lk 1:39-56

Exaltation of the Cross

1	Nm 21:4b-9
2	Phil 2:6-11
3	Jn 3:13-17

All Saints

1	Rev 7:2-4, 9-14
2	1 Jn 3:1-3
3	Mt 5:1-12a

Commemoration of the Faithful Departed

1	Wis 3:1-9 or Wis 4:7-15 or Is 25:6-9
2	Rom 5:5-11 or Rom 5:17-21 or Rom 6:3-9 or Rom 8:14-23 or Rom 8:31b-35, 37-39 or Rom 14:7-9, 10c-12 or 1 Cor 15:20-28 or 1 Cor 15:51-57 or 2 Cor 4:14–5:1 or 2 Cor 5:1, 6-10 or Phil 3:20-21 or 1 Thes 4:13-18 or 2 Tm 2:8-13
3	Mt 5:1-12a or Mt 11:25-30 or Mt 25:31-46 or Lk 7:11-17 or Lk 23:44-46, 50, 52-53; 24:1-6a or Lk 24:13-16, 28-35 or Jn 5:24-29 or Jn 6:37-40 or Jn 6:51-59 or Jn 11:17-27 or Jn 11:32-45 or Jn 14:1-6

Dedication of the Lateran Basilica

1	Ez 47:1-2, 8-9, 12
2	1 Cor 3:9c-11, 16-17
3	Jn 2:13-22

Immaculate Conception

1	Gn 3:9-15, 20
2	Eph 1:3-6, 11-12
3	Lk 1:26-38

Contributors

Mary Elsbernd, O.S.F., is professor of pastoral studies in social ethics and graduate program director for the MA in Social Justice at the Institute of Pastoral Studies, Loyola University Chicago. Her work is focused on Catholic social teachings, social justice, human rights, and leadership. She is a Franciscan Sister of Dubuque, Iowa.

Leslie J. Hoppe, O.F.M., is an adjunct professor of Old Testament studies at Catholic Theological Union. He is a member of the editorial board of *The Bible Today* and is author of several books on Old Testament studies. He is currently the Provincial Minister of the Assumption Province Franciscans.

Irene Nowell, O.S.B., is a Benedictine of Mount St. Scholastica in Atchison, Kansas. She is an adjunct professor at St. John's University School of Theology, has published two books and numerous articles, and is a past president of the Catholic Biblical Association. She is also a member of the Committee on Illuminations and Texts for *The Saint John's Bible.*

Catherine Upchurch serves as the director of Little Rock Scripture Study. Her work in adult faith formation involves writing, editing, lecturing, and leading retreats and days of reflection. She is the editor of *A Year of Sundays* and an associate editor of *The Bible Today*, a journal of biblical spirituality.

Macrina Wiederkehr, O.S.B., author and retreat leader, is a monastic of St. Scholastica Monastery in Fort Smith, Arkansas. In addition to her published books, she writes a regular column for Stepping Stones, the online newsletter of Little Rock Scripture Study. Visit her website: www.Macrina Wiederkehr.com.

Ronald D. Witherup, S.S., is superior general of the Sulpicians and lives in Paris, France. He holds a doctorate in biblical studies and is the author of numerous books and articles on Scripture. His current interest is in the letters of Saint Paul and the Acts of the Apostles.

Illustration Credits

Index

Index

The complete cycle of Sunday readings can be found on pages 273–83. Additional lists of readings may be found in the article "The Bible and Liturgy" on pages 267–72. These include Advent Sunday readings, Lenten Sunday readings, Old Testament readings in the Sunday lectionary, and prophetic readings in the Sunday Lectionary.